CHILDREN AND THEIR ART

Methods for the Elementary School

Seventh Edition

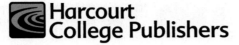

Harcourt College Publishers

Where Learning Comes to Life

TECHNOLOGY

Technology is changing the learning experience, by increasing the power of your textbook and other learning materials; by allowing you to access more information, more quickly; and by bringing a wider array of choices in your course and content information sources.

Harcourt College Publishers has developed the most comprehensive Web sites, e-books, and electronic learning materials on the market to help you use technology to achieve your goals.

PARTNERS IN LEARNING

Harcourt partners with other companies to make technology work for you and to supply the learning resources you want and need. More importantly, Harcourt and its partners provide avenues to help you reduce your research time of numerous information sources.

Harcourt College Publishers and its partners offer increased opportunities to enhance your learning resources and address your learning style. With quick access to chapter-specific Web sites and e-books . . . from interactive study materials to quizzing, testing, and career advice . . . Harcourt and its partners bring learning to life.

Harcourt's partnership with Digital:Convergence™ brings :CRQ™ technology and the :CueCat™ reader to you and allows Harcourt to provide you with a complete and dynamic list of resources designed to help you achieve your learning goals. You can download the free :CRQ software from www.crq.com. Visit any of the 7,100 RadioShack stores nationwide to obtain a free :CueCat reader. Just swipe the cue with the :CueCat reader to view a list of Harcourt's partners and Harcourt's print and electronic learning solutions.

http://www.harcourtcollege.com/partners

CHILDREN AND THEIR ART

Methods for the Elementary School

Seventh Edition

Al Hurwitz
Maryland Institute, College of Art

Michael Day
Brigham Young University

HARCOURT COLLEGE PUBLISHERS

Fort Worth   Philadelphia   San Diego   New York   Orlando   Austin   San Antonio
Toronto   Montreal   London   Sydney   Tokyo

Publisher	Earl McPeek
Executive Editor	David Tatom
Acquisitions Editor	John Swanson
Market Strategist	Steve Drummond
Developmental Editor	Stacey Sims
Project Editor	Laura J. Hanna
Art Director	April Eubanks
Production Manager	Serena Sipho

ISBN: 0-15-507438-5
Library of Congress Catalog Card Number: 00-108350

Address for Domestic Orders
Harcourt College Publishers, 6277 Sea Harbor Drive, Orlando, FL 32887-6777
800-782-4479

Address for International Orders
International Customer Service
Harcourt, Inc., 6277 Sea Harbor Drive, Orlando, FL 32887-6777
407-345-3800   (fax) 407-345-4060
(e-mail) hbintl@harcourt.com

Address for Editorial Correspondence
Harcourt College Publishers, 301 Commerce Street, Suite 3700, Fort Worth, TX 76102

Web Site Address
http://www.harcourtcollege.com

Harcourt College Publishers will provide complimentary supplements or supplement packages to those adopters qualified under our adoption policy. Please contact your sales representative to learn how you qualify. If as an adopter or potential user you receive supplements you do not need, please return them to your sales representative or send them to: Attn: Returns Department, Troy Warehouse, 465 South Lincoln Drive, Troy, MO 63379.

Printed in the United States of America

1 2 3 4 5 6 7 8 9   048   9 8 7 6 5 4 3 2

Harcourt College Publishers

The authors have been blessed not only with great children,
but also with their children's spouses who continue to enrich our lives.
We are happy to dedicate this book to them.
Richard Jones
Mami Kato
Melinda Mann
Susan Puciel
Bill Pullman
Amy Reeve
David Tuckfield

PREFACE

On the occasion of this new edition of *Children and Their Art*, the first of the new century and new millennium, the authors express appreciation to the publisher for unparalleled support over many years. Few texts reach seven editions, and few continue to be published over a period of more than four decades. That *Children and Their Art* has reached this status is a testimonial to the consistent commitment of the publisher, both to the topic of the book and to the authors.

The world has changed greatly since 1958, the date of the first edition of this book, and the authors have made every attempt to keep each new edition up to date and current with the best theories and practices of art education. It seems that change in education has accelerated with other aspects of life in the computer age. This new edition of *Children and Their Art* reflects significant changes in art education while maintaining the solid foundation of values that have been consistent from the beginning. These values include a strong belief in the contributions of art in the education of all children, the significant role of teachers, the centrality of art centered content including creative art expression, and the importance of sound instruction in a supportive learning environment.

The past six years (since publication of the previous edition) have produced major changes in art education, most of which can be viewed as progress for the field. The National Standards for the Visual Arts have been adopted and implemented in some form in most states. Nearly two hundred teachers have become National Board Certified (NBC) in art by the National Board for Professional Teaching Standards (NBPTS). The National Art Education Association (NAEA) has published Standards for Art Teacher Preparation, which will increase the likelihood that new art teachers will be competent and successful in their classrooms. After a twenty-year hiatus, the National Assessment of Educational Progress (NAEP) conducted and reported an assessment in the arts. The report revealed strengths and weaknesses in art education, noting particularly that many students still do not receive regular instruction in art.

Studies by the National Center for Education Statistics (NCES) and NAEA indicate that, although art is not universally implemented in public elementary, middle level, and secondary schools in the United States, much progress has been made. The study of art is institutionalized within school systems at an unprecedented level, and art is increasingly regarded as an essential subject within a balanced curriculum. Art is recognized for its intrinsic educational value as well as for its role in facilitating learning in the general curriculum.

CHANGES IN THE NEW EDITION

The most obvious change in the seventh edition of *Children and Their Art* is the format for the book itself. We have increased the size of the book and moved to a four-color, two-column design that allows us to better showcase the numerous examples of children's art found throughout the book. The new edition includes over 300 illustrations, and over sixty new images have been added in this edition to provide examples of new media and better representation of postmodern artforms and works by women and minority artists.

Some of the changes experienced readers of the book will note are as follows:

- increased attention to the use of computers as learning tools and as a medium for making art
- addition of a section in Chapter 2 on the postmodern era in art and implications for art education
- introduction of Internet addresses and references following each chapter and to the resources presented in the appendices wherever applicable.
- addition of new art reproductions, examples of child art, and photographs of teaching and learning situations.

We have much to learn from countries we have visited—Russia, People's Republic of China, Israel, Japan, France,

Netherlands, Germany, Qatar, Austria, Republic of South Africa, Korea, Taiwan, Kenya, Jamaica, and Egypt. While children in all cultures will create images of their own accord, it is through cultural support, schooling, and teaching that they are able to realize their real potential. We are concerned in this book with assisting teachers to provide the best support for children as they progress in their artistic expression and in their understanding of art.

No one country has all the answers for the ideal art program nor can any one society be cited for maintaining a full or adequate array of support for the aesthetic development of all its children. To study art education beyond the borders of one's own country is to reaffirm one's sense of mission as an art educator.

ACKNOWLEDGMENTS

Many individuals, including art teachers and students, assisted the authors as they prepared the seventh edition. We thank the following colleagues for their insightful reviews of the previous edition: Joe Fry, Kent State University; Gaye Green, Western Washington University; Christopher Greenman, Alabama State University; Michael Smith, University of North Florida; and Mary Zahner, University of Dayton.

We would also like to thank Joseph Germaine, Max Klager, Margaret Peeno, Sharon Seim, Susan Mudle, Susan Hazelroth, Kay Alexander, Bridgette Tuckfield, Xie Li-fang, Tom Anderson, for their contributions of child art and photographs and Val Brinkerhoff and David Hawkinson, both professional photographers, for permission to use their works.

Dr. Virgie Day made significant contributions with her discussion of postmodernism in Chapter 2 and editorial support for the entire manuscript. She spent countless hours on the computer to provide all the Internet addresses and references, a major addition to the book.

The following people also provided valuable assistance: Ben Manas for photography, Helen Hurwitz for typing, Kevin Tavin of the Art Institute of Chicago. We would also like to thank the Philadelphia Museum of Art, Walters Art Gallery, and The Baltimore Museum of Art for permission to use their collections.

We thank Janet Hart, Heather Young, and Linh Nguyen and the Brigham Young University Department of Visual Arts for mailing, telephone, and secretarial assistance.

Finally, we wish to thank the editorial and production staff at Harcourt College Publishers, in particular, John Swanson, acquisitions editor; Stacey Sims, senior developmental editor; and Laura J. Hanna, senior project editor. We also wish to thank Serena Sipho, senior production manager, April Eubanks, art director, and Shirley Webster, pictures and rights editor, and Susan Holtz, photo researcher. The combined efforts of everyone at Harcourt have resulted in the best edition yet of *Children and Their Art*.

ABOUT THE AUTHORS
Al Hurwitz

Al Hurwitz is Chair Emeritus in Art Education at the Maryland Institute College of Art. He taught at the elementary and secondary levels in Miami-Dade County, Florida, before his appointment as art supervisor. He was Director of Visual and Performing Arts for Newton, Massachusetts, schools and taught art education at Harvard University Graduate School of Education, Ohio State University, Teachers' College, Columbia University, Brandeis University, and the Massachusetts College of Art.

He has also written, coauthored or edited 12 books on art education, served as president of the International Society for Education Through Art (InSEA) and the United States Society for Education Through Art (USSEA). His national and international awards include the Distinguished Alumnus Award of Pennsylvania State University, the Edmund Ziegfeld Award, the Distinguished Alumnus Award, Maryland Institute College of Art, the Sir Herbert Read and Mahmoud El Bassiouny Awards, and the National Art Educator Award from the National Art Education Association (NAEA). He received his doctorate from Pennsylvania State University and holds the MFA from Yale Drama School.

Dr. Hurwitz served on the planning committee of the National Board for Professional Teaching Standards (NBPTS), the national certification program for art teachers. He has evaluated programs in art education for the Corcoran School of Art, and Teachers' College of Columbia University, and conducted workshops for the Hirshhorn, Whitney, and the Los Angeles County Museums of Art.

The Hurwitz Study Center for Art Education has been created in his name at the Maryland Institute, College of Art.

Michael Day

Michael Day is Professor and former Chair of the Department of Visual Arts at Brigham Young University. He taught middle and high school art in California prior to heading the art education programs at the University of South Carolina and the University of Minnesota. A widely published author and researcher, Professor Day is recipient of the Manuel Barkan Award for published research from the National Art Education Association (NAEA). He has directed national curriculum development institutes and national professional development seminars for the Getty Education Institute for the Arts. In 1993, he was named the Getty Institute's first Visiting Scholar.

Professor Day has consulted for college art departments, state departments of education and school districts in 25 states and has served on national panels, editorial boards for national scholarly publications, and art museum boards. He was invited to the former Soviet Union in a scholarly exchange sponsored by the International Research and Exchanges Board, and in 1998 he was one of five scholars invited to Beijing, in a delegation sponsored by the Getty Education Institute and the Ministry of Education of the People's Republic of China.

Dr. Day served as President of the NAEA from 1997–1999. His continued interest in art teacher preparation resulted in his 1997 book, *Preparing Teachers of Art,* and in the development and publication in 2000 of the NAEA *Standards for Art Teacher Preparation,* completed under the aegis of his presidency.

CONTENTS

CHILDREN AND THEIR ART

Methods for the Elementary School

Seventh Edition

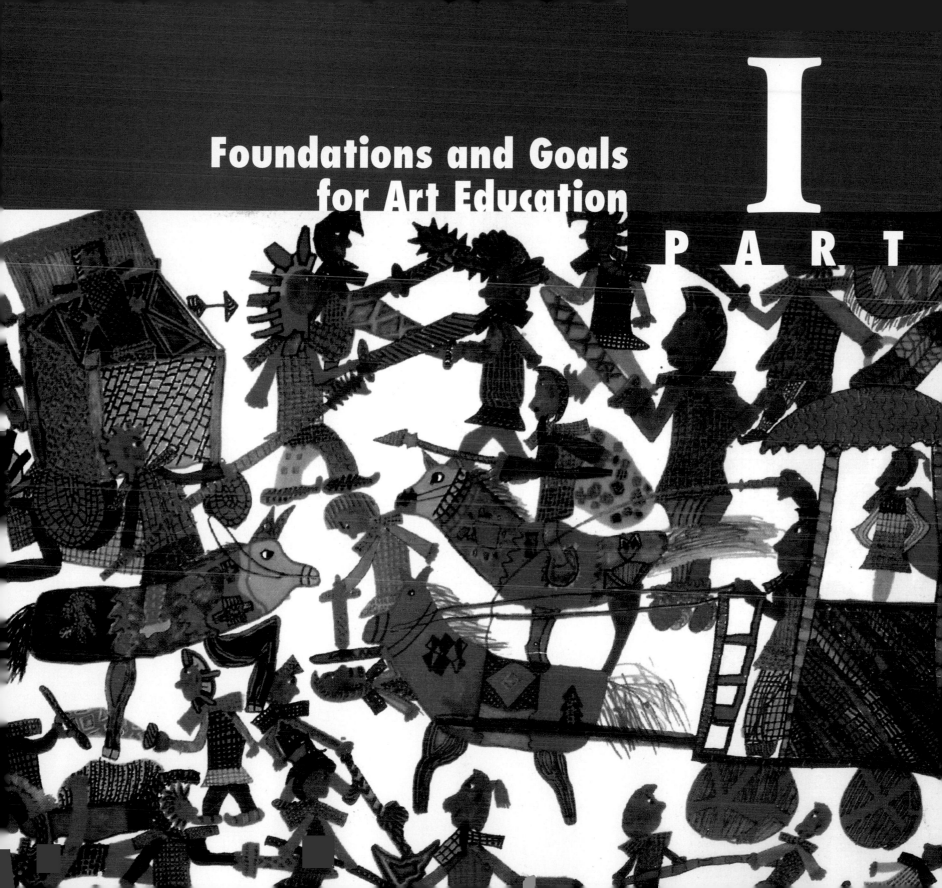

Foundations and Goals
for Art Education

I

PART

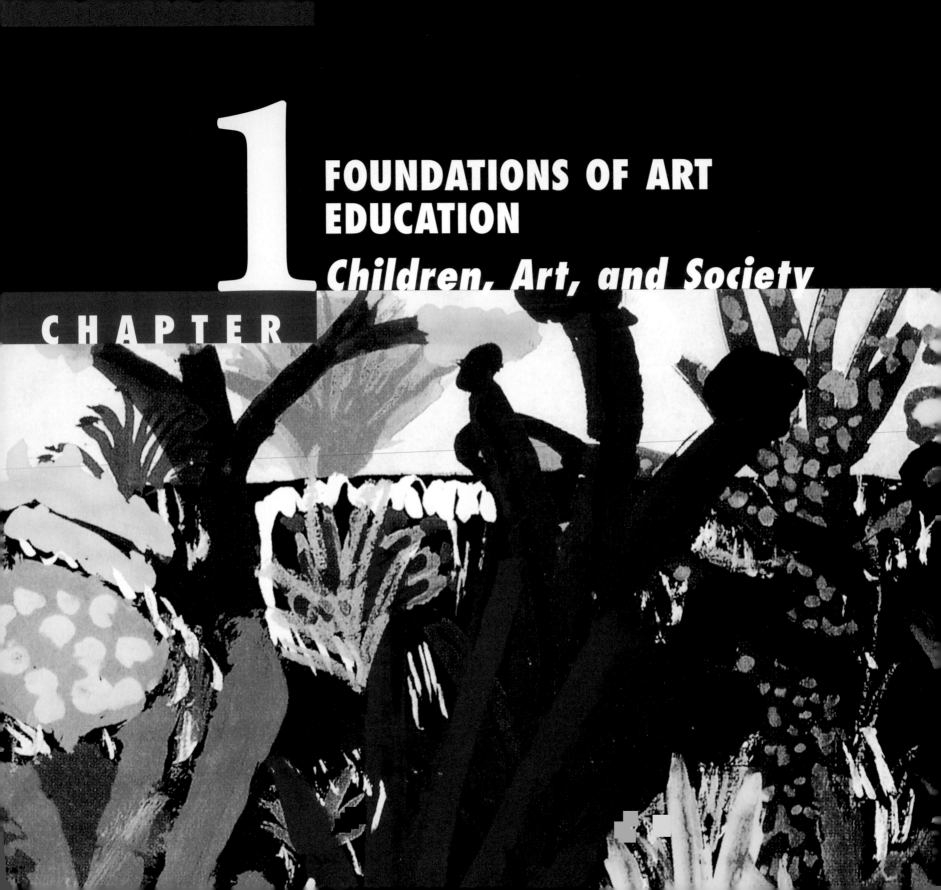

CHAPTER 1

FOUNDATIONS OF ART EDUCATION

Children, Art, and Society

One function of education is to maintain the culture—its values, ideals, and patterns of living—through the training of succeeding generations. In art, this maintenance is difficult because the arts have not been generally recognized as central in our culture. We must set up objectives for art education in a society that surrounds itself with art forms, but that is generally unaware of the aesthetic qualities. We must work with many people who have negative feelings about artists and designers, so we cannot derive all our values about art education from the general public.[1]

—June King McFee

Any person who would educate others faces three fundamental factors. The first basic factor is the nature of those who will learn. Second, every educator needs to consider the content to be taught and learned. And third, the values of the society in which education is to take place cannot be ignored.[2] For this discussion, then, the prospective educator needs to consider the dynamic *nature of the visual arts,* various *conceptions of the learner* that will guide education practices, and the *values of the society* in which the educational program exists. These three factors must be addressed whether the educational setting is a public school district, a private school, a home school, or any setting where formal art education is the goal.

NATURE OF THE VISUAL ARTS

To obtain a basic understanding of art, we might imagine ourselves back in time, even before the age of cave paintings. From this vantage we may recognize the importance of one early achievement: the invention of containers. The seemingly simple realization that a hollow space would allow someone to store water or grain must have been one of the wonders of primitive technology. Eventually, someone must have noticed that if greater attention were given to the *shape* of a vessel as well as to the thickness of its walls, the container would somehow be more satisfactory. In perfecting the form in order to improve the function, that anonymous fabricator was working on the level of enlightened craftsmanship.

Later, a person making a container, or pot, must have experimented with the *surface* of the vessel, although this had nothing at all to do with its *function*—that is, with how much the pot can carry or how much wear it can survive. Decoration can only make the handling and the seeing of the object more *pleasurable* experiences. This development of the idea

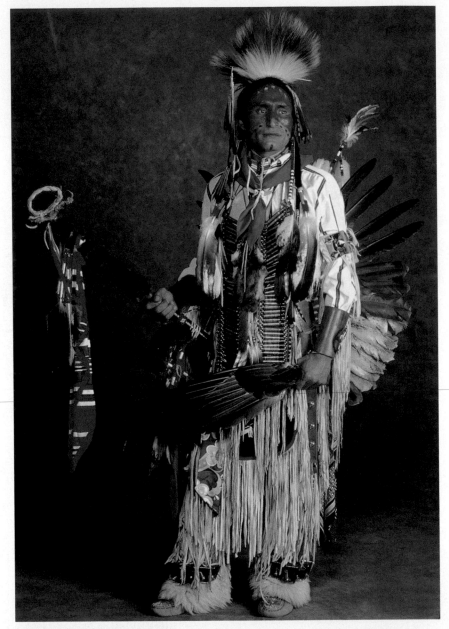

Peter Anthony (Sky Eagle), Shuswap, interior British Columbia, Canada, traditional dance regalia. From *Pow Wow* by Ben Marra. Photo © 1996 Ben Marra.

The finest examples of clothing are works of applied art and often express cultural meanings and values. Clothing in most cultures is used to convey cultural roles, establish status in society, and express individual personalities. These aesthetic functions require the skills and sensitivities of artists in their creation. The concept of clothing extends far beyond the obvious needs for covering, protection, and warmth to notions of uniform, fashion, and beauty. The variety of colorful materials and the associations children have with Native Americans make the study of Pow Wow regalia a subject with strong inherent values.

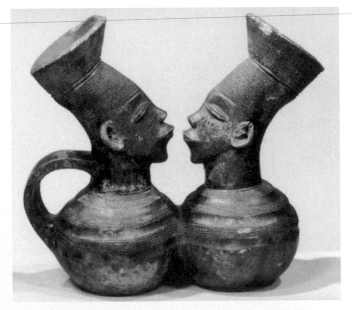

Double-bowled Pot, Mangbetu style, Africa, collected about 1910, ceramic, American Museum of Natural History. This exquisite double pot features incised decoration, a beautifully integrated handle, and two sculptured heads with head coverings indicating social or political rank. Ceramic clay is one of the most universal art media: Note the range of time, culture, and place exemplified by ceramic pieces displayed in this book.

of decoration provided the potter with unlimited options for technique and design. Once the object was formed, shapes could be inscribed or painted in patterns that might include swirls, loops, straight lines, or combinations of any of these.

These early craftspersons discovered that decoration could have *meaning,* that signs could stand for ideas. They found that symbols not only might express fears, dreams, and fantasies but could communicate their states of mind to other people.[3] Cave paintings reflect this function, for in these the animals depicted are more than recognizable shapes taken from the experiences of the group—they probably represent rituals whereby hunters could record concern for survival.[4] Decoration now moved into the more profound sphere of the image as metaphor, and not every member of the tribe was capable of making such a transference. Those who could we now call *artists.*[5]

As art moved beyond utilitarian functions and as attention was centered on appearance as well as use, the notion of *aesthetic* response evolved. A painting or a fine vessel might be valued as an investment or as historical data, but central to its existence as a work of art is the power to provide pleasure or stimulation as distinctive in its way as musical compositions or poetry. When we view art objects from various cultures, we can respond to the aesthetic "vibrations" of the work despite a lack of knowledge of conditions surrounding the creation of the object. When available, historical and cultural information can extend and intensify our responses to an artwork and greatly increase our understanding of it.

As we discuss the visual arts in this book, we refer to a fascinating array of different art traditions and forms. The traditional *fine arts,* including drawing, painting, sculpture, and printmaking, have existed for many centuries. Today the fine arts embrace a boisterous set of contemporary contenders based in such technologies as photography, video, and computer-generated imagery. The newer concepts of environmental art, performance art, conceptual art, and installation contribute to the diversity of the visual arts.

Included also are the *applied arts* that surround us every day, such as architecture, interior design, weaving, ceramics, fashion design, and a host of other applications. The *folk arts,* works by naive or untutored artists, and the *arts of indigenous peoples* emerge in many forms from the vital creative impulses and social functions within cultures that only art can satisfy. *Popular art* forms, such as posters, comic books, body decoration, and graffiti, add to the vital and dynamic definition of *the visual arts.* This broad, inclusive view of the

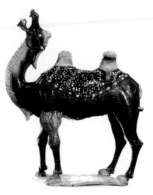

Tomb Figure, Camel, Chinese, T'ang Dynasty (618–906 C.E.), glazed ceramic, 35" × 28" × 9". Portland Art Museum, Oregon, gift of Friends of the Museum. From the times of prehistoric cave painters, artists of virtually all cultures, times, and locations have created images of animals. This expressive, beautifully formed, glazed ceramic camel, more than a thousand years old, is one of the prime examples of animal art from China.

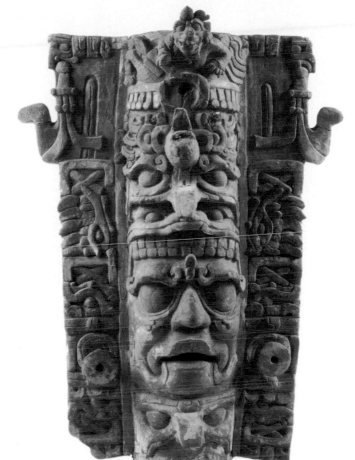

Flanged Cylinder, Chiapas, Palenque, Mexico, c. 690, ceramic 28 in. high, Instituto de Cultura de Tabasco, Dirección de Patrimonio Cultural, Museo Regional de Antropología "Carlos Pellicer Cámara." Photo commissioned by the Metropolitan Museum, Encuadre: Gerardo Suter-Lourdes Almeida. Numerous cultures of the past have vanished from the earth, leaving behind artifacts, some of which are works of art as this magnificently formed ceramic sculpture from Mexico. Art historians and archeologists study objects such as this and learn about religious, social, political, and other practices and values of the objects' creators. Significant artworks often express a great deal about past societies, just as the contemporary arts of our society reflect our social and cultural values.

visual arts is postmodern in scope and is consistent with the postmodern era in which we reside.

As educators concerned with the nature of art, we might study the visual arts of many cultures, including western European, Egyptian, Asian, African, pre-Columbian, Mexican, Native American, Polynesian, and many other traditions. The visual arts, ranging from prehistoric to contemporary

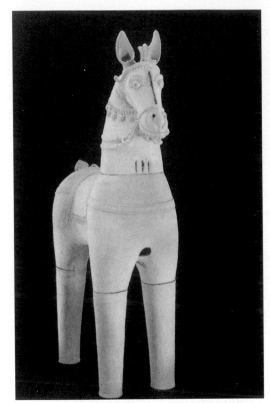

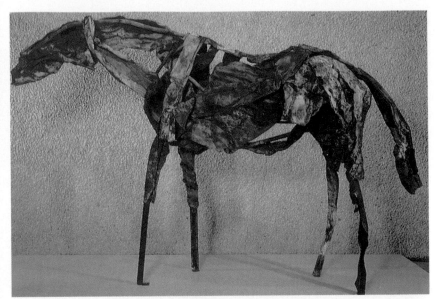

One way to study culture is to note differences in treatment of the same subject across cultures. Compare the differences (clockwise from top left) among a terracotta horse from India Freer Gallery of Art, Arthur M. Sackler Gallery, S1986.551. Deborah Butterfield's *Horse*, 1985, constructed of painted and rusted steel (Hirshhorn Museum and Sculpture Garden, Smithsonian Institution. Thomas M. Evans, Jerome L. Greene, Joseph H. Hirshhorn, and Sydney and Frances Lewis Purchase Fund, 1985. Photograph by Lee Stalsworth.); Divination cup, early-late 20th century, Yoruba peoples, Ekiti-igbomina region, Nigeria. Wood, pigment, 27.5 cm high, gift of Dr. and Mrs. Robert Kuhn, 92-10-1. (Eliot Elisofon Photographic Archives, National Museum of African Art, Smithsonian Institution, Washington, D.C. Photo Franko Khoury.); and Elie Nadelman, *Horse*, Hirshhorn Museum and Sculpture Garden, Smithsonian Institution, gift of Joseph H. Hirshhorn, 1966.

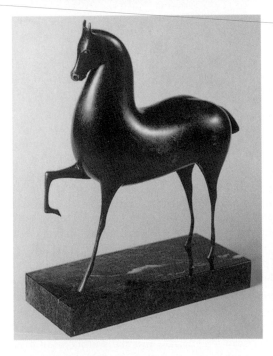

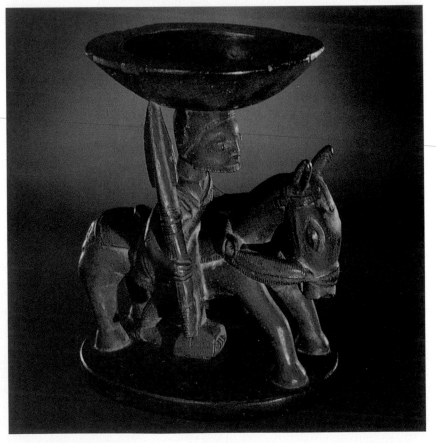

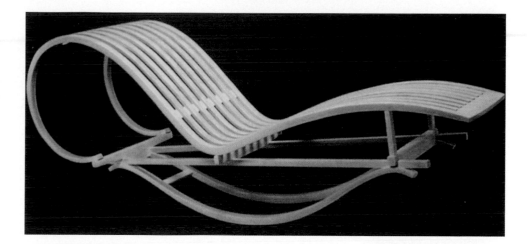

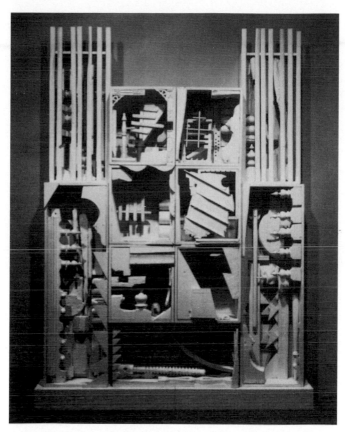

Louise Nevelson, *Dawn's Wedding Chapel II*, 1959. White painted wood, 116″ × 83″ × 10″ Collection of Whitney Museum of American Art, purchase, with funds from the Howard and Jean Lipman Foundation, Inc. 70.68 a-m. © 2000 Estate of Louise Nevelson/Artists Rights Society/ARS, New York. The artist collected and fashioned a wide variety of wood pieces and boxes from which she constructed this very large, totally white sculpture. The whiteness of the wood emphasizes the role of light and shadow for definition of three-dimensional form.

times, are worthy of study, including the ancient, medieval, Renaissance, and modern periods. Within the ranges of cultures and periods are numerous styles of art, such as Chinese T'ang dynasty, archaic Greek, African Benin, Italian baroque, surrealism, pop art, and neoexpressionism, that can provide fascinating insights into the nature of art on a worldwide basis.

Over time, as art has become increasingly complex and diverse, professions have grown out of needs to preserve, study, interpret, and judge artworks of today and from the past. A complex system of art museums, galleries, publications, markets, laws, and private and governmental agencies that support and oversee the art community has evolved. This system employs numerous art professionals, such as art edu-

cators, gallery directors, art dealers, museum curators, conservators, producers of art reproductions, and many more.

Four art disciplines provide the basic expertise that, in various combinations, endow most art professionals with the knowledge and skills necessary for their specific functions. These are the disciplines practiced by artists, art critics, art historians, and aestheticians. Each of these four disciplines or fields reflects many other influences, such as the political, anthropological, social, philosophical, and psychological.[6]

As they have for centuries, artists of today continue to create a wide range of art objects that vary in purpose, quality, and influence. Art critics respond to artworks as they perceive, describe, interpret, and judge them for the professional art world and the lay public. Art historians preserve, study, classify, interpret, and write about important art objects from the past. Aestheticians employ philosophical methods of inquiry and discourse to examine fundamental issues about the nature of art, such as its definition, questions of quality and value, and issues of creation and response to art.[7]

This book provides chapters that explore each of these art disciplines in greater detail (see Chapters 6–13).

Michael Hurwitz, *Rocking Chaise*, 1990. National Museum of American Art, Smithsonian Institution, gift of Anne and Ronald Abramson, the James Renwick Alliance and museum purchase made possible by the Smithsonian Institution Collections Acquisitions Program, Washington, D.C., U.S.A. © 1989 Michael Hurwitz. Art Resource, N.Y. Traditional distinctions between fine and applied art can be discerned in comparison of Nevelson's and Hurwitz's uses of wood as medium. The sculpture is considered fine art because it is free of any constraints other than those created by the artist. The elegantly designed wooden rocker falls into the applied art category because its design has limitations placed upon it by its functional character.

CONCEPTIONS OF THE LEARNER

Is the mind of a child a blank tablet waiting to receive the imprint of the teacher? Are learners passive receivers, active seekers, or some combination of both? Does learning take place most efficiently by using all the senses? Are drill and repetition necessary? Are there different learning styles? To what extent does learning transfer from one task or problem

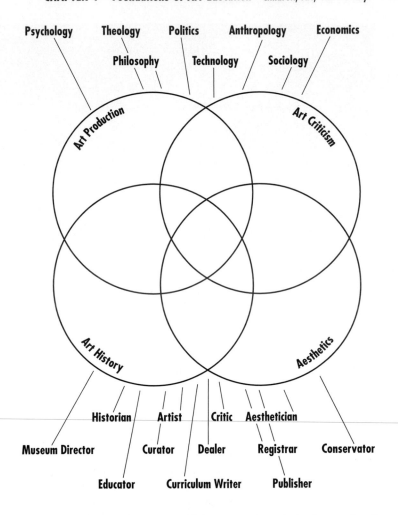

The four art disciplines, their interrelationships, and their relationships with the art professors.

Early Influences of Philosophy and Psychology

An eighteenth-century philosopher whose ideas influenced early childhood education, Jean-Jacques Rousseau, advocated that teaching should be related to childhood interests and that education should be concerned with the everyday life of the child.[8] Let children be children, Rousseau advocated, and let them learn through self-initiated activities.

Rousseau's ideas about the nature of children as learners were carried forth by fellow Europeans, such as Johann Pestalozzi, Johann Friedrich Herbart, and Friedrich Fröbel.[9] These powerful educators emphasized active engagement by learners in their surroundings, hands-on manipulation of materials, such as the basic geometric forms, and systematic ways to develop plans for instruction. The beginnings of the discourse that shapes the field of art education today can be traced to these pioneers and their many colleagues around the world.

An even stronger influence on education is to be found in the development of psychological thought. Although a detailed discussion is not possible here, these influences are too important to ignore. Interested readers are encouraged to study further what is only suggested on these pages.

Known as the father of progressive education, American philosopher John Dewey became a force in education early in the twentieth century, when children's desks were bolted to the classroom floor in straight rows and rote learning was a primary school activity. Dewey was greatly concerned with the relationship of learners to their environment and to the society in which they live.

Dewey regarded education as the "continuing re-creation of experience."[10] According to Dewey, education involves the direction and control of experience, and a meaningful experience implies active participation and control on the part of learners. Knowledge is not static, he insisted, nor is it gained in a static environment to be used in a static society. Dewey believed that education should be seen not as a preparation for life, but as life itself. Many of Dewey's ideas from a century in the past still ring true in today's dialogue in art education.[11]

A contemporary of Dewey, psychologist E. L. Thorndike, developed what came to be known as the *stimulus-response theory,* which held that learning consists of the establishment of a series of connections, or pathways, in the brain resulting from a specific response to stimulus.[12] His studies led Thorndike to believe that learning, to a large extent, was a matter of repetitive drill. Translated to school practice, this would result in the breaking down of a school subject into minute parts to be practiced and learned by students.[13]

to another? Is learning self-determined, or is it the result of influences from the environment? Obviously the views a teacher holds on these and other issues in learning theory will influence educational practice. Whether the various conceptions of learning are developed by individual educators or are implied by psychological investigation, their practical influence cannot be overlooked.

Contemporary education, like modern art, is not a product of the last three or four decades. Many of the basic ideas found both in aesthetics and teaching theory today may be traced to ideas held by philosophers and teachers who lived long ago, as well as to psychologists of more recent years.

Contemporary art education, then, is a field fed by the history of art and of general education. The development of current practice in art education is also supported by the investigation of psychologists into learning processes.

Almost opposite in emphasis to this theory, the system of psychology called *Gestalt* has had a strong influence on art education. Gestalt psychologists maintained that wholes are primary and parts derive their properties and behavior from them. The learner acquires knowledge by achieving "insight"— that is, by understanding the relationships among the various aspects of the learning situation.

Rudolf Arnheim, in his book *Art and Visual Perception* and other writings, provided art teachers with the clearest and most completely stated view of Gestalt psychology.[14] Works of art, as Gestalts or complete functional units, must be viewed as wholes. Within works of visual art, each part affects all the other parts simultaneously, so if one aspect is altered, such as the area or brightness of a color, the entire work is changed. In art and in Gestalt psychology, the whole is more than the sum of its parts.

Another influential view of learning in the twentieth century was that of behavioral psychology, in the work of B. F. Skinner and others.[15] Behaviorists considered the learner to be a relatively passive organism governed by stimuli supplied by the external environment. Through proper control of environmental stimuli, the learner's behavior could be, to a significant extent, predicted. This study of behavior as an objective science resulted in such developments as programmed instruction, which informed early uses of computers for instruction.

Influences of behavioral psychology on education are significant. In addition to early developments of computer-assisted instruction, behaviorism provided foundations for the writing of behavioral objectives for all aspects of the school curriculum, as well as practices of educational evaluation, measurement, and testing. Recurring periods of the accountability movement in education rely on behaviorist concepts. Critics of behaviorism in art education cite the theory's failure to fully account for the idiosyncratic, intuitive, and creative manifestations of human experience.[16]

These personal aspects of life and learning, however, are the primary focus of the humanistic psychologists, such as Abraham Maslow and Carl Rogers.[17] The humanists considered the learner free to make choices, and behavior as only the observable expression of an essentially private, inner world of being. The individual exists uniquely within a subjective world of feelings, emotions, and perceptions, many of which may not be acted out in behavior.

Much of the humanists' research took the form of clinical work with individual subjects, to provide therapy and gain understanding. The goal of education, according to Rogers, must be the facilitation of learning, for only the person who has learned how to learn, to adapt, and to change is an edu-

cated person. The humanistic view of education resonates with art educators who would emphasize the creative and expressive facets of the human personality.

Contemporary Views of the Learner

The work of Swiss psychologists Jean Piaget and Barbel Inhelder became influential worldwide beginning in the late 1950s.[18] Their theories in cognitive and developmental psychology had an extensive impact on education. Piaget and Inhelder examined such topics as the evolution of language and thought in children; the child's conceptions of the world, of number, time, and space; and other aspects of a child's intellectual development.

Piaget outlined three major stages or *periods* in the child's cognitive development: the sensorimotor period, the period of concrete operations, and the period of formal operations. According to Piaget, the child neither "flowers," as described by Rousseau, nor is "programmed" in the manner Skinner discussed. Rather, the child develops sequentially through Piaget's three stages. Intellectually, a child is qualitatively different from an adult, and this difference varies according to age and to progress within the three stages. For educators, this implies that knowledge of the learner's characteristics is essential to curricular and instructional decision making.[19]

Current research in cognitive psychology, as it is applied in education, emphasizes interactions between knowledge and various levels of thinking. Resnick and Klopfer point out that

> Before knowledge becomes truly generative—knowledge that can be used to interpret new situations, to solve problems, to think and reason, and to learn—students must elaborate and question what they are told, examine the new information in relation to other information, and build new knowledge structures.[20]

This view recognizes that learners require a certain *amount* of knowledge in order to use knowledge flexibly or creatively and that learning is easier once a generative knowledge base has been established. This poses for educators the problem of how to get students started in developing their base of generative knowledge so they can learn more easily and independently.

In art education this view of a "thinking curriculum" correlates well with the use of content and methods of inquiry derived from the four art disciplines. Art teachers can engage students in thinking and reasoning about art, questioning ideas about art, solving problems through active engagement, and being involved in their own creation of, response to, and examination of art objects. The art curriculum has the potential, as well, to engage students in several ways: through refined perceptions of aesthetic qualities of artworks; through analysis and interpretation of meanings, often metaphorical, embedded in works of art; through inquiry into social, political, and other contexts that give rise to artistic creation; and through pondering and discussing important perennial questions about the nature of art, art appreciation, and the creation of art.

As contemporary educators continue their pursuit of understanding learners, of how and why they learn, two major areas of scholarly research and theory have captured their attention. Howard Gardner's theory of multiple intelligences, published in 1985, has burgeoned as a topic for educational theory and practice.[21] More recently, and concurrently, an explosion of research in neuroscience has exciting implications for our understanding of learning.

Multiple Intelligences

Gardner's theory is based on knowledge of multiple and differentiated capacities of the brain as well as on scientific observation and analysis of the historical record of the range of human accomplishment. In place of the unitary view of intelligence represented by the intelligence quotient (IQ) scores, Gardner describes eight distinctive intelligences. Each person has all intelligences to some degree, and some persons develop one or more intelligences to high levels.

The important point is that all eight intelligences are valuable and can be developed within a comprehensive educational program. The traditional emphasis in schools on the linguistic and logical-mathematical intelligences, in Gardner's view, is too narrow and leaves many potentialities undeveloped in students.

During the past decade, many educators and school systems have applied the principles of Multiple Intelligence (MI) theory in attempts to broaden opportunities of all students to learn and develop.[22] Gardner encourages applications of his theory, but cautions that MI is not a quick solution for problems in education. "Educators who thoughtfully use the theory to support their larger educational goals find that it is a worthy partner in creating schools of excellence."[23]

This broader view of intelligence recognizes contributions of the arts for significant learning in schools. Prominent theoretician Elliot Eisner suggests a more comprehensive view of knowledge, and particularly the kind that comes out of the arts. "What we try to do when we take multiple or artistic intelligences seriously is to broaden the array of resources that are brought to bear on topics students study. Varied resources that provide different kinds of opportunities for youngsters with different proclivities (different intelligences) enable them to secure forms of understanding that would not be available without those resources."[24]

Brain Research

During the 1970s, research into the functions of the right and left hemispheres of the human brain sparked much discussion among educators. Studies supported the notion that the right and left brain hemispheres are somewhat specialized in their functions, with the left brain as the site of analytical, rational, logical, and linear thinking and the right brain as nonrational, intuitive, and holistic. This research lent support to the belief that the traditional narrow focus of education, with almost exclusive emphasis on logical-mathematical and verbal learning, overlooks significant abilities in students that could and should be developed in schools.[25] Through this discussion the notions of multiple intelligences and artistic intelligences were cited in support of more emphasis on the arts, where intuition and the nonrational, nonverbal aspects of thought and expression are valued.

Study of the brain has progressed far from these early studies of brain hemispheres. Following a resolution from the United States Congress in 1989, President George Bush officially proclaimed the 1990s the "Decade of the Brain." The promise of this proclamation has been met with an unprecedented explosion of knowledge on how the human brain works. With the aid of new electronic technologies that can map brain activity, "we have learned more about the brain in the past five years than in the past hundred years."[26]

How can knowledge of brain physiology and function influence education, which is traditionally informed by issues of philosophy, psychology, and economics? Philosophy and psychology often deal with broad questions of human values and potentials, yet historically they have been influenced as well by understandings of human physiology. Neuroscience is a specialized field separate from education, yet the new brain research promises to extend understanding of learning in ways that, at the very least, suggest more efficient and appropriate educational practices for learners of all ages.

Some of the findings of the neuroscientists are particularly relevant to arts educators. The study of music, especially, has proven to be fruitful. The work of researcher Frances Rauscher, for example, made connections between music and spatial task performance.[27] Other studies linked music and

The Intelligences, in Gardner's Words

- Linguistic intelligence is the capacity to use language, your native language, and perhaps other languages, to express what's on your mind and to understand other people. Poets really specialize in linguistic intelligence, but any kind of writer, orator, speaker, lawyer, or a person for whom language is an important stock in trade highlights linguistic intelligence.

- People with a highly developed logical-mathematical intelligence understand the underlying principles of some kind of a causal system, the way a scientist or a logician does; or can manipulate numbers, quantities, and operations, the way a mathematician does.

- Spatial intelligence refers to the ability to represent the spatial world internally in your mind—the way a sailor or airplane pilot navigates the large spatial world, or the way a chess player or sculptor represents a more circumscribed spatial world. Spatial intelligence can be used in the arts or in the sciences. If you are spatially intelligent and oriented toward the arts, you are more likely to become a painter or a sculptor or an architect than, say, a musician or a writer. Similarly, certain sciences like anatomy or topology emphasize spatial intelligence.

- Bodily kinesthetic intelligence is the capacity to use your whole body or parts of your body—your hand, your fingers, your arms—to solve a problem, make something, or put on some kind of a production. The most evident examples are people in athletics or the performing arts, particularly dance or acting.

- Musical intelligence is the capacity to think in music, to be able to hear patterns, recognize them, remember them, and perhaps manipulate them. People who have a strong musical intelligence don't just remember music easily—they can't get it out of their minds, it's so omnipresent. Now, some people will say, "Yes, music is important, but it's a talent, not an intelligence." And I say, "Fine, let's call it a talent." But, then we have to leave the word *intelligent* out of *all* discussions of human abilities. You know, Mozart was very smart!

- Interpersonal intelligence is understanding other people. It's an ability we all need, but is at a premium if you are a teacher, clinician, salesperson, or politician. Anybody who deals with other people has to be skilled in the interpersonal sphere.

- Intrapersonal intelligence refers to having an understanding of yourself, of knowing who you are, what you can do, what you want to do, how you react to things, which things to avoid, and which things to gravitate toward. We are drawn to people who have a good understanding of themselves because those people tend not to screw up. They tend to know what they can do. They tend to know what they can't do. And they tend to know where to go if they need help.

- Naturalist intelligence designates the human ability to discriminate among living things (plants, animals) as well as sensitivity to other features of the natural world (clouds, rock configurations). This ability was clearly of value in our evolutionary past as hunters, gatherers, and farmers; it continues to be central in such roles as botanist or chef. I also speculate that much of our consumer society exploits the naturalist intelligences, which can be mobilized in the discrimination among cars, sneakers, kinds of makeup, and the like. The kind of pattern recognition valued in certain of the sciences may also draw upon naturalist intelligence.

SOURCE: Kathy Checkley, "The First Seven . . . and the Eighth: A Conversation with Howard Gardner," *Educational Leadership* 55, no. 1 (November 1997): 8–13.

learning and documented actual changes in brain physiology in professional musicians.[28]

Four general findings of brain research appear to have implications for learning and, therefore, for teaching, curriculum, and education in general:[29]

> Finding One: *The brain changes physiologically as a result of experience. The environment in which a brain operates determines to a large degree the functioning ability of that brain.*

For parents, caregivers, and educators, the finding that the electrical activity of brain cells changes the physical structure of the brain is perhaps the most significant discovery of neuroscience. The first three years of a child's life are apparently even more important than many have supposed. Major capacities of each child's brain are shaped and reinforced during the first ten years of life. These findings underscore the importance of hands-on parenting, of finding the time to cuddle a baby, talk with a toddler, and provide a young child with stimulating experiences.

By the age of three, a child who is neglected or abused bears marks that, if not indelible, are exceedingly difficult to erase.[30] The positive corollary, that a rich and caring environment also makes a difference for children, is encouraging for parents and teachers. Education has a major influence on the learner and, therefore, changes not only the mind, but the brain itself. The richness of the educational environment can have a positive effect on each child's capacity to learn.

> Finding Two: *IQ is not fixed at birth.*

At birth a baby's brain contains about 100 billion neurons, virtually all the nerve cells it will ever have. But the pattern of wiring between them has yet to stabilize. Up to this point, says neurobiologist Carla Shatz, "what the brain has done is lay out circuits that are its best guess about what's required for vision, for language, for whatever." From birth onward, it is up to neural activity, driven by a flood of sensory experiences, to take this rough blueprint and progressively refine it.[31]

> Finding Three: *Some abilities are acquired more easily during certain sensitive periods, or "windows of opportunity."*

Some of the brain study findings are truly amazing and will revise our views of the capabilities of very young children with respect to their motor, cognitive, and emotional development. For example, according to neuroscientists, an infant's brain can perceive every possible sound from every language. By ten months, babies have learned to screen out foreign sounds and to focus on the sounds of their native language.[32] This window for language development is wide open for infants during the period when they must learn language. Then the window gradually closes, although it will never completely shut.

These windows of opportunity represent critical periods when the brain demands certain types of input to create or consolidate neural networks, such as for acquiring language and emotional control. "Certainly one can learn new information and skills at any age. But what the child learned *during* that window period will strongly influence what is learned after the window closes."[33]

The brain's greatest growth spurt declines around age ten, when the balance between synapse creation and atrophy abruptly shifts. Over the next several years, during a period of "use it or lose it," the brain will ruthlessly destroy its weakest synapses, preserving only those that have been transformed by experience. By the end of adolescence, around age eighteen, the brain has declined in plasticity but increased in power. Abilities that have been nurtured and reinforced are ready to blossom.[34]

> Finding Four: *Learning is strongly influenced by emotion.*

Researchers have verified what many teachers already know—that the stronger the emotion connected with an experience, the stronger the memory of that experience. Through chemical processes, the brain recognizes the connection between emotion and learning. When teachers are able to add emotional input to learning experiences to make them more meaningful and exciting, the brain deems the information more important and retention is increased. At the same time, emotions of threat or fear can sidetrack learning.

The role of emotion in learning is another concept that has been discussed for years by educators and psychological theorists.[35] At one point, theorists attempted to separate cognition and affect for development of educational objectives.[36] Now, brain research has focused attention on the essential role of emotion in learning and the concept of "emotional intelligence" has entered the discourse of psychologists and educators.[37]

Researcher Marian Diamond believes that enriched environments unmistakably influence the brain's growth and learning. According to Diamond, an enriched environment for children:

- Includes a steady source of positive emotional support;
- Provides a nutritious diet with enough protein, vitamins, minerals, and calories;

- Stimulates all the senses (but not necessarily all at once!);
- Has an atmosphere free of undue pressure and stress but suffused with a degree of pleasurable intensity;
- Presents a series of novel challenges that are neither too easy nor too difficult for the child at his or her stage of development;
- Allows social interaction for a significant percentage of activities;
- Promotes the development of a broad range of skills and interests that are mental, physical, aesthetic, social, and emotional;
- Gives the child an opportunity to choose many of his or her efforts and to modify them;
- Provides an enjoyable atmosphere that promotes exploration and the fun of learning; and
- Allows the child to be an active participant rather than a passive observer.[38]

This blueprint for a happy and healthy learning environment for children reinforces many of the ideas held by educators and psychologists mentioned earlier. Many teachers have come to similar conclusions after years of experience working closely with children and observing how they learn.

Brain research also provides support for the notion of multiple intelligences and definitely underlines the importance of the arts in the education of every child, beginning in the very earliest years. Educator and writer on brain research Robert Sylwester writes:

> Evidence from the brain sciences and evolutionary psychology increasingly suggests that the arts (along with such functions as language and math) play an important role in brain development and maintenance—so it's a serious matter for schools to deny children direct curricular access to the arts.[39]

Education writer Pat Wolfe counsels educators to reflect on their practice, engage in substantive dialogue about teaching and learning, and study new research findings to determine for themselves the relevance for education. She adds, "Brain research is not a program to be implemented in the schools; neuroscience does not prove that any particular strategy or method works. Rather, the research is adding to our knowledge base, helping us better understand how the brain learns—or doesn't learn—and why."[40]

The brain research is new, exciting, and apparently redolent with heady implications. Nevertheless, as scientists and educators alike caution, the road between the scientific laboratory and the school classroom can be long and winding with many detours. Educators must always maintain the professional autonomy and integrity that accompany the great responsibility they have to children. This means that educators should carefully and critically assess recommendations that derive from the neurosciences, relying, as always, on their own training, experience, and good professional judgment.

VALUES OF SOCIETY

Educators' concerns with the nature of art and their conceptions of how young people learn are balanced, in the process of education, by the values of society. In a democracy these values are brought to bear on education by the taxpaying public, usually through community school systems, election of school boards, and hiring of school administrators, faculty, and staff to carry out the wishes of the electorate. Public schools in the United States have been responsive also to the needs and values of the larger society, sometimes on a national level. Changes in education brought about by space exploration, the civil rights movement, the need for safe drivers on our streets and highways, the problems of alcohol and drug abuse, and the threat of AIDS are only a few examples of how the needs and values of society influence what occurs in school classrooms.

Art education in the United States has been influenced no less by societal values than by innovations in art or advances in psychology. The programs of art instruction initiated by Walter Smith, for example, were motivated by the business community's need to design goods that could compete on an international basis. The creativity and self-expression emphasis of Viktor Lowenfeld was based on a particular view of child development. The position taken by this book emphasizes a content program based on the works and methods of inquiry of artists, art critics, art historians, and aestheticians.

The art program is an especially appropriate and effective place in the general school curriculum to deal with social issues, problems, and values. This is precisely because the history of art is replete with the most vivid images of social values, such as Picasso's masterpiece protesting war and violence, *Guernica;* an Indian statue of a contemplative *Buddha;* Judy Chicago's feminist statement, *The Dinner Party;* or a Navajo wedding basket. The art of any cultural or ethnic group often reveals values held by that group. Understanding of art created within a particular culture requires knowledge of the purposes, functions, and meanings of artworks within the context of their creation.

The history of art education includes significant emphasis on democratic values. The freedom necessary for the success of an aesthetic act cannot be separated from the freedom of thought and action that is the prerogative of individuals living in a democracy. Art educators have been among the pioneers in developing a pedagogy compatible with democratic practices.[41] What assisted them as much as anything else was their understanding that art could not be taught successfully unless it was presented in an atmosphere designed to develop individual, and at times possibly nonconformist, expression. It is the emphasis that art education places on personal decision making that often separates art classes from many others.

As individuals we become involved in interpersonal relationships and in social or political events. As citizens we learn to respect and live with our neighbors in various social contexts. Good citizens often improve the quality of everyone's life by taking appropriate actions to affect the broad social and environmental issues confronting the community at large.[42] These broad social concerns are present as themes in many significant works of art. They become relevant whenever art education extends our view beyond the concerns of individuals to the values of society.[43]

Even aesthetic values have become the focus of social issues. Beginning in the 1920s, critics expressed serious concern about the general level of aesthetic taste in the United States. As early as 1934, Dewey asked, "Why is the architecture of our cities so unworthy of a fine civilization? It is not from lack of materials nor lack of technical capacity … yet it is not merely slums but the apartments of the well-to-do that are aesthetically repellent."[44]

Statements like this offered a challenge to education, for such condemnation referred indirectly to the masses of people educated in public schools. The inference was that the art education program was not effective in developing the ability to recognize good design from bad. Art educators continue to seriously consider methods of developing critical thinking and aesthetic sensitivity in children. Aesthetic issues continue to be central to the social and environmental needs of society. The impact of the mass media, the changing faces of cities, forms of suburbia, and the pollution of natural resources are factors of modern living in all parts of the world and need to be brought to the attention of children. How effective art teachers can be in their attempts to create visual sensitivity is still a matter of speculation. One thing is certain: The future designers and planners who share the task of creating environments that humanize and enhance our lives are students in our schools at this very moment.

Public Attitudes in the Schools

The influences of democracy and freedom already discussed are fundamental and have been in operation since the founding of this country. Other values and attitudes toward art perpetuated from early times have not all been beneficial to art education. Unlike citizens of countries with longstanding cultural accomplishments, American pioneers did not grow up in the midst of artistic and architectural traditions. Aesthetic and artistic concerns often were low in priority, because the tasks of survival and practical living required much time and energy. In place of an aristocracy, the traditional patrons of the arts, our thriving democracy produced business leaders and politicians. Because business and politics are often based in practicality, only when the arts could be viewed as making a profitable contribution were they placed higher in priority. The attitude that art is a frill to be turned to only after the "real work" is done is still quite evident and is largely the reason that art has yet to achieve a place in the school curriculum comparable to the "three Rs," science, and social studies. Nevertheless, art education has progressed in theory and in professional practice to the point where enlightened educators view it as an essential rather than as a peripheral aspect of a balanced curriculum.[45]

Recent research reports very significant gains for art as a regular subject in the school curriculum. In his report of a study conducted in 1989, Leonhard stated that the offering of art is "almost universal in elementary schools and over 80 percent of elementary schools with art programs have a written curriculum for each grade." In comparison to results of a similar study in 1962, "art education has developed impressively and merits the high level of parental support it garners."[46]

A 1995 national study by the National Center for Education Statistics (NCES) reported that the visual arts are offered in 85 percent of public elementary schools and 89 percent of secondary schools. The majority of public elementary schools indicated that a specially equipped space is provided for art instruction.[47]

These positive attitudes toward art education might well be the result of the dedicated service of thousands of art teachers during the past fifty years. At least the positive change in attitude toward the arts—as verified by attendance records for art museums, theaters, concerts, and so on—directly correlates with the increased attention paid to the teaching of art in the schools.

The quality of art programs varies widely from state to state and from school district to school district according to the values of legislators, school leaders, and communities, and according to varying degrees of financial stability. Art educators often are called upon to advocate support for their programs from parents and from school and community groups. One effect of the seemingly constant need to justify art education is the development of art programs based on well-articulated, convincing rationales.[48]

CHANGE IN ART EDUCATION

The history of art education is a fascinating, ongoing tapestry of interwoven threads that form a complex design. Three of the most prominent threads—the nature of art, conceptions of the learner, and the values of society—have already been discussed. Others represent the works of individual artists, writers, and teachers, and the advances in technology, curriculum projects, and even legislation. It is difficult to gain a clear view of the emerging pattern while the design is still being developed.[49] The following brief discussion is an attempt to identify some of the more prominent threads in the historical development of art education.

In the United States, for instance, the origins of art education in the schools are related to the requirements of business and industry or the goals of society in mid-nineteenth-century New England. American business leaders witnessed how the English had raised their standards of industrial design in order to compete favorably with European business in taste, style, and beauty. England's schools of design were revitalized in the 1850s, and they produced a corps of skilled designers for industry. In the United States, a few shrewd business leaders noted cause and effect and urged skeptical merchants and manufacturers to see the practical necessity of art education for competition in world trade markets. Following the British example, the Americans recruited Walter Smith, a graduate of England's South Kensington School, and appointed him concurrently director of drawing in the public schools of Boston and state director of art education for Massachusetts. Smith began his monumental task in 1871, just a few months after the Massachusetts legislature passed the first law in the United States making drawing a required subject in the public schools.

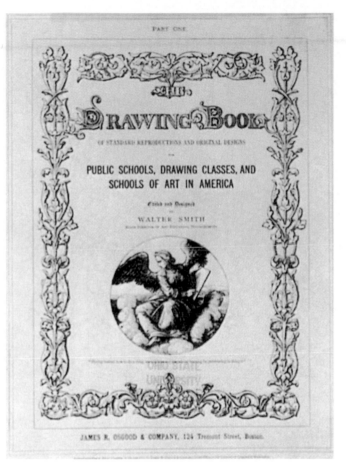

Title page of Walter Smith's plan for art education in American schools.

Walter Smith approached his work with great vision and vitality and began the development of a sequential curriculum for industrial drawing. Within nine years, he had founded and directed the Massachusetts Normal Art School, the first in the country (now the Massachusetts College of Art and still the only state-supported art school in the country), and had implemented his curriculum in all Massachusetts primary grades up to high school. In addition, Smith's writings and the teachers trained at the Normal School extended Smith's influence across the country. Smith's publications included a volume entitled *Art Education, Scholastic and Industrial* and many series of drawing books for instructional purposes. In format, the series of drawing books were very similar. Usually the purpose of a series was "the laying of a good foundation for more advanced art training." The following statements about the particular aims of the books are typical:

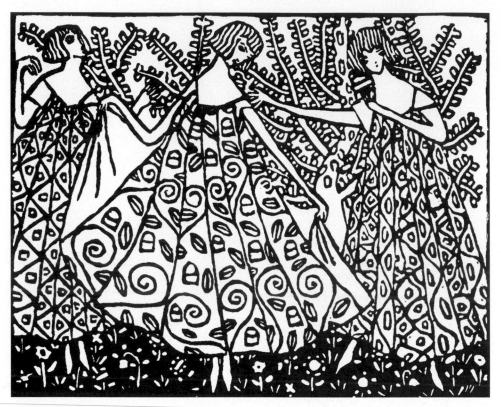

Example of a linoleum block print by a student in Franz Cizek's class in Vienna.

1. To train the eye in the accurate perception of form, size, and proportion and to exactness in the measurement of distances and angles

2. To train the hand to freedom and rapidity of execution

3. To train the memory to accurate recollection of the forms and arrangements of objects

4. To cultivate and refine the taste by the study, delineation, and recollection of beautiful forms

This beginning of art education was quite different from what we experience today. Smith's instruction led teachers and children through a rather rigid sequence of freehand, model, memory, and geometric and perspective drawing. Rote learning, copying, and repetition were common aspects of the sequential curriculum.

Smith's method of presenting the content depended upon class instructions and relied heavily upon the use of the blackboard, from which the students copied the problem the teacher drew. Prints and drawings were also copied by the students. Smith justified copy work in two ways: that it was

the only rational way to learn, since drawing was essentially copying; and that it was the only practical way to teach, since classes were large and only a very limited amount of time was allotted in the school week to drawing.[50]

Although we would reject this type of art program today, Smith's accomplishments were well ahead of his time. His program broke new ground and gave art education in the United States a firm foundation on which to build, a status the subject had never before had, and a precedent that could never be ignored.[51]

Cizek and Children's Artistic Expression

Until the advent of expressionism or emphasis on children's creative art production, art education remained remarkably aloof from artistic tradition. Expressionism first had its effect on art education largely through the work of one outstanding teacher, Franz Cizek. Cizek, an Austrian, went to Vienna in 1865 to study art. In 1904 he accepted the position of chief of the Department of Experimentation and Research at the Vienna School of Applied Arts. His now-famous art classes for children were developed in this department.

Cizek eliminated certain activities from these classes, such as making color charts and photographic drawing of natural objects. Instead, he encouraged children to present, in visual form, their personal reactions to happenings in their lives.[52] In the output produced under his guidance—much of which has been preserved—the children depicted themselves at play and doing the things that naturally engage the attention and interest of the young. Cizek always maintained that it was not his aim to develop artists. Instead, he held as his one goal the development of the creative power that he found in all children and that he felt could blossom in accordance with "natural laws."[53]

Much of the work produced in Cizek's classrooms reveals the charm of expression of which children, under sympathetic teachers, are capable. Some of the output may now seem sentimental, overdirected, and disclosing of pretty mannerisms, such as a profusion of stars in the sky areas of compositions or a stylized expression of childish innocence in the faces. These mannerisms imply that some of the classes may have been highly structured by today's standards and that the artistic development of the children was brought about more by Cizek's teachers than by the "natural laws" that Cizek advocated. Nevertheless, Cizek is an important figure in art education, and his work deserves the widespread admiration it has received. The contemporary belief that children, under certain conditions, are capable of expressing themselves in a personal, creative, and acceptable manner derives largely from his demonstrations in Vienna. Cizek's ideas contrasted completely with those of Walter Smith.

The Teachers of Art

Other threads appear in the warp and weft of the history of art education. Great teachers emerged, such as Arthur Wesley Dow of Columbia University, Walter Sargent of the University of Chicago, and Royal B. Farnum of the Rhode Island School of Design.[54] Dow was concerned with analyzing the structure of art and sought to develop a systematic way in which it could be taught. He developed and taught what we know today as the elements and principles of design. Within this formalist view, the artist works with line, value, and color, composing these elements to create symmetry, repetition, unity, transition, and subordination, which can be controlled to achieve harmonious relationships. Concepts and language developed by Dow are considered essential fundamentals, and many contemporary art curricula are still organized purely on the basis of a list of design elements and principles.

Walter Sargent's contribution to art education came from his focus on the process by which children learn to draw. He described in acceptable terms three factors that he believed influence children's ability to draw. First, children must want to say something, must have some idea or image to express through drawing. Second, children need to work from devices, such as three-dimensional models or pictures, in making drawings. Finally, children often learn to draw one thing well but not others, so that skill in drawing is specific; a person could be good at drawing houses or boats and not good at drawing horses or cows.

It is a tribute to Sargent that these three points are echoed in the literature of art education, such as the work of Brent and Marjorie Wilson:

> The process of losing innocence in art involves the acquisition of artistic conventions—this imitative process which has for too long remained hidden . . . this borrowing and working from pre-existing images sometimes began before the age of six.
>
> Individuals employ a separate program for each object which they depict. . . . In the case of those objects that are well drawn, they have repeatedly played essentially the same program sharpening their ability to recall the desired configuration easily from memory.[55]

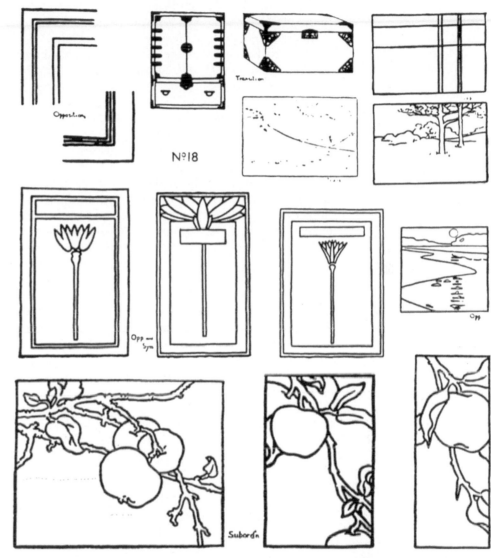

Arthur Wesley Dow's debt to Japanese handling of placement of form in composition is evident in this illustration from his book *Composition*, 1899. Courtesy University of California Press.

Following Cizek's focus on creative art activity for young children and the values of the progressive education movement inspired by Dewey, art educators in the United States, such as Margaret Mathias and Belle Boas, were influential in shaping the field through their teaching, writing, and professional activism. Mathias wrote of the natural growth of children's expression through art and also affirmed her belief in the value of art appreciation "for understanding the art of others." In this she anticipated the work of Farnum and others who directed attention to the viewing of art by professional artists. At the same time, Boas projected the earlier work of Dow while she called attention in her book to development of "good taste" and aesthetic judgment in the lives of children through their study of design principles.[56]

Royal B. Farnum was one of the many art educators involved in the *picture study* movement during the 1920s. When it became possible through advances in printing technology to produce inexpensive color reproductions of paintings, many art educators of that era took the opportunity to present children with lessons in art appreciation. It was characteristic that the pictures chosen for study were not contemporary with the time, presented a narrow standard of "beauty," and often carried a religious or moral message. In his book *Education through Pictures: The Practical Picture Study Course,* published in 1931, Farnum lists no works of art by Picasso, Kollwitz, Cezanne, van Gogh, or even Monet or Cassatt.[57] Instead, the works are chosen from earlier times, with at least fourteen of the total of eighty being pictures on religious themes.

Although it is easy to be critical of early attempts at art appreciation, we must recognize the pioneering nature of this type of art education. Nevertheless, as Eisner pointed out, "Until very recently art education as a field has been quite unresponsive to contemporary developments in the world of art. Art education until as late as the middle of the twentieth century was more a reflection of lay artistic tastes than it was a leader in shaping those tastes and in enabling students to experience the work of the artistic frontiers of their day."[58]

The Owatonna Project

The Owatonna Art Project in Minnesota was the most successful of several community art projects funded by the federal government in the 1930s. The object of the Owatonna Project was to create art activities based on the aesthetic interests of community members. The project promoted "home decoration, school and public park plantings [and] visually interesting window displays in commercial areas."[59] The idea was to apply principles of art in everyday life for a richer experience. The Owatonna Project was a successful cooperative effort that involved many sectors of the community, the local schools, and the University of Minnesota. Unfortunately, it was interrupted by the outbreak of World War II and never achieved the impact it might have had under different circumstances. Although art existed in the regular school program, the Owatonna Project was community rather than studio centered. In this regard, it represented a

move away from the child-centered approach of Franz Cizek, as Cizek rejected the vocational goals of Walter Smith.

The Bauhaus

Another influence in the late 1930s was the Bauhaus, a German professional art school committed to integrating the technology of its day into the artist's work. As a result of its influence, modern art materials, photography, and visual investigation involving sensory awareness found their way into the secondary school art program. Interest in the technology of art (notably in the communications media), concern for the elements of design, and an adventurous attitude toward new materials are all consistent with the Bauhaus attitude. The Bauhaus stimulated a growing interest in a multi-sensory approach to art, as well as a tendency to incorporate aesthetic concerns into environmental and industrial design, especially in secondary schools.

Teachers who were influenced by the Bauhaus regarded design in a much broader, more inclusive way than did Dow or Sargent. Bauhaus teachers and their students who moved to America were some of the "gifts" this country inherited from Nazi Germany.

Creativity and Art Education

Art educators' interest in the development of creativity is well documented by the titles of prominent books published in the field, especially during the 1940s and 1950s. Victor D'Amico's *Creative Teaching in Art,* Viktor Lowenfeld's *Creative and Mental Growth* and, later, Manuel Barkan's *Through Art to Creativity* were three of the most influential.[60] Long an interest of art educators, creativity was also the focus of considerable attention and study by psychologists. The progressive education movement of the 1920s had laid a groundwork for this interest by relating the free and expressive aspects of art creativity to a theory of personality development.

When the movement declined in the late 1950s, members of the American Psychological Association, acting on the suggestion of their president, J. P. Guilford assumed leadership in applying more rigorous research techniques to such problems as the analysis of creative behavior and the identification of characteristic behaviors of professionals in both the arts and sciences.[61] Within a decade, what had formerly existed on the level of a philosophical mystique was replaced by scientific inquiry.

The research tools of psychologists of the time—tests, measurements, computers, and clinical methods—were brought to bear on the processes of artistic creation. In considering the creative process, psychologists went beyond the visual arts and established commonalities of experience among all types of people involved in solutions to creative problems. Creativity in the schools was no longer the private preserve of the art room. As a result of discovering how the creative process served teachers of other subjects, ideas emerged that would permit art teachers to view their profession with new understanding. Art teachers have long suspected that art, taught under proper conditions, can promote values that transcend the boundaries of the art lesson.

The work of Viktor Lowenfeld emerged as the single most influential force in shaping the field of art education from the early 1950s into the 1980s. Lowenfeld was head of a large doctoral program in art education at Pennsylvania State University. Many of the graduates from his program became established in other colleges and universities around the country and in positions at state and school-district levels. *Creative and Mental Growth* became the classic work in art education, was translated into other languages, and continued to be published in numerous editions, even after Lowenfeld's death in 1960.

Lowenfeld espoused many of the views of art education that we have noted from the time of Pestalozzi through the era of progressive education. He combined a primary emphasis on the development of creativity with his theory of personality integration through art activities. This involved such areas of personality growth as physical, social, creative, and mental. Almost exclusive emphasis was placed on art production activities, beginning at very early ages and involving a wide range of art materials to encourage children to explore and create. Lowenfeld emphasized the supportive and motivational roles of teachers more than explicit instruction. Teachers were counseled to beware of imposing adult concepts and views on children, who were encouraged to develop their natural creative powers.

Cognitive researchers are currently reexamining creativity. In addition, new insights are emerging from brain research and sociology. Creativity theories are emerging that combine ideas from these three major areas of research.

Toward Art Content

The creativity rationale for art education and the interest in personality development so strongly advocated by Lowenfeld

and others dominated the field well into the 1960s, when a new generation of scholars and educators began to suggest, for the first time, that the study of art was worthwhile per se. Attention was focused on art as a body of knowledge that could be learned by children. Justifications for art in the schools arose from art's value to other areas of concern, such as the development of competent industrial designers, the development of perception, achievement of general educational goals, or cultural literacy. Content-centered writers justified the study of art on the basis of what functions art performs in society and why it is important to understand those functions.[62] This position, as Eisner pointed out, "emphasizes the kinds of contributions to human experience and understanding that only art can provide; it emphasizes what is indigenous and unique to art."[63]

Many contemporary art programs recognize a body of art knowledge that fosters understanding art and responding to art as well as activities that result primarily in art making. Students are exposed to the visual arts of the ancient and modern eras through films, slides, and reproductions, as well as through actual art objects in galleries, studios, and museums, when possible. Awareness of the world of art and of the concepts, language, and approaches used in responding to art not only helps students understand and appreciate the art of others but also increases students' sensitivity to their own artwork.

Many art educators today advocate a teaching philosophy that encourages students to think about the relationship of art, ecology, and community, following the earlier work of June King McFee and others.[64] They emphasize a curriculum that is interdisciplinary, action oriented, and based on social values. Teaching is aimed at fostering awareness of interconnections between community and environment and focuses on concepts of environmental design, ecological art, and involvement with community. As we can see, the three fundamental emphases for any program of education—content centered, child centered, and society centered—continue to be advocated and implemented within the diversity of contemporary art education.

SOME BASIC BELIEFS IN CONTEMPORARY ART EDUCATION

Art education today is still very much a composite of what has gone before. It is not difficult to identify the many threads in the pattern that we have discussed. The development of strong professional associations, such as the National Art

Education Association (NAEA) in the United States, Canadian Society for Education through Art (CSEA) in Canada, the National Society for Education in Art and Design (NSEAD) in the United Kingdom, and the International Society for Education through Art (InSEA) as a world organization (see Appendix B); the publication of an impressive body of literature in the field, including burgeoning research literature; and the emergence of well-founded teacher-education programs in colleges and universities have led to an enlightened group of art educators. This increased level of professional communication has not resulted in a narrow unanimity of thought about the goals of art education in contemporary society, although some points are agreed on by most art educators.

The development of national standards for the arts was accomplished in 1994 in response to the Goals 2000: Educate America legislation passed by the U.S. Congress and signed by President William Jefferson Clinton. The voluntary standards provide a general guideline for states and local school districts to adapt, adopt, or reject. The introduction to the national standards included the following general statements of values, which were accepted by the national organizations for art, music, theatre, and dance education.[65]

- The arts have both intrinsic and instrumental value; that is, they have worth in and of themselves and can also be used to achieve a multitude of purposes.

- The arts play a valued role in creating cultures and building civilizations. Although each arts discipline makes its unique contributions to culture, society, and the lives of individuals, their connections to each other enable the arts disciplines to produce more than any of them could produce alone.
- The arts are a way of knowing. Students grow in their ability to apprehend their world when they learn the arts. As they create artworks, they learn how to express themselves and how to communicate with others.
- The arts have value and significance for daily life. They provide personal fulfillment, whether in vocational settings, avocational pursuits, or leisure.
- Lifelong participation in the arts is a valuable part of a life fully lived and should be cultivated.
- No one can claim to be truly educated who lacks basic knowledge and skills in the arts.
- The arts should be an integral part of a program of general education for all students.

In addition to these views about the arts in education, many art educators share the belief that all children possess both innate creative and appreciative abilities that can be nurtured through art instruction.

Of course, views expressed in this book are subjects for dialogue within the teaching profession. Awareness of issues will assist teachers in evaluating their own experiences.

NOTES

1. June King McFee, *Preparation for Art* (San Francisco: Wadsworth, 1961), p. 170.

2. Ralph Tyler, *Basic Principles of Curriculum and Instruction* (Chicago: University of Chicago Press, 1950).

3. Ellen Dissanayake has explored in depth the origins and functions of the arts in human culture in her book, *What Is Art For?* (Seattle: University of Washington Press, 1988). She speculates that the arts evolved through making socially significant activities memorable and special and are therefore essential to human survival.

4. Albert Elsen, *Purposes of Art*, 2d ed. (New York: Holt, Rinehart and Winston, 1968).

5. Edmund Feldman, *The Artist* (Englewood Cliffs, NJ: Prentice-Hall, Inc., 1982).

6. Gilbert Clark, Michael Day, and Dwaine Greer, "Discipline-based Art Education: Becoming Students of Art," in *Discipline-based Art Education: Origins, Meaning, and Development*, ed. Ralph Smith (Urbana: University of Illinois Press, 1989).

7. For discussions of each of these four art disciplines as sources for art curricula, see the essays by Frederick Spratt, Eugene Kleinbauer, Howard Risatti, and Donald Crawford in *Discipline-based Art Education*, ed. Ralph Smith, op. cit.

8. Jean-Jacques Rousseau, *Emile*, trans. Barbara Foxley (London: J. M. Dent and Sons, 1977).

9. See Pestalozzi's novel, *Leonard and Gertrude* (1781), and his book on education, *How Gertrude Teaches Her Children*

(1801). Herbart wrote *ABC of Sense Perception* to explain Pestalozzi's views. See Herbart's *Text Book of Psychology* (1816) and *Outlines of Educational Doctrine* (1835).

10. John Dewey, *Philosophy in Civilization* (New York: Minton, Balch and Co., 1931).

11. John Dewey, *Art As Experience* (New York: Capricorn Books, G. P. Putnam's Sons, 1934).

12. In 1913 and 1914 Thorndike published his three-volume *Educational Psychology,* comprising vol. I, *The Original Nature of Man;* vol. II, *The Psychology of Learning;* and vol. III, *Work, Fatigue, and Individual Differences.*

13. E. L. Thorndike, *Educational Psychology: Briefer Course* (New York: Teacher's College, 1914), p. 173.

14. Rudolf Arnheim, *Art and Visual Perception,* 4th ed. (Berkeley: University of California Press, 1964).

15. Examples of B. F. Skinner's writings include *Walden Two* (New York: Macmillan, 1948); *Science and Human Behavior* (New York: Macmillan, 1953); and *Beyond Freedom and Dignity* (New York: Knopf, 1971).

16. Frank Milhollan and Bill Forisha, *From Skinner to Rogers: Contrasting Approaches to Education* (Lincoln, NE: Professional Educators, 1972), p. 46.

17. Abraham H. Maslow, "Existential Psychology—What's In It for Us?" in *Existential Psychology,* ed. Rollo May (New York: Random House, 1961); and Carl R. Rogers, *Freedom to Learn* (Columbus, OH: Merrill, 1969).

18. See, for example, Barbel Inhelder and Jean Piaget, *The Growth of Logical Thinking from Childhood to Adolescence* (New York: Basic Books, 1958), and *The Early Growth of Logic in the Child* (New York: Norton, 1964); and Jean Piaget, *Science of Education and the Psychology of the Child* (New York: Viking, 1971).

19. Kenneth Lansing, "The Research of Jean Piaget and Its Implications for Art Education in the Elementary School," *Studies in Art Education* 7, no. 2 (spring 1966).

20. Lauren B. Resnick and Leopold E. Klopfer, eds., *Toward the Thinking Curriculum: Current Cognitive Research* (Alexandria, VA: Yearbook of the Association for Supervision and Curriculum Development, 1989). See also Robert Marzano et al., *Dimensions of Thinking: A Framework for Curriculum and Instruction* (Alexandria, VA: Association for Supervision and Curriculum Development, 1988).

21. Howard Gardner, *Frames of Mind: The Theory of Multiple Intelligences* (New York: Basic Books, 1983); and Howard Gardner, *Multiple Intelligences: The Theory in Practice* (New York: Basic Books, 1993).

22. Carol Reid, and Brenda Romanoff, "Using Multiple Intelligence Theory to Identify Gifted Children," *Educational Leadership* 55, no. 1 (November 1997): 71–74; Andrew Latham, "Quantifying MI's Gains," *Educational Leadership* 55, no. 1 (November 1997): 84–85; and Linda Campbell, "Variations on a Theme: How Teachers Interpret MI Theory," *Educational Leadership* 55, no. 1 (November 1997): 14–19.

23. Howard Gardner, "Multiple Intelligences As a Partner in School Improvement," *Educational Leadership* 55, no. 1 (November 1997): 20–21.

24. Elliot Eisner, "Implications of Artistic Intelligences for Education," in *Artistic Intelligences: Implications for Education,* ed. William J. Moody (New York: Teachers College Press, 1990), p. 37.

25. A sample of articles includes Madeline Hunter, "Right-Brained Kids in Left-Brained Schools," *Today's Education* (November–December 1976); Elliot Eisner, "The Impoverished Mind," *Educational Leadership* 35, no. 8 (May 1978); and Evelyn Virsheys, *Right Brain People in a Left Brain World* (Los Angeles: Guild of Tutors, 1978).

26. Pat Wolfe, and Ron Brandt, "What Do We Know from Brain Research?" *Educational Leadership* 56, no. 3 (November 1998): 8–13.

27. Frances Rauscher, et al., "Music Training Causes Long-Term Enhancement of Preschool Children's Spatial-Temporal Reasoning," *Neurological Research* 19 (1997): 2–8.

28. Debra Viadero, "Research: Music on the Mind," *Education Week* (April 8, 1998): 25–27.

29. Wolfe and Brandt, "What Do We Know?"

30. Madeleine Nash, "Fertile Minds," *Time,* February 3, 1997, 48–56.

31. Ibid.

32. Shannon Brownlee, "Baby Talk: Learning Language Is an Astonishing Act of Brain Computation," *U.S. News & World Report,* June 15, 1998, 48–55.

33. David Sousa, "Is the Fuss about Brain Research Justified?" *Education Week* (December 16, 1998): 35, 52.

34. Renate Nummela Caine and Geoffrey Caine, *Teaching and the Human Brain* (Alexandria, VA: Association for Supervision and Curriculum Development, 1991).

35. George Geahigan, "The Arts in Education: A Historical Perspective," in *The Arts, Education, and Aesthetic Knowing: Ninety-first Yearbook of the National Society for the Study of Education,* eds. Bennett Reimer and Ralph Smith (Chicago: University of Chicago Press, 1992).

36. Benjamin Bloom, ed., *Taxonomy of Educational Objectives: Cognitive Domain* (New York: David McKay, 1956) and *Affective Domain* (1964); and Robert Mager, *Preparing Instructional Objectives* (Palo Alto: Fearon, 1962).

37. Daniel Goleman, *Emotional Intelligence: Why It Can Matter More Than IQ* (New York: Bantam, 1995).

38. Marian Diamond and Janet Hopson, *Magic Trees of the Mind: How to Nurture Your Child's Intelligence, Creativity, and Healthy Emotions from Birth through Adolescence* (New York: Dutton, 1998). A practical book on brain research for parents and teachers. An excellent mix of clearly explained scientific research and solid advice on how to create stimulating home and school environments.

39. Robert Sylwester, "Art for the Brain's Sake," *Educational Leadership* 56, no. 3 (November 1998): 31–35.

40. Pat Wolfe, "Revisiting Effective Teaching," *Educational Leadership* 56, no. 3 (November 1998): 64.

41. Italo De Francesco, *Art Education: Its Means and Ends* (New York: Harper & Row, 1958).

42. June McFee, *Preparation for Art* (Belmont, CA: Wadsworth, 1961).

43. June McFee and Rogena Degge, *Art, Culture, and Environment* (Dubuque, IA: Kendall-Hunt, 1980).

44. Dewey, *Art As Experience,* p. 344.

45. Endorsements of art as an essential component in general education are on record from many professional education groups, such as the Association for Supervision and Curriculum Development, the College Board, the National Endowment for the Arts, the Council for Basic Education, the National Art Education Association, and the National Parent and Teachers Association.

46. Charles Leonhard, *The Status of Arts Education in American Public Schools* (Urbana, IL: Council for Research in Music Education, 1991), p. 204.

47. National Center for Education Statistics, *Arts Education in Public Elementary and Secondary Schools,* Statistical Analysis Report, (Washington, DC: Office of Educational Research and Improvement, U.S. Department of Education, October 1995), Statistical Analysis Report, NCES 95-082

48. Illinois Art Education Association, *Excellence and Equity in Art Education: Toward Exemplary Practices in the Schools of Illinois* (Champaign: University of Illinois Press, 1995).

49. Arthur Efland, *A History of Art Education* (New York: Teachers College Press, 1990).

50. Harry Green, "Walter Smith: The Forgotten Man," *Art Education* 19, no. 1 (January 1966).

51. Foster Wygant, *Art in American Schools in the Nineteenth Century* (Cincinnati: Interwood Press, 1983).

52. Peter Smith, "Franz Cizek: The Patriarch," *Art Education* (March 1985).

53. W. Viola, *Child Art and Franz Cizek* (New York: Reynal and Hitchcock, 1936).

54. Stephen Dobbs, "The Paradox of Art Education in the Public Schools: A Brief History of Influences," ERIC Publication ED 049 196 (1971).

55. Brent Wilson and Marjorie Wilson, "An Iconoclastic View of the Imagery Sources in the Drawings of Young People," *Art Education* (January 1977): 5,9.

56. Frederick M. Logan, *Growth of Art in American Schools* (New York: Harper and Brothers, 1955). See also Logan's "Update '75, Growth in American Art Education," *Studies in Art Education* 17, no. 1 (1975).

57. Royal B. Farnum, *Education through Pictures* (Westport, CT: Art Extension Press, 1931).

58. Elliot Eisner and David Ecker, eds., *Readings in Art Education* (Waltham, MA: Blaisdell, 1966).

59. Dobbs, "The Paradox of Art Education," p. 24.

60. Victor D'Amico, *Creative Teaching in Art* (Scranton, PA: International Textbook, 1942); Viktor Lowenfeld, *Creative and Mental Growth* (New York: Macmillan, 1947); and Manuel Barkan, *Through Art to Creativity* (Boston: Allyn & Bacon, 1960).

61. J. P. Guilford, "The Nature of Creative Thinking," *American Psychologist* (September 1950).

62. For example, see Ralph Smith, ed., *Aesthetics and Criticism in Art Education* (Chicago: Rand McNally, 1966), and Edmund Feldman, *Art As Image and Idea* (Englewood Cliffs, NJ: Prentice-Hall, 1967).

63. Elliot Eisner, *Educating Artistic Vision* (New York: Macmillan, 1972).

64. See, for example, Louis Lankford, "Ecological Stewardship in Art Education," *Art Education* 50, no. 6 (1997): 47–53; Ronald Neperud, *Context, Content, and Community in Art Education* (New York: Teachers College Press, 1995); and Theresa Marche, "Looking Outward, Looking In: Community in Art Education," *Art Education* 51, no. 3 (1998): 6–13.

65. Consortium of National Arts Education Associations, *National Standards for Arts Education: What Every Young American Should Know and Be Able to Do in the Arts* (Reston, VA: Music Educators National Conference, 1994).

ACTIVITIES FOR THE READER

1. Visit an art museum and find examples of works that are representative of purposes art has served, as discussed in this chapter. See "Nature of the Visual Arts." A textbook in art history or a World Wide Web museum site (see below) may be used if a museum is not available. Find examples of the following:
   a. An object created to serve a particular function.
   b. An object enhanced with decorative elements or created in a unique shape to provide a pleasurable experience.
   c. An object whose decoration includes symbols that express ideas or values related to its origin.
   d. An object that elicits an aesthetic response from the viewer.
2. Visit an elementary school and observe instruction and learning activities in art. From your observations answer the following questions:
   a. Is valid art content being taught?
   b. Is the art learning part of a sequential curriculum?
   c. Do the children have an opportunity to engage in creative art making?
   d. Is the art of children displayed in the classroom?
   e. Does learning include analysis and interpretation of meaning in art?

   f. What evidence is there that children are learning about art history?
3. As you spend time observing in an elementary classroom, can you detect if the emphasis is child centered, content centered, or society centered? Or, do you note a combination of these approaches?
4. Visit a gallery or art museum and identify examples of art that might be classified according to the discussion in this chapter (see "Nature of the Visual Arts"). A textbook in art history or a World Wide Web museum site may be used if a museum is not available. Find examples of the following:
   a. Traditional fine arts, such as painting, sculpture, and printmaking.
   b. Applied arts, such as furniture, interiors, weaving, pottery, silver, or quilts.
   c. Works by indigenous artists from North and South America, Asia, Africa, and so on.
   d. Works by naive or self-educated artists.
5. Compare a historical period of art education to similar developments in the field of education. See "Change in Art Education" in this chapter.
6. Turn to the historical framework of art education in Appendix A. Add to the framework any events or persons you think should be included.

SUGGESTED READINGS

Nature of the Visual Arts

Dissanayake, Ellen. *What Is Art For?* Seattle: University of Washington Press, 1988. This text presents an anthropological view of art, its origins, and its functions in society.

Russell, Stella Pandell. *Art in the World.* 4th ed. Chicago: Harcourt Brace College Publishers, 1997. An excellent resource for elementary-school teachers and art educators who wish to increase their appreciation of art. This informative and well-illustrated book provides an excellent introduction to the visual arts, covering the nature of artistic creation, functions of art, and media and techniques employed in creating art forms—including photography, film, design, and craft in addition to drawing, painting, sculpture, and architecture. The book includes a succinct discussion of major periods of Western and non-Western art.

Stokstad, Marilyn, et al. *Art History.* Rev. ed. New York: Harry N. Abrams, 1999. Provides a highly visual survey of art history worldwide, reaching beyond the Western canon to include an examination of the arts of other regions and cultures. The two volumes include 1,350 photographs, more than half in color, and some not previously published.

Tansey, Richard G., and Fred S. Kleiner. *Gardner's Art through the Ages.* 11th ed. 2 vols. Fort Worth: Harcourt College Publishers, 2001. Still one of the best general art history textbooks. Includes a pronunciation guide to artists' names and an extensive glossary.

Yenawine, Philip. *Key Art Terms for Beginners.* New York: Harry N. Abrams, 1995. Attractive reference—not just for beginners.

Conceptions of the Learner

The authors recommend the following texts for further study on multiple intelligences, cognition, and brain research, and their implications for today's classrooms:

Armstrong, Thomas. *Multiple Intelligences in the Classroom.* Alexandria, VA: Association for Supervision and Curriculum Development, 1994.

Arnheim, Rudolf. *Thoughts on Art Education.* Los Angeles: Getty Center for Education in the Arts, 1989.

Caine, Renate Nummela, and Geoffrey Caine. *Education on the Edge of Possibility.* Alexandria, VA: Association for Supervision and Curriculum Development, 1997. Translates brain research into useful educational theory.

Gardner, Howard. *Multiple Intelligences: The Theory in Practice.* New York: Basic Books, 1993. Gardner's own explanation of his theory and its implications.

Sylwester, R. *A Celebration of Neurons: An Educator's Guide to the Human Brain.* Alexandria, VA: Association for Supervision and Curriculum Development, 1995.

Values of Society

The following works discuss the relationship and contributions of art education to culture, society, and community.

Kaagan, Stephen S. *Aesthetic Persuasion: Pressing the Cause of Arts Education in American Schools.* Los Angeles: Getty Center for Education in the Arts, 1990. Presents a compelling argument for inclusion of a comprehensive art education program in today's schools that counters common cultural biases against it.

McFee, June King. *Cultural Diversity and the Structure and Practice of Art Education.* Reston, VA: National Art Education Association, 1998. Provides a historical reflection on changing social conditions, cultures, and aesthetic trends and looks at art education practices from a sociology perspective.

National School Boards Association. *More Than Pumpkins in October: Visual Literacy in the 21st Century.* Alexandria, VA: National School Boards Association, 1992. Provides a rationale for art education.

Neperud, Ronald W., ed. *Context, Content, and Community in Art Education: Beyond Postmodernism.* New York: Teachers College Press, 1995. Various articles discuss the appropriateness of art education as a means to empower community and achieve other social goals.

Wolf, Dennie Palmer, and Mary Burger. "More Than Minor Disturbances: The Place of Arts in American Education." In Stephen Benedict, ed., *Public Money and the Muse.* New York: W. W. Norton, 1991.

Change in Art Education

Amburgy, Patricia M., et al., eds. *The History of Art Education: Proceedings from the Second Penn State Conference.* Reston, VA: National Art Education Association, 1992.

Clark, Gilbert A., Michael D. Day, and W. Duane Greer. "Discipline-based Art Education: Becoming Students of Art." In Ralph A. Smith, ed., *Discipline-based Art Education: Origins, Meaning, Development.* Urbana: University of Illinois Press, 1989. An essential and authentic source about the tenets of discipline-based art education.

Dobbs, Stephen M. *Learning in and through Art: A Guide to Discipline-based Art Education.* Los Angeles: Getty Education Institute for the Arts, 1998. A review of the theory and practice of discipline-based art education.

Efland, Arthur. *A History of Art Education: Intellectual and Social Currents in Teaching the Visual Arts.* New York: Teachers College Press, 1990.

Geahigan, George. "The Arts in Education: A Historical Perspective." In Bennett Reimer and Ralph A. Smith, eds., *The Arts, Education, and Aesthetic Knowing.* Chicago: University of Chicago Press, 1992.

Soucy, Donald, and Mary Ann Stankiewicz, eds. *Framing the Past: Essays on Art Education.* Reston, VA: National Art Education Association, 1990.

Basic Beliefs

The authors recommend the following texts to acquaint art educators and elementary-school teachers with old and new classics of the field.

Broudy, Harry S. *The Role of Imagery in Learning.* Los Angeles: Getty Center for Education in the Arts, 1987.

Dewey, John. *Art As Experience.* New York: Putnam, 1958. The classic text by the great philosopher of education. Essential for art educators.

Eisner, Elliot W. *Educating Artistic Vision.* New York: Macmillan, 1972. Reprinted in 1998 by the National Art Education Association. A classic text in art education.

Gardner, Howard. *The Disciplined Mind: What All Students Should Understand.* New York: Simon and Schuster, 1999.

Smith, Ralph Alexander, and the National Art Education Association. *Excellence II: The Continuing Quest in Art Education.* Reston, VA: National Art Education Association, 1995.

WORLD WIDE WEB RESOURCES

Almost every major museum in the world has created a Web site that provides images of artworks from their collections as well as educational material. A good way to become acquainted with this resource is to begin at ArtsEdNet, the Web site for the Getty Institute for Education in the Arts, and open "Web gateways." Select "museum and image resources" from the list of categories and prepare to be amazed at the depth of resources available to teachers and students of art. Another good place to begin is the National Museum of American Art at the Smithsonian Institution. Web addresses for these sites are:

ArtsEdNet: <http://www.artsednet.getty.edu/>

National Museum of American Art:
   <http://www.nmaa.si.edu/>

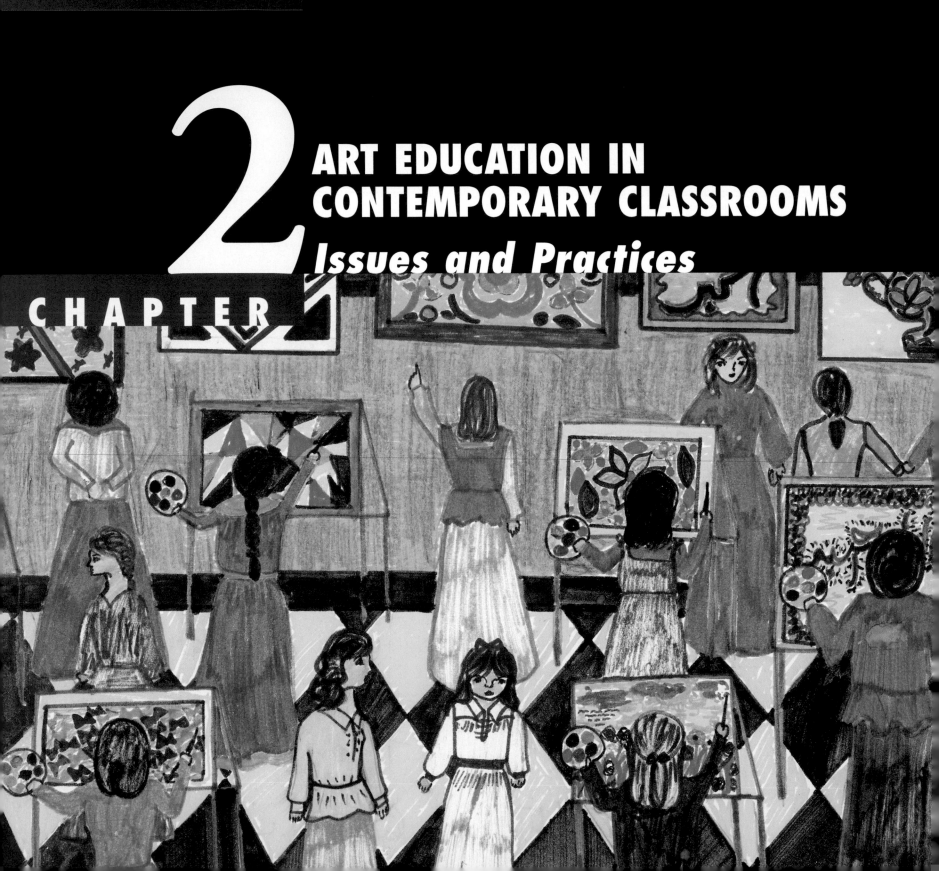

2 ART EDUCATION IN CONTEMPORARY CLASSROOMS
Issues and Practices

CHAPTER

No one can claim to be truly educated who lacks basic knowledge and skills in the arts.[1]

—National Standards for Arts Education

Art Is Necessary, Not Just "Nice"

Noted philosopher of education Harry Broudy has raised and commented eloquently on the question, "What is the role of art in general education?"[2] He pointed out that if art is an essential component for a balanced education, then there should be no question of its inclusion in the regular curriculum of elementary and secondary schools. If art is only something "fun" or "nice" for the children to have after "serious" schoolwork, then, says Broudy, it has no place in the curriculum. There are numerous nice experiences for children to have, and any of them will do.

However, if the state or school-district board of education promises a quality, balanced education for all students, then art must be offered if that promise is to be redeemed. Art becomes a basic subject required within any curriculum of excellence.

The history of art education reveals that sometimes too many promises or claims have been made for art as a subject in school. We can note in the literature claims that art will increase creativity, enhance personality development, improve school attendance, enhance reading skills, and stimulate the right side of the brain. Each of these claims has a valid foundation, sometimes based on educational research. None of these benefits, however, is unique to

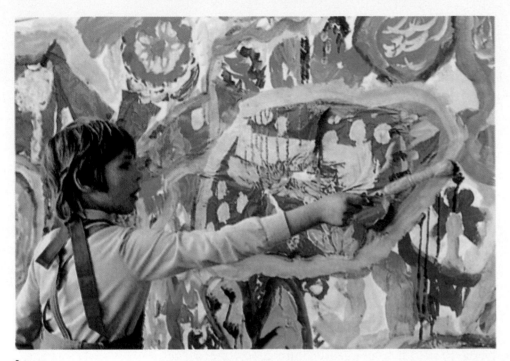

Germany

the study of art; each can be achieved through other areas of the curriculum as well as through art class.

The rationale for art in the schools is based on the essential contributions that come from studying art. Art is taught because, like science, language, and mathematics, the study of art is essential for an educated understanding of the world. Art as well as science provides a fundamental lens of understanding through which we can view and interpret the world in which we live.[3] Children who do not receive a sound art education are denied a balanced, well-rounded general education and are excluded from much of educated discourse. A person who has never seen the Emanuel Leutze painting *Washington Crossing the Delaware,* which has become a cultural icon, will not catch the humor in Gary Larson's cartoon *Washington Crossing the Street.*

The rationale for art as an essential subject is founded on much more than an ability to understand a joke, as noted in the following statements by distinguished writers and scholars:

> In saying: "This is who I am," in revealing oneself, the (artist) can help others to become aware of who they are. As a means

Art images such as Emanuel Leutze's *Washington Crossing the Delaware,* 1851, become cultural referents—the prior knowledge that we need in order to understand everyday experience and educated discourse. (The Metropolitan Museum of Art, New York.)

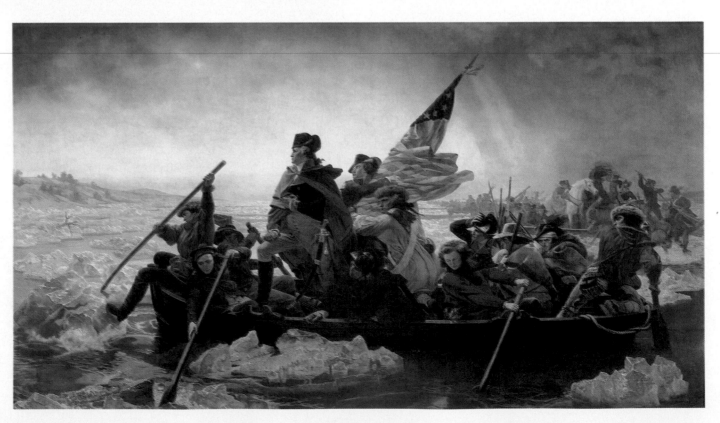

of revealing collective identity, art should be considered an article of prime necessity, not a luxury.[4]

—*Eduardo Galeano, Uruguayan writer*

The goal of the new, more globally inclusive curricula being forged amid heated debate is the perception of Western civilization as one of many worth studying in a multicultural nation, where white students will be encouraged to see themselves as simply another Other.[5]

—*Lucy Lippard, critic*

Art is humanity's most essential, most universal language. It is not a frill, but a necessary part of communication. We must give our children knowledge and understanding of civilization's most profound works.[6]

—*Ernest Boyer, former president, Carnegie Foundation for the Advancement of Teaching*

Arts education is a requisite and integrated component of the entire educational process.[7]

—*Nelson Goodman, Harvard Graduate School of Education*

What views might we have, then, of the characteristics and outcomes of sound programs of art education? When art is implemented as a regular part of the basic curriculum, what might we expect as outcomes in the lives of the children? What does a sound program of art education look like? How much time in the school week does it require? How does it relate to the rest of the curriculum? Who should teach art? These questions represent the threads that make up the constantly changing tapestry of art education. As the threads change color and texture across the years, the design of the tapestry is altered subtly or drastically, according to the times.

As we have learned from the brief history of art education in Chapter 1, many views about the contributions of art in education and its implementation in schools exist. It is neither possible nor desirable to present single answers to any of the questions just posed. Rather, we present here a view generally accepted in the field of art education, with expectations that there are many valid variations of that view.

A BALANCED PROGRAM OF ART EDUCATION

For the first time, art educators, along with colleagues in music, theatre, and dance education, have access to the guidance of national standards. The *National Standards for Arts*

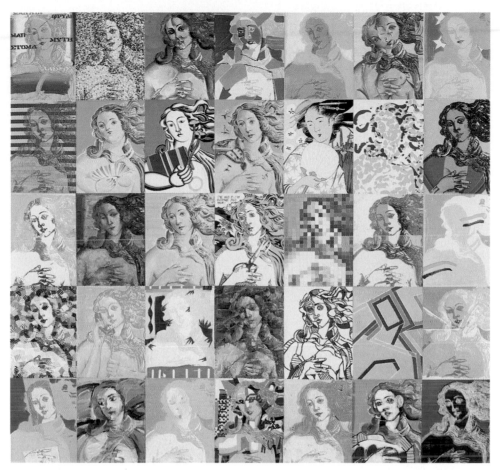

Paul Giovanopoulos, *Venus II,* © 1989 Paul Giovanopoulos.

The artist has appropriated the famous image of Botticelli's Venus and rendered it in a number of styles appropriated from well-known artists. How many artists' styles can you identify in this work?

Education provide general directions that can be adopted or adapted voluntarily at the state and local levels. The standards insist that art education is not a hit-or-miss effort but a sequenced and comprehensive enterprise of learning. Art instruction takes a hands-on orientation in that students are continually involved in the work, practice, and study required for effective and creative engagement.

In a classroom where art is taught, we expect to see children's artwork displayed. The work of children reflects the individuality of expression fundamental to art, but also exhibits what children have learned in class.

A visitor to a contemporary classroom sees children learning ways to discuss and respond to works of art (originals whenever possible), reading and writing about art (sometimes correlated with language instruction), investigating questions about art (through class discussion, library research, and the

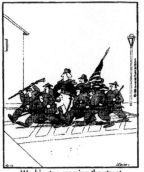

Washington crossing the street

Cartoonist Gary Larson's humorous takeoff on Leutze's serious painting is an example of parody. Without knowledge of the original image we simply would not get the joke. *Washington Crossing the Street,* Gary Larson, 1986, *The Far Side,* Universal Press Syndicate.

Internet), as well as making their own art. Students are enthusiastic and interested in all these learning activities.

Outcomes of a Quality Art Program

Often, children enjoy their overall school experience more because art touches on areas not addressed in other classes. Being able to make art is very important to many children, and some may attend school more regularly when there is a good art program.

It is often during art instruction that children have opportunities to express ideas, opinions, and judgments, either through their own art production or discussion of other works. In art class, children are often praised for the uniqueness of their work rather than its uniformity to a predetermined standard or response. In art, each student might successfully complete an assignment based on the concept of "landscape," but each student's landscape painting is unique.

A young person who participates in a quality art program throughout the elementary grades will have the following experiences:

1. The student will create drawings, paintings, and other artwork from observation, memory, and imagination. The child will progress through stages of symbol formation and elaboration and will develop relatively sophisticated levels of art-making skills. The child will

gain an understanding of art as a means for expressing ideas, feelings, and ideals.

2. The student will have access to an expanding store of visual art images, referred to by Broudy as the "imagic store." The child will see, during the years from kindergarten through grades six, seven, or eight, literally hundreds of exemplary works of fine, folk, and applied visual arts. This "imagic store" is a source of imagination.

3. The student will gain a basic understanding of the range of the visual arts throughout history and across many cultures. The child will be conversant with art terms and concepts from the history of art, as well as with many particular landmark works and the artists or cultures that produced them. The child will develop preferences for some types or styles of art.

4. The student will learn about a range of world cultures through study of artworks, their contexts, purposes, and cultural values. The child will appreciate his or her own cultural heritage and that of many of the distinctive cultural groups of the United States, Canada, and other countries.

5. The student will investigate ways the visual arts are influenced by the contexts of their creation, such as psychological factors in an artist's life, political events, social values, or changes in technology. The child will learn how art expresses cultural values and, in turn, influences society.

6. The child will use the library, Internet, and other sources to seek specific information about art and artists.

7. The student will discuss the very nature of art, including issues that surround the making, displaying, buying and selling, and interpreting of works of art.

The fortunate children who experience such a program of art will have exercised their creative abilities in art; thought deeply about art; and responded to and learned about art, artists, and their contexts. They will have developed the aesthetic lens of the visual arts that empowers them to view their world with added meaning and significance. They will have taken one of the essential steps toward achieving a well-rounded, balanced general education that is the right of every child in this society and a requirement for an enlightened citizenry.

Students can work well together on painting assignments in the classroom setting. These students are working on a large painting made possible by the large tables in the art room. Note the tray holder for paints and brushes and the stools which give students easy access to exit to the painting area. The expansive hand and arm motions of the two boys are typical when children have opportunity to work on a large scale.

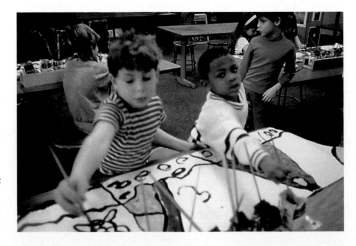

Integrating Art with the Elementary Curriculum

Integrating art with other subjects is not a new idea. Leon Loyal Winslow wrote *The Integrated School Art Program* in 1938, and since that time, the topic has reappeared regularly and not without justification. The history of art relates naturally to *historical topics* usually studied at various grade levels. Most history texts, in fact, are illustrated with works of art, providing a ready means for integration. *Social issues* are often expressed by means of powerful art images. Artists of many cultures and eras have dealt with virtually every universal social issue and human value, and teachers have access to the images they have produced.

Language instruction can be readily integrated with and enhanced by the art curriculum. Art criticism uses visual concepts and terms (vocabulary) in discussing art. Children learn systematic ways to talk and write about art. Visual art images are intrinsically interesting and provide issues and topics that fascinate children and motivate them to speak and write. Art criticism can take children beyond descriptive use of language to formal analysis and interpretation of meaning in art.

A current concern in general education has to do with *levels of thinking* that are fostered within all subjects in the curriculum.[8] Too much of children's time is spent with lower levels of thinking involving rote memorization, identification, and recall, and too few complex thinking skills are developed. Some educators are surprised to learn that the art curriculum is one of the easiest and most direct means to engage children in more challenging thinking. Art criticism, for instance, involves forming hypotheses for interpretations of meaning in visual works and discussion, debate, and defense of different interpretations based on visual evidence in the work itself.

Children routinely make judgments about the relationships of each element that they introduce in their own artwork to the totality of the work. A child's tentative decision to introduce hot reds and yellows in a painting that is composed of cool colors requires the child to make sophisticated perceptions, weigh options, interpret implications, and judge appropriateness in relation to intended expression. The child must decide, for example, if red and yellow fit with the overall character of the painting. Few subjects in the curriculum provide such ready means for children to engage in this type of decision making and problem solving.

Children can deal with fundamental issues in art, often using reason, logic, and careful definition of terms in the process of discourse. Each time a new artwork is introduced in the classroom, an aesthetics issue is introduced. For example, when a teacher shows a slide of a pot by the Native American artist Maria Martinez, the question might arise, "Is a simple clay pot art?" Children often come up with numerous questions that address fundamental issues, such as, "If this pot is art, does that mean that all pots are art?" or "Why is this pot in the art museum and others are not?" When teachers are confronted with these difficult questions and others that inevitably seem to follow, they usually wish to find some way to deal with them in an educationally productive way.

When questions arise in the classroom that address such topics as the nature of art, how quality is determined, or how one becomes an artist, teachers and students become involved in aesthetics discourses at levels appropriate for the age and understanding of the children. This type of discourse is almost always conducted using more complete and challenging levels of thinking so valued by those concerned with general education.

INFLUENCES ON POSTMODERN THOUGHT

Every time we make an educational decision we carry out a philosophical act that arises from a cultural context and has cultural implications. The more we understand the cultural contexts and implications of educational decisions the better able we are to create an effective learning environment for all students. Many of the issues educators are involved with today are part of a movement or cultural period known as postmodernism. Postmodernism is now a worldwide movement in all the arts and disciplines, and, according to cultural critic Charles Jencks, we are well past the age when we can merely accept or reject it as a new "ism." "It is too omnipresent and important for either approach."[9] Rather, Jencks claims, we must understand it before we decide to selectively support or criticize aspects of it. Accordingly, understanding the philosophical ideas of postmodernism provides a context for thinking about current issues and trends in art education. The discussion that follows is necessarily brief; see the Suggested Readings for sources that provide a more in-depth treatment of the subject.

In art and art education, postmodernism is "a new paradigm" that has emerged to challenge ideas that arose during the modern era.[10] It is therefore best understood by contrasting its premises with those of the modern age—known as modernism. A product of Western European thought, modernism includes the philosophical movement known as the Enlightenment, which occurred from about 1680 to 1780. The modern age continued to about 1950, to be succeeded by what is generally called the postmodern era.

Modernism

Many aspects of modernist philosophy evolved from Enlightenment thinkers who "had the extravagant expectation that the arts and sciences would promote not only the control of natural forces but also understanding of the world and of the self, moral progress, the justice of institutions and even the happiness of human beings."[11] Modernism is a vast and complex phenomenon that covers many beliefs. In time, however, these beliefs developed into "metanarratives," or great themes that some believe influenced the course of history, guided major social movements, and shaped theory in the academic disciplines. Metanarratives that shaped thought in the West include:

- Belief that history is shadowed by logic;
- Belief in a universal and coherent foundation of truth;
- Belief in reason as a force for a just and egalitarian social order;
- Belief in moral progress and the perfectibility of humankind;
- Belief in progression of knowledge;
- Belief that elimination of worldwide poverty, despotism, ignorance, and superstition is achievable through application of science; and
- Belief in the power of (Western) art to elevate and refine humanity.[12]

A central link among these metanarratives is the idea of *progress*—in knowledge, in technology, in human freedom, in morality, in education, and in the arts. Time was interpreted as linear and progressive, and history was seen as a series of linear events that eventually would culminate in an endpoint of perfection. Disciplines of knowledge, even art history and education, were imbued with belief in progress

and improvement through change, and change was generally equated with progress.

Another link among modernism's tenets is found in an abiding *faith in science*. Indeed, the belief that nature could be brought under control through the systematic application of science became so powerful that it has dominated modern culture.[13] This belief has influenced thought in all fields of study, including education and art, giving rise to the elevation of empirical science as the only way of knowing.

Scientific systems of classification were applied to many fields of study, including art. Art historians developed methodologies for classifying art into categories based on historical periods, styles, and formal properties. In art, music, and literature, human values were discounted in favor of a focus on formal structure. Eventually form and formal elements in art were elevated to the position of universals that transcended any historical, cultural, or ethnic consideration.[14]

As modernism continued into the twentieth century, it is best understood as "a cultural movement relating directly to . . . the social condition of living in an urban, fast changing, progressivist world governed by instrumental reason. This in turn stems from modernization (continual economic growth dependent on industrialization and progressive technology)."[15] Modernism's ideals are illustrated in the history of art and its role in society.

Modern Art

Modern theories in art developed sometime after the philosophy of modernism was established. "Artistic modernism" refers both to the styles of art and to the ideologies of art that were produced from about 1880 to 1970. Certain central assumptions or beliefs about art developed as part of modernism:

- Belief in progress in the history of art and that art must constantly move toward the new and innovative;
- Belief that works exist that are superior representatives of a period, school, or style;
- Belief that art has the power to apprehend, depict, and influence social norms;
- Belief that content and meaning reside in the work of art;
- Belief that quality is a property intrinsic to the work itself; and

- Belief that art is accessible to all regardless of context or culture and that all persons respond similarly to the visual properties of art.[16]

Progress in Art

Modern art assumed a progressive course in which each generation of artists pushed ahead to find new expressions. Artistic progress was viewed as a series of stylistic revolutions, "a process that typically dispatched earlier styles to history."[17] Using the concept of evolving styles, art historians identified particular works and artists as stylistic signposts, enabling them to create the appearance of an ordered past. For example, we mark progress toward "abstraction" in art through the styles of impressionism, cubism, and abstract expression.

The theory of historical progress in art was established and maintained through university courses and textbooks, and, eventually, in school classrooms. In art museums, exhibitions and collections were organized to illustrate the history and progress of art. Because of this, art museums were viewed by some as social instruments used to maintain and reinforce modernism's theories and beliefs.[18]

In education and art education, modernism's vision of progress was equated to continual shifting from one paradigm, style, or philosophy of teaching to another. Art education has responded to larger movements and trends in both the field of education and in the art world.[19] Chapter 1 of this textbook describes the various approaches that shaped the teaching of art during the modern era.

The Role of Art in Social Progress

Modernism's assumption that art had the power to apprehend and depict evolving social norms as well as influence them is reflected in the teachings of philosopher John Dewey, who believed that aesthetic experience had the capacity to influence morality.[20] A belief in the power of art to bring about individual and cultural refinement was widespread in the classrooms of the United States during the Picture Study Movement in the 1920s.

Many art museums still reflect these goals in their mission statements and education programs. For example, during the 1960s, art museums received government funds to offer museum tours emphasizing masterpieces of Western art to disadvantaged students.[21] However, the notion that mere exposure to works of art can confer a moral benefit on the viewer has fallen to low repute—a view consistent with postmodernism.

Canon of Great Works

A *canon* is a list of works accepted by scholars and connoisseurs as superior representatives of a period, style, or school, and which "provides a standard against which new work can be judged."[22] This is a highly selective list of works, or "masterpieces," that have shaped art-world values and influenced the direction of art history. Through formal study the canon is internalized by new generations of artists, art educators, and art historians. The canon is familiar to all educated persons who usually are exposed to it in college courses on Western civilization. The canon of traditionally accepted masterpieces receives further sanction through its presentation in art history textbooks, museum exhibitions, visual resources (such as reproductions and slides), and art curricula.

Formalism

Another theory of modernism asserts that in principle it is possible for individuals to reach agreement about the interpretation and judgment of artworks. This assumes that the capacity for aesthetic feelings is common to humankind; that response to art is universal; and that the visual aspects of art "have the power to move all humans in a similar way."[23]

The quest for a universal language that "lies at the core of all understanding" led to the articulation of elements and principles of design or "form." What mattered was form, not content—consequently the label "formalism." Formalism became prevalent in higher education programs in art and entered the field of art education at the turn of the twentieth century. Knowledge of design and composition was considered foundational to making art that could be experienced aesthetically in any culture, any place, and any time. Prospective art teachers received their art training in studio classes organized around media and processes. The elements and principles of design were assiduously studied and practiced in art schools and art departments.[24] Formalist design content is found even today in many elementary-school art curricula.

Autonomy of the Artwork

The notion that a work of art is equally accessible to all people, regardless of context or culture, comes from modernism's belief that what is aesthetically relevant about the work is determined by the work itself and not by the context. This modernist theory holds that a work of art is capable of overcoming social, cultural, and temporal boundaries.

Belief in the autonomy of the artwork (from context or culture) supports the art world's long-held notions that quality resides in the work and that judgments of art's quality are not affected by shifting cultural and social conditions. Art historians and other connoisseurs of art have traditionally claimed the capacity to make objective judgments about the relative worth and visual merit of works of art. From a postmodernist point of view, this practice has come under criticism on grounds that all judgments are subjective and are relative to and conditioned by the social context in which they are made.

Modern Art and the Quest for Originality

Although modernist theories began earlier, the actual works that came to be known as Modern Art date from about 1880 through 1970. Modernism's value of the new and experimental in art resulted in a host of artistic styles, for example, impressionism, fauvism, surrealism, and abstract expression. Modern Art was characterized by the imperative to seek new solutions and leave behind the old. The new was constantly being overcome and made obsolete through the discovery of the next new event. Innovation was stressed over all other criteria. Stylistic innovation has defined art in the modernist period, art in the schools, and students' progress in the university classroom.

Additional attributes of Modern Art included rebellion against the establishment; repudiation of naturalism as a principle of art; and preoccupation with the media and properties of the work, such as color, shape, rhythm, line, balance, and composition. The preoccupation with media and the elements and principles of design dominated art education for decades.

Barrett reminded us that "although Modernism is now old and perhaps over, it was once new and very progressive, bringing a new art for a new age."[25] Not all theorists believe that modernism is over. Some even say that postmodernism is simply a continuation of modernism's vision of social emancipation, with old metanarratives being revised or rejected in place of their proliferation.

Postmodernism

Although it is generally recognized that we live in an era characterized as postmodern, the term itself has defied definition.

Postmodernism is not a coherent philosophical movement but rather a collective name for a multiplicity of philosophical stances and theories. Although postmodernism is often thought of as the era following modernism, scholars have not agreed whether an actual break with the modern era occurred.[26]

Postmodern theorists maintain that postmodernism marks a breakdown in the beliefs developed during the modern era. The political calamities and barbarisms of the twentieth century—totalitarianism, genocide, and possible nuclear annihilation—led to a loss of faith in the perfectibility of humankind. Deeply held beliefs in universal justice and equality were challenged by contemporary social structures and the persistent existence of an underclass. The notion of consequence-free technological domination of nature was shaken by pollution and other environmental ills.[27] Postmodern theories developed as challenges to traditional Western assumptions of reality. Much postmodernist thought was aimed at deconstructing Western metanarratives and the "ethnocentrism implicit in the European view of history as the unilinear progress of universal reason."[28]

Postmodern Theory in Art and Art Education

Two particular influences have informed postmodern theory in art and art education. The first is Marxism and the related social movements of feminism and multiculturalism. The second influence comes from linguistic theory and includes structuralism, post-structuralism, deconstruction, and semiotics.

Marxism was developed in the mid-nineteenth century based on writings of Karl Marx, a German philosopher. Marxist theory addressed issues of social domination and subservience, political inclusion and exclusion, and the economics of a social structure that is characterized as class oppression.[29] Contemporary Marxist theory considers, in addition to economics, multiple spheres of domination and power, including religious, aesthetic, ethical, legal, and other cultural systems. Marxist theory holds that societies and their institutions have developed in ways that privilege and benefit particular groups. A major focus, therefore, is to pierce the veils that disguise hidden structures that conceal economic, political, and social elements. The term *Marxism* often has pejorative connotations, so many scholars use terms for modes of inquiry developed *from* Marxist theory— that is, *critical theory, ideological criticism,* or *social theory.* For the sake of simplicity, this text will continue to use the term *Marxism.*

Marxism and Art Education

Contemporary Marxist theory in art is aimed at understanding the role of art in society and the influence of society on art. Institutions, such as museums and schools, are thought to perpetuate the interests of the powerful and wealthy by controlling the kinds of knowledge, skills, and attitudes available to people of different classes. The theory holds that upper classes achieve power and often maintain it through the sphere of high culture, which includes only those with intellectual and economic access. Art museums are often implicated as tools for maintaining systems of class, race, and gender. Power and control are achieved in ways that make such domination seem natural or inevitable.[30]

Postmodern assumptions based on Marxist theory and prevalent in discussions of education and art include the following:

- Certain groups in any society are privileged over others, and this advantage is most effective when subordinates accept their social status as natural, necessary, or inevitable.
- All thought is mediated by power relations that are socially and historically based.
- Some education practices tend to reinforce systems of class, race, and gender discrimination.

Marxist View of the Art World

Postmodern critics maintain that power and elitism in the art world were created and maintained during the era of modernism. The values of modern art dominated the art world and were understood by those who had access. Knowledge and practices developed that privileged museum curators, art historians, and other experts in the art world and allowed them to perpetuate their control and authority. Two postmodern movements aimed at revealing power structures are those known as feminism and multiculturalism. These movements sought to expose hidden power structures in society, culture, and related institutions that privilege a viewpoint that excluded women and marginalized all but European culture.

Feminism and Art Theory

The discourse of art history, art criticism, and the operations of art institutions are subjects of feminist criticism. Feminist scholars questioned the lack of representation of women artists in art history and sought to redefine the discourse of art history. A plethora of new studies and books were published as feminist scholars exposed a dominant masculinist element in traditional art and art history.[31] Women's experience, as distinct from men's, became equally legitimate as subject for art and discourse about art. Traditional masculine ways of depicting women in art were questioned and critiqued by scholars and artists. Feminist scholars, writers, and artists strove to obtain gender equity, or at least a better gender balance, in museum and gallery exhibitions, funding, and scholarly pursuits.[32]

Scholars in art education have sought not just to bring the feminist agenda to the field, but also to offer constructive ways to recognize and incorporate women's contributions and viewpoints into all aspects of art learning. Laura Chapman pointed out that "the persuasiveness of gender bias is not limited to *whose* art has been judged historically important. It extends to the traditional structure of schooling, and the kind of knowledge valued in schools, museums, and other institutions in society. It influences styles of interacting with students and conventional ways of evaluating learning."[33]

This text will address feminism and art education more completely in the chapters that deal with art content, teaching, and classroom management.

Multiculturalism

The traditional ways in which non-Western cultures have been presented in art history, art museums, and art education curricula too often reflected a Eurocentric bias that appeared exclusionary to many. The Western view of non-Western culture was incomplete at best and racist at worst. Cultural groups—Native Americans, African Americans, Latinos, Asian Americans, and others—looked at the art world and education and saw a distorted record of their contributions. What is portrayed, what is written and communicated, whose voices are included and whose are silenced are issues addressed by multicultural criticism. Postmodern multicultural theory exposed biased accounts and skewed visual presentations of the cultural histories of non-European peoples. Scholars sought for more authenticity in presentation of diverse cultures in schools, museum exhibitions, and history texts. In the art world, redress was sought for artists of color and women, who had not enjoyed the same opportunities and benefits as white male artists and whose work had previously been excluded from consideration because of its incompatibility with Western aesthetic ideals.

Multicultural studies challenged modernism's concept of quality in art. Lucy Lippard pointed out that exclusion of women and artists of color "is balanced on a notion of

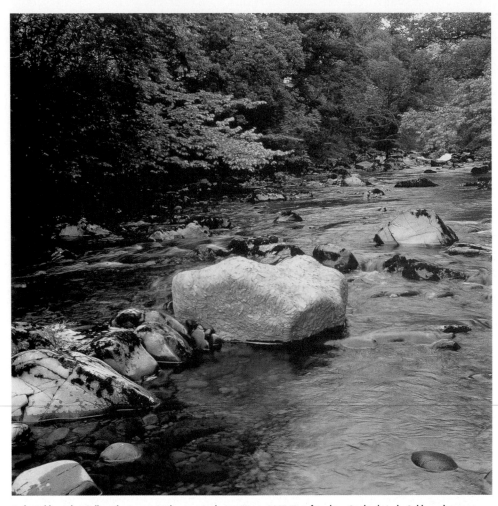

Andy Goldsworthy, *Yellow Elm Leaves Laid over a Rock, Low Water,* 1991, Dumfriesshire, Scotland. Andy Goldsworthy, courtesy Galerie Lelong.

One of the favorite artists of young students, Goldsworthy creates unique and complex works that might be classified as environmental art. The artist uses no man-made objects or materials, relying solely on nature to provide the materials for his expression. He goes out into nature and creates visually and intellectually appealing works out of leaves, sand, wood, stones, water, ice, snow, sticks, and virtually any natural object he encounters. Although his works return to nature, sometimes very quickly he records them photographically in order that they might be shared with others.

"refocused art educators on the historical, contextual, evaluative, and definitive *content* in art as well as on individual expression."[35] The disciplines of art history, art criticism, aesthetics, and educational theory have broadened to accommodate feminist and multicultural viewpoints. Content-based art curricula and educational resources have been created to support art educators in the classroom. The official research agenda of the National Art Education Association is inclusive of multicultural and feminist issues.[36]

Community and Social Values

Awareness of multicultural issues has led to more concern about what community means. Many art educators today advocate a teaching philosophy that encourages students to think about relationships of art, ecology, and community.[37] Art making may be interdisciplinary, action-oriented, and based on social values. Rather than focusing exclusively on form in art, studio teaching often fosters interconnections among art, community, and environment. Working with concepts of environmental design and ecological art "can empower students with the understanding that they, as creative individuals, can have an active voice in protecting their environment and changing current devastating ecological trends."[38]

A curriculum based on social responsibility and ecological attunement requires an approach that broadens the content of art learning as well as pedagogy. Lankford suggested a curriculum that includes (a) the study of art from an ecological perspective, (b) artistic production guided by ecological awareness and responsiveness, and (c) interdisciplinary learning centered on ecological stewardship.[39] Aesthetics may involve consideration of ecological art, created by Andy Goldsworthy and others working in this medium, as well as appropriateness of local public art. Art criticism learning might focus on environmental design problems, such as the relationship between landscape, ecology, and community. Art making may involve an interdisciplinary and collaborative approach that brings groups of students together to work on projects involving issues of land use, environmental science, landscape design, and public art.

The *Art in Action* video series, for example, includes a curriculum unit that addresses social and ecological issues.[40] *Commentary Islands* is an integrated unit of art curriculum developed by an art teacher. The unit involved students working in teams to create three-dimensional statements about the environment. The sculptural pieces were made on thick styrofoam bases that would float on the water like islands—thus the title of the unit. On the occasion of launching the "islands"

Quality . . . identifiable only by those in power" who claim racism has nothing to do with art judgment.[34] The notion of quality, Lippard claimed, has been the most effective tool in sustaining the homogeneity of Western art.

The field of art education has accommodated multiculturalism in numerous ways. Tom Anderson pointed out that discipline-based art education must be credited for "opening the door" to postmodern approaches in art education that on a nearby pond,* students read statements they had written in support of maintaining the natural environment of Earth. These students created artworks that conveyed messages about which they cared deeply.

Cognitive Structure of Art

The second strand of postmodern theory comes from the field of linguistics and includes contemporary methods of inquiry known as post-structuralism, semiotics, and deconstruction. It is not within the scope of this textbook to discuss and define each of these disciplines. See the Suggested Readings at the end of this chapter for more material. However, a brief explanation of semiotics and deconstruction and their relationship to art education is offered here.

Semiotics

Semiotics is the study of how images, as opposed to words, produce meaning. The modernist viewpoint held that meaning was created by individuals and communicated by them to others using words with already fixed meanings. Semiotics views images as sign systems. The essence of semiotic theory holds that the interpretation of an "object" or work of art cannot be accomplished solely on the material nature of the object alone. A work of art would have a meaning that has been socially constructed and assigned to it. This means that the work of art functions as a sign, which stands for something in the social context. Interpretation of signs or images is performed within a cultural and social context. "The meaning of a picture is never inscribed on its surface as brushstrokes are; meaning arises in the collaboration between signs (visual and verbal) and interpreters."[41]

The employment of semiotic theory affects the way one thinks about the aesthetic status and value of a work of art. Semiotic theory rejects the notion that aesthetic values exist as inherent qualities of the work of art. Valuing a work of art is affected by the social and cultural context of the person who is making a judgment. What one period or culture finds aesthetically significant or valuable is not necessarily what another culture or period will regard highly. The concept of a universally recognized canon of great art is rejected and replaced with the belief that each generation will value art based on its particular political and cultural interests.

Semiotic theory relates to aesthetic issues in the elementary art classroom. Marilyn Stewart asserted that "those of us who

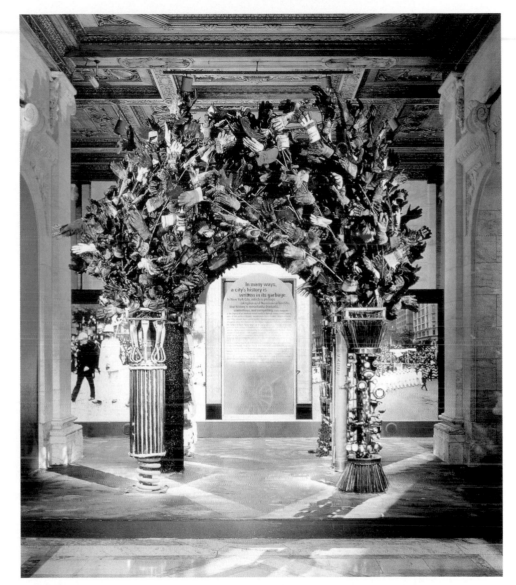

Mierle Ukeles, Ceremonial Art Honoring Service Workers in the New Service Economy, 1988, steel arch with materials donated from New York City agencies, including gloves, lights, grass, straps, springs and asphalt, 11 × 8 ft. × 8.5 in.

More than a visual arrangement, this installation carries a strong social message from the artist. Postmodern elements include collaboration, use of nontraditional materials, social theme, and the installation method. Most temporary installations are photographed for purposes of documentation and to make possible the continued impact of the work.

have taught art in the schools know that our students often wonder why certain works have merit and others seem not to."[42] Anderson claimed that all art teachers are involved with aesthetic content. "Determining the definitions, meaning, and

---

* Note: The islands were held by nylon lines to keep them from floating away and polluting the environment.

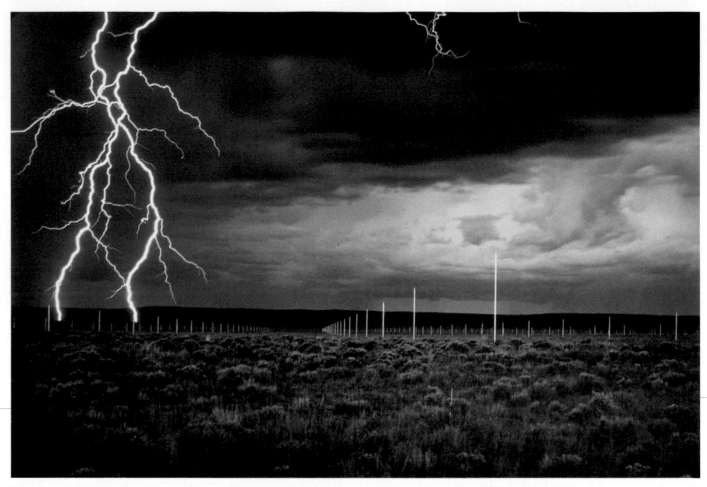

Walter De Marie, Lightning Field, 1974–77, stainless steel poles, near Quemado, NM, average height of poles is 20.5 ft., overall dimensions: 5290 × 3300 ft (1 mile × 1 kilometer).

As the dark, rolling thunderheads roll across the open New Mexico plains, active lightning flashes can be seen for miles. When the dark clouds pass over Lightning Field, electric bolts arc between earth and sky through the numerous stainless steel poles positioned for that very purpose. This orchestrated display of nature's dramatic power exemplifies several characteristics of postmodern art: It is an installation and a work that cannot become part of the commercial system for buying and selling art. It is an environmental work, utilizing natural forms and phenomenon. And, it is ecologically harmless in this remote location.

values of art and deciding how art is to be approached are core issues of aesthetics."[43]

Deconstruction

Deconstruction proponents have little or no faith that language can refer to reality. They hold that meaning does not exist autonomously in the world to be expressed in language or visual images. Therefore, one can never know an artist's meaning, or accurately interpret the symbols operating in a particular time or place, or understand what a work of art might have meant to a particular audience. Meaning is actually produced by a reader or viewer (interpreter) and, therefore, exists only as an intellectual construct for each individual.[44]

Ideas, concepts, and objects are viewed as texts, or mental constructs, which, because they are generated by the structures of language, can be deconstructed. Deconstruction refers to a mental taking apart or unbuilding of a concept or text (verbal or visual) in order to find and understand hidden assumptions. Deconstructionism is generally not motivated by destructive purposes but, rather, is the careful study of language and the relationship of language to meaning. Deconstructionism is a type of interpretation and reinterpretation at a deep level.

The following concepts from deconstruction theory are relevant for art education:

- Greater importance is attached to the viewer and the process of interpretation.
- The notion that the viewer is a passive recipient of knowledge created and served by experts who have discovered the true meaning of a work of art is not valid.
- Interpretation and meaning-making are creative endeavors.
- Meaning exists as an intellectual construct and is individual.

Deconstruction and Art Education

Art educators generally agree that meaning is central to teaching about art and is both unavoidable and desirable. Postmodern notions about the construction of meaning can encourage students to place artworks in a rich context for interpretation. Deconstruction can raise a number of questions for classroom art criticism practice, such as: Are there ever conclusive meanings about artworks? Will meaning change with every viewer? How are artworks given social meaning?[45] Art criticism is reconceived as something more than an activity subsidiary to artworks; rather, it is a creative process resulting in its own linguistic "works of art."

Hyperreality: A Postmodern Condition

A third strand of influence occurring during our postmodern era is the advent of hyperreality. *Hyperreality* is a term used to describe an information society saturated with ever-increasing forms of representation: film, photography, video, CD-ROM, electronic media, and the Internet. These visual media have a profound effect on the construction of cultural narratives that shape our identities.[46] Mechanically produced images collapse the distinction between authentic experiences and those we experience through hypermedia. Hyperreality utilizes new forms of literacy that do not depend on traditional modes of learning but, rather, on proficiency in the use of multiple forms of media.[47]

The computer is so revolutionary that it will eventually affect the way all knowledge is acquired and created. In art, the computer is creating interdisciplinary effects "whose promise we are only beginning to fathom."[48] The implications for artmaking are also profound—allowing for interactive multimedia, interactivity with viewers, and collaborative works. Internet hypertext allows multiple connections to images, text, and other media.

Beyond making art, changes in the relationship between the viewer and the artwork offer a multitude of opportunities to educators. Computer technology in art education makes it possible for a whole range of meanings, related to a single object or artwork, to co-exist. Interactive hypermedia do not depend on a linear or a hierarchical structure and are particularly well suited to both art making and art criticism. Samples of curricula involving hypermedia and hyperlinks are available on the Getty Art Education World Wide Web site. Chapter 10, *Newer Media,* relates hypermedia to art education and the elementary classroom.

SUMMARY

There is much in postmodernism that is both attractive and disturbing to art educators. Educators generally welcome the broadening of the art world to multiculturalism, exposure of bias in educational materials, placement of greater value on students' interpretations, and connections students have with art they make. On the other hand, it is difficult to give up established traditions that have shaped the meanings of art in the past and contributed to a cultural viewpoint. We learn from postmodernism a measure of modesty about our claims and a sense of the historical character of our understanding of art. The problem for most of us "is not whether to accept modernism or postmodernism, but how to strike the right balance between those approaches and to take from them what is most valuable to us. . . . Teaching has always been the attempt to pass on our best understanding of the present so that our students will make sense of the future. Postmodernism shows us how important and difficult that task has become."[49]

NOTES

1. *National Standards for Arts Education: What Every Young American Should Know and Be Able to Do in the Arts* (Reston, VA: MENC, 1994).

2. Harry S. Broudy, "Arts Education—Necessary or Just Nice?" *Phi Delta Kappan* 60, no. 5 (January 1979): 347–350.

3. Harry S. Broudy, *The Role of Art in General Education* (Los Angeles: The Getty Center for Education in the Arts, videotape of Broudy lecture, 1987).

4. Rick Simonson and Scott Walker, eds., *The Graywolf Annual Five: Multi-Cultural Literacy* (Saint Paul, MN: Graywolf Press, 1988), p. 116.

5. Lucy Lippard, *Mixed Blessings: New Art in a Multicultural America* (New York: Pantheon Books, 1990), p. 23.

6. Ernest Boyer, *Toward Civilization: A Report on Arts Education* (National Endowment for the Arts, 1988), p. 14.

7. Nelson Goodman, "Aims and Claims," in *Art, Mind, and Education,* ed. Howard Gardner and D. N. Perkins (Urbana: University of Illinois Press, 1989), p. 1.

8. Lauren Resnick and Leopold E. Klopfer, "Toward the Thinking Curriculum: An Overview," in *Toward the Thinking Curriculum: Current Cognitive Research* (Reston, VA: Association for Supervision and Curriculum Development, 1989).

9. Charles Jencks, *What Is Post-Modernism?* 4th ed. (New York: Academy Editions, 1996).

10. James Hutchens and Marianne Suggs, eds., *Art Education: Content and Practice in a Postmodern Era* (Reston, VA: National Art Education Association, 1997).

11. Jurgen Habermas, "Modernity versus Postmodernity," in *Postmodern Perspectives: Issues in Contemporary Art,* ed. Howard Risatti (Upper Saddle River, NJ: Prentice-Hall, 1998), pp. 53–64.

12. See, for example, Terry Barrett, "Modernism and Postmodernism: An Overview with Art Examples," in Hutchens and Suggs, *Art Education,* 17–30; Arthur Efland, Kerry J. Freedman, and Patricia L. Stuhr, *Postmodern Art Education: An Approach to Curriculum* (Reston, VA: National Art Education Association, 1996); and D. Hebdige, "A Report from the Western Front," in *Postmodernism,* ed. N. Wakefield (London: Pluto Press, 1986).

13. Daniel Bell, "Modernism, Postmodernism, and the Decline of Moral Order," in *Culture and Society: Contemporary Debates,* ed. Jeffrey C. Alexander and Steven Seidman (New York: Cambridge University Press, 1990), pp. 319–329.

14. Howard Risatti, *Postmodern Perspectives: Issues in Contemporary Art* (Upper Saddle River, NJ: Prentice-Hall, 1998).

15. Jencks, *What Is Post-Modernism?* p. 8.

16. Terry Barrett, *Criticizing Art: Understanding the Contemporary* (Mountain View, CA: Mayfield, 1994).

17. Efland et al., *Postmodern Art Education.*

18. Donald Preziosi, *Rethinking ART History: Meditations on a Coy Science* (New Haven, CT: Yale University Press, 1989).

19. Efland et al., *Postmodern Art Education.*

20. Albert William Levi and Ralph A. Smith, *Art Education: A Critical Necessity, and Disciplines in Art Education: Contexts of Understanding* (Urbana: University of Illinois Press, 1991).

21. Barbara Newson and Adele Silver, eds., *The Art Museum As Educator* (Berkeley, CA: University of California Press, 1978).

22. Eric Fernie, *Art History and Its Methods: A Critical Anthology* (London: Phaidon Press, 1995).

23. Michael J. Parsons and H. Gene Blocker, *Aesthetics and Education: Disciplines in Art Education* (Urbana: University of Illinois Press, 1993).

24. Hutchens and Suggs, *Art Education.*

25. Barrett, *Criticizing Art.* p. 112.

26. Charles Jencks, "The Post-Avant-Garde," in *The Post-Modern Reader,* ed. Charles Jencks (London: Academy Editions, 1992).

27. Jean-Francois Lyotard, "The Postmodern Condition," in Alexander and Seidman, eds., *Culture and Society,* pp. 330–341.

28. Norman Wakefield, *Postmodernism* (London: Pluto Press, 1990).

29. Susan M. Pearce, ed., *Interpreting Objects and Collections,* Leicester Readers in Museum Studies (London: Routledge, 1994).

30. Carol Duncan, *Civilizing Rituals: Inside Public Art Museums* (New York: Routledge, 1995).

31. For example, see: Norma Broude and Mary Garrard, eds., *The Power of Feminist Art* (New York: Harry N. Abrams, 1994); Carol Duncan, "The MoMA's Hot Mamas," in

The Aesthetics of Power: Essays in Critical Art History (New York: Cambridge University Press, 1993), pp. 189–207; and Guerrilla Girls, *Confessions of the Guerrilla Girls* (New York: HarperCollins, 1995).

32. Elizabeth A. Ament, "Using Feminist Perspectives in Art Education," *Art Education* 51, no. 5 (1998): 56–61; and Heidi Hein, "Refining Feminist Theory: Lessons from Aesthetics," in *Aesthetics in Feminist Perspective,* ed. Heidi Hein and C. Korsmeyer (Bloomington: Indiana University Press, 1993), pp. 3–20.

33. Laura Chapman, foreword to *Gender Issues in Art Education: Content, Contexts, and Strategies,* ed. Georgia Collins and Renee Sandell (Reston, VA: National Art Education Association, 1996).

34. Lippard, *Mixed Blessings.*

35. Tom Anderson, "Toward a Postmodern Approach to Art Education," in Hutchens and Suggs, *Art Education,* pp. 62–73.

36. NAEA Commission on Research in Art Education, *Art Education: Creating a Visual Arts Research Agenda toward the 21st Century* (Reston, VA: National Art Education Association, 1994).

37. Louis E. Lankford, "Ecological Stewardship in Art Education," *Art Education* 50, no. 6 (1997): 47–53.

38. Cynthia L. Hollis, "On Developing an Art and Ecology Curriculum," *Art Education* 50, no. 6 (1997): 21–24.

39. Lankford, "Ecological Stewardship."

40. Getty Center for Education in the Arts, "Episode A: Student Social Commentary," *Art Education in Action,* No. 2 (Los Angeles: The J. Paul Getty Trust, 1995).

41. Norman Bryson, "Semiology and Visual Interpretation," in *Visual Theory: Painting and Interpretation,* ed. Norman Bryson and K. Moxey (New York: HarperCollins, 1991), p. 10.

42. Marilyn Galvin Stewart, "Aesthetics and the Art Curriculum," *Journal of Aesthetic Education* 28, no. 3 (1994): 77–88.

43. Anderson, "Toward a Postmodern Approach."

44. Ellen Dissanayake, *Homo Aesthetics: Where Art Comes From and Why?* (New York: The Free Press, 1992).

45. Sydney Walker, "Postmodern Theory and Classroom Art Criticism: Why Bother?" in Hutchens and Suggs, *Art Education,* pp. 111–121.

46. "e-Life: How the Internet Is Changing America," *Newsweek,* September 20, 1999.

47. Joe L. Kincheloe and Peter L. McLaren, "Rethinking Critical Theory and Qualitative Research," in *Handbook of Quantitative Research,* ed. Norman K. Denzin and Yvonna S. Lincoln (Thousand Oaks, CA: Sage, 1994), pp. 138–157.

48. Margot Lovejoy, *Postmodern Currents: Art and Artists in the Age of Electronic Media* (Upper Saddle River, NJ: Prentice-Hall, 1997), p. 160.

49. Parsons and Blocker, *Aesthetics and Education*, p. 65.

ACTIVITIES FOR THE READER

1. Write a letter advocating the inclusion of art in the elementary school curriculum. Use resources from Suggested Readings for this chapter and World Wide Web resources. The reader is directed to Web sites, which follow.

2. Evaluate art education curricula. How are postmodern issues integrated in art history, art criticism, aesthetics and art making? What evidence is there that the curriculum includes multicultural resources? Are women artists represented? Does the curriculum recognize a diversity of art forms, such as folk art and public art?

3. *Art Education: The Journal of the National Art Education Association* includes a section titled "Instructional Resources" in each issue. Example: Volume 50, no. 4 (July 1997) published "Children Ask Questions About West African Art." Review "Instructional Resources" in several issues of this publication for features on multicultural art and art made by women. University libraries generally subscribe to the journal.

4. Use the World Wide Web to locate curriculum resources on multicultural art and women's art. Make a list of works and include name and World Wide Web address (URL) of the site where located. Many sites allow viewers to print copies of art images.

SUGGESTED READINGS

Art Is Necessary, Not Just "Nice"

The following publications offer cogent and compelling explanations for the necessity of art education for every child.

Broudy, Harry S. *Enlightened Cherishing: An Essay on Aesthetic Education.* Urbana: University of Illinois Press, 1972. A delightful philosophical essay on the benefits of arts in education.

————. "Cultural Literacy and General Education." In Ralph A. Smith, ed., *Cultural Literacy and Arts Education.* Chicago: University of Illinois Press, 1991, pp. 7–16.

Gee, E. Gordon, and Constance Bumgarner Gee. "Arts Education for a Lifetime of Wonder." *ArtsEdNet.* Available http://www.artsednet.getty.edu/ArtsEdNet/Advocacy/Life/wonder.html

Getty Center for Education in the Arts. "Beyond the Three Rs: Student Achievement through the Arts." *Educational Leadership* 53, no. 2 (1995): Insert.

Levi, Albert William, and Ralph A. Smith. "Art Education: A Critical Necessity." *Disciplines in Art Education: Contexts of Understanding.* Urbana: University of Illinois Press, 1991.

National Endowment for the Arts and Gary O. Larson. *American Canvas: An Arts Legacy for Our Communities.* Washington, DC: National Endowment for the Arts, 1997. Online version available: http://arts.endow.gov/pub/AmCan/

Harold Williams. *The Language of Civilization: The Vital Role of the Arts in Education.* Washington, DC: President's Committee on the Arts and Humanities, 1991.

Issues and Topics in Art Education: Postmodernism

The following texts provide discussions on the application of postmodern theory to education and art education.

Postmodernism and Art Education

Efland, Arthur, Kerry J. Freedman, and Patricia L. Stuhr, eds. *Postmodern Art Education: An Approach to Curriculum.* Reston, VA: National Art Education Association, 1996. Provides an excellent discussion of postmodern theory and attendant curriculum problems, supplemented with examples of postmodern art curricula.

Hutchens, James, and Marianne Suggs, eds. *Art Education: Content and Practice in a Postmodern Era.* Reston, VA: National Art Education Association, 1997. This text emphasizes economic, political, social, and cultural influences in the art world. Includes a section calling for rethinking the "elements and principles of design" orientation to curriculum.

Neperud, Ronald, ed. *Context, Content, and Community in Art Education: Beyond Postmodernism.* New York: Teachers College Press, 1995.

Smith-Shank, "Semiotic Pedagogy and Art Education." *Studies in Art Education* 36, no. 4. (1995).

Feminist Theory and Art Education

American Association of University Women. "Gender Gaps: Where Schools Still Fail Our Children." Available http://www.aauw.org/2000/research.html

Collins, Georgia, and Renee Sandell, eds. *Gender Issues in Art Education: Content, Contexts, and Strategies.* Reston, VA: National Art Education Association, 1996. Insightful presentation of issues related to feminism and strategies for improving understanding of gender.

Nochlin, Linda. *Women, Art, and Power and Other Essays.* New York: Harper & Row, 1988.

Sandell, Renee, and Peg Speirs. "Feminist Concerns and Gender Issues in Art Education." *Translations: From Theory to Practice* 8, no. 1 (1999). Written to be helpful to classroom teachers as well as theorists.

Multicultural Theory and Art Education

Chalmers, F. Graeme. *Celebrating Pluralism: Art, Education, and Cultural Diversity.* Occasional Paper 5. Santa Monica, CA: Getty Center for Education in the Arts, 1996. Presents a case for multiculturalism as a means to strengthen commonalities of human experience.

Delacruz, Elizabeth Manley. "Multiculturalism and Art Education: Myths, Misconceptions, Misdirections." *Art Education* 48, no. 3 (1995): 57–61.

McFee, June King. *Cultural Diversity and the Structure and Practice of Art Education.* Reston, VA: National Art Education Association, 1998. Reflects on the civil rights and women's movements and their influence on education reforms.

Saunders, Robert J., ed. *Beyond the Traditional in Art: Facing a Pluralistic Society.* Reston, VA: National Art Education Association, 1998. Clarifies multicultural terminology involved in art criticism and aesthetics. Includes a proposal for a multicultural art canon. Provides strategies and help in planning a multicultural curriculum.

Young, Bernard, ed. *Art, Culture and Ethnicity.* Reston, VA: National Art Education Association, 1990. Called a landmark study, this text addresses the need to focus on the cultural heritage of a multicultural society. Includes discussions related to teaching disadvantaged youth.

WORLD WIDE WEB RESOURCES

Advocacy

The Arts Education Partnership, *Task Forces and Advocacy.* <http:/aep-arts.org/tfadvoc/tfadvocacy.html> September 9, 1999. Advocacy resources and links to other sites.

Getty Education Institute for the Arts, *ArtsEdNet.* "Winning Support for Arts Education." <http://www.artsednet.getty. edu/ArtsEdNet/Advocacy> September 9, 1999. Speeches, conference reports, articles and other publications, and links to other sites.

John F. Kennedy Center for the Performing Arts, *ArtsEdge,* "Advocacy Web Resources." <http://artsedge.kennedy-center.org/ir/advocacy.html> September 9, 1999. Articles, resources, and links to other sites.

National Art Education Association, *Publications.* <http://www.naea-reston.org/> September 1999. Publications and links to other sites.

National Endowment for the Arts. <http://arts.endow.gov> September 1999. Arts programs, publications, resources for advocacy, and links to other sites.

Multicultural Art and Women's Art Images and Resources

Getty Institute for Education in the Arts, *ArtsEdNet.* <http://www.artsednet.getty.edu/> September 1999. Curriculum, resources, images, publications, and links to other sites.

Fowler Museum of Cultural History, UCLA. <http://www.arts.ucla.edu/museums/fowler> September 1999.

Los Angeles County Museum of Art. <http://www. lacma.org>

Museum of Latin American Art. <http://www.molaa.com/>

National Museum of African Art. <http://www.si.edu/nmafa/nmafa.htm>

National Museum of American Art. <http://www.nmaa.si. edu/>

National Museum of the American Indian. <http://www. si.edu/nmai/nav.htm>

National Museum for Women in the Arts. <http://www. nmwa.org>

The Arthur M. Sackler Gallery and Freer Gallery of Art, Smithsonian Institution, The National Museum of Asian Arts for the United States. <http://www.si.edu/Asia/>

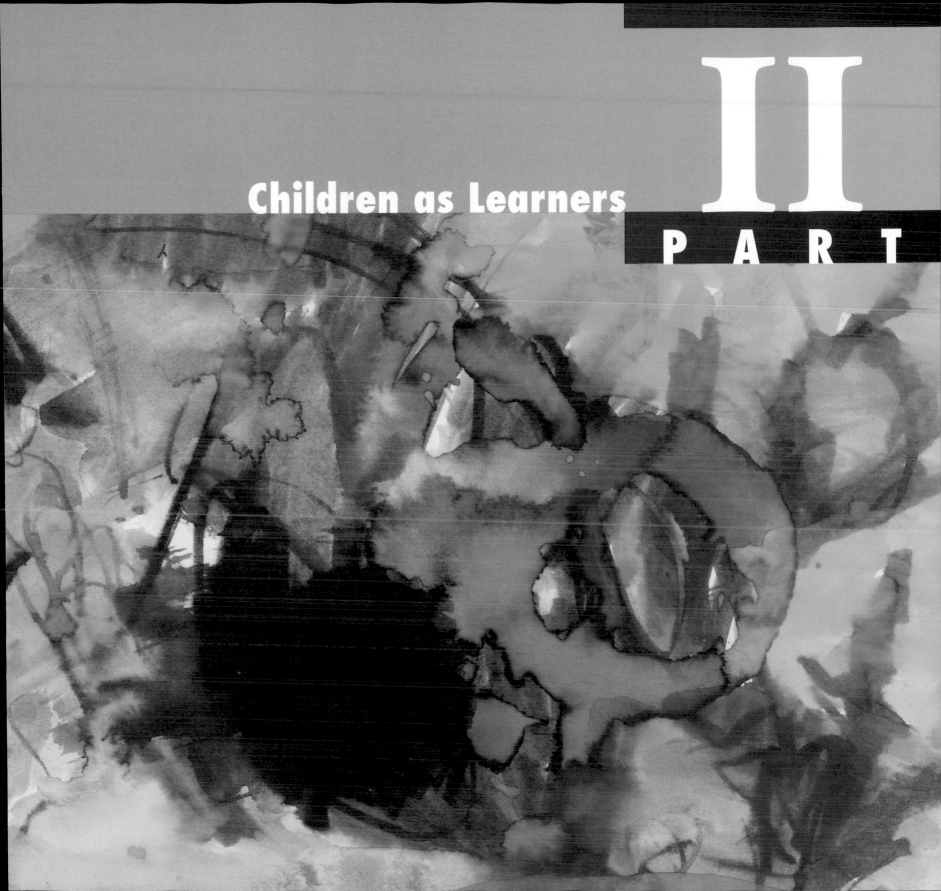

Children as Learners

II

PART

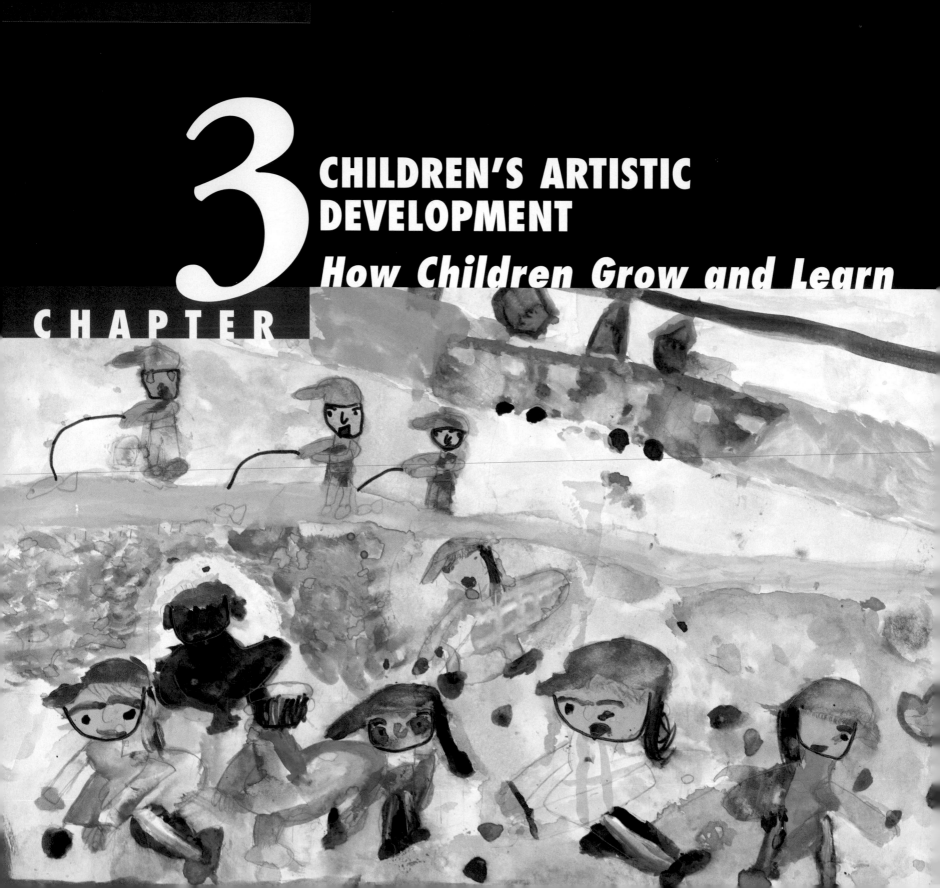

I admire the mind's capacity to derive a pertinent order from the chaos of experience. This dramatic struggle starts at birth, and the art of children is an essential instrument of this need to recognize and create meaningful order.[1]

—Rudolf Arnheim

For many years adults have been fascinated with drawings, paintings, and other art objects made by children. Psychologists, educators, parents, and other interested adults have studied children's art from several vantages. Analysis of art products of children has been viewed as a means to look into their young minds and hearts, to learn what they are interested in, what they know, and how they think. Children's art has been studied as an expression of their emotional lives or personality development. Some scholars have used the apparent changes in the ways children draw and paint as they grow older as a basis for theories of mental development. More recently, ways that children understand what art is, how it is made by artists, and how it is judged and valued have been studied by researchers. This chapter discusses the emotional, developmental, and cognitive aspects of children's development in art and investigates relationships between children's art products and the works of adult artists.

Very young children, even before age two, enjoy the process of making marks by whatever means are available. The kinesthetic experience of rhythmic movement coupled with the observable results of their actions provide

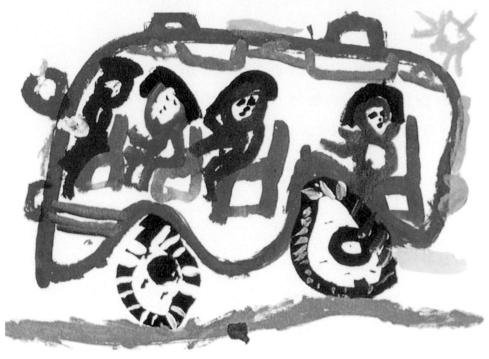

Japan

symbols that represent persons, animals, and objects extends the range of what they can communicate in their art and increases the likelihood that knowledgeable adults can interpret meaning from the art of children.

In the normal course of living prior to formal school experiences, children often relate and explore events in their lives that are emotionally important to them. Relationships with parents, siblings, family pets, or even fantasy characters often are depicted and explored in drawings, paintings, and clay. Children frequently are able to integrate the worlds of imagination, fantasy, and reality in their artistic creations. Sometimes children's understanding of how parts of the real world function can be seen in their artwork, as when they draw family members engaged in activities; when they draw animals, houses, cars, or airplanes; and when they deal with their personal fears or aspirations.

Because young children have naive abilities to draw and paint about their emotional lives in uninhibited ways, adults understandably have been very interested in their artwork. Children at early ages tend to draw and paint the people and events in their lives—both happy and sad. This seems to be a very natural and healthy practice exhibited by children from all parts of the world. Knowledgeable teachers of art recognize this and encourage children in their natural interests as they gradually assist them to enlarge their understanding of the world of art.

Some psychologists and educators are especially interested in children's art as a window into their thoughts and feelings, especially those children who might be emotionally disturbed or who have experienced traumas of some sort. The subject matter of drawings, paintings, and sculptures by such children, ways they represent themselves and others in their works, and even the manner by which they create with art materials can sometimes provide clues to their emotional lives. This is the area of special concern for art therapists.

An example of this type of revelation can be seen in the drawings and paintings of refugee children from strife-torn countries who witnessed the horrors and violence of war and later immigrated to North America and entered American and Canadian schools. Similarly, children who experience personal trauma sometimes focus on these topics in their art production and, through the process of dealing with the traumatic event in a safe, nonthreatening medium over which they have control, gain some resolution for themselves. The abilities of children to represent, manipulate, and control their worlds through art, and thus to deal with difficult life situations, are the source of the therapeutic dimension of art.

reinforcement for children to draw and paint. As they grow older and develop their cognitive, social, and psychomotor skills, children are able to express their ideas and feelings in their artwork.

As children develop individual symbol systems, their art becomes a personal language for many of them, although much of what they communicate may not be accessible to others. Indeed, because children of ages two, three, and four are not concerned with producing an art object, as adults perceive art, they often draw or paint directly over one graphic idea with a subsequent image that might in turn suggest a second or third idea. There might be layers of a child's thought and emotion buried within what to many adults might appear to be scribbles or a mess of paint. Researchers who have observed and listened to young children during this process have noted their flexibility in moving from one idea or theme to another, often talking to themselves or singing as they draw, paint, or work with clay.[2]

As children grow older, into the preschool and kindergarten ages, the result of their artwork often becomes more readily discernible and easier to interpret, especially as verbal skills increase, so they can explain their images, interests, and intentions. The development of children's abilities to create

Many art educators emphasize this capacity of art in their educational programs for very young children. Regardless of programmatic emphasis, it would be unwise for teachers to ignore or in any way diminish the spontaneous interest in making art that characterizes children everywhere.

It is not the art teacher's role to attempt to render psychological interpretations of particular children by analyzing their art products. This chapter discusses some of the normal characteristics in children's drawings and paintings. This knowledge will assist teachers to note gross variations from the norm on the part of particular children. Very unusual art products can be clues that teachers can share with appropriate school personnel, such as other teachers, school counselors, or school psychologists. This information can be useful in helping school officials provide the best educational opportunities for each child. The following chapter deals with problems related to atypical children.

STAGES OF GRAPHIC REPRESENTATION

Teachers who work with children come to know a great deal about how children behave at particular age levels. A good deal of "teacher talk" or professional shoptalk in faculty lounges is concerned with these behavioral characteristics and with the noticeable gains in maturity as children move from grade to grade. Major proportions of the fields of developmental psychology and cognitive psychology are dedicated to the study of these maturational or developmental changes in children. Educators are concerned with these studies and continuously attempt to make school learning environments more appropriate for the developmental characteristics of children. For example, the organization of learning centers for use by a few children in the classroom while others are working in reading groups or other activities is very different from earlier practices in which desks were bolted to the floor in rows and all students participated in rote lessons copied from the blackboard. The organization of middle schools is motivated in large part by recognition of developmental differences of children as they progress from the elementary-school years toward the more independent life of high-school students.

Children's capacities to make and understand art develop parallel to changes in the cognitive, emotional, social, and physical dimensions of their lives. The notion that children progress through stages of development in these various areas is central to the field of developmental psychology and the writings of Lowenfeld, Piaget, Gardner, and others.[3] Developmental or stage theory associated with art is based on the assumption of *untutored progression,* accounted for primarily by qualitative differences in the minds of children and the results of their life experiences as they grow older.

Although problems are inherent with this assumption, when we take the position that children should be educated in art, the basic information available through the study of stages or changes in the ways children make and think about art can be very valuable.[4] Knowledge of developmental stages in art can provide teachers with insights about what children are attempting in their artwork and ways that appropriate motivation and instruction might be provided.

Children grow and develop in generally predictable ways, with extensive variations within an age norm or a stage. Just as reading levels vary widely in an average class of twenty-five or thirty children (and the variation increases with each grade level), so abilities in art vary widely as well. This means that teachers can come to know, generally, what to expect and plan for when they are preparing their art programs, but they must be aware of the unique educational needs of each child.

We present a simplified version of stage theory that describes three general stages of children's graphic development, known here as the *manipulative stage* (ages two through five), the *symbol-making stage* (ages six through nine), and the *preadolescent stage* (ages ten through thirteen). Important differences in artistic development are noted among the stages, which are also quite broad.

Some of the characteristics of children's artwork are altered when they are given instruction and when they learn more about the adult world of art. Rather than viewing these alterations of the natural as negative, we view them as the normal outcome in any area of learning in the school curriculum. When we accept the obligation to provide art education as an essential component in the general education of all children, we accept the fact that education will alter the way children think and act. The moral and ethical requirement for teachers is to assure that changes they bring about in the lives of children are positive, enabling, and life-enhancing.

The first stage is one at which children manipulate materials, initially in an exploratory, seemingly random fashion. Later in this stage the manipulation becomes increasingly organized until the children give a title to the marks they make. During the next stage, the children develop a series of distinct symbols that stand for objects in their experience. These symbols are eventually related to an environment

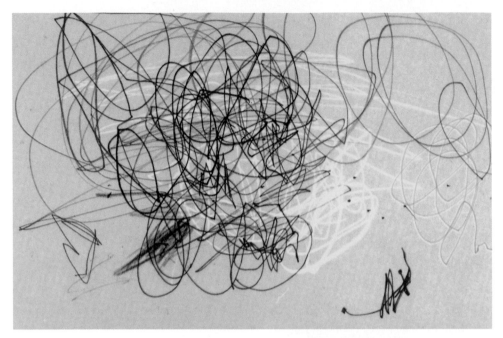

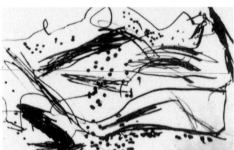
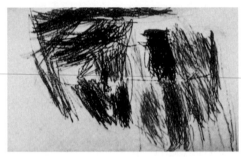

Children who scribble (preschematic investigation) develop a repertoire of lines and marks they will use later. As these examples show, there is considerable development even within this stage from the seemingly random and exploratory (top) to an increased sense of organization (bottom left) to the use of color and a more conscious connection between parts of the whole configuration (bottom right).

within the drawing. Finally comes a preadolescent stage, at which the children become critical of their work and express themselves in a more self-conscious manner. The fact that these stages appear in the work of most children in no way detracts from the unique qualities of each child's work. Indeed, within the framework of the recognized stages of expression, the individuality of children stands out more clearly. *Stages of artistic development are useful norms that can enlighten the teacher, but they should not be considered as goals for education.*

The Manipulative Stage
(Ages 2–5, Early Childhood)

Drawing is a natural and virtually universal activity for children. From infancy onward, children mark, scribble, and draw with whatever materials are available. As soon as they can grasp a marking instrument of some sort—a crayon, a pencil, or even a lipstick or piece of charcoal—children make marks and scribbles. Some adults discourage this behavior in their offspring, especially when it occurs on walls, floors, and other surfaces not intended for graphic purposes, and they are relieved when their children outgrow the tendency to engage in scribbling.

These parents, and often teachers, too, do not realize that what we call scribbling can be a worthwhile learning activity for very young children.[5] By scribbling, an infant literally "makes a mark on the world" in one of the earliest examples of personal causation: Children come to realize in physical and visual terms that they can exercise control over their environment. Before the age of two, infants are fascinated by their abilities to make oral noises—babblings, cries, gurgles, and laughs. All these sounds cease instantly on completion. Graphic marks that the infant makes remain, however, and provide evidence of the marking behavior. The child marks and sees the marks with the dawning awareness that he or she can alter them and add to them. This is a significant realization for such a tiny person and, as Elliot Eisner explains, is also a source of pleasure:

> The rhythmic movement of the arm and wrist, the stimulation of watching lines appear where none existed before are themselves satisfying and self-justifying. They are intrinsic sources of satisfaction.[6]

Through their preschematic efforts, children aged one through three or four develop a repertoire or vocabulary of graphic marks, which they create primarily for the kinesthetic rewards inherent in the manipulation of lines, colors, and textures.

Scribbled marks are precursors to the visual symbol system of drawing that each child develops independently and uses in her or his own way. Children who have opportunities to scribble produce a wide variety of lines, marks, dots, and shapes during the first two or three years of life. This repertoire of graphic marks is utilized later for the invention of visual symbols in the form of drawings. The child who develops a variety of graphic marks during the scribbling years will manifest this visual vocabulary to produce symbolic drawings that increase in richness and sophistication as the child matures. Children who rarely engage in early graphic activities usually exhibit a narrower vocabulary in their drawings and require considerable encouragement to continue drawing.

This initial stage of artistic production is referred to here as the *manipulative stage* and can last through ages four or five in many children. The term *manipulative* implies a general stage of initial exploration and experimentation with any new materials, including clay, blocks, and so on. The manipulative stage usually lasts until the children are in kindergarten.

As time goes on, seemingly random drawings are increasingly controlled; they become more purposeful and rhythmic. Eventually, many children tend to resolve their marks into large circular patterns, and they learn to vary their lines so they are sweeping, rippling, delicate, or bold. When a child can return a moving line to its point of inception, a sense of control is vastly increased, leading to the creation of the *mandala*.

The great variety of circular patterns, or "mandalas," according to Rhoda Kellogg's analysis of thousands of children's drawings, appears as a final stage between scribbling and representation.[7] The term *mandala* is usually used to describe a circle divided into quarters by two crossed lines. Carl Jung and Rudolf Arnheim viewed the mandala as a universal, culture-free symbol that evolves out of a physical condition (that is, as a basic property of the nervous system) as well as a psychological need.[8] It is interesting that the mandala, like other manifestations of children's early drawing, appears readily among children around the world.

As they experiment with materials and gain experience, normal children progress through the manipulative stage. They develop a greater variety of marks, and use them in varying combinations. Random manipulation becomes more controlled as children invent and repeat patterns and combinations of marks. Lines of all types are used by children in their marking, including vertical, horizontal, diagonal, curved, wavy, and zigzag lines. Some children will attend to drawing intently for periods of thirty minutes or more and will produce a series of a dozen or more drawings within a brief time.

Children aged two to five learn about qualities of art materials around them, the multitude of textures, colors, smells, tastes, weights, and other properties. They are interested in art materials because of the intrinsic visual and tactile properties. They can manipulate art materials and can even transform their characteristics. With a brush they can make paint into a line or a shape or various textures. How thrilling it is for the child to learn that colors change when mixed together—and that he or she can make this happen. Similarly, the child can make a piece of clay into a coil or pinch it into small flat shapes or scratch it with an object to create an inter-

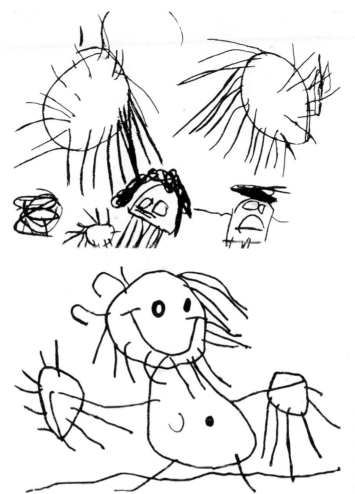

The mandalas at the top served as models for the head and hands of the figure at the bottom. The mandala is one of the rudiments of graphic vocabulary that can be used by children for various purposes.

esting texture. Children experience the same exploratory process with other media, such as scraps of wood or cardboard boxes.

Picture making in general comes naturally to children at a surprisingly early age. Some children will grasp a crayon and make marks with it before they are fifteen months old. Children's bodily movements are overall movements and result in a broad rhythmic action. When very young children paint, they do so from their fingertips to the ends of their toes. Not until they grow older and gain control of the smaller muscles do their muscular actions in art become localized to hand, arm, and shoulder.

As well as exhibiting an ability to design in two dimensions, the preschool child often learns to produce three-dimensional designs. By the time some children have reached

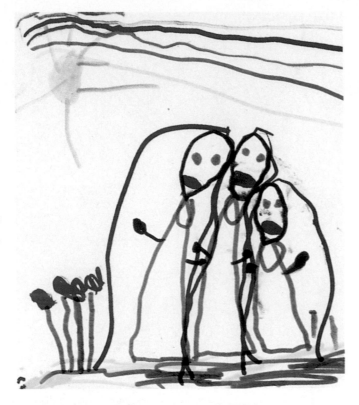

Once established, children will use schematic representation in a number of circumstances, retaining some portions as other ideas are included. These two remarkable drawings were created by the same girl at ages 4 and 10. The theme of both works is "Friends." As the child, Maria, has grown and developed perceptually, her schemata have progressed accordingly from early undifferentiated representations of the figure, arms, and face. At age 10 she demonstrates her ability to draw figures in proportion and to create a wide variety of costumes and hair styles as she depicts her nine- and ten-year-old friends.

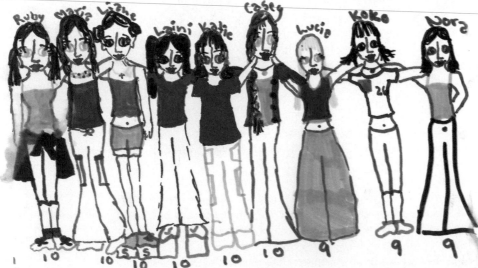

age three, they have experimented with sand and—sometimes to their parents' horror—mud. They are capable of joining together scraps of wood and cardboard boxes or using building blocks to bring about the semblance of an organized three-dimensional form. The interaction between child and materials is a vital aspect of this stage.

Burton describes three types of conceptual learning accomplished by children in the manipulative stage. When children are able to grasp the outstanding features of lines, shapes, and textures and when they learn that materials can be organized in many different ways, they have formed *visual concepts*. *Relational concepts* are formed when children can construct relationships of order and comparison and when they can apply these relationships knowledgeably.

> For example, when organizing a painting, children make careful decisions about the placement of their lines and shapes, whether they are to be close together or far apart, positioned in the middle, top or bottom of the page, or enclosed within each other.[9]

Expressive concepts are formed when children recognize the connections between their actions with art materials and the visual outcomes and sensations these actions cause. Children begin to describe lines as "fast" or "wiggly" and shapes as "fat" or "pointy." The fact the child can control and select the qualities and organize them in ways that express happiness, bounciness, or tiredness represents significant artistic development. It means the child has developed a graphic language with which he or she can begin to express and communicate ideas and feelings.

Up to this point children may or may not have established a theme or expression nor given a title to their work. Because drawing is an emotional and social as well as cognitive (intellectual) process, children will often accompany their work with appropriate sounds. Eventually, however, children will lift their eyes from their work and say, "It's me," or "It's a window," or even "That's Daddy driving his car." The manipulative process has at last reached the stage at which the product may be given a title.

We cannot overemphasize the importance of the "naming of a scribble" in the life and development of a child. Naming—matching a word with an image—can precede the drawing experience when parents read to children from illustrated books. Many parents watch with great anticipation and record the exact age when their child takes the first step; the child's first word is another memorable occasion, but neither is as intellectually significant as the child's own invention of a graphic symbol, for this act places the child far ahead of all other mammals and reveals the tremendous mental potential of human beings.

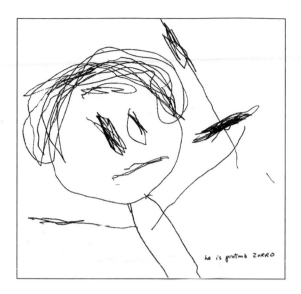

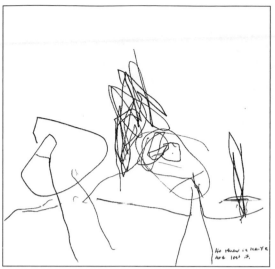

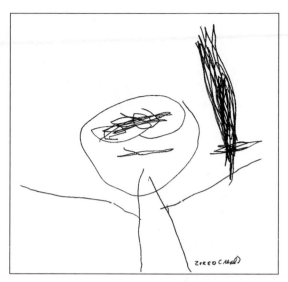

We do not know precisely how children arrive at such pictorial-verbal equivalents. On the one hand, it has been suggested that the shapes they produce in their controlled manipulations remind them of objects in their environment. On the other hand, the dawning realization that marks or shapes can convey meaning, together with a newly acquired skill to produce them at will, may prompt children to create their own symbols. Perhaps the symbol appears as a result of both mental processes, varying in degree according to the personality of its author. Whatever the process may be, the ability to produce symbols constitutes an enormous advance in the child's educational history. By the first grade, the child has developed her or his own means of expression and communication that are definitive, personal, and flexible.

The first-named scribble is usually a circular or generally round shape. The child sees the shape as it appears among random marks and learns to repeat the shape at will. The production of symbols demands a relatively high degree of precision because a symbol, unlike most of the results of manipulation, is a precise statement of a fact or an event in experience.

On entering kindergarten at the age of four or five, even those children who have had practice at home with art materials and who have produced pleasing designs tend to regress. The causes of such a condition are not hard to find. In the first place, the children are passing through a period of adjustment to a new social setting. Many of them are away from the protection of their parents and their homes for the first

time. Unfamiliar faces and situations surround them, including a new and powerful adult in the form of a teacher. Also, many are passing through a new phase of artistic development. From the scribble or manipulative stage they are progressing into the stage of symbols. In the *symbolic* stage, marks can no longer be placed at random on a sheet of paper but rather must be set down with increased precision. Not until they feel more at home in their new environment will qualities of spontaneity and directness return. Regressions in ability occur with each child from time to time and may be observed at any level of development. Absence from school, illness, or temporary emotional upsets can be reflected in the artwork of any child.

Although normal children progress beyond it, *no one leaves the manipulative stage entirely.* Even when confronted as adults with an unfamiliar substance or a new tool, we are likely to perform some manipulation before we begin to work in earnest. After buying a new pen, for example, we generally scribble a few marks with it before settling down to write a letter. Artists who purchase a new kind of paint will in all likelihood experiment with it before they paint seriously. Indeed, the manipulation of paint was one of the chief characteristics of abstract expressionist painting. Moreover, the painterly surface is one of the hallmarks of all romantic art, much as the repression of painterly effects is a distinguishing characteristic of classicism. Surface manipulation plays the same role in sculpture. The teacher should realize that manipulation is not a waste of educational time and materials; it is a highly educative process. The interaction between ideas and materials

After viewing the movie, *The Mask of Zorro,* a three-year-old boy made a distinction between a "pretend" Zorro (figure A) and the real Zorro (figure C), who wears a mask. In (figure B) Zorro loses his knife in the midst of a sword fight.

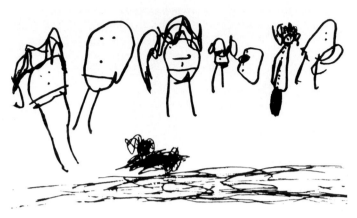

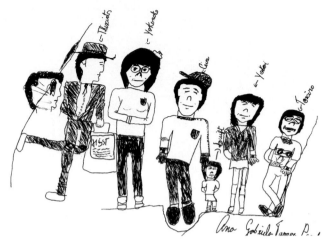

Illustrating a range in children's degrees of differentiation, the top drawing by a four-year-old Australian shows a family as a series of tadpole-like figures emerging at the end of the scribble stage, while the lower drawing by a ten-year-old Brazilian exhibits the stage of realism, around two years in advance of her age level.

The most intresting stage the child becomes alot more visual

that the children gain through manipulation allows them to enter more easily into the symbolic phase of expression.

Parents and teachers might be tempted to rush a child into the next stage of development prematurely, but children follow their own timetable. It is well to bear in mind that elaboration precedes advancement. Like many artists, children prefer to exhaust the possibilities of one stage before proceeding to the next.

The Symbol-Making Stage
(Ages 6–9, Grades 1–4)

When the normal child makes a connection between image and idea, assigning meaning to a drawn shape, the shape becomes a symbol. Initially, this shape is used to stand for whatever the child chooses. A shape designated as "Mommy" might appear very similar to another shape that the child calls "house." The early symbol is, in the terms of psychologist Rudolf Arnheim, *undifferentiated.* It serves the child by standing for many objects. A parallel use in the verbal symbol system is demonstrated when a young child who has learned to say "doggie" in relation to the family pet points to a sheep, cow, or other furry four-legged animal and says "doggie." Adults correct the child and introduce the appropriate term. The child then has a more differentiated symbol to apply: "doggie" for one kind of animal, "sheep" for another, and so on.

A similar process develops with children's drawings. The initial primitive symbol can stand for whatever the child chooses it to represent. As the child's symbol-making ability progresses, the child produces more-sophisticated graphic symbols. This can be seen especially in children's early representations of the human figure. The primitive circular shape stands for "Mommy." Later, a line and two marks inside the shape are "Mommy" with eyes and mouth. The primitive shape is differentiated further by the addition of two lines that represent legs, two lines for arms, and a scribble that stands for hair.

It is at this point that a fundamental misunderstanding of children's graphic representation can occur. Most adults view these early drawings of people as heads with arms and legs protruding, termed "tadpole" figures. The question is asked, "Why do children draw figures this way?" Those who are experienced with children at this level realize that the children understand human anatomy much differently than their drawings would suggest. They know the parts of the body, and they know that arms do not protrude from the head—they are aware of shoulders, chest, and stomach. Why, then, do these early drawings appear to represent heads with arms and legs and no torso? Arnheim's explanation is eminently logical and useful:

> Representation never produces a replica of the object but its structural equivalent in a given medium. . . . The young child spontaneously discovers and accepts the fact that a visual object on paper can stand for an enormously different one in nature.[10]

This means that the child's primitive symbol, the circular shape, stands for the entire person, not just the head. This is a person with eyes and a mouth, a person with hair. It does not represent only the head of a person with inappropriately placed appendages. This interpretation eliminates the apparent

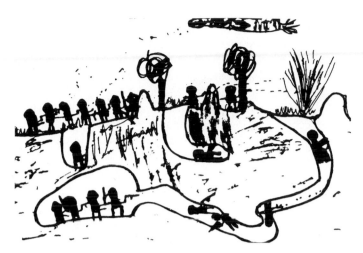

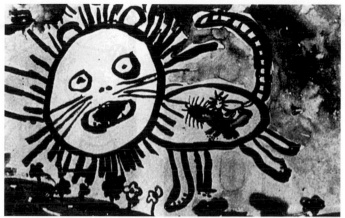

Examples of the results when children draw what they know rather than what they see are shown in these X-ray views (top) of an eight-year-old Australian child's conception of armies using a tunnel, and an interior view of a lion by an eight-year-old Korean child.

discrepancy between what children draw and paint and their understanding of the world around them, especially the human figure. We must recognize that children's symbols are not replicas of the world and that the materials used by children will influence their symbol making. In other words, *children at this stage draw what they know, not what they see.*

As children grow and develop from this early symbolic behavior into the symbol-making stage, they produce increasingly differentiated representations. The human figure appears with more details, such as feet, hands, fingers, nose, teeth, and perhaps clothing. It is interesting to note again how children create equivalents rather than replicas of their subjects. Hair might be represented by a few lines or by an active scribble. Fingers are often shown as a series of lines protruding from the hands with a "fingerness" quality, but with little regard for exact number.

Eventually a body is drawn with the head attached and with arms and legs in the appropriate location. This more true-to-life figure drawing is usually achieved through a process of experimentation with the medium. Sometimes the space between two long legs becomes the body. Some children add another larger circular shape for the body and draw the head on top. Once the child's representation of the human figure has reached the point where all the body parts are explicitly included, the symbol can be used and elaborated upon in many significant ways. The child can draw men and women, boys and girls, and people with different costumes and occupations. Most children also develop symbols for other objects in the world, including animals and birds, houses and other buildings, cars, trucks, and other vehicles, and in general anything that interests the child.

Claire Golomb suggests that children's conventions for representing three dimensions in drawings, such as transparencies and mixed views from front and side, are "a record of the child's problem-solving strategies and also reflect the child's lack of familiarity with the so-called 'tricks of the trade' that create the appearance of three-dimensional space."[11] Golomb's detailed studies of children's work in clay provide useful comparisons between performance in two- and three-dimensional media.

Relating Symbols to an Environment

Whenever pupils produce two or more symbols related in thought within the same composition, they have demonstrated an advance in visual communication, for they have realized that a relationship of objects and events exists in the world. The problems that confront them at this point revolve around a search for a personal means of expressing satisfactory relationships among symbols, ideas, experience, and environment. In striving for such connections they are engaged in the main task of all artists. This development can occur only if educational conditions are right. Unfortunately, during these delicate developmental stages, problems may develop if adults view children's art as a crude version of adult work. Children's work up to this point sometimes appears to the eye of the uninitiated as untidy, disorderly, and often unintelligible. To make children's work neater or clearer, adults sometimes inappropriately use certain "devices," such as outlining objects for them to color or giving them the work of others to copy and trace. The problem with many of these devices is that they are devoid of educational value and ignore the child's point of view. Because of this, adult

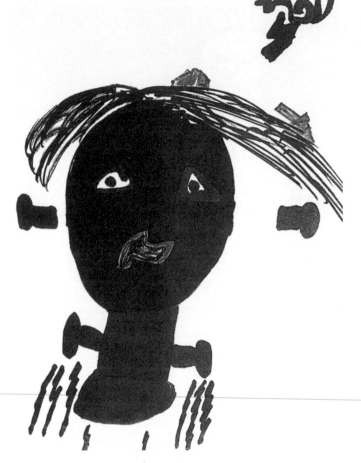

The story behind a drawing can be far more complex than the work itself. The comments which follow were transcribed by the father after the drawing was completed: "This is a picture of a monster. His hands are like lightning and they are used to change other people into the same monster. The neck is lava; the neck is strong. The ears on the side of the monster's head go out to kill people and then they return. The eyes and mouth are angry and so is the shape of the eyes and mouth. The hair is dangerous because it contains electricity and it kills people. The red in the hair are lasers which give strength to the brain which give strength to the body. The monster is very bad. It comes from space." (Israel)

Children As Storytellers

Frequently, children weave into one composition events that occur at different times. In a sense, they may treat the subject of a painting as they do that of a written composition. For example, in a painting entitled *Shopping with Mother,* they may show themselves and their mother driving to a shopping center, making various purchases, and finally unpacking the parcels at home. This becomes a story in three paragraphs with all the items placed on one painting surface.

Expression based on vicarious experiences—stories told or read to them, events they have seen on television or in the movies—may appear in children's art. Brent and Marjorie Wilson studied the themes of children's drawings and described the surprisingly broad range of thought and feeling depicted by them. To encourage children to draw stories, the Wilsons provided paper divided into frames and made the following request:

> Have you ever drawn pictures to tell stories? Have you ever drawn adventures that you, or heroes, or animals might have? Have you drawn stories about strange creatures in strange worlds? Have you ever drawn stories of battles or machines, even of plants and insects? Have you ever drawn stories about sports or vacations or holiday celebrations? Have you drawn stories about everyday things that happen to people? Please draw a story using boxes to show what first happens in your story, what happens next, and how things finally turn out.[12]

In analyzing many children's graphic narratives (story drawings), the Wilsons found about twenty different themes.

models can discourage some children from developing their own ideas.

Children may begin relating a symbol to its environment by simple means. They may render in paint, clay, or some other suitable medium two similar symbols for human beings, to which they give the title *Me and My Mother.* Soon they begin to put together symbols for diverse objects that have a relationship in their thought. Their work may be given such titles as the following:

Our House Has Windows
My Dog Fetching a Stick
I Am Watching Television
I Am Learning to Use a Computer
Riding to School with My Friends
Throwing the Ball to Maria
Mommy and I Are Cooking

Children continually draw *quests* ranging from space odysseys to mountain climbing; *trials* depicting tests of strength, courage, and perseverance; and they show *contests* and *conflicts* in which individuals and groups engage in battles, sports contests, and fights. The process of *survival* is a persistent theme, where children depict evasive actions, but here the characters make little effort to fight back. Little fish are eaten by big fish, and people eat the big fish. Children show *bonding,* love or affection between individuals, animals, plants (and even shoes) in any combination. The process of *creation* is shown through all kinds of depictions of constructing and making, such as building a house, arranging a bouquet, or modeling a sculpture. Sometimes creation is followed by *destruction* of plants, animals, and people as well as objects. They are eaten, swallowed, or killed. Quite a number of story drawings deal with *death*. Children are no more immune to contemplations of death than any other group.[13]

Other themes included growth, failure, success, freedom, and daily rhythms; the slice-of-life themes of going to school, going on a picnic and returning, or going to the playground. Although children may first depict nothing but the objects they mention in the titles of their work, when encouraged, they begin to provide a setting or background for objects and even produce graphic narratives.

These topics are universal themes found in all the arts, from poetry and literature to music and the visual arts. Teachers can channel children's innate interests in these themes and ideas toward integrated learning about art as the children make their own art, view works of art by adult artists based on the same themes, and learn about the history and circumstances that caused artists from many cultures to share the same ideas and feelings. As we will note in Chapter 16 on curriculum, themes provide a very useful means by which to organize art learning for school programs.

Children's Use of Space

As children's use of symbols broadens and their expression consequently grows in complexity, the task of finding adequate graphic techniques to make their meaning clear becomes increasingly difficult. Their strong desire to express ideas with clarity leads them to invent or adopt many curious artistic conventions. The ingenuity exhibited by children in overcoming their lack of technical skills and in developing expressive devices of their own is fascinating to behold.

Children are confronted with unavoidable spatial problems in their drawings and other two-dimensional work. At first, objects and symbols are not related to each other. There is no up or down or surface on which people or objects are made to stand. For the child, the sheet of paper (picture space) is a place, and all the objects are together. Children often *vary the relative sizes of the symbols* used in their work. A symbol having emotional or intellectual importance may be made larger. "Mother," for example, may be depicted as being larger than a house; or, perhaps more frequently, children—who are generally egocentric at this stage—will delineate themselves as towering over their associates. Children employ this device in connection with all the familiar art materials, but it is especially noticeable in their painting. When children paint, they not only give a greater size to the object that appeals most to them but also may paint it in a favorite color. *Color is often chosen for its emotional appeal* rather than for its resemblance to a natural object. Soon, of course, the children's observation of the world affects their choice of color— sky becomes blue and grass green. When this happens, at

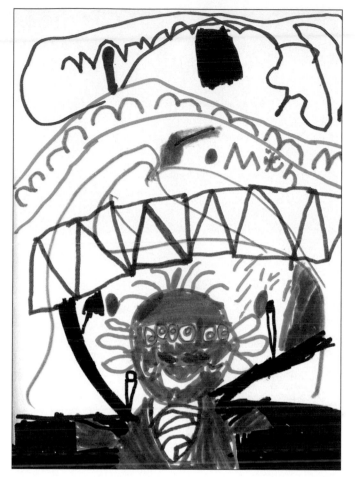

This seven-year-old boy's drawing for a six-eyed monster reflects two uses of the imagination: the specific rendering of a subject, and an expressive use of lines and shapes above the monster's head that reflect the artist's attitude towards his subject.

about seven years of age, their paintings tend to lose some of their naiveté.

Even though young children lack technical skills for making art, many are extraordinarily inventive in devising relatively complicated means to present their emotional and intellectual reactions to life. As they grow and learn, children become increasingly aware of relationships among the images they create. They want to make objects or people "stand up" or stand together, and they seek a place that will serve to support them. The bottom edge of the paper often is chosen to perform this function, and people, houses, and trees are lined up nicely along this initial *baseline*. Before long, other baselines are drawn higher on the paper, usually horizontal to match the bottom edge. Sometimes *multiple baselines* are drawn, and objects are lined up on each of them.

The baseline represents the relationships of objects in the real three-dimensional world, at least for the child at this level

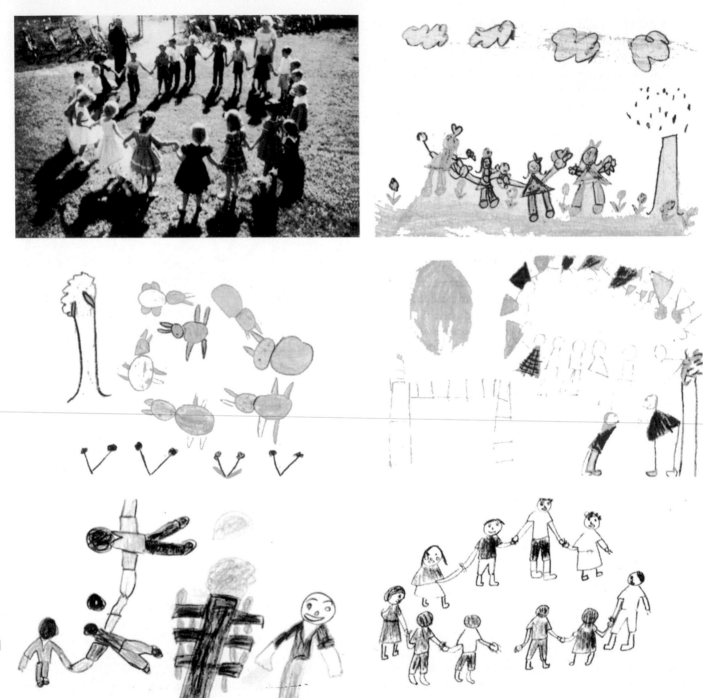

After they played circle games, first graders were asked to draw their favorite games. Note the treatment of people in a circle. Note also the wide range of expression as each child extracted that part of the experience which had the most meaning. To one child, it was a fashion parade; to another, the game Rabbit Run was meant to be taken literally. Another child, evicted from the games for misbehaving, shows himself sulking on the jungle gym, while a fourth child, likewise ostracized, was obviously less disturbed by the situation. The fifth child is interested in the problem of shifting views of people standing on the playground. Physical involvement may have destroyed the baseline and expanded the use of space.

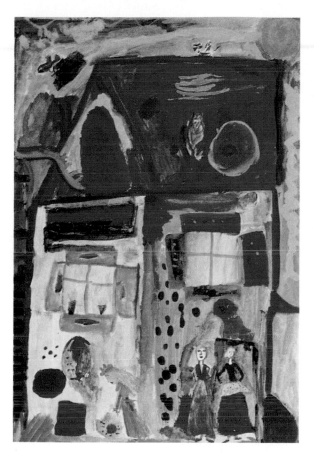

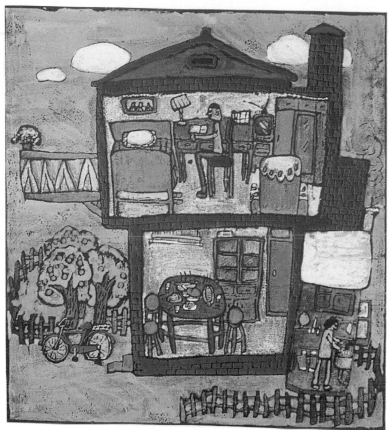

"Summer Day" by Russian child (Sherbakovva Zgenja 7, Vladivostok, Russia). House interior by Chinese child.

Teachers should recognize the potential of early schema for picture making. In figure A, a Russian child of 7 years allows us to peer behind exterior walls of a house. A Chinese child had created a similar X-ray view of a house in figure B. The Russian example is executed in tempera and is more realistic than the Chinese work. The Chinese child worked with mixed media to create this imaginative scene.

of development. At the same stage that children develop baselines, it is not unusual for them to place a strip of color or line at the top of the paper to represent the sky. Between the sky and the ground is air, which it is not necessary to represent because it is invisible. Often accompanying the strip of color as sky is a symbol for the sun, which is frequently depicted as a circular shape with radiating lines. Starlike shapes are sometimes added as a further indication of sky. These symbols may persist for years, and the sky does not appear as a solid mass of color touching the earth until the child has developed greater maturity of expression, either as a result of sensitive art instruction or, eventually, because of maturation.

Another spatial problem that must be dealt with by young symbol makers is *overlap*. Because children realize that two objects cannot occupy the same space at the same time, they typically avoid overlapping objects in their drawings. Because the paper is flat, unlike the real world, overlapping appears to be inconsistent in drawings. Nevertheless, children often

represent houses with people inside or show a baby inside the mother's stomach in apparent *X-ray views*. This convention is a logical one to solve a difficult artistic problem—how to represent the interior of a closed object. It is similar to the theatre stage, where one side of the set is open to allow the audience to look in.

As children become less egocentric and more interested in how the world functions, the subject matter of their art often becomes more complex. They encounter numerous representational problems, such as how to include many parts of an event or how to represent a comprehensive view. Children often solve such representational problems by utilizing a *bird's-eye view*, a *foldover view*, or *multiple views* in one drawing or painting. For example, in a drawing of a football game, the symbol-making child might draw the field's yardlines striped from a bird's-eye view to depict the space on which the players run. The football players are drawn from a side view, which is more useful for pictorial purposes than the bird's-eye view and is also easier to represent. Even in drawing

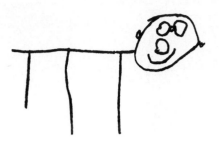

4 years — A circle head with circle ears, eyes, nose and mouth.

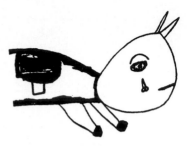

4 years/6 months — Features partially in side position: eye and nose centered, mouth attached to the outline. Diagonal lines are discovered and describe the ears.

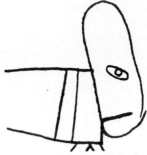

4 years/11 months — The circular head elongates into an oval as experiment toward a "more horse-like" head. The eye is also an oval.

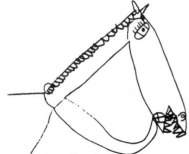

5 years — With diagonal lines, head and neck become one. The oval eye is perpendicular to the line of the nose and remains so for eight years.

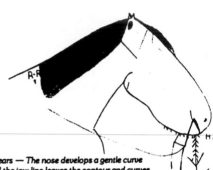

6 years — The nose develops a gentle curve and the jaw line leaves the contour and curves over the throat. This is Heidi's first concern with facial differences.

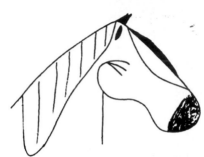

7 years — The curve of the jaw is exaggerated into a half circle ending in three wrinkles. A blaze and dark muzzle enhance the head.

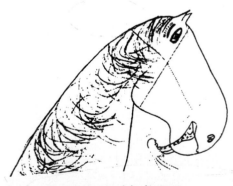

8 years — The head is broadened, the chin groove more indented!. The mane is freely drawn, eye and bit are decorated

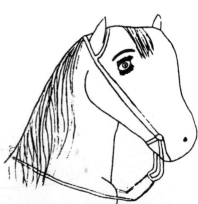

10 years — First attempt to turn the head to a three-quarter position. The ears are widely separated. The right eye moves away from the forward edge of the head, and the bony prominence over the left eye is noted.

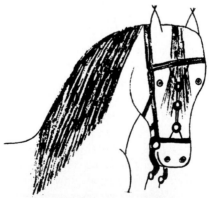

11 years — Both eyes, made visible by the almost frontal position of the head, revert temporarily to their circular formation. The nostrils are tight spirals. The bridle, forelock and ear tips are generously treated.

Overview of one girl's changes in the depiction of her favorite subject from symbolic to preadolescent stage. From *Heidi's Horse* by Sylvia Fein, Exelrod Press, 1984.

a single figure, it is not unusual for children to combine profile and front views to best represent the sitting or moving posture of the person.[14]

In a picture of a hockey game or of people seated around a table, some of the participants may appear to be lying flat or to be standing on their heads. The many children who produce compositions of this type usually do so by moving their picture in a circular fashion as they delineate objects or people. Thus, a child may draw a table and place Mother or Father at the head of it. Then, by turning the paper slightly, the child may place Brother in the now-upright position. This process continues until all are shown seated at the table. As an alternative to moving the drawing or painting surface, children may walk around the work, drawing as they go.

The foldover view is an interesting phenomenon seen in the drawings and paintings of numerous children. Again, it is a logical solution to a difficult representational problem. For example, the child wishes to draw a scene including a street, with sidewalks and buildings on both sides. The child draws the street and sidewalks using a bird's-eye view. The buildings on one side of the street are drawn up from the sidewalk, and the sky is above the buildings. The child then turns the paper around and draws the buildings and sky on the other side of the street up from the sidewalk. The drawing appears to have half the buildings right-side up and the other half upside down. There is sky at the top and at the bottom of the picture. The logic of this can be demonstrated by folding the picture on both sides of the street at the base of the buildings and tipping the buildings up vertically. Now the scene is like a diorama, and a person walking down the street could look left or right and see buildings and sky in proper placement.

Adult artists from various times, places, and cultures have all dealt with these problems associated with spatial representation. Egyptian art is typified by a rigid convention for the human figure, with particular representations of the eye, the profile head, hair, and so on. Chinese artists developed conventional ways to represent mountains rising from the mist, bamboo plants, and the human figure. Renaissance artists developed the conventions of linear perspective, which is one way artists deal systematically with the problems of representing the three-dimensional world on a two-dimensional surface. Artists of every era learn the artistic conventions of their culture and use them, reject them, or develop new solutions to problems, which in turn become another set of artistic conventions. Artists learn the conventions of their cultures and apply them in unique and expres-

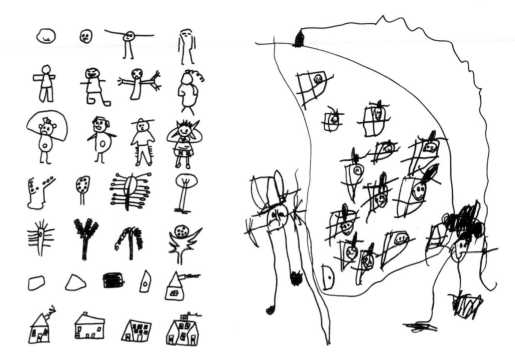

sive ways in their own work. This process of learning conventions, applying them, and innovating with them is useful also for children, especially as they approach adolescence, when their critical awareness becomes more acute.

The Schema and the Stereotype

Symbol-making children develop ways of drawing objects or figures so they become graphic equivalents of what they represent. A *schema* is a drawing (or painting or clay form) developed by a child that *has a degree of resemblance to an actual object*. The arms of a man, for example, are drawn differently from the branches of a tree. Children use these simple drawings consistently again and again to designate the same objects.[15] To create a schema, "the child not only has to fashion a graphic equivalent of objects in the world, but also has to design each solution so as to differentiate the marks from others that she makes."[16] In this sense, schema are a later form of the principle of differentiation.

Children learn to render the petals of a flower or the parts of people and animals in ways that serve their purposes. Children who develop their own schemata naturally understand them and are able to use them in flexible ways. A child who has developed a schema for the figure of a girl, for example,

Diagrams on the left show symbols that represent people, trees, and houses, proceeding (left to right) from the simple to the complex. These are the work of kindergarten children.

The drawing (to the right) of a schoolhouse shows a range of ideas in advance of the level of drawing, such as relative sizes of people, an inside-out relationship, subjects connected to each other, filling of the entire space, and the use of smoke to indicate a specific function.

The child doesn't care if the fence is not finished he is more intrested in shawing the action of throwing a ball and running!

is able to draw girls with different clothing or different hair or different poses. The basic schema for *girl* remains fairly uniform, but the child can accomplish reasonable variations. Sometimes children will alter their schema by leaving parts out or by exaggerating significant parts. Drawings are sometimes left unfinished, or some parts are obviously unattended to by the child. These variations should serve to remind adults that children often are more interested in the process of drawing or painting than they are in the result of their efforts as a work of art. The child who draws a picture of his interaction with the neighborhood bully is emotionally more involved with the situation than with the outcome of the drawing as a finished piece. In the child's depiction of the story, it matters little if the fence is not completed—the child knows it is there. The legs that are running and the arm that is throwing are the essential and emotionally significant parts that receive the child's careful attention. Children's art does not so much make visual statements as make experience visible.

Children who continue to make art as they progress through the typical symbol-making ages of six, seven, and eight usually construct a number of schemata that gain in sophistication and detail as the children's understanding progresses. Some children focus almost exclusively on the human figure; others draw many objects. Because of the time and effort required to develop an advanced schema, most children (and adults) are able to draw some objects much better than others, depending on what each person has developed during the schematic years. This explains why several levels of depiction might appear within a single drawing.

Children in the primary grades approach art as though it were their own private discovery, working freely and unselfconsciously, despite the profusion of visual influences around them. Allowing children in this stage to use a coloring book opens the door to self-doubt, because they are dramatically confronted with the gap between an adult's image and their own. In attempting to draw a clown at a later time, they may recall a "grown-up" clown they had once colored and either try unsuccessfully to emulate it or suddenly become dissatisfied with their own rendering.

Artistic *stereotypes* are images children repeat from another source without real understanding. Because children do not understand the stereotypes, they can only repeat them inflexibly and often incorrectly or inappropriately. A pervasive example is the looped V-shape that represents birds in flight. This was developed by artists to represent birds in the distance, where the details of body, tail, head, and feet are not distinguishable.

Variations of the looped V-shape and the concurrent understandings are not available to children who pick up the stereotype for flying birds and apply it inappropriately. Children demonstrate their lack of understanding of the meaning and origin of the stereotype in drawings where the looped V is upside down and the birds are apparently flapping their wings upward instead of downward. Sometimes the children's marks look more like the letter *M*.

In any case, bird symbols allow the child to suggest flocks of birds. Were the child to attempt to render a bird with its component parts of head, bill, body, wings, and tail, it would not be possible to give the impression of groups of birds. The child has a need for a shorthand version of a bird image.

Many stereotypes are available to children through television, advertising, and cartoon strips in newspapers and comic books. Others are passed on from child to child. Two problems arise with children's use of stereotypes. First, children cannot utilize stereotypes for the central purposes of their artistic development because the stereotypes are not their own. Second, reliance on copying stereotypes robs children of the confidence required to develop their own schemata.

The pervasiveness of adult graphic images (potential stereotypes) in most children's environments suggests that there is no sure way to protect children from these influences if, indeed, protection is warranted. Children will continue to be influenced by smiley-face buttons, cartoon characters, and the like, regardless of what adults do or say. When copying tends to stultify or limit individual expression, however, it is harmful. In dealing with children who are involved with copying, the teacher can help them identify what they might learn from their efforts and how they might apply this learning in their own original artwork.

Because it is inevitable that children will be exposed to adult graphic images, many of which may be of low artistic quality, it makes good sense for teachers to expose children to high-quality artworks. Slides, reproductions, films, and books of great variety are readily available. Just as in literature, music, or mathematics, children should become aware of the best the world has to offer in art. Children are much less likely to rely on stereotypes when they are aware of a variety of graphic options.

The Preadolescent Stage (Ages 10–13, Grades 5–8)

The preadolescent stage includes children from approximately the fourth to the seventh grades and even into the eighth grade. It is well to acknowledge again the wide variation in rates of maturity among children. This range can be seen quite obviously in sixth- and seventh-grade classrooms, where girls are usually more physically mature than boys, and in the eighth and ninth grades, where some boys have reached puberty and others are still a year or two away from it. Teachers at each higher grade level must deal with the continuously widening intellectual range among students.

The physical, mental, and social changes that occur during these years set preadolescent children apart from younger children in the symbol-making stage. Although preadolescent children are still naturally inquisitive and creative, they have learned to be more cautious. Younger children work in art with abandon and will often try anything the teacher suggests in their art. For the younger children practically every art experience is a new one, and they enjoy working on unfamiliar ground. During the years of the preadolescent stage, however, children become more socially aware and sensitive to peer opinion.

The range of topics that interest preadolescent children expands significantly during these years as they become more conceptually sophisticated and more aware of the teen world. Preadolescent boys and girls increasingly turn to the adolescent culture of popular music; interests in television, movies, and music videos; ways of dressing and grooming; and adolescent language that varies with each new generation. Just prior to adolescence, boys and girls tend to stay separated and often pursue separate interests and activities. As they near the onset of puberty, and for the remainder of their school careers, boys and girls become involved more and more in social interactions between the sexes.

The age range from ten to thirteen is crucial from the standpoint of art education. It is during these years that most children cease to be significantly involved in making art. Indeed, when asked to make a drawing, the majority of adults will refer back to images they made before reaching the teen years. Drawings of human figures made by adults are very often difficult to distinguish from the figure drawings of preadolescent children. This is because when individuals give up drawing, their development is virtually arrested at that level. With the development of critical skills at about age eleven, children become acutely aware of the qualities of their own art products. If their own drawings and paintings appear "childlike" to them, they become self-conscious and dissatisfied with their artwork and tend to produce less or quit altogether.

With the possible exception of urban graffiti, spontaneous drawing has virtually disappeared at this age. If art activity is to continue, it will do so in the art class rather than on the playground. This is a time to appeal to students' interests as a point of departure, including comic books, cartoons, videos, or T-shirt designs. Nine- or ten-year-old children's dissatisfaction with their own best efforts to make art heralds the beginning of a representational stage, when children desire to become more skillful and competent.

The solution to the problem of decline in art production prior to the teen years seems relatively clear. The preadolescent years are critical in the artistic development of children. They must make enough progress during this period so, when they become capable of self-criticism, they will not find their own work too wanting. If children are to continue artistic production during adulthood, they must work with diligence, mastering the technical and expressive conventions of adult art that provide a bridge between the art worlds of the child and the adult. As with skills of reading or math, unless instruction is provided, many children will not advance in their own art making and appreciation.

The role of the art teacher changes during students' preadolescent years. Students are more receptive to instruction in competencies of drawing; of color and design principles; of technical skills in painting, printmaking, and sculpture; and of other modes of art making. Children want to know how artists handle the problems of overlap, size, and placement relationships, and of convergence of lines for representing space and depth in drawings and paintings. They are receptive to instruction in many technical aspects of art and are motivated to become skilled in making art that passes their own critical judgment and that of their peers. They are ready to learn more about what artists of the past have created and what contemporary artists are doing and why.

Teachers can draw on the full range of the visual arts, including applied arts, such as graphic design and illustration. Students become increasingly interested in social, political, and personal influences in art and respond to themes that will engage them in discussion as well as production. These years can be tremendously rich and exciting for children and for their teachers as the world of art unfolds before them. The child's gaze is directed toward the teen and adult years, and it is there that much of the content of art as a subject lies.

WHY CHILDREN MAKE ART

The virtually universal participation of children in marking and graphic symbol making strongly suggests that basic reasons exist for these behaviors. Children must gain satisfaction

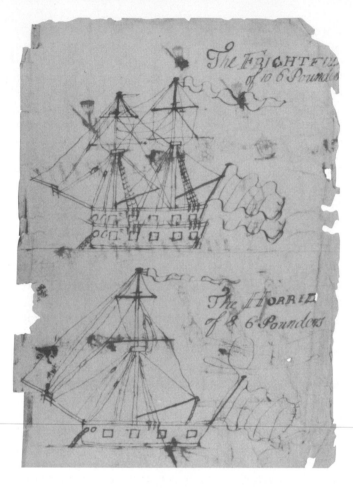

A Fresh View of the Presidency. From *The Diary of John Quincy Adams*. In 1780, a thirteen year-old John Quincy Adams accompanied his father to Paris. Although an avid sightseer, young Adams found time to fill his journal with drawings, two of which are shown here. Adams designed his own ships (the Horrid and the Frightful) and was particularly concerned about the correct way for a flag to unfurl. To save time and space he portrayed the enlisted men as stick figures, reserving his acuteness of observation for the uniforms of the officers.

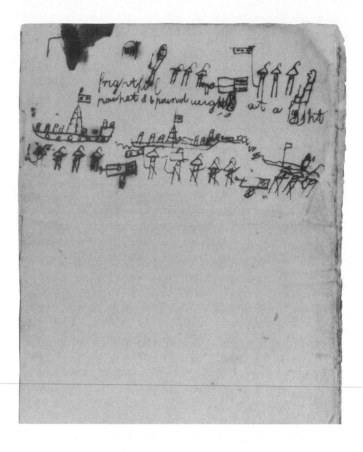

from these activities, or they would not engage in them spontaneously. On this topic, however, writers and educators must speculate, because they are unable either to communicate sufficiently well with young children or to recall their own early art experiences. Nevertheless, through lengthy and careful observation of children and through the application of useful psychological theory, it is possible to speculate with some confidence.[17]

For children, art is a means to engage all their senses for learning and expression. Creating art heightens children's sensitivity to the physical world and provides a means of expressing both emotional and imaginative states of mind in ways unique to art.

The effects of art activity on children's self-concept and general personality development can be very beneficial. Art can provide a means for children to develop their inherent creative abilities and, in the process, to integrate their emotional, social,

and aesthetic selves. Children's art is often seen as instrumental in fostering and preserving each individual's identity, uniqueness, self-esteem, and personal accomplishment.

In addition, some educators claim that art activity contributes to cognitive development. More than sixty years ago, John Dewey stated:

> To think effectively in terms of relations of qualities is as severe a demand upon thought as to think in terms of symbols, verbal and mathematical. Indeed, since words are easily manipulated in mechanical ways, the production of a work of genuine art probably demands more intelligence than does most of the so-called thinking that goes on among those who pride themselves on being "intellectuals."[18]

Children's early graphic behavior—the making, scribbling, and manipulation of materials—appears to be intrinsically valued. As they move into the symbol-making phase, these psychomotor and kinesthetic rewards are reinforced by children's newly developed ability to conceive and convey meanings. This power to use the images they create as symbols for the world allows children to construct their own knowable world and to convey what they know to others.

As we watch children draw or paint, we are often struck by their concentration and involvement. Children frequently talk as they draw, and it is only through close observation that an adult can gain understanding of what has been created by a particular child. For example, through discussion with her four-year-old boy, a mother learned that his drawing was a picture of the family. The figure on the right with lots of dark hair is the mother; the short figure is the father; next is the child who drew the picture. The small figure next to the boy is his baby sister. When asked by his mother where his brother (a sibling rival) was, the child quickly made the scribble on the left and said, "Here he is; he is hiding behind a bush." In this drawing we see several things:

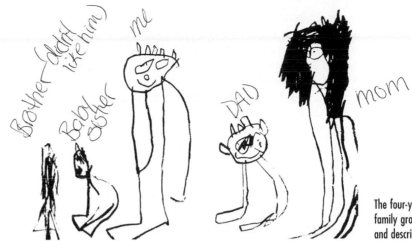

The four-year-old boy who drew this family group was able to identify and describe the figures.

1. The child is developing symbols for the human figure and can make basic differentiations to represent specific individuals.
2. The child is able not only to represent figures but also to consider family relationships in his drawing.
3. The emotions of the child are important and obvious in his drawing. Mother is most important in his life and is made prominent in the drawing. His own figure is large. The brother with whom he feels competitive is conveniently left out of the picture. Later he is represented only in a hurried scribble.

One of the fascinating and charming aspects of children's art is that it can often serve as a window into the minds and emotions of the children. A series of drawings was done by a seven-year-old girl as a response to her experience at school. The first drawing shows the girl admiring a classmate who has pretty curls and is neat and prim. The child artist is an active girl, her hair is stringy, and she is disheveled. Her classmates note these characteristics and comment unfavorably. This motivates the girl to ask her mother to give her a permanent wave. She has the permanent and puts ribbons in her neat hair. However, after a few hours at school running and playing, her hair is stringy and the ribbons are untied. The pretty classmate is as neat as ever.

This art product reveals the following:

1. The child is very aware of peer social relationships at school, and she is concerned about her appearance.
2. She is able to reconstruct the series of events in her drawings and to identify her feelings.
3. She is able to tell her story with graphic images in a direct and effective way.

The therapeutic value of making these drawings is not possible to determine. The child was motivated to make them, however, and she did sort out the experience through her art.

In similar ways, children deal with many of life's concerns, joys, and trials through their art. A child is afraid of fire and

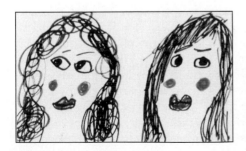
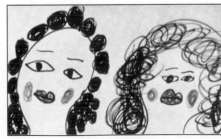
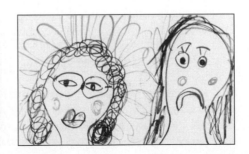

This series of portraits provides a spontaneous narrative of a personal experience by a seven-year-old girl (described on this page) and shows her awareness of social relationships and the level of her ability to tell a story.

paints a picture of someone escaping from a burning building. A child is fascinated with sports, invents team players, and draws them in action; the favorite team wins. A child hears a fairly tale and draws a picture illustrating the story. A child visits a grandparent and makes a painting of the experience. The list of possible subjects for child art is as endless as the list of life experiences. Through their art, children can create new worlds as they investigate concepts, relationships, understandings, and models of behavior.

Children can create fantasies and stories through plays and songs as well as through the visual arts, although drawing seems to be a very significant medium for such accomplishments. As children create visual representations, they are required to combine the elements of design into structures with meaning and then to judge the adequacy and quality of their own work. Then they must proceed on the basis of their own judgments. The flexibility of art activity, where even the purpose of the process can change on the basis of the individual's judgment, is very different from activities that emphasize linear thinking and convergent learning where all students arrive at a single correct answer.

As children enter the preadolescent stage, their interest in art moves from using it solely for personal expression to consciously improving the quality of visual forms. Children become interested in the visual properties of their works—composition, the elements of design—and in the technical aspects of materials and processes. Very few activities available to people of any age allow the personal control from initiation to completion typical of art activity.

Artistic behavior seen from a broad perspective suggests a reciprocal action between art making and responding to art. The imagination can be as intensely engaged in studying artworks as in their creation. The sensory appeal of color as children apply it in a painting can also draw them into a still life by Pierre Bonnard, a color-field painting by Helen Frankenthaler, or a fourteenth-century Japanese ceramic figure. The process of engagement with the world of artworks can be as absorbing and satisfying as the process of their creation.

CHILDREN'S CONCEPTUAL DEVELOPMENT IN ART

It is clear that the intellect is involved in the making of art. It is also clear that children progress in their abilities to understand art, to perceive art and respond to it, to relate art to their own life experiences, and to ponder fundamental questions about art. Understanding of art in these areas is not necessarily developed simply through art making. Gardner suggests that "there are separate developmental sagas which govern skills of perception, reflection, and critical judgment" in art.[19]

In one study of children's understanding about art, researchers learned that children of different age levels held widely differing views about basic art topics.[20] They interviewed children from ages four through sixteen, showed them reproductions of artworks, and asked them questions about where art comes from, how one becomes an artist, what can count as art, how one recognizes quality, and who is able to make judgments about art.

The researchers learned that misconceptions about art were common, especially among younger children. For example, some believed that art could be created by animals or that animals could not paint only because they could not hold a brush. When questions were asked having to do with how works of art are judged for quality and how they are selected for exhibit in a gallery or museum, different misconceptions emerged. Even some teenagers demonstrated limited understanding about the basic notions surrounding the creation of, response to, and judgment of art.

This study encourages teachers to learn more about what their students think and understand about art. Children who are unaware of why original art is different from reproductions, for example, cannot fully appreciate a visit to a museum. The appreciation of art requires understanding that enriches experience.

Teachers of all subjects in the school curriculum should carefully consider the conceptual levels of their students. For example, very young children have limited conceptions of time; the notion of a decade or a century might not be within their intellectual grasp. The historical fact that Rembrandt was a sixteenth-century artist, therefore, might not be relevant when a teacher is showing students the artist's drawings or paintings. Most often, errors of aiming too high or too low conceptually can be avoided if teachers engage their students in discussions of what they are seeing and learning. Beyond simple factual items, are basic questions about art that can be discussed fruitfully over and over as students progress from grade level to grade level. One such question is, "How is quality in art determined?" This question can be discussed in terms simple enough for a first grader—"Some people (such as art critics or gallery directors) study and devote their lives to judging art"—or for an eighth-grade student—"Judgment of quality depends on one's aesthetic position, or beliefs about the nature of art."

Teachers should also take care that they do not aim too low in their assessments of what children at particular ages can do. Teachers need to continue to challenge the fastest students in the class in order to keep their interest and involvement, while concurrently accommodating the needs of slower and special learners. Subsequent chapters on curriculum and instruction and evaluation will discuss these issues in greater depth.

ARTISTS AND CHILDREN'S ART

It has been the goal of many adult artists to capture the freshness, spontaneity, and directness so apparent in the art of children. Examples of artistic conventions commonly used by children can be seen in artworks from many cultures and times. Enlargement of important figures in painting and sculpture is a common device in early Christian art. The placement of mountains and trees in Chinese landscapes is similar in many respects to ways children manipulate space in their drawings and paintings. The cubist painters consciously depicted multiple views of objects, flattened space, and distorted images—devices that children typically accomplish in the course of their natural development in art. Such artists as Jean Dubuffet, Paul Klee, and Jean Michel Basquiat took great pains to eliminate all vestiges of adult conventions from their works in order to achieve the expressiveness associated with children's art. According to Gardner, it is the child's approach to art, "his preconscious sense of form, his willingness to explore and to solve problems that arise, his capacity to take risks, his affective needs which must be worked out in a symbolic realm," that many adult artists wish to emulate.[21]

Is the art of children, then, to be considered in the same way as the work of mature artists, and in what ways are they different?

In the case of naive painters (sometimes referred to as intuitive, or folk artists), such as Grandma Moses, Horace Pippin, and Henri Rousseau, whose works contain distinctively childlike qualities, similarities with children's work is unplanned. Naive artists, by definition, lack professional training and enjoy an independence from the mainstream of art that places them in a situation similar to that of children, who have not yet developed adult conventions and techniques. Nevertheless, as with the work of children, some naive artists have created works of aesthetic merit, almost always accompanied by strong emotional involvement with the subject matter of the works.

Some mature artists in the Western tradition actively have sought to achieve a semblance of the spontaneity often found in the works of children. These artists, such as Picasso and the cubists or Matisse and the fauvists, were well grounded and expert in the standard art techniques of their times but chose to ignore or reject those techniques in order to achieve expressive purposes. Others, such as Paul Klee, pursued what is seen by the innocent eye, uncorrupted by a technological society. He left us a body of work noted for its remarkable range—humorous, delicate, and mystical—drawing its strength from the shapes and symbols of the four- to six-year-old child.

Important differences exist, however, between the art of children and the art of adult professional artists. Small children paint the sky yellow and the tree red because they have not yet developed the conventions of local color, of making objects approximate their appearance, or of controlling the mixing of hues, values, and intensities. Adult artists might disregard the conventions of local color, with which they are quite familiar, for their own expressive purposes. Unlike the child, adult artists have developed considerable facility with materials and techniques; they have trained eye and hand to a sophisticated level; and they have the capacity to plan ahead and follow through over a considerable period of time. Adult artists know the works of other artists, how they were made, and their place within culture and tradition.

Beyond this technical and expressive dimension of art is also the development of the adult artist's personality, which is unavailable to the child because of a lack of experience. Life's events, crises, responsibilities, hardships, and satisfactions are the stuff of which art is made, and it is the person with the most developed feeling for life who is most likely to create art that will speak with significance.

Given these differences, we can celebrate the art of children as well as the art of adults. We can be delighted by the work of children, and we can see in their art production the crucial seeds of future achievement. The value of children's art varies according to the point of view of the observer. The educator may view it as one route to the development of the aesthetic lens; the psychologist, as a key to understanding behavior; and the artist, as the child's most direct confrontation with the inner world of sensation and feeling. But educator, psychologist, and artist all view children's artistic development as a unique and essential component of their general education.

NOTES

1. Rudolf Arnheim, "A Look At a Century of Growth," in *Child Development in Art,* ed. Anna Kindler (Reston VA: National Art Education Association, 1997), p. 12.

2. Claire Golomb, "Representational Concepts in Clay: The Development of Sculpture," in Kindler, *Child Development in Art,* pp. 131–142.

3. Viktor Lowenfeld and Lambert Brittain, *Creative and Mental Growth,* 8th ed. (New York: Macmillan, 1987); Jean Piaget, *The Origins of Intelligence in Children* (New York: Norton, 1963); and Howard Gardner, *Artful Scribbles: The Significance of Children's Drawings* (New York: Basic Books, 1980).

4. For a discussion of problems inherent in the assumption of untutored progression, see Anna Kindler, ed., *Child Development in Art* (Reston, VA: National Art Education Association, 1997).

5. Although the term "scribble" has been accepted by psychologists and art educators in relation to children's drawing, it is in fact a misnomer. Children's scribbles are not the hasty, careless, or meaningless marks defined in the dictionary. The marks that children make are more accurately described as "pre-symbolic graphic investigation." As Judith Burton of Teacher's College, Columbia University, has noted, the word "scribbling" intimates behavior that is not serious or order-seeking, behavior that must be overcome as soon as possible so the serious business of symbolization can begin. We err when "we mistake the swirls and swooshes and speeds of pre-symbolic action as hurried, mindless, and meaningless. Nothing could be further from the truth" (personal correspondence with author).

6. Elliot Eisner, "What Do Children Learn When They Paint?" *Art Education* 31, no. 3 (March 1978): 6.

7. Rhoda Kellogg, *Analyzing Children's Art* (Palo Alto, CA: National Press Books, 1969).

8. Carl Jung, *Psychology and Religion* (New Haven: Yale University Press, 1960); and Rudolf Arnheim, *Art and Visual Perception* (Berkeley: University of California Press, 1967).

9. Judith Burton, "Beginnings of Artistic Language," *School Arts,* September 1980, p. 9.

10. Arnheim, *Art and Visual Perception,* p. 162.

11. Golomb, "Representational Concepts in Clay," p. 141.

12. Brent Wilson and Marjorie Wilson, "Drawing Realities: The Themes of Children's Story Drawings," *School Arts,* May 1979, p. 16.

13. Ibid., p. 15.

14. Judith M. Burton, "Representing Experience from Imagination and Observation," *School Arts,* December 1980.

15. Betty Lark-Horovitz, Hilda P. Lewis, and Mark Luca, *Understanding Children's Art for Better Teaching* (Columbus, OH: Charles E. Merrill, 1967), p. 7.

16. Gardner, *Artful Scribbles,* p. 67.

17. Claire Golomb, *The Child's Creation of a Pictorial World* (Berkeley: University of California Press, 1992).

18. John Dewey, *Art As Experience* (New York: G. P. Putnam's Sons, 1938), p. 46.

19. Howard Gardner, "Toward More Effective Arts Education," *Art, Mind and Education* (Urbana: University of Illinois Press, 1989), p. 160.

20. Howard Gardner, Ellen Winner, and Mary Kircher, "Children's Conceptions of the Arts," *Journal of Aesthetic Education* (July 1985).

21. Gardner, *Artful Scribbles,* p. 269.

ACTIVITIES FOR THE READER

1. Collect from a kindergarten and a first-grade class a series of drawings and paintings that illustrate the three types of concepts of the manipulative stage.

2. Collect some drawings or paintings by a single child to illustrate the development of a symbol, such as that for "person," "toy," or "animal."

3. Collect from several children in the first to third grades a series of drawings and paintings that illustrate developments in symbolic expression.

4. Collect from pupils enrolled in the third to sixth grades drawings and paintings that illustrate some of the major developments in the preadolescent stage.

5. Make one collection of drawings and paintings representative of artistic development from kindergarten to the end of sixth grade.

6. Collect work in three-dimensional materials, such as clay or paper, from the pupils in situations identical with, and for purposes similar to, those mentioned in the first five activities.

7. Show children an original painting or a good-quality reproduction. Discuss with each child various questions about the origins, creation, and expressive qualities of the artwork.

8. Ask college students or older adults to draw a human figure in a pose of their choice. Observe the developmental

level of the drawing, and ask the persons when and where they learned to draw as they did. At what age did each person stop drawing?

9. Ask an adult and a ten-year-old child each to draw a picture of a person in action. If the adult holds a Ph.D., the comparison can be even more interesting.

SUGGESTED READINGS

Arnheim, Rudolf. *Thoughts on Art Education.* Los Angeles: Getty Center for Education in the Arts, 1989. Addresses, among other topics, the role of art in education and the nature and methods of teaching.

Bredenkamp, Sue, and Carol Copple, eds. *Developmentally Appropriate Practice in Early Childhood.* Washington, DC: National Association for the Education of Young Children, 1997.

Day, Michael. "Child Art, School Art, and the Real World of Art." In *Art Education and Back to Basics,* ed. Stephen M. Dobbs. Reston, VA: National Art Education Association, 1979. Clearly written and useful discussion comparing school art projects with real child art and how both relate to the real world of art.

Engel, Brenda. *Considering Children's Art: Why and How to Value Their Works.* Washington, DC: National Association for the Education of Young Children, 1995.

Fein, Sylvia. *Heidi's Horse.* Pleasant Hills, CA: Axelrod Press, 1984. A fascinating account of the drawings of a child, Heidi, over several years of her life.

Gardner, Howard. *Artful Scribbles: The Significance of Children's Drawings.* New York: Basic Books, 1980. A leading psychologist discusses all the issues mentioned in this chapter, adding case studies, a discussion of Picasso's *Guernica,* and a personal perspective.

————. *Creating Minds.* New York: Basic Books, 1993.

Gardner, Howard, and Getty Center for Education in the Arts. *Art Education and Human Development.* Occasional Paper 3. Los Angeles: Getty Center for Education in the Arts, 1990.

Golomb, Claire. *The Child's Creation of a Pictorial World.* Berkeley: University of California Press, 1992.

Johnson, Andra, ed. *Art Education: Elementary.* Reston, VA: National Art Education Association, 1992.

Kellogg, Rhoda. *Analyzing Children's Art.* Palo Alto, CA: National Press Books, 1969. Clearly written and profusely illustrated coverage of early years of children's art.

Kindler, Anna M., ed. *Child Development in Art.* Reston, VA: National Art Education Association, 1997. A comprehensive look at current theory about artistic and aesthetic development in children.

Lark-Horovitz, Betty, Hilda P. Lewis, and Mark Luca. *Understanding Children's Art for Better Teaching.* Columbus, OH: Charles E. Merrill, 1967. Helpful from a historical point of view.

Lowenfeld, Viktor. *Creative and Mental Growth.* New York: Macmillan, 1952. Classic work on the nature of artistic development and its role in child development.

Olson, David R., and Nancy Torrance. *The Handbook of Education and Human Development: New Models of Learning, Teaching, and Schooling.* Malden, MA: Blackwell, 1998. Complete review of theory and issues related to early childhood education.

Parsons, Michael. *How We Understand Art: A Cognitive Developmental Account of Aesthetic Experience.* Cambridge: Cambridge University Press, 1987.

Thompson, Christine Marmé, ed. *The Visual Arts and Early Childhood Learning.* Reston, VA: National Art Education Association, 1995. Topics include developmentally appropriate practices, historical and critical understanding, and introduction to multiculturalism for young learners.

WORLD WIDE WEB RESOURCES

Learn more about children's artistic development on the World Wide Web. The authors suggest the following sites:

AskERIC: Education Information with the Personal Touch. <http://ericir.syr.edu/>

Task Force on Children's Learning and the Arts. "Young Children and the Arts: Making Creative Connections." *Arts Education Partnership.* 1998. <http://aeparts.org/tfadvoc/taskforces/youngchildren.pdf http://aep-arts.org/>

Wolf Trap Education Institute for Early Learning through the Arts. 1999. <http://www.wolf-trap.org/institute/>

Getty Institute for Education in the Arts. *ArtsEdNet.* 1999. <http://www.artsednet.getty.edu/>. Use Search feature.

National Association for Education of Young Children. 1999. <http://www.naeyc.org/>. Look for *Resources.*

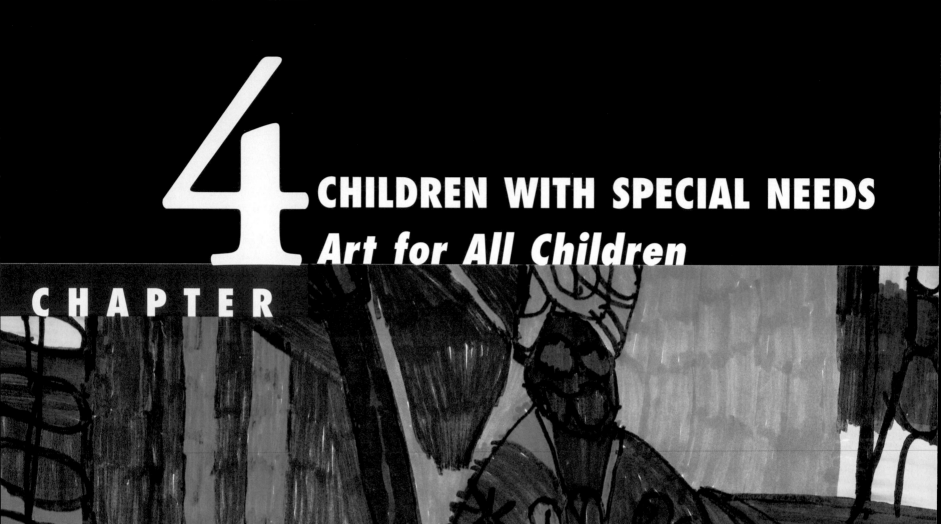

4

CHILDREN WITH SPECIAL NEEDS
Art for All Children

CHAPTER

They took away what should have been my eyes,
(But I remembered Milton's Paradise).
They took away what should have been my ears,
(Beethoven came and wiped away my tears).
They took away what should have been my tongue,
(But I had talked with God when I was young).
He would not let them take away my soul—
Possessing that, I still possess the whole.[1]

—Helen Keller

In a middle-class suburban K–5 elementary school (570 students), the first- and second-grade children are gathered in a spacious area outside their open classrooms. They begin their daily assembly this morning with patriotic songs.

Boisterously, if a bit off-key, the group of 100 or so belts out traditional favorites. But they quiet to a hush when country crooner Lee Greenwood's *God Bless the U.S.A.* begins to blare from the stereo, and their 2nd grade teacher announces that they will perform the song in sign language.

It takes a few lines before most of the students can synchronize their sweeping motions to keep pace with the lyrics, but soon the children are signing the words as passionately as they sang a few moments earlier.

Every student takes part in some way, including a grinning boy with Down's syndrome sitting to one side of the group and a girl with cerebral palsy nearby. Toward the back of the group, a boy who uses a wheelchair and computerized audio device to speak cannot lift his arms to sign, yet he follows his schoolmates with his eyes.[2]

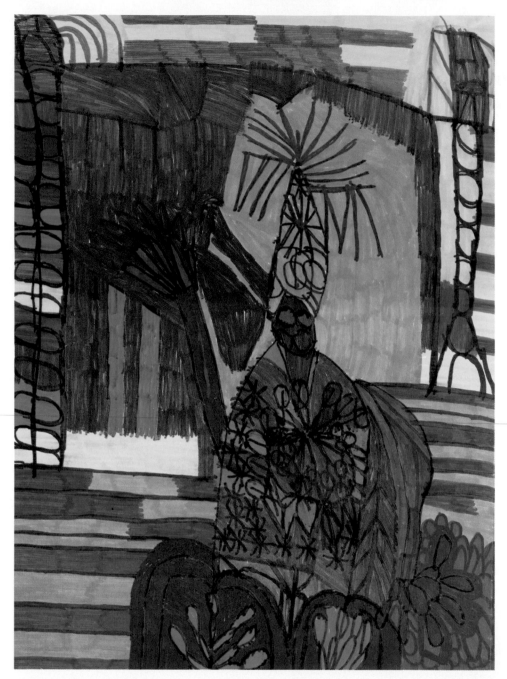

Germany, mentally retarded student

rience in mainstreaming will carry through after the assembly disperses, as nearly all disabled students are taught alongside their nondisabled classmates. And, according to teachers' and administrators' observations and pupils' grades, "not only have the disabled students made noticeable improvement in academic and social performance, but other students also have become more caring and tolerant."[3]

This is one school's response to the intent of the Individuals with Disabilities Education Act (IDEA), which has been in place in the United States for a quarter century. The goal of this federal legislation is to provide equity in education for all students, a very complicated task given the variations in abilities and learning styles of students. We begin the new millennium with approximately six million students with disabilities in American schools. This means that all teachers must be ready to teach all children who enter their classrooms in a mainstreamed environment. Art teachers traditionally have accommodated special learners very effectively in their classes.

The language of special education changes as new categories, concepts, and sensitivities emerge in professional discourse. The first distinctions that should be made are between all-inclusive references, such as *challenged, handicapped,* and *disabled,* and those that refer to specific conditions, such as *mentally retarded, emotionally disturbed,* or *orthopedically impaired.* The box on page 73 presents terms and definitions found in the current IDEA legislation. The term *special needs* has been retained for the discussion in this chapter because it addresses the complete range of learners.

Through classroom experience with many children, teachers come to recognize and respect diversities among students. Some disabilities are permanent, while others, such as severe periods of emotional disturbance, might be temporary. In light of the concept of multiple intelligences, teachers note that a child experiencing a disability might excel in other areas of schooling. A child with a specific learning disability, for example, might excel physically or socially.

General education is intended to accommodate the broad range of students who can benefit from regular schooling. This encompasses the entire spectrum of learning types, including children who, for various reasons, are handicapped or challenged learners. Children who are mentally retarded, physically or emotionally challenged, or who speak English as a second language (ESL) increasingly are "mainstreamed" in regular classrooms, where they associate with all their peers rather than remain with a limited subgroup related to their particular challenge. The inclusion of special students in regular classrooms

The scene described here took place at a model full-inclusion elementary school, where students with disabilities spend almost all their days in regular classes and study the same curriculum as their nondisabled peers. The morning's expe-

Definitions of Disability Terms*

Autism means a developmental disability significantly affecting verbal and nonverbal communication and social interaction, generally evident before age 3.

Deaf-blindness means concomitant hearing and visual impairments, the combination of which causes such severe communication and other developmental and educational needs that they cannot be accommodated in special education programs solely for children with deafness or children with blindness.

Deafness means a hearing impairment that is so severe that the child is impaired in processing linguistic information through hearing, with or without amplification.

Emotional disturbance is defined as:
  a. An inability to learn that cannot be explained by intellectual, sensory, or health factors;
  b. An inability to build or maintain satisfactory interpersonal relationships with peers and teachers.
  c. Inappropriate types of behavior or feelings under normal circumstances.
  d. A general pervasive mood of unhappiness or depression.
  e. A tendency to develop physical symptoms or fears associated with personal or school problems.

Hearing impairment means an impairment in hearing, whether permanent or fluctuating, existing concurrently with deficits in adaptive behavior and manifested during the developmental period.

Mental retardation means significantly subaverage general intellectual functioning, existing concurrently with deficits in adaptive behavior and manifested during the developmental period.

Multiple disabilities means concomitant impairments (such as mental retardation-blindness, mental retardation-orthopedic impairment, etc.), the combination of which causes such severe educational needs that they cannot be accommodated in special education programs solely for one of the impairments.

Orthopedic impairment means a severe orthopedic impairment, including impairments caused by congenital anomaly, impairments caused by disease, and impairments from other causes.

Other health impairment means having limited strength, vitality or alertness, including a heightened alertness to environmental stimuli, that results in limited alertness with respect to the educational environment.

Specific learning disability means a disorder in one or more of the basic psychological processes involved in understanding or in using language, spoken or written, that may manifest itself in an imperfect ability to listen, think, speak, read, write, spell, or to do mathematical calculations.

Speech or language impairment means a communication disorder, such as stuttering, impaired articulation, a language impairment or voice impairment.

Traumatic brain injury means an acquired injury to the brain caused by an external physical force, resulting in total or partial functional disability or psychosocial impairment, or both.

Visual impairment including blindness means an impairment in vision that, even with correction, adversely affects a child's educational performance.

SOURCE: "IDEA 1997 Final Regulations: Subpart A—General," *Federal Register*, September 1998. <http://www.ideapractices.org/regs/SubpartA.htm#sec300.7c>

---

*To qualify for IDEA each definition is followed by the phrase "that adversely affects a child's educational performance."

has, in many instances, improved their educational opportunities and broadened their social contacts. At the same time, teachers are challenged by the broad range of learners and special learning needs of their students and must be prepared to educate all children who are assigned to their classes.

When we consider the wide range of learning styles and abilities among learners, the average class size in elementary and middle-school classrooms, the inclusion of one or more special learners in most classrooms, and the charge to regard each child as an individual, we can gain some appreciation for the complexity of being an effective teacher. School programs typically employ trained experts who work with special groups of students. Classroom teachers rely on these experts for support and assistance with special students. All teachers, however, must gain a basic understanding of the needs of special learners and develop ways to adapt their instructional programs to these needs.[4]

The goals of general education are usually appropriate for all learners, regardless of their special status. For example, we attempt to teach all students to read, although some will learn to do so very slowly and with great difficulty. Reading instruction must be adapted for visually impaired learners or for those who do not yet speak English, but the goal to teach reading remains unchanged. The same is true with general education goals for writing, mathematics, social studies, and the arts. The goals and learning activities for art education outlined in Chapters 1 and 2 are valid for nearly all students but must be adapted according to the levels and abilities of individual special learners.

One of the improvements in special education is the attitude that encourages special learners of all types to advance as far as their capabilities will allow. An example of this attitude can be seen in the case of Down syndrome children, many of whom have progressed much further educationally than was previously believed possible.[5] Events for these students, such as the Special Olympics and Very Special Arts (now VSA arts), have sensitized many people to the needs, capabilities, and contributions of persons with disabilities or challenges.[6] Teachers should be in the forefront of those who are dedicated to assisting special learners to enjoy as full and productive a life as possible.

Legislation in the United States has drawn attention to the need for educational programs for the challenged. Federal Chapter 766 mandated the "mainstreaming" of children with special needs into integrated situations with "normal" children. The goal is to meet the educational needs of every student experiencing disability on an individual basis, while at the same time integrating (mainstreaming) such students into the normal schoolday's activities, so each child has as much contact as possible with children who do not share his or her problems.

Through state-run festivals, teacher-training symposiums, and exhibits, the importance of arts programs for children with special needs is gaining public attention. Research has emphasized the value of arts instruction in special education. Federal and state funding (in Canada, provincial funding) has opened professional opportunities within the public sector in the fields of special education and of art, integrated arts, dance, and music therapy. As these approaches become accepted, their balance of visual, manipulative, and kinesthetic expression aids children whose learning styles are visual, manipulative, auditory, and kinesthetic—as well as verbal.

Doris Guay points to the challenges for art teachers to employ creative problem solving for planning and teaching.

> With increased diversity in art class, we can no longer assume that the methods and materials of past practice apply. Teachers must learn to use instructional practices that maximize individual student learning. These include cooperative grouping methods, task analysis, and partial participation. Teachers must also develop effective techniques for individualization, motivation, student empowerment, and classroom management. The creation of normalized opportunities for personal expression and response in art, for a range of student ability, challenges creativity and inventiveness.[7]

CONTRIBUTIONS OF ART FOR SPECIAL LEARNERS

The art program in many schools traditionally has been viewed as a particularly favorable setting for educating special learners, for several reasons. Children in art are able to interact with such materials as paint or clay in direct response to their senses of sight, sound, smell, and touch. The materials of art are sensory, concrete, and manipulable in direct ways that are unique within the school curriculum. All the senses can be brought into interaction, providing opportunities to adapt art-making activities for students who have some sensory or motor impairment. For example, even totally blind children can form expressive objects with clay. Hearing-impaired children can visually observe a demonstration of color mixing with paint and can try the process with immediately verifiable results, and children with motor difficulties can work with finger paints or with large brushes for painting.

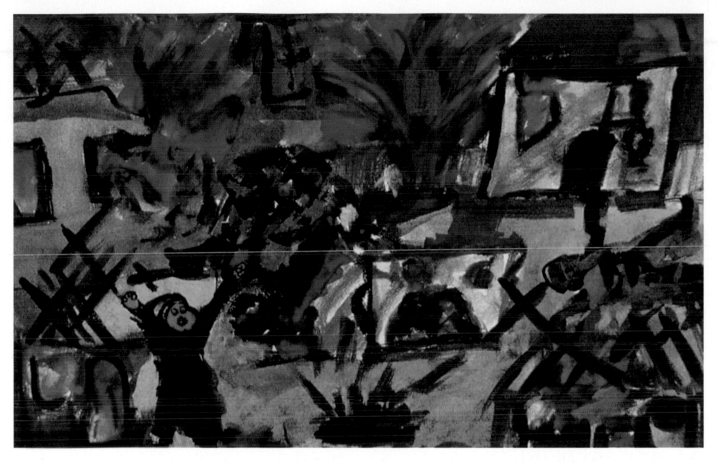

Children often prefer to convey their impressions of experiences that disturb them by drawing or painting rather than by writing or even talking about the event. This example by a Croatian child tells us much about personal expressiveness on both a therapeutic and artistic level.

Another reason why art class is often a supportive place for special learners has to do with the tradition of personal expression in art. Even when all students are engaged in the same task, such as painting a self-portrait, the outcome for each child can be unique. Each can paint his or her own version of a self-portrait with a stipulated context, yet each one can express a different mood or point of view. This opportunity for individuality within an assigned task is readily provided by sensitive art instruction.

The comprehensive program of art education we describe in this book is especially adaptable to the needs of special learners (as well as to varying learning styles among all students) because of the wide range of possible art activities. A balanced art program includes the sensory, cognitive, and manipulative activities of art production as well as activities that emphasize visual perception, discussion of artworks, investigation of culture and history, and questioning of fundamental ideas about art. It is unlikely any student will be able

to do *all* these activities with equal facility, but it *is* likely that all students, including special learners of all types, will find that they will be able to do, enjoy, and learn from many of these activities. The breadth and variety of valid art learning activities are one more characteristic of the art program that makes art education especially valuable for special learners.

Art As Therapy

Participation in art activities can have therapeutic effects for many special learners. Engaging in art production might serve a therapeutic function in a general sense, in fact, for almost any person.[8] The same might be said for any educational pursuit that requires total involvement, such as a scientific experiment, a cooking activity, or participation in a sports event. However, the aspect of art activity that provides so much therapeutic potential is the creative and expressive dimension. Art, according to Susanne Langer, is "the objectification of human feeling."[9] Verbal language, says Langer, is inadequate for the expression of the life of feeling all human beings share. These feelings can be adequately expressed only through the arts.

Art therapists are able to engage their clients or patients in arts activities that encourage free expression of emotions. Acts of artistic expression, such as drawing or painting, can result in communication of feelings that goes beyond and is apart from verbal expression. Once the art object has been created, once the feelings have been objectified as an artwork, they can then be viewed and discussed. Thus, art activity assists the therapist and client in two ways. First, creation of the art object can be an expressive release for the patient, providing feelings of profound satisfaction. Second, the object becomes a focus for discussion between therapist and patient, often leading to helpful revelations of the person's emotional life. Trained professional art therapists are capable of helping individuals to interpret meanings from their artworks and use this knowledge to improve patients' mental or emotional health.

Therapeutic aspects of art education can occur in classrooms with regular students and, more particularly, with students who have fewer or less-developed communication skills. Any person with strong emotions and limited ways of expressing them might benefit from artistic expression. In numerous cases of mentally retarded children, of immigrant students with little English capability, of children who have experienced traumatic events, and of others, artistic expression has provided a desperately needed means for expression. The art objects these children produce often provide sensitive teachers with insights into the mental and emotional lives of the children. *Teachers, however, are not professionally trained art therapists and should not attempt to fulfill that role.* Insights that teachers glean through children's art activities and products should be shared with professional school personnel, such as psychologists or therapists. Working together, school teams of counselors, psychologists, administrators, parents, and teachers can best develop and provide the educational opportunities needed for each individual learner.

A distinction is made between exceptional children who receive special schooling and slow-learning or retarded children who are capable of functioning within normal school situations. The retarded are those who make considerably lower-than-average scores on intelligence tests and who progress in academic subjects at a pace manifestly slower than that displayed by the majority of their fellow students.[10] As the work of German art educator Max Klager attests, a sen-

sitive teacher can attain remarkable artistic results with slow learners. His longitudinal studies of several mentally retarded individuals demonstrated that the subjects' personalities, as well as the visual quality of their work, showed remarkable progress with proper supervision.[11]

The current policy is to move special-needs children out of specialized schools and into regular schools. As a result, all teachers must be prepared to teach these students. Teachers need to examine each subject area in search of more effective means for dealing with the gifted, the emotionally disturbed, the physically impaired, and the mentally retarded.

TEACHING MENTALLY RETARDED CHILDREN

According to the American Association on Mental Retardation, an individual is considered to have mental retardation based on three criteria: "intellectual functioning level (IQ) is below 70–75; significant limitations exist in two or more adaptive skill areas; and the condition is present from childhood, defined as age 18 or less."[12]

Mental retardation is ten times more common than cerebral palsy and affects twenty-five times as many people as blindness. "Mental retardation cuts across the lines of racial, ethnic, educational, social and economic backgrounds. It can occur in any family. One out of ten American families is directly affected by mental retardation."[13]

The effects of mental retardation vary considerably among people. According to recent statistics,

about 87 percent will be mildly affected and will be only a little slower than average in learning new information and skills. As children, their mental retardation is not readily apparent and may not be identified until they enter school. As adults, many will be able to lead independent lives in the community and will no longer be viewed as having mental retardation.[14]

The remaining 13 percent of the mentally retarded, those with IQs under 50, "will have serious limitations in functioning. However, with early intervention, a functional education, and appropriate supports as an adult, all can lead satisfying lives in the community."[15]

The causes for retardation should be noted. While some children may indeed be suffering from cerebral or neurological dysfunctions, the deficiency of others may be due to a lack of personal attention (loving, touching, and playing) or to general sensory and environmental deprivation.

Approximately 1 in 800 newborns has mental retardation caused by Down syndrome (the presence of forty-seven chromosomes instead of the normal forty-six). In today's society many Down syndrome children, usually in the 40 to 70 IQ range, commonly go to regular schools, live in group homes, and work at jobs. With good health care and access to current therapies, 80 percent of the Down syndrome adults will live past age fifty-five (in past decades, only 50 percent lived past age ten). The success and visibility of such people as Chris Burke, a Down syndrome young man who acted in a weekly network television program, has helped to increase the general acceptance and understanding of mentally retarded persons.

Both Donald Uhlin and Zaidee Lindsay view the sensory nature of art experiences as a positive factor in the development of a sense of self in the child.[16] Art experiences, and crafts in particular, can involve the student in learning situations that are tactile, sensory, and stimulating physically as well as mentally.

Identifying the causes for retardation are best accomplished through a team approach when the art or classroom teacher has a psychologist, physician, or psychiatrist to consult. School districts have Individual Educational Program (IEP) committees that determine "if a student meets eligibility criteria as a handicapped child and then determines if this handicapping condition is adversely affecting the child's ability to benefit from education."[17] The arts specialists often interact with these committees to develop the educational plan best suited to each student's needs.

Slow learners enrolled in a regular classroom begin their artistic career, like normal children, by manipulating art materials rather than by drawing or modeling recognizable objects. They are sometimes slower than normal children in interacting with the materials given to them and may not initially explore their possibilities fully. However, with patience and encouragement, the repetition of skills will enable the child to feel more comfortable with new media. Even so, the child's symbol formation will reflect his or her developmental level. Thus, a child of chronological age fifteen whose developmental age is four can be expected to create symbols appropriate to a four-year-old child.

Whereas a normal five-year-old may arrive at the symbol stage within three weeks to six months, the five-year-old slow learner may not reach this stage for a year or more. In time, however, slow learners arrive at the symbol stage in a manner resembling that of nondisabled children. Once the symbol stage has been reached, several symbols may appear in quick succession.

Because of their greater chronological age, mentally retarded children often possess physical coordination superior to that of normal children of the same mental age. These physical abilities, of course, help them to master drawing skills more readily and allow them to repeat a recently developed symbol without much practice. Retarded children are as slow to make progress in the stage of symbols as they are to pass through the period of manipulation. Nevertheless, a slow learner, like all children, will sometimes surprise a teacher with a burst of progress.

As noted earlier, regression from the symbol stage to that of manipulation will sometimes occur as a result of such factors as fatigue, ill health, temporary emotional disturbances, periods of intense concentration, interruptions of various kinds, absence from school, or faulty teaching methods. Reversion of this kind occurs more frequently with mentally retarded children.

Gradually, learners with cognitive disabilities come to spend more time on their work and thus begin to add details to their symbols. Sometimes they learn to relate their symbols to one another. The progress they make depends largely, of course, on the attention they give to their work. Slow learners' attention spans tend to increase with both their chronological age and their mental age. As with all children, slow learners should be encouraged to explore with art materials and to devise their own images rather than rely on stereotypes that have no real meaning in the context of their artwork.

Many of the conventions, conceptions, and misconceptions associated with children's artistic development are discussed in Chapter 3. This discussion applies as well to slow learners, with appropriate adjustment for mental ages rather than chronological ages of the children. The differences in mental capabilities of a retarded eleven-year-old, however, along with more extensive life experiences and different interests, will often show up in the child's artwork.

The teacher's attitude in approaching children with special needs is of utmost importance. Patience helps to develop trust. Accepting the children as they are and guiding them to progress at their own rate will enable children to work with confidence. An awareness of the particular learning style of each child will aid the teacher in developing a program of appropriate activities. As the teacher helps the child to expand

and broaden a sensory vocabulary, the child's ability to grasp abstract concepts can deepen.

Slow learners can benefit from the visual and verbal aspects of a comprehensive art program, as well as from participating in art making. One fourth-grade teacher introduced her students to art criticism by teaching them to name objects depicted in paintings (using good-quality color reproductions). She taught them to name colors, types of lines, and shapes and then introduced visual concepts, such as contrast and balance. At a parent's night at the school, a mother approached the teacher and asked what she had done so successfully to stimulate her Down syndrome daughter's language development. "When Susie comes home after school, she loves to open a picture book, point to the pictures, and describe what she sees. We have encouraged this and have noticed much progress in her language abilities."[18]

As indicated earlier, all children who have the aptitude to do so pass through the normal stages of pictorial expression mentioned in Chapter 3—the manipulation, symbol, and preadolescent stages. The child with a mental age of around three and a chronological age of six will not go beyond manipulating materials; however, the child with the same chronological age and a mental age of four or more may begin to enter the symbol stage. With a mental age of five, the child will even place symbols within his or her environment.

Once they progress beyond the stage of manipulation, slow learners discover subject matter for expression in their own experiences. Many of the titles they give to their works are barely different from those selected by their nondisabled classmates. The titles describe events that occur at home, at school, at play, or in the community. The following are representative:

Where I Live
Our Class Went to Visit a Farm
I Saw a Big Fire
My Favorite Foods
A Movie I Like

Subjects such as these are appropriate for the late symbol or preadolescent stage of expression. The titles are concise, and, in most of them, the children have identified themselves with their environment. The less able the learners, the less inclined they are to relate themselves to the world in which they live. In other words, an ability to identify oneself with the environment seems to vary directly with intelligence.[19]

Subject Matter

The themes many mentally retarded children select are often closely connected with small, intimate events in life. A normal child might overlook them, or, having touched on them once or twice, would then find other interests. Many slow learners, on the other hand, seem to find constant interest in pictures of this nature. Some subjects in addition to those listed earlier are

I Sat on Our Steps
The Birds Are in the Trees
Our School Bus

Many children frequently like to depict their reactions to vicarious experience, even though they are more attracted to actual experience. Dramatized versions of familiar stories and events may excite them to visual expression. However, the teacher should, whenever possible, connect the physical experiences of the children and their drawings. Situations that deal with personal accidents ("falling down," "bumping my head") make effective sources for drawing, as do activities such as rolling or bouncing balls and using playground equipment.

METHODS OF TEACHING

To teach students experiencing disabilities, a teacher must possess a number of commendable personal qualities and professional abilities. The teacher must above all be patient, for children often progress slowly in their work. The teacher must, furthermore, be able to stimulate children to maximize their potential, but at the same time not hurry them into work beyond their abilities. Finally, the teacher must treat every slow learner as a unique person. A study of their output in art offers a striking illustration of the fact that the personalities of slow learners differ widely.

If in her classroom the teacher finds one or two particularly slow learners in art who require special attention, this should not create problems. Since all successful teaching in art demands that the teacher treat all pupils as individuals, the fact that the slow learners are afforded certain special attention should in no sense make them unique in the eyes of their fellows. Every child in the class, whether disabled, normal, or gifted, will require individual treatment. If the teacher is placed in charge of an entire class of slow learners, similar educational principles apply. Although every member of the group may be disabled, no two children will react in an identical manner to art. Here, as elsewhere, every child must be offered an educational program tailored to individual needs and capacities.

Step-by-step teaching practices, while rarely of value to normal pupils because they present little challenge, may often give the slower learner a valuable and necessary sense of achievement. Frequently, attention to the structure of a lesson may lead slow learners into more creative endeavors. Approved teaching methods are, to a large extent, also effective when used with students experiencing disabilities. Teaching learners with cognitive/academic disabilities does not require as much reorientation on the part of the teacher as one might suppose. It can require teaching in sequential concrete terms—hence, the importance of demonstrating art processes, of simplifying, of slowing down verbal instructions, of having the patience to repeat directions, and of breaking down the learning experience into manageable stages.

In her study of accomplished art teachers, Doris Guay observed a number of strategies that led to success with disabled students. She found that teachers:

> maintained expectations in a caring classroom atmosphere through the use of verbal praise, hand-over-hand assistance, and the invention of adaptive devices. Teachers generally moved throughout their classroom, providing reinforcement and encouragement. They sought to maintain a calm, personal approach, keeping individuals on task by personal closeness. They never appeared to be rushed. As they found both students with and without disabilities needing assistance, most teachers routinely asked table peers to provide help.[20]

The teachers assisted through questioning students' intentions and reminding students of technical concepts taught previously. And, without exception, these teachers revealed an enjoyment of students through their easy humor and quiet laughter. Table 4-1 was developed by Guay as a guide to assist teachers to improve the learning environment for students experiencing disabilities.[21]

Using Museums

Innovative approaches, such as taking children with disabilities to art museums, have proved valuable in stimulating perceptual awareness and in developing an appreciation of the larger artistic world. Most art museums are barrier free and welcome patrons with disabilities, and many art museums offer learning materials developed especially for school-

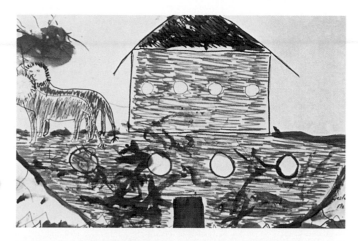

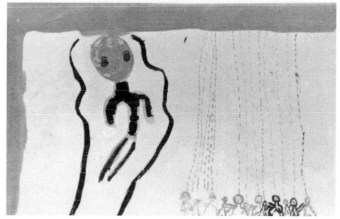

Top: The illustration for the story of Noah's ark was drawn by the attendant of a boy who was incapacitated in speech and movement. His nurse developed the picture from whatever sounds the boy conveyed. The boy's desire to contribute personally was so strong that a brush was strapped to his wrist so that he could add his own concluding touches in watercolor—an example of the will to create, which cannot be stifled even under the most limiting circumstances.

Bottom: Another version of the Noah story, by a twelve-year-old retarded Hungarian child. His conception of God as well as the idea of each person as a victim of his own private thunderstorm is strikingly original.

children. These materials explain the museum's major collections and exhibitions and often include slides or other color reproductions of artworks. The art and artists are usually placed in the context of their time and culture. When children are made aware in the classroom of the art they will see at the museum, they often are thrilled when they experience the original versions.

A number of teaching and learning strategies work well with visits to art museums. From the simplest to the most complex, these methods and games are effective with a range of learning styles and abilities. Museum visits are discussed more completely in Chapter 12 of this book.

Suitable Individual Activities

Stimulating an art vocabulary in each student is an important step in developing an art program for the disabled.

TABLE 4-1   Self-Questioning to Stimulate Problem-Solving Ideas

Student Disability Characteristics	The Instructional/Learning Environment				
	How can I help the STUDENT EXPERIENCING DISABILITY (SED) to:	How can CLASS PEERS be encouraged to:	How can I create an ENVIRONMENT that:	How can I design CURRICULUM/LESSONS that:	As ART TEACHER, how can I:
Cognitive/Academic	-independently find creative problem solutions? -use, but not copy, models? -use effective learning strategies? -experience success?	-work in cooperative groups with SED? -use a cue hierarchy? -model processes? -communicate with SED? -value differences?	-displays/illustrates examples of concepts? -displays examples of art in everyday life? -extends into the community? -encourages interaction?	-provide a variety of sensory involvement? -allow students to create in a variety of media? -are flexible and adaptable? -provide alternatives?	-support SED positively? -communicate SED's needs to parents and teachers? -inform parents of community resources in art? -inventory SED strengths and task requirements?
Behavioral/Managerial	-self-monitor behavior? -follow the example of peer behavior models? -share ideas and feelings? -understand and follow rules?	-model appropriate behaviors? -work cooperatively? -ignore inappropriate behaviors? -follow class rules?	-facilitates integration? -eliminates distractions? -is organized for easy access? -is noncompetitive and cooperative?	-use student interests? -are developmentally/creatively appropriate? -are organized into manageable segments? -use nonfrustrating media?	-learn more about SED and behavior management? -allow more choices as long as work is completed? -establish noncompetitive and cooperative environment?
Motivational/Attentional	-use personal ideas and interests in creating? -contract with contingency reward? -systematically monitor on-task behavior? -set personal goals?	-attend to own work? -share ideas when appropriate? -clarify, explain, and demonstrate to the class if asked?	-values SED's artwork? -extends beyond the classroom walls? -allows for productive movement? -is individualized for maximum learning?	-use high status materials? -include motivating games? -include use of video, film, visuals, and works of art?	-increase personal teaching and planning skills? -create a positive assessment system? -provide feedback quickly? -organize content for efficient learning?
Physical/Coordination	-participate in routines? -adapt media for self? -partially participate? -use a buddy to assist?	-offer assistance? -assist when needed? -communicate positively?	-provides quality tools? -gives access to media, sinks, closets, etc.? -allows free flow of movement?	-allow a variety of media? -can be accomplished with adapted tools? -include experiences using large muscle groups?	-invent/create tools and adaptations? -inventory SED skills and curriculum requirements? -develop cue hierarchies? -analyze for accessibility?
Sensory	-organize personal environment? -express needs? -adapt for self when possible?	-assist when asked? -communicate with SED?	-is organized for maximum sight/hearing?	-use sensory strengths? -can be completed without complication after class?	-invite communication? -use SED's sensory strengths in teaching? -clarify and support? -create touch/sight models?

SOURCE: Doris Guay, "Cross-Site Analysis of Teaching Practices: Visual Art Education with Students Experiencing Disabilities, *Studies in Art Education* 34, no. 4 (summer 1993): 61.

Children whose cognitive ability is limited to concrete thinking will need more visual, kinesthetic, and manipulative activities to aid them in experiencing the world. As their sensory experience is broadened, their expressive ability and self-confidence in the art-making process will increase.

Most art activities have proved to be sufficiently flexible to be performed by slow learners either in special classes or in regular classrooms. These activities include some types of drawing and painting, some forms of paper and cardboard work, sculpture and pottery, and printmaking. Simple perceptual and verbal activities can be adapted for slow learners, and the children also enjoy hearing stories about the lives and works of artists.

Basic Activities

Media and Techniques

In drawing and painting, learners with cognitive disabilities may use the standard tools and equipment recommended for other pupils. Hence, wax and oil-based crayons, tempera paint, the usual types of brushes and papers, and so on may be employed. Most of these pupils also achieve success when cut paper is used as a medium for two-dimensional pictures. Some pupils, however, may begin to build their pictures into three dimensions. Nearly all children enjoy box sculpture, and many seem capable of doing some freestanding paper sculpture. Many slow learners can use molds to make simple masks, and nearly all of them can work successfully with papier-mâché if it is prepared in advance for them.

Carving in wood and other substances might be difficult for some slow learners. The tools required in much of this work are too dangerous for them, and the technique is beyond their ability. Simple forms of modeling and ceramics, however, are recommended. The direct nature of modeling pleases these pupils, and the expressive potential of ceramics makes this activity highly suitable. Vegetable printing is also a useful technique, largely because it is repetitive, while stencil and linoleum work may be too difficult for all to master.

With all the basic activities just mentioned, the teacher of slow learners must modify classroom techniques to suit the abilities of these pupils. A step-by-step approach becomes necessary not only in the work itself but also in the selection of tools and media. Some preadolescent slow learners experience difficulty when confronted by a wide range of color or by the problems of mixing tints, shades, and even sec-

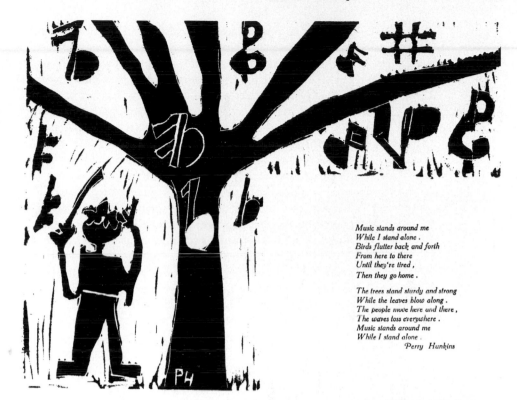

Music stands around me
While I stand alone .
Birds flutter back and forth
From here to there
Until they're tired ,
Then they go home .

The trees stand sturdy and strong
While the leaves blow along .
The people move here and there ,
The waves toss everywhere .
Music stands around me
While I stand alone .
Perry Hunkins

An example of graphic design combining poetry, printmaking, and typography to create a limited edition of booklets for parents. Francis Perkins School.

ondary hues. Chalk and charcoal also might create difficulties for some slow learners. In assisting students, teachers should provide the least amount of help to effect the greatest learning.

When three-dimensional work, such as pottery or box sculpture, is being taught, the teacher would be wise to analyze the process from start to finish in terms of separate operations. Then, before the pupils begin work, they should be shown a finished object, so they know what to expect at the end of their work. After that, however, demonstrations and general teaching might be performed only one operation at a time. The pupils should select the tools only for the one operation, complete the operation, and then return the tools. This process should then be repeated until all the necessary operations have been mastered.

History and Criticism

Slow learners can participate in all types of art activities if they are adapted to their ability levels. For example, postcard images of artworks are readily available from art museums and commercial publishers. Children can sort these images according to simple categories, such as subject matter (trees, animals, persons), art mode (picture of buildings, of furniture), color (name hues, possibly distinguish warm and cool), mood (happy, frightening), and many others. Color cards can be made using watercolors and paints and then sorted, mixed, and matched by the children according to basic color theory.

Children can enjoy stories about artists, seeing pictures of them (photographs or self-portraits), hearing stories of their lives and work, and looking at and reading children's books about art. Like most children, mentally retarded learners can enjoy seeing pictures of the people who created the art and learning how these artifacts were used. A balanced art program can provide rich opportunities for learning for mentally retarded children as well as for normal and gifted children. The full educational resources—including art reproductions, games, films and videos, slides, books, magazines, and objects for handling (such as museum replicas)—should be brought to bear for the art education of all children.

Group Activities

Pupils with mental retardation often have difficulty participating in class or group art activities, largely because of considerable differences in the mental and chronological ages of individual members of the group, even among pupils in special classes for the retarded. Group activity presents some difficulties for many people; for the mentally retarded the group activity must be very carefully chosen and supervised, if it is to succeed.

One recommended group activity is puppetry. This activity allows the child to work both as an individual and as a member of a group. Only the simplest of puppets need be made for a successful group performance. Stick and fist puppets are suitable for most slow learners. The child's subjects, cut in cardboard and tacked to sticks, or doll-like creatures made from old socks or paper bags and manipulated with the fingers, will serve as suitable characters for a play. A large cardboard carton provides a simple stage. The spoken lines and the action of the play may be derived from a well-liked story or based on some experience in the children's lives.

Because mural making demands a high level of group cooperation and organization, this activity must be adapted for slow learners. The quasi-group activity, in which the general plan is discussed and decided on by a group but in which each child works independently on a section of the display, is practical for slow learners, as it is for young chil-

dren. Some slow learners may not be able to grasp the overall design concept of a mural, but working on a large scale is a pleasurable experience. Many partly cooperative activities of this type may be carried out in clay or in other modeling or building materials, including empty boxes and odd pieces of wood. A service station, a farm, a village, or a playground are subjects slow learners might be interested in developing.

When only one or two noticeable slow learners are found in a class, the challenges arising from group work are different, since these pupils must participate and attempt to hold their own with their classmates. The problem of having all pupils purposefully occupied is not too great when the whole class is engaged in a group activity such as puppetry. That activity involves a variety of tasks, such as assembling the stage or hemming curtains, to which slow learners can contribute if given some guidance. In the more difficult activities involving only a few major tasks, such as, say, mural making, the slow learners' relative lack of ability tends to become conspicuous. Obviously, they cannot be asked to do only such menial jobs as washing brushes or cleaning paint tins. They must be given more important jobs, if they are to retain their sense of self-esteem.

The gains to be derived for slow learners working in art may be summarized by the following seven points:

1. Through art activity, students often create products that are not noticeably inferior to those of their neighbors. Their efforts need not suffer by comparison. Quality of product, in any case, is of secondary importance.

2. The process of concept-formation through art takes place for pupils with cognitive disabilities as it does for average and above-average children. Through art, slow learners can present ideas that may otherwise be denied expression because of limited ability in handling language skills.

3. For the trained observer, the artwork may provide diagnostic clues to emotional difficulties that sometimes accompany retardation.

4. Art activity can function as therapy, providing a unique source of satisfaction and stability to children who have a history of failure.

5. Working in art provides vital sensory and motor experiences that involve the total mental and physical capabilities of the children. The integration of physical and mental operations in turn facilitates the union of

thought and feeling. In this respect, art serves the same unifying function for children of all abilities.

6. Artistic activity provides slow learners with experience in decision making and problem solving, which are socially useful skills.

7. The art room can provide a nonthreatening atmosphere in which to begin the mainstreaming process of integrating normal children and those with special needs.

OTHER KINDS OF DISABILITIES

Although this chapter has focused on art and mental retardation, teachers may be faced with other kinds of disabilities, as children with disabilities are mainstreamed from special-learning situations into the regular classroom. Teachers cannot become instant authorities on all disabilities, but they can continue to be informed and work with special educators and other experts for the benefit of students with disabilities. Special education authorities urge us to view a disability not as a defect but rather as a difference through which teachers can discover the potential for a specific and unique mode of experience and through which other sensory modes may even be heightened.

> As we opened ourselves to their [blind children's] unique ways of being, we learned to value their otherness, to treasure the ways in which they sensitized us. The children expanded our sensory awareness by referring to "clay that smells like candy," "markers," or "soft paper." They tuned us in to sounds, like Billy, who took intense pleasure in "a marker that squeaks a whole lot . . . that makes a whole lotta noise." Although one would not have chosen a felt-tip marker as the most appropriate tool for a boy with no vision, Billy taught us not to allow our own preconceptions to interfere with what media we might offer a handicapped child.
>
> Through their sensitive use of their hands, those who could see nothing taught us about a kind of "free-floating tactile attention" in their approach to shape, form, and texture. . . . They seemed to know where to position their wood-scraps, suggesting a "tactile aesthetic" different from a visual one.[22]

One educator tells how a child with limited vision experienced a "kind of 'color shock'" from the intense hues of tempera paint. "And Terry, a deaf-blind child, literally jumped for joy when she accidentally discovered that wet clay pressed on the white paper made a visible mark. . . . The art program . . . opened our eyes to the need and capacity for joy. . . . The

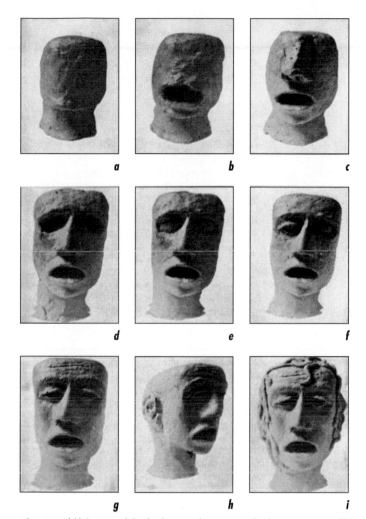

Viktor Lowenfeld documented the development of a portrait in clay by a sixteen-year-old blind girl. The project shown here develops from a general outline (a) to the finished head (i). Although known mostly for his work on artistic development, Lowenfeld began his career working with children and adults with special needs to develop this theory of visual and haptic types. These classifications, which he likened to expressionist and impressionist modes of art, are consistent with both normal and special-needs children.

Pain. Visual-blind sculpture. Congenitally blind sixteen-year-old girl.
a General outline
b Cavity of the mouth is formed
c Nose is added
d Eye sockets are hollowed out
e Eyeballs are put in
f Lids are pulled over
g Wrinkles are formed
h Ears are added
i The head is finished. All features are incorporated into a unified surface. Typical for the visual type.

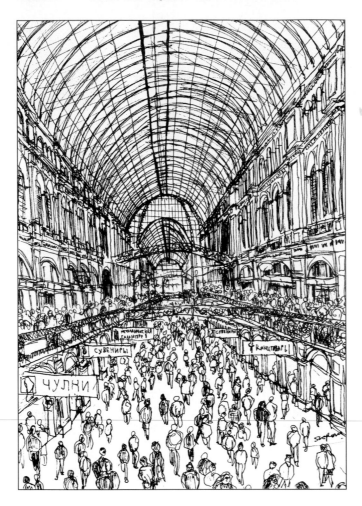

Autistic children may be extremely withdrawn, rigid, and inflexible in their habits and may also demonstrate impairment in both speech and social relationships. They can also be exceptionally gifted in art. This drawing of Gum's department store in Moscow was drawn by Steven Wiltshire at the age of twelve. Steven, who is as obsessed by architecture as was Nadia with horses (see Chapter 5), began this drawing from observation but completed it from memory.

intensity of the children's sensory-motor pleasure in the art experience was inescapable."[23]

Severely mentally retarded children make advances in behavior, speech, and language through arts programs that include other art forms. Through creative drama, deaf children can shed the fear of using words. Music can help to develop a rhythmical sense in handicapped children, as well as aid them in relaxing their muscles, and movement activities can help blind children gain the freedom to extend their sense of personal space.

In another study, a curriculum was "designed so that the students actually were exposed to language concepts within the process of making art objects. Through a concrete method, abstract verbal concepts were learned and integrated into each student's life." A multisensory approach can foster greater understanding of abstract concepts. "A highly visual curriculum which attempts to unify the total learning experience of the hearing impaired child" can often be achieved through arts activities. Using the visual, tactile, and linguistic modes results in a "greater concept attainment."[24]

What a child is not able to do is often offset by a heretofore-neglected area of ability. Once this becomes apparent, the teacher should be certain the parent is informed and the ability noted on the student's record. For example, a student who retreats from working on a large scale may perform very well with a smaller format; or, the child who cannot manipulate art materials may excel in responding to art.

We need to keep in mind that the art education program is comprehensive and broad, with a range of learning activities, including reading and writing about art, viewing and responding to art, studying and doing research about art and artists, as well as a rich series of art-making activities. And, as Blandy reminds us, "There can no longer be one type of art education for those who are disabled and another type for those who are not. . . . Environments in which art education takes place will need to become flexible, dynamic, and adaptable to meet the needs of all participants."[25]

NOTES

1. Helen Keller, "On Herself," *The Faith of Helen Keller,* ed. Jack Belck (Kansas City, MO: Hallmark Editions, 1967).

2. Joetta Sack, "More Schools Are Educating Students with Disabilities in Regular Classrooms. Are Teachers Ready?" *Education Week* 17, no. 28 (March 25, 1998): 32.

3. Ibid., 34.

4. G. Wallace and J. M. Kauffman, *Teaching Students with Learning and Behavior Problems,* 3rd ed. (Columbus, OH: Merrill, 1986).

5. Cindy Yorks, "Moving Up," *USA Weekend,* November 24–26, 1989.

6. For more information, write to VSA Arts, 1300 Connecticut Avenue NW, Suite 700, Washington, DC 20036, or go to their Web site at vsarts.org.

7. Doris M. Pfeuffer Guay, "Normalization in Art with

Extra Challenged Students: A Problem Solving Framework," *Art Education,* January 1993, p. 58.

8. Edith Kramer, "Art Therapy and Art Education: Overlapping Functions," *Art Education,* April 1980.

9. Susanne Langer, *Mind: An Essay on Human Feeling,* vol. 1 (Baltimore: The Johns Hopkins Press, 1967), p. 87.

10. See, for example, Frances E. Anderson, *Art-Centered Education and Therapy for Children with Disabilities* (Springfield, IL: C. C. Thomas, 1994) pp. xv, 268; and R. J. Morris and B. Blatt, *Special Education: Research and Trends* (New York: Pergamon, 1990).

11. Max Klager, *Jane C.—Symbolisches Denken in Bildern und Sprache* (Munchen, Basel: Ernst Reinhardt Verlag, 1978).

12. American Association on Mental Retardation, *Mental Retardation: Definition, Classification, and Systems of Supports,* 9th ed. (Washington, DC: 1992).

13. Association of Retarded Citizens (The Arc), *Introduction to Mental Retardation.* Publication #101-2, 1998, p.1 <http://www.thearc.org/faqs/mrqa.html>

14. Ibid.

15. Ibid.

16. Donald Uhlin, *Art for Exceptional Children* (Dubuque, IA: Wm. C. Brown, 1972), Chapter 3, "The Mentally Deficient Personality in Art"; and Zaidee Lindsay, *Art and the Handicapped Child* (New York: Van Nostrand Reinhold, 1972), pp. 18–45.

17. Joye H. Thorne, "Mainstreaming Procedures: Eligibility and Placement," *NAEA Advisory* (Reston, VA: National Art Education Association, spring 1990).

18. This anecdote was related in personal conversation with the authors.

19. For more assistance in understanding appropriate activities for special learners, see Andra L. Nyman and Anne M. Jenkins, eds., *Issues and Approaches to Art for Students with Special Needs* (Reston, VA: National Art Education Association, 1999); and Richard A. Villa and Jacqueline S. Thousand, eds., *Creating an Inclusive School* (Alexandria, VA: Association for Supervision and Curriculum Development, 1995).

20. Doris Guay, "Cross-Site Analysis of Teaching Practices: Visual Art Education with Students Experiencing Disabilities," *Studies in Art Education* 34, no. 4 (summer 1993): 222–232.

21. Ibid., p. 61.

22. Personal conversation with authors.

23. Judith Rubin, "Growing through Art with the Multiple Handicapped," *Viewpoints: Dialogue in Art Education, 1976.*

24. J. Craig Greene and T. S. Hasselbrings, "The Acquisition of Language Concepts by Hearing Impaired Children through Selected Aspects of Experimental Core Art Curriculum," *Studies in Art Education* 22, no. 2 (1981).

25. Doug Blandy, "Assuming Responsibility: Disability Rights and the Preparation of Art Educators," *Studies in Art Education* 35, no. 3 (spring 1994): 184.

ACTIVITIES FOR THE READER

1. Visit an art class that includes students of diverse disabilities.
   a. Compare drawings and paintings of slow learners with those of normal learners.
   b. Compare the work habits of particular disabled children with those of normal children.
   c. Observe what physical arrangements have been made to accommodate disabled students.
   d. Observe what adjustments have been made in curriculum, materials, and methods to accommodate disabled students.

2. Technology has improved learning opportunities for disabled children. What assistive technology might an art class provide for the following disabilities? (a) Autism; (b) Hearing impairment; (c) Visual impairment; (d) ADD; and (e) Muscular dystrophy. See the World Wide Web Resources list for up-to-date information.

3. Develop a plan to demonstrate and teach techniques involved in the following activities to a class of mentally retarded children: (a) making a tempera painting; (b) making a clay pot by the coil method; (c) making a simple weaving.

4. Develop a plan to take a class of visually impaired students to an art museum. What special accommodations might the museum make to provide access to these students and to enhance their experience with art?

5. Discover resources available to classroom teachers and art educators through the World Wide Web. The sites listed here specialize in education of disabled and exceptional children.

SUGGESTED READINGS

Anderson, Frances E. *Art-Centered Education and Therapy for Children with Disabilities.* Springfield, IL: C. C. Thomas, 1994.

Arnheim, Rudolf. "Perceptual Aspects of Art for the Blind." *Journal of Aesthetic Education* 24, no. 3 (1990).

Buck, G. H. "Creative Arts: Visual, Music, Dance, and Drama." *Strategies for Teaching Learners with Special Needs,* ed. E. A. Polloway and J. A. Patton. Upper Saddle River, NJ: Prentice-Hall, 1997, pp. 401–427.

Carrigan, Jeanne. "Attitudes about Persons with Disabilities: A Pilot Program." *Art Education* 47, no. 6 (1994).

Cohen, Jane G., and Marilyn Wannamaker. *Expressive Arts for the Very Disabled and Handicapped.* 2d ed. Springfield, IL: Charles C. Thomas, 1996.

Cohen, Libby G. *Children with Exceptional Needs in Regular Classrooms.* Washington, DC: NEA Professional Library, 1992.

Golomb, Claire, and Jill Schmeling. "Drawing Development in Autistic and Mentally Retarded Children." *Visual Arts Research* 22, no. 44 (1996): 5–18.

Guay, Doris M. "Art Educators Integrate: A Challenge for Teacher Preparation." *Teacher Education and Special Education* 17, no. 3 (1994).

————. "Students with Disabilities in the Art Classroom: How Prepared Are We?" *Studies in Art Education* 36, no. 1 (1994): 44–56.

Henly, David. *Exceptional Children, Exceptional Art: Teaching Art to Special Needs.* Worcester, MA: Davis Publications, 1992.

Loesl, Susan. *Insights: Art in Special Education—Educating the Handicapped Through Art.* Reston, VA: National Art Education Association, 1993.

Nyman, Andra L., and Anne M. Jenkins, eds. *Issues and Approaches to Art for Students with Special Needs.* Reston, VA: National Art Education Association, 1999. Up-to-date and comprehensive treatment of art for special learners.

Peter, Melanie. *Art for All: Developing Art in the Curriculum with Pupils with Special Educational Needs.* London: David Fulton, 1996.

Villa, Richard A., and Jacqueline S. Thousand, eds. *Creating an Inclusive School.* Alexandria, VA: Association for Supervision and Curriculum Development, 1995.

VSA Arts (Very Special Arts). *Start with the Arts.* Washington, DC: VSA Arts. John F. Kennedy Center. Instructional program for four-, five-, and six-year-olds that uses the arts to assist young children, including those with disabilities, in exploring themes commonly taught in early childhood classrooms.

VSA Arts (Very Special Arts). *Express Diversity!* Washington, DC: VSA Arts. John F. Kennedy Center. Instructional materials for disability awareness training through arts, adaptable for multiple grade levels.

Willard-Holt, Colleen. *Dual Exceptionalities.* ERIC Clearinghouse on Disabilities and Gifted Education (ERIC EC), 1999.

Witten, Susan Washam. "Students with Special Needs: Creating an Equal Opportunity Classroom." In *Middle School Art: Issues of Curriculum and Instruction,* ed. Carole Henry. Reston, VA: National Art Education Association, 1996.

WORLD WIDE WEB RESOURCES

Council on Exceptional Children (CEC). <http://www.cec.sped.org/> (September 1999). CEC is the largest professional organization dedicated to educating individuals with exceptionalities, students with disabilities, and/or the gifted. Excellent links to other WWW sites, including those specific to individual disabilities.

ERIC Clearinghouse on Disabilities and Gifted Education. "Selected Internet Resources for the Arts and Disabilities." <http://ericec.org> (September 1999). Provides access to numerous reports, articles, curriculum, and other resources. Special links to education and arts organizations with resources for disabilities education.

Internet Resources for Special Children (IRSC). <http://www.irsc.org/> (September 1999). The IRSC Web site is dedicated to communicating information relating to the needs of children with disabilities. Includes educational resources and links to other sites.

National Arts and Disabilities Center. <http://nadc.ucla.edu/>(September 1999). Develops technology to assist disabled persons and provides information pertaining to improving school environments.

National Center to Improve Practice (NCIP). <http://www2.edc.org/NCIP/> (September 1999). Dedicated to enhancement of education for students with disabilities through technology.

U.S. Department of Education, Office of Special Education and Rehabilitative Services (OSERS). "IDEA '97 Amendments Final Regulations." Individual Disabilities Education Act (IDEA). 1997. <http://www.ed.gov/offices/ OSERS/ IDEA/regs.html> (August 19, 1999). Site contains full text, summary, and index. Act includes legal definitions of various disabilities.

VSA Arts (formerly Very Special Arts). <http://www.vsarts.org/> (September 1999). VSA Arts is an international nonprofit organization dedicated to promoting the creative power in people with disabilities. Programs, resources, art images, and links to affiliated organizations. The VSA Arts Online Gallery presents art by emerging and established artists with disabilities.

Online Journal Articles and Reports*

"Assistive Technology and the Visual Arts." National Arts and Disabilities Center. March 1999. <http://nadc.ucla.edu/ata.htm> Identifies programs that utilize assistive technology.

Getty Institute for the Arts Newsletter. "Assistive Technology and the Arts: New Keys to Creativity," no. 11 (spring 1993). Online: ArtsEdNet. <http://www.artsednet.getty.edu/ArtsEdNet/Read/Newsletters/>

Joan D. Lewis, "How the Internet Expands Educational Options." *Teaching Exceptional Children TEC Online*, vol. 30, no. 5 (May/June 1998). <http://www.nscee.edu/unlv/Colleges/Education/ERC>

*Note: Online versions of journals are becoming more prevalent. Check your university library Web site for availability.

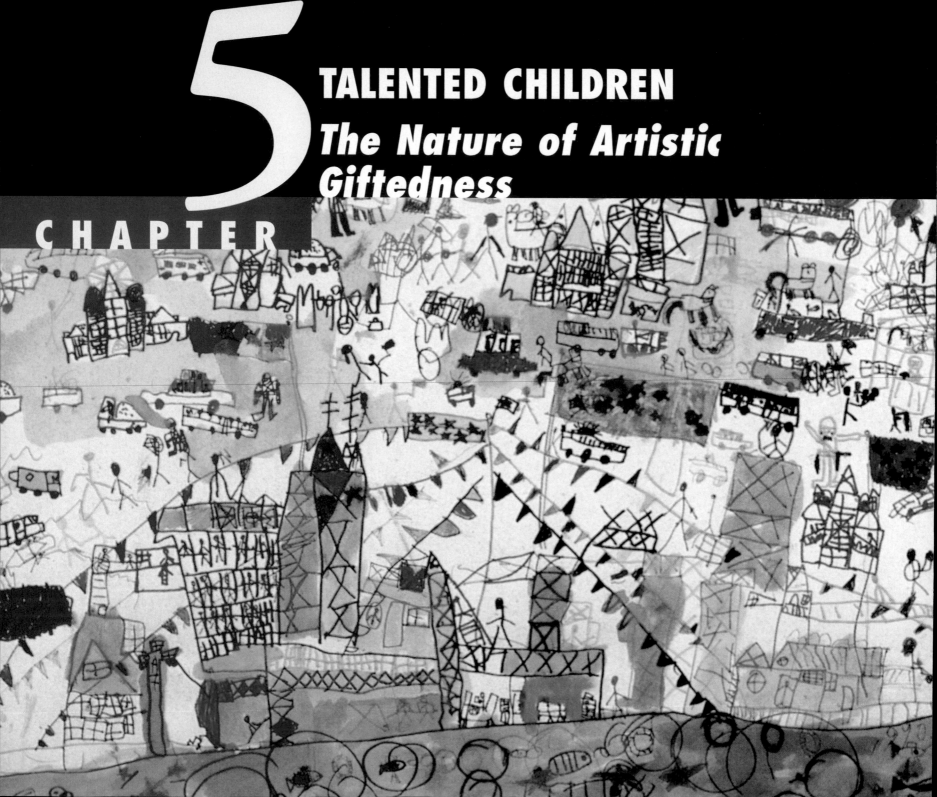

5 TALENTED CHILDREN
The Nature of Artistic Giftedness

The United States is squandering one of its most precious resources—the gifts, talents, and high interests of many of its students. In a broad range of intellectual and artistic endeavors, these youngsters are not challenged to do their best work. This problem is especially severe among economically disadvantaged and minority students, who have access to fewer advanced educational opportunities and whose talents often go unnoticed.[1]

—Pat O'Connell Ross

Every child has a profile of mental and physical strengths and weaknesses. Some children are physically well coordinated and others excel in mathematics or learn to read quickly. Some children are musically inclined, or are verbally adept, or have an ability to make others laugh. In the area of art, some children can draw well at early ages, and others are especially able to appreciate and understand works of art. Each and every child has a combination of the multitude of human abilities and a profile of interests that makes him or her a unique individual.

Our education system has in the past been more successful with general education for students in the normal range of abilities than it has in providing for the needs of gifted and talented children.

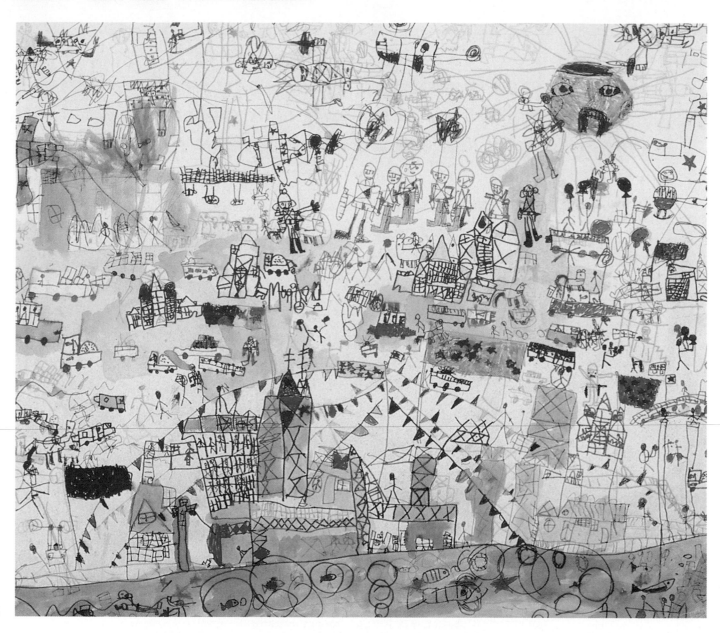

China (Shanghai), age 5

Neglect of these students cannot be excused on the grounds that gifted children are able to make satisfactory progress without help. On the contrary, much evidence shows that cases of failure, delinquency, apparent laziness, and general maladjustment easily occur among gifted children as a result of neglect. A major part of this neglect is the failure of teachers to provide challenges that interest fast learners and channel their creative energies in positive directions. The lot of academically gifted children has improved through the addition of special programs, grouping for ability levels, team teaching, and use of paraprofessionals and volunteers. Children who are gifted in art, however, typically have not been as readily identified or as well provided for.

This chapter deals with three main topics: how to identify children gifted in art, what types of educational programs and practices are needed for their support, and how gifted children can be encouraged to continue in their development.[2]

IDENTIFYING GIFTED CHILDREN

It seems to be more difficult to identify artistically talented children than academically gifted students. With the latter, educators can rely to a large extent on pupils' scores on IQ and other standardized tests, along with reports of their interests, activities, and performance in the area of interest. The identification of artistic talent is even more difficult. Although the results of some studies suggest that children gifted in art often score high on IQ tests, not every child with high IQ scores possesses artistic talent. Some, indeed, with exceptionally high IQs may appear to be lacking in even normal artistic skills and sensibilities.

One of the greatest difficulties in discovering artistic talent arises from the fact that no reliable measures exist to judge either art production or appreciation. Whatever beliefs we may hold about a particular child's abilities in art are usually based on personal appraisal rather than on data gathered objectively. Most experts hold that subjective appraisals are not so important in reading, spelling, and number work, where fundamental abilities can be measured fairly accurately, and, as a consequence, talent can be identified. We might suspect, however, that the expressive and appreciative aspects of even these academic fields are no more amenable to a reliable measurement than they are in art.

Because most teachers depend on subjective means to identify artistically talented youngsters, their estimate of the children's artistic future can be relied on only with reservations. Nevertheless, the pooled opinion of informed people has frequently led to surprisingly accurate judgments concerning artistic talent.

Most researchers agree that there are different ways to be intelligent and different ways that exceptional talent is demonstrated. There is general agreement that children should not be rigidly labeled and that more attention should be focused on the processes of developing potential in children.[3]

A U.S. Department of Education publication offers the following official definition of children with outstanding talent. This is based on the definition used in the federal Javits Gifted and Talented Education Act:

> Children and youth with outstanding talent perform or show the potential for performing at remarkably high levels of accomplishment when compared with others of their age, experience, or environment.
>
> These children and youth exhibit high performance capability in intellectual, creative, and/or artistic areas, possess an

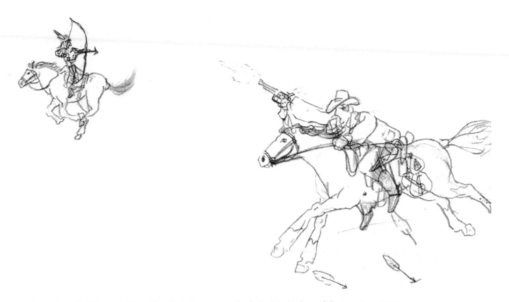

Kai, the sixth-grade "class artist" in a Shanghai elementary school, displays his love of the American West.

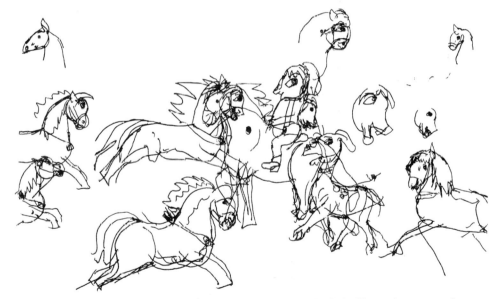

Great Britain. Nadia, the most celebrated of visually gifted autistic children, drew hundreds of horses. This group was drawn when she was three years and five months old.

unusual leadership capacity, or excel in specific academic fields. They require services or activities not ordinarily provided by the schools.

> Outstanding talents are present in children and youth from all cultural groups, across all economic strata, and in all areas of human endeavor.[4]

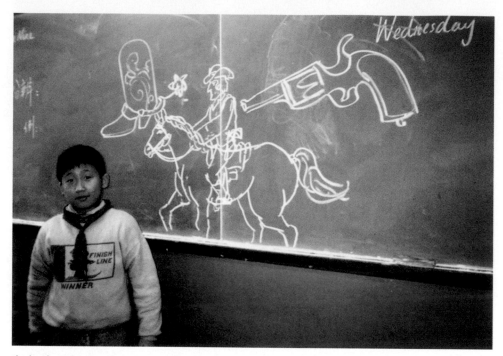

This boy from Shanghai, China, is the "class artist." His interest in the American West, cowboys, boots, and spurs is evident.

Research indicates several categories of talented children who are particularly neglected in programs for top students. These include culturally different children, minority and disadvantaged students, females, children with disabilities, underachieving high potential students, and students with artistic talents.

One school district, typical of many others, has developed procedures for admitting children to gifted programs that combine teacher nominations, test scores, examples of work, and interviews, while another relies largely on the judgment of parents and teachers. No tests, reviews, grades, portfolios, or requirements are utilized. Sometimes a system for identifying gifted children is criticized for bias in selecting only certain types of children and eliminating others, possibly from particular ethnic or socioeconomic groups. In some cases resources for gifted programs are limited, and parents are anxious to have their children identified in this category, leading to a competitive atmosphere and potential hard feelings. For these reasons and others, the best systems for identifying students who might benefit from special programs for the gifted and talented are usually developed on the local level in response to local needs and resources.

The U.S. Department of Education urges schools to develop a system for identifying gifted and talented students that:

- Seeks variety—looks throughout a range of disciplines for students with diverse talents;

- Uses many assessment measures—uses a variety of appraisals so that schools can find students in different talent areas and at different ages;

- Is free of bias—provides students of all backgrounds with equal access to appropriate opportunities;

- Is fluid—uses assessment procedures that can accommodate students who develop at different rates and whose interests may change as they mature;

- Identifies potential—discovers talents that are not readily apparent in students, as well as those that are obvious; and

- Assesses motivation—takes into account the drive and passion that play a key role in accomplishment.

SOURCE: Pat O'Connell Ross, *National Excellence: A Case for Developing America's Talent* (Washington, DC: U.S. Department of Education, Office of Educational Research and Improvement, October 1993), p. 3.

Characteristics of Gifted Children

Several authorities have made the study of artistically gifted children a special concern. One of the earliest efforts to characterize the special capacity for art was made by Norman Meier, a psychologist whose interest in the subject led him to design tests to assess the degree and kind of artistic talent among children. Meier claimed that gifted children derive their artistic ability from superior manual skill, energy, aesthetic intelligence, perceptual facility, and creative imagination. His study of gifted and average children led him to conclude that, since youngsters with the greatest artistic aptitude had a greater number of artists in their family histories, the genetic factor played a major role in determining artistic abilities.

The lists of characteristics of gifted children vary from one writer to another. Using points on which there is greatest consensus, we might construct a profile of a gifted child as follows: A child gifted in art observes acutely and has a vivid memory, is adept at handling problems requiring imagination, and, although open to new experiences, prefers to delve deeply into a limited area. The child takes art seriously and derives great personal satisfaction from the work, is persistent, and spends much time making and learning about

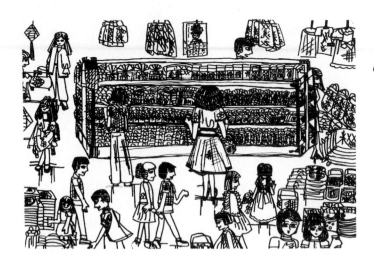

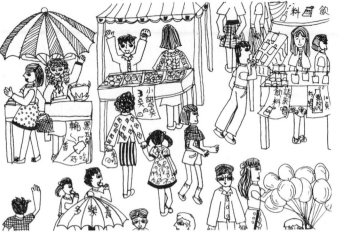

These two drawings represent the general level of drawing in one sixth-grade class in Taiwan. Because of the consistently high level of the students in this class, one speculates about the relation of talent to instruction. The teacher, who has been selected to give drawing work-shops to other teachers, has, it would appear, developed a "sys-tem" of instruction that is consid-ered effective in his country. Two questions come to mind in studying the drawings: How would American children respond to what appears to be such a rigorous approach to drawing, and what effect, if any, has the method had on the stu-dents' sense of individuality?

art. Indeed, the gifted child may sometimes be obsessive or compulsive about artwork, neglecting other areas of study for it.

As special programs for artistically gifted children have grown in number in both schools and museums, teachers have come to realize that many traits of creative behavior are shared by average or nonartistic as well as gifted children. Attitudes toward art, such as self-direction and commitment, merit attention and are best noted through observation. The following list of characteristics, both general and artistic, has been divided into categories of behavior relevant to artistic talent.[5]

General Characteristics

Precocity Children who are gifted in art usually begin at an early age—in many cases, before starting school and often as early as age three. A classic example is Yani's monkeys. Yani, a Chinese child, was six years old when this was painted.

Focus on Drawing Giftedness first evinces itself through drawing and for the most part will remain in this realm until the child tries other forms of expression or becomes bored with drawing. Drawing dominates not only because it is accessible but also because it fulfills the need for rendering detail.

Rapidity of Development All children progress through certain stages of visual development. The gifted child may traverse such stages at an accelerated pace, often condensing a year's progress into months or weeks.

Extended Concentration Visually gifted children stay with an artistic problem longer than others, because they both derive greater pleasure from it and see more possibilities in it.

Self-directedness Gifted children are highly self-motivated and have the drive to work on their own.

Possible Inconsistency with Creative Behavior The behavior of the artistically gifted is not necessarily consistent with

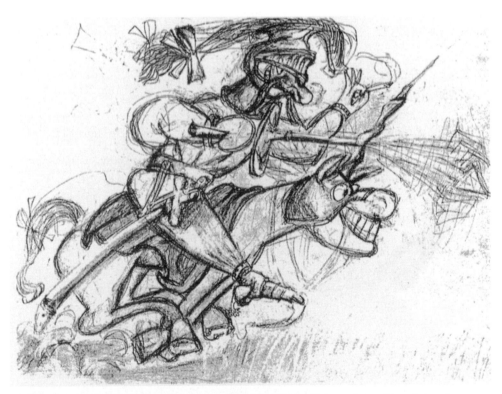

Visual fluency is a marked characteristic of this nine-year-old Russian émigré child. As a caricature, this work shows humor without relying upon the context of cartoons. For this child, drawing is a means to an end rather than an end in itself.

characteristics usually associated with creativity; in many cases the opposite may be true. The success won through long hours of practice is not easily relinquished in favor of journeys into the unknown. Young people's reluctance to make fools of themselves, to appear ridiculous, or to lose face before their peers tends to instill attitudes of extreme caution when confronting new problems.

Characteristics of the Gifted

The following characteristics are common but not universal:

- Shows superior abilities to reason, generalize, or problem solve.
- Shows persistent intellectual curiosity.
- Has a wide range of interests; develops one or more interests to considerable depth.
- Produces superior written work or has a large vocabulary.
- Reads avidly.
- Learns quickly and retains what is learned.
- Grasps mathematical or scientific concepts readily.
- Shows creative ability or imaginative expression in the arts.
- Sustains concentration for lengthy periods on topics or activities of interest.
- Sets high standards for self.
- Shows initiative, originality, or flexibility in thinking.
- Observes keenly and is responsive to new ideas.
- Shows social poise or an ability to communicate with adults in a mature way.
- Enjoys intellectual challenge; shows an alert and subtle sense of humor.

These characteristics can lead to conflicts in the regular classroom, as the gifted child may:

- Get bored with routine tasks.
- Resist changing away from interesting topics or activities.
- Be overly critical of self and others, impatient with failure, perfectionistic.
- Disagree vocally with others, argue with teachers.
- Make jokes or puns at times adults consider inappropriate.
- Be so emotionally sensitive and empathetic that adults consider it overreaction, may get angry, or cry when things go wrong or seem unfair.
- Ignore details, turn in messy work.
- Reject authority, be nonconforming, stubborn.
- Dominate or withdraw in cooperative learning situations.
- Be highly sensitive to environmental stimuli, such as lights or noises.

SOURCE: Based on Steven M. Nordby, "A Glossary of Gifted Education" <svennord/ed/GiftedGlossary.htm> (1998), p. 3.

Art As an Escape The gifted child may use art as a retreat from responsibility and spend more than a normal amount of time drawing. This is often accompanied by the kind of fantasizing reflected in the artwork. No talent, however impressive, is beneficial when used as an escape from other realities, and precocity in and of itself should not absolve a child from fulfilling the same responsibilities required of others.

Characteristics of Work

Verisimilitude, Being True to Life Although most children develop the desire to depict people and other subjects from their environment in the upper elementary years, gifted children develop both the skills and the inclination at an earlier age.

Visual Fluency Perhaps the most significant of all, this characteristic is most similar to that of the trained artist. Visually fluent children may have more ideas than they have time to depict. Asked to draw a still life, they will include details missed by others; given a story to illustrate, they present many episodes rather than just one. They draw as spontaneously as most people talk, because through drawing they maintain a dialogue with the world.

Complexity and Elaboration In their drawings, most children create "schemas" that are adequate to their needs; the gifted child goes beyond these and elaborates on them, sometimes as an adjunct of storytelling or fantasizing and sometimes for the sheer fun of adding details of clothes, body parts, or objects related to the schema. Wholes are related to parts as powers of recollection are tested and transformed into a growing repertoire of images.

Sensitivity to Art Media Because one of the characteristics of giftedness is the ability of one to immerse oneself in an art activity, it is logical to assume that through hours of practice the child will master any media of particular interest. Where most fourth graders are content to use a color straight out of the box or tube, a gifted one may become quickly bored with packaged color and combine several colors to achieve desired effects. A child may be instinctively sensitive to what a particular medium can do or may consciously try to attain mastery through practice. Older children (ages ten to twelve) are more apt to do this than are younger ones.

Random Improvisation Gifted children often doodle—they improvise with lines, shapes, and patterns; seem conscious of negative areas or spaces between the lines; and are absorbed with the effects of lines. They transfer this interest to subjects such as the human face; like cartoonists, they experiment with the influence of minute changes on facial expression, noting the differences that the slightest shift in the direction of a line can make.

Some psychologists, such as Howard Gardner, believe that educators have accepted a limited view of intelligence that neglects the importance of other mental capacities. Gardner's theory of multiple intelligences includes "logical," "mathematical," and "language" as traits (from which most conventional ideas of intelligence are drawn) but also includes "musical" and "personal" abilities.[6] "Spatial" intelligence relates to artistic ability. When a teacher engages in a discussion of aesthetics or asks a child to write or talk about art, the child extends not only the subject matter of art but also exercises other modes of intelligence. Artistic or spatial intelligence can also be distributed or divided into categories that draw on other modes mentioned by Gardner. As an example, an art director may begin as an artist (spatial) but call on abilities that relate to mathematical, language, and personal skills, for without these abilities, it would be impossible to give a client a cost estimate, write copy, or work as part of a planning team. Although certain kinds of intelligence are genetic or inherited, all can be strengthened if the desire for improvement is sufficiently strong.

Case History of Two Students

Strong indications of the nature of talent may sometimes be found in case histories of artistically gifted people, but it is often difficult to unearth actual evidence of their early work. A child's art is usually lost, and both parents and teachers are generally unable to recall accurately the child's early behavior. For some cases, however, reasonably detailed and apparently accurate data exist.

Among these cases are the histories of two girls of the same age from upper-middle-class homes, Susan McF and Mary M. These girls showed promise of talent in art very early in their lives. A study of their work shows that both of them began drawing just before they were one year old and that they had passed beyond the stage of manipulation before their second birthdays. Around fifteen months Susan was naming the marks she was producing in crayons. Mary did the same when she was sixteen months old. Around this age Mary began to use some spoken words clearly, but Susan was slower to learn to speak and instead was producing sounds such as "rrr," which consistently stood for "automobile," and "goong"

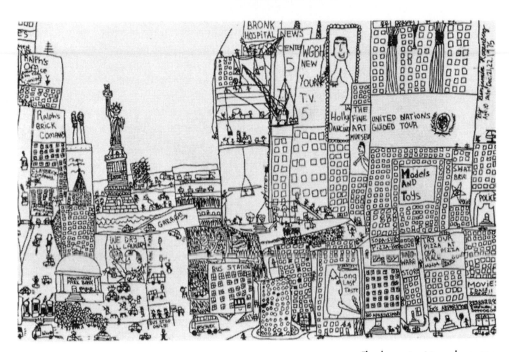

The class cartoonist may have more wit, inventiveness, and persistence than the "serious" artist. The ten-year-old boy who made this drawing had been interested in cartoons since the age of six. His drawing shows a keen observation of people, places, and events.

for "duck." When she depicted such objects in her paintings by the use of symbols, she named them in this vocabulary. When twenty-five months old, Susan produced an attractive montage with sticky tape and colored paper. Around twenty-seven months of age, both girls could delineate many different symbols and give them some relationship in the same composition.

Both children led normal, active lives, and during warm weather neglected their art for outdoor games. A study of their work (which their parents carefully dated) reveals, however, that inactivity in art did not seem to interfere with their continuous development. By the time both children were three years old, they were overlapping objects in their drawings and paintings, and at four Mary seemed to recognize texture as an expressive element of design. By six, they were skilled in a variety of techniques—mixing colors, devising textural effects, and inventing outstanding compositions. Before she was seven, Mary even gave hints of linear perspective in her work. It is important to note that both girls attended elementary schools that apparently provided progressive and highly regarded art programs.

By the time Susan was ten years old and Mary ten years and eight months, their work had lost most of its childlike qualities. Each girl passed through a realistic stage in which objects were rendered rather photographically. Then Susan's work became distinctly mannered in its rhythms, and Mary's output became reminiscent of that of several artists. In quick succession, she went through an Aubrey Beardsley period, followed by one reflecting the influence of Degas and later Matisse. When they were twelve years old, the girls met and became friends. They attended the same art classes in high school and produced paintings in a style obviously derived from that of the impressionists.

Fortunately, their secondary school art program proved almost as effective as that of the elementary school. After a time their work became noticeably more personal. Eventually both girls attended special classes for children with artistic talent, where they remained for four years, and where they produced paintings and sculpture in forms that continued to be recognizably personal. Both girls went on to attend a college of art where, according to their teachers, they gave evidence of outstanding artistic ability.

There seems to be little doubt that Mary and Susan were talented. What characteristics common to both might identify them as such? First, they expressed an almost lifelong preoccupation with art. Although their interest in art was at times intermittent, their production of art forms was for the most part uninterrupted. Second, both girls came from homes in which the parents enjoyed artistic interests. Both environment and biological inheritance often contribute to talent. Children of musical or artistic parents have the double advantage of both "nature" and "nurture" often denied the children of parents who lack these interests and abilities.[7]

Third, the progress of Mary and Susan throughout the phases of their childlike expression was both richer and more rapid than normal. Although both girls developed skills in handling tools and materials that were obviously above average, neither allowed her skills to assume paramount importance in her output. Again, at one period the girls' artwork apparently was dominated by technique, and the work of other artists whom they admired strongly influenced their output. Fortunately, however, their insight into artistic processes and their personal integrity, intellectual vigor, and vision were sufficient to overcome these powerful influences, which can be very seductive to the gifted young person who seeks a satisfying means of artistic expression.

Artists Examining Their Past

Another form of case history may be gathered from listening to the earliest memories of adult artists. When asked to reflect on their earliest artistic experiences, artists seem to have remarkable powers of recall. Much of what they describe, however, may on first reading appear to have little to do with conventional views of art.

Milton Glaser, a top graphic designer, is precise about an incident that occurred at the age of five.

> I have a precise picture of the moment I wanted to become an artist . . . it happened when I was five and my cousin, who probably was ten or fifteen years older than I was, came into the house with a brown paper bag, and he said, "Do you want to see a pigeon?" I thought he had a pigeon in the bag and said, "Yes." He took a pencil out of his pocket, and he drew a pigeon on the side of a bag. Two things occurred. One was the expectation of seeing somebody draw a pigeon; and two, it was the first time I had actually observed someone make a drawing that looked like the actual object—as opposed to my own rudimentary drawing. I was literally struck speechless. It seemed a miraculous occurrence, the creation of life, and I have never recovered from that experience.[8]

The noted artist Judy Chicago has recollections that begin even earlier, at age three, and, like many success stories, begin with the sympathy and support of a parent—in this case, her mother.

> When I was three, I began drawing, and my mother, who had wanted to be a dancer, gave me a lot of encouragement. . . . Throughout my childhood, she told me colorful tales about the creative life, particularly when I was sick in bed, and these stories contributed to my developing interest in art, for, from the time I was young, I wanted to be an artist. My father, on the other hand, could never relate to my artistic impulse, so it was to my mother that I brought my artistic achievements and to my father that I brought my intellectual ones.[9]

As the following excerpt reveals, Louise Nevelson not only knew she wanted to be an artist but also a particular kind of artist, a sculptor.

> I claim for myself I was born this way. From earliest childhood I knew I was going to be an artist. I *felt* like an artist. You feel it, just like you feel you're a singer if you have a voice. So I have that blessing, and there was never a time that I questioned it or doubted it. . . . The librarian asked me what I was going to be, and of course I said, "I'm going to be an artist." "No," I added, "I want to be a sculptor, I don't want color to help me." I got so frightened, I ran home crying. How did I know that when I never thought of it before in my life?[10]

Were one to generalize about major influences on artistic talent, one might conclude from the sources just cited that the role played by parents, literature (storytelling), and exposure to models of artistic behavior all contribute to the advancement of the creative lives of gifted children.

Many artists have other memories in common—parents who were ignorant of art yet sympathetic to their children's interests; an impulse to copy; and an affinity for realism. First experiences with museums are largely positive, and, as with many writers and actors, their childhoods were particularly rich in fantasy, daydreams, and love of and pursuit of stories. Faith Ringgold is particularly eloquent in this regard when recalling her childhood in her video *Faith Ringgold: The Last Story Quilt*.[11]

IDENTIFYING THE TALENTED CHILD

The teacher who suspects a child of possessing unusual artistic talent might be wise to enlist the opinions of others, including artists and art teachers. Opinions of such well-informed people, furthermore, might be sought over a relatively long period. A sudden appearance of talent may later prove to be merely a remarkable but temporary development of skill. Again, what appears to be artistic talent in early years may disappear as the child develops other interests into which energies and abilities are channeled.

When teachers want information on a particular aspect of talent, they can devise certain tasks to reveal specific skills. Characteristics to be studied in the area of art might include observational ability; color sensitivity; ability to fuse drawing and imagination; emotional expressiveness; memory; handling of space; and sensitivity to media.

Teachers might also notice the interests children have for looking at art, especially original art in galleries and museums, and for reading about art and artists. They might note, as well, children who seem to be adept at discussing works of art, making interesting interpretations of meaning, relating to other artworks, and generally appearing knowledgeable and comfortable in the presence of art and talk about art.

The problem of assessing giftedness continues throughout a child's school career. Those who are most concerned with its identification are the admissions personnel of art schools. While the traditional means of admission rests on the applicant's portfolio (which reflects the child's capabilities in draw-

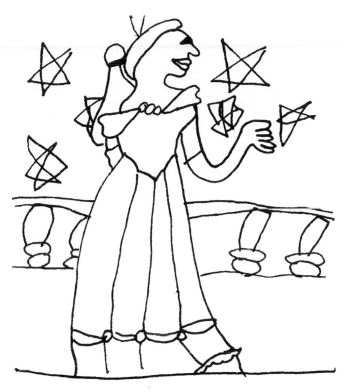

This drawing by Will, who is six years old, shows an advance in execution through the handling of proportion, the use of the profile, and in the variety of shapes used in portraying the subject. Such spatial awareness is often overlooked in favor of the subject of the drawing.

ing, color, or design), many art schools have for some time used other criteria for admission, such as problem-solving abilities, evidence of creative thinking, and personality traits assessed through personal interviews. In other words, an alert student with a flexible and inventive mind may now have an advantage over an applicant whose main talent lies in skillful watercolors.

The system of identification that is based on both time and the opinions of several specialists seems to function with reasonable efficiency. Pupils are selected for advanced art instruction by peer and teacher recommendations based on apparent art production abilities, interest, and general school success. Students might move into or out of the advanced class according to their self-evaluations and observations of progress by the art teacher.

In some special art classes offered to children, a major criterion for admission was commitment to art rather than talent as such. These special classes demonstrated that skill does indeed improve in many instances, once children work in an environment of peers who share their enthusiasm. The classes were specifically designed for those whose hunger for art was simply not satisfied by the amount of activity the normal

These two drawings are small segments from a team drawing by two brothers, ages 5 and 7. The complete work has literally dozens of situations and fragments of stories. The sheer number of ideas rather than evidence of conventional drawing skills reflects a high level of fluency. The whole drawing is 18 X 24 inches on cardboard and included hundreds of figures, buildings, imaginary animals, and so on.

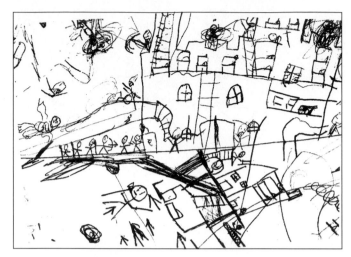

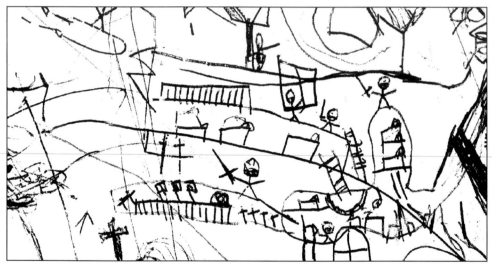

time from other obligations to work in art. The danger here is that the classroom teacher might not be equipped to provide special help, or that excusing the child from nonart activities to work in art might arouse adverse reactions from the rest of the class. We also must bear in mind the negative attitudes many teachers exhibit toward children who are particularly nonconformist in their creative behavior.

Another arrangement for helping the gifted is the "special class," in which only talented children are enrolled. Such classes may be offered during school hours, after school, or on Saturday mornings. Many educators believe these classes provide the best solution to the problem of meeting the needs of the gifted. Teachers can be engaged who possess capabilities in special artistic fields. Much as a sympathetic teacher of general education may help a gifted child in art, a specialist can provide even more assistance. In the special classes the need to provide for individual differences will be even more apparent.

Whatever special arrangements are made for the child with artistic talent, two considerations of paramount importance to the child's future development must be kept in mind. In the first place, on no account should the child's artistic development be unduly hastened into adult forms of expression. In the elementary school, the talented youngster is still a youngster, and artistic growth must occur with due respect for this fact. Even so, in the second place, every talented child must be provided with sufficient challenge to work to capacity. Unless this condition prevails, the gifted pupil may lose interest in the work, and considerable energies and abilities may be dissipated in less worthwhile ways.

Under what circumstances will talent flourish? To begin with, parents should, at best, encourage an interest in art and, at worst, not discourage it. A sympathetic home environment is extremely stimulating. The home that provides art supplies, art books, and a place to work, together with loving and intelligent parents to admire the work being produced and to encourage further production, will aid substantially in fostering talent. Next, the elementary and secondary schools that the gifted pupil attends should provide a sufficiently stimulating and challenging art program. Finally, somewhere along the line of artistic progress, the gifted pupil should be afforded special opportunities for the cultivation of talent and should have the opportunity to encounter a supportive teacher who is sensitive to any capabilities that set the gifted child apart from other pupils. Some questions teachers and administrators

school could allow. In other words, it is possible to hunger for art without the ability to produce artwork of outstanding quality.

SPECIAL ARRANGEMENTS IN ART FOR GIFTED CHILDREN

When gifted children have been identified, a problem arises concerning suitable educational treatment for them. An "enriched" program may be offered by the classroom teacher or art consultant, whereby the pupil is assigned advanced work, given special materials, and allowed to take might ask themselves when identifying and planning for gifted children are the following:

- Have I notified the parents that their child has special talents that deserve support?
- Have I investigated any sources of additional help from the community, such as special classes in museums?
- In dealing with gifted children, am I being overly solicitous—giving more attention than needed?
- Am I adding an appreciative or critical dimension to the activities by showing and discussing artworks related to studio activities?
- Do I have rapport with the children? Do they respect my opinions?
- Has their ability in self-appraisal improved?
- Do I know how to deal with and interpret negative attitudes sometimes displayed by gifted children?
- Am I an effective model for a gifted child? How does my behavior reflect my own love of art?

The word *talent* is a general term covering four levels of ability. There are those with an aptitude for art, those of minimal talent who nevertheless enjoy making art, those whose attitudes and skills set them above their classmates, and those who combine skill, intellect, imagination, and drive. It is especially important that the teacher has credibility with these students, particularly in the upper grades.

SUGGESTED ART ACTIVITIES

It is unwise to offer the gifted a curriculum oriented exclusively toward media. The talented child can be challenged by ideas as well as by materials in special classes. Moreover, students should have opportunities to work in one area in depth. A conceptual approach to art activities begins with an idea and then asks the child to use materials as a means of solving a problem. The problem may be stated as follows: "One characteristic of humans is that they design their environment for pleasure and for aesthetic purposes, as well as for function and utility. In creating your own environment, take into consideration purpose, scale, and materials." Stating the problem in this manner opens up a number of choices for the student and encourages decision making different from what results when the child is told. "On the table you will find cardboard, pins, knives, and rulers. These are the materials to be used in making a scale model of a vacation home."

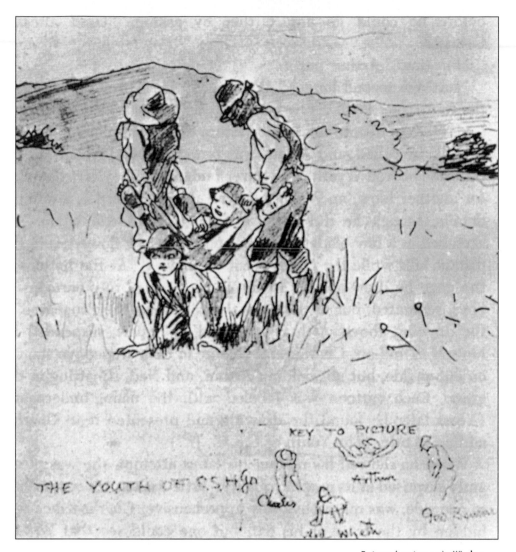

Eminent American artist Winslow Homer made this drawing at age 11. Note the four structural studies at the bottom of the page, a member of the Wyeth family among them. Winslow Homer, *Beetle n' Wedge* (from *Winslow Homer: A Portrait*, by Jean Gould, Dodd Mead and Company, 1962).

The teacher of the special class or the art consultant teaching in an after-school program should take an inventory of art activities offered prior to the special class in order to better plan the new program. Thus, a child who is interested in sculpture but has worked only in clay might try a large-scale plaster or wood carving. In printmaking, a child who has worked only in linoleum may try a woodcut, or one who has handled both of these could attempt a multicolor silkscreen or any other problem beyond the capabilities of the other children. These activities extend the range of the child's experience and compensate for the relatively limited exposure to art in the regular school program.

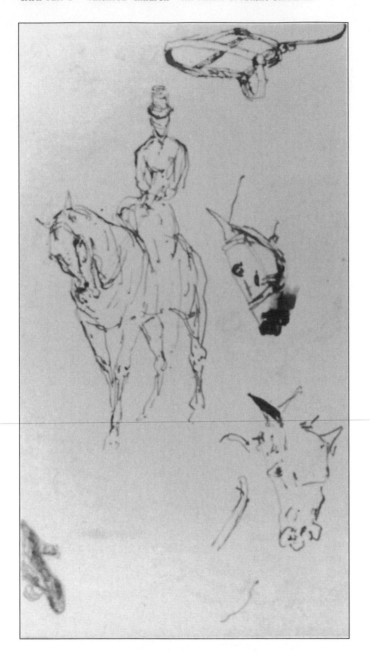

Drawing by Henri de Toulouse-Lautrec, Chevaux, 1875–1876. (Henri was 11–12 years old.)

not be as promising as classmates with lesser abilities. A difficult, but necessary, task of the teacher is to make a new material, process, or idea so challenging that the student will be willing to suspend the results that have earned him or her acclaim.

Gifted children are particularly curious about the lives and works of exemplary artists. Children interested in making a wood or clay sculpture, for example, should have access to books, filmstrips, videos, or slides that show how different artists approach this process. They might learn how some artists make preparatory sketches of their ideas for a sculpture, selecting the most promising idea and then assembling the materials needed to carry out the idea. They might learn that other artists make sketches, usually in small scale, from the same materials used for the final sculpture. Gifted boys and girls should learn that women as well as men create sculpture. They should become familiar with sculptural pieces from their own country and time, done by living artists, as well as with the heritage of sculpture from other times and places. They should learn that sculpture can be representational or abstract or nonobjective, depending on the expressive purposes of artists. Gifted children should have experiences that help them to understand that artists make sculptures that express meaning and feeling, and they should gain skills in reading meaning from art.

General Activities

Gifted children may demonstrate a number of peculiarities in their selection of art activities. Their interests in such basic types of artwork as cartooning, portraiture, and sculpture develop early, and they appear to find greater challenge and deeper satisfaction in these than they do in some of the crafts, such as weaving a paper construction. While they may occasionally turn to crafts for their novelty, they generally return with renewed interest to what might be described as the more traditional art forms, possibly because these afford an opportunity to display the children's special brand of precocity.

Gifted children usually prefer to work at art by themselves rather than to participate in group endeavors. Although as a group the gifted are socially inclined, they seem to recognize in art a subject that demands sustained individual deliberation and effort. They are not entirely averse to participating in puppet shows, mural making, and other art forms requiring a pooled effort, but most are happiest when submerged as individuals in their own artistic agenda.

Highly gifted students have their own agenda, which often reflects a repetition of past successes. When a child has been praised by teachers and peers for the ability to draw in a realistic fashion, why should the student relinquish flattering responses for new and unknown realms of expression? When it comes to openness to new experience, such children might

Painting in Oils

Painting in oils is a good example of a special activity suitable for the gifted. It offers the student an effective means of identifying with "real artists." The oils are rich and sensual in color and are far more versatile than most water-based paints. The slow-drying quality of oil paint makes it suitable for art projects undertaken over a period of time. By the time they reach preadolescence, gifted children should have had an opportunity to work with it. However, not even the most gifted children can use it effectively until they have had experience with many other types of paint. (See Appendix D for possible health hazards involving solvents.)

Other Media for Drawing and Painting

Gifted pupils in the preadolescent stage will find several other challenging media that may not be available in the regular art program. Some of the more expensive colored drawing inks, for example, might be used in conjunction with india ink or in some of the mixed-media techniques previously mentioned. Work with felt pens and pointed brushes might be explored. Charcoal pastels, and conté crayon in black and brown can also be used fairly extensively, either in quick sketching or in more deliberate drawing. Some of this line drawing might lead to more advanced graphic processes like serigraphy and lithography.

Some gifted children in the preadolescent stage become proficient in the use of various types of watercolor. In the opinion of many painters, transparent watercolor is one of the most subtle and difficult of media. It must be used with precision and speed, and its "wetness," or watery character, should be reflected in the finished work. Good watercolor paints, brushes, and especially papers are relatively expensive. The pigments in tubes are more convenient to use than those in cake form. When gifted pupils begin to paint seriously in watercolors, they should be provided with materials of a higher quality than is usually found in the school art program. The many acrylic paints on the market offer colors as intense as oils, as well as quick-drying properties.

In the contemporary educational climate, with technical innovations becoming increasingly available, it would be a mistake to ignore the creative possibilities of the computer. Many children in today's schools started using computers in preschool. With graphics, painting, and animation programs available in computer software, it is not uncommon for elementary-school children to make art on the computer. Gifted and talented children can benefit immensely through their access to computers, both as a research tool on the World Wide Web and as a medium for creating their own art.

Regardless of the medium, the emphasis should be on the nature of the art problem (more challenging), on the instruction (more specific, where needed), and on the creation of additional time, preferably with a group of their peers. Teachers should require more of gifted children, set higher standards of work, and be more directive when the occasion demands it. Instruction, therefore, differs as much in intensity as in kind.

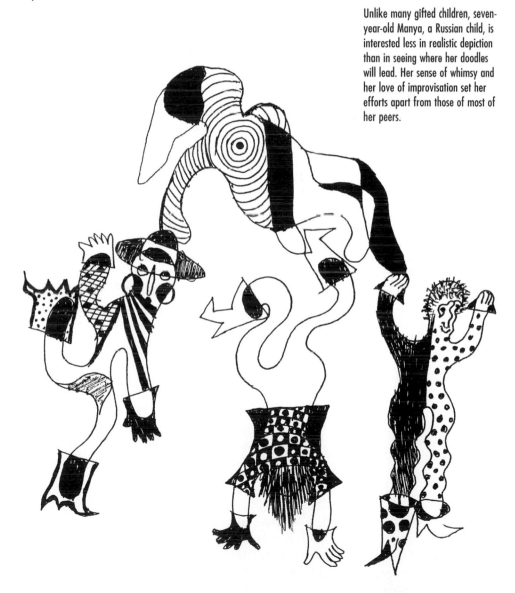

Unlike many gifted children, seven-year-old Manya, a Russian child, is interested less in realistic depiction than in seeing where her doodles will lead. Her sense of whimsy and her love of improvisation set her efforts apart from those of most of her peers.

TEACHING THE GIFTED CHILD

The young gifted child will, of course, make use of the usual materials and perform the basic activities mentioned in earlier chapters in connection with the general art program for normal children. Because the gifted may be recognized only over a period of time, they must obviously take part in the art program designed for all until their talent is noted. When it is clear that individuals possess gifts above the ordinary, the teacher should help them to progress at their optimum level of accomplishment. Progress in art occurs when the worker keeps producing art. Mere quantity of production or repetition of forms previously created is not progress, but production that leads to improved skill, more penetrating insight, and greater mastery of media can help to develop a child's talent.

The principle of teaching in response to the needs of the learner is emphasized throughout this book. The preceding chapter observed that, in order to profit from art at all, some slow learners need to follow a step-by-step method of instruction. With the gifted the reverse is necessary. Here the teacher is faced with the necessity for what might be described as "under-teaching." Every attempt must be made to challenge the greater abilities of gifted children. Whenever they can learn a fact or a technique for themselves, they should be encouraged to do so. Assistance must in general be withheld until the children have explored their own avenues for solutions to their problems. Gifted pupils who are given this type of educational treatment thrive on it, and so does their art.

Although artistically gifted children are normally motivated to express themselves with drawing and painting media, they should always have access to fine works of art in the media of their choice or, failing the actual works, good reproductions of them. The teacher should suggest certain outstanding works for them to study at art galleries and museums. Talented children can be assumed to be capable of extending their passion for creating works of art to the appreciation or criticism of art. *Artworks should be discussed—both for their own sake and for the problems they pose as regards the work currently in progress.*

The teacher will have to make special efforts with gifted pupils from underprivileged homes to encourage them to see the best art and to read good books on art. Gifted children from well-endowed homes generally have opportunities to add to their knowledge of art. Underprivileged children enjoy few, if any, such opportunities. Indeed, their gift must often be an especially vital one. In their case, the teacher's duty is to supply the inspiration and sources of knowledge that their home environment has denied them.

As one authority has noted:

> Art teachers should recognize that gifted education in art, whether it be for the academically or the artistically gifted— or both—must be as rich in ideas as it is in studio experiences. Likewise, the experiences should emphasize looking at and responding to works of art as well as creating images and objects. What is clearly apparent from practice is that bright students respond quickly and adeptly to art instruction. On the other hand, those with artistic gifts often need to be challenged to use their image-making abilities to think about and explore the world of ideas which reside in the history of art and in the realm of aesthetics.[12]

NOTES

1. Pat O'Connell Ross, *National Excellence: A Case for Developing America's Talent* (Washington DC: U.S. Department of Education, Office of Educational Research and Improvement, October 1993).

2. In much educational writing *gifted* refers to children with a high general intelligence, while *talented* refers to a special capability in one field of endeavor. This differentiation of meaning is by no means universal and has not been adopted here. In this chapter the words are used interchangeably.

3. Ross, *National Excellence,* Part 3, p. 1.

4. Ibid., p. 3

5. Al Hurwitz, *The Gifted and Talented in Art: A Guide to Program Planning* (Worcester, MA: Davis Publications, 1983).

6. Howard Gardner, *Multiple Intelligences: The Theory in Practice* (New York: Basic Books, 1993).

7. Because each girl had highly educated parents who are especially interested in art, records of their art were preserved. The parents systematically filed the children's

work after writing comments about each piece on its reverse side. Both children eventually enrolled in classes for gifted children, at which time the parents disclosed the girls' records. The girls' IQ scores were 120 (Mary) and 130 (Susan).

8. Milton Glaser, *School Arts Magazine,* May 1993, p. 60.

9. Judy Chicago, *Through the Flower: My Struggle as a Woman Artist,* (New York: Doubleday, 1993), pp. 3–4.

10. Louise Nevelson, *Dawns and Dusks* (New York: Scribner, 1976), pp. 1, 14.

11. *Faith Ringgold: The Last Story Quilt,* prod. Linda Freeman, 28 min., L & S Video, 1992, videocassette.

12. Karen Lee Carroll, *Towards a Fuller Conception of Giftedness: Art in Gifted Education and the Gifted in Art Education* (Ph.D. diss., Teachers College, Columbia University, 1987).

ACTIVITIES FOR THE READER

1. Study some children considered to be artistically gifted. Make a note of their outstanding personal qualities and work habits and of their attitudes toward their contemporaries.

2. Make a collection of drawings and paintings by artistically gifted children. Analyze works for subject matter, design, and technique. Compare this collection with works of normal children of the same chronological ages as those in the gifted group.

3. Study the home environment of several artistically gifted pupils. How does this environment rate culturally and economically?

4. Contact some artists and request that they lend you a drawing from their school days, if one still exists. Ask several artists to recount their earliest recollections of interest in art.

5. Compare the entrance requirements of at least two programs for gifted children (museums, art schools, etc.).

6. How would you describe levels of giftedness? *Example:* Cleverness as opposed to the highest level of ability.

7. A fairly significant percentage of college students have been involved in gifted and talented programs during their K–12 education. Interview your classmates and friends who have this experience. Ask them to describe and evaluate the programs they were in.

SUGGESTED READINGS

Callahan, Carolyn M., and Jay A. McIntire. *Identifying Outstanding Talent in American Indian and Alaska Native Students.* Washington, DC: U.S. Dept. of Education, Office of Educational Research and Improvement, Javits Gifted and Talented Education Program, 1994.

Clark, Gilbert A., and Enid Zimmerman. "Issues and Practices Related to Identification of Gifted Students in the Visual Arts." *Translations: From Theory to Practice* 2, no. 2. Reston, VA: National Art Education Association, 1992.

———. "Nurturing the Arts in Programs for Gifted and Talented Students." *Phi Delta Kappan* 79, no. 10 (1998).

———. *Resources for Educating Artistically Talented Students.* Syracuse, NY: Syracuse University Press, 1987.

Gardner, Howard. *Creating Minds.* New York: Basic Books, 1993.

———. "Multiple Intelligences: Implications for Art and Creativity." *In Artistic Intelligences: Implications for Education,* ed. William J. Moody. New York: Teachers College, 1990, pages 11–27.

———*Multiple Intelligences: The Theory in Practice.* New York: Basic Books, 1993.

Golomb, Claire. *The Development of Artistically Gifted Children: Selected Case Studies.* Hillsdale, NJ: L. Erlbaum, 1995.

Hurwitz, Al. *The Gifted and Talented in Art.* Worchester, MA: Davis Publications, 1983.

Porath, Marion. "A Developmental Model of Artistic Giftedness in Middle Childhood." *Journal for the Education of the Gifted* 20, no. 3 (1997): 201–223.

Salome, Richard A. "Research Pertaining to the Gifted in Art." *Translations: From Theory to Practice* 2, no. 1. Reston, VA: National Art Education Association, 1992.

Zimmerman, Enid. "Factors Influencing the Art Education of Artistically Talented Girls." *Journal of Secondary Gifted Education* 6, no. 2 (1995): 103–112.

WORLD WIDE WEB SITES

Advanced Network and Services, Inc. "ThinkQuest Library: Art." *ThinkQuest.* <http://www.thinkquest.org/> Think-Quest is a classroom-based program that promotes active use of computers and technology as learning and collaboration tools. The site presents exemplary models of student-directed, project-based learning and includes numerous comprehensive art projects.

Council for Exceptional Children. <http://www.cec.sped.org/> The Council for Exceptional Children (CEC) is the largest professional organization dedicated to educating individuals with exceptionalities—students with disabilities and/or the gifted. The CEC Web site provides diverse resources for gifted education, including advocacy material.

KidSource OnLine, Inc. "Education: Gifted and Talented Students." <http://www.kidsource.com/kidsource/pages/ed.gifted.html> Annotated bibliography and other educational resources.

National Association for Gifted Children. <http://www.rmplc.co.uk/orgs/nagc/> United Kingdom Web site for gifted and talented children, families, and educators. Presents resource material and links to international gifted and talented organizations.

National Research Center on the Gifted and Talented. *Center for Gifted Education and Talent Development.* <http://www.gifted.uconn.edu/> Sponsored by the U.S. Department of Education, the mission of the National Research Center on the Gifted and Talented is to plan and conduct research and disseminate information to persons and groups that have a stake in the education of high-potential youth from preschool through post-secondary levels. Offers high-quality resources in a variety of media—some available on the Internet and others available through ordering.

Northwestern University. "Online Publications and Resources." *Center for Talent Development.* <http://ctdnet.acns.nwu.edu/> Online articles, listservs on gifted education, excellent annotated bibliography, and links to other sites.

U.S. Department of Education and Office of Educational Research and Improvement. *Jacob K. Javits Gifted and Talented Students Education Program.* <http://www.ed.gov/prog_info/Javits/> To support the development of talent in the United States, the U.S. Congress passed the Jacob K. Javits Gifted and Talented Students Education Act of 1994. This Web site presents the legislation authorizing funding for gifted and talented education and explains the programs created to support it.

U.S. Department of Education and National Library of Education. *ERIC Clearinghouse on Disabilities and Gifted Education* (ERIC EC). 1997. <http://ericec.org/> Searchable database of articles, curricula, digests, fact sheets, and bibliographies, with a new full-text library featuring journal articles, books, and other resources from across the Internet. Links to discussion groups and other professional information related to gifted education.

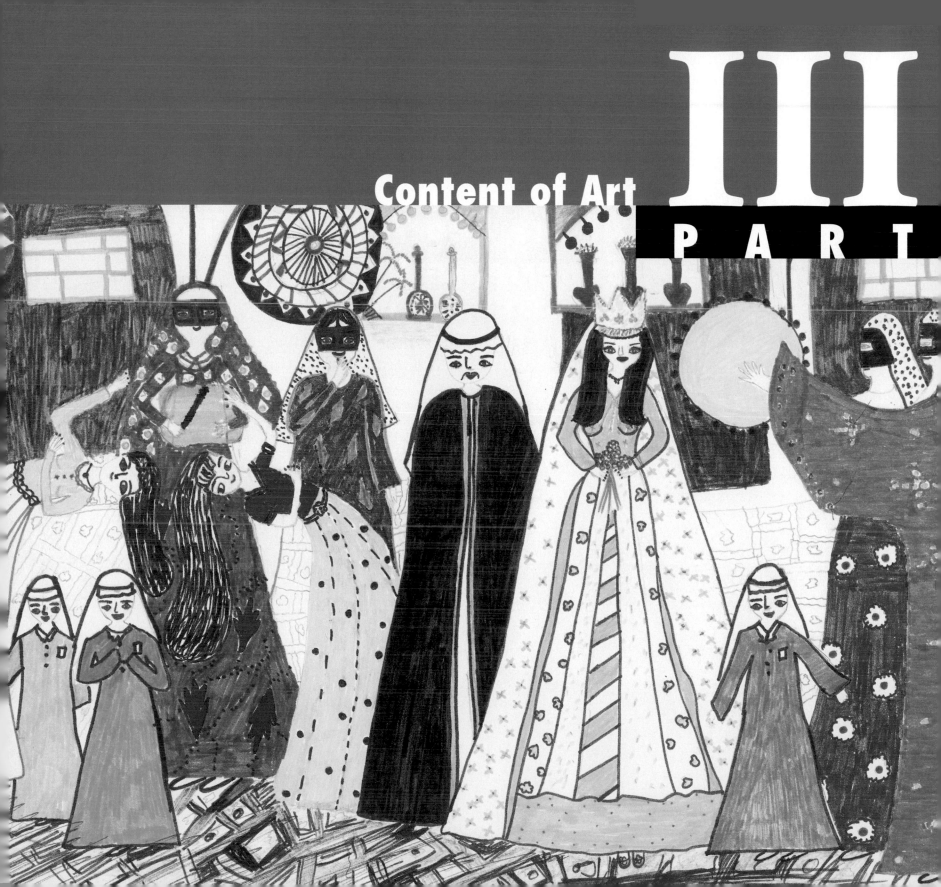

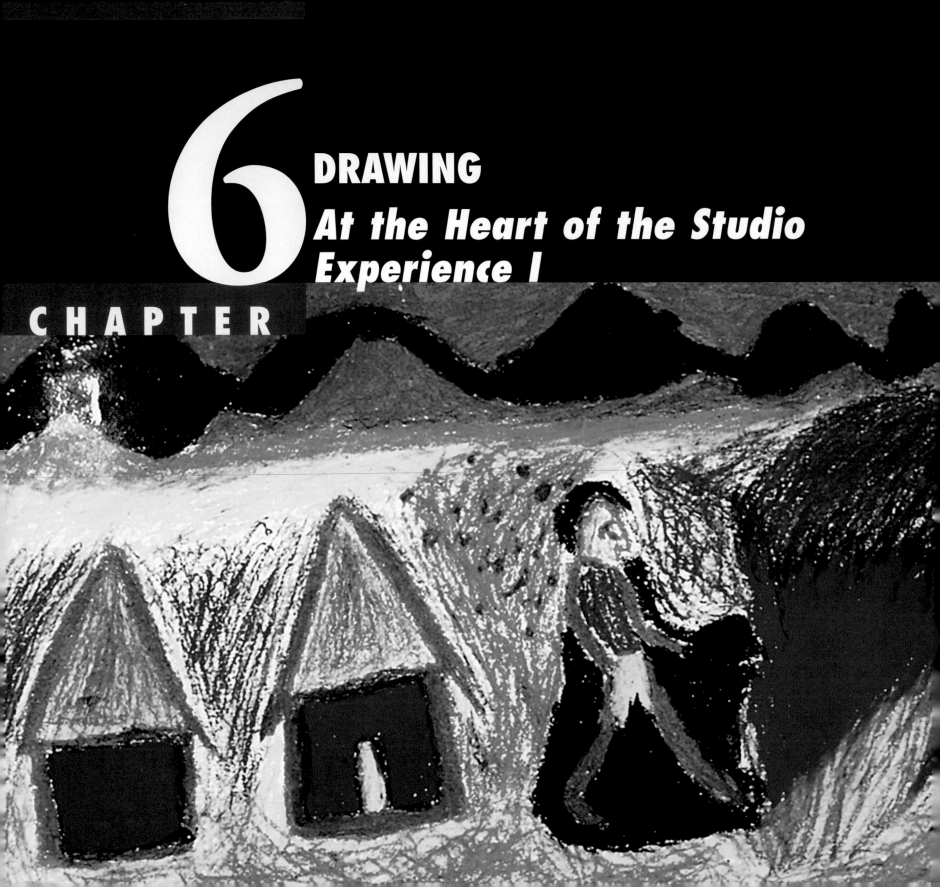

6 DRAWING

At the Heart of the Studio Experience I

CHAPTER

Learning to draw will put you in touch with a long and respected tradition that begins in Prehistoric times. Drawing remains a natural way for creative people to visually express their attitudes about the world around them.[1]

—Wayne Enstice and Melody Peters

Drawing and painting are probably the most pervasive of all art activities engaged in by children. Through these two modes of art making, children participate in the exploration of media, the creation of symbols, the development of narrative themes, and the solving of visual problems. The emphasis in contemporary art education is on the expressive aspects of both responsive and creative experience, with support and instruction by the teacher appropriate for the levels of development of the children.

Children produce drawings and paintings that say something about their reactions to experience and heighten their abilities to observe. Drawing activity is also a precursor to the development of writing skills. The correlation between drawing and lettering is particularly effective in China and Japan, where practice in calligraphy enlivens the quality of line. Certainly, when taught effectively, drawing and painting activities are universally enjoyed and provide a very flexible and practical means of expression for the young at all stages of artistic development.

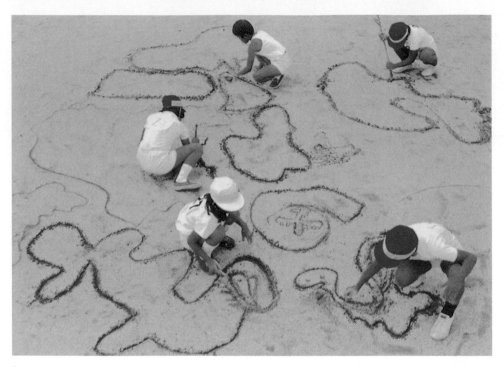

Japan

This chapter will describe tools and materials for drawing and will comment on its use at various developmental levels. We will also refer to certain problems related to the teaching of drawing and painting, such as dealing with spatial relationships; producing figure, landscape, portrait, and still-life compositions; using mixed media; and improving pictorial composition. Included in our discussions are comments that refer to the historical, critical, and cultural dimensions of art.

The chief purposes in encouraging preschool children to draw and paint are, first, to allow them to become familiar with the materials associated with picture making and, second, to help them develop their own ideas more readily. As previously noted in the chapter on artistic development, children draw and paint for many reasons, and these reasons change as children grow and mature. From the manipulation of materials to the creation of symbols to an emerging interest in aesthetic qualities and meaning in works of art, children make and respond to art in dynamic ways. Very young children may require little or no external motivation to engage in art activities, but as they grow older and become more aware of their capacities and more critical of their abilities, children can benefit increasingly from the guidance of a knowledgeable and sensitive instructor. Numerous suggestions are provided in this chapter to help teachers foster artistic growth in their students. Before reading this chapter, review the material in Chapter 3, "Children's Artistic Development."

THE MANIPULATIVE STAGE (AGES 2–5)
Media and Techniques

In selecting media for children who are in the manipulative stage (grades one and two), the teacher must keep in mind the children's working methods and their natural inclination to work quickly and spontaneously. For beginners, soft chalk and charcoal are dusty and tend to smear and break too easily. These media are more acceptable when the child has progressed well into the symbol stage, in about the second grade.[2]

Young children who are beginning to draw seem to prefer felt-tip pens and oil-based crayons to other media. The crayons should be firm enough not to break but soft enough for the color to adhere to the paper without undue pressure. Felt-tip pens are especially popular because of their vivid colors and ease of handling. They are available in a variety of sizes, colors, and prices and can be very stimulating for all age groups. Young children will sometimes draw in great detail with fine-point pens and soft pencils and should not be limited to drawing implements with large points.

Crayon-pastels combine the soft, richly colored qualities of pastels (colored chalks) with the dustless quality of crayons. These are usually more expensive than crayons but are well received as art media by all groups because of the potency of color. Always select safe, nontoxic art materials for use by children.

A wide variety of papers are appropriate for drawing, and a range of sizes and shapes of paper provides interesting alternatives for young artists. Regular 9-by-12-inch white drawing paper is standard. Manila paper is inexpensive and has sufficient "tooth" for crayon. Newsprint is also suitable, but although it is cheaper than manila paper, its texture is too smooth and it tears easily.

THE SYMBOL-MAKING STAGE: (GRADES 1–4)

Media and Techniques

In earlier art sessions, little or no chalk is used, but in the symbol-making stage, with their newly acquired skills, most children will be ready to use soft chalk, or "pastels," as they are sometimes called. "Dustless" chalk, while lacking in color potency, leaves less residue on children's clothing. Pressed charcoal in hard sticks is better than the "willow vine" variety, which breaks easily. Chalk and charcoal can be used conveniently on manila and some newsprint papers, which should be large, about 12 by 18 inches.

Teaching

From primary grades on, drawings and paintings represent subject matter derived directly from the child's experiences in life, as well as imaginative subjects and illustrations for stories, with priority given to the child's interests. The student may also want to combine painting with collage or to draw from observation.

The teacher may from time to time assist the children in recalling the important facts and features of the depicted objects. For example, for children developing symbols for "man" or "woman," the teacher could draw attention to such activities as running, jumping, climbing, brushing teeth, wearing shoes, combing hair, and washing hands. If the children act out these activities, the concept inherent in the symbol is expressed more completely. Judicious questioning by the teacher concerning both the appearance of the symbol in the children's work and its actual appearance as observed by the children in their environment might also be effective. These teaching methods, it should be noted, are not suggested for the purpose of producing "realistic" work but rather to help the children concentrate on an item of experience so their statements concerning it may grow more complete.

THE PREADOLESCENT STAGE (GRADES 4–6)

Preadolescent children are ready to develop specific competencies in drawing and painting activities.[3] By the time children reach the fourth and fifth grades, they will probably have

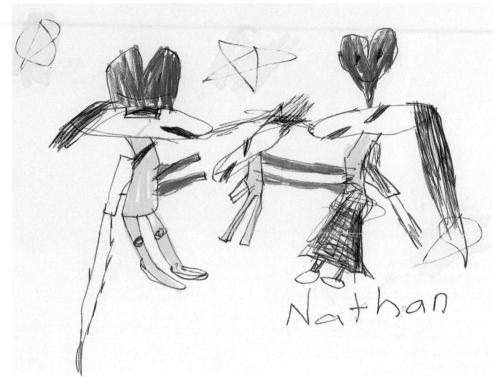

This imaginative "Family of Aliens" was created by an eight-year-old boy with pen and crayon on heavy cardboard. Subjects taken from the culture of the child need not lead to the use of stereotypes. The subject of aliens from outer space can prove to be a liberating force for the imagination as shown in this drawing of an alien child and its parents.

had considerable experience with art media and will have developed many skills in their use. A brush or crayon should now do what the child wants it to do in order to develop an idea.

Handling of Space

Students in the lower grades will accept their handling of space, but, around the middle grades, some will become dissatisfied with their efforts. These children are ready for instruction that deals with basic problems of perspective. Following are five conventions of perspective that children can begin to use very early and in which they can gain competency as they grow and progress:

1. *Overlapping* causes one object to appear to be in front of another in space. Draw anything that involves a grouping of objects. You can begin with pieces of fruit or any scene where objects overlap.

2. *Diminishing size* of objects gives them the appearance of being farther from the viewer. Draw the same subject

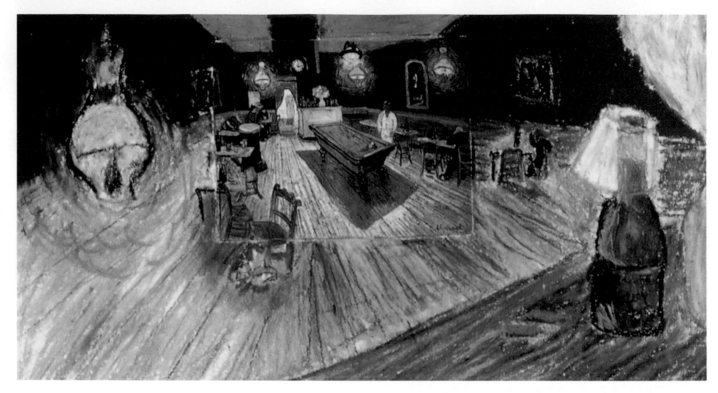

By placing a postcard of an artwork or fragment of a photograph in the center of a piece of drawing paper and using the image for cues to fill the entire page by extending the artwork, students can develop a better understanding of perspective. In this case, a sixth grader extended Vincent van Gogh's *The Night Cafe,* 1888. (Yale University Art Gallery. Bequest of Stephen Carlton Clark, B.A. 1903.)

as in number 1, making the objects in front larger and the objects that are overlapped smaller.

3. *Placement* of objects on the picture space implies distance. For objects on the ground (or floor, table, etc.), closest objects are near the bottom of the picture space. As the object is moved upwards it appears to recede in the distance. Combined with diminishing size, this convention is very effective.

4. If we stand directly in front of a building, the sides will not be visible. When we move to the right or left, the sides begin to appear and the top edges of the *sides* of the building *appear to slope downward.* This is actually a manifestation of diminishing size. Ask students to test this concept at home, in the neighborhood, or at school. A culminating activity for these four principles might be to trace evidence of each directly on a photograph (architectural or home magazines are good sources) or to paint directly on the window of the room if buildings are seen.

5. Although *details are less distinct* with distance, do not expect to see this unless great distance is involved. The edges and colors of close subjects, such as the backyard, are clearer than the mountains on the horizon or the distant view of a city. Have students plan a drawing of overlapping city forms, such as skyscrapers, blurring details with distance to achieve a sense of space.

Any instruction beyond this point would require a more formal application of the conventions of linear perspective using *horizon lines, vanishing points,* and *guide lines* for constructing the illusion of three dimensions on a two-dimensional surface. Students who are ready for this advanced level of instruction and investigation should observe their environment as well as the works of artists who employ the rules of perspective.

Developing Skills in Drawing from Observation

Many art educators now make a distinction among three categories of activity: *imaginative self-expression, observation,* and *appreciation.* In terms of child development, self-expression has greater implications for the lower elementary grades, and observation is more relevant to the capabilities of children in the upper elementary grades. Directed perception satisfies a strong desire among older children to depict subject matter.[4]

Good drawing occurs when artists select, interpret, and present in a personal, aesthetically coherent composition those items of experience that move them, regardless of whether or not the presentation is realistic. Weak drawing occurs when the forms used are drawn merely to fill gaps in the pictorial surface with scribbles and stereotypes.

There is little merit in encouraging children of any age to draw with photographic accuracy. But a distinction must be made between requiring children to work for realism in drawing and using certain drawing techniques to heighten their visual acuity. Few teachers who use nature as a model really believe they are forcing their students to conform to photographic realism. In the first place, this kind of professional skill is impossible to achieve on the elementary level, and, second, there would be very little point to such a goal, even if it were possible to attain.

The question a teacher must inevitably ask is, What can the child learn from drawing activities? Drawing activities can fulfill the following goals:

1. To see freshly through close observation
2. To exercise imaginative powers
3. To develop skills of concentration
4. To exercise memory and be able to use recall ability as a basis in drawing
5. To provide pleasurable art activity that allows children to attain a degree of success
6. To offer an opportunity to study works of outstanding professional artists from many cultures
7. To direct children away from stereotypes toward their personal means of expression
8. To provide children with skills that may be employed in other art activities and other subjects, such as science and language arts

Sources of Observation

Good drawing depends in no small measure on the producer's experience of the things drawn. Such experience depends not only on the eye but also on a total reaction of the artist, involving, ideally, all the senses. Often in the fifth and sixth grades, good drawing may be developed through the use of some time-honored subjects that demand personal reactions to experience. Using sources grounded in experience, the child may produce drawings of the human face and figure, landscapes, and still-life subjects. According to what subjects, materials, visual references, and motivating forces the teacher selects, drawing can be an exciting and pleasurable activity or an academic and inhibiting one.

As far as is practical, the children should be responsible for arranging their sources of observation. For example, they should have some control in posing the model for life drawing. The teacher, of course, will have to oversee the lighting and set reasonable time limits for poses. Artificial lighting by one or more spotlights can be used, and these lights must be moved until anatomical details are clearly revealed and an interesting pattern of the elements, especially line and light

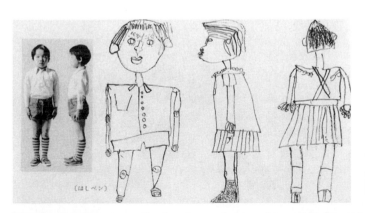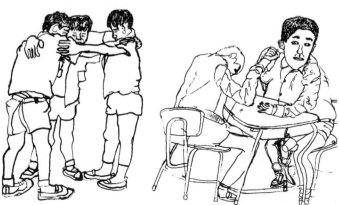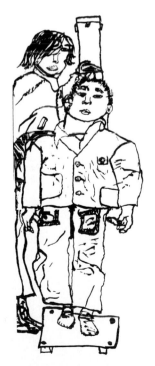

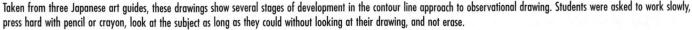
Taken from three Japanese art guides, these drawings show several stages of development in the contour line approach to observational drawing. Students were asked to work slowly, press hard with pencil or crayon, look at the subject as long as they could without looking at their drawing, and not erase.

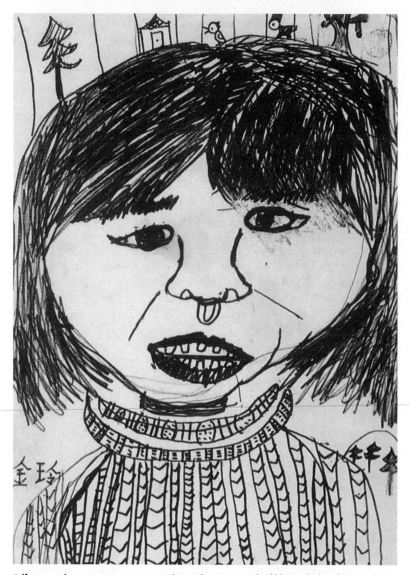

Self-portraits have a strong intrinsic appeal to students. Mirrors should be on the list of requests that teachers send to parents. This example is the work of a ten-year-old Chinese child.

and shade, is visible. Models must not be asked to pose for too long (usually ten minutes is a lifetime). The teacher, of course, should remember the pose in case the pupil forgets it. Chalk marks to indicate the position of the feet often help the model to resume the pose after a rest.

In producing life drawings and portraits, older pupils will be assisted by study both of pertinent relationships among parts of the body and of approximate sizes of parts of the figure. The pupil who is maturing physiologically often shows an interest in the human body by drawing certain anatomical details in a rather pronounced manner. The teacher should point out the nature of the mechanically independent body blocks—the head, the torso, and the pelvic girdle.

The human figure lends itself to interpretation. Once the children have closely examined the figure, they might be asked to interpret it in terms of fantasy or qualities of mood—joy, doom, strength, violence. Such subjects can be drawn from observation as well as imagination, for students can be posed displaying these moods.[5]

In still-life work, the pupils should not only arrange their own groups of objects, but they should also be given the opportunity to become thoroughly familiar with each item. By handling the objects, they may make note of differences in textures and degrees of hardness and softness. Sole dependence on the eye in artwork limits unnecessarily the experience of the creator.

Selection of still-life material is another instance of the need for the teacher to plan a program with the pupils' preferences in mind and to have a challenging variety of objects with diverse types of contrasting surfaces, such as the textures found in glass, fur, metal, cloth, and wood. Contrast in the shapes of objects also must be arresting. The other elements—line, space, light and shade, texture, and color—should be considered for the variety they can bring to a still-life arrangement. As the objects are assembled, however, they should be brought together into a unified composition.

Once the objects of the still life have been selected and arranged, the teacher must establish some visual points of reference with which the pupils can work. These might include getting them to use objects that have inherent interest (masks, dolls, toys) and that have simple shapes.

1. Search for size relationships among various objects.

2. Concentrate on the edges of objects (contour drawing).

3. Use crayon to indicate shadows.

4. Use one object (an ink bottle, a wine bottle, a hammer) to arrange repeated shapes, overlapping portions of the object to obtain a pleasing flow of forms.

5. Concentrate only on shape by drawing the forms, each on a different color paper, cutting them out, and pasting them on neutral-toned paper in overlapping planes.

6. Relate the objects to the size and shape of the paper. Students will find they can work on rectangular surfaces

(12 by 18 inches), on squares, and even on circular shapes; they can draw small objects many times their size and reduce large objects to paper size.

In general, landscapes selected for outdoor drawing or for preliminary studies to be finished in the classroom should have a reasonable number of objects in them that can be used as a basis for composition. By having many objects before them, the pupils may select items that they think will make an interesting composition. Children can be sent outside the classroom to bring back sketches of the environment for their classmates to identify. A simple homework assignment is to have the students bring in drawings of their homes that show the surrounding areas.

The work in these activities need not be of long duration. Some pupils, however, may wish to produce a more finished work and, of course, should be encouraged to do so.

Contour Drawing As a Basis for Observation

Contour-line drawing, which can be applied to landscape, figures, or objects, is considered by many educators to be a sound basis of perception. *The contour approach requires the children to focus their visual attention on the edges of a form and to note detail and structure; they are thus encouraged to move away from visual clichés to a fresh regard for subjects they may have lived with but never truly examined.* The following teaching session demonstrates how one teacher went about introducing this method of drawing.

TEACHER: . . . I need someone . . . to pose. Michael, how about you? (*Michael is chosen because he is the tallest boy with the tightest pants. He will do very well for the purpose of the lesson. The teacher has him sit above eye level in a chair placed on a table.*) Now listen carefully. First, is there anyone here who is not able to draw a picture of Michael in the air by following the edge of his body with your finger? . . . Then let's try it. (*The teacher closes his right eye and slowly follows the outer edge of the subject in the air. The class follows, feeling fairly certain of success, at least at this stage.*) Very good. That wasn't too bad, was it?

PAUL: But that's not drawing.

TEACHER: Let's wait and see. Now, suppose I had a pane of glass hanging from the ceiling and some white paint. Couldn't you *trace* the lines in Michael's body right on the glass? (*They think about this for a moment.*) After all, it's the next thing to drawing a line in the air, isn't it?

ALICE: We don't have any glass.

TEACHER: True. I wish we did. But if we did you could do it, couldn't you? (*All agree they could.*) O.K.—then if you can follow the lines through the glass, you can *see* them. If I ask you to put them on your paper instead, what will your problem be?

ANDY: How can we look at Michael and at our paper at the same time?

TEACHER: Andy is right. We can't do it, so we just won't look at our paper. . . . May I show you what I mean? (*The class heartily approves of this. The teacher goes to the chalkboard.*) Now I'm not going to look at the chalkboard, because I'm more interested in training my eye than in making a pretty picture. I'm going to concentrate just on following the edge. Do you know what the word *concentrate* means? Who knows?

ALICE: To think very hard about something.

TEACHER: Exactly. So I'm going to think very hard—to concentrate—on the outside edges of Michael. We call this *contour-line drawing.* (*Writes it on chalkboard.*) Contours are edges of shapes. You don't see *lines* in nature as a rule. . . . What you see mostly are dark shapes against light shapes, and where they meet you have *lines.* Who can see some in this room? (*Among those mentioned are where walls meet the ceiling, where books touch one another, and where the dark silhouette of the plants meets the light sky.*) Very good, you get the idea. We start with edges—or contours—then. Another example is my arm. (*He puts it up against the chalkboard.*) If I ask you to draw my arm from *memory,* you might come up with something that looks like this (*draws several schematic arms—a sausage shape; a stick arm; a segmented form divided into finger, hand, forearm, and upper arm; and so on. The class is visibly amused*). Now, watch this carefully and see what happens when I concentrate on the contour of my arm. (*With his right hand he follows the top contour and the underside of his arm. As he removes his arm from the chalkboard the class is delighted to see a line drawing of the teacher's arm remain on the board.*)

VERNON: I used to draw around my fingers that way.

TEACHER: Well, it's kind of hard to trace around every object you'll ever want to draw, and even if you could, would that teach you how to look?

VERNON: But you just did it on the chalkboard.

TEACHER: What was I trying to show you?

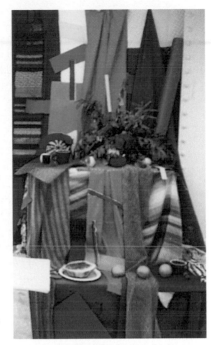

One way to instill interest in observational drawing is to create a still life that is rich in color, pattern, and variety of form. Problems of design take care of themselves through the selection of subject.

ALICE: You were trying to show what the *eye* is supposed to do.

TEACHER: Exactly. I showed you what the eye must do *without* a subject to feel. What did the eye show me about my arm? (*The class notes wrinkles, the separation of shirt-sleeve and wristwatch and hand.*) I'll bet you didn't realize there were so many dips and squiggles in just one arm, even without shading—that is, without dark and light. Once a contour drawing is finished, the eye fills in *between* the lines. Now, let me try Michael. (*As he draws he describes what is happening.*) Now, I'm starting at the top of his head, working down to his toe, I'm going up over the ear, down to the neck, and on to the collar. Now I move away, along the shoulder, and here the line turns down the arm. (*He continues in this manner until the line reaches the foot of the model, then starts the process over again, moving the line down the opposite side of the figure.*)

The discussion points made by the teacher in the dialogue were arrived at after careful study of the kinds of problems children face when attempting contour-line drawing. Their confusion arises in part from the necessity to coordinate eye and hand in analytic drawing skills. Because the contour-line drawing focuses on only one aspect of form—that of the edges of the subject—it cannot be expected that the relationship of parts will follow. This problem should be taken up as a second stage in the activity of contour-line drawing. The method described here is recommended for students who suffer from the "I can't draw" syndrome, particularly in the preadolescent stage. All students are sincere in their desire to draw; the contour method is an effective way to begin.

Developing Methods of Mixing Media

Children can mix media from an early age, so by the time they reach the higher elementary grades, they may achieve some outstandingly successful results by this means. The use of *resist* techniques, for example, is practical for preadolescents and tends to maintain their interest in their work.

The technique of using resists relies on the fact that waxy media will shed liquid color if the color has been sufficiently thinned with water. A reasonably heavy paper or cardboard having a matte, or nonshiny, surface is required. Crayons or oil pastels are suitable and may be used with watercolor, thinned tempera paint, or colored inks. The last are particularly pleasant to use with this technique. In producing a picture, the pupil first makes a drawing with wax crayon and then lays down a wash of color or colors. To provide accents in the work, thicker paint or india ink may be used. The ink may be applied with either a pen or a brush or with both tools.

In using a scratchboard, the pupil scratches away an overall dark coating to expose selected parts of an undersurface. Scratchboard may be either purchased or made by the pupils. The surface of heavy (80 lb.) white paper is prepared by covering it with a heavy coat of wax crayons in light colors. A coating of tempera paint or india ink sufficiently thick to cover the wax should then be applied and left to dry. Later, the drawing may be made with a variety of tools, including pen points, pins, scissors, and so on. A careful handling of black, white, and textured areas has highly dramatic effects.

The techniques described above are basic and may be expanded in several ways. For example, white wax crayon may be used in the resist painting, with paint providing color. Another resist technique is to "paint" the design with rubber cement and then float tempera or watercolor over the surface. The next day the cement can be peeled off, revealing broken white areas against the color ground.

Lines in dark ink or tempera work well over collages of colored tissues, and rich effects can be obtained by covering thick tempera paintings with india ink and washing the ink away under a faucet. The danger of mixing media lies in a tendency toward gimmickry, but often the use of combined materials can solve special design problems. We should not consider these techniques as merely child's play. Many reputable artists have used them to produce significant drawings and paintings.

Other forms of mixed media are as follows:

- India ink and watercolor. The child may draw in ink first, then add color or reverse the procedure.
- Watercolor washes over crayon drawings. This is a way of increasing an awareness of "negative space" or background areas.
- Black tempera or india ink over crayon or colored chalk. Here the black paint settles in the uncolored areas. The student can wash away the paint, controlling the amount left on the surface of the colored areas.
- Photocopies of photographs or drawings with addition of inks, markers, watercolors, or other media.
- Color photocopies of collages with a variety of materials. Translations of three-dimensional materials to two dimensions and color are often very satisfactory.

THE DEVELOPMENT OF PICTORIAL COMPOSITION

Some assistance in pictorial composition must occasionally be offered if the children are to realize their goals of expression. This means that children should be helped toward an understanding of the meaning of design and a feeling for it, largely in connection with their general picture making (see Chapter 11). As they gain experience with the elements of design, children should be praised for any discoveries they make, and any obvious advances might be discussed informally by the class. Professional work emphasizing certain elements of design can be brought to the attention even of pupils who are still in the early symbol stage. The works of Picasso, Wyeth, Frankenthaler, Ringgold, and others may be viewed by children with much pleasure and considerable profit if related to their own acts of expression. The teacher should also use slides and originals of work by the children to demonstrate the possibilities of design on their own level for interaction between studio experience and critical skill. Artwork of illustrators can be useful for reference and study, particularly when the literary works are known and liked.

Form and Idea

Questions directed at the children are valuable for yielding visual information that can lead to more satisfactory picture making. When this technique is used, the teacher should try to establish the connection between *ideas* and *pictorial form.* This can begin when the children are at an early age by playing a *memory game.* Here the teacher simply draws a large rectangle on the chalkboard and asks someone in the class to draw a subject in the center, say, a turtle. The teacher then draws a second rectangle next to the first and puts the same subject in it. What then follows is a series of questions about the turtle. The children answer the questions by coming up and adding details to the turtle in the second rectangle. As shapes, ideas, and forms are added, the picture becomes enriched, and the space *around* the turtle is filled as a result of the information acquired. When the picture is finished, the first one looks quite barren by comparison. The questions surrounding the subject might be posed as follows:

Q. Where does a turtle live?
A. In and around the water.
Q. How will we know it's water?

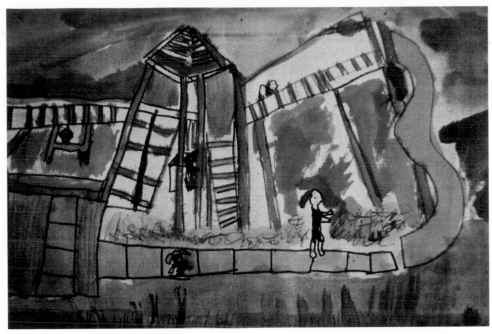

A. Water has waves and fishes.
Q. How will we know there is land next to the water?
A. There is grass, rocks, and trees.
Q. What does a turtle eat? Wheaties? Canned pineapple? Peanut butter? What does she eat?
A. She eats insects, bugs.
A. She can eat her food from a can, too.
Q. Think hard now: Where are there interesting designs on a turtle?
A. On her shell. . . .

Composition is thus approached through the grouping and arranging of forms and ideas. As each answer provides additional visual information, the picture takes on a life of its own by the relation of *memory* to drawing. The teacher can play this simple game with third graders, and it can provide a way of thinking about picture making.

Another important task for the teacher is the development of a vocabulary of design terms. Some teachers have been eminently successful in assisting children to use words about design with precise meaning. They have done so, of course, with due regard for the fact that art learning should not be primarily verbal but should consist of visual, cognitive, and tactile experiences. These teachers have made sure that, if not at first, then eventually, the terms are used with understanding and precision. Thus, although the

This drawing by a second-grade child deals with complex problems of space relationships. The child has used several artistic conventions to depict the playground path, fence around the area, and the playground equipment. Several figures are placed in the work using conventions of perspective including size reduction and overlap. Above all, the child has been aware of the composition of the picture and was very likely satisfied with the results.

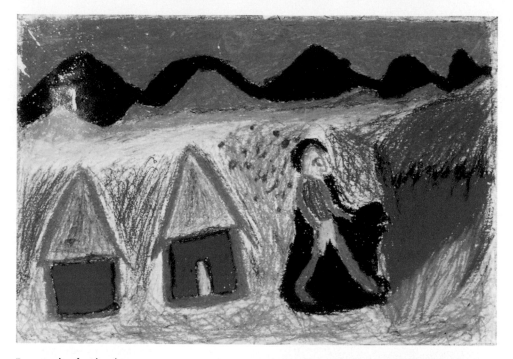

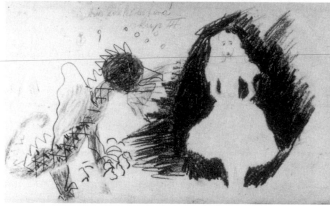

Two examples of art based upon internal sources of the child. (1) An 11-year-old Zulu boy recalls a fire that destroyed his village. (2) Doris Zdekauerova, an inmate of Terezin who later perished in Auschwitz, renders a state of apprehension in this self-portrait with a dragon-like beast hovering on the edge of a dark area in the center of which stands the artist.

teacher might at first compliment a child on the rhythmic flow of lines in a composition by saying that the quality of line was like the "blowing of the wind," later the teacher would use the word *rhythm*. In this incidental but natural manner, the vocabulary of even the youngest child can be developed.

If continual attention has been paid to vocabulary building, pupils may develop a reasonably adequate command of art terms that will enable them to participate in a more formal program of composition and art appreciation. It is necessary for pupils to have a working vocabulary in art before

they reach adolescence. At that period in their development, they are often ready and eager to approach design in a more intellectual manner. Without a basic art vocabulary, they will have difficulty engaging in the type of art activities their stage of development requires. Art terms, such as *contrast, shading, perspective,* and *proportion,* can be used by older children and identified in artworks.

Memory and Drawing

Actors must memorize their lines, musicians their notes, and orchestral conductors a complex array of instrumentation. Writers rely on memory of their own personal histories, dancers display choreographic memory, and artists develop a kind of visual encyclopedia of images and forms they have encountered. Most of us do this casually—on the run, so to speak—but the memory of an artist is trained as conscientiously as a pianist practices the scales. It is important that children become aware of the powers of their own memories in order to depict them later and to gain the insight memory can give to their own sense of self.[6] The process of "becoming" is more fulfilling if we retain some sense of continuity with former states of being.

If asked to work in the abstract, children rely on visual judgment, both conscious and intuitive. When asked to deal with a subject from their own lives, such as a visit to the doctor, they must deal not only with the memory of form but also with its surrounding knowledge. Preschool children are content with graphic symbols, but older children are often frustrated by their inability to capture memory and match it with form as they know it. To be able to recall the shape of a tractor and to describe it is one thing, but to find the right lines and shapes to depict it does not come as easily. Here are ten suggestions to help children develop memory abilities.

1. Divide the class into pairs, and have the children study their partners closely for two minutes. Everyone then turns around and makes some change or adjustment in clothing, hair, facial expression, and so on. Turning back to each other, the partners are asked to note the changes.

2. Before going on a field trip, discuss things to look for; call attention to shapes, patterns, and colors, and tell the class before leaving that they will be expected to draw what they have seen. This will sharpen their perceptions.

3. Have each child in the class draw a scene from his or her neighborhood to send to a class in a foreign country. Remind the children that those receiving the collection may not read English and that art, as a universal language, will have to tell the story of life in their country.

4. Prepare a still life of contrasting shapes, and have the class draw it from observation, putting in as many details as they can. Take the still life away and ask the children to draw it from memory. Check these drawings against the original. What was not included?

5. Ask the children to draw a picture of their very first memory of school. Again, they are to put in as many details as possible. How early can memory be pushed back? What details remain?

6. Take the class outside to study a tree or house. Discuss the characteristics that make the object special. Return to the classroom and draw the object from memory.

7. Have the children close their eyes. Describe a scene with which the class is familiar. Be precise with large things such as buildings and streets, and do not worry about details. Ask the children to build up the picture in their minds as it is described and then to draw it or paint it.

8. Show a slide of a painting—one with a strong composition that is not too complex. Let the class study it for three minutes, then turn on the lights, and ask them to draw it. Do this several times with pictures of increasing complexity of design.

9. Ask the children to pretend they are on the back of a giant bird that will fly them to school. How many street corners, stores, streets, and the like will they see from the air? Have them draw a diagram of the aerial view just as they would walk it.

10. To demonstrate how conscious a process memorization can be, have the children draw the entrance to their house, extending the doorway and its surroundings to both sides of the paper. Then ask the children to either draw the same subject from observation or to study it consciously with an eye for another memory drawing the following day.

WORKING WITH NARRATIVES: STORYTELLING

Another approach is exemplified in the studies by Wilson, Hurwitz, and Wilson.[7] Their emphasis is on narrative drawing, graphic storytelling, and the creation of new and exciting worlds by children. Their ideas have centered on the ways children learn to draw from the graphic models of other children, of adults, and of the media, and on the way children use their drawings to tell stories—stories that motivate them to depict people and action and events.

The five-frame story drawing on this page, collected by the Wilsons, is an example of the influence of stories and images derived from the entertainment media. In response to a request to tell a story with drawings within the frame format, this sixth grader chose to represent a simple vignette based on a television commercial for a fast-food chain. Quite simply, the story deals with the typical advertising theme of initial deprivation and ultimate acquisition—the character in the story is suffering a "Big Mac attack." He breaks through the wall of the restaurant in his haste to obtain and eventually bite into the desired hamburger. Television has also taught the young boy the sophisticated devices of the closeup—witness the lusciously drippy, well-packed sandwich in the second frame—and the long shot—in the next frame—as well as the ability to zoom in and out of the action.

Children like to tell as well as listen to stories. Narrative art encourages both visual and ideational fluency. One picture becomes a beginning for an entire scenario rather than an end in itself, as one image and event set the stage for succeeding ones.

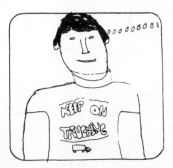 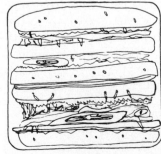 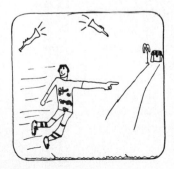 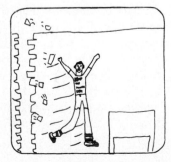 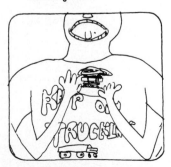

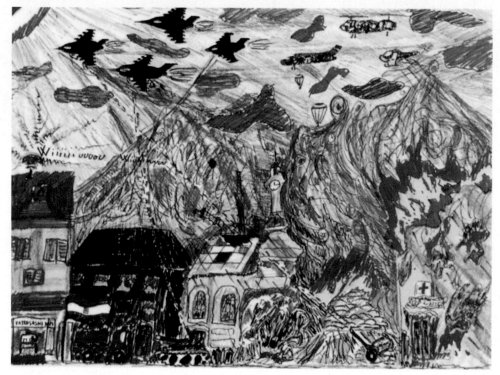

"War" (p. 13) from *I Dream of Peace; Images of War by Children of Former Yugoslavia* with Preface by Maurice Sendak. Copyright © 1994 UNICEF. Reprinted by permission of HarperCollins. When Harvard psychologist Robert Coles was asked at a P.T.A. meeting why he used so many drawings in his book *Children of Darkness,* he reminded the audience that children often say things in their drawings that are not dealt with in their writing or speaking. This drawing by a boy in Sarajevo not only conveys information about the disastrous effects of war but provides a moving record of an emotional response.

the child in producing satisfying and meaningful drawings. Following are several of the exercises:

1. Ask children to draw as many versions of a single object as possible. Examples might be different types of people, shoes, cars, trees, insects, and so on.

2. Ask children to think of a person, such as a dancer, an acrobat, a sports player, or a superhero, who goes through lots of motions. On a long strip of paper, show the figure going through its action as it moves from side to side across the paper.

3. Ask the children to think about extremities of form and then to draw people who are very tall or very thin, situations that are too bad or too weird, and so on.

4. Using the concept of metamorphosis, ask children to start with one object, such as a car, and to gradually change it in a series of steps untill it looks like something else, perhaps an elephant.

5. Ask children to draw a face and then to draw the same face with a series of expressions, such as sad, happy, excited, or frightened. Have them project the face into the future and imagine how age will transform it.

6. Working with teams, have a member pretend he or she is a police artist. How well can the student draw from a verbal description?

The writers have developed several methods for encouraging children to develop graphic skills. These skills are viewed as a graphic vocabulary and grammar, and they assist

NOTES

1. Wayne Enstice and Melody Peters, *Drawing: Space, Form, Expression* (Englewood Cliffs, NJ: Prentice-Hall, 1990), p. 1.

2. In the use of all art materials and processes, teachers must take care to select safe materials for student use and to explicitly teach safe methods with appropriate health precautions. See Charles Qualley, *Safety in the Artroom* (Worcester, MA: Davis Publications, 1986).

3. See drawing books, such as Ted Rose, *Discovering Drawing* (Worcester, MA: Davis Publications, 1990; Bert Dodson, *Keys to Drawing* (Cincinnati: North Light Publishers, 1985); and Nathan Goldstein, *The Art of Responsive Drawing,* 4th ed. (Englewood Cliffs, NJ: Prentice-Hall, 1992).

4. Karl Larsen, *See & Draw: Drawing from Observation* (Worcester, MA: Davis Publications, 1992).

5. See the classic drawing text by Daniel Mendelowitz and Duane Wakeham, *A Guide to Drawing,* 5th ed. (Fort Worth, TX: Harcourt Brace Jovanovich, 1993).

6. Bill Martin, *The Joy of Drawing* (New York): Watson-Guptill, 1993).

7. Brent Wilson, Al Hurwitz, and Marjorie Wilson, *Teaching Drawing from Art* (Worcester, MA: Davis Publications, 1987). See Chapter 13.

ACTIVITIES FOR THE READER

Teachers should be thoroughly familiar with the tools, media, and techniques they will use in the classroom. The following activities are suggested to help them gain this familiarity. Because knowledge of the processes of art, in this instance, is more important than the art produced, teachers should not feel hampered by technical inabilities. Experience with art media is what counts at this stage.

1. Select some objects you think are interesting and use them to make a still-life arrangement. Sketch the arrangement with wax crayons, using light, bright color where you see the highlights at their brightest and using dark-colored crayons where you see the darkest shadows.

2. Using heavy drawing pencil, try to draw the following subjects in a strictly accurate, photographically correct manner. (Remember that lines below the horizon line rise to this level; lines above fall to this level; all lines meet at the horizon line.)

   a. A sidewalk or passageway as though you were standing in the center.

   b. A cup and saucer on a table below your eye level.

   c. A chimney stack, silo, or gas storage tank, the top of which is above your eye level.

   d. A group of various-sized boxes piled on a table or on the floor. (It is easier to draw if you first paint the boxes one unifying color, such as gray or white.)

3. Sketch a house or a collection of houses or other objects with crayon or heavy pencil, following the rules of linear perspective. In another drawing, rearrange the areas you drew to change the patterns of masses and spaces. Carry the lines through each other, taking liberties with the spaces between the lines. Notice how this freedom gives your picture more variety.

4. Have a friend pose for you. On manila or newsprint measuring at least 12 by 18 inches, make contour drawings in conté crayon or heavy pencil. Draw quickly, taking no longer than three to five minutes for each sketch. Do not erase mistakes—simply draw new lines. Make many drawings of this type, based on standing, sitting, and reclining poses.

   Now begin to draw more carefully, thinking of places where bones are close to the surface and where flesh is thicker. Heavy pressure with the drawing medium will indicate shadows; the reverse will indicate light areas. Think also of the torso, the head, and the pelvic region as moving somewhat independently of each other. Begin to check body proportions.

   Later make drawings with ink and a sable brush. Always work quickly and fearlessly. Try using some of the suggested visual references for drawing listed in the section "Sources of Observation," p. 111.

5. Place yourself before a mirror for a self-portrait. Study the different flat areas, or planes, of your face. Notice the position of prominent features (especially eyes, which are about halfway between the top of your head and the bottom of your chin). Quickly draw a life-size head in charcoal, crayon, or chalk. When your features have become more familiar to you, try some other media, such as ink or paint. Try a self-portrait that is many times larger than life-size.

6. Who are the greatest creators of drawings in history? Visit the library and browse bookstores looking for the best examples of drawings by many artists. Beginning with cave drawings and rock art, collect drawings from all cultures and times as well as drawings by contemporary artists. Using quality copy and color copy machines, you can compile an excellent collection that can be used in many teaching situations with all age groups. Does your collection include some of the great women artists?

7. Collect drawings by children of various ages. Ask each child to "draw a person as well as you can." A second request might be "Draw what you draw best." Be sure to label each drawing on the back with the child's name and age in years and months. Bring your collection of drawings to class and discuss them. Can you and your fellow students arrange the drawings according to age levels of children? What can you learn about individual differences of children of the same age? Can you see the results of art teaching and learning in any of the drawings? Where do children get their ideas for "what they draw best"?

SUGGESTED READINGS

Brommer, Gerald F. *Exploring Drawing.* Worcester, MA: Davis Publishing, 1987.

Brookes, Mona. *Drawing with Children: A Creative Method for Adult Beginners, Too.* New York: G. P. Putnam's, 1996.

Cole, Alison, Tony Rann, and Ann Kay. *Eyewitness Art: Perspective.* New York: DK Publishing, 1993.

Cox, Maureen V. *Children's Drawings of the Human Figure. Essays in Developmental Psychology.* Hove; Hillsdale, NJ: L. Erlbaum, 1993.

————. *Drawings of People by the Under-5s.* London; Bristol, PA: Falmer Press, 1997.

Edwards, Betty. *The New Drawing on the Right Side of the Brain.* New York: J. P. Tarcher, 1999.

Finley, Carol. *Art of the Far North: Inuit Sculpture, Drawing, and Printmaking.* Lerner Publications, 1998.

Gardner, Howard. *Artful Scribbles: The Significance of Children's Drawings.* New York: Basic Books, 1980.

Goldman, Paul. *Looking at Prints, Drawings and Watercolors: A Guide to Technical Terms.* Los Angeles: J. Paul Getty Museum, 1989.

Golomb, Claire. *The Child's Creation of a Pictorial World.* Berkeley: University of California Press, 1992.

Mendelowitz, Daniel, and Duane Wakeham. *A Guide to Drawing.* 5th ed. Fort Worth, TX: Harcourt Brace, 1993.

Shardin, Richard L. *Design and Drawing: An Applied Approach.* Worcester, MA: Davis Publishing, 1992.

Wilson, Mark. *Drawing with Computers.* New York: Perigee Books, 1985.

WORLD WIDE WEB RESOURCES

Collections and Exhibitions

MoMA: The Museum of Modern Art, New York. "The Collection: Drawings." <http://www.moma.org/docs/collection/drawings/index.htm> The Museum of Modern Art holds one of the most comprehensive collections of twentieth-century drawings anywhere and includes a historical range of drawings in pencil, ink, and charcoal, as well as watercolors, gouaches, collages, and works in mixed mediums. This Web site includes enlarged views and curatorial commentary on works presented.

National Museum of American Art. "Drawing." Collections and Exhibitions. <http://nmaa-ryder.si.edu/collections/index.html> Extensive online database of the collection. Search by subject, media, and artist categories.

Lesson Plans and Curriculum Resources

AskERIC Visual Arts Lesson Plans. <http://ericir.syr.edu/> The Educational Resources Information Center has a fully searchable database of lessons. Once on the main page, click on "search" and choose "Search the AskERIC World Wide Web site," then click the button in front of "Search the AskERIC Lesson Plans only." Once on the search page, type in "painting," "sculpture," "drawing," or other specific keywords for resources relevant to these areas of the curriculum.

California Consortium for Arts Education. "Fritz Scholder, Human in Nature #11, 1990." *Discipline-Based Art Education Lesson.* <http://www.sac-co.k12.ca.us/ccae/Lesson/scholder/scholderesson.html> This curriculum unit includes art production (drawing), art history, art criticism, and aesthetics. The site features a number of comprehensive DBAE curriculum units.

Davis Publications. *Adventures in Art: Lesson Supplements.* (Grades 1–6.) <http://www.davis-art.com/webresr.htm> This site provides new lessons to supplement the *Adventures in Art* curriculum. Each lesson has WWW links intended to enrich the material. The site has other teaching resources, such as "Artists' Bibliographies" and "Web Tips for Teachers."

Delahunt, Michael R. "Drawing." *ArtLex.* <http://www.artlex.com/ArtLex/d/drawing.html> Visual arts dictionary for artists, students, and educators in art production, criticism, history, aesthetics, and education.

Definitions of terms, along with numerous illustrations, pronunciation notes, great quotations, and links to other resources on the Web.

Kennedy Center. "Making Connections between Art and Music." *ArtsEdge Curriculum Studio.* http://artsedge. <kennedy-center.org/cs/curric/artmusic.html> Interdisciplinary unit with lessons designed to engage students in critical and art-making activities. Features drawing.

The National Society for Education in Art and Design (UK). *Arteducation.co.uk: Your Personal Art Teaching Assistant.* <http://arteducation.co.uk> A growing resource of over six hundred pages of art lessons, art projects, and ideas about teaching art. Written by leading art educators in the United Kingdom with primary, secondary, and K–12 teachers in mind.

Walker Art Center, Weisman Art Museum, and The Minneapolis Institute. "Drawing"; "Perspective What's Your Point of View?" *ArtsNetMinnesota.* <http://www. artsnetmn.org/actmedia.html> *ArtsNetMinnesota* features information about artists and their works, classroom and museum resources, and multidisciplinary classroom curriculum.

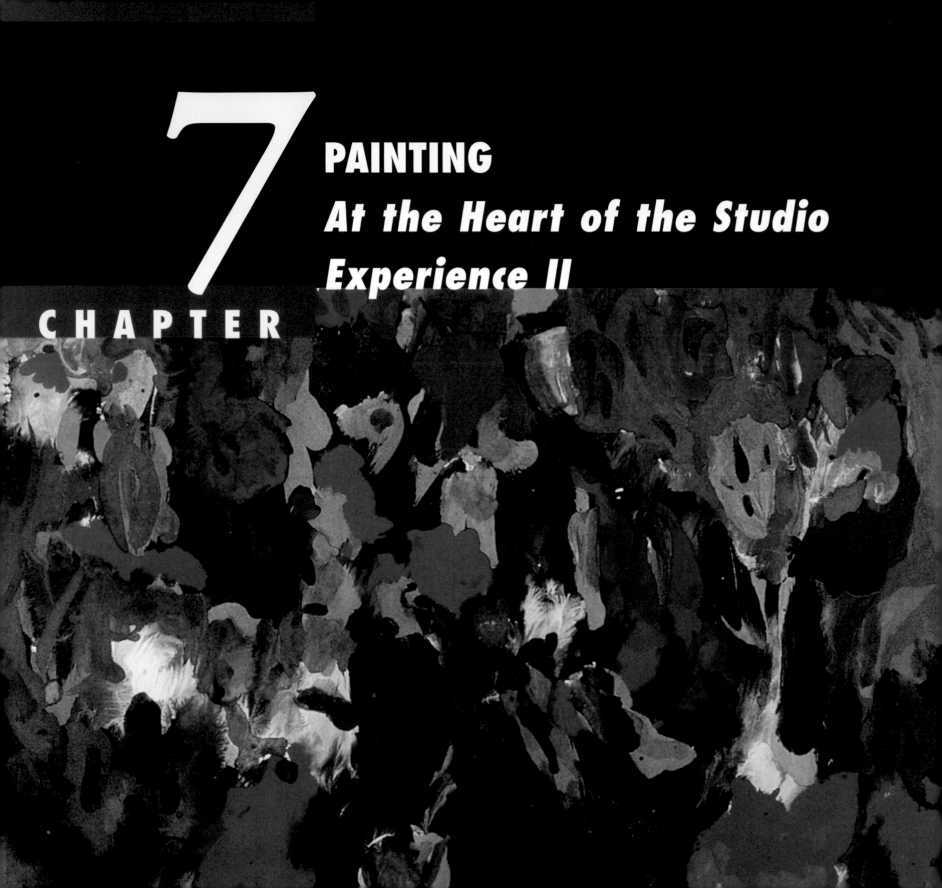

7

CHAPTER

PAINTING

At the Heart of the Studio

Experience II

I found that I could say things with color and shapes that I had no words for.[1]

—Georgia O'Keeffe

Painting, like drawing, is at the heart of the studio experience, both in terms of children's participation and the history of art.[2] Although there are numerous modes of art production, it seems that even from prehistoric times drawing and painting were practiced. The marks of drawing and colors of painting are found on virtually every natural and fabricated object that provides an appropriate surface, from marks cut into tree bark and paintings on cave walls to painted pottery, painted dwellings, and graffiti currently found on every available surface in many of our cities.

Color is exciting for everyone but is especially delightful and interesting for children. As they have opportunity to manipulate, explore, and control color through painting, children can learn and grow in their artistic expression. You will benefit from reading Chapter 6 on drawing prior to this chapter to gain a better knowledge of developmental stages that children progress through from kindergarten to sixth grade. This chapter is organized according to progressively more advanced learning experiences for young painters but does not replicate the discussion of stages from Chapter 6. In general, this chapter discusses children's early explorations and discoveries with painting, the development of painting skills and conventions, the study of paintings from history and other cultures, and older children's empowerment as artists when they eventually conceive of painting in relation to concepts, issues, and communication.

In general, children produce paintings that say something about their reactions to experience. Certainly, when taught effectively, painting activities are universally enjoyed and provide a very flexible and practical means of expression for the young at all stages of artistic development.

Some children entering kindergarten already have a wide range of experience with art. Some have looked at many good-quality picture books with their parents, other adults, or older siblings. Some have worked with paints and brushes and might even have some skills in identifying and mixing colors. A few children might come from families in which someone is an artist, or they might have visited art museums. Other children will come to the teacher with none of this background. Regardless of their prior experiences and advantages or lack of advantages, nearly all children will be receptive to the delights of pure colors and to the use of paints and brushes on a painting surface.

When stating a preference for one painting over another, the attraction of color and subject matter will prevail. Thus children will often respond favorably to the bright color of Henri Matisse and the dreamy landscapes of April Gornik.

PAINTING MEDIA AND TECHNIQUES

The most suitable paint for the beginner is an opaque medium usually called *tempera,* which may be purchased in several forms, the most inexpensive being powder, which must be mixed with water before it is used. (With beginning pupils, the teacher or adult volunteer must mix all the paint.) Powdered tempera has one advantage over liquid tempera: Its textural qualities can be varied as desired. The liquid paint tends to go on with a uniform smoothness, whereas the powdered variety can be applied with varying degrees of roughness or smoothness, depending on how much water is mixed with it. School-quality acrylic paints are also available.

The broad, muscular fashion in which young children naturally work is even more noticeable with paint than with crayon. Large sheets of paper (18 by 24 inches) allow for young painters' large strokes and exuberant movements. The teacher should use a variety of paper and brush sizes so the children can explore different ways of controlling the paint. Newsprint and manila paper are both suitable, as are the thicker papers such as Bogus and kraft. The children can also use colored poster paper and brown mural paper.

Paintbrushes are usually flat or round, and the coarseness of the bristles varies from very stiff to very soft. Cost is always a factor in purchasing art materials for schools, but it is inconsiderate to ask children to express themselves with materials that even an experienced adult could not control. The poorest-quality brushes, although usually the least expensive, might not be the best value in the long run. With cheap brushes, bristles can fall out in the process of painting and will not stand up to rigorous cleaning. It is better to invest in decent-quality paintbrushes for better service and less frequent replacement. Purchase a variety of brushes, particularly large bristle brushes (10-inch handle, ½-inch flat bristles) for young children. After use, wash brushes in water and store in jars with the bristles up to avoid warping.

Very young children are usually anxious to experiment with media and will use whatever crayons, paint, and paper they find within reach. Their attention span is short, however, so within five minutes some may exhaust their interest in one kind of work and seek a new activity. The more children experiment with art media, the longer their attention span becomes, and some children remain involved in art activities for extended periods.

When children first use paint, it is wise to offer them only one color. When they have gained some familiarity with the manipulation of the paint, the teacher can give them two colors, then three, then four. By providing children with the primary hues—red, yellow, and blue—plus black and white paints, the teacher can encourage them to discover the basics of color mixing at a very early age. Colors will mix at first by accident (the red and yellow miraculously turning orange can be quite exciting). Accidents with color mixing should be encouraged and explored.

Paint should be distributed in small containers, such as plastic jars, coffee cans, milk cartons, or juice cans. Place these containers firmly in a wire basket or a cardboard or wooden box to prevent accidents. Very young children should have one brush for each color, because they cannot at first be expected to wash their equipment between changes of color. The teacher can give simple demonstrations on how to clean brushes in water and how to mix or lighten colors.

Teaching

From the beginning of the children's experience with paint, the teacher should attempt to enlarge their color vocabulary. This can occur naturally by naming colors as they are used.

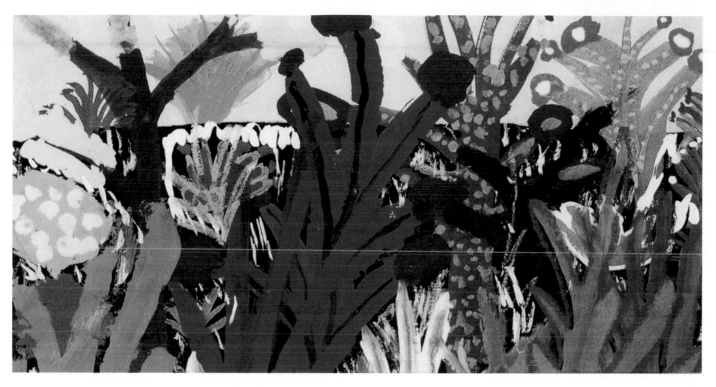

The child who created this exuberant painting employed a combination of approaches, with imaginative use of color and pattern applied to plant and tree forms observed in nature. USA

Children learn about color most effectively by using it, talking about it, and identifying color terms in artworks.

Because many children come to school with a linear orientation to picture making, their first experiments in painting during both the manipulative and symbolic stages are likely to be brush drawings. Picture making in its early stages is generally a matter of enclosing images with lines rather than the more sophisticated work of placing areas of color next to each other. Even if they begin as painters, children may often complete their work by going over it with black lines to lend greater clarity to the shapes. The teacher should accept whatever strategies the children happen to use but keep an eye on their work habits and handling of materials and get them to talk about their work during the evaluation period.

When the children are familiar with crayons, paints, and brushes, the teacher may try a few simple methods to encourage them and perhaps to help them improve their technique. Sometimes background music helps children improve the rhythm of their lines or color areas. When certain children in the group make discoveries, such as stipple or dry-brush effects, the teacher might draw the attention of the entire class to these discoveries. The teacher should also, in a general way, praise each child's industry or some other broad aspect of the child's endeavor.

One technique used to provide children with a painting direction is to ask them to imagine a scene or an experience that the teacher describes in great detail, such as "riding in a boat, rocking rhythmically on the waves and feeling the spray, smelling the salt air as the bright sun shines down and reflects on the water" (you get the idea). Then children are asked to paint their responses to this imaginary experience.

Another technique is to provide children with a real-life experience, such as a walk on the school grounds, during which different types of trees are carefully observed, with attention to the way they are shaped when seen from a distance, how much of the trunk is visible, how branches are smaller than the trunk, and differences in types of foliage. Children move close to the trees, feel the texture of the bark, put their arms around the trunk, collect and examine leaves, and note how the trees respond to the breeze. With this type of sensory experience as source and motivation, children usually are able to paint more interesting, detailed, and expressive paintings.

The teacher should encourage children to talk about the subject matter of their painting. In so doing, the pupils tend to clarify their ideas and thus progress into further stages of development. The relation among ideas, language, and images is very intense at early ages and should be encouraged. Whatever learning takes place at the stage of manipulation, however,

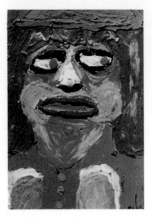

Israel

depends largely on the children. *At this age the teacher's main task is to help children carry out and improve their own ideas.* A pleasant working environment and one in which suitable materials are readily at hand are essential ingredients of a successful program during this stage of expression. The teacher must give much thought to preparing and distributing supplies and equipment and must work out satisfactory procedures for collecting work and cleaning up after each session.

It is possible to use transparent watercolor for painting, but the teacher must realize that it is more difficult to control than tempera and must proceed accordingly. Watercolors require more instruction and more structured supervision for children to use them successfully. Some teachers prefer to wait until children are older before introducing watercolor painting.

When the children relate their symbols to the settings of their paintings, their chief difficulty often arises from an inability to make the symbol sufficiently distinct from the background of a picture. The following dialogue between a teacher and a third-grade pupil relates to such a problem.

TEACHER: Mark, it looks as if you're about finished. What do you think?
MARK: I don't like it.
TEACHER: What's the matter with it?
MARK: I don't know.
TEACHER: You know, there comes a time when every artist has to stop and look at his work. You notice things you don't see up close. (*Tacks painting on easel.*) Now look at it hard.
MARK: You can't see it too clear—
TEACHER: You mean the tent?
MARK: It doesn't show up.
TEACHER: What we need is a way to make the subject— that is, the tent—stand out. What can you do? I can think of something right off.
MARK: I know—paint stripes on it.
TEACHER: Try it and see what happens. You can paint over it if you don't like it.

There could have been other solutions, such as using an outline or increasing the size of the tent. The important point of this dialogue is that the teacher got Mark to discover his own solution without requiring him to give a single correct answer.

As students become older and more experienced, the teacher should provide a wide variety of brushes, ranging from about size 4 to size 10 of the soft, pointed type made of sable or camel hair, and should also make available the bristle-type brush in long flat, short flat, and round types and in all sizes from ⅛ inch to 1 inch in width. Since children

in upper grades usually can use tints and shades of color, it is sometimes a good idea to provide a neutral-toned paper to make the tonalities of paint more effective.

The discussion that follows will focus on several important techniques that preadolescents are expected to develop— techniques involving facility in use of color, understanding of space, skills in painting from observation, and ability to mix media. Because the teacher's role is central to the process of developing these techniques, comments on how to teach them are incorporated into this discussion rather than set forth in a separate section.

DEVELOPING COLOR AWARENESS

In the early preadolescent stage, children might be concerned with the relationship of background to foreground. This concern, together with their interest in the effects of light and shade, involves them in problems related to color. By learning more about mixing colors, children increase their choices, thereby using a wider range. They also learn how to lower color intensity by adding small amounts of the complementary color and how to lighten color by adding white.[3]

Once it is decided that pupils will mix colors themselves, the physical arrangements in the classroom for the distribution of pigments must be carefully planned. The "cafeteria" system allows the pupils to select their colors from jars of tempera. Using a spoon or wooden paddle, they place the desired quantity of each color in a school-quality palette or a muffin tin. The mixing of colors can be done directly in the palettes or tins. Because children sometimes waste paint, the teacher should tell them to take only enough pigment for their painting. They should be cautioned not to mix too large a quantity. By adding stronger colors to weaker, such as blue to yellow to make green, or red to white to make pink, they can save paint.

A variety of ways exist to alter the standard hues. Mixing black with a standard tempera color creates a shade, while adding white to a color produces a tint. If watercolor is used, adding black creates a shade, but the white paper showing through the watered-down pigment creates the tint. Light areas must be carefully planned in advance, but an area can be lightened by dabbing it with a damp towel or by diluting it with more water. The ability to mix tints and shades and thus arrive at different values greatly broadens pupils' ability to use color. Preadolescent children can also alter hues without undue difficulty by mixing the standard hue with its complement. Hence, when a small amount of green is added to red, the character of red is altered; the more green added, the greater the change in the red, until finally it turns a brownish gray. Grays achieved this way have a varied character and are different from those achieved by mixing black and white. When used in a composition, these grays give dramatic emphasis to the areas of bright color.

Children in the upper elementary-school grades are capable not only of looking analytically at how color behaves, as with the color wheel, but also of using what they learn about color in their paintings. This is not as true of children who have not yet reached the preadolescent stage, since young children tend to work intuitively; the works of first graders often exhibit exciting, "painterly" qualities. But the upper grader, being more cautious and less spontaneous in expression, requires stronger and more specific motivation. Color activities built around problems posed by the teacher enable the student to learn more about the interaction of color, as well as to arrive at a more personal, expressive use of color.

Here are some suggestions to develop general color awareness.

1. Questions that sensitize students to color in the environment:
   - How many colors can you see in this room?
   - Would everyone who is wearing red please stand together?
   - Name the colors you see outside the window. Can you grade them according to brightness or dullness?

2. Problems relating to color investigation:
   - First make a painting with just three primary colors—red, yellow, and blue. Mix them any way you like. In a second painting, add black and white to the three colors.
   - Compare the brown in the paint jar with a brown of your own, made by mixing the primaries. Which do you like better?
   - Mix your own orange, and compare it with the prepared orange in the bottle. Which do you prefer?

3. Problems relating to the nature of pigment:
   - What happens when you use color on wet paper?
   - What happens when you use color on black paper?
   - What happens when you combine painting and collage? Notice how a separation of color and texture appears. How can you bring the painted part and the collage section together?

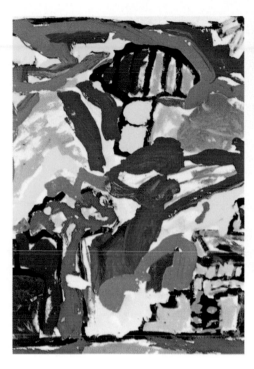
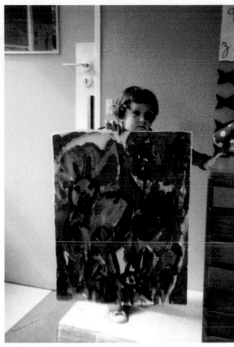

Paintings by two six-year-olds, one from the United States, the other from France. Children in the primary grades normally do not fill the pictorial space as completely as they have here. For children at this age, art largely is a graphic—that is, drawing—process. Paintings first emerge as brush drawings, which then may be filled in with areas of color. The teachers of these children have made a conscious attempt to direct attention to certain "painterly" approaches, such as color against color, color and moving lines, and forms that cover the complete surface of the paper.

4. Problems relating to the emotive power of color:
   - Mix a group of colors suitable for a painting about a hurricane, a picnic, and a carnival.
   - Prepare little "families" or related groups of color around specific ideas, and see how close you can get to what you are trying to express. For example, for a blazing house, you might group red, black, and orange; for an autumn scene, yellow, red, brown, and orange.

5. Colors may differ according to their relation to other colors. For a homework assignment, have everyone bring in anything that they think is red. All examples should be no larger than the palm of their hand. Paste all contributions randomly, making certain the selections touch each other. Assign a different color each day or session, and ask teams of students to prepare the color collage. When the color blue is assigned, have a reproduction of one of Picasso's blue period works, and ask the class to point out the tones that match most closely. The exercise, when completed, will be an attractive introduction to the possibilities of abstract art and collage. If the presentation is mounted behind a circular opening, its appearance will improve.

Spontaneous brush strokes and the textural quality of the paint are evident in this large abstract expressionist work by American artist Joan Mitchell.

Field for Skyes, Joan Mitchell, 1973. Height each: 110 in. Width: A(L) & C(r) each: 70⅞; B(c) 63 in. Hirshhorn Museum and Sculpture Garden, Smithsonian Institution.

6. To make color mixing more dramatic, fill jars half with water and add color inks or tempera. When the teacher pours one jar of colored water into another, the effect of the art teacher as "mad chemist" will not soon be forgotten.

7. Give each student a small section (2 by 2 inches) of a reproduction, and see how close they can come to matching the colors on a larger, 4-by-4-inch scale. Use a color-centered work from the fauvist, expressionist, or Blau Reiter schools. The effect, when assembled, will be striking.

8. Ask the students to select one of their contour-line drawings and to fill in separate areas with hues taken from their color vocabulary.

Color and Art History

Another way to study color is to use works of art as a frame of reference or as an organizing factor.[4] There is *symbolic* use of colors, as in the case of red and blue used for Madonna figures of the Renaissance or of Native American symbols painted on shields; *realistic* color use, based on the actual color of the subject (blue skies, green grass, etc.); *flat* application of color, as in minimal or hard-edged painting; and color directed at specific *moods,* as in the case of theatre set designs. Color can be bold, bright, and painterly, as in the

case of the *expressionists;* linked to light, as in the work of the *impressionists;* or limited and restrained, as in the early work of the *cubists.* When discussions of such differences are illustrated with examples, students should be able to identify works by different artists, art movements, and cultures in examples that are new to them.

By the third grade, children can easily master basic color vocabulary—especially if some imagination is used in reinforcing the terms. The following exercise requires students to mix colors within an interesting context based on the history of costume design.

1. Ask the students to select a costume from history (it might be European, Asian, Native American, contemporary American, etc.). The costume should have clearly separated areas, such as a hat, cape, or shawl, and so forth.

2. Working from the costume or picture of a costume, ask students to make a contour-line drawing of the subject.

3. In each outlined area students are to write a number.

4. On the chalkboard write numbers followed by the color terms you have been studying, such as *primary, complementary, analogous, warm, cool,* etc.

5. The students' task is to fill in each numbered area with the corresponding color concept listed on the chalkboard. If paint is used, students can blend from one area to another, such as "warm" into "cool" colors.

Such problems may be viewed as ends unto themselves or as exercises. They can lead into the area of art appreciation when the children are asked to relate their class activities to the solutions developed by artists. Thus, in conjunction with exercises in the emotive power of color, the teacher may refer to El Greco's *View of Toledo,* O'Keeffe's *Red Poppy,* Bearden's *Patchwork Quilt,* and Picasso's blue period paintings.

Perspective

Masses and Shapes in Space

The problem of rendering space often frustrates the older child, who will require the help of the teacher. Teaching perspective is similar to teaching sensitivity to color, in that in neither case does an *intellectual* approach assure that personally expressive use will follow. Children can have their attention directed to the fact that distance may be achieved through overlapping, diminution of size, consistency of vertical edges, atmospheric perspective or neutralization of receding color, and convergence of lines. This knowledge, however, has only limited value if the children are not able to see the many ways perspective may be used; indeed, effective pictorial expression may occur without recourse to linear perspective. The works of such painters as van Gogh, Braque, Cassatt, and Hockney, as well as traditional paintings from China, should be studied as examples of ways artists have distorted, adjusted, and exaggerated the principles of perspective for particular artistic ends. The teacher should have on hand art reproductions (from books, magazines, or other sources) that demonstrate different ways space has been treated by artists. Such examples from the history of art are:

1. Chinese or Persian placement of objects, which usually disregards the deep, penetrating space of Western art;

2. Renaissance use of linear perspective, with its vanishing points and diminishing verticals and horizontals;

3. Cubist dissolution of Renaissance-type space, with its substitution of multiple views, shifting planes, and disregard of "local" or realistic color;

4. Photographic techniques using aerial views, linear perspective, and unusual points of view in landscape subjects;

5. Renewed interest in spatial relationships by contemporary realists, such as Richard Estes, who applies the rules of perspective to city scenes, and David Hockney, who investigates ideas first seen in the works of the cubists through his use of fragmented Polaroid collages.

Space may also be studied by examining color in nonobjective paintings, where no objects exist to distract the viewer from perceiving the artist's use of color in the painting. Children can describe which colors seem to come forward and which recede, which ones "fight" with each other and which are harmonious. Abstract painter Hans Hofmann referred to the tensions of color as a process of "push and pull."

In teaching perspective, as in teaching about color and drawing, the teacher should keep in mind that children may produce successful work without using linear perspective. Linear perspective is a system developed during the Renaissance that provides a set of rules or guidelines for rendering objects and buildings with an appearance of three dimensions. There are many guides that provide the accepted diagrams that art students have traditionally used, and children, while eager and able to use such guides, do not always understand the connection between what they copy and what they see in the real world.

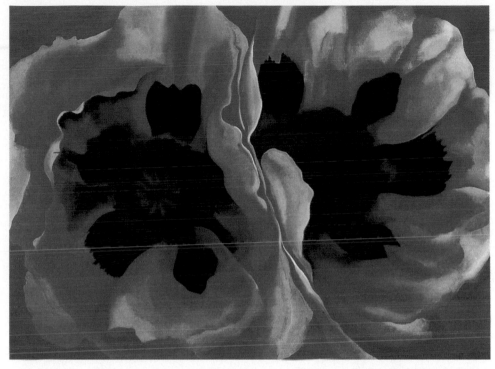

Oriental Poppies, Georgia O'Keeffe, 1928, oil on canvas. © 2000 The Georgia O'Keeffe Foundation/Artists Rights Society (ARS), New York. Brilliant use of limited color unfolds in this close-up of flowers. By bringing the viewer close to the flowers, the artist can fill the canvas with the vibrant color of the petals. Blowing up a detail such as this can be used in several contexts. The close-up format is seen extensively in contemporary cinema.

With appropriate instruction from the teacher, who has access to visual materials such as slides, art prints, books, videos, and filmstrips to enrich class presentations, students can make marked progress. With appropriate instruction and time for practice, students can master color theory so they are able to mix whatever hue, intensity, and value they choose in the course of making a painting. They have learned to render objects with paint so they appear solid through the use of chiaroscuro. Students can paint a landscape, for example, with a foreground, middleground, and background, and they can control color value and intensity to make objects in the distance recede and objects in the foreground advance. They have learned how to paint background areas first, then to paint opaquely on top to make objects contrast. They have experimented with abstract and nonobjective painting; they have tried painting moods, still lifes, landscapes, and figures. They have attempted imaginary (fantasy) paintings. As young artists, they have developed a repertoire of painting skills from which to choose in expressing their own ideas creatively.

In the process of all this learning about painting over the years of art instruction, beginning in kindergarten, older elementary children have also studied and enjoyed many paintings by mature artists. They are familiar with major names in the history of Western painting, such as Michelangelo, Rembrandt,

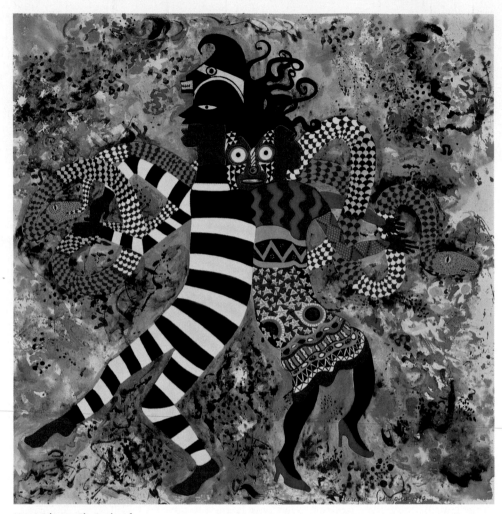

Miriam Schapiro, *The Garden of Eden*, 1990, acrylic on canvas, 95" square. Courtesy Bernice Steinbaum Gallery, Miami, Florida.

This painting on the origin theme appears to combine the traditional Christian story with Native American patterns and symbols that relate to a different origin story. Compare this work by Schapiro with the Paradise sculpture by Tolson (see page 140).

appropriately, in conjunction with other studies in their school curriculum. They can view works by artists whose subject is related to these issues, such as Käthe Kollwitz's statements about war and suffering, Leon Golub's paintings of poverty and brutality, and Faith Ringgold's quilts/paintings about her experiences growing up in a black community. Students can create their own paintings on social issues about which they have strong feelings or beliefs, possibly environmental pollution, saving the rain forest, or gang violence.

2. A number of universal themes run through the history of art across cultures and across the centuries. One pervasive theme in art is "mother and child," seen in Christian art as Madonna and Child, but noted in virtually every culture that developed art forms by which such a theme could be conveyed. Other themes deal with occupations and work; genre scenes of everyday life; and celebrations of special events, such as weddings, harvest, war and battle, birth, death, and many more. These themes can provide students with much grist for their creative mills.

3. Many children are interested in fantasy, or the life of the imagination, which is one of the primary sources for much art. Traditional works by Bosch, Bruegel, Dali, Kahlo, and other artists can be studied and used as sources of inspiration for fantasy painting. Contemporary fantasy artists illustrate science-fiction books, make movie posters, create fantasy paintings, and most recently, do computer animation as seen in such movies as *Toy Story* or *Tarzan*. The realm of the imagination remains a strong thread in the fabric of world art.

Gentileschi, van Gogh, and many others. They have examined paintings from other cultures, including Japanese, Chinese, Native American, Mexican, African, and others. They are familiar with names and works by contemporary American artists, such as Wyeth, Bearden, Neel, Fish, Bartlett, Johns, de Kooning, Scholder, Frankenthaler, and many others.

At this level of experience and accomplishment, many students have developed what will become a lifelong propensity for aesthetic enjoyment in the appreciation of works of art, most particularly paintings. Many students are ready for another level of accomplishment in their own art production. They are ready, as fifth- and sixth-grade students or older, to emulate the adult artist as a communicator of concepts, issues, and ideas.

1. Students can study the political and social issues of the day through the newspapers and television and, most

4. Students enjoy recognizing styles of painting and can become very accomplished in recognizing historical influences. They can explore art styles in their own work, attempting to emulate impressionism, cubism, realism, surrealism, abstract expressionism, or pop art. At this age level and with appropriate guidance from the teacher, deriving ideas from art styles can be very educational, as students must spend a good deal of time analyzing what they see, exploring painting media and techniques, and attempting to apply a particular style in their own work. This process provides students with an ever-increasing repertoire of skills and concepts in painting and can be very instrumental in developing appreciation for a variety of art styles.

5. Many artists work from an attitude of introspection, gaining much of their inspiration from their own internal

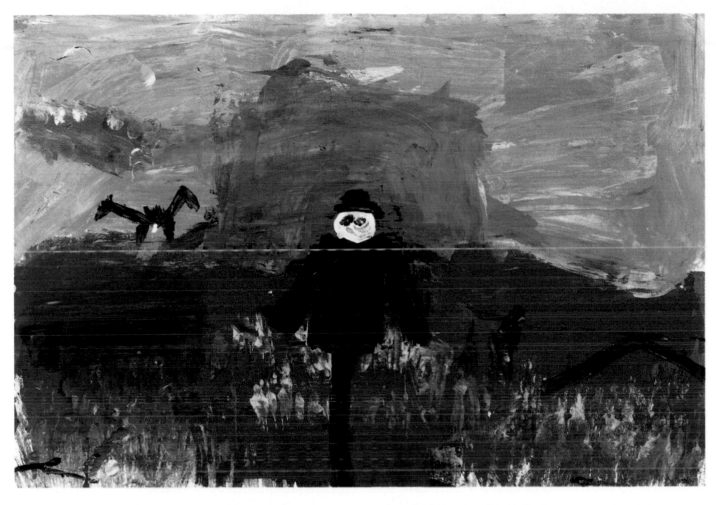

Is this painting of the loneliness of a scarecrow, or does it signify the state of mind of the ten-year-old Australian boy who painted it?

thought processes and moods. The long history of self-portraits is one example of artists turning to their own resources for a subject and idea. Students can be encouraged to examine their own psychological states, moods, preferences, and aspirations as subject for their paintings. In some cases this might lead to study of the abstract expressionists, who relied not at all on the external visual world but created their paintings from personal resources and immediate responses to the process of painting.

Many other traditions and sources for painting arise from the history of world art and from many cultures, all available within the art classroom to catalyze the interest and progress of young artists with appropriate guidance from their teachers. As students learn more about painting and how to gain inspiration and knowledge from the works of others, their potentials as painters and appreciators of painting will continue to expand.

NOTES

1. Georgia O'Keeffe, *Beyond Creating* (J. Paul Getty Trust, Los Angeles, 1985).

2. Lucy Micklethwait, *A Child's Book of Art: Discover Great Paintings* (New York: DK Publishing, 1999).

3. Alison Cole, *Eyewitness Art: Color* (New York: DK Publishing, 1993).

4. Muriel Silberstein-Storfer, with Mablen Jones, *Doing Art Together* (New York: Metropolitan Museum of Art, 1997).

ACTIVITIES FOR THE READER

1. Using a large-bristle brush for broad work, paint in tempera an interesting arrangement of color areas on a sheet of dark paper. Try to develop varied textural effects over these areas in the following ways:

   a. *By using dry-brush:* Dip the brush in paint, and rub it nearly dry on a piece of scrap paper. Then "dry-brush" an area where the new color will show.

   b. *By stippling:* Holding a nearly dry brush upright so the bristles strike the paper vertically, stamp it lightly so a stipple pattern of paint shows.

   c. *By brush drawing:* Select a sable brush and load it with paint. Paint a pattern over a color area with wavy or crisscrossed lines, small circles, or some other marks to give a rougher-looking texture than is found in surrounding areas.

   d. *By using powdered paint:* Apply liberal amounts of powdered paint mixed with very little water to your composition to obtain some rough areas. (Add sawdust or sand to liquid tempera if you have no powdered tempera.)

   e. *By using a sponge:* Paint the surface of the sponge, or dip it into the paint, and rub the sponge on your composition.

   f. *By using a brayer:* Roll the brayer in paint, and pull it over cut-paper forms. Experiment with the roller by using the edge or by wrapping string around it. Place small pools of color next to each other, and pull the brayer over them, changing directions until you have blocks of broken color that lock into each other.

2. The following formal exercises can help you develop technique.

   a. Draw about a dozen 2-by-2-inch squares, one below the other. Paint the top square a standard hue; leave the bottom one white. Make a gradation of color areas ranging from the standard hue to white by progressively adding white to the standard hue. The "jumps" between areas should appear even.

   b. Repeat part a, using some other hues. Use transparent watercolor as well as tempera for some exercises, adding water instead of white paint to the watercolor pigment.

   c. Repeat, this time adding the complementary color to the first one chosen. Now the gradations will go from standard to gray rather than to white.

   d. Add black progressively to a standard hue to obtain twelve "jumps" from standard to black.

   e. Try shading about six 3-inch-square areas with conté crayon, charcoal, or heavy pencil so you progress from very light gray to very dark gray.

   f. Draw textures in four 3-inch-square areas so each square appears "rougher" than the next. Crisscrossed lines, wavy lines, circles, dots, and crosses are some devices to use. India ink and a writing pen are useful tools in this exercise.

   g. Using the side of a crayon, take a series of "rubbings" from such surfaces as wood, sidewalks, rough walls, and so on. Create a design using the rubbings you have collected.

3. Using art magazines, color copies, art postcards, or other color art reproductions, begin a collection of paintings that exemplify color concepts you will teach. For example, many artists from various cultures, times, and places have recognized the power of the primary colors in their work. When viewing an array of adult works by renowned artists, children can see the validity of art concepts and skills they are learning in elementary school.

4. Use your collection of painting reproductions to create teaching aids for a target age level. Children learn visually as well as by making their own art. Teach visually by using the wealth of art teaching resources for virtually any concept you decide to teach.

SUGGESTED READINGS

Borzello, Frances. *Seeing Ourselves: Women's Self-Portraits.* New York: Abrams, 1998.

Brody, J. J., and School of American Research. *Pueblo Indian Painting: Tradition and Modernism in New Mexico, 1900–1930.* Seattle: School of American Research Press and University of Washington Press, 1997.

Brommer, Gerald F., *Understanding Transparent Watercolor.* Worcester, MA: Davis Publishing, 1993.

Brommer, Gerald F. and Nancy K. Kline. *Exploring Painting: A Guide for Teachers.* Worcester, MA: Davis Publications, 1995.

Brown, Maurice, and Diana Korzenik. *Art Making and Education.* Urbana: University of Illinois Press, 1993.

Carr, Dawson W., and Mark Leonard. *Looking at Paintings.* Malibu, CA: J. Paul Getty Museum, 1992.

Chaet, Bernard. *An Artist's Notebook.* New York: Holt, Rinehart and Winston, 1979.

Cikanove, Karla. *Teaching Children to Paint.* Craftsman House, 1994.

Fineberg, Jonathan. *The Innocent Eye: Children's Art and the Modern Artist.* Princeton, NJ: Princeton University Press, 1997.

Frohardt, Darcie Clark. *Teaching Art with Books Kids Love: Teaching Art Appreciation, Elements of Art, and Principles of Design with Award-Winning Children's Books.* Fulcrum Publishers, 1999.

Gentle, Keith. *Teaching Painting in the Primary School.* London; New York: Cassell, 1993.

Richardson, Joy, and Charlotte Voake. *Looking at Pictures: An Introduction to Art for Young People.* New York: Harry N. Abrams, 1997.

Smith, Nancy R., et al. *Experience and Art: Teaching Children to Paint.* 2d ed. New York: Teachers College Press, 1993.

Topal, Cathy Weisman. *Children and Painting.* Worcester, MA: Davis Publishing, 1992.

Welton, Jude. *Eyewitness Art: Looking at Paintings.* New York: DK Publishing, 1994.

Wilson, Brent. "Studio-Based Scholarship: Making Art to Know Art." In *Collected Papers: Pennsylvania's Symposium on the Role of Studio in Art Education,* edited by Joseph B. DeAngelis. Harrisburg: Pennsylvania Department of Education, 1989.

Yenawine, Philip. *Key Art Terms for Beginners.* New York: Harry N. Abrams, 1995.

WORLD WIDE WEB RESOURCES

Collections and Exhibitions

Heard Museum. *Native Cultures and Art.* Exhibits. <http://www.heard.org/> "Contemporary Fine Art" features an exceptional array of leading artists of the Native American Fine Art Movement from the museum's collection. "Imaging the World through Native Painting" features works by renowned Latin American artists. Web site presents American Indian and Latin American art and culture.

Georgia O'Keeffe Museum. "Georgia O'Keeffe: The Poetry of Things." *Exhibitions.* 1999. <http://www.okeeffemuseum.org/exhibitions.html> This museum site specializes in the work of O'Keeffe, a major figure in American Art, and her contemporaries.

Nicolas Pioch. Famous Paintings Exhibition. *Web Museum, Paris.* 1996–1999. <http://www.iem.ac.ru/wm/paint/> *Web Museum, Paris* is an extensive online database of images and information. Search capability with links to internal information and external Web sites. This site presents a massive database of world art and art history information.

Studio Museum of Harlem. Permanent Collection: Nineteenth- and Twentieth-Century African-American Art. SMH on the Web. 1999. <http://www.studiomuseuminharlem.org/> Presents nineteenth- and twentieth-century African-American art; twentieth-century Caribbean and African art; and traditional African art and artifacts.

Lesson Plans and Curriculum Resources

Davis Publications. *Adventures in Art: Lesson Supplements* (Grades 1–6). 1998. <http://www.davis-art.com/webresr.htm> "Styles of Painting: A View Out the Window" discusses how artists work in many different styles by taking a look at impressionism and expressionism. Features work by Matisse and Bonnard. "Styles of Art: Painting a Still Life" focuses on realism, cubism, and pop art. "Expressing Ideas in Art: Landscape" explores paintings by Georgia O'Keeffe. Complete lessons with relevant links to other Web sites.

Getty Art Education Web Site. "Telling Stories in Art." *ArtsEdNet, Resources.* 1999. <http://www.artsednet.getty.edu/ArtsEdNet/Resources/Stories/html> This material is intended to build students' awareness of how stories can be told visually and how the effective use of such elements as color, light, gesture, and composition are central to the telling. Adaptable to elementary grades.

Walker Art Center, Weisman Art Museum, and the Minneapolis Institute. "Painting." *ArtsNetMinnesota.* 1999. <http://www.artsnetmn.org/actmedia.html> Features information about artists and their works, classroom and museum resources, and multidisciplinary classroom curriculum.

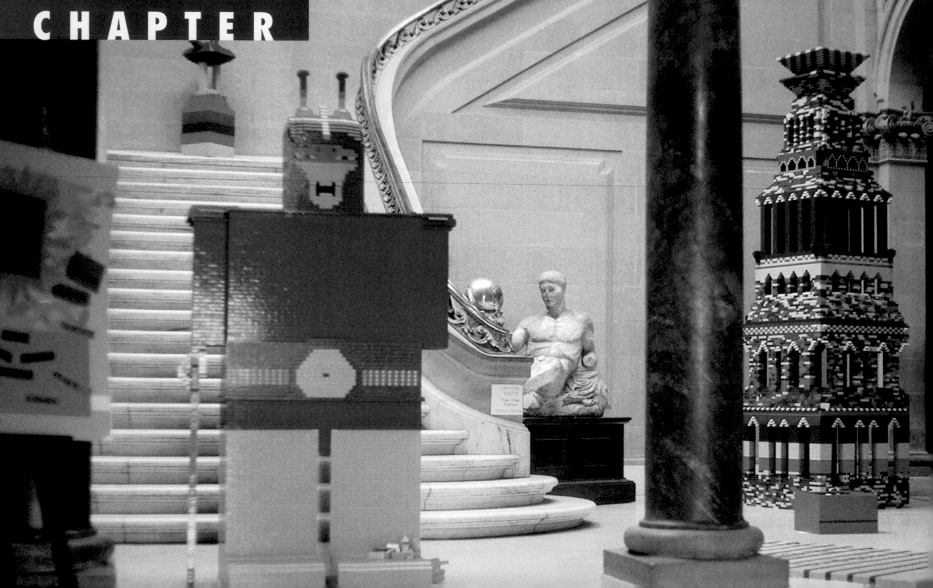

8 SCULPTURE, CERAMICS, AND OTHER THREE-DIMENSIONAL ART FORMS

Creating works of art in three dimensions is of particular significance. Human beings experience the world in three dimensions. Men, women, and children establish scale in accordance with their own bodies. Each of us is three dimensional in a three-dimensional world.[1]

—Wayne Higby

Drawing and painting, as previously examined in Chapters 6 and 7, are accomplished primarily on two-dimensional surfaces, usually paper, canvas, or board. Art that extends into the third dimension includes sculpture and ceramics, which in some ways overlap as art modes. Some sculpture, for example, is made of fired clay and can be considered ceramic sculpture. Ceramics includes pottery made of fired clay, and even it overlaps with sculpture, as some pots exhibit fine sculpture qualities, some are purposely nonfunctional, and sometimes pots are used as components in sculpture. Ceramic pottery is an ancient art mode and also one of the most universal; pots are found that were created far back in time and in all parts of the world. Sculpture is discussed first in this chapter, with attention paid to media and methods for its creation and with suggestions for teaching children and young people about sculpture. Discussion of ceramics follows, with special attention to the area of pottery and including references to historical and critical learning that accompany the making of ceramics.

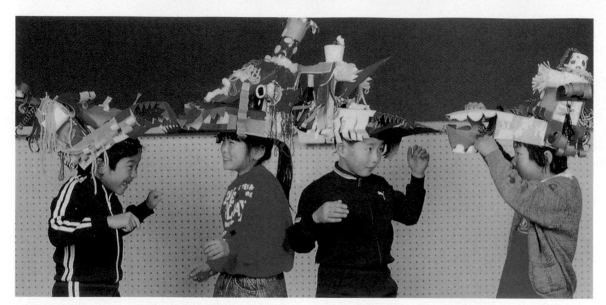

Japan

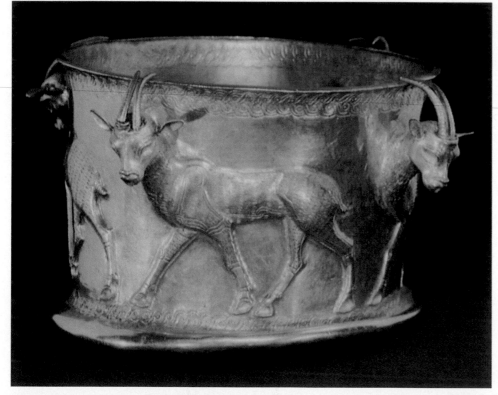

This very old and beautiful gold cup, made in Iran about three thousand years ago, is an example of relief sculpture. The gazelles can be seen only from one side, although their heads and horns are actually "in the round." The cup is also an example of a utilitarian object that has been raised to the level of fine art by its decorative and sculptural work. (The Metropolitan Museum of Art, New York)

SCULPTURE: BASIC MODES OF FORMING AND CONSTRUCTION

When we consider the beginnings of sculpture, we think of very ancient, even prehistoric, examples created before the great sculptures from Egypt that date back nearly six thousand years. Yet the art of sculpture continues today as one of the most highly respected and dynamic of the art modes. Sculpture is often classified as either freestanding or relief. Free-standing sculpture, or sculpture in the round, is the type that can be viewed from many angles, such as a statue of a person or an animal that a person might walk around. Relief sculpture is usually viewed from the front, like a painting, and is often seen on walls or other surfaces that cannot be viewed from behind.

As is the case with all significant works of art, sculptures reflect ideas, values, and practices of the artists who created them and the societies and cultures to which the artists belong. Ancient Egyptian art, for example, was commissioned by the powerful rulers of the time and served purposes profoundly influenced by the religious beliefs of the culture. In contrast, contemporary art is influenced by the individuality of artists. Yet even the highly individual work of today's sculptors reflects the society in which they live.[2] These relationships can be seen in the carved wooden figures of the Yoruba peoples of Nigeria, the bronze sculptures of sacred bulls from India, and the mobiles (moving sculptures) of Calder that, incidentally, add another category to sculpture—that which moves while the viewer remains stationary.

Modeling, carving, and constructing are typical processes involved in making sculpture. Modeling involves building up a form from material, such as clay, and then adding and shaping the material. For example, when a head is modeled in clay, the basic form is modeled, and then more clay is added and shaped to develop the nose, hair, ears, and other features. *Modeling*, then, is usually an additive process. *Carving* is typically a subtractive process, in which the material, such as wood or plaster, is carved or chipped away until the desired sculptural form emerges. Sculpture also involves a process of *constructing*, in which the materials are cut or shaped or found and bound together with appropriate materials. Welded metal, nailed or glued wood, and a limitless array of materials, from sheet plastic and glass to driftwood and junk, can all be used to construct sculpture. Constructing is usually an additive process.

Today's art requires a rather broad definition of sculpture, one that takes into account the mixed-media approach and the interrelation of art and technology. "Shaped canvases" can be viewed as painted sculpture or as painting that moves into space. In *assemblage,* artists create unusual contexts for mundane "found objects."[3] The artist Marisol combines whimsical and traditional drawing with carved and geometric forms. Jean Tinguely animates his constructions with intricate mechanical devices; other artists experiment with sound and light as components of the total sculptural experience. Because children respond positively to many of the concepts inherent in sculpture today, problems of both a traditional and a contemporary nature should be considered when planning activities built around forming, shaping, and constructing.

In the traditional sense, carving and modeling are activities in which raw materials from the earth and the forest are directly manipulated by the artist. In modeling, artists may approach clay with few tools other than their bare hands, while in carving wood and other media, a tool as primitive as a knife allows artists to pit their skill against the material. If the artist shows respect for it, the primary characteristics of the original material remain in the finished product. Wood remains wood, clay remains clay, and each substance clearly demonstrates its influence on the art form into which it was fashioned.

Children in all stages of development can work successfully in modeling clay. Only older preadolescents, however, are able to carve wood and plaster of paris, because the skills involved are beyond the ability of younger children, and some of the tools required are too dangerous for them to use. It is important when considering the appropriateness of art activities for various grade levels to make a distinction between *media* and *techniques.* Instead of arbitrarily relegating any one type of material to a particular grade level, the teacher should examine the material in terms of the specific problem to be explored. Although it is true that the range of manual control varies with the age of children, some techniques associated with a particular medium are within children's capability on every grade level. For instance, even elementary-school children engaged in making animal figures can be encouraged to "pull out the shapes" and to "piece the figure together so the parts don't fall off." They can practice maintaining uniform thickness of the side of a pinch pot and can press patterns of found objects into clay tiles. These ideas might be presented to the children with such remarks as:

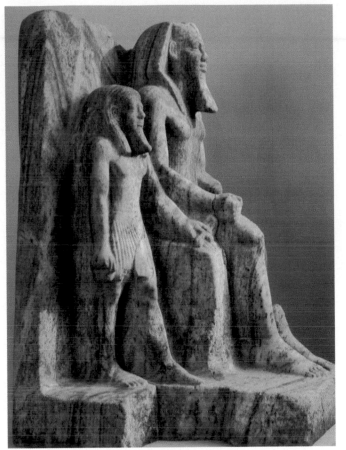

This stone sculpture is nearly 4,500 years old. The larger figure represents an Egyptian king and the smaller one an Egyptian deity, juxtaposing political authority and religious beliefs in one artwork. Children can learn about such cultural contexts and the purposes of artworks in order to better understand and appreciate them. (The Metropolitan Museum of Art, New York)

- "There are many ways of making sculpture. As all artists do, choose one that is most comfortable for you."
- "Some kinds of modeling (or sculpture) require practice, just like learning a musical instrument or handling a ball. It may be difficult at first, but practice will help you to make something you will want to keep."
- "Even a flat piece of sculpture (relief) can be made to catch light. Then it will make interesting surface patterns."
- "An animal form is trapped in this piece of clay. Can you help it come out, so we can see what it is?"

Sculpture has a universal appeal, and the problems of creating forms in space and of merging materials and processes with ideas engage the interest of people of all age groups. Indeed, the ideas discussed in this chapter are as useful to senior high school or even college students as they are to elementary school students. The children who make their first

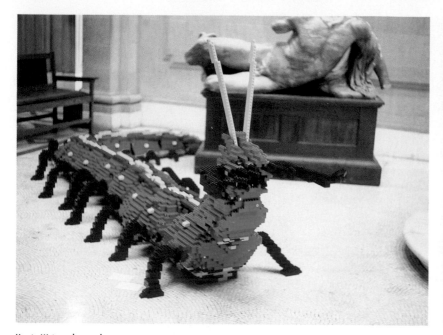

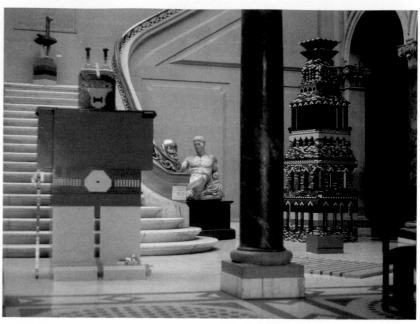

Howie Weiss, who teaches a course called "Play" at the Maryland Institute College of Art, uses simple children's toys to make large sculptural constructions. In some classes, students work alone and with others in teams or in small groups. To obtain the thousands of LEGO units needed, Weiss rented them from a recreation department of the city of Baltimore.

papier-mâché masks and the team of teenagers involved in carving totemic figures out of discarded telephone poles can benefit equally from the practical suggestions found here.

Sculpture can be taught using simple materials, such as paper or boxes or wood blocks, or more sophisticated and difficult materials and techniques, such as those required for wood carving. Ceramic clay methods can be taught to all age groups. The following pages deal primarily with techniques for a variety of sculpture media and applications appropriate for children. We do not attempt to present a lesson or unit for each technique, but expect that teachers will develop their own learning objectives, themes, and goals with their own students in mind. For more on lesson and unit development, see Chapter 17 on curriculum planning.

SCULPTURE WITH PAPER

Paper is one of the most accessible, least expensive, and most versatile materials for the making of art. Not only is paper used as a surface on which to draw, paint, print, and make collage, but also it is an art medium in its own right. Paper can be cut into intricate patterns, built into sturdy and detailed sculptures, or folded, expanded, curled, twisted, torn, rolled, laminated, creped, and scored. The art world has undergone a resurgence in the use of paper as a medium of artistic expres-

sion. Prominent artists such as Chuck Close and Sam Gilliam have produced works of art from handmade paper.[4]

Because paper has so many uses as a medium of art expression, there are no firm rules about when paper work should be offered in the art program. Paper can be used in sculpture or as part of a mixed media process. The teacher should encourage children to test paper and to get some sense of its special qualities of strength, tension, and resilience. Children should learn that if they tear paper, it offers little resistance; yet if they pull it, another kind of force is involved. The many different types of paper, from heavy cardboard to delicate rice paper, and its numerous forms, such as boxes, cans, cups, and cartons, make paper an ideal medium for experimentation by children. More sophisticated paper projects continue to interest children even into their adolescent years. The fact that mature artists use paper as a medium lends validity and integrity to its use in the school art program.

Box Sculpture

Media and Techniques

Probably the simplest type of sculpture for very young children is made with paper or cardboard boxes. The only supplies necessary are an assortment of small cardboard containers, masking tape or other sticky paper tape, and possibly white glue.

Tempera paint and suitable brushes can also be supplied. The containers should vary in shape and range in size from, say, about 1 inch to 1 foot on each side. If possible, cardboard tubes of different diameters and lengths and perhaps a few empty thread spools should also be provided.

The beginning of this activity is very much like building with blocks.[5] Young children are able to innovate and learn as they stack the boxes and watch them tumble down. Then the children can use masking tape to secure the paper containers and build a permanent structure. For a more stable sculpture, children can glue the boxes and secure them with tape until the glue dries.

Young children delight in gluing containers together to build shapes at random, and later they like to paint them. As might be expected, they first build without apparent plan or subject matter in mind. Very quickly, however, children begin to name their constructions. "This is a bridge," says five-year-old Peter to his classmates, describing an object that faintly resembles such a structure. "This is my dad's factory," says José, who has placed a chimneylike object on top of a box. "I guess it's a castle," says Mary, describing a gaily painted construction. This parallels the naming stage in drawing that occurs at an earlier age.

Soon children begin to make plans before starting their work. One child might decide to make a boat; another, to construct a house, paint it red, and build a garden around it. Others may enjoy creating forms without any realistic associations. Thus, when working in sculpture, children tend to progress through the usual stages of manipulation and symbolic expression. When sculptures are complete, the students should discuss the choices that await them: to unify the forms by painting them a single color, to decorate the forms in color, or to add additional shapes and textures using paper or cardboard.

Teaching

For children in the primary grades, little teaching is required, apart from the usual general encouragement and an attempt to keep the children free of glue and paint. Children should have ample opportunity to discuss their symbols with the teacher and with one another. In this way their work will grow in clarity and completeness. The teacher should encourage children in this stage to add significant details in cut paper and in paint.

Older children construct marvelous sculptural forms using paper containers. These sculptures can become quite large—even taller than the student—and still remain light-weight and easy to move. The teacher can provide motivation by showing pictures or slides of sculpture. Modern, nonobjective, or abstract sculptures interest children and, at the same time, expose them to the real world of art. The sculptural forms of other cultures can be studied—for example, the monumental sculpture of ancient Egypt or the abstract forms of African carvings. The following text describes how to implement a paper sculpture project based on the totem poles of the Indians of North America.

The teacher might begin by asking students what they know about totem poles—where they are found, how large they are, what they are made of, and what their purposes are. Pictures of totem poles can be shown, studied, and discussed. When the children have become sufficiently knowledgeable about totem poles to understand a related project, the teacher suggests that they make totem poles out of paper and cardboard containers. Depending on the ages in the group and the level of detail desired by the teacher, the children might begin planning totem poles based on ideas learned through their studies of Pacific Northwest tribes. They might give symbolic meaning to each figure and a definite order for the figures from bottom to top, just as real totems have. One of the central goals of such a curriculum unit might be multicultural knowledge and appreciation. In such a project, it is often desirable to encourage the children to work in groups of three or four.

The students begin construction by gathering a variety of rectangular, round, and unusually shaped containers and stacking them to create a pole-like form. Flexible cardboard can be cut and shaped into tubes, triangular forms, and so on, according to need. The pieces are taped together as the pole takes shape. At this point the class should decide what holes and notches to cut with a knife or scissors to make facial features and what shapes to add to make wings, arms, and headpieces fabricated from paper and taped onto the pole.

When the basic pole is completed, surface decorations of cut colored paper can be glued on or tempera paint applied. The entire construction and decoration can follow a traditional Native American theme or can be a contemporary adaptation of the totem concept. The results are often striking and impressive in their size and visual presence. In this type of project, children learn not only about an art medium, design, and technique but also about the art of another culture.

As always, the teacher should take care not to trivialize the art of any people or culture. A preponderance of world art is based on religious or supernatural beliefs held within the

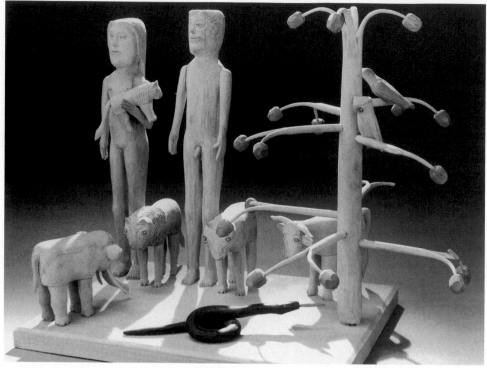

Edgar Tolson, *Paradise*,1968, carved and painted white elm with pencil, 12 7/8" × 10". National Museum of American Art, Smithsonian Institution, Washington, D.C., U.S.A. Art Resource, N.Y. Gift of Herbert Waide Hemphill, Jr. and museum purchase made possible by Ralph Cross Johnson. This innocent view of Eden includes Adam and Eve, the birds and animals, the serpent, and the fruited tree. Both rural and urban America have produced passionate, though untrained, folk artists. A section of the National Museum of American Art exhibits the delightful and insightful works of naive artists.

cultures that produced the art. The goals for art activities such as this are increased cultural understanding and respect as well as conceptual and creative learning. A rich selection of visual art teaching resources is available to assist with multicultural art education.

Stabiles and Other Freestanding Forms

Children in the upper elementary grades find stabiles and other freestanding forms of paper sculpture challenging. The supplies required for such sculpture include the usual scissors, knife, construction paper, and cardboard; odds and ends of colored paper, tape, and glue; and a vast array of miscellaneous articles, such as drinking straws, toothpicks, and pins with colored heads.

Media and Techniques

The chief problem in developing freestanding forms in paper lies in the necessity to develop a shape that will support the completed object. A tentlike form is perhaps the first such shape children will devise. Later they may fashion a paper tube or cone strong enough to support whatever details they plan to add. In constructing a figure, for example, the children might make a cylinder of paper for the head, body, and legs. The arms might be cut from flat paper and glued to the sides of the cylinder. A hat could be made in a conical shape from more paper. Details of features and clothing might then be added with either paint or more paper.

For older children, rolled paper to construct objects can be used. Old newspapers may be used together with glue, tape, and sometimes wire. Children who begin this work obviously must possess some ability to make plans in advance of production. Their plans must include an idea of the nature and size of the object to be fashioned. What will be its general shape? When this is decided, the underlying structure is easily developed. When making a human figure, for example, arms, legs, body, and head may all be produced from rolled newspapers. A

Fifth graders achieved these three-dimensional effects by cutting, scoring, and folding. (Photo by Rick Steadry). At right are some ways of developing three-dimensional forms in paper:

a folding and bending,
b frilling,
c pleating,
d stretching,
e scoring, and
f twisting.

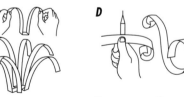
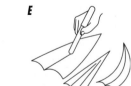
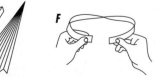
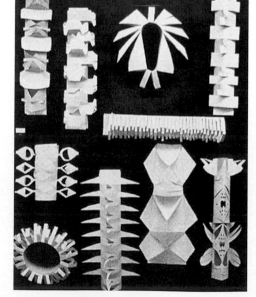

chief component, say, the body, should be taped at several places and other components taped to it. Should one part of the creation tend to be flimsy because of extreme length, it can be reinforced by wire or strips of cardboard or wood.

When the main structure is complete, it is strengthened by carefully wrapping 1-inch-wide strips of newspaper, dipped in art paste, around all parts of the object—until it looks like an Egyptian mummy. While it is still wet, the children can add details, such as eyes, ears, and nose made of other objects. Wheat paste is not recommended because of possible allergic reactions, the difficulty in storing the wheat paste and water solution, and its attraction for insect and animal pests. Vinyl wallpaper pastes are generally superior.

Teaching

The teacher will often find it necessary to demonstrate the techniques involved in general freestanding paper sculpture and rolled-paper sculpture. *It is important that teachers always try art projects themselves before introducing them to students.* This is the best way to anticipate problems and the need for demonstrations. As a project progresses, teachers should observe each pupil and be ready to make suggestions, so an otherwise impractical improvisation in a paper technique can be successfully altered.

As the pupils gain experience, the teacher must emphasize the necessity of making reasonably detailed plans in advance. The pupils might make sketches of the basic shape of a figure so it can be accurately cut out. Even a sketch of a rolled-paper figure, in which some indication of proportions and reinforcement points is given, is occasionally helpful. In fact, the pupils and teacher together might well go through all stages of using a medium in advance of individual construction.

Papier-Mâché

Papier-mâché, or mashed paper, has been used as a modeling medium for centuries. Chinese soldiers of antiquity are said to have made their armor with this material. Mashed paper is strong and may be put to many uses in an art class. To prepare this claylike medium, tear newsprint into small pieces. (Do not use magazine paper with a glazed surface, because fibers do not break down as readily into a mash.) Leave the torn paper to soak overnight in water. It is possible to use an electric blender to mash the paper in water but it is not necessary. Instead, mash the paper in a strainer to remove the water, or wring it in a cotton cloth. Four sheets of newspapers shredded will need four tablespoons of white glue as a binder.

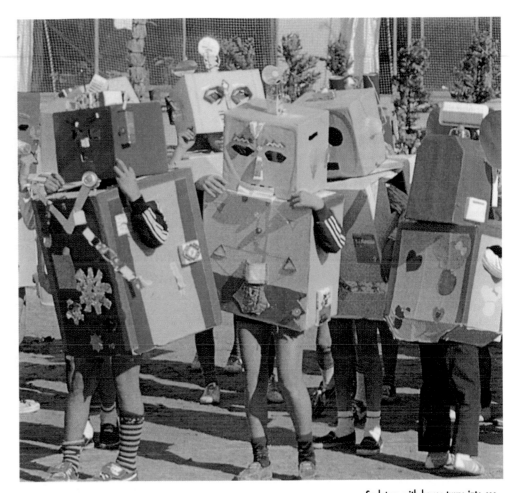

Sculpture with boxes turns into costumes as these eleven-year-olds become robots for a school play. The simple processes of pasting, joining, painting, and collage can be used to create sculpture, stage properties, or costumes. Japan, grade 6.

Stir until the pulp has a claylike consistency. If desired, a spoonful of linseed oil for smoothness and a few drops of oil of cloves or wintergreen as a preservative can be added. This mixture can be wrapped in plastic and stored in the refrigerator. The teacher can also purchase commercially prepared mixtures of papier-mâché that require only the addition of water.

Children can roll papier-mâché, model it, and produce subjects such as vegetables and fruits. After the mashed paper has dried—a process that takes about a week—it can be worked with hand tools. The dried papier-mâché forms can be sandpapered; holes can be bored in it; it can be carved and painted. Acrylic paint is particularly useful, both for its brilliant color and its protective qualities. Objects painted with other types of paint should be shellacked, if possible.

Papier-mâché can also be used as a casting process for anything from balloons to masks that have been modeled in

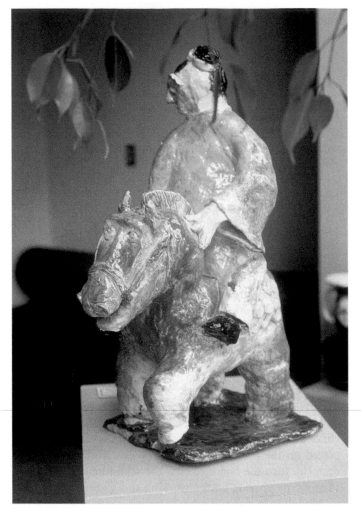 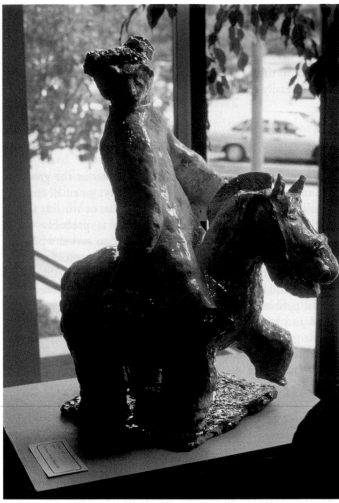

This glazed ceramic sculpture of a horse and rider is nearly two feet high! The child artist worked with the coil method, allowing the lower part to become firm before adding additional coils and weight. The fifth-grade child who created the sculpture studied ancient art from China in conjunction with an exhibit in a local museum. The art museum exhibited a group of ceramic sculptures from the elementary school, including this piece.

nothing in particular. In a sense, an object made at this stage is a record of an investigation: a kind of scribble in clay. Later, the children may give a name to shapes of this kind. Still later, the symbols associated with drawing and painting may appear in the clay in three-dimensional form. Finally, preadolescents refine their symbols, aiming at greater detail and realistic proportion. Younger children are less concerned about the permanence of their objects than are older ones, who want to see their pieces fired and carried to completion through the use of glazes.

There is no one technique recommended for modeling. Children begin to model naturally with considerable energy, enthusiasm, and, generally, dexterity. Given a piece of clay weighing from one-half pound for kindergarten and first-grade pupils to two pounds for those in higher grades, children will squeeze, stroke, pinch, and pat it to get a satisfactory result. Whereas younger children may pull out their subject from a central mass of clay, they seldom draw this way, preferring to assemble objects out of separate parts. When demonstrating, it is recommended that both additive and modeling from a central mass of clay be offered as options.

The finished product in clay must be a solid, compact composition. As they gain confidence in the medium, children attempt to form slender protuberances. These usually fall off, and children quickly learn not to draw out the clay too far from the central mass. They may add little pellets of clay for, say, eyes and buttons, but even these must be kept reasonably flat if they are to adhere to the main body of the clay. It is important to understand that clay shrinks as it dries, so if a wet piece is adhered to a drier piece, the wet one will shrink more in drying and will break off. Pieces to be joined must be similar in moisture content. The use of watery clay, or *slip,* may help children fix these extra pieces. Slip is prepared by mixing some of the clay used in the modeling with water until the mixture has the consistency of thick cream. The child *scores,* or roughens, the two surfaces to be stuck together with the teeth of a comb, a knitting needle, or a pointed stick, and then paints or dabs on the slip with the fingers before pressing the pieces together.

If worked on too long, clay becomes too dry to manipulate. In order for it to be kept sufficiently moist from one day to the next, it should be wrapped in a damp cloth, over which is wrapped a plastic sheet, and, if possible, the whole should be placed in a covered tin until it is to be worked again. When the work is finished and left on a shelf to dry, it should be dampened from time to time with water applied with a paintbrush. The small protuberances will thus be prevented from cracking or dropping off before the main body of the work has dried.

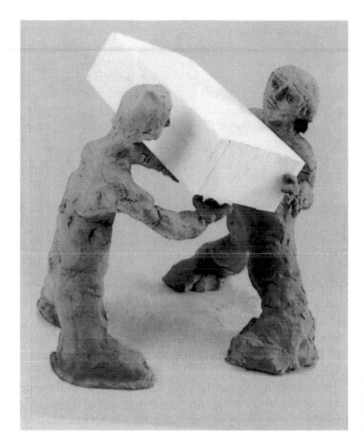

A sense of animation can be readily achieved when the human figure is involved in handling an object. Japan, grade 4.

Teaching

The teacher must be concerned with the preparation of the clay, the physical arrangements for handling it in the classroom, and the subject matter selected by the children.

For the youngest children the teacher must prepare the clay. For the older children, step-by-step instructions and then careful supervision of their preparation of the medium are needed. The clay must be prepared correctly if the work is to be successful. The room and its furnishings must be adequately protected from clay dust and particles. The teacher should ask each child to spread newspaper on the floor under the work area. Desks or tables on which the work is performed should be covered with oilcloth, rubber, or plastic sheeting, or with more paper. Many cleaning cloths dampened with water should be readily at hand, and the pupils should be taught to use them both when the work is in progress and when it is finished. The pupils must also learn to pick up the protective coverings carefully so clay particles are not left on the desks or floor.

Good teachers will see that adequate shelves are provided for storing clay work. Teachers should carefully supervise as each child stores the work and should make sure the products are in no way damaged during the storage process.

Subject matter for modeling in clay is somewhat restricted. Usually it involves one person or thing, or at the most two persons or things resolved into a closely knit composition. Only objects or shapes that are chunky and solid can be successfully rendered. Thus the human figure and certain animals, such as owls, squirrels, or pigs, which can be successfully stylized into a solid form, are more suitable subjects than naturally spindly creatures, such as giraffes, spiders, and flamingos. Students should discuss and select a subject in keeping with the nature of clay before they begin work.

Working from a posed figure can be a desirable activity for the upper grades. Positioning the human body and interpreting its general proportions can be exciting art experiences when carried through in both the flat and the in-the-

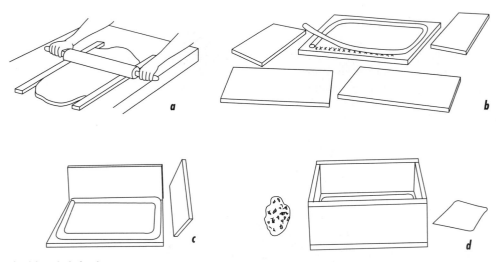

The slab method of making pottery:
a preparing the clay,
b placing the supporting coil on the base,
c applying the sides or other vertical forms, and
d smoothing the sides with sponge and sandpaper.

FINISHING PROCESSES
Media and Techniques

Several techniques may be used to decorate objects made of clay. These include glazing, incising, pressing with various objects, painting with *engobe* (colored slip), and a technique of incising through engobe known as *sgraffito*.

The successful glazing of clay requires skill and experience. First, the raw clay must be very carefully wedged to remove air bubbles. Next, after the modeling is done, the object must be dried thoroughly. Then a kiln or oven must be stacked with the pieces for preliminary or bisque firing. When the first firing has been successfully completed, the glazes (of which there are at least five distinct types) must be applied. Always check a prepared glaze to be certain it does not contain lead. The kiln is stacked in such a way as to prevent the glazes on one object from touching another, and the second process of firing and cooling is completed. Although it produces lovely results, glazing is a complicated process, and few people learn to do it merely by reading a book on the subject.

Incising involves scoring the clay with various objects. The clay must be partly dry before incising can be done. Any one of a number of objects, ranging from nails and knitting needles to keys and pieces of comb, can be repeatedly pressed into fairly moist clay to make an interesting pattern.

Engobe, or colored slip, is underglaze pigment. Commercially prepared engobe is available from school supply houses.

The engobe is painted on nearly dry (leather-hard) clay with a sable brush. When the painted clay is dry, it must be fired as described earlier. A second firing is required if transparent glaze is applied over the bisque-fired engobe.

Sgraffito combines both incising and painting with engobe. Engobe is painted onto the partially dried object. In order to get thorough coverage and to avoid streaks, two coats should be applied—the first by brushing consistently in one direction, the second by brushing consistently in another direction. When the engobe coats have almost dried, lines are incised through them—usually with a stick—to the clay before firing the object.

A number of teachers are experimenting with approaches to surface decoration, which may include polymer acrylics or even tempera paint. In the latter case, when the paint is dry it may be left matte (nonglossy) or covered with a protective coating of shellac. Polymer paints, unlike tempera, will not come off when the object is handled. Shoe polish gives a pleasing surface tone and may be used in place of paint; it comes in a surprising range of colors. In all cases the clay should be bisque fired before a coating is applied.

It is not necessary to think of clay as something that must be fired to be complete. The process of forming is more important than finishing the surface. In Israel, a widely used modeling material is colored plastecene.

Teaching

Finishing clay objects produced by elementary-school children places the teacher in an educational and artistic dilemma. Glazing is the most acceptable finish for clay. Although clay will take paint, which may in turn be covered with shellac or varnish to give it a shine, such a finish tends to make even the best work look cheap. On the other hand, children can paint clay easily enough, but most of them cannot successfully fire it without help from the teacher.

Teachers have attempted to solve the dilemma arising from the finishing of clay products in several ways. Some tell the children it is impossible for them to fire and glaze their work at the present time, but they might instead try pressing or incising a design into it. The decorated object is then preserved in its natural form. Often teachers glaze for each child one or two products finished in engobe, sgraffito, or another technique the teacher has demonstrated. Others show the children how to coat the work with shellac and explain that this is merely a makeshift process. Still other teachers, having explained that not all the steps in glazing can be performed by the children themselves, go ahead with glazing but take every opportunity to let the children do whatever lies within their competence. Thus, a young child might at first only paint a bowl with engobe but later might help to stack the kiln. None of these alternatives is wholly satisfactory, but perhaps the last provides the children with the most insight into and experience with the craft of pottery.

THE EMERGENCE OF NEW FORMS IN SCULPTURE AND CERAMICS

The art teacher will occasionally be unable to relate sculpture and ceramic activities in an elementary program to the work of some professionals. Materials and methods are difficult to duplicate in fields where contemporary artists work with such diverse means as synthetics, electricity, and control of the atmosphere. In general, teachers should be cautioned against concentrating on any extreme approach for the sake of living out their own personal interests. A teacher's indiscriminate pursuit of the avant-garde may have as little meaning to fifth graders as a stubborn reverence for traditional forms. On the other hand, students should not be denied the pleasure of seeing sculptural forms that they are unable to create.

Sculpture and ceramics, like any art form, should challenge a child within the boundaries of enthusiasm and capability, providing experience in depth and breadth. As in drawing, there is a time to work from observation and a time to work from one's imagination; a time for ideas that move quickly and a time for extended sequential approaches. Children may carve and model as artists have done for ages, or they may combine assembled constructions with light and motion. They may also take a functional form—such as a container—and endow it with some human attribute. When ideas become as important as form, then pottery moves closer to sculpture. In a broad sense, sculpture in particular may be said to encompass many kinds of volumes and masses organized within a spatial context. It can be created with boxes, junk, papier-mâché, clay, or plaster. During the course of six or seven years in an elementary school, a child should have the pleasure of working with many approaches.

Although a conscientious teacher plans for most of the activities, a portion of the program should be left open for the unexpected—a windfall of unusual materials, a trip to a gallery, a magazine article, or an acquaintance with a great

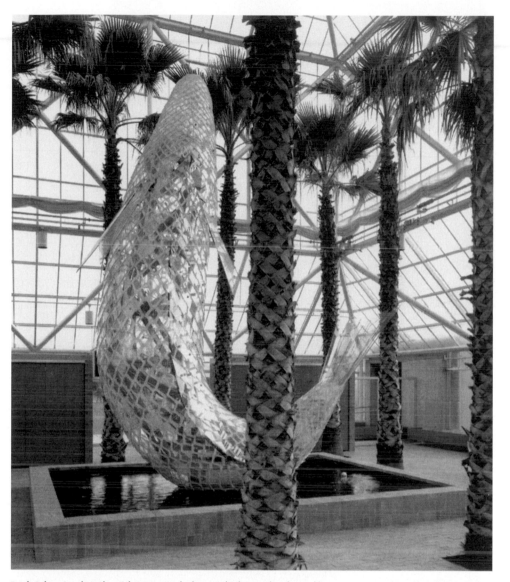

Frank Gehry, *Standing Glass Fish,* 1986. Wood, glass, steel, silicone, plexiglass, rubber, 264″ × 168″ × 102″. Collection Walker Art Center, Minneapolis, gift of Anne Pierce Rogers in honor of her grandchildren, Anne and Will Rogers, 1986. This huge (approximately 15 feet high), leaping fish is made primarily of glass on a wooden framework and is installed with a pool of water as a pedestal. It is part of an extensive sculpture garden featuring works by contemporary artists, who employ a wide range of materials in their creations.

artist could capture the interest of both students and teacher in a new activity.

A fourth-grade class decided to create the environment of a tropical rain forest. The walls were covered with murals, vine-like treatments of paper hung from the ceiling, and papier-mâché and stuffed paper sculptures of animals and

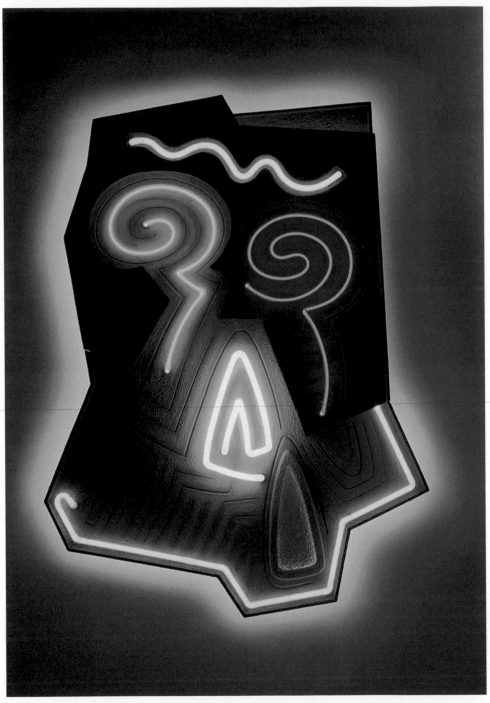

Ganrinis, Quentin Mosely, 1998, acrylic on wood with neon and argon tubes, 45 in. × 34 in. × 6 in. Maryland Institute, College of Art, Decker & Meyerhoff Galleries. Mosely's work is a unique combination of traditional painting, sculpture, iconic imagery, and contemporary use of technology. It challenges accepted boundaries among several forms of art as it emanates a mystical, magical presence.

birds were attached to both murals and the ceiling. Such installations can include any and all art forms and media, so long as they are generated by an idea or theme. If the work is idea-centered, it is closer to what is known as an installation; if the work's emphasis is on a particular place rather than a concept or an idea, it is an environment. This is an example of the difficulty of categorizing works that overlap in media and intent. Since *Tropical Rain Forest* is a collaborative effort that exists in space and utilizes three-dimensional form, it can also be viewed as an activity that could not have existed at the turn of the century when art education was focused primarily on drawing. If such a phenomenon as the "cutting edge" of sculpture occurs within the limitations of art in the schools, it probably lies in the realm of environments and installations.

NOTES

1. Wayne Higby, "Viewing the Launching Pad: The Arts, Clay, and Education," in "The Case for Clay in Art Education," Gerry Williams, ed., symposium report in *Studio Potter* 16, no. 2 (1988).

2. C. Rubinstein, *American Women Sculptors: A History of Women Working in Three Dimensions* (Boston: G. K. Hall, 1990).

3. Cathy Weisman, Topal and Lella Gandini, *Beautiful Stuff!: Learning with Found Materials* (Worcester, MA: Davis Publishing, 1999).

4. Nicholas Roukes, *Sculpture in Paper* (Worcester, MA: Davis Publishing, 1993).

5. For example, see the works of modern sculptor David Smith, who created an entire series of works based on the cube. Stephen Polcari, *Abstract Expressionism and the Modern Experience* (Cambridge: Cambridge University Press, 1991).

6. Maxwell Museum of Anthropology, *Seven Families in Pueblo Pottery* (Albuquerque: University of New Mexico Press, 1974), p. 43.

ACTIVITIES FOR THE READER

1. Survey the district around your school for materials suitable for sculpture and pottery. Can you find any clay, wood, or wire? Test the materials according to the suggestions found in this chapter under the subheadings "Media and Techniques."

2. Glue scraps of wood together to form a piece of sculpture. Smooth the surfaces of the sculpture with medium and then fine sandpaper. Wax the sculpture, and polish it with a soft cloth until it glows. Ordinary solid floor wax is suitable.

3. View the installation by Sandy Skoglund on page 256, Note also the work of Christo on page 223, and study about installations from art publications. Working as a group with several colleagues, create an installation related to one of these works. First, find an available space for the installation, establish a theme, list materials you will need, collect the materials, and work collaboratively to create the installation. Consider holding an "opening" for the installation with invitations and refreshments. Plan when and how you will remove the installation and how you will dispose of or distribute materials.

4. Roll a slab of clay big enough to wrap around an oatmeal box. Press rows of designs into the clay with hard-edged objects, such as seed pods, coins, tools, wood ends, and the like. Keep a balance of large and small shapes and deep and shallow marks. Wrap the slab around the oatmeal box, and seal the joined edges by pinching them. Remove the oatmeal box. Add a clay base, and fire the object. You will have a unique container.

5. Visit a local bookstore or library and find books on ceramics. Browse through books with ceramics work from various countries and cultures, for example, Native American, African, Chinese, pre-Columbian, and others. Look for examples of ceramic art that suggest teaching and learning activities for you and your students. Make copies, color copies, or slides, to begin a file of teaching resources. Follow the same procedure for sculpture from many times, places, and cultures.

6. Make freestanding figures of animals or people, based on each of the following basic forms: (a) a tent made with one simple fold; (b) a cylinder; and (c) a cone that may be cut to shape after twisting and gluing. Heads and legs should be devised by cutting and shaping paper and gluing it in place. Add features and details of clothing by gluing cut-paper pieces to the basic shape.

7. Make an object out of rolled newspaper. Roll the newspaper into a tight cylinder for the body, and tie it with string in three or four places. For arms and legs, make thinner cylinders of newspaper also tied with string. Tie the arms and legs to the body. Next the neck and head should either be modeled separately and attached to the body or be bent under as an extension of the body cylinder. Dip strips of newspaper or paper toweling about 1-inch wide into paste, and wrap them around the figure. When the object is dry, add details with colored paper, scraps of fur, and so on. Finish with paint and shellac.

SUGGESTED READINGS

Golomb, Claire, and Maureen McCormick. "Sculpture: The Development of Three-Dimensional Representation in Clay." *Visual Arts Research* 21, no. 1(1995): 35–50.

Gregory, Ian. *Sculptural Ceramics.* New York: Overlook Press, 1999.

Hedgecoe, John. *A Monumental Vision: The Sculpture of Henry Moore.* New York: Collins & Brown, 1998.

Heller, Jules. *Papermaking.* New York: Watson-Guptill, 1978. An articulate text on the topic, with excellent illustrations and beautiful color reproductions of paper works by contemporary artists.

Kong, Ellen. *The Great Clay Adventure: Creative Handbuilding Projects for Young Artists.* Worcester, MA: Davis Publishing, 1999.

Kraus, William, and Toni Sikes. *The Guild: A Sourcebook of American Craft Artists.* New York: Kraus Sikes, 1987. This book has hundreds of color photographs of contemporary sculpture, ceramics, and crafts.

Shilo-Cohen, Nurit. *Stork Stork, How Is Our Land?* Israel Museum, 1993.

Simpson, Michael W. *Making Native American Pottery.* Happy Camp, CA: Naturegraph Publishers, 1991.

Topal, Cathy Weisman. *Children, Clay and Sculpture.* Worcester, MA: Davis Publishing, 1998.

Verhelst, Wilbert. *Sculpture: Tools, Materials, and Techniques.* 2d ed. Englewood Cliffs, NJ: Prentice-Hall, 1988. A thorough guide to advanced sculpture methods of use in teaching children about how professional artists create sculpture.

Watson-Jones, R. *Contemporary American Women Sculptors.* Phoenix, AZ: Oryx Press, 1986.

Williams, Arthur. *Sculpture: Technique, Form, Content.* Worcester, MA: Davis Publishing, 1995.

WORLD WIDE WEB RESOURCES

Sculpture Collections

Smithsonian Institution Hirshhorn Museum and Sculpture Garden. <http://www.si.edu/hirshhorn/> Study guides, slides, and other teaching resources.

International Sculpture Society. <http://www.sculpture.org/> Contemporary works and education resources, including an online gallery and archive featuring contemporary and historical sculptors.

Minneapolis Sculpture Center, Walker Art Center. <http://www.walkerart.org/resources/>

Teaching Resources and Curriculum

ArtsEdNet: The Getty's Art Education Web Site. "Trajan's Rome: The Man, the City, the Empire: Analyzing Roman Statements of Power through Monumental Sculpture." *Lesson Plans and Curriculum Ideas.* 1998. <http://www.artsednet.getty.edu/ArtsEdNet/Resources/Trajan/> Interdisciplinary middle school curriculum unit that includes historical background and compares two triumphal arches.

ArtsEdNet: The Getty's Art Education Web Site. "Weaving Granite: The Sculpture of Jesús Moroles," and "Common Threads: An Integrated Unit Comparing *Granite Weaving*

and *Navajo Blanket.*" *Lesson Plans and Curriculum Ideas. Online Exhibitions.* 1996. <http://www.artsednet.getty.edu/ArtsEdNet/Resources/Moroles/> "Weaving Granite" includes an online exhibition of Jesús Moroles's sculpture with additional reading material about Moroles and his work. "Common Threads" is a comprehensive DBAE unit that focuses on *Granite Weaving,* a work by Moroles currently on display at the National Museum of American Art, and a Navajo weaving on display at the Southwest Museum in Los Angeles.

ArtsEdNet: The Getty's Art Education Web Site. "Sandy Skoglund: Teaching Contemporary Art." *Lesson Plans and Curriculum* Ideas. 1996. <http://www.artsednet.getty.edu/ArtsEdNet/Resources/Skoglund/> DBAE teaching and learning activities focus on Skoglund's sculpture.

Heritage Preservation. "SOS/4KIDS." *Save Outdoor Sculpture.* 1999. <http://www.heritagepreservation.org/PROGRAMS//S4KHOME> Program that teaches kids how to look at sculpture and how to value it.

Michael C. Carlos Museum. "Odyssey Online." August 1999. <http://www.cc.emory.edu/CARLOS/ODYSSEY/> Presents Near Eastern, Egyptian, Greek, Roman, and sub-Saharan

African art and cultures. Along with museum objects you'll find puzzles, games, worksheets, and other education resources for elementary school. Features sculpture.

Smithsonian Institution. "Smithsonian Resources." *Smithsonian Education*. March 1999. <http://educate.si.edu/resources/> Teaching guides, posters, resource lists, study guides, slides and cassettes, and other resources.

Publications and Articles

Ceramics Monthly. <http://www.ceramicsmonthly.org/> Informative articles and photographs.

Sculpture Magazine Online. <http://www.sculpture.org/documents/main.htm>

Chaiklin, Amy. "Why Paper?" *Web Special Archives*. International Sculpture Society. June 1999. <http://www.sculpture.org/documents/webspec/>

Paul, Christiane. "Fluid Borders: The Aesthetic Evolution of Digital Sculpture" *ISC Newsletter (Online)*. International Sculpture Society. September 1999. <http://www.sculpture.org/documents/main.htm>.

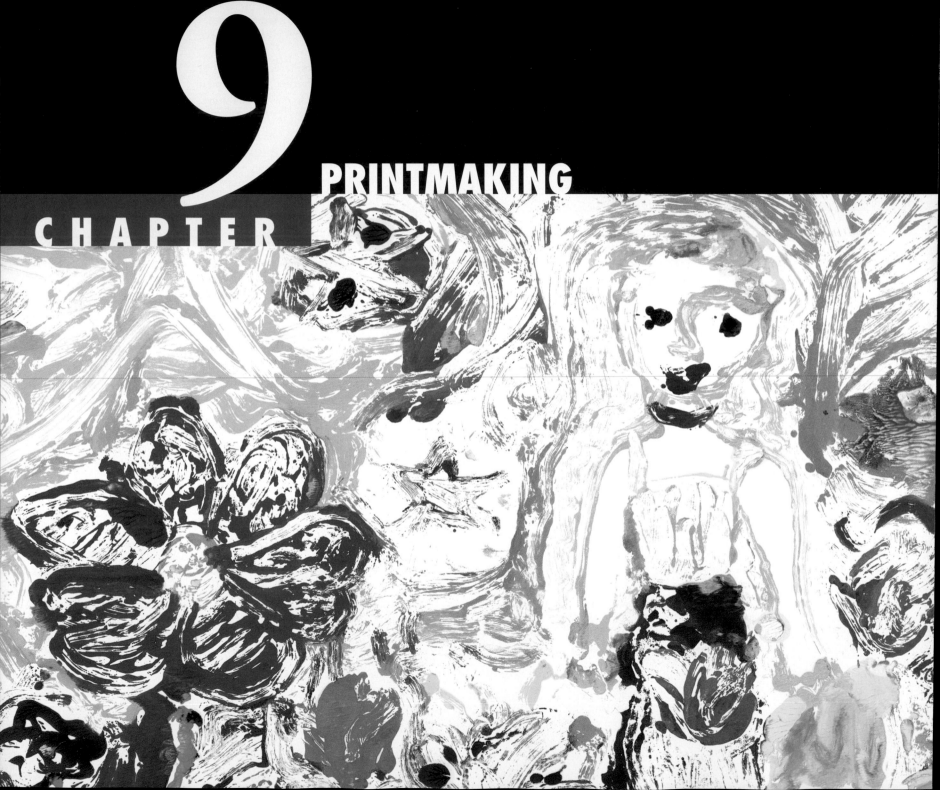

CHAPTER **9**

PRINTMAKING

A fine print may be produced lovingly and patiently, or violently and impetuously— dependent upon the "climate" of the printmaker. From a fleeting idea wrested from the complex of human experience, worked through to the final visual image on paper, the print is employed as a medium in its own right. It is utilized by the printmaker for what it alone can accomplish in serving his particular needs. This precious sheet of paper bears the autographic trace of the printmaker on its surface; in his own "handwriting," then, we read the record of his dreams, his hopes, aspirations, play, loves, and fears.[1]

—Jules Heller

Drawing, painting, sculpture, and ceramics are very old modes of art, whose origins exist prior to historical records. Printmaking might have occurred during these early times, when our distant ancestors colored the palms of their hands with pigments and pressed them against cave walls. However, the art of printmaking as we know it today required a technological innovation that is less than two thousand years old. This innovation was the invention of paper, which is required for the making of prints. Paper, not to be confused with the much older Egyptian material, *papyrus*, was invented in A.D. 105 by a Chinese eunuch, Ts'ai Lun, in the court of Ho Ti. One of Ts'ai Lun's duties was to salvage scraps of silk from cuttings of material in the emperor's court:

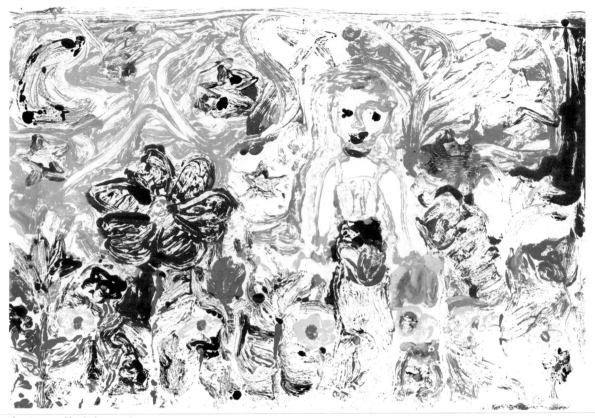

The nine-year-old girl who created this monoprint gave it the title, "Myself in a Garden." She used a bristle brush and a wide range of color to attain the rich texture typical of the monotype process. The print is 17 × 24 inches.

not as well known as other print forms, monoprinting has a stronger historical background than most teachers realize. Giovanni Castiglione first used the process, and Rembrandt used a monoprint technique in making his copper plates. By the mid-1890s, Degas was a leader in this technique. Monoprinting has enjoyed a recent revival of interest among printmakers, some of whom wipe away color from a surface (subtractive method) and some of whom prefer to add color to the plate (additive).[6]

Media and Techniques

The supplies required include a sheet of glass with the edges taped so the children cannot cut their hands. Instead of glass, a piece of linoleum or masonite may be used, measuring about 6 by 8 inches and preferably glued to a slab of wood. In the lower elementary grades, finger paint or tempera may be used directly on the table, since it is easily cleaned with a damp cloth or sponge. Brayers, brushes, pieces of stiff cardboard, or fingers may all be used, depending on the desired effect. Water-soluble ink and paint in a wide range of colors are available, as are newsprint and other reasonably absorbent papers.

texture but also a means of attuning them to the "skin" of the environment.

The paper should be lightweight so it does not tear easily and white enough to provide high contrast. (Ordinary typing paper is adequate for small objects.) When they use crayons, students should be encouraged to blend colors. Large primary-color crayons are fine for this activity, but if the budget will allow, Japanese rice paper and crayon pastels offer the most handsome results. In taking rubbings of raised type—as on manhole covers—students can improvise with the image by rearranging the pattern of form, repeating it, or changing the position of the paper.

MONOTYPES

The printing technique most closely allied to drawing and painting, and to which any child may transfer some picture-making ability, is called *monoprinting*. Although

The process is begun by squeezing the ink from the tube onto the surface of the glass or linoleum and then rolling evenly over the surface. More than one color may be used if desired. If two colors are used, for example, they may be dabbed onto the glass and then blended with the brayer. Another method is to mix the colors lightly with a palette knife before rolling. Each technique produces its own effect.

A drawing can be produced with almost any implement that can make a strong mark directly into the ink. The eraser end of a pencil, a piece of cardboard, and a broad pen point are but a few of the suitable tools. The drawing, which is made directly in the ink, must be kept bold because the inked surfaces do not show fine details. Only the ink that is left on the surface will be recorded in the final printing.

For the printing, a sheet of paper should be placed gently over the prepared inky surface and pressed to it with the tips of the fingers. A clean brayer rolled evenly over the paper also produces a good print. The completed print may then be gently peeled away. Sometimes two or three impressions may be taken from one drawing. By using papers with varying textures, an interesting variety of prints can be obtained. Although newsprint is recommended because it is cheap and absorbent, other papers should be tried also, such as colored tissue, construction and poster papers, and even the coated stock found in magazine advertisements.

In another method of monoprinting, the glass is covered with ink in the usual manner. The paper is then placed gently over the inked glass. Next the pupil draws with a pencil on the upper side of the paper, taking care not to drag the side of the hand on the paper. The resulting print is a composition of dark lines with some imprint of ink on the background areas. Since children have a tendency to over-ink the plate, they should try a test mark on the corner and lift the paper to see if the line is visible.

Drawing in monoprint creates an arresting line quality—soft, rich, and slightly blurred. Because of this, it is particularly appropriate as an adjunct of contour-line drawing in the upper grades.

Another variation of monoprinting is the *paper stop out* method. Paper forms are cut or torn and then placed in a desired pattern on the inked plate. The impression is made by putting fresh paper on the arrangement and rolling it with the brayer. The cut-paper forms beneath serve to "stop out" the ink, and the areas they cover will appear as a negative pattern (that is, as the color of the paper) in the finished print.

Teaching

Four main tasks confront the teacher of monoprinting. The first is to arrange tools and supplies so printing may be done conveniently; the second is to see that the ink does not get all over the children; the third is to give stimulating demonstrations and continued encouragement; and the fourth is to make certain that an area is cleared for wet prints to hang or otherwise be stored until they dry.

Printing should be done on a long table covered with newspapers or oilcloth. At one end or at several points on the table, the teacher should arrange the glass, brayers, and inks. Because it would be uneconomical for each pupil to have a separate set of printing tools, the pupils should be given an order in which to work. Those who are not printing should know what other activities are available. As each print is completed, the child should place it carefully on the remaining table space. When all the children have finished, the teacher should encourage them to select the prints they consider most interesting. When wet, the prints can be hung

with clothespins on an improvised clothesline and then, when dry, pressed between the leaves of a heavy book such as an almanac or a telephone book. When possible, clear a wall on which to mount new prints for drying.

As can be imagined, a large amount of ink comes off on the children's hands. The teacher should make sure that the children either wash their hands often or at least wipe them on a damp cloth. Unless the classroom has a sink, the teacher must provide pails of water, soap, and towels or damp cloths.

The teacher should efficiently demonstrate all methods of monoprinting. Although the techniques are simple enough, monoprinting can be very messy unless the teacher has had some previous experience with the work.

Pupils find monoprinting challenging and stimulating. Once they know how to begin, they are eager to discover all the possibilities of this technique. It is a valuable activity not only because it permits spontaneous work but also because it gives children a reasonably accurate idea of the printmaking process in general. Any form of printmaking works well for small groups, especially when they try it for the first time.

POTATO AND STICK PRINTING

All children can produce potato prints, and nearly every child in the primary grades can print with sticks.

Media and Techniques

For potato printing, children should select pieces with a hard consistency. The pieces should be large enough for the children to grasp easily and should be cut flat on one side or end. All the children need do is dip the flat side of the potato into watercolor, tempera paint, or colored ink and then press it on a sheet of newsprint. The child in kindergarten at first dabs at random but later controls the pattern and develops a rhythmic order of units. Scraps of sponge may also be used in this type of printing.

The next step is to control the design by cutting into the end of the potato. The potato should be sliced in half and the design cut into the flat side. If a design of a different shape is wanted, the printing surface can be trimmed into a square. Tempera may then be painted over the designed end, after which printing on paper may begin.

In addition to potatoes, interesting shapes may be obtained by using a variety of wood scraps. If the wood is

Print the design on paper in repeated patterns in the manner indicated in activity 5.

9. Take a plank of wood and make a print of the grain. Use light colors and overlap the grain or turn the wood to create patterns. If the pattern of the grain suggests anything to you, cut away a few sections of the wood to make the movement of the pattern even stronger.

10. Make a collograph by cutting out cardboard shapes, gluing them to a base, inking the surface, and taking a print. The thicker the cardboard, the greater the play of light around the edges of shapes in the print.

11. Obtain a Styrofoam meat tray from the local supermarket. Using a ballpoint pen or blunt pencil, draw on the tray. Then, using a brayer, ink the drawn area and print the image on paper cut to fit the tray.

12. Decide how you would explain the differences among other graphic techniques, such as intaglio, lithography, photography, and silkscreen.

13. Make a color copy of a collograph, a monotype, or a collage. How do the two versions compare? If the work is to your liking, would you consider making a limited numbered series of color copies?

14. Browse through several school art supply catalogs and explore the tools and materials available for elementary-school printmaking. As a class project, order a sample of interesting materials and experiment with them to determine their best uses for elementary students. How do the materials correspond to the skills of children? Are the results acceptable? Are the costs reasonable and feasible for a school art program? Keep records and samples of the best materials and the sources for ordering.

SUGGESTED READINGS

Field, Richard S., Ruth Fine, and Mount Holyoke College Art Museum. *A Graphic Muse: Prints by Contemporary American Women.* New York: Hudson Hills Press in association with the Mount Holyoke College Art Museum, 1987.

Gascoigne, Bamber. *How to Identify Prints: A Complete Guide to Manual and Mechanical Processes from Woodcut to Ink Jet.* New York: Thames and Hudson, 1995.

Goldman, Paul. *Looking at Prints, Drawings and Watercolors: A Guide to Technical Terms.* Los Angeles: J. Paul Getty Museum, 1989.

Martin, Judy. *The Encyclopedia of Printmaking Techniques.* Philadelphia: Running Press, 1993.

Printmaking Workshop. *Strategies of Narration: Mel Edwards, Faith Ringgold, Juan Sánchez. Michelle Stuart, Kay Walkingstick.* New York: Printmaking Workshop, 1994.

Ross, John, et al. *The Complete Printmaker: Techniques, Traditions, Innovations.* Rev. and expanded ed. New York; London: Free Press; Collier Macmillan Publishers, 1990.

Tallman, Susan. *The Contemporary Print from Pre-pop to Postmodern.* New York: Thames and Hudson, 1996.

Toale, Bernard. *Basic Printmaking Techniques.* Worcester MA: Davis Publishing, 1992.

WORLD WIDE WEB RESOURCES

Collections and Exhibitions

Fine Arts Museum of San Francisco. *Art Imagebase.* <http://www.thinker.org/> Art Imagebase is a searchable catalog of prints, paintings, drawings, sculpture, and decorative arts. The database is indexed and provides for searches by artist, title, country, period, or subject matter.

National Gallery of Art. "Selections from John James Audubon's *The Birds of America (1827–1838)*"; "Mary Cassatt—Selected Color Prints"; "M. C. Escher—Life and Work." *The Collection.* 1999. <http://www.nga.gov/collection/gallery/> Online tour. Slide programs, teaching packets, films, videocassettes, and videodiscs are available.

Lesson Plans and Curriculum

The @rt Room. 1999. <http://www.arts.ufl.edu/> The mission of the @rt room is to provide a virtual learning environment for exploring the world of art. Designed with kids in mind (age 8 and up), it also provides resources, lessons, activities, and information useful to teachers. Printmaking unit included.

Getty Center for Education in the Arts. "Printmaking with a Japanese Influence: Integrating Art History and Art Criticism"; "Art Education in Action: Making Art, Video Footnotes." *Art Education in Action Video Series.* 1995. ArtsEdNet: The Getty Art Education Web Site. Lesson Plans and Curriculum Ideas. <http://www.artsednet.getty.edu/ArtsEdNet/Resources> Complete DBAE curriculum on printmaking.

Kinderart.com. "Printmaking." 1999. <http://www.bconnex.net/~jarea/printmaking/> Site contains lesson plans and links to other educational resources.

National Society for Education in Art and Design (UK). *Arteducation.co.uk: Your Personal Art Teaching Assistant.* 1999. <http://arteducation.co.uk> A growing resource of over 600 pages of art lessons, art projects, and ideas about teaching art. Written by leading art educators in the United Kingdom with primary, secondary, and K–12 teachers in mind.

Walker Art Center, Weisman Art Museum, and the Minneapolis Institute. "Graphic Arts." Activity: Art Media. *ArtsNetMinnesota.* <http://www.artsnetmn.org/actmedia.html> Also features information about artists and their works, classroom and museum resources, and multidisciplinary classroom curriculum.

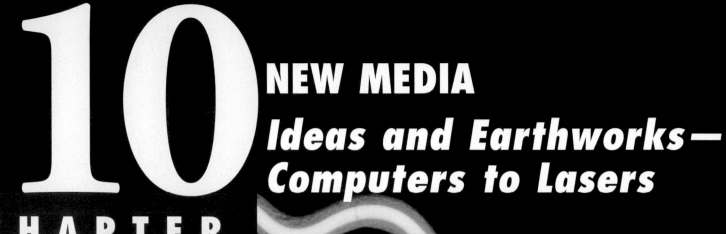

10

CHAPTER

NEW MEDIA

Ideas and Earthworks—
Computers to Lasers

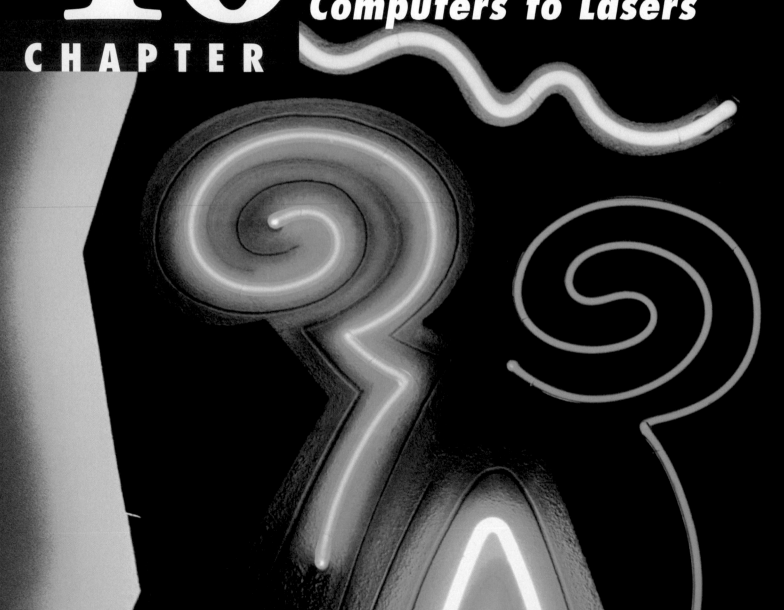

Art is not possible without technology. Nevertheless, art does not reflect how powerful technology is, but how powerfully it serves the artist's artistic means.[1]

—Mihai Nadin

The invention of oil paint in the fifteenth century changed the art of painting forever. Before that time artists had to paint on fast-drying plaster (fresco) or use tempera pigments mixed with water or egg yolk. With the new slow-drying oil paints, artists could take time to blend colors carefully and develop images more deliberately. And, if properly applied, the oils improved the longevity of paintings.

Many other technical advances have greatly influenced what artists attempt and what they are able to accomplish. We mentioned in Chapter 9 the invention of lithography and the making of paper as technical advances in the art of printmaking. During the past century, technical advances have occurred at a startling and accelerating rate. Artists today have a range of art media that their predecessors a hundred years ago never dreamed of. Contemporary artists also use materials in new and unusual ways that would not have been accepted or understood in the past. In this chapter we will sample a few of the ideas and media that mark the current art scene, and we will suggest ways elementary-school children might learn about art beyond the traditions of drawing and painting.

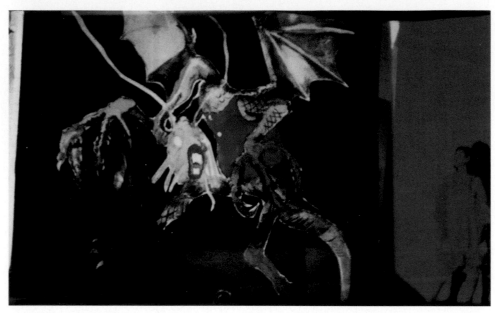

U.S.A.

NEW IDEAS, NEW MEDIA

The invention of photography in the nineteenth century made a tremendous impact on the visual arts that continues to the present. At first, many artists moved away from realistic representation in drawing and painting because the camera could accomplish that quickly and accurately. Instead, artists developed ideas that the camera could not accomplish. The impressionists developed a painterly style, creating images that expressed mood without great detail. The cubists moved in another direction with greater abstraction, using the real visual world only as a starting point and manipulating the concept of reality in art. The fauvists rejected the notion of local or realistic color and painted in ways that the camera could not duplicate.

Later, other artists began using photographic images as reference material for their drawings, paintings, prints, and sculptures. Instead of rejecting the photographic image, some artists began to use the camera to assist them. Gradually, photography became more than a technical process, and photographers entered the realm of art. Photographers found ways to distort images, alter colors at will, print double or triple images, and generally be as expressive as painters. Currently the lines between photography and painting or printmaking are blurred, as artists often combine media. For example, instead of painting, drawing, or sculpting a portrait

of the art collector Ethel Scull, Andy Warhol asked her to sit in a coin-operated photo booth and pose for a large number of pictures. He then used a selection of the photographs to make a photoserigraph showing Scull in a variety of views and moods, creating a much more revealing portrait of her than any single view could.

From the beginning days of photography, we have moved ahead to the technologies of cinema, video, and computer-generated images. Each of these technologies has become an artistic medium, and, as with photography, new modes of making art have come into being. The entire movie industry has resulted from that invention, and many films are considered works of fine art—collected and screened in museums of art. Films are made not only by Hollywood studios but also by a growing coterie of independent filmmakers worldwide. Videocassette recorders (VCRs) are becoming common in many households around the world, creating a large market for videocassettes. Many individuals now use video camcorders to make the equivalent of home movies that were common during the previous generation.

Not yet as common or accessible, but developing at a rapid rate, is the technology of computer-generated images. Even personal computer users can purchase programs for "drawing" and "painting" on the computer. A new generation of artists has chosen the computer as its art medium. Most college art departments offer courses that teach students to create expressive art images with the computer. In the commercial art fields, computer art is well established. Many of the images in television advertising are computer generated, as are an increasing number of movies, such as the pioneering feature film *Tron* and numerous animated films. The tremendous popularity of commercial movies, such as *Jurassic Park, Toy Story,* and *Titanic,* can be attributed largely to the amazing capabilities of computer-generated imagery. Technology is advancing rapidly in the computer area, and it is safe to say that the computer will become increasingly significant as a tool for generating art images.

Virtually every innovation in technology makes an impact in the art area as artists appropriate new media to create images previously not feasible. In the area of metals, for example, we are seeing sculptures cast from stainless steel, welded with corten steel, constructed of lightweight expanded aluminium, and suspended with high-tensile-strength wire cable. Artists have created light shows, using colored beams of laser light on a large scale at night, often in conjunction with architectural forms. Others, perhaps after a visit to Las Vegas, have made sculpture from neon tubing of different colors and sizes.

An entire range of kinetic sculpture has been developed, including sculptures moved by energy produced by water, wind, electricity, gasoline engines, magnets, and so on.

Perhaps as important as new technologies are the new ideas artists continually develop. During the second half of the twentieth century, we witnessed the initiation of conceptual art, environmental art, and art performances. All these new ideas have resulted in an expansion of acceptable materials for art, such as the 24-mile-long *Running Fence* created by Christo and Jeanne-Claude in California of 18-foot-high white nylon material hung from steel poles and more than 100 miles of steel cable.[2] The fence existed only two weeks, after which it was dismantled as planned and the materials given to the ranchers on whose lands the fence was constructed. *Running Fence* was an example of conceptual art, in that the idea of a fence uniting the land that had been divided by state jurisdictions, county boundaries, and individual landowners was central to the project. It was environmental art because of its scope and the importance of the environment to its success. In some ways it was also performance art, as an excellent documentary film was made of the project. The film remains years after the fence itself ceased to exist. More recently, the artists completed an international work with hundreds of huge umbrellas installed concurrently in Japan and California, making a visual reference to the beauty of both locations and to the interrelationships between the United States and Japan physically, culturally, economically, and as Pacific-rim trading partners. The 1,340 blue umbrellas in Japan and 1,760 yellow umbrellas in California were nearly 20 feet high with a diameter of 28 feet. They were on display for 18 days in 1991 before being dismantled as planned.

Some artists have taken that most basic and ancient of environments, the earth itself, as an art medium. One artist, Walter De Maria, chose a flat, semi-arid basin in New Mexico to create the environmental work known as *Lightning Field*. He installed 400 stainless steel poles (2 inches in diameter) in an area known for its thunderstorms, for the specific purpose of attracting lightning strikes. The work covers nearly a square mile with poles installed in rows 225 feet apart. De Maria planned *Lightning Field* as a means to celebrate the power and visual splendor of this aspect of nature.[3]

Another artist (Robert Smithson) created a spiral of rock and dirt that extended into the Great Salt Lake in Utah. While the *Spiral Jetty* remained in place over the months and years, the colors of the water changed around the spiral as communication with the lake, water depths, and temperatures

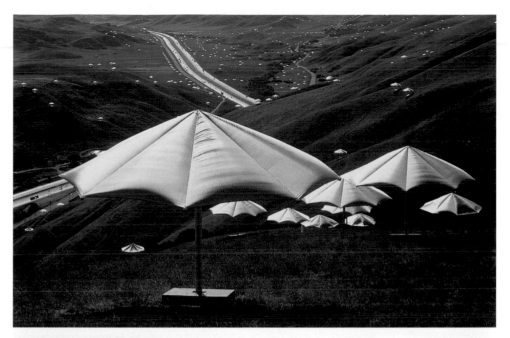

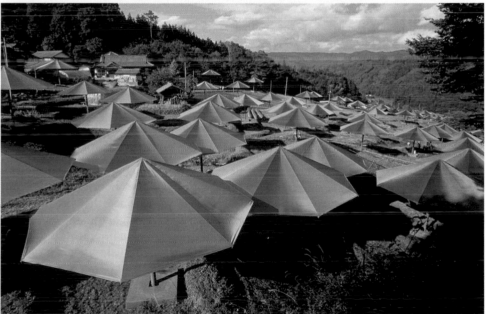

Christo and Jeanne-Claude's 1991 Umbrella project integrated his work with the landscapes of California and Japan and connected the two countries conceptually and aesthetically. What is the value of works of art such as Christo's that are temporary and cannot be owned, bought, or sold?

Christo and Jeanne-Claude, *The Umbrellas*, Japan-USA, 1984–1991. 1,340 blue umbrellas in Japan, 1,760 yellow umbrellas in California, 20' high, 28' in diameter. Prior to being dismantled, as planned, the umbrellas were on display for 18 days. © 1991 Christo. Photo Wolfgang Volz. Christo and Jeanne-Claude raise all the money with their own work and pay all the expenses for their projects themselves, without any sponsorship.

are left in nature to disintegrate and change with the season and the weather. His photographs of the works are the only record of their existence. Goldsworthy speaks little about the meaning of his art. He has said: "I have become aware of how nature is in a state of change, and that change is the key to understanding. I want my art to be sensitive and alert to changes in material, season and weather."[9]

Goldsworthy's approach is eminently available to children, who are always interested in nature and the environment. Following his lead, children might:

- Look for leaves with different colors caused by the seasonal changes. Arrange leaves from the same type of tree according to color changes, such as light yellow, yellow, yellow green, green, dark green. Clear a path on the ground and create a line of leaves that change colors gradually and subtly from one extreme to the other. Make the line several inches wide in a curved or zigzag direction.

- Find an area with sand. Using a tool from nature, such as a stick or rock, make a series of wavy lines in the sand to see how it responds. Is it too dry to hold its shape? Is water available to wet the sand? Create shapes or patterns using repetitions of marks with the natural tools at your disposal.

- Using Goldsworthy's work *Yellow Elm Leaves Laid over a Rock, Low Water* as inspiration, find a location with leaves, rocks, and water. Select and arrange leaves according to colors and cover one or more rocks with leaves using the water to hold the leaves in place. Try some variations: several smaller rocks, each a different color; one large rock blended from one color to another; one large rock a single color; or any variation you wish to try.

- Find a location with lots of small, smooth rocks, like a creek bed or gravel pit. Collect a large number of rocks and separate them according to sizes and colors.

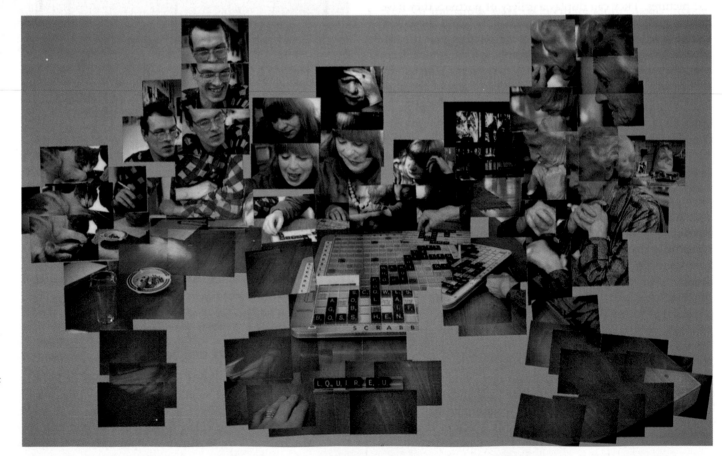

The Scrabble Game, Jan. 1, 1983 #10, David Hockney, 1983, Photographic collage, 30 × 58 in. © 1983, 2000 David Hockney.

The artist made multiple images of a scene with a Polaroid camera, then combined the photographs in ways similar to the collages of cubist artists Picasso and Braque.

Then create a series of concentric circles using variations of rock size and color. Stop when you think the design appears complete.

- Remember to bring cameras to the sites and record your efforts and your finished works of art. The art will remain on site and the photographs will be your record and your reminder of the beauty you saw in nature. Like Goldsworthy's, your art is a collaboration with nature.

Polaroid Photography As an Art Medium

Prominent artist David Hockney has explored the Polaroid camera as a tool for making art. He is also interested in the cubism of Picasso and Braque, in which multiple views of the same subject are presented in a single painting, producing distortions but also revealing more information than is possible with only one view (note the similarity with Warhol's idea for the Ethel Scull portrait). Hockney has taken this idea and applied it with unusual results using the Polaroid camera.

Polaroid cameras are very common, and, if the school does not have one, one can usually be obtained for temporary use from parents or friends of the school. Ask children to select a scene that they like, such as their own classroom, a local park, or an interesting building. Working in teams according to how many cameras you have or by taking turns with one camera, have the children take pictures of the selected subject from different points of view. When all the pictures are completed, ask the children to select the ones that are most interesting and best express what they feel about the subject. Then they can assemble the pictures and mount them on a firm surface such as poster board. If they work in teams, they might make several Polaroid works.

When you display the Polaroid "collages," you might include the work of Hockney, along with some information about his life and work. You might even relate the work to the idea of cubism. Statements by the children about what they were trying to capture and communicate in the photographs would add greatly to the display.

Working in a similar way, the children might take pictures of a person (maybe the principal) and assemble a portrait using Warhol's approach. They might add drawings or paintings of the person to achieve another dimension of insight and interest.

Art from Everything

It is the attitude of artists that determines what materials they will use to create art. This attitude has changed recently to allow virtually any (safe) materials to be used in the creation of works of art.

Ask children to collect many items that they no longer want or need, such as old toys, dishes, plastic items, even small

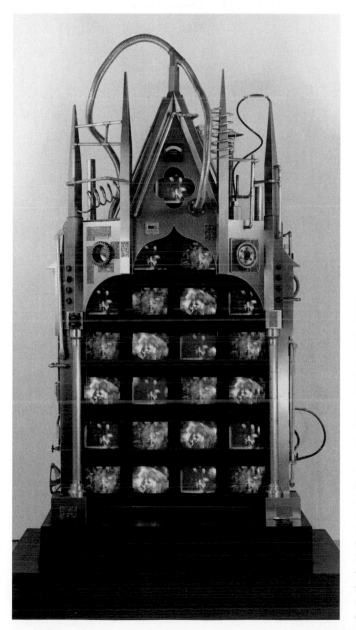

Nam June Paik, *Technology*, 1991, 25 video monitors, 3 laser disc players with unique 3 discs in cabinet (side view). National Museum of American Art, Smithsonian Institution, Washington, D.C., U.S.A. Art Resource, N.Y.

Nam June Paik is considered the father of video art, having developed this new direction for four decades. His integration of technology and visual art exemplifies one major thrust of the postmodern era. Dozens, or even hundreds, of video monitors in Paik's works are computer programmed with video sequences, sometimes projecting independently, sometimes in sequences, and sometimes in unison. The result is a series of dynamic works that seem to have a life of their own.

appliances or lamps no longer in use. Supplement what they bring with a trip to a local surplus warehouse or thrift store, and purchase (or ask for the donation of) interesting items. Collect wood scraps from the high-school wood shop, from the local lumberyard, or from parents who do woodwork. It

Xeroxes of the same subject encourage variations as students work directly on the images. (France)

is possible to collect one or more television sets that still work, although sometimes not very well, among the items.

Tell the children they are going to work together to make a sculpture out of the collected materials. They can discuss what mood they might want to express: funny, frightening, exciting, beautiful, and so on. Then they can begin selecting objects and try them together to see if they "work" in interesting ways. The children will also need to decide at the appropriate time what colors will be best for expressing the mood they have chosen. Individual items will need to be painted before combining them with other objects.

One major problem is how to combine the objects so they do not fall apart. Children might need a hammer and nails, good-quality glue, screws and a screwdriver, clamps, and whatever other means they can devise. Decide in advance if the sculpture will actually have working parts. When the sculpture is assembled and stabilized so it will not fall apart, decide what colors would be most appropriate for the final painting. When the work is completed, the students will have a contemporary sculpture, and, if they have included anything electrical that works, they can turn it on and admire the sight, movement, and sound of their work.

Fax Friendships

Artist David Hockney sent an entire mural by fax from California to the Walker Art Center in Minneapolis. The mural image was generated by computer, and each page of printout was a segment of the whole. After Hockney printed out the total image, which required many sheets of paper, he transmitted each sheet across the country by fax. The separate sheets were then assembled on a huge wall in the Art Center, creating the mural. Show students what a fax message looks like, and explain how the fax machine works: Words or images on a sheet of paper are transmitted by telephone as bits of sound, received by another fax machine, and reconstructed on another page at the receiving site in the form of the original image.

Suggested activity: Explain that students will work in groups to create messages in the form of graphic art that they will send to selected potential friends in another location. Find a willing recipient of student art messages by fax. These messages could be an exchange with a sister city in another country or with another school in the district, or they could be messages to a politician, the superintendent of schools (one way to promote the art program), a corporation, or a celebrity. Remind students that, in order to be transmitted, their work must be of high quality. Tell them to think about it and have fun.

Primary assessment would focus on the success of the project: Did students create appropriate and good-quality graphic art messages? Were the messages successfully transmitted and received? Did you receive acknowledgment in response to students' works? In what ways was this a positive experience? Did students become more aware of the uses of technology and art for communication in contemporary life?

Copy Technology for Learning about Art

Most schools have photocopy machines, and some school districts have access to color copy machines. Many of the uses for such machines are not very expensive. For example, after discussing and analyzing van Gogh's *The Starry Night,* the teacher can make a copy of the reproduction for every child. Children would then be asked to perform such tasks as these: "Use your red crayon to outline the shapes of the trees" or "With your black crayon, show the swirling lines in the sky, the trees, and the foreground" or "With your blue crayon, make an X on the spots the artist has made most interesting to look at (centers of interest)." The teacher can adapt this idea for any types of responses as children study and understand a particular work of art.

Artists are beginning to use color copy machines as another addition to printmaking technology. These machines can enlarge, reduce, distort, change color emphasis, and do other interesting operations, giving the artist immediate results and ideas for more changes. When the artist has created the final image, it can be duplicated on the machine for whatever edition is wanted. Color slides can also be duplicated on color copy machines, making it possible to print from slides, alter the print with crayons, paints, or inks, and then print the results.

Using the regular copy machine, children can make drawings that can be duplicated and colored or painted on in different ways without destroying the original. The drawing can be enlarged or reduced, and several versions can be cut and pasted together, like Hockney does with Polaroid shots, to create a collage of multiple versions of a single image drawn by the child. Children can learn about the fluency afforded artists with modern technology as they experiment with the copy machine. They can also learn to manipulate their own ideas in ways that would not be possible without the copy machine.

MEDIA FOR INSTRUCTION

The hardware of media are considerably more than mechanical gadgets for presenting information; they are linked to the very shape and structure of the content being imparted and thus represent different modes of learning. Let us consider for a moment the many ways instructional media are able to extend students' perceptions of a subject such as painting:

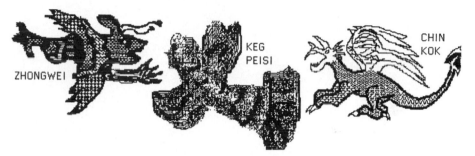

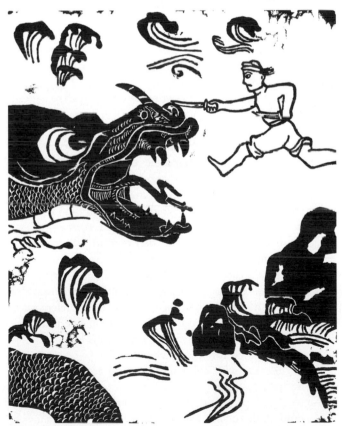

Two views of a dragon: The group of three is computer designed and the other example is a linoleum print from a children's art center in Beijing, People's Republic of China. These images demonstrate the effect of media upon subject. Jane Chia and Bimu Dutli taught the computer lesson.

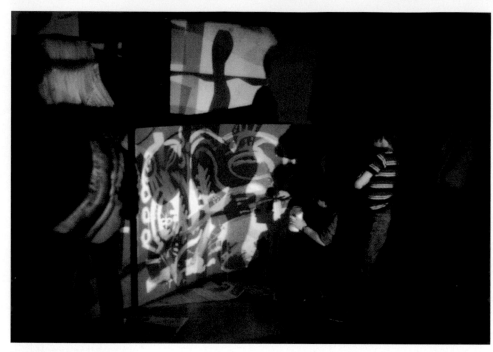

In making an animated film, students photograph shapes as they are positioned on a flat surface. If the shapes are transparent, they can be projected on a large scale through the use of an overhead projector.

- A *film* or *video* about a particular artist can show something of the process of change and maturation in an individual.
- A *comparison of slides* of works of art can lead to a group discussion of likenesses and differences in style and content of art objects.
- Packets of small *reproductions* allow students to investigate at their own pace the visual components of a series of paintings.
- A *filmstrip* can provide an inexpensive collection of slides centered on a single idea. For commentary, there is usually an accompanying record or lecture notes; students can also work from their own impressions.
- A *live television lesson* from a public network can bring a professional artist to the class for a single performance.
- A *portable videotape machine* can play back a demonstration by a visiting artist recorded for future reference or for classes that could not attend the original performance.
- A *tape recording* of an interview with a local art critic can be stored for future reference.
- A *computer* with color monitor and compact disc can be used to retrieve color images of any artist, style, or work and present them on the screen. A single disc can hold thousands of art images.

- There is no limit in sight for the information about art available on the Internet, including museum sites, exhibits of artists' works, commentaries by critics and historians, and color images that can be downloaded. The range of sites is worldwide.

Teachers might not have access to all these modes of instruction, but, with time, knowledge, and equipment, teachers can significantly extend their own style of teaching, the pupils' scope of learning, and the range of subject matter. In all modes of media, limitations are offset by the advantages.

Environmental Influences

Children today are both eager and prepared to engage in media activities. Their visual sense is oriented to motion because of early exposure to television, films, and video and computer games. They accept condensed time-space concepts because they view live coverage of news events, and they have never doubted, for instance, that they could breakfast in one part of the world and lunch in another.

The art teacher who is truly sensitive to what is happening outside the classroom will give serious thought to incorporating newer media into the art program, realizing that there is no inherent contradiction in goals or philosophy between creating in either the new or the traditional media. Both kinds of materials provide excitement and challenge in the areas of design, including color and drawing; both elicit original solutions on the part of the child and call for a high level of creative ingenuity. Newer media have simply added such increasingly relevant ingredients as time, motion, and light to the elements of color, space, mass, line, texture, and shade. According to one art teacher:

> Computers have the potential of expanding the possibilities of creative expression. They provide a playground for ideas and images. . . . Risk taking, experimentation, exploration, and play—are all essential to the artistic process, and are all possible with computers.[10]

Teachers will be shortsighted indeed should they fail to capitalize on the built-in motivations provided by the excitement of matching sound to light or image to movement. They will also deprive themselves of a logical means of combining other arts, such as music, dance, and choral reading.

The activities described in this chapter range from simple projects that can be carried out in one learning session to more complex operations requiring several sessions. In most

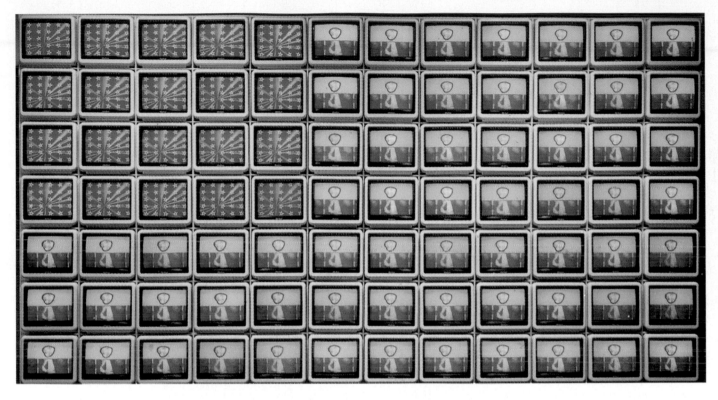

Nam June Paik, *Video Flag z*, 1986, Television sets, videodisc players, videodiscs, plexiglass modular cabinet, 74" × 133" × 18". Los Angeles County Museum of Art. Copyright © 1993 Museum Associates, Los Angeles County Museum of Art, gift of the Arm Museum Council. All rights reserved.

In this work, the artist combined multi-monitor VCRs in a wall installation with eighty-four TV screens programmed in the configuration of the American flag. Images on the screen move constantly, providing a dynamic version of the flag. The viewer can see the entire display as a unified work or concentrate on each screen individually.

cases, the amount of time spent on the project depends on how deeply the teacher wants to probe the subject.

Most schools have slide and overhead projectors, and schools with a drama program usually have transparent color gels. Simultaneous use of projected images combined with handmade slides can be very effective, particularly when used on different subjects, for example, a white sheet draped over a collection of large objects. This form of multimedia is about thirty years old, but still allows students to cover large areas with light and color in a relatively short time.

Experiences with a Camera

If a camera is available, whether handmade or on loan from a friend or family, it can be used as an instrument for observation and personal commentary. The treatment of one subject in two or more greatly contrasted media (as in sculpture, painting, and photography) is an effective way of attuning children to the possibilities and limitations of art media. The following tasks for the beginning photographer are also worth trying in drawing (and writing).

- Make a "living comic strip." Tell a story in a series of pictures using real people.
- Photograph an autobiography. Tell about yourself by taking pictures of your favorite things, your family, where you live, yourself.
- Document your neighborhood. Take pictures of people at work and play, people of different ages, and buildings where you and others live, work, and spend time.
- Define a word or a feeling with a picture or series of pictures (happiness, sadness, cold, hot, hard, soft).
- Pretend you are a bug or a giant. Photograph the world through their eyes.
- Illustrate a song or a poem or a short story with your own photos.
- Look for patterns. Find repeated designs in the environment, like picket fences, railroad tracks, or bricks.

The Storyboard

The storyboard is a transdisciplinary activity that draws in varying degrees on narrative skill, the linking of image to story, and the use of drawing. It can also prepare children to

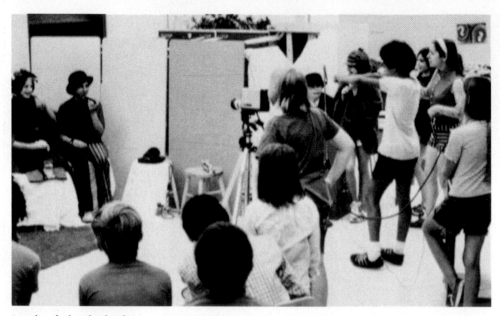

A number of roles related to the video production are in evidence here: actors, camera crew, director, and studio audience. Writers and sound technicians are less evident. During the course of production, students will change roles.

better understand how filmmakers, animators, and even writers of commercials think on paper.

A storyboard is a sequence of pictures that tells a story or relates to a given problem. Some students may choose to draw their sequences; others may compile them or paste them up from news or magazine photos.

The storyboard can be used to plan a film or video or it can be an activity in itself. Specific homework assignments can be made. For example, children in the upper elementary grades are capable of studying a one-minute television commercial by reducing it to a sequence of storyboard frames, thereby recording the timing of shots, distinguishing among tight shots (very close), long shots (at a distance), close-ups, and so on. In making a storyboard, students can apply the basic vocabulary of film and video to extend their own picture making. Storyboards are the middle ground between the realm of the communications media and the traditional forms of picture making.

A wonderful example of visual narrative that all ages can appreciate is the award-winning children's book *Tuesday,* by David Wiesner.[11] This delightful story demonstrates all the techniques of the storyboard.

Video

The portable videocassette recorder (VCR) and camcorder are gaining popularity in the schools at a rapid rate. How-

ever, the VCR has still to gain wide acceptance as part of the art program, and its position at this time is similar to that of the camera a generation ago. If we examine the creative possibilities of video recording dispassionately, we must admit that it is a truly revolutionary instrument. To children, it means that they can, in a sense, control the very machine that for so many years has dominated their leisure hours. The tables are suddenly turned, and they as viewers are in command, becoming producer, director, or actor. Their new domain is a television studio in miniature, consisting of camera, television monitor, and computer. It is now possible for formerly passive observers to control the camera, create the image, and get immediate feedback on the monitor. Nor do they have to limit their activities to the school; they can extend their control to the playground, the neighborhood—anywhere the camcorder can be carried.

As with photography, technical aspects of video cameras are best learned in a workshop. It is, however, worth noting some of the ways one art teacher with special training went about building a sequence of activities around the VCR. During a summer workshop, the children, working in rotating groups, did the following:

- Designed and presented their own commercials. This involved designing the package, writing copy, and delivering the "message," as well as recording the entire experience on tape.
- Designed and assembled several settings for short plays, which were developed from a series of improvisations. Sets were constructed of large sheets of cardboard and included cast-off furniture.
- Studied the effects of light and change of scale by examining miniature sets on camera.
- Critiqued commercial programming viewed on the monitor.
- Role-played various social situations derived from their school and home experiences.
- Acted as television art teachers by demonstrating a simple process such as potato printing, stenciling, or collography.
- Took turns as camera operator, director, performer, designer, and producer. They also learned the basic operation and nomenclature of the equipment.[12]

The use of video in the art program has become commonplace in many schools. A review of the activities just listed might make a curious teacher speculate about the many possibilities offered by the VCR and camcorder as a means of extending the children's visual awareness.

With the current quality of digital video cameras (camcorders), very high-quality videos can be achieved. After shooting video segments, scenes can be fed into a personal computer with editing software. The higher-level cameras and software programs allow for all types of editing, special effects, titles, and sound. Digital video cameras and personal computers are becoming increasingly common in homes in the United States as well as in schools.

New technology is available; the problem is to get it into the classroom—or to get the students to the equipment. The use of photocopying machines—in both black and white and color—suggests an array of new images. Teachers should bear in mind, however, that new technology is always possible if not easily accessible, and that if Leonardo da Vinci were alive today, he certainly would have used any means at his disposal capable of extending his unique vision. With his voracious curiosity, he would have embraced every means of expression available to him through the advance of technology.

Computer Technologies in the Art Classroom

The range of art learning and teaching that can be accomplished through uses of computer, video, VCR, and CD-ROM technologies is truly mind boggling. Virtually anything we can think of to do as teachers can be done now, and computer capabilities are still emerging from this extremely rapidly developing field. Moving from the simple to the more sophisticated uses, it is now possible for students to:

- Create black-and-white or color artwork on computers in the art classroom, using school computers and readily available graphics software packages.
- Experiment with their art images, altering the color, form, and composition of their work while saving the original image in case they "ruin" an experimental version.
- Print out their computer drawings or paintings in black and white or color.
- Transfer images from a video camera to the computer screen, where they can be altered and transformed by using graphics software packages.
- Transfer student art images from the computer screen to a television monitor and record on a videotape.

- Take photographs with a handheld digital camera that uses a small videodisc instead of traditional film, then place the disc in a VCR to view on the television monitor, and, if desired, transfer (scan) the images to the computer screen, where they can be artistically altered and used as components of an artwork.
- Transfer virtually any image, including their own drawings and paintings or photographs, to the computer screen, where they can alter them or incorporate them in their artwork.
- Gain access to color images of entire museum collections captured on videodiscs and browse through the collection, calling up images of works by artist, style, title, or other keywords.

These potentialities might seem very exciting to many of us, but relatively few teachers are involved in any but the simplest applications mentioned. Why haven't more teachers of art moved into the realm of computer technologies, when the possibilities seem to be tailored almost perfectly for comprehensive art programs that feature a range of art images, both historical and critical inquiry, and that value the type of creativity in art production possible with computers? Among the most likely reasons are school district budgets that do not allow for the purchase of necessary computer hardware and software programs or a reluctance on the part of teachers to learn about computers as tools for teaching art. Some might not accept computers as valid media for the creation of art.

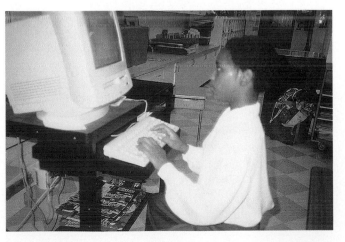

Elementary and middle-level schools are making computers more and more accessible to students. Some schools have computer labs which are used by different classes according to a schedule, similar to use of the library or gymnasium. Basic graphics programs are increasingly available for making art and design work with computers, and color printers are becoming more common in schools.

Whatever the reasons, it is likely that most of them will diminish quickly in validity as computer technologies advance, as prices for previously expensive items fall to an affordable level, and as computers, CD ROMs, VCRs, digital cameras, and other items become more and more common in schools and in homes of students and teachers. For example, in just a few years, the capabilities of computers and laser printers have increased exponentially as prices have dropped drastically. The number of CD ROMs more than doubled between 1991 and 1993, and they now are being included as standard components in computers. Soon, the interconnection of the major electronic devices, including telephone, cellular phone, satellite access, telefax, radio, television, VCR, and computers will do nothing but increase the potentials of newer media for teaching and learning. And electronic network systems will open the art classroom windows for innumerable learning programs and opportunities. Art programs, as well as the entire school system, will benefit through intelligent and judicious use of this unlimited potential.

However, as with all technological innovations, these tools will be only as effective as the teacher who selects and organizes them in a well-founded art curriculum with clear direction and valid goals. It will be even more important for teachers to distinguish between what content will be educationally significant and what will be merely entertaining.

Teachers interested in developing computer skills often have access to classes in computer operation through school districts, adult education programs, and college or university classes. In addition, some computer companies offer regular workshops and intensive two- to five-day seminars for increasing computer skills and knowledge of specific software programs. Teachers seeking information about hardware and software have many published sources that address computer applications for elementary, secondary, and higher education. Such publications discuss educational applications of all forms of advanced electronic technologies. Some states have developed written materials available to all school districts and teachers for the purpose of encouraging computer use in all subject areas, including the arts.

NOTES

1. Mihai Nadin, "Emergent Aesthetics—Aesthetic Issues in Computer Arts," *Leonardo,* Supplemental Issue, 1989, p. 47.

2. For more on *Running Fence, Umbrellas,* and the artists, see Jacob Baal-Teshuva, *Christo and Jeanne-Claude* (New York: Christo, 1995).

3. For more on *Lightning Fields* and De Maria, see John Beardsley, *Earthworks and Beyond,* 3rd ed. (New York: Abbeville Press, 1998).

4. For more on *Spiral Jetty* and Smithson, see Beardsley, *Earthworks and Beyond.*

5. A picture of *Radioactive Cats* and information about the artist appear in Randy Rosen, Catherine Brawer et al., *Making Their Mark: Women Artists Move into the Mainstream, 1970—1985* (New York: Abbeville Press, 1989), p. 86.

6. Ibid., p. 84.

7. For more on *Radioactive Cats,* see *ArtsEdNet: The Getty Art Education Web Site,* "Sandy Skoglund: Teaching Contemporary Art," <http://www.artsednet.getty.edu/ArtsEdNet/Images/Skoglund/>

8. Rosen, Brawer, et al., *Making Their Mark,* p. 138.

9. Beardsley, *Earthworks and Beyond,* p. 206.

10. Deborah Greh, *Computers in the Artroom: A Handbook for Teachers* (Worcester, MA: Davis Publications, 1990), p. 10.

11. David Wiesner, *Tuesday* (New York: Clarion Books, 1991).

12. This special workshop for fifth and sixth graders was offered by the Newton Creative Arts Summer Program, Newton, MA.

ACTIVITIES FOR THE READER

The chapter itself describes many activities to try with the instruments of light, motion, and nature. Here are some:

1. Run two films simultaneously, but eliminate the sound of one and the image of the other. Now try to create connections between the image of the one film and the sound track of the other.

2. Work with colleagues to create simple "how to" instructional videos on such topics as pulling a print, wedging clay, mixing colors, doing formal analysis of a painting or library research on an artist, or others. Make each video segment brief and easy to understand, and make sure it works with the intended age group of students.

3. Any series of still pictures will give the illusion of motion when viewed in sequence. Create a sequence of "flip cards" by working on one side of a group of index cards. By slightly changing the position of the image from card to card, it is possible to create the illusion of a ball flying off the page, a ship sinking into the sea, a smile appearing on a face, or Dr. Jekyll turning into Mr. Hyde.

4. Using a simple computer animation program, try the "flip card" activity described in suggestion 3.

5. Using Adobe Illustrator or a comparable computer graphics program, make teaching aids for concepts of color, design, art history, and other topics in the curriculum for elementary grades.

6. Experiment with methods of correlating music and media. Select some music, and create abstract images on glass slides in any manner suggested by the music. Such elements as line, color, and mass should all reflect the mood of the music. The slides can be grouped according to their relation to the changes in the mood and pace of the music. A roughly synchronized slide production can be made if two projectors are used and if the image of one is faded into the image of the other by adjusting the focusing mechanism of the projectors.

7. Use photographs in combination with art materials, such as colored markers, colored pencils, paints, or inks, and create a collage or poster with the goal of making a color photocopy as the final product. Note how versatile the photocopy medium is.

8. Wrap two students in muslin or a cotton sheet and project a picture of a well-known painting or building upon the wrapped figures. See how this transforms a familiar image.

9. Ask the theatre department of your school or a nearby secondary school for any sheets of transparent colored gels used for lighting that are about to be discarded. Cut the gels into strips or geometric shapes. If you arrange these on an overhead projector, large spaces ranging from a movie screen to an entire wall can quickly be filled with color. Try overlapping different colors. For black silhouettes, cut any piece of opaque paper in shapes that relate to the transparent colored forms.

SUGGESTED READINGS

For up-to-date commentary on contemporary artists with images of their work, see such periodicals as *Contemporanea, ARTnews,* and *Art in America.* Online versions are available at addresses cited in the World Wide Web Resources section.

Beardsley, John. *Earthworks and Beyond.* 3rd ed. New York: Abbeville Press, 1998.

Druin, Allison, ed. *The Design of Children's Technology.* New York: Academic Press/Morgan Kaufmann, 1998.

Erhlich, Linda. "Animation for Children." *Art Education* 48, no. 2 (1995): 24–27.

Freedman, Kerry. "Visual Art/Virtual Art: Teaching Technology for Meaning." *Art Education* 50, no. 4 (1997): 6–12.

Leigh Green, Gaye. "Installation Art: A Bit of the Spoiled Brat or Provocative Pedagogy." *Art Education* 49, no. 2 (1996): 16–19.

Gregory, Diane C., ed. *New Technologies and Art Education: Implications for Theory, Research, and Practice.* Reston, VA: National Art Education Association, 1997.

Knapp, Stephen. *Digital Design: The New Computer Graphics.* Rockport MA: Rockport Publishing, 1998.

Lovejoy, Margot. *Postmodern Currents: Art and Artists in the Age of Electronic Media.* Upper Saddle River, NJ: Prentice-Hall, 1997.

Matthews, Jonathan C., and ERIC Clearinghouse for Social Studies/Social Science Education. *Computers and*

Art Education. Bloomington: Clearinghouse for Social Studies/Social Science Education, Indiana University, 1997.

O'Brien, Michael, and Norman Sibley. *The Photographic Eye: Learning to See with a Camera.* Worcester, MA: Davis Publishing 1991.

Stroh, Charles. "Basic Color Theory and Color in Computers." *Art Education* 50, no. 4 (1997): 17–22.

Wagstaff, Sean. *Animation on the Web.* Berkeley, CA: Peachpit Press, 1999.

WORLD WIDE WEB RESOURCES

Collections and Exhibitions

Digital Art

Guggenheim Museum. "Virtual Projects." *Guggenheim Virtual Museum.* 1998. <http://www.guggenheim.org/virtual/index_fst.html> The Guggenheim Museum's Virtual Museum commissions, acquires, and displays works of digital art on this WWW site.

Museum of Computer Art. *Images for a New Millennium.* 1999. <http://www.donarcher.com/moca/index.html> The Museum of Computer Art features works by artists of technical and artistic interest.

Walker Art Center. "The Shock of the View: Artists, Audiences, Museums in the Digital Age." *Gallery 9: New Media Initiates.* 1998. <http://www.walkerart.org/salons/shockoftheview/sv_front.html> Features a series of curated online exhibitions and dialogue about art and technology.

Mixed Media and Photography

Getty Education Institute for the Arts, ArtsEdNet. "Kids Framing Kids: More Than Just a Pretty Picture." 1997. *ArtsEdNet. Lesson Plans and Curriculum Ideas.* <http://www.artsednet.getty.edu/ArtsEdNet/Exhibitions/Kids/> The children of Shelley Elementary School are the artists and subjects of the photographs in this exhibition. Teaching methodology and other resources are included.

ArtsEdNet: The Getty Art Education Web Site. "Sandy Skoglund: Teaching Contemporary Art." *Online Exhibition. Image Galleries and Exhibitions.* 1996. <http://www.artsednet.getty.edu/ArtsEdNet/Images/Skoglund/> Artworks by Sandy Skoglund, internationally known installation artist and photographer, are presented. In addition to the online exhibition, curriculum resources, discussions with the artist and art educators, lesson plans, and activities are included.

Curriculum Resources and Lesson Plans

Photography

Eastman Kodak Company. "K–12 Resources: Lesson Plans." *Enhancing Learning through Imaging.* 1999. <http://www.kodak.com/US/en/digital/edu/> Lesson plans include: A Glossary of Photographic Terms; Beginnings of Photographic Composition; The Language of Light; Darkroom Design for Amateur Photographers; and Digital Photography.

University of Arizona. "Teaching from the Collection: Educator's Guides." *Center for Creative Photography.* <http://dizzy.library.arizona.edu/branches/ccp/> The Center for Creative Photography is a museum and research center devoted to photography as an art form. This site presents a series of guides for educators with images and instruction on incorporating photography into elementary-school curricula.

University of California, Riverside. "Kids Lessons." *California Museum of Photography.* 1999. <http://cmp1.ucr.edu/exhibitions/education/vidkids/lessons.html> Lessons focus on a "low-tech" approach to creation of moving pictures and an introduction to video and television.

Digital Art and Animation

Illusion Works, L.L.C. 1997. <http://www.illusionworks.com/> This site includes interactive demonstrations, scientific explanations, school projects, illusion artwork, interactive puzzles, 3D graphics, suggested reading lists, bibliographies, perception links, and much more.

Advanced Network and Services. *ThinkQuest.* 1999. <http://www.thinkquest.org/thinkquestjr.html> *ThinkQuest,* an Internet-based education program, is one of the best Internet media sites for art teachers and students. *ThinkQuest* sponsors projects created for the Internet by teams of students, teachers, and coaches and presents them on this site. Among those on art are several on digital art and computer graphics. The art projects are innovative and informative and model the technological possibilities of the Internet.

Warner Brothers. "Animation 101." 1998. <http://wbanimation.warnerbros.com/cmp/ani_04if.html> Interactive site for students interested in animation.

Publications

<http://www.ed.gov/Technology/> The Web site of the U.S. Department of Education Office of Technology provides up-to-date information and resources for teachers about acquiring and implementing technology in the classroom. The site features online publications and links to other education technology sites.

North Central Regional Education Laboratory. *Technology Connections for School Improvement Planners' Handbook.* 1999. <http://www.ncrel.org/tplan/tplanB.html> Useful tool for educators involved in planning for and acquiring technology resources.

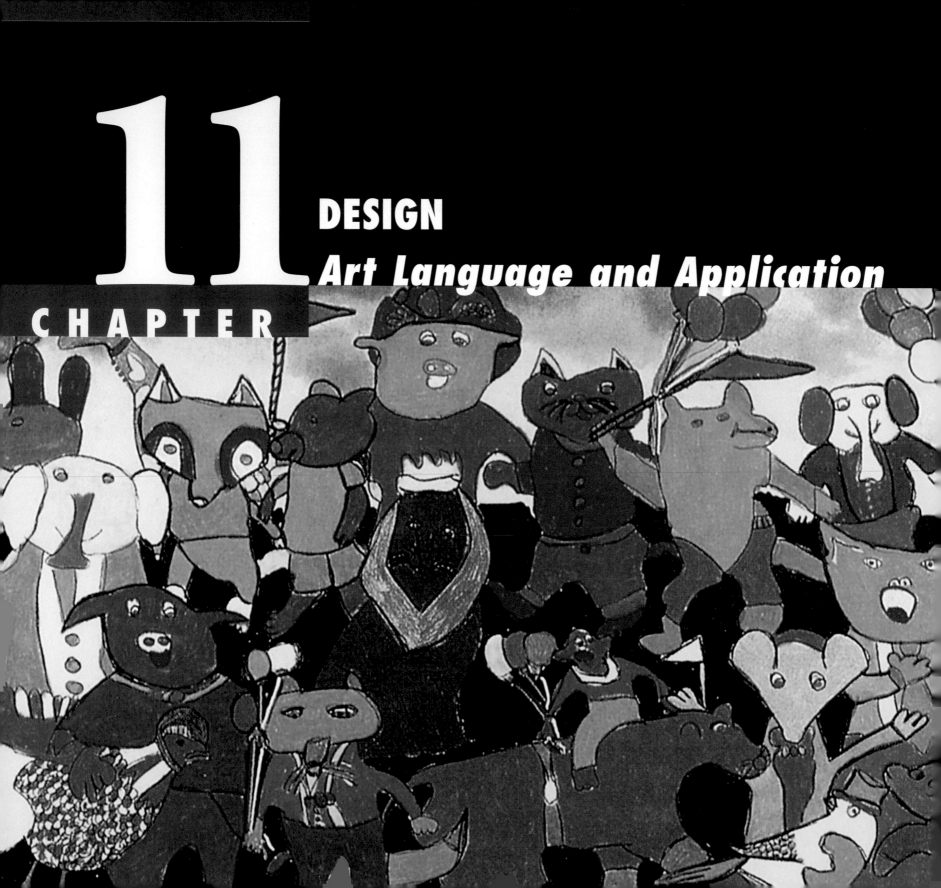

CHAPTER 11

DESIGN
Art Language and Application

Precisely what is formal in sculpture today? One answer would be that it is those material-optical-tactile features of sculpture which can be identified and logically examined as separate physical entities. The formal qualities are those that still give form in the original classical sense: shape, proportions, scale, structure, texture, color, context—those aspects of visual reality to which we turn for our nonliterary meanings in objects.[1]

— Jack Burnham

The term *design* is used today instead of *composition,* which is now considered to have a more limited meaning. We can speak of the composition of a tree and describe the relation of the whole (the trunk) to its parts (branches), but a tree has not been planned or *designed* with some aesthetic or functional intent in mind. Design is not a separate and distinct area of art; it is an integral part of any art form. The message a creative person wishes to convey is automatically made apparent by the formal organization of any work of art, whether by a child or an adult. A piece of clay sculpture by a child in the first grade, a Chinese stoneware vase, a painting by Cassatt, a symphony by Beethoven, or a play by Arthur Miller all involve design, structure, and the relation of subsidiary elements to a unified whole.

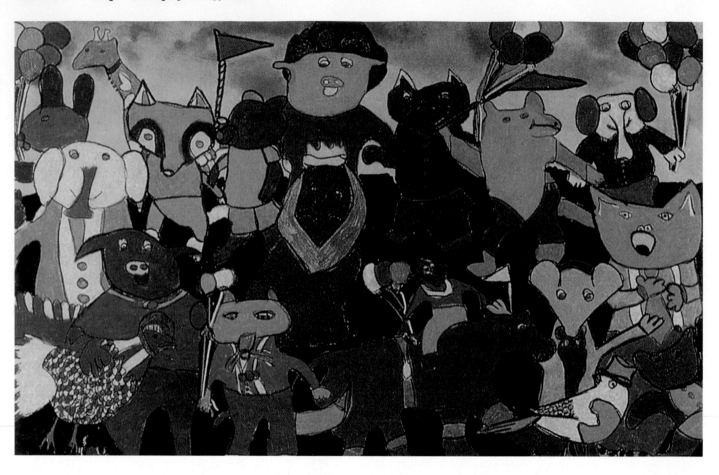

U.S.A.

Design, therefore, is presented in all art forms and may be intuitively achieved or consciously dealt with. One function of art education is to develop a child's awareness of design. In this chapter we will discuss design as it applies to visual forms of expression, including an analysis of the parts, or elements, that make up design and an outline of the methods employed by artists to use these elements coherently. The teacher without a knowledge of design is handicapped when the need arises to instruct and assist children with their own artwork and with understanding the work of others. The information in this chapter is presented as professional background knowledge with suggestions for practical classroom applications.

THE ELEMENTS OF DESIGN

Design is the organization of parts into a coherent whole. Visual design is the organization of *materials* and *forms* for a

specific *purpose*. The designs of accomplished artists should convey the feeling that nothing in the designs could be changed without violating their structure. All the elements of design in use should make a complete and harmonious whole.

The act of designing is common to all human beings. Early peoples brought order and coherence to their environments while constructing their villages. Homemakers follow the desire for order in arranging furniture in their living rooms, lawmakers bring order to a legislative session, and gardeners bring order to their gardens. Because the desire for order is universal, artistic acts—which demand that a form, composition, or design be achieved—have potential significance for us all.

A distinction can be made between designers who begin with practical functions and use the principles and elements of visual organization to make their solutions as aesthetically pleasing as possible and artists who use the same elements in nonfunctional ways for purely aesthetic purposes.

Those who have attempted to isolate the elements of design for definition have reached only partial agreement. Nevertheless, nearly all agree that the elements of design include *line, shape, color, texture,* and *space.* Design in three dimensions includes the element of *mass,* which is analogous to two-dimensional *shape.* The term *form* has two major meanings in art and design. Form is

1. The underlying structure or *composition* in a work of art.

2. The shape or outline of something.

These elements of art are, in effect, the building blocks of all visual art; they are all the artist has to work with. The elements will be discussed individually so teachers may not only acquire some insight into design as it appears in the work of children but also develop a vocabulary for this segment of art education. The vocabulary of form is the foundation of the formal analysis process and provides student and teacher with the language needed to discuss the work of artists as well as students.

Each element discussed can be seen in both nature and art. It is the teacher's task to assemble the sources to teach children to recognize the elements and principles and to reinforce students' understanding with art activities derived from those sources.

Contemporary artists, such as Frank Stella and Judy Pfaff, have worked against what they feel are static effects, such as symmetry, balance, and classic proportion. Instead, they have placed a premium on accident, on spontaneity of execution, and on deliberate avoidance of a "closed" image. Despite this change in the concept of design, the elements exist in all styles, and for purposes of elementary instruction, we can use design vocabulary in referring to both the child's work and the work of professionals. The language of design provides a basis for discussing the work of students, which can begin as soon as a child understands—through use and recognition—the meaning of the vocabulary.

Design also has another meaning worth noting. *Design* as a verb can refer to the planning of useful or decorative objects, such as fabrics, appliances, automobiles, or interiors. We can therefore design a container or create a painting wherein elements and principles of design operate effectively. The *principles* of design refer to generalizations in the structure of forms, be they from fine arts or commercial design.[2] When elements interact they make up *principles.* Since it is important to convey to young children the meaning of the elements (line, shape, color, texture, and space) as well as the princi-

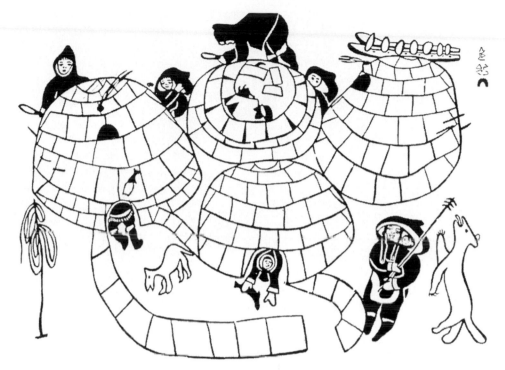

Ashoona Pitseolak, *Winter Camp Scene,* 1969, Cape Dorset, Northwest Territories. © Pitseolak Ashoona, 1969. Reproduced with permission of the West Baffin Eskimo Co-operative, Ltd., Cape Dorset, Northwest Territories, Canada.

Inuit artists depicted scenes of life in the frozen North in sensitive prints made from stone blocks.

ples, this chapter will discuss both sets of terms. The danger in planning activities related to the design elements is that too often teachers neglect the second, vital stage of making the connections between principles and elements. The ultimate goal of design education is to become aware of this important interaction, in both the children's work and that of professional artists. Teacher and pupil must share some common language, and the terminology of design constitutes the beginning of a mode of discourse that can be referred to during the entire span of the elementary art program.

Line

Most of us have entered the world of art through the lines we have created. *Line* is the path traced by a moving point and is perhaps the most flexible and revealing element of design. If we are angry and doodle a line, our anger is clearly revealed in the marks we make. If we are placid, calm, or pleased, our line takes on a different character. Artists readily express their feelings by means of line. In communicating hatred of war and brutality in general, an artist may use slashing, angular, abrupt lines; presenting feelings about the beauty of a summer landscape, the artist's lines might be gently undulating and flowing.

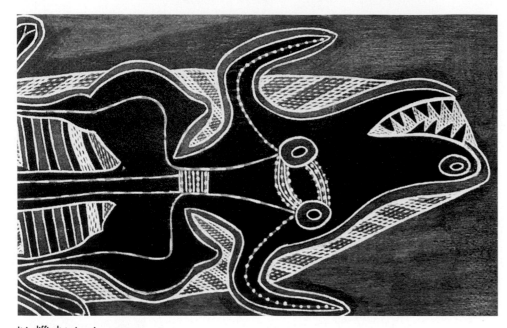

It is difficult to imagine any program of art education without referring to art's early sources—be they the cave walls of Altamira or, as in the case of this illustration, the bark drawings from northern Australia. Such images record our earliest interests in the use of pictographs with magical associations. Although survival played a part in the creation of symbolic images, the pleasure given to both artist and viewer was surely a part of the process. Aboriginal bark paintings (Australia) provide exceptionally clear references to art terms, such as symmetry, line, repetition, and rhythm. (From *The Australian Aboriginal Heritage*, Ronald Bernatt and E. S. Phillips.)

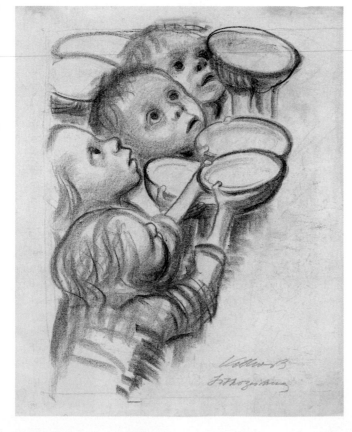

Käthe Kollwitz, *Germany's Children are Starving*, 1924. Kollwitz's use of bold emphatic lines for the lithograph reinforce the tragic content of her subject. © Bildarchiv Preussischer Kulturbesitz, Berlin.

Line may be used strongly and directly. German artist Käthe Kollwitz used line as a primary means to achieve her end; the strong, powerful line supports both her rage at society and her compassion for its victims. The sensitively drawn lines of Inuit printmakers define objects, figures, and animals and lead the eye around the picture. The quality of line is integral to the meaning of both works. Artists may also imply line—that is, convey it indirectly—by forming edges of contrasting tones that move from one part of a painting to another.

Line has sometimes been called the "nervous system" of a work of art. For most of us, linear experience is our first contact with art—if only because of the availability of pencil, pen, or crayon. The study of line is particularly effective with elementary-school children, because they usually have experienced a number of ways of drawing lines with a variety of tools, such as pencils, crayons, and felt-tip pens. Children will often find their own words to distinguish among "scratchy" lines, "funny" lines, or the "squiggly" character of some lines. This sort of discussion provides a basis on which to build the vocabulary of art. The study of line need not be limited to drawing or painting, for line can be observed and enjoyed in architecture and sculpture, as well as in nature, when we observe cracks in a sidewalk or branches against a sky.

Shape and Mass

The term *shape* refers to the general outline of something. Shapes can be drawn with lines, painted, or cut out of paper or other two-dimensional materials. They can be categorized as geometric or natural. Geometric shapes include squares, rectangles, circles, and triangles, whereas natural or organic shapes are those found in nature, such as rocks, trees, clouds, and the shapes of animal and plant life. Geometric shapes are also found in nature, as in honeycombs, some seashells, and cellular structures. Artists such as Barbara Hepworth or Henry Moore, for example, use the natural biomorphic shapes that suggest natural forms without making specific reference to shapes that occur in nature. Also, the shape of a pyramid in silhouette is a triangle, but the same shape may exist beneath the outward form of a Madonna and Child.

Mass, as discussed earlier, is the three-dimensional equivalent of shape, although it may be found in artworks that give an illusion of mass, such as Michelangelo's paintings in the Sistine Chapel. The cube, pyramid, and sphere are the three-dimensional equivalents of the geometric square, triangle, and circle. *Mass* refers to the volume or bulk of objects in a work of art, and *space* refers to the areas that surround mass. The aesthetic effect of mass is most readily grasped in architecture and sculpture. The great mass of an office building and the delicate mass of a church spire have the power to move us in different ways. In sculpture, we can be affected by the weight, shape, and balance of the masses created by the sculptor.

Color

Because of the complexity of *color*, artists and scientists both have for years tried to arrive at a theoretical basis for its use. Feldman has noted:

> Color theory provides speculative answers to questions which are not often asked in the course of examining works of art. Some color systems seem related to the physiology of perception more than to the aesthetics or psychology of perception. Others may have evolved from industrial needs for the classification and description of dyes, pigments and colored objects. At any rate, artists work with color—pigment, to be exact—more on an intuitive than a scientific basis.[3]

In teaching children about the nature of color, the teacher may vary the methods, using intuitive approaches in the primary grades and gradually introducing color terminology and its application in the middle and upper grades.

Color is a powerful element, and it serves to emphasize the extent to which all the elements are interdependent. Although the elements have been discussed here separately, in reality they cannot be dissociated. The moment we make a mark on paper with a black crayon, line and space are involved. If paint has been applied, color is present. As soon as a shape is drawn, it interacts with the space around it. Only for the sake of convenience have we treated these elements as separate entities.

Color functions on two levels. On the cognitive level, color conveys information in purely descriptive terms, as when leaves change color in the fall, and in symbolic terms, as in flags or traffic signals. On the level of feeling (or affective level), color evokes psychological associations and thereby creates moods and feelings. As any industrial design consultant or theatre designer is aware, color affects us emotionally as well as psychologically and can be discussed in terms of the wavelengths of light as legitimately as in terms of the interaction of pigments. Indeed, so pervasive are col-

or's effects that the vocabulary of color theory can be used metaphorically in a wide variety of contexts—such as in music, when we refer to tone color, or in writing, when we speak of "purple prose."

Color also has been used symbolically within and sometimes across cultures, from early Renaissance painters to Navajo weavers. As with texture, color can be based on real events (green leaves and blue skies) or used expressively, as in the still-life paintings of Janet Fish and the landscapes of April Gornik.

The Language of Color

Scientists may define color as an effect of physical forces on our nervous system through impact on the retina. To painters, however, color is far more complex: It is a vital element closely related to all the other design elements. The sensitivity with which painters use color can convey a personal style and the meaning of a particular work. Ultimately it can influence the varied responses of viewers to a work of art.

The painter's color terminology also differs from the physicist's, whose primary reference is light rather than pigment. In art, a consistent terminology has come to be accepted as a means of discussing and using color, both in looking at works of art and in producing them. The following definitions provide some guidelines for instruction in painting, design, and the appreciation of art.

Hue is another word for color, as in the phrase "the varied hues of the spectrum." Scientifically, a hue is determined by the wavelength of light reflected from an object. As the wavelengths change, we note those distinct qualities that we call *hues*. Hues, therefore, are identifiable segments of light waves even though everyone may not see or receive them in exactly the same way. Computers have actually expanded our conception of color. Computers can generate subtle variations of color that result in an almost unlimited number of color choices for the graphic artist.[4]

To the painter working with pigment, the primary colors are red, yellow, and blue. Most children can recognize and work with the painter's primaries, as well as violet, green, and orange (secondary colors) because they can be created by mixing the primaries. The tertiary colors result from mixing primary and secondary colors and may be more difficult for children to achieve, since they require a greater control of paint (see the color wheel on page 197). The use of tertiaries can provide richer hues than the simple mixing of black and white will yield.

Value refers to the degree of darkness or lightness of a hue. The lighter a color, the higher its value; the darker the color, the lower its value. Hence, if white is added, the value is heightened; if black is added, the value is lowered. When most of the pigment is white, the resulting color is called a *tint.* The addition of black produces *shades.* Hues also may be changed by the use of a *glaze,* or a veil of thin transparent color, which is brushed over the hue. This method of changing a color was much favored during the Renaissance.

Chiaroscuro is the technique used in drawing and painting to create the effects of light and shadow in the natural world. This entails shading objects from light to dark to give the appearance of three dimensions. In Rembrandt's work, the light appears to glow from within the subject. Monet bathes his haystacks in light, and contemporary abstract painter Helen Frankenthaler uses veils of color for dramatic emotional effects. Children enjoy the vivid interaction that only opposites can provide.

Architects and sculptors control the light-and-dark composition of their work, not by mixing pigments as in painting or shading with pencil or crayon as in drawings, but by planning the way light and shadow interact. A building may be designed with deep recesses to produce shadows in contrast to a facade that catches the light, and sculptors take great pains to control the "hollows" (negative areas) and "bumps" (positive areas) they make so light and shade are used to their best advantage. A portrait sculptor, for example, in order to achieve the very dark center of the human eye, makes a deep recess that becomes dark shadow.

Intensity indicates the freedom from admixture with another color—in other words, the ultimate purity of a color. Any hue that has not been mixed with another color is considered to be at its maximum intensity. Although a color can be made more intense by the addition of another color (as in the addition of some oranges to some reds), the original color may lose its distinctive identity as mixing is carried beyond a certain point.

Complementary is a term that refers to the relationship between primary and secondary colors on a color wheel. On the wheel, these colors are in opposition to one another, as red is to green, blue to orange, and yellow to violet. The complementaries are antagonistic in the sense that neither color in a pair possesses any property in common with the other. Complementary pairs, however, are complete in the sense that together they contain all three primaries. For example, the complement of red is green, which is made of yellow and blue. Browns and blacks are obtained by mixing the three primaries in some ratio. Mixing two complementary hues has the same effect as mixing the primaries. Artists make great use of the fact that complementary pairs neutralize each other, creating a wide range of grays, which are potentially more interesting than grays composed of black and white.

Analogous colors are intermediate hues on the color wheel and may be explained to children in terms of families of color. Analogous colors can be likened to a family in which a red man and a blue woman produce a violet child. Analogous colors always get along; it is the complementary colors that often disagree.

Warm and *cool* refer to the psychological properties of certain colors. We normally call reds, yellows, and oranges warm colors, which we generally perceive as coming forward, or "advancing," in a field of color. Blues and greens are usually identified as cool and "receding" colors. The movement forward or backward of any color, however, depends entirely on its relationship to the surrounding hues. A red with a touch of blue can appear even cooler than it would by itself and, when placed next to an intense orange, may well recede behind it, while yellow with a touch of green, normally warm, will seem very cool when placed next to red-orange, which will advance. Experimentation with recession and advancement of color is of special interest to the hard-edge and color-field painters.

Color wheels, referred to in the preceding definitions, are chiefly useful as guides to understanding the terminology of color relationships. Teachers should not restrict pupils to the schematized set of relationships shown on the wheel. If color wheels have any virtue, it is to enlarge the options available to pupils, rather than narrow them.

Many art forms are produced in which color is lacking—black-and-white films, most forms of sculpture, many of the etching processes, and drawings in which black-and-white media are used. Color, then, is a complex element—at once dependent, powerful, and moving in its sensual appeal. As for the interests of children, teachers will discover that color has an appeal far in excess of the other elements of design.

Texture

Texture is the degree of roughness or smoothness of surface. Every surface has a texture; a pebble on the seashore, a veined leaf, the wrinkled face of an old man, a brick wall, and a sheet of glass all display varying kinds and degrees of texture. We derive a sensuous enjoyment from texture. We like to run our hands lightly over the surface of a tweed jacket or a fur coat; we enjoy holding a smooth stone lightly in our hands or gently stroking a baby's hair. We enjoy textures visually, too, through the sense of touch. Architects plan surface textures for visual contrast, variety, and unity, as well as for practical concerns.

Texture appeals to people for both aesthetic and sensuous reasons, although it is doubtful if the two can be entirely separated. The texture that artists use may be actual or simulated. Paper for watercolor paintings is carefully chosen for its textural qualities. Some painters create effects with gesso on a surface before painting on it with tempera or oils. The paint itself may be applied with careful regard for its textural effects. Paint applied thickly has a degree of roughness, but it can also be put on with silky smoothness. In drawing and painting, artists represent textures as well as employ them with roughened painting surfaces or impasto. Richard Estes is known for the photorealistic quality of his city scenes, in which he represents concrete buildings, plate-glass windows with reflective surfaces, asphalt pavement, shiny automobiles, brick facades, and natural textures such as foliage and grass. Sculptors work directly with textures inherent in the materials of their art. Deborah Butterfield has created a series of horses in materials ranging from plaster and bronze to sticks, mud, and wire. The materials she selects often determine the textures of the sculptures and the moods they express.

Children delight in surface qualities in drawing, painting, sculpture, and collage activities. Teachers can assist children to explore the possibilities of expression through the use of textures in their own artwork. And, teachers can help children develop visual and tactile sensitivity by discussing the treatment of texture and surface in such objects as a Japanese tea bowl, a monumental Egyptian sculpture, a Native American woven basket, a modern automobile, and paintings by Hans Hofmann (textured surface) and William Harnett (realistic illusion of objects of varied surfaces). Since texture is a major avenue of aesthetic awareness for sightless students, some museums now have a special collection of "please touch" objects that children are encouraged to handle.

Space

In art there are two types of space: actual space and pictorial space. *Actual space* is two-dimensional, as in drawings, paintings, or prints produced on flat surfaces, or three-dimensional, as in sculpture, architecture, or ceramics. Artists have learned

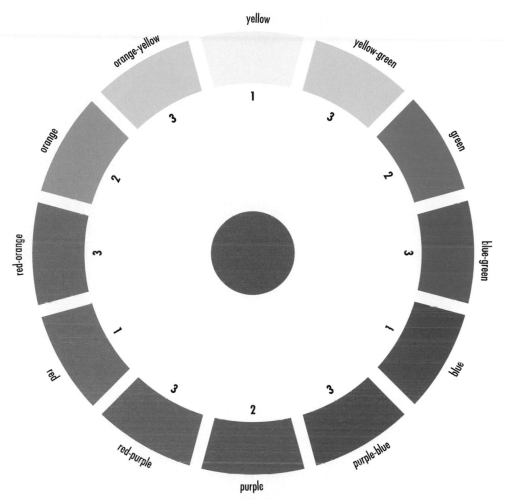

A color wheel is a useful visual aid for teaching color mixing theory with watercolor, tempera, oil, acrylic, pastels, or other forms of pigments. Students who learn about the relationships of colors (hue, value, intensity) and their effects when mixed or juxtaposed greatly enhance their technical and expressive capabilities with painting media.

to be as sensitive to the organization of space as they are to line and shape. As soon as a line or a shape is placed on paper or canvas, it sets up a dynamic with the surrounding space. When a second line or shape is added to the composition, other spatial relationships are created. Two shapes can be close together or far apart, above and below, side by side, or crowded in a corner. The possibilities multiply as each new shape or line is added to the composition.

Sculpture is three-dimensional and exists in actual space as it relates to surrounding areas. The sculptor is aware of these relationships and makes purposeful decisions to pierce

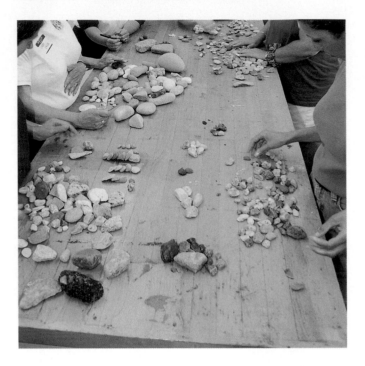

Sensitivity to the nuances of form can begin with sorting exercises such as sorting pebbles and stones for specified visual characteristics.

space with sculptural forms and to cause forms to move in space—as with mobiles or kinetic sculpture.

Pictorial space is the flat surface of the paper, canvas, or other material and is known also as the *picture plane.* On this surface artists often create the illusion of three-dimensional space. For example, a landscape picture often has a *foreground* of objects that appear near to the viewer, a *middle ground* farther away, and a *background,* such as the sky or distant hills, that is behind most of the objects in the picture. To achieve this illusion, the artist can overlap objects in the background and make them smaller than similar objects in the foreground.

Linear perspective is a system developed by artists of the Renaissance that approximates the visual phenomenon of apparently diminishing size of objects as their distance from the viewer increases. This system, which utilizes a horizon line and one or more vanishing points, is rarely learned spontaneously and usually requires instruction and practice for mastery. Pictorial space is not limited to linear perspectives and can also be created in a totally abstract and nonobjective painting through the use of shapes and colors that recede or advance.

Whatever line or shape is placed on the picture plane immediately creates a *figure-ground relationship,* in which the mark or shape is the "figure" and the surrounding area is the "ground." With three-dimensional works of art, the object is the figure, and the space behind or around it is the background, or just the ground. The placement of any figure in a pictorial space shapes the ground. Every shape and mass is surrounded by the element of space. As an example of the use of space in architecture, consider the courtyards separating the buildings in a modern housing development. Here the architect has carefully planned the amount of space that should be provided between one building and another. If the space had been planned smaller, the buildings might appear to be huddled together; if the space had been planned wider, the buildings might not appear to belong to a coherent plan.

The artist working in two dimensions must also regulate the spaces between shapes. Children can learn to appreciate these qualities when they create designs by pasting pieces of dark paper on a white background.

Tension is a design concept that does not fall easily into the categories of elements or principles. When Cezanne painted an apple on the edge of a table, his use of tension is easy for children to sense, but when portions of a work are intended to convey tenseness or a sense of straining between opposing forces, the tension is too difficult for an untrained, immature student to understand—particularly if the work is abstract.

Children should be made aware of the action that takes place among all elements of a picture, and one way to call their attention to it is by showing them how artists deal with the problem of shape and space.

THE PRINCIPLES OF DESIGN

It would be convenient to offer a formula for the production of satisfactory designs, but, of course, if designs were subject to rules and regulations, art would cease to exist. Every good design is different from every other good design, and all artists have unique ways of using the elements and principles of art.

Artists in non-Western societies may not be aware of the elements and principles as described here, but they still make use of design concepts. When an Aboriginal artist creates a bark or rock drawing, line is the dominant aspect, and when a Dogon sculptor carves rows of marching figures on a granary door, then repetition becomes an outstanding factor in the door's design. We will now discuss individually those principles mentioned earlier: *unity, rhythm, proportion,* and *balance,* in which the elements have a role to play.

Unity

We have already mentioned the integrated nature of design. We described design in terms of order and coherence, and we considered it analogous to a world of stability. These are the most obvious characteristics that result from a successful art form, whether musical, dramatic, literary, or graphic. Each element is so arranged that it contributes to a desirable oneness or wholeness. In a drawing, a line ripples across a certain area to be caught up elsewhere; shapes and spaces set up beats and measures in a kind of visual music. Colors, textures, and areas of light and shade all contribute to the orchestration of the visual pattern. This oneness or wholeness we call *unity.*

Without oversimplifying or intellectualizing a process that is largely one of feeling, we may analyze to some extent how unity is achieved in a visual design. Three aspects of design that contribute to the unity of a work of art are the rhythms, the balances, and the centers of interest established.

Rhythm

The controlled movements to be found in all good designs are called *rhythms.* They may be established through the use of any of the elements of design—lines, areas of light and shade, spots of color, repetitions of shapes and spaces, or textured surfaces. For example, in a particular work of art, a line may ripple in one direction, then undulate in another. This movement may be momentarily halted by an obstructive, brightly colored shape before it darts away elsewhere along a pathway formed by areas of light and shade. Rhythm is used by artists to give movement to the manner in which our eyes move over a work of art and to control the pace at which our gaze travels.

At least two main types of rhythm appear to occur in works of art. The first has the character of a flow and is usually achieved either by lines or the elongation of forms. (The work of El Greco is an outstanding example.) The second type has the character of a beat. An element may be used in one area of a work and repeated elsewhere, either as an exact duplication of the original theme or motif or as only an echo of it. In traditional paintings we are more likely to find reminiscences than duplications of an original motif. The undulating stripe paintings of Bridget Riley are examples of visual rhythm and visual beat. In many crafts, such as weaving or tole ware, repetition is used purely for decorative purposes.

Proportion

The size relationships within a composition refer to its *proportion.* Proportion often involves an ideal relationship that the artist strives for. Things that are "out of proportion" are often awkward or disturbing, such as an oversized sofa in a small room, a tiny painting hung alone on a broad expanse of wall, or a part of a figure or other object that is too large or small for the other parts. The ancient Greeks developed an elaborate system of proportion by which they built temples and other edifices.

> The proportions of a classical Greek temple . . . were rigidly prescribed in a formula that can be stated mathematically as $a{:}b = b{:}(a + b)$. Thus, if a is the width of a temple and b the length, the relationship between the two sides becomes apparent. Similar rules governed the height of the temple, the distance between columns, and so forth. When we look at a Greek temple today, even without being aware of the formula, we sense that its proportions are somehow supremely "right," totally satisfying. The same mean rectangle that determined the floor plan of the temple has been found to circumscribe Greek vases and sculpture as well.[5]

Some artists adhere to systems of proportion to achieve their expressive aims. Others convey ideas and feelings by distorting proportion or controlling it in other ways. To children, proportion is largely a matter of appropriate size relationships.

Balance

Closely related to the aspect of proportion in design is *balance.* When the eye is attracted equally to the various

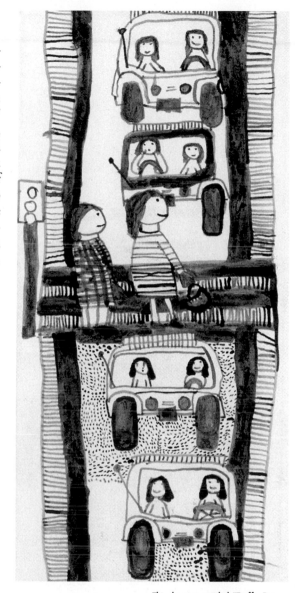

This drawing entitled "Traffic Patterns" demonstrates the student's sensitivity to the relationship between positive and negative forms. South Africa, 11 years.

imaginary axes of a composition, the design is considered to be in balance.

Many writers, particularly those associated with the postimpressionist movement, attempted to explain balance in terms of physics, usually referring to the figure of a seesaw. Unfortunately, the concept is not quite accurate, since physical balance and aesthetic balance, although related, are not synonymous. Balance in aesthetics should be considered as attraction to the eye, or visual interest, rather than as simple gravitational pull. Aesthetic balance refers to all parts of a picture—the top and bottom—and not only to the sides, as the seesaw analogy suggests. The sizes of the shapes, moreover, while having some influence on aesthetic balance, may easily be compensated and, indeed, outweighed by a strong contrast of elements. A small, bright spot of color, for example, has great visual weight in a gray area, as does an area of deep shade next to a highlight.

In many books on art there is still discussion about "formal" versus "informal" balance. The arrangement of a composition with one well-defined figure placed centrally and with balancing elements placed on either side of this center, as in a front view of a Haida totem pole, is called *formal* or *symmetrical* balance. All other arrangements are called *informal* or *asymmetrical*.

Attraction to one kind of balance or another is also dictated by the ebb and flow of artistic fashion. The history of art shows us that most civilizations (including the Hindu, Aztec, and Japanese) have gone through a symmetrical design phase. The high Renaissance prized symmetry and was followed by the mannerists, who rejected the limitations of two-point perspective. The dadaists of the 1920s and abstract expressionists of the 1950s discarded all semblance of conventional visual order; yet during the 1960s, many hard-edge painters and pop artists revived it for the simplicity and directness of its impact on the viewer. Neoexpressionist artists opt for more dynamic, informal compositions.

Broad Implications of the Design Process

It is possible to produce a design that has all the attributes of unity but is neither interesting nor distinguished. A checkerboard, for example, has a rhythmic beat and a balance, but as a design it is unsatisfactory because it is monotonous and lacks tension and a center of interest. Likewise, a picket fence, a line of identical telephone poles, and a railway track are as uninteresting as the ticking of a clock. A stone wall, however, might have great design interest because of the variety of its units. Even in a brick wall, in which shapes are similar, people generally prefer the random colors, tones, and textures found in old, used brick.

Although the perceptual process, as we have noted, seeks closure, or completeness, educated vision demands that in art, at least, a degree of complexity be attained if our attention is to be held. Every element, therefore, must be employed to bring about a desirable variety within unity.

This variety within unity is, in fact, an expression of life. Philosophers have postulated that design, or form, is a manifestation of our deepest and most moving experiences. In the designs they produce, people are said to express their relationship to the universe. In *Art As Experience,* Dewey mentioned the mighty rhythms of nature—the course of the seasons and the cycle of lunar changes—together with those movements and phases of the human body, including the pulsing of the blood, appetite and satiety, and birth

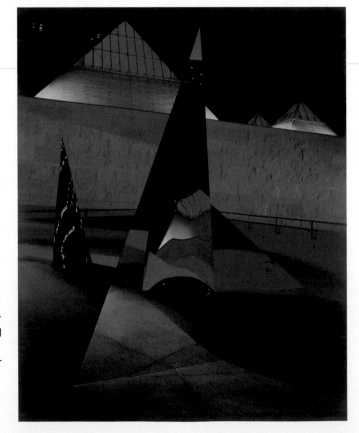

An imaginative photographic artwork depicts a work of contemporary architecture. Barbara Kasten's 1986 cibachrome photograph *Architectural Site 10* provides an exciting and colorful interpretation of architect Arata Isozaki's Museum of Contemporary Art, Los Angeles. Does this museum structure seem appropriately contemporary to house the art of today?

and death, as basic human experiences from which design may arise.[6]

Sir Herbert Read, commenting on Platonic doctrine, tells us that

> the universality of the aesthetic principle is Plato's philosophy: the fact that it pervades not only man-made things in so far as these are beautiful, but also living bodies and all plants, nature and the universe itself. It is because the harmony is all pervading, the very principle of coherence in the universe, that this principle should be the basis of education.[7]

Dewey, Plato, and Read would, then, seem to assert that the search for order, which the design impulse seeks to fulfill, is important not only for an individual's artwork but also as a reflection of that person's larger integrative relationship with life itself and can indeed be viewed as a metaphor for life.

THE ATTITUDES AND CREATIVE PROCESSES OF THE ARTIST

What do artists think and feel when they create? How do they know when their work is "right"? Views are divergent on this subject. Some artists feel that the act of designing is a feat of intellect; some hold that it is an emotional adventure. The Gestalt psychologists point out, however, that the human organism acts in totality: When people are occupied with an act of artistic expression, both their feelings (impulses) and intellect (ideas) are involved.

It is true that creative people in different art careers tend to have particular orientations: Architects and industrial designers lean toward an intellectual approach to design, whereas painters and poets generally lean toward imaginative and intuitive approaches. Nevertheless, both intellectually and intuitively inclined artists apparently alternate between feeling and thinking. "I feel that this should be done" is followed by "I think this is right," or vice versa. Thus, emotion enlivens an artistic statement, and intellect tempers it. Exactly when intellect is the dominant force in artistic acts, or precisely when feeling replaces intellect, is difficult to detect. Often, creative people themselves are unable to or refuse to analyze their approach.

In producing a design for functional purposes, such as a design for a building, a piece of pottery, or an item of furniture, designers must give some consideration to practical requirements. In such a case, designers' decisions are governed by a respect not only for the materials used but also for the purpose to which they are put. Efficiency cannot, of course, always be identical with aesthetic quality, since extreme functionalism, as required in airplanes, must place limitations on the personal choices necessary to artistic acts.

Thus, one important difference between "fine" artists and industrial or commercial designers is the amount of autonomy enjoyed by the former. Unless their work is commissioned, fine artists answer only to themselves; they are members of no team, responsible to no board of directors, and subject to no limitations of time or budget imposed by others. The blessings of freedom, needless to say, place other burdens on them, but it is through this state of freedom that artists periodically produce unique, authentic, and innovative works.

As the distinctions between categories of art continue to erode, it is possible to regard a piece of furniture as well as a painting as possessing qualities described above. Factors related to quality also have a way of eroding categories of expression. Most people, as an example, would prefer an exciting, well-designed poster (graphic design) to a tired, trite rendering of a still life.

Changing Attitudes toward Design

Art does not lend itself readily to rules and regulations, and any statement concerning principles must be outlined with caution. Should learners come to rely on the principles they have developed from their experiences to such an extent that they cease to look for new, deeper meanings in art, their thinking will become stale. Whatever universal beliefs we may hold about art must, it seems, be subject to continued revision and further inquiry. General truths about art, in short, must always be regarded in a pragmatic light. An accepted principle may seem outmoded once we have enjoyed new experiences and gained new insights into design.

The attitude toward honesty in the use of materials reflects this idea. If we were to hold to the idea that artists must respect the integrity of their materials and work from the accepted definitions of painting and sculpture, what are we to say of George Sugarman, who paints his sculpture, or of Marisol, who includes both drawing and painting in her sculptures? Should we adhere to the "rules" and reject their work, or should we keep ourselves open to the elements of surprise and amusement when confronted with such combinations? Obviously, today's children should be prepared for the art of their time, and there is no reason why their life cannot have room for both a fresco by Michelangelo and the multimedia assemblages of Betye Saar. (We must bear in mind that in the opinion of many of his contemporaries, Michelangelo violated the integrity of the human figure by distorting human proportions.)

Each learner arrives at a personal statement of principles that reflects insights born of personal experience.

THE USES OF DESIGN

The language of design as discussed in this chapter provides us with a vocabulary to talk about art more effectively. When *design* is used as a verb, as in "design a house," the term implies using the principles and elements for practical purposes (we do not say to a painter, "design a painting"). Design, in its broadest sense, deals with the organization of the elements of art for functional purposes. In the "living" or "applied" arts, design shows us its practical side. This can be better understood by studying the diagram that follows, which likens design functions to a concentric scheme, with the individual at the center and the community at its outermost layer.

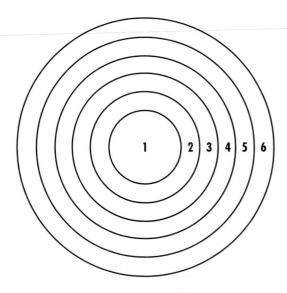

1. Individual uses: clothing, jewelry, tattoos, uniforms
2. Objects used by individuals: appliances, automobiles, tools
3. The interiors we live in: furniture, fabrics, wall coverings
4. Dwellings: apartments, houses, houses of worship
5. Neighborhoods: from established urban areas to housing developments
6. New towns and cities: Columbia, Maryland, to Brasilia

Environmental design, such as landscaping, has its own parameters and extends through circles 4, 5, and 6.

Although this book addresses the personally expressive side of art—that is, art that exists only for what it can provide by way of pleasure or intellectual stimulation—we must keep in mind that art for most people exists to serve other human needs. Something basic to our nature makes us designers. An object as simple as a toothpick has undergone so many changes that an example from the turn of the twentieth century looks quite different from one purchased today.

Of course, interesting crossovers occur from one function to another, as in one-of-a-kind buildings, articles of clothing, furniture, or jewelry that not only serve practical needs but also are cherished for their high aesthetic value. When a museum prefers to add a table by George Nakashima to its collection rather than the dozens of paintings and sculptures that have been offered, then the line that traditionally separates useful art from fine art has been blurred.

A wide range of applications of design exists, much too broad to discuss here. The following (partial) list of careers in the applied arts will provide a hint of the extent of these fields.[8]

architecture	film and television
interior and display design	theatre and stage design
graphic design	editorial design and illustration
industrial design	photography
fashion design	crafts design

Keep in mind that each of these fields of design has numerous parts and permutations involving many other careers. For example, under graphic design we will find, among others:

advertising designer	layout artist
corporate art director	letterer, calligrapher, type
graphic designer	designer
computer graphics	outdoor advertising designer
designer	record jacket designer

We will briefly discuss the fields of graphic design, design for entertainment, and architecture; the latter will be the subject of suggested classroom applications.

Graphic Design: Art for Communication and Persuasion

The means used to persuade consumers to use one product over another involve every sort of printed media, from handbills to posters and from newspapers to billboards. Sometimes graphic designers also produce public symbols promoting civic responsibility, as in the case of traffic and safety hazard signs.[9] Two goals are uppermost in the minds of the graphic designer: to communicate quickly and to find the proper match between word and image—hence, the importance of typography. Of the careers mentioned, the one that connects most closely to the task of the art teacher is that of the poster designer. The teacher must be wary that the art program not end up as a service pursuit, producing posters for PTAs, community causes, national campaigns, and school functions. One thing is clear: As long as methods of reproduction on a mass scale are available, graphic designers will produce for a mass market. The more underdeveloped the society, the lesser the need for the graphic designer.

When we consider the extent to which children as well as adults are exposed to the influence of graphic design, and the general pervasiveness of the applied arts in our lives, we can gain an appreciation of the importance of including design fundamentals in a comprehensive school art program. When young people become familiar with the principles, practices, and motives behind much of graphic design, they will, it is hoped, become more selective rather than be manipulated by such influences.

Design in the Entertainment Media

Artists and designers in the electronic media occupy a category of their own. The role played in our lives by television alone is as influential as that of graphic design. Artists in film, video, and stage design usually work in concert with other artists and technicians. In live theatre, set designers, lighting designers, and makeup and costume designers work with

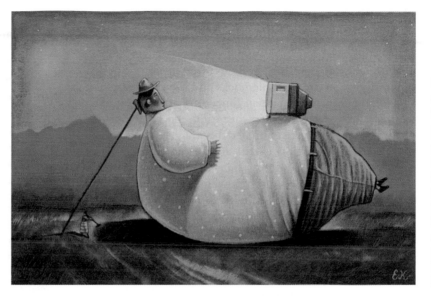

Earl Keleny, *Obesity in Men Linked to TV Viewing*, 1989, watercolor and oil on paper.

Humor and art have long been companions. This is the image of the ultimate "couch potato" (notice the spots on his shirt). Who is the woman making ready to dislodge the long pole that supports his head? What will happen then? How can art be used to convey a serious point through a whimsical image? Can you find other examples of humor in art?

writers, directors, musicians, and actors to create the final presentation. In television, advertising designers often include visual graphics, animation, music, drama, and dance in a thirty-second commercial.

The field of music videos is another example of collaboration, of how hazy the line is between the fine and applied arts. Many music videos are artworks in their own right and might become a contemporary version of the type of collaborations inherent in opera, which some view as the ultimate art form.

The applied arts, including the design areas, are often considered in different categories from the fine arts. Russia, for example, would be unlikely to hold an art exhibit on a national level without including the works of theatrical, film, and book designers. In the United States it is less likely that the work of such artists would appear in a similar situation. Illustrators and graphic designers have their own recognition and award systems that often result in yearbook publications of the best works in the various fields. The design fields in the entertainment and advertising industries each have their own cultural histories, and, because such works can be examined for their social and philosophical contexts, they have a legitimate place in a balanced art program. To include areas other than drawing, painting, and sculpture in the art program, teachers require access to visual resources, along with an adequate background of understanding of the applied arts.

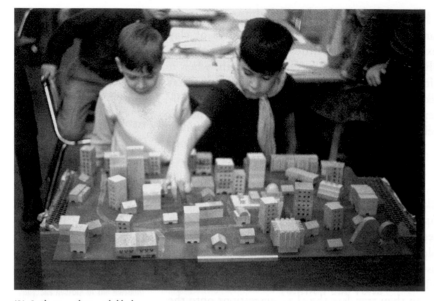

(1) Students working with blocks. Begin with group blocks to establish basic relationships among elements, such as living and commercial areas versus private spaces.

(3) Model community. For upper grades, the factor of accurate scale is dealt with, bringing art closer to mathematics. In this example, class members used the community in which they live as a point of reference. Photograph by Kay Alexander © Ken Burris, Shelburne, Vermont.

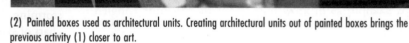

(2) Painted boxes used as architectural units. Creating architectural units out of painted boxes brings the previous activity (1) closer to art.

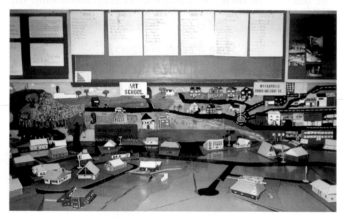

models that may be discarded after use. These can be an introduction to the use of scale and the variety of materials used in models, such as sandpaper (roofs and driveways), dyed bits of sponge (trees and bushes), balsa wood (walls), and so forth.

Homework (Historical)

Copy a facade of a building from another country or historical period and mount it on a time line. Or, ask students for small drawings and mount them alongside a map of the world with arrows leading to the point of origin.

Street Making (Brainstorming)

Have everyone bring in one box to be turned into a house. (Changes or additions to the basic rectangle may be added.) Group the boxes together, and see what it would take to turn them into a neighborhood.

Reconstruction through Memory

Ask the students to suppose they are birds flying from home to school. What would the earth look like? How many streets can they remember?

Form Analysis (Developing Critical Skills)

Show an architectural slide that is out of focus, and ask the students to use the sides of small pieces of crayon to indicate the shadow areas of the volumes of form. Increase the focus two more times and ask them to use the point of the crayon.

For all these architecture activities, see the World Wide Web Resources listed at the end of the chapter. These and other sites will provide images and information that will enrich student learning.

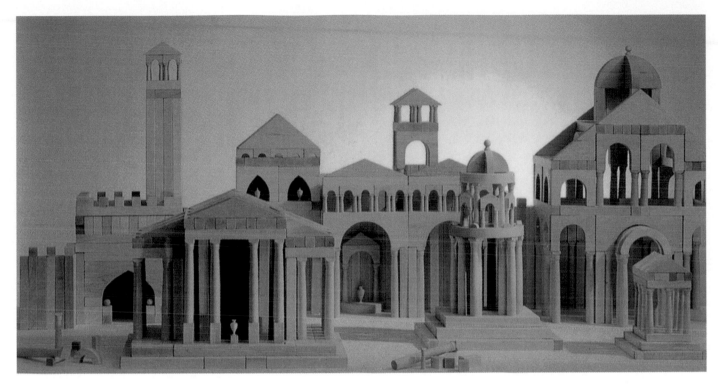

This example of an architectural "toy" shows how far designers have come since building blocks were introduced. Archiblocks and other block sets encourage improvisation of form and instill an awareness of the history of architecture.

NOTES

1. Jack Burnham, *Beyond Modern Sculpture* (New York: George Braziller).
2. Steven Heller, and Anne Fink, *Less Is More: The New Simplicity in Graphic Design* (Cincinnati: North Light Books, 1999).
3. Edmund B. Feldman, *Art As Image and Idea* (Englewood Cliffs, NJ: Prentice-Hall, 1967), Chapter 9.
4. Charles Stroh, "Basic Color Theory and Color in Computers," *Art Education* 50, no. 4 (July 1997): 17–22.
5. Marjorie Elliott Bevlin, *Design through Discovery* (New York: Holt Rinehart and Winston, 1977), p. 130.
6. John Dewey, *Art As Experience* (New York: Capricorn, 1937). See Chapter 1 in this book.
7. Herbert Read, *Education through Art,* rev. ed. (New York: Pantheon, 1958), p. 64.
8. The Consortium for Design and Construction Careers and FutureScan (see address under World Wide Web Resources). Other Internet sources provide additional information regarding the many careers in art and design.
9. Kevin Gatta, *Foundations of Graphic Design* (Worcester, MA: Davis Publications, 1991).

ACTIVITIES FOR THE READER

Activities Emphasizing Line

1. Select black chalk and a sheet of inexpensive paper, such as newsprint, measuring about 18 by 24 inches. Play some stimulating music and begin to draw a line, not to depict an object but rather to develop a nonobjective arrangement. Draw the line freely, without attempting to

produce a particular effect. Repeat the operation, but now consider the variety of the line. See that it swoops and glides, ripples and pauses. Repeat again, this time thinking of the unity of the composition produced. Play music of a completely different mood, and produce some further compositions in line.

2. Study the paintings and sculpture of such recognized masters as Picasso, Rembrandt, and Barbara Hepworth. Make a linear analysis of one of the works. Such an analysis should emphasize the main flows of line in the composition rather than copying the objects themselves. Pen and ink, soft lead pencil, and crayon are suitable media.

3. Take a small subject, such as a piece of popcorn, a bit of crumpled paper, or some nuts and bolts. Using a brush, try to blow up the detail on a sheet of mural paper that measures at least 3 by 4 feet. Consider the space between the lines and how the figure (the object) relates to the ground (the surrounding space).

Activities Emphasizing Shape, Mass, and Space

1. Cut some rectangular shapes from paper of various tones but generally neutral in color. Move these shapes on a piece of white cardboard until a satisfactory arrangement of the shapes and spaces has been found, then glue them in place. Take similar shapes, and drop them from above the cardboard so they fall in an accidental pattern. Continue this procedure until you come upon an arrangement that pleases you. Compare the "found" design with the planned one. Which do you prefer and why? Does the accident offer an element of surprise that the planned design seems to need?

2. Take toothpicks or balsa strips, and glue them together to form a nonobjective three-dimensional construction having interesting internal space relationships.

3. Using pieces of cardboard or wood scraps, make the same type of construction described in activity 2. Concentrate on the way flat planes work with internal relationships—confirming them, allowing one space to flow into another, and so on. If this sculptural approach to mass and space has caught your interest, try combining the lines of the balsa strips with the planes of the cardboard. You can further articulate your space by connecting one area to another with string and by cutting the cardboard for a colored glass or cellophane insert.

4. Work a mass of clay (at least 5 pounds) into a block. With simple tools, scoop out sections of the clay, and then note how light and shade can be manipulated. Think of mass

as "positive" areas and space as "negative." When you have established a relationship between shallow and deep areas and the surface of the clay, take a flashlight and study how the character of your work changes as the light source moves. Think of this in relation to architecture as well as to sculpture. Notice how this problem overlaps with the next category, light and shade.

5. To investigate line and space, try the "exploding" design. Divide a sheet of dark paper into sections and place the sections on white background. Observe how pulling the sections apart creates everything from a thin white line to a dominant segment of white. Do this also with curving lines that bisect the paper.

Activities Emphasizing Light and Shade

1. Paint six or seven containers found around the house (cereal boxes, tea tins, cigar boxes, soup cans) a single unifying tone of white. Group these before you on a table, and draw them with black chalk on gray paper, using white chalk for the planes that attract the light. Let the color of the paper play through for middle tones, and reserve the white and black for the extreme values. Try one view with the flat side of your chalk and another with the point, carefully building your tones by massing strokes and lines.

2. Place the three pieces of sculpture produced to illustrate problems of mass and space in the path of a strong light. Manipulate them until the shadows and highlights on the objects themselves, together with the shadows cast from one object to another, form an acceptable unity. Observe the pattern of the shadows behind the sculpture.

3. Project a slide of a group of buildings on a sheet of light paper. Forget you are dealing with buildings, and fill in the image with dark and light patterns. As a follow-up, take your sketch outdoors, and see if this exercise in concentration on pattern and mass and light and shade has aided you in seeing (and drawing) an actual building.

Activities Emphasizing Texture

1. Cut pieces from printed pages that utilize various kinds and arrangements of type. Paste the pieces on cardboard or paper so an interesting textural arrangement is developed.

2. Roll out a slab of clay, and cut it into various shapes—square, round, rectangular, triangular. Create textural patterns on the surface by pressing found objects (coins, scissors, nuts, wood scraps) into the clay. With

softer materials, such as sponge, burlap, combs, and string, make patterns even closer to the surface. Use your imagination to think of items other than the ones suggested.

3. Crumple a piece of paper, and spray it with black paint from one angle only. Let the paper dry, and press it flat. Notice the startling dimensional quality of the texture.

4. Create a collage that changes texturally in one direction from glassy smoothness to extreme roughness. Feel it with your eyes closed, and compare it with those of your classmates. Vary the feel by adjusting the size and location of your textural samples. Visually disabled children will enjoy touching these.

Activities Emphasizing Color

1. Paint freely with a large brush, noting the apparent changes in hues as one color is placed next to another. How do the adjacent colors affect each other? Cut out various-sized windows in black paper, and move them about your painting, noticing the variety of possible compositions and color interactions.

2. Dampen a sheet of heavy white drawing paper and drip tempera paint or watercolors so different hues run and blend. Note the new colors so formed.

3. Join the class in bringing in a swatch of color you think is red. When placed next to one another, the swatches of reddish paper, paint, and cloth will produce a surprising range of tone and value in a subtly modulated monochromatic collage. Try other colors as well, including black and white. Notice in each case how the surface texture contributes to the effect of the color. Each week, choose a particular "color."

4. Cut out six squares of any single color and paste on them circles of six different colors. Notice how each of the circular background colors changes the nature of the constant foreground color. Is color a fixed entity, or does it have relative characteristics?

Activities Emphasizing Function and Adequate Use of Materials

1. Collect for study pictures of families of similar objects, such as automobiles, chairs, yachts, and kitchen equipment. Compare one brand with another from the point of view of function. How does a Porsche, for example, compare with a Cadillac or a Toyota in this respect? What concessions have the manufacturers made to style at the expense of function? Why have they done so? To what

extent are they justified in doing so? Start a scrapbook that concentrates on the most poorly designed products.

2. Find a number of objects in which a certain material has been processed to resemble another, such as cardboard to resemble leather or plastic to look like woven cloth. Why has the manufacturer resorted to such practices? What are the opinions of designers and critics about them?

Other Activities

1. *Emphasizing analogies:* Take a photo of an actual familiar object, and draw a different object that the first one appears to resemble. For instance, a fence may remind you of teeth, a fireplug of a robot, and a rock of a loaf of bread.

2. *Emphasizing positive and negative patterns of dark and light:* Draw a group of shapes of common objects, such as scissors, tableware, or an ink bottle, that overlap. Where the forms overlap, switch back and forth from black to white, so the objects are fragmented and the viewer becomes engaged in reestablishing the form of the object.

3. *Emphasizing variety within a single form:* Select any geometric shape as a working module. Using any medium you like, create an arrangement based on your shape, obtaining variety in the design by adjustment of the size or color of the shape, by overlapping, and by other effects.

4. Gather as many images as you can from the media that can indicate the design categories discussed. What examples are the most difficult to obtain? Industrial design? Illustration? Theatre design?

5. After watching the credits at the conclusion of a film, make a list of every job title you feel is art-related.

6. Watch any situation comedy (including commercials), and list every art-related career. Eliminate these from the show, and try to imagine how it would appear.

7. List some of the kinds of graphic design that are part of the world of the child.

Activities for Studying Architecture

1. *Exercising preference and judgment:* What is the least attractive building in the community? The most attractive? Is there a very ugly building in your town? What makes a building ugly?

2. *Guests:* Most cities have a branch of the AIA (American Institute of Architects). Branches often have an educational committee with volunteers who will talk to a class that requests them.

3. *Aesthetic decision making:* Suppose you had a certain amount of money to build an arts center. If you started

from scratch, you would have everything you need. If you restored an old factory, you might have to make some compromises in parking, flow of visitor traffic, or desirability of location. What factors would influence your decision?

4. *Imagining:*
   a. Design a tree house for a private hideaway.
   b. Plan a children's center so attractive in appearance and function that no one can resist attending it.

   c. A room of your own is being added to your apartment or home. What will it offer in the way of convenience of work or leisure, hobbies, and so on? What will it look like? Draw each wall separately on cardboard, then stand them vertically on a clay base.
   d. Design a doghouse or a birdhouse using a historical period or culture as a model: classical, Victorian, or thatched hut.

SUGGESTED READINGS

Carpenter, William, and Dan Hoffman. *Learning by Building: Design and Construction in Architectural Education.* New York: Van Nostrand Reinhold, 1997.

Conway, Hazel, and Rowan Roenisch. *Understanding Architecture: An Introduction to Architecture and Architectural History.* New York: Routledge, 1994.

Dyson, Anthony. *Looking, Making, and Learning: Thinking about Art and Design in the Primary School.* London: Beekman Publishers, 1989.

Frohardt, Darcie Clark. *Teaching Art with Books Kids Love: Teaching Art Appreciation, Elements of Art, and Principles of Design with Award-Winning Children's Books.* Golden, CO: Fulcrum Publishers, 1999.

Glenn, Patricia Brown, and Joe Stites, illus. *Discover America's Favorite Architects.* New York: John Wiley and Sons, 1996.

Johnson, Mia. "The Elements and Principles of Design: Written in Finger Jello?" *Art Education* 48, no. 1 (1995): 57–61.

Klaustermeier, Del. *Art Projects by Design: A Guide for the Classroom.* Englewood, CO: Teacher Ideas Press, 1997.

Marschalek, Douglas. "A Guide to Curriculum Development in Design Education." *Art Education* 48, no. 1 (1995): 14–20.

Miller, Anistatia R., and Jared M. Brown. *Graphic Design Speak: A Visual Dictionary for Designers and Clients.* Cincinnati, OH: North Light Books, 1999.

Prince Claus Fund. *The Art of African Fashion.* The Hague; New Trenton, NJ: Prince Claus Fund; Africa World Press, 1998.

Riggs, Jennifer. *Architecture and Construction: Building Pyramids, Log Cabins, Castles, Igloos, Bridges and Skyscrapers. Scholastic Voyages of Discovery.* New York: Scholastic, 1995.

Thorne-Thomsen, Kathleen. *Frank Lloyd Wright for Kids: His Life and Ideas.* Chicago: Chicago Review Press, 1994.

Ulrich, Karl T., and Steven D. Eppinger. *Product Design and Development.* New York: McGraw-Hill, 1995.

Wong, Wucius. *Principles of Form and Design.* New York: Van Nostrand Reinhold, 1993.

———. *Principles of Color and Design.* 2d ed. New York: Van Nostrand Reinhold, 1997.

WORLD WIDE WEB RESOURCES

Design

Think Quest, Inc. *Understanding Color and How It Affects Your World.* 1999. <http://library.advanced.org/50065/color/index.html>
This site examines the properties, theories, meanings, and effects of color and the role it plays in our lives. It offers a cross-curricular approach by making connections between the art, the science, the psychology, and the sociology of color.

ArtsEdge: J. F. Kennedy Center. "Design Arts." *Curriculum Studio.* <http://artsedge.kennedy-center.org/cs/desarts. html>
Classroom resources and lessons on design.

Architecture

ArtsEdNet: The Getty's Art Education Web Site. "Cultural Heritage Sites: Teaching About Architecture and Art." *Lesson Plans & Curriculum Ideas. ArtsEdNet: Resources.* <http://www.artsednet.getty.edu/ArtsEdNet/Resources/Maps/Sites/>

An innovative tool for teaching students about the architectural, artistic, and cultural context of the following cultural heritage sites: Pueblo Bonito in Chaco Canyon, New Mexico; the Sydney Opera House in Australia; Katsura Villa in Kyoto, Japan; the Great Mosque in Djenné, Mali, Africa; and Trajan's Forum in Rome, Italy.

The Consortium for Design and Construction Careers and FutureScan. *I Want to Be an Architect.* 1999. <http://www.futurescan.com:80/architect/>

This Web site is designed to inform young people about the art and science of architecture and its related fields. The site features interviews with architects and discusses a variety of projects. Related links are included.

Artifice, Inc. *The Great Building Collection.* 1997–1999. <http://www.greatbuildings.com/gbc.html> Great Buildings Online documents hundreds of buildings and leading architects with 3D models, photographic images, and architectural drawings, plus commentaries, bibliographies, and Web links, for famous designers and structures of all kinds. Loaded with information.

The Getty Center for Education in the Arts. "Spaces and Places: An Introduction to Architecture." *Discipline-Based Art Education: A Curriculum Sampler,* 1991. Online Version Available ArtsEdNet: The Getty's Art Education Web Site. <http://www.artsednet.getty.edu/ArtsEdNet/Resources/Sampler/>

This curriculum unit examines some of the many factors that influence the design of architecture, including environmental, emotional, cultural, and personal effects.

Foundation for Architecture in Philadelphia. *Architecture in Education.* 1996–1999. <http://www.whyy.org/aie/>

AIE's mission is to help young people understand what it takes to make buildings and communities work for the people who live in them. This Web site is designed primarily for educators and features projects and activities related to teaching children about architecture. Lessons include: Mapping the Community; Designing a Native American Village; Designing a Community Ten Years in the Future; Architecture around the World; and Culture and Community.

SiliconGraphics. *CitySpace.* 1999. <://www.cityspace.org/> *CitySpace* is a virtual city environment built collaboratively by kids, educators, and media artists across the Internet. This innovative site uses technology to promote interactivity and creative problem solving.

CUBE: Center for Understanding the Built Environment. *Architectural Activities.* <http://www.cubekc.org/architivities.html>

This site provides information for educators about architectural design, preservation, and planning. Teachers can adapt curriculum for any grade level. Among the curriculum units are Box City; Frank Lloyd Wright; and Women in Architecture.

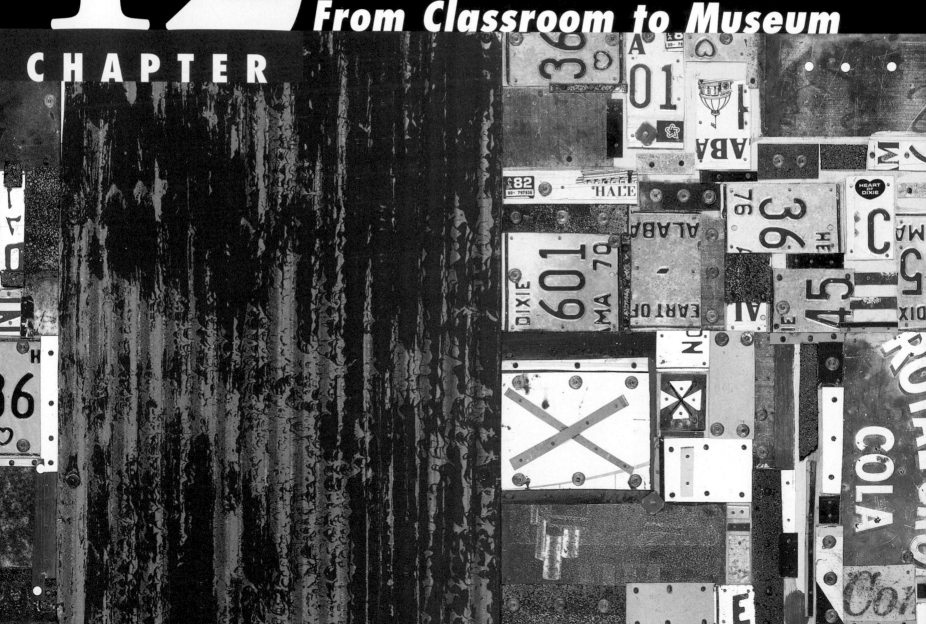

12

CHAPTER

ART CRITICISM
From Classroom to Museum

What a joy and relief to hear art discussed in terms of qualities and values instead of fashion, personalities, or auction sales records! To see it analyzed as a human activity involving the full range of mankind's passions and delights. To have it acknowledged not so much as something beautiful or valuable to own, but as an infinitely varied mode of expression, as one of humanity's finest and most effective ways of communicating and sharing.[1]

—Theodore Wolff

Up to this point, we have considered problems arising from creating art forms. We must now turn to another aspect of art education, that of developing the pupils' appreciation of art through critical skills. The purpose of this chapter is to move the aesthetic response of a child from a "glance" to more sustained engagements.

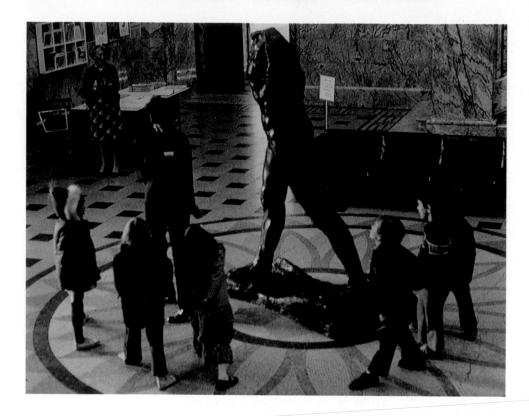

THE NATURE OF ART APPRECIATION AND CRITICISM

Art appreciation, although an outmoded term associated with the picture-study movement of the early 1920s, still has some validity. The word *appreciate* means "valuing" or having a sense of an object's worth through the familiarity one gains by sustained, guided study. Appreciation also involves the acquisition of knowledge related to the object, the artist, the materials used, the historical and stylistic setting, and the development of a critical sense. If we accept the fact that critics as well as artists can be models for artistic study, we must think about how critics operate. There are journalistic critics who write for the general public and who avoid the more profound level of writing, and there are critics who work for art journals who are knowledgeable in history and aesthetics and use language in such a way that criticism itself becomes an art form. The goal of all critics is the same: to provide the readers with information regarding an artist or an exhibit and, beyond that, to help the readers to increase their understanding by viewing art through the informed eye that good critics are assumed to possess.

A good way to understand the phases of criticism is to read an art review to see how the reviewer goes about discussing either an exhibition or a single work.

If we study excerpts from the following review, we can gain a clearer idea of the kinds of content that occupy critics. The painting under discussion is Vincent van Gogh's *The Starry Night.* Key passages have been selected from the review to distinguish four phases of discussion: descriptive, analytical, interpretative, and historical. The *judgment* about the work's quality is implicit in the critic's choice of this painting. We begin with a statement by the artist, van Gogh, which provides historical context.

> *Historical:* "I devour nature ceaselessly. I exaggerate, sometimes I make changes in the subject, but still I don't invent the whole picture, on the contrary I find it already there; it is a question of picking out what one wants from nature."[2]

In a discussion of the painting, we find illustration of the other three modes of critical approach to the artwork.

> *Descriptive:* "Look at van Gogh's painting, *The Starry Night.* You can easily recognize village, trees, moon, stars; but clearly this is not the point."
>
> *Analytical:* "We can point to certain qualities of the brushwork and relate them to the impact of the total work. The individual strokes are 'rough,' they vary, although they hold to a definite scale or size. . . . These patterns are in themselves dynamic and they are insistently repeated."
>
> *Interpretative:* ". . . you are at once impressed by a grand, almost hypnotic rhythm which binds all the representational elements together into a kind of cosmic unity . . . van Gogh lays bare his very act of painting and it is partly through the suggestion of his physical activity that we share his emotion."[3]

When we utilize a knowledge base in art, we deal with information surrounding a work (names, dates, places), as well as facts concerning physical details taken from the work itself (subject matter, media, colors). Knowledge also includes those concepts of design, technique, and style that the teacher feels can enable the student to "read" a painting. Being able to recognize these factors in an artwork begins in our natural, untrained powers of perception but requires guided experience in order to make them operable.[4]

Appreciation can begin in a spontaneous, intuitive reaction, but it does not end there. One way to arrive at a deeper level of response is to understand the difference between looking and seeing, and, in order to do this, we can employ a process used by professional art critics, as illustrated in the review cited here. The goal of the critical phase of the larger appreciative process is to be able to respond more fully to an artwork and to defend one's opinion regarding it.

Knowledge, however, is not a precondition for deriving pleasure from works of art—if it were, people would not collect African or Asian art or anything else about which they know little but which nevertheless has the power to capture and hold their attention. Although we can be drawn to a cathedral because of its sense of grandeur and its use of light, knowing that the use of the exterior flying buttresses is what creates the passage of light through stained-glass windows or being aware that lives have been lost as churches collapsed before buttresses were conceived is historical knowledge that can enhance our appreciation and heighten our initial intuitive response. The role that historical information and other forms of knowledge play in our responses is also an authentic issue and is dealt with more fully in Chapter 13.

Criticism as part of the broader issue of appreciation focuses our attention more intensely on the kinds of knowledge that can be obtained from the object itself rather than on the circumstances that surround it. There is probably much truth in the old saw about "a picture judging a person" rather than the reverse. What a person is emotionally, intellectually, and socially will determine the nature of his or her appreciation. Although this ability seems to be built around innate qualities, so that some of us are able to acquire it more quickly than others, as teachers we must assume that art appreciation can also be the result of education.

One German literary critic sums it up as follows:

> Criticism ranges from journalism to scholarship, and in rare moments of glory, it becomes literature in its own right. Above all, the task of criticism is to *mediate*. The critic stands between author (artist) and reader (viewer), mediating between art and society. In this regard his function is primarily educational. The objection often made in regard to the critic—that he has a touch of the schoolmaster—is absolutely justified. Whom do critics wish to instruct? . . . The critic wants to instruct the readers, to point out to them what is good and why it is so. By the same token this means that a critic is obliged to point out what is bad and why.[5]

Postmodern Perspectives for Criticism

In his book *Postmodern Perspectives: Issues in Contemporary Art,* Howard Risatti emphasized the plurality of approaches common in postmodern criticism.[6] Among the most promi-

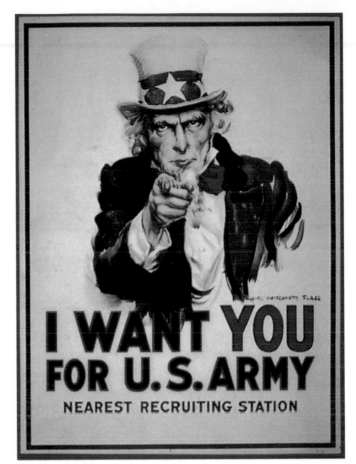

James M. Flagg, "I Want You," recruiting poster. This classic recruiting poster has a firm place in American history. Children can learn about the events that led to the creation of this poster, its use during World Wars I and II, its place as an American icon, and how images become icons. They can interpret the emotional qualities of the image and what ideas it conveys, and they can debate whether this image should be considered art. Evaluation in a balanced art program will consider children's progress in art production, and their learning of concepts and skills from art history, art criticism, and aesthetics. (National Museum of American History, Smithsonian Institution)

nent approaches we find traditional formalist criticism, feminist criticism, ideological or Marxist views, and psychoanalytical criticism based on concepts originating with Sigmund Freud's work. A good deal of emphasis is placed on the context of the work: when, where, and how the work was created, its function within the culture of origin, relationships with other prominent works or movements in art, and values of the society from which the work emerged. The study of context includes details of influential events in the artist's life that might shed light on his or her artistic creations.

In addition to these four prominent approaches to art criticism, numerous others can be pursued, including economic, religious, technical, and other perspectives, each of which might illuminate our understanding of the work(s) in question. Postmodern approaches lend credence, as well, to the views of individuals as they bring their unique backgrounds of experience to the encounter with art. Criticism becomes

TABLE 12-1   A Comparison of Past and Present Methods of Developing Appreciation through Critical Skills and Art History

Past	Present
Rarely went beyond immediate reactions to a work of art.	Defers judgment until the art object has been examined.
Instruction was primarily verbal and teacher-centered.	Instruction may be based on verbalization, contextual and perceptual investigation, studio activity, or combinations of these.
Relied primarily on reproductions.	Utilizes a wide range of instructional media—slides, books, reproductions, videos, films, and, most important, original works of art, visits to museums and galleries, and visits from local artists.
Based primarily on painting, because of its "storytelling" qualities.	May encompass the complete range of visual form from fine arts (painting, sculpture) to applied arts (industrial design, architecture, and crafts). May also include print media, television, advertising, films, and magazine layouts.
Used literary and sentimental associations as basis for discussion. Concentrated on such elements as beauty and morality to the exclusion of formal qualities and social issues.	Bases discussion on formal qualities of the artwork. Recognizes beauty and other sensuously gratifying qualities as only one part of the aesthetic experience; also recognizes abrasive and shocking images as legitimate expressions of psychological and political motives.
Neglected the contributions of women artists and representatives of growing minority populations, such as African American, Hispanic, and Asian.	Utilizes references to the past; shows respect for artistic efforts of all epochs. Strives for gender balance. Is no longer exclusively Western European in its sources.
Spent much time in anecdotal accounts of artist's life.	Minimizes life of the artist and concentrates instead on the work in its societal context.
Concentrated on a "great works" approach, to the exclusion of "lesser" works that have a special contribution to make.	Adopts a broader view of art objects and can include craft, illustration, media, or industrial arts, and comic books, as well as fine arts. Plays down "great works" approach.

more democratic and less authoritarian than was perceived in the writings of modernist critics, such as Clement Greenberg and Harold Rosenberg, whose writings helped to establish abstract expressionism as the dominant art movement in the United States following World War II.

TEACHING METHODS TO DEVELOP CRITICAL SKILLS

The freshness, honesty, and directness that characterize the artwork of primary pupils, and the imaginative and intuitive capabilities of most children on the elementary level, combine to provide a positive learning climate for their critical-appreciative activities. The increased verbal skill of children in the upper elementary grades can also compensate

for the self-consciousness some may feel in certain studio activities and can often provide highly verbal children with an opportunity to excel in activities that are not studio oriented.

When we ask children to verbalize, to use linguistic as well as visual forms of expression, we are using skills developed in the language arts program for our own ends. While children may engage in art activities for an hour a week, they will have had two hours of reading and writing on a daily basis since the first grade. *Critical activities are the meeting ground between art and language arts, and it is because of the students' familiarity with the latter that they take so readily to applying language to the understanding of artworks.*

An extraordinary amount of nonsense has been perpetrated in many classrooms through formal lessons in art appreciation, in which irrelevant questions are asked about certain works of art. When the questions become artistically remote from the work and include sentimental or literary ideas—"Isn't she a pretty little girl?" or "Do you think she is happy?" or "Why isn't she wearing shoes? Will it rain?"—critical understanding can never occur. Such questions simply lead the children away from the essence, the inner life of the work, into irrelevant and distracting directions. Perhaps the most compelling argument for using a phased approach to discussing art is that it is an effective means of keeping children in the presence of artworks for longer periods than is normally allotted—usually a matter of seconds.

Studio Involvement

Critical skills also can be developed in close relationship to art activities. According to this method, a teacher seizes every practical opportunity to introduce the subject of appreciation, not only of drawing and painting, but also of three-dimensional work, such as sculpture, pottery, and architecture. This studio- or activity-centered method is based on the belief that one should not divorce expression from appreciation. When working with a medium, we become conscious of the problems, needs, and goals that have influenced our own expressive acts.

In commenting on the reciprocity between the creative and critical processes in television art instruction, Manuel Barkan and Laura Chapman stated:

> The most sensitive making of art cannot lead to rich comprehension if it is not accompanied by observation of works of art and reflective thought about them. Neither can observation and reflection alone call for the nuances of feeling nor develop the commitment that can result from personal involvement in making works of art. The reciprocal relationship between learning to make art and learning to recognize, attend to, and understand art should guide the planning of art instruction.[7]

The Phased Approach to the Critical Act

The method that follows is a form of analysis related to the distinctions critics make in writing about art. Awareness of formal structure requires children to be acquainted with the components of artworks and the teacher to be sensitive to children's perceptual, linguistic, and creative capabilities. It includes processes whereby students may engage in studio, historical, and critical activities, gaining relevant information

while discussing works of art, and suggests deferring judgment and interpretation until the work has been examined and discussed.

One of the goals of critical activity is the development and use of the language of art. Children will not compare a photorealist work and a van Gogh in terms of "painterly" textures unless this term has been pointed out to them. Even fourth graders are capable of such distinctions if their attention has been directed specifically to nuances of surface, or if they have been brought to discover it for themselves. Consistent examples should be selected for art terms that you expect children to learn.

Description

Although the descriptive level focuses on aspects most of us generally perceive commonly, it can also lead to some heated discussions, since what you see as red, your neighbor may see as orange; one person may see square shapes, another trapezoidal. In any case, it is through description that we make language more precise.

From the middle grades on, the teacher should make a distinction between *objective* description, items with which no one will disagree (such as a house, two people walking, a sky that takes up more than half the space, etc.), and *personalized* or *evocative* description ("sloppily" painted may be described by someone else as "loosely" painted, and the color

Criticism is an extension of Chapter 11 (Design) in that the language of art should be applied when discussing artworks. The example shown is the entrance to an exhibition centered around the term *texture*. Each rubber glove contains different contents of varying textures ranging from soft (fur and water) to hard (sand, gravel, pebbles, etc.). Participants literally shake hands with many variations of the same concept. (Ruth Youth Wing of the Israel Museum)

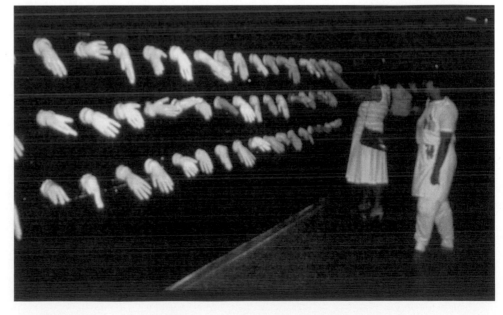

red may appear as more orange to another). A scientist may describe a horse by Delacroix as a four-legged quadruped; a critic or a poet may note its "noble bearing" or observe that it "moves like the wind." Evocative description usually involves adjectives. It can be imaginative in nature, and, although it should be encouraged, students should be made aware of the difference between the two approaches.

The descriptive level can be made more interesting if it is personalized or treated as narrative. Taking inventory in a purely objective, detached way of what we see can seem mechanical and devoid of human association. Something quite different happens to the process when one's observations are personalized through prefacing with a sentence such as, "As I entered the room (or 'walked down the street'), I was surprised to see . . ."[8]

Formal Analysis

Although formal analysis also has a perceptual basis, it takes the descriptive stage a step further by requiring the child to discuss the structure or composition of an artwork. The child who can distinguish between symmetry and asymmetry, identify the artist's media, and be sensitive to the qualities of color and line can discuss the form of an artwork or how it is put together. This is the stage in which the teacher discovers whether the children can use the language of design discussed in Chapter 11.

Once students are able to identify elements and principles, they can move on to search for the ways in which the

José Clemente Orozco, *Zapatistas*, 1931. The striking contrasts of light and dark in this work can be a starting point for a discussion of ends in painting. Related terms for the students to learn here are *contrast, repetition, diagonal, stylize, selective realism,* and *rhythm.* (Collection, The Museum of Modern Art, New York. Given anonymously.)

elements of art (or design) interact. A student can easily point to a circle of red, but may not be aware of the role the circle plays in relation to the rest of the composition.

The discussions initiated at both descriptive and formal-analytic stages bring about that intense, sustained visual concentration necessary for the critical act. They also set the stage for the development of the interpretation that follows. Description and analysis do not accept premature judgments, requiring, instead, that the student defer certain opinions until they can be handled with that degree of detachment we call "distancing." When we "distance," we put a temporary hold on our emotions and our judgments.

Interpretation

In the interpretative stage, the student moves to more imaginative levels and is invited to speculate about the meaning embodied in a work or the purpose the artist may have had in mind. To do this, the child is asked to establish some connection between the structure that can be discerned and the direction in which the artist is taking him or her. For example, if the class has agreed that Orozco in his *Zapatistas* used sharp contrasts of dark and light and strong directional forces, the question that follows is, "To what end?" Would the meaning have been as clear had the artist used the more delicate colors and softer brushwork of impressionism? At this point, the class is getting at the painter's use of compositional elements for a specific end—in *Zapatistas,* compositional elements reinforce Orozco's attitude toward the revolution in Mexico. How does Renoir's sensuous and pleasing color relate to *his* feelings regarding motherhood and courtship? How do de Kooning's fragmented shapes and strident colors tie in with his attitudes regarding certain types of women? Such questions characterize discussion in the interpretative stage, which is open—a time and place without right and wrong answers.

Judgment and Informed Preference

The critical process normally ends with a judgment—that is, a conclusion regarding the success or failure of an artwork and its ranking with other artworks. Judgment, in this sense, will not be discussed because it is more the province of professional critics and connoisseurs than elementary students. Judgment, in the mind of a child, is synonymous with preference. A child's opinion regarding the position of Dürer's etchings in the canon of graphic art would not be terribly enlightening, but the same child's defense of personal acceptance or rejection of Dürer's work should be encouraged, provided such opinions are open to discussion and have relevance to the preceding critical phases.

It is useful to recognize the distinction between preference and judgment in response to works of art. Preferences are not subject to correction by authority or persuasion since one's personal liking or disliking of an artwork is an aspect of one's individuality. Such reactions as "like/dislike," "it stinks," and "wow" are psychological reactions and by their very nature discourage further discussion. Judgment, however, is subject to argumentation and persuasion. For example, a person might be convinced, on the basis of nutritional evidence, that asparagus is a fine food but still dislike asparagus.

When someone makes a statement such as, "That is a very strong painting" or "That is a poor example of raku pottery," it is reasonable for someone else to ask, "Why do you say that?" and request some justification for the judgment. If the justification is weak or controversial, then the floor is open to discussion. One goal of critical activity is to move students from closed to open minds, from instantaneous preference to a state of deferred judgment.

It is perfectly reasonable to say, "I know this drawing is not of high quality, but I like it nevertheless." Conversely, it is appropriate to remark, "I know this is an excellent sculpture, but I really don't like it." In most instances, however, we are more apt to like a work of art if we understand it and have spent some time with it. In most cases we prefer works that we judge to be of high quality to those that we judge to be of low quality. Another goal of art appreciation is accepting that preference and judgment are not finite, that they can change over time. Even the greatest critics maintain their personal likes and dislikes. We find, however, as we learn more about art, that our tastes change and expand as our acceptance of artworks increases.

The stage of informed preference is the culminating and most demanding phase of formal criticism. It invites students to render their opinions regarding the worth of an object, provided their opinions are based on what they have learned in the previous stages. Such questions as the following are asked: "Are you moved by this work of art?" "How do you feel about it?" "Would you like to own it or hang it in your room?" "Does it leave you cold?" "Do you dislike it?" "Why?" Most viewers instinctively begin at the level of preference: The process of criticism as set forth here attempts to *defer preference until the matter has been given sustained thought and attention.*

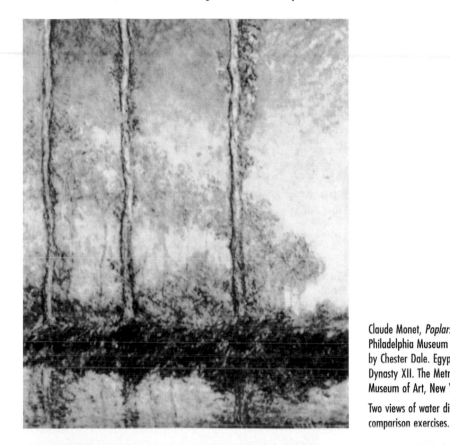

Claude Monet, *Poplars,* 1891. Philadelphia Museum of Art, given by Chester Dale. Egyptian fresco, Dynasty XII. The Metropolitan Museum of Art, New York.

Two views of water discussed in the comparison exercises.

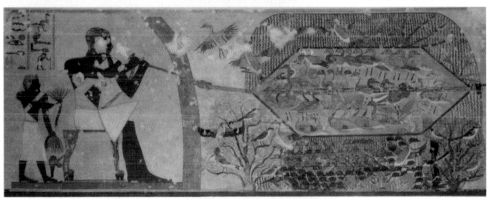

Children view criticism as a visual-verbal game and will participate with enthusiasm if the discussions are not too lengthy (a half-hour seems to be an outside limit). Works with strong color, interesting subject matter, and a clear compositional structure seem to elicit the most positive responses.

STUDENT: Above—we're above it.

DR. A: How about the ducks?

STUDENT: You're in front of them.

DR. A: Good. Then we might say that in one way the Egyptian artist used his space and subjects with a lot more freedom than the other artist. But what does the impressionist painting offer us instead of different points of view in the same picture?

STUDENT: You can see more . . . more details . . . more real . . .

DR. A: Would you agree with me that there are many ways of being "true"; that the Egyptian painting shows us the way we know things to be and the impressionist more the way we are likely to react?

TABLE 12-3	Sample Questions Utilizing the Terminology of Art	
Terminology	**Painting**	**Question**
Depth	*The Last Supper* (Leonardo da Vinci)	In this wall painting, what gives you the feeling of depth? A. The direction of the lines in the construction of the room. B. The strong and bright colors. C. Both A and B.
Paint Quality (Technique)	*Lady with a Parasol* (Auguste Renoir)	The edges of the objects in this painting are *mostly*: A. Unclear and fuzzy. B. Sharp and exact. C. Both A and B.
Line Quality	*Killed in Action* (Käthe Kollwitz)	We can describe the line in this print as: A. Delicate and soft. B. Strong and bold. C. Both A and B.
Meaning	*Killed in Action* (Käthe Kollwitz)	Which statement *best* describes what is going on in this print? A. A mother is resting with her children. B. A mother is expressing misery in front of her children. C. A mother is playing with her children.
Style	*Zapatistas* (José Orozco)	The style (the artist's own way of painting) of this picture is called: A. Realism (looks lifelike). B. Selective realism (partly real). C. Abstract (unrecognizable shapes).
Composition	*Poplars* (Claude Monet)	The trees dominate this painting. Monet makes them stand out by: A. Emphasizing the texture of the trees. B. Making the trees large and placing them centrally in the picture. C. Focusing attention on strong vertical shapes.

Applying a Discovery Method

In the teacher's follow-up on the lesson, Dr. Ackerman's ideas were used to lead the children to discover a basis for criticism for themselves. The children were shown four reproductions and asked to name the differences they could detect among the works. The paintings were Raphael's *Madonna and Child,* Kollwitz's *Killed in Action,* de Kooning's *Marilyn Monroe,* and Kandinsky's *Improvisation 28.* The children began by agreeing that the four pictures had easily definable differences. As these were noted, the teacher wrote them on the blackboard in columns, according to whether they related to materials, subject, meaning, form, or style. When the children's powers of observation were apparently exhausted, the teacher wrote the category headings above the columns, pointing out that what the class had really done was create its own critical system or categories of discussion (see Table 12-2, page 221). Such an ordering of concepts demonstrated to the children that there were many ways to discuss works of art. Instead of providing them with answers *before* the discussion, the teacher sought to elicit responses by posing questions that centered on a single conceptual problem—the ways artists differ in their work (see Table 12-3). In order to deal with such a problem, the children had to engage in such conceptual processes as ordering, comparing, classifying, and making generalizations.[10]

During this discovery discussion, the teacher translated the naive vocabulary of the class into an art-centered vocabulary, adding important characteristics that were missed. This discussion laid the groundwork for lessons that followed. The "materials" column provided the background for a visiting artist to demonstrate the difference between oil and watercolors; the "meaning" classification prepared the class for a lesson in comparison of styles, in which they were shown a variety of paintings, each with a different stylistic approach to the same theme. Let us now note other activities that can develop art appreciation.

WORKING WITH LANGUAGE

Begin by listing art terms that are to be learned by lesson, by unit, and by year, and try to avoid using any word unless it has a clear equivalent in an artwork. This can be accomplished with students at any age, as long as the concepts can be clearly illustrated in an artwork. Once having learned a word, students should be expected to use it from then on, whenever it is exemplified in work under discussion.

New critical language also provides the teacher with a way to evaluate learning. The following words suggest three levels of complexity. Terms may overlap categories and can include formal qualities, subjects, media, and even emotional states or qualities of feeling.

Level I: Lower Elementary

portrait	shape	contrast	sketch
still life	color	paint	sculpture
landscape	line	art	contour
cartoon			

Level II: Middle Elementary

abstract	watercolor	assemblage	composition
realism	pastel	collage	shading
nonobjective	print	contour	texture
modeling	repetition		

Level III: Upper Elementary and Middle School

style	agitated	technical	symbols
proportion	balance	expressive	theme
perspective	dominance	emphasis	genre
crosshatch	subject	gradation	fantasy
pattern	formal	variation	painterly

Teachers can construct their own lists of terms, suggesting increasing complexity, sequenced instruction, and cumulative learning. After a word is learned on one level, it is then added to the ones on the next. This also opens the door to making variations of key words. As an example, the author showed a group of seventh graders a reproduction of a painting by Jackson Pollock and asked someone to point to the presence of lines. The immediate reaction was to deny the existence of lines. The class was urged to keep looking until the use of line was detected. Within a few minutes, it was discovered that Pollock used several ways of creating lines; he dripped, he brushed, and he painted them. Pollock's method was then related to his general approach to painting, which, in turn, emerged as a key to understanding the movement known as abstract expressionism. One term—*line*—thus provided an entry into a major style of this century, or, to put it another way, the *microcosmic* opened the door to the *macrocosmic*.

Word Matching

Number every word on the vocabulary list on a piece of cardboard with one side cut like an arrowhead. Hand each student a vocabulary card, and have him or her place it on or close to the matching section of a large reproduction. (Use Velcro or felt backing or a tack to keep it in place.) Or, place the reproduction on the lip of the chalkboard, and have students write the new terms on the board, using color-coded chalk to keep categories separate (red for formal elements, blue for principles of design, white for expressive characteristics, and so on).

Visualizing Words Relating to Feelings

Write the following words on cards, and distribute them randomly: angry, nervous, quiet, and joyous. Each student then creates a drawing, painting, or piece of sculpture that conveys the essence of the word. On completion, display them, and ask the class if they can recognize the words. If the words are sufficiently varied, this should be simple.

The next question is: What do the "quiet" words show us that "angry" words do not? The final task is to see how the mood of the word is reflected in art. (The teacher can select the words from the reproductions that happen to be on hand.)

Dreaming Artworks

To get the imaginative juices flowing, ask each student to select a painting from an array of examples and write a few paragraphs beginning with the sentence: "Last night I had the strangest dream."

One variation is to have the class respond to the same artwork. This will call attention to students' individual responses. "Dreaming" can be used in classrooms with art reproductions, but it is more effective with original works in museums or galleries. Younger children who cannot write can participate in an oral version of this activity.[11]

FURTHER SUGGESTIONS FOR STUDY
The Artist of the Week

A lesson need not take up the full art period. An effective learning situation can occur in five to ten minutes. Each art class could begin with an introduction to the "Artist of the

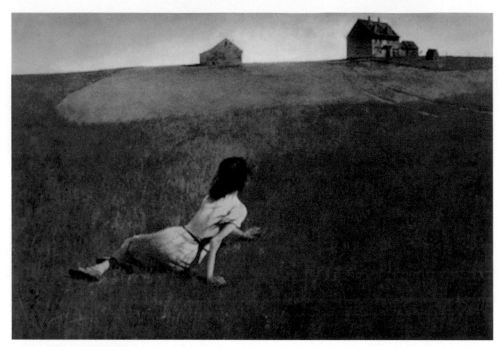

Andrew Wyeth, *Christina's World,* 1948. Tempera on gessoed panel, 32 1/4″ × 47 3/4″. The Museum of Modern Art, New York, purchase.

Questions of interpretation the teacher might pose: What is Christina's relaionship to the house? Does it mean something special to her? Does her position on the ground or her infirmity bear on these questions?

Week," the teacher providing some interesting information about the artist and his or her work, posing some questions of a descriptive, analytical, or interpretive nature, and displaying the picture as part of an expanding exhibit.

Thematic Displays

Teachers can teach critical skills visually as well as verbally by displaying works that are connected to each other in some way. For example, three photographs of sculptures are placed on the bulletin board: the head of an Egyptian, an African, and an Aztec. After the pictures have been on display for a few days, the teacher asks, "What have you learned by looking at these sculpture heads?" Discussion might include concepts of sculpture, the idea of portraiture, differences in style, similarities, and interpretations.

Connecting with Studio Activity

As previously mentioned, whenever possible, teaching for art appreciation should take place in conjunction with studio art projects. When students are working on a visual or technical problem in their own art, they are more receptive to learn-

ing from other artists who have confronted similar problems. For example, children are working on a collage, and several are using pictures and fragments of pictures from magazines. They might be shown collages by Braque and Bearden and the story quilts of Ringgold.

Aware of their apparent interest in fantasy, the teacher shows the children pictures of works by artists who specialize in fantasy, such as Dali, Magritte, Klee, or Kahlo. Children can thus gain empathy by explicitly trying what artists have tried. In another example, the teacher's goal is to help the children understand why the impressionists are called "painters of light"—that is, why and how they captured so much sunlight in their work and why their colors are "broken" rather than "solid." The teacher takes the students outdoors on a sunny day to do landscape pictures with craypas. The children are encouraged to capture the colors they see in sunlit areas. When they return to the classroom, they discuss how working outdoors is different from working in the classroom. Then they view and discuss the impressionists' works a second time and share insights.

It is through a studio experience that students can role-play the artist. Although copying is not creative, it can enable a student to empathize with an artist's technique and expressive content. An attempt to duplicate a drawing by Seurat can for the moment place the student in Seurat's presence.

WORKING FOR TOTAL GROUP INVOLVEMENT

Instruments of Engagement and Evaluation

Teaching for the critical phase of appreciation, however, poses distinct problems. The role of dialogue has already been mentioned; although verbalizing about art is central to criticism, nonverbal activities also must be considered. Since children vary in their inclinations and abilities to speak about art, class discussions are too often dominated by the articulate and outgoing students. Moreover, since there is rarely enough time for each member of the class to give his or her opinion, several verbal and nonverbal instruments (task sheets) are described that suggest how to achieve total class involvement. Each sheet should be related to what may reasonably be expected of children in the area of art appreciation, and each of the instruments attempts to reach one of four goals:

1. To enable the children to discuss artworks with a knowledge of art terminology and to be able to identify the design, meaning, and media as these elements function in particular works of art.
2. To extend the students' range of preference or acceptance of artworks.
3. To sharpen or refine the students' powers of perception of visual elements in artworks.
4. To develop the students' ability to speculate, to imagine, and to form a hypothesis based on what has been observed.

Statement Matching

One way a teacher can involve a full class in working toward the first goal is to have them respond to multiple-choice questions while they progress through a series of slides or reproductions. The questions should be based on the terminology and concepts the teacher deems valuable. Notice that some questions given are purposely more open-ended than others to permit more extended discussion after the test. Thus, as the children see their first Wyeth painting, the teacher may want to emphasize the uses of composition and placement of objects:

> This painting is called *Christina's World.* You notice that the artist has used a high rather than a low horizon line (point to line). Now study it carefully. If you think he did it because the house just happened to be located there, put down *A.* If you think he did it because it allows for more space between the girl and the house, put down *B.* If you think he did it because it would look that way if the scene were photographed by a camera, put down *C.* All right, how many put down *A? B? C?* How many put down more than one reason? Paul, I notice you didn't raise your hand at all—can't you decide? Mary, you voted for *B.* How about trying to convince Paul why you voted that way?

Formal Analysis

Another way to involve the whole class in identifying components of design is to give each child a reproduction or photocopy of the same painting and a sheet of tracing paper. The

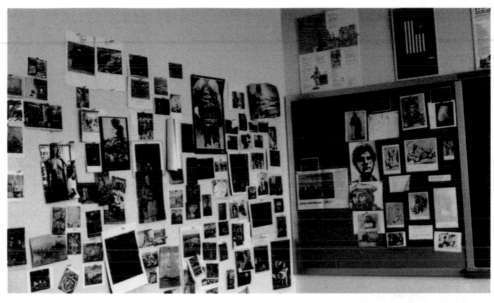

One section of a room can be designated as a picture wall to provide the teacher with a ready reference for comparisons, identification of artists, styles, subjects, and art vocabulary. The picture wall can be assembled from museum cards, magazines, or commercially prepared reproductions. It should be used flexibly, from making comparisons and creating connections to studying cross-cultural and chronological contexts.

paper is placed over the reproduction, and the class is asked to seek out and define such compositional devices as balance, center of interest, directional movement, and "hidden" structure. This method of searching for what lies beneath the form of a subject or composition will be most effective if first demonstrated on an overhead projector.

A variation of this method is to project a slide of an artwork on mural paper or on the chalkboard. The teacher begins by chalking a directional line directly on the projected image. Every child must then come up and add his or her own "invisible" line, such as a triangular shape of a mountain in a Chinese landscape or a prominent curve in an O'Keeffe flower painting (colored chalks may be used to make the final effect more vivid). When the lights are turned on, the class is confronted with the "skeleton," or substructure, of the work, which has been reduced to an abstraction of the original.

If children trace around a subject, they "lose" and must return to their seats to wait for the next round. The final result will show the relationship between the abstract structure hidden from view and realistic forms that are first seen.

A Pre- and Post-Preference Instrument

In order to assess the degree and nature of change in children's preference of artworks, the teacher can use a simple assessment based on all the slides and reproductions to be used dur-

of works, such as hands, background, portraits, handling of light sources, and so on. Many times just one work can provide enough information for study. For example, Flemish tapestries have a great variety of types of clothing that can be copied, counted, and compared. Although such inventorying is considered a lower order of learning, while students are involved, they will note other parts of the work.

Museum Treasure Hunt

The Impressionists
Rooms 7 and 8

CAN YOU FIND IT?

Can you find each of these in the paintings of the impressionist artists in Rooms 7 and 8 of the museum? As you find each one, write the name of the artist and the title of the painting in which it appears.

1. A black top hat _____

2. A yellow flower _____

3. A lighthouse _____

4. A newspaper _____

5. A green parasol _____

6. A sky full of stars _____

7. A hat with fluffy blue feathers _____

8. A broom _____

9. Water lilies _____

10. A mandolin hanging on the wall _____

A "treasure hunt" or study sheet that students can use to independently observe artworks in a gallery or museum.

- Ask everyone to bring a sketchbook, and assign one or two exercises based on work done in class. If you have taught action drawing, ask students to draw a complex composition in a free, loose, gestural style. In the case of sculpture in the round, draw it from three different points of view.

- Try to have enough funds to purchase for all students one postcard at the end of the visit that they have selected for themselves. This will put them in the position of thinking before selecting. Ask them to look at their postcard just before going to bed and to make it the first thing they see on awaking. After a week, ask them to draw it from memory.

- Ask the students to suppose a fire started. Which work(s) would each one save? Why? Ask them to suppose they had a choice of saving that work or the life of a vandal who had slashed and smashed artworks just before the flames engulfed the gallery. Which would they save and why?

- Prepare a study sheet or visual "treasure hunt" based on the example shown to the left and give each student a copy to work on independently.

- Select a painting that suggests a narrative (some element of storytelling) and ask the students: "What happened before and after this particular moment?"

- Have students pretend they are describing a work to someone who is blind. Have the rest of the class turn their backs to the work or blindfold them. What happens when a visual experience is transformed into a verbal record? Do this at least three times, and note how the descriptive process gains in acuteness.

- Ask the children to imagine what the portraits might say to each other at night when the lights go out and the guards depart.

- Interview the subject of a portrait.

- Visit the museum in advance of the class visit, and learn one story (usually from mythology or history) related to a particular work; tell the story to the class later in the presence of the art object. This advance visit should also include information of historical interest.

- Employ word associations by placing a pile of words lettered on large (6-by-12-inch) pieces of paper in the middle of the floor. Have each student pick up two or three and place them on the floor by the work that he or she feels is the most appropriate. Use such words as *realistic, abstract, nonobjective, hot, cold, active,* and *quiet.* Base words on vocabulary studied in class.

- Find out the estimated value of one of the museum's most precious works. Ask students why they think it costs so much. What would this amount buy in the non-art world? A Porsche can cost $85,000. How does that relate to the $17 million that Jasper Johns's work brought in 1989? What are the social and political issues related to the economics of art?
- Describe a journey that is suggested by a representation painting, perhaps a landscape or interior. (Where would you enter and where would you exit?) Emphasize the senses by asking students what they are seeing, hearing, smelling, and feeling on their journey.

Museum Resources

Many contemporary art museums provide excellent programs, materials, and support for school art programs. Here are some examples:

- The Museum of Fine Arts, Boston, is particularly mindful of students with disabilities who wish to visit the museum. Their publication *Stories in Art: A Resource for Teachers of Young People with Disabilities* provides meaningful suggestions that will assist teachers during the museum visit and in the classroom.[14]
- The Smithsonian Office of Education offers *Museums and Learning: A Guide for Family Visits,* aimed to assist families and teachers who plan to visit any of the fine Smithsonian museums in Washington, D.C. Another periodical publication, *Art to Zoo: Teaching with the Power of Objects,* features in one issue "Landscape Painting: Artists Who Love the Land."[15]

- The J. Paul Getty Museum in Los Angeles welcomes students and teachers. The museum's educational resources division produces interpretive materials, including printed publications, a random-access CD-ROM audioguide, the museum orientation film, and videos to orient school groups in their classrooms before they visit.
- The Brandywine River Museum in Pennsylvania features the work of the Wyeth family of artists in its collection of American art. The museum's *Family Guide: A Museum Activity Book* offers suggestions and activities intended to enhance the experience of children and adults during their visits.[16]
- The Denver Art Museum is visitor friendly and offers a range of school and teacher programs. One interesting program is the "Sleepover for 8–12-year-olds." Children are asked to "make your way through the museum by snooping out works that show how artists have fun. Get crazy at this far-out sleepover, and solve the mystery of the missing art."[17]
- A three-year exhibition at the Art Institute of Chicago was mounted especially for the 200,000 children who visit the museum each year. The publication *Telling Images: Stories in Art* presents the story of the exhibition and how it was created.[18]
- The Museum of Contemporary Art in Los Angeles offers *Contemporary Art Start®,* a curriculum-based education program that introduces contemporary art and culture to elementary- and secondary-school students and teachers.[19] Like those of many art museums around the country, many of MOCA's materials are published in two languages.

These examples are typical of art museums in many cities and towns around the country. Millions of children, young people, teachers, and parents visit the nation's art museums each year for learning and enjoyment.[20]

NOTES

1. Theodore Wolff, "Encounter with Committed Teachers Renews Faith in the Value of Art," *The Christian Science Monitor,* September 8, 1989.

2. John Rewald, *Post-Impressionism from van Gogh to Gauguin* (New York: Museum of Modern Art, 1956), p. 218.

3. Leonard Freedman, ed., *Looking at Modern Painting* (New York: W. W. Norton, 1961), p. 17.

4. For an excellent book of art criticism essays, see Theodore Wolff, *The Many Masks of Modern Art* (Boston: The Christian Science Monitor, 1989).

5. Marcel Reoch-Ranicki, in an interview for Lufthansa's *Germany* magazine, vol. 33 (February 1988), p. 26.

6. Howard Risatti, *Postmodern Perspectives: Issues in Contemporary Art* (Englewood Cliffs, NJ: Prentice-Hall, 1998).

7. Manuel Barkan and Laura Chapman, *Guidelines for Art Instruction through Television for Elementary Schools* (Bloomington, IN: National Center for School and College Television, 1967), p. 7.

8. Presenting students with open-ended sentences is a useful teaching strategy as well as a means to elicit personal responses for purposes of assessment.

9. Dr. James Ackerman is former chair of the department of fine arts, Harvard University. Because of the length of the tape, excerpts have been interspersed with descriptions of what occurred. This discussion emphasizes the point that art critical skills are employed by many art professionals, including, in this case, an art historian.

10. As mentioned in Chapter 1, educators are seeking ways to engage children in higher levels of thinking. Critical and philosophical discussions about works of art are occasions for such thinking. See, for example, David Perkins, *The Intelligent Eye: Learning to Think by Looking at Art* (Los Angeles: J. Paul Getty Trust, 1994).

11. The authors are indebted to the education department of the Art Institute of Chicago for this activity.

12. See Appendix B at the end of this book for addresses of companies that produce films, videos, and other art teaching resources.

13. André Malraux, *The Voices of Silence* (Princeton, NJ: Princeton University Press, 1978), p. 13.

14. Division of Education and Public Programs, *Stories in Art: A Resource for Teachers of Young People with Disabilities* (Boston: Museum of Fine Arts, 1999).

15. Wilma Prudhum Greene, *Museums and Learning: A Guide for Family Visits* (Washington, DC: Smithsonian Institution, 1998); and "Landscape Painting: Artists Who Love the Land," in *Art to Zoo: Teaching with the Power of Objects* (Washington, DC: Smithsonian Institution, March/April 1996).

16. Brandywine River Museum, *Family Guide: A Museum Activity Book* (Chadds Ford, PA: Brandywine Conservancy, 1996).

17. Family and Kids Programs, Denver Art Museum, 100 West 14th Ave. Parkway, Denver CO 80204.

18. Jean Sousa, *Telling Images: Stories in Art* (Chicago: The Art Institute of Chicago, 1997).

19. The Museum of Contemporary Art in Los Angeles, *Contemporary ArtStart®, a Curriculum-based Education Program* (Los Angeles: MOCA, 1999).

20. Mary Ann Stankiewicz, ed., Special Theme Issue: Art Museum/School Collaborations, *Art Education* 51, no. 2 (March 1998).

ACTIVITIES FOR THE READER

1. Clip an example of art criticism from the newspaper and paste it on a sheet of paper, allowing at least three-inch margins. Indicate in the margins the various ways the critic deals with the subject, such as historical, descriptive, analytic, interpretative, judgmental, or formal.

2. Outline some teaching procedures for helping fifth-grade children to appreciate each of the following:
   a. a mural by a well-known painter;
   b. the design of a frying pan;
   c. the design of living-room curtains;
   d. a wood sculpture by a well-known artist

3. Create a visual reduction game by collecting about twenty reproductions and dividing them into subcategories. Directions for such a game might read as follows:
   a. Divide this group of reproductions into two piles, one nonobjective and one realistic.
   b. Now divide the nonobjective pile into two more piles, one emphasizing line and the other solid masses.
   c. Divide the realistic group into two sets, one sentimental in nature and the other aesthetic.

4. In Emile Zola's *L'Assommoir*, the author describes the first visit to the Louvre by a group of working-class Parisians

in 1875. Art critic Linda Nochlin, in discussing this passage, intersperses Zola's writing with her own comments. (The italics are from Zola.) "The little group, an amusing spectacle for the artists and regular museum-goers, *trailing all the hand-me-downs of poor people's fashions,* trouped dutifully through the endless halls of the great palace of art. They were somewhat taken aback by the Assyrian Gallery and thought the statues very ugly: nowadays a good stonecarver could do a lot better job than that. . . . *It was with great respect, walking as softly as they could, that they entered the French Gallery.* In the Gallery of Apollo, they were amazed at the sheen of the floor, as shiny as a mirror; in the Salon Carré . . . some of the less-mannerly wedding guests tittered at the naked women, especially impressed by the thighs of Antiope . . . *a jumble of people and things in glaring colors began to give them a headache. . . . Centuries of art passed before their bewildered ignorance, the fine rigidity of the early Italians, the splendor of the Venetians, the sleek and sunny life of the Dutchman. But what interested them the most were the copyists, with their easels set up in the midst of the people, painting away undisturbed.*

. . . Little by little, the new visitors began to lose their enthusiasm. . . . The wedding party, tired out and losing their respect for things, dragged their hobnailed shoes along, clattering over the sounding floor with the noise of a herd in confusion. . . . For relief, their guide led them to Rubens' *Kermesse,* before which the women screamed and blushed and the men pointed out the dirty details. . . . At last, in complete rout, lost and terrified, they found a doorkeeper to *take them in charge and show them the way to one of the doors. Once in the courtyard of the Louvre . . . they breathed again. . . . All the party affected to be very much pleased to have seen it all.*" Questions for consideration: Could this passage be used in a school curriculum, and if so, in what way? If you wanted to see how consistent the reactions and behaviors of Zola's viewers were with those of today, how would you go about comparing the two groups?

5. How would it be possible to describe an abstract painting to a blind person? Find examples of abstract paintings in contrasting styles, for example, one of Barnett Newman's minimalist stripe paintings and a colorful painterly work by Joan Mitchell.

SUGGESTED READINGS

Anderson, Tom. "Defining and Structuring Art Criticism for Education." *Studies in Art Education* 34, no. 4 (1993): 199–208.

Anderson, Tom. "Toward a Cross-Cultural Approach to Art Criticism." *Studies in Art Education* 36, no. 4 (1995): 198–209.

Archer, Michael. *Art since 1960.* London: Thames and Hudson, 1997.

Atkins, Robert. *Art Speak.* New York: Abbeville Press, 1997.

Barrett, Terry. *Criticizing Art: Understanding the Contemporary.* Mountain View, CA: Mayfield, 1994.

Broude, Norma, and Mary Garrard, eds. *The Power of Feminist Art.* New York: Harry N. Abrams, 1994.

Danto, Arthur Coleman. *After the End of Art: Contemporary Art and the Pale of History.* The A. W. Mellon Lectures in the Fine Arts, 1995. Princeton, NJ: Princeton University Press, 1997.

De Oliveira, Nicolas, Nicola Oxley, and Michael Petry. *Installation Art.* London: Thames and Hudson, 1994.

Feldman, Edmund. *Practical Art Criticism.* Englewood Cliffs, NJ: Prentice-Hall, 1993.

Gablik, Suzi. *The Reenchantment of Art.* New York: Thames and Hudson, 1991.

Getty Center for Education in the Arts. Viewer's Guide by Michael D. Day. *School Museum Collaboration: Episode A: "A Focus on Original Art"; Episode B: "Interacting with a Contemporary Artist."* Video. Santa Monica, CA: Getty Center for Education in the Arts, 1995.

Guerrilla Girls. *Confessions of the Guerrilla Girls.* New York: HarperCollins, 1995.

Hurwitz, Al, and Stanley Madeja. *The Joyous Vision: A Source Book for Elementary Art Appreciation.* Englewood Cliffs, NJ: Prentice-Hall, 1977. Concentrates on methods of teaching art criticism and examples of units of instruction.

Lippard, Lucy. *Mixed Blessings: New Art in Multicultural America.* New York: Pantheon Books, 1990.

Nochlin, Linda. *Women, Art, and Power and Other Essays.* New York: Harper & Row, 1988.

Risatti, Howard. *Postmodern Perspectives: Issues in Contemporary Art.* Englewood Cliffs, NJ: Prentice-Hall, 1998.

Wolff, Theodore F. *The Many Masks of Modern Art.* Boston: The Christian Science Monitor, 1989.

WORLD WIDE WEB RESOURCES

Art Critics and Art Criticism

New York Times. *Arts* (*Daily Arts and Arts and Leisure*). <http://www.nytimes.com/yr/mo/day/artleisure/> Art criticism of current exhibitions and art; extensive archive.

University of California, Berkeley. Berkeley Art Museum/Pacific Film Archive. *MATRIX*. 1999. <http://www.bampfa.berkeley.edu/exhibits/matrix/matrix.html> *MATRIX* is an ongoing exhibition program at the Berkeley Art Museum/Pacific Film Archive, created as a showcase for the newest, most innovative, and inspirational art. The online exhibition provides commentary by curators, critics, and art historians. The archive covers twenty years of contemporary art and commentary.

Teaching Resources and Curriculum

Erickson, Mary. "Critics and Collectors: African American Art." *Worlds of Art*. 1999. <http://www.artsednet.getty.edu/ArtsEdNet/Resources/Worlds/index.html> *Worlds of Art*, developed by art educator Mary Erickson, takes an innovative, interdisciplinary approach by using the Internet to bring art into classrooms. This curriculum is multicultural and comprehensive. Students learn about art critics and perform their own criticism in "Critics and Collectors: African American Art."

Marmillion, Valsin A., et al. *Art Education in Action*. Santa Monica, CA: The Getty Center for Education in the Arts, 1995. 5 videocassettes. Video Footnotes by Michael D. Day. Each video features an aspect of DBAE curriculum, developed and taught by classroom teachers. The video series provides a model for comprehensive curriculum as well as a model for exemplary teaching. Footnotes elaborate on and explain lesson content and teaching methodology.

Online version is available at *ArtsEdNet: The Getty Art Education Web Site*. 1999. <http://www.artsednet.getty.edu/> See the following episodes from "Lesson Plans and Curriculum Ideas" for art criticism content:

"Integrating Art History and Art Criticism." <http://www.artsednet.getty.edu/ArtsEdNet/Resources/Aeia/history-vf.html>

"Interpreting Contemporary Art: Mona Lisa: What's Behind Her Smile?" <http://www.artsednet.getty.edu/ArtsEdNet/Resources/Aeia/interp-lp.html>

North Texas Institute for Educators on the Visual Arts. *Curriculum Resources: Art Criticism*. 1995–1999. <http://www.art.unt.edu/ntieva/artcurr/crit/index1.htm> Comprehensive curriculum resources for classroom teachers and art educators. Art criticism units include: art criticism activities, instructions on using art reproductions in the classroom, instructions on using Internet resources, and museum activities.

Pacific-Bell, Knowledge Network Explorer. *Eyes on Art: A Learning to Look Curriculum*. 1998. <http://www.kn.pacbell.com/wired/art2/> Comprehensive and interactive, this lesson follows a DBAE framework and is well written.

Publications

The State University of New York at Stony Brook. *Critical Review*. 1998. <http://www.creview.com/> *Critical Review* is an electronic magazine devoted to writing on current art exhibitions in the United States. It includes reviews and critiques of exhibitions by such artists as Bill Viola, Frank Stella, and Cindy Sherman. *Critical Review* has no ideology outside of a desire to present well-written reviews and to provide a meaningful context for thoughtful discourse. Readers may send in their own comments to the discussion board, and there is an archive of previous reviews. The electronic journal publishes a wide range of viewpoints, including those by younger critics as well as more established writers.

Critical Review hosts the journal *Art Criticism: A Journal of Contemporary Writing*. This journal can be accessed through *Critical Review*'s home page.

Dobbs, Stephen Mark. *Learning in and through Art: A Guide to Discipline-Based Art Education*. Los Angeles, CA: The Getty Education Institute for the Arts, 1997. Available

"Reading Room and Publications." *ArtsEdNet: The Getty Art Education Web Site*. 1999. <http://www.artsednet. getty.edu/> For art criticism, open *Learning in and through Art*. Open "The Disciplines of Art," and select "Art Criticism."

13

ART HISTORY
Other Times and Places

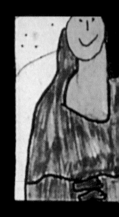
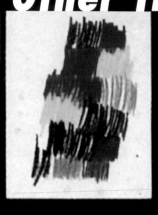
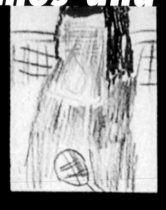
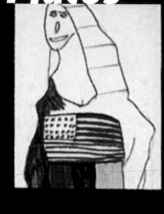
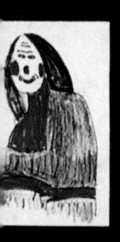
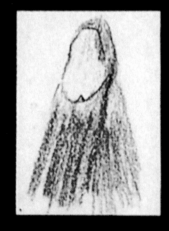
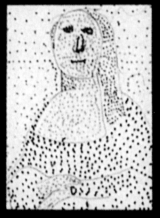
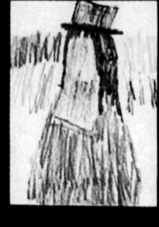
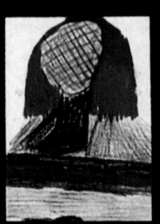
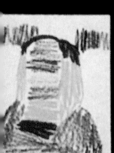
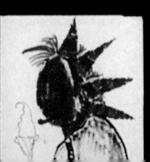
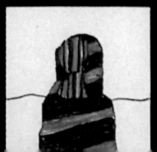
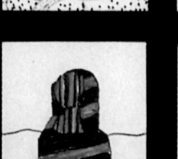
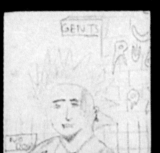
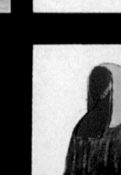

Art history is a keystone enterprise in making the visible legible.[1]

—Donald Preziosi

The first account of art history, at least in the Western world, was written by the Florentine architect and painter Giorgio Vasari, whose contemporaries included the great Italian artists Raphael, Andrea del Sarto, Leonardo da Vinci, and Michelangelo, with whom he was well acquainted. Vasari tells the story of how he happened to undertake the task of writing *Lives of the Artists.* He was involved with a painting commission for the church in Rome under the patronage of Cardinal Farnese. In the evenings he would often join the cardinal for dinner and conversation with other men of arts and letters. During these evenings the idea was initiated that a catalog of all the artists and their works would be a marvelous possession of great interest, and it was suggested that Vasari, who had for years filled his notebooks with drawings of great art and notes about the artists, undertake the project. Vasari wrote:

> This I readily promised to do, as best I could, though I knew it was really beyond my powers. And so I started to look through my memoranda and notes, which I had been gathering on this subject since my childhood as a pastime and because of the affection I bore towards the memory of our artists, every scrap of information about whom was precious to me.[2]

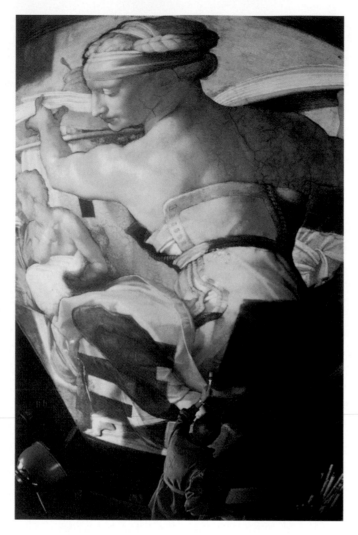

A highly trained art conservator cleans the figure of the *Libyan Sibyl,* part of the great fresco painting by Michelangelo on the ceiling of the Sistine Chapel in the Vatican, Rome, 1508–1512. The entire mural was cleaned of years of grime, candle smoke, and air pollution, revealing colors more bright and vivid than anyone had imagined. Conservators applied all the scientific and artistic knowledge and skill at their disposal to assure that the masterwork would not be harmed in any way. Photo © Nippon Television Network.

With this book Vasari began a tradition that has been multiplied in importance, complexity, and participation by thousands of professional art historians, many of whom share Vasari's love of art and affection for the memory of great artists. As we can see from the quote at the beginning of this chapter, the contemporary field of art history ranges far beyond the scope of Vasari's relatively simple beginning. Art historians today employ technical tools from the physical sciences and methods of inquiry from the social sciences that were unknown in the sixteenth century.

Vasari wrote of the lives of Italian painters, sculptors, and architects from Cimabue, born in 1240, to Michelangelo, who died in 1564. Art historians today study art and artists from all continents of the world, from a multitude of cultures, and from a range of art modes, including printmaking, ceramics, decorative arts (including furniture design), and photography, cinema, and video, which have emerged only during the past century.

ART HISTORY CONTENT: A BRIEF SURVEY OF WORLD ART

The intent of art history, especially as we approach it in art education, is to provide information and insights that will enlighten our understanding and appreciation of artworks and their significance and meaning. Often this means learning about the peoples and cultures from which the artworks came and the purposes of the art within those cultures. Art historians have studied the art of the world created not only since Vasari's time but also back into prehistory and the several thousand years of Sumerian and Egyptian culture. One of the contributions of art historians has been their categorization of art into styles and historical periods, providing us with conceptual handles to grasp meaning and significance in the art we see. We find art history organized in numerous ways, each of which presents a different emphasis and provides a different insight. For example, art historians have studied and written about art according to periods (the Middle Ages, the age of baroque), styles (romanticism, cubism), cultures (Egyptian, Native American), religions (Christian, Islamic), locations or countries (royal Benin art, art of the Andes), themes (the figure, nature), purposes (images of authority, imaginative art), and other categories. More recently the field of art history has broadened to include approaches that emphasize cultural, political, economic, and social issues. New insights are also gained from writers who employ post-Marxist, feminist, and psychoanalytical methods and perspectives. Educators can follow and benefit from this range of approaches and should adapt different approaches for different educational goals.

The following very brief survey of world art is only a suggestion of the vast and rich content for the study of art. It is necessarily incomplete and simplified and is included here to demonstrate the range of content for systematic study appropriate for children in a regular art program. The massive body of world art from prehistory to contemporary times can be almost overwhelming for curriculum organizers. Questions of emphasis, theme, culture, mode, period, works, and artists for study become very difficult when every decision to include one item means the elimination of many equally valid competing items. The scope and balance of art content from different cultures and times might vary according to local resources, populations, and educational goals. The traditional emphasis on Western European art in North American schools has evolved in many locations to a more balanced study of the arts from many cultures. Recognition of excellence in art contributions from many cultures seems appropriate for a democracy with a multicultural population. Some teachers believe that art history should begin in their own communities, with the buildings and monuments that exist in the immediate world of the students.

This survey has been organized according to historical periods often used by art historians: the ancient world, the classical world, the Middle Ages, Renaissance and baroque, the modern world, and contemporary art. Because of the great complexity of art and its relationship to culture, this system of organization, like any other, has certain limitations. For example, the arts of China cross many of these chronological periods, while Byzantine art resides within a narrower time frame. Some teachers prefer to relate art-history content to the topics of social studies curricula in their schools. References to art objects can extend students' art learning and integrate art with their other studies.

The Ancient World

Prehistoric Art

The earliest art provides the major part of our knowledge of prehistoric humans. Although cave paintings and other artifacts that have survived are extremely old, some dating back fifty thousand years, some are surprisingly sophisticated and rich in aesthetic as well as cultural value. *Paleolithic art* is the art of the last ice age, the time when massive glaciers covered much of Europe and North America. Cave paintings of animals and humans have survived in France and Spain, as have small stone sculptures of female figures, such as the well-known *Venus of Willendorf.* The great stone monument at Stonehenge in England was created primarily during the *Neolithic* period, which ranged from 1800 to 1400 B.C.

The Art of Egypt

When we think of the art and culture of Egypt, it is usually in the context of very ancient times. Indeed, in discussing Egyptian art, we speak in terms of many centuries, going back five thousand years. Early wall paintings date to 3500 B.C., and the latest (New Kingdom) period lasted until nearly

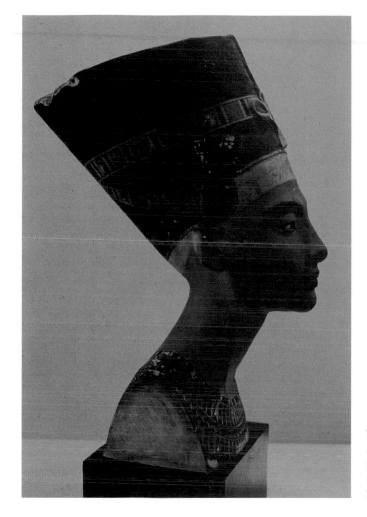

This painted limestone sculpture of Queen Nefertiti typifies the simplified form of Egyptian sculpture. (Ägyptisches Museum, Berlin) Scala/Art Resource, N.Y.

1000 B.C., a span of twenty-five hundred years of clearly recognizable Egyptian artistic style. When we consider the pace of contemporary life, with amazing events occurring in all parts of the world, scientific advances that significantly influence our lives within a generation, and political events that drastically alter systems of government for entire continents, all of which become known to us almost instantaneously via television, it is difficult for us to comprehend the continuity of Egyptian culture. When we compare this continuity to changes in more recent periods—such styles as impressionism, which began about 150 years ago, or pop art, which emerged less than 50 years ago—we gain some perspective. Life in Egypt evidently changed very slowly, and time was a plentiful commodity for Egyptian leaders, who envisioned grand accomplishments that took decades to complete.

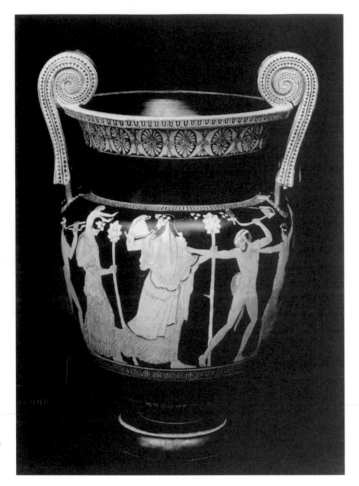

Red-figure Volute Krater, attributed to the Methyse Painter, 455–450 B.C., painted ceramic vessel. (The Minneapolis Institute of Arts)

This exquisite Greek vessel is functional and decorative, but also provides a surface for a highly developed painting style. The shape and size of the vessel, style of decoration, and content of the painting all have cultural significance. This object demonstrates some of the contradictions that occur when critics or aestheticians attempt to make distinctions between craft and art.

The Middle Ages

Christian Art

Dominating Europe for centuries, Christian art began during the fourth century. Early *Byzantine* art blended influences from the Roman traditions with Eastern conventions from Constantinople (Byzantium or modern Istanbul). One of the monuments of the Byzantine era (400–1453) is the church of San Vitale in Ravenna, Italy. This spacious and well-lit church was built on an octagonal plan different from most European cathedrals and is noted for the beautiful mosaics that decorate its walls and ceilings.

Romanesque architecture emerged as an important style "quite suddenly when a medieval prophecy foretelling the end of the world in 1000 failed to come true."[13] Christians set out to show their gratitude by building churches across Europe in Italy, Spain, Germany, and France. The Romanesque style was a revival of Roman forms of architecture, as churches were built with a central nave and side aisles. Because of the need to build strong walls to support the broad vaults, the churches were quite dark, with few small windows. *Gothic* cathedrals were then built with even higher walls and arches. Exterior buttresses to support the high walls made large stained-glass windows possible and led to the exquisite development of this art form. The Notre Dame cathedral in Paris and the Chartres cathedral are two prime examples of the glories of Gothic architecture still in existence.

Rome conquered Greece and most of the Western world beginning about 30 B.C. and maintained the Roman Empire until nearly A.D. 500. Roman art followed closely the traditions of Greek art but related more to the political and military aspects of the culture than to religious beliefs. Architecture on a grand scale produced the Colosseum, the Pantheon, the Arch of Constantine, and many beautifully proportioned Roman villas. Roman sculptures of human figures were often startlingly realistic, rather than idealized like the Greek figures. Roman portrait sculptures provide accurate records of a number of leaders of the time:

> Although much Roman art is derived in style from that of Greece, its portrait sculpture originated in a tradition that was wholly Italian. It is in this sculpture that we witness Rome's unique contribution to the arts—that of *realism*.[12]

Islamic Art

Art by the followers of Mohammed (beginning early in the seventh century) crosses boundaries among Asia, Africa, and Europe. Throughout the Islamic world, the Muslims built mosques as houses of worship. From the minarets, or towers, the faithful were called to pray five times daily. Because Muslim tradition forbids representation of the human figure, sculpture, though not unknown, did not develop as in other cultures and religions. Islamic art is magnificent, however, in the development of nonrepresentational decoration using geometric and natural forms as motifs. One of the best-known examples of Islamic architecture is the *Taj Mahal* in Agra, India.

The aesthetic attitudes developed in Asia and the forms and conventions of Eastern artistic creation differed significantly from those common in Western art. Eastern and

African art influenced European artists greatly in the late nineteenth and the twentieth centuries.

The Art of Oceania

This diverse category includes Australia, New Zealand, New Guinea, and major Pacific island groups. Because warfare among the island peoples was frequent, numerous groups devised distinctive war clubs made of wood, stone, and seashells. Many of the decorated objects relate to religious ceremonies, including masks, costumes, and body decoration used in conjunction with dancing. The Maori people of New Zealand created a distinctive style of the sculpted human figure with curvilinear designs and overall patterns. Intricate carvings and decorations are found on huts, canoes, coffins, staffs, and facial tattoos.

The famous monoliths of volcanic stone on Easter Island in Polynesia remain a puzzle. These large, brooding sculptures, originally set on ceremonial stone platforms, were discovered on an Easter Sunday by nineteenth-century missionaries. More than six hundred of these huge heads and half-length figures survive, some of which are up to sixty feet tall. Because the people who created these sculptures left no records, archaeologists speculate that they symbolized the spiritual and political power that chieftains were thought to derive from the gods.

Pre-Columbian Art

The Native Americans of Mexico, Central America, and South America shared knowledge needed to cultivate such crops as maize, squash, beans, cotton, and tobacco; they used irrigation systems in agriculture and developed weaponry, metalwork, featherwork, basketry, and textiles. Several groups became proficient in astronomy and developed the calendar, mathematics, metallurgy, hieroglyphic writing, amazingly precise architecture, and painting and sculpture. Evidence shows that some peoples accomplished surgery. The Mayan peoples, the Incas, and the Aztecs were three major cultures that left behind a wealth of marvelous art objects, including their extensive cities and magnificent temples. As with many early cultures, a major impetus for pre-Columbian art was religious belief.

The plentiful availability of gold and silver, which eventually contributed to the decline of these peoples at the hands of Spanish conquerors, is evident in many pre-Columbian objects. Following is a commentary about a tapestry tunic with golden spangles from the Chimu culture, woven about 1200:

> It may seem unnecessary to our eyes to have added the gold to this tawny-toned tapestry tunic, such is the charm of the tapestry design itself, but perhaps the gold carries status which no textile design could equal. The representation is a row of trees with monkeys in the limbs above plucking fruit for the aide below who holds the bag. . . . The technique of the textile is slit tapestry with alpaca weft and cotton warp, with the golden-toned autumn colors which are characteristic of the fabrics from the north coast of Peru.[14]

It is apparent that very sophisticated and accomplished cultures have disappeared in the jungles of Mexico and Central and South America, leaving behind intriguing evidences of their thought and customs.[15] Excavations on a number of sites are being conducted currently in hopes of learning more about the arts and sciences of these early civilizations.

Native North American art is similar in many ways to that of Central and South America, except that most natives in the northern continent were nomads and did not build permanent cities. Some of the exceptions to this are the Hopi mesas in Arizona, which are among the oldest continuously inhabited dwellings on the continent. They were inhabited before Europeans came to this land. Also in Arizona and in Colorado and New Mexico, in the Canyon de Chelly and other locations, are the ruins of cliff dwellings built in small communities high in the steep canyon walls by the Anasazi, the "ancient ones." Petroglyphs painted and carved by very old Native American cultures, and similar in some ways to the prehistoric cave paintings of Europe, are still found in many isolated canyons in Arizona, Colorado, and Utah.

Many of the points made in the discussion of African peoples apply as well to Native American arts and culture. This is a large continent, and the various tribal nations lived in very different climatic, political, and social conditions. The Navajos and Hopis of the Southwest lived in a hot, dry, and, in many ways, inhospitable climate; the Sioux, Plains Indians of the Dakotas and Nebraska, roamed on horses, taking

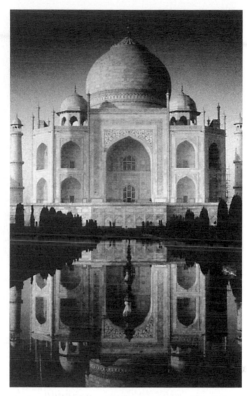

Taj Mahal, commissioned by Shah Jahan, Agra, India, 1623–1643. One of the world's best-known buildings, the *Taj Mahal* was created as a memorial and symbol of the Shah's love for his deceased wife. It demonstrates how architecture can be personally and culturally significant as well as metaphorically expressive, just as other modes of art. © Trevor Wood/Tony Stone Worldwide.

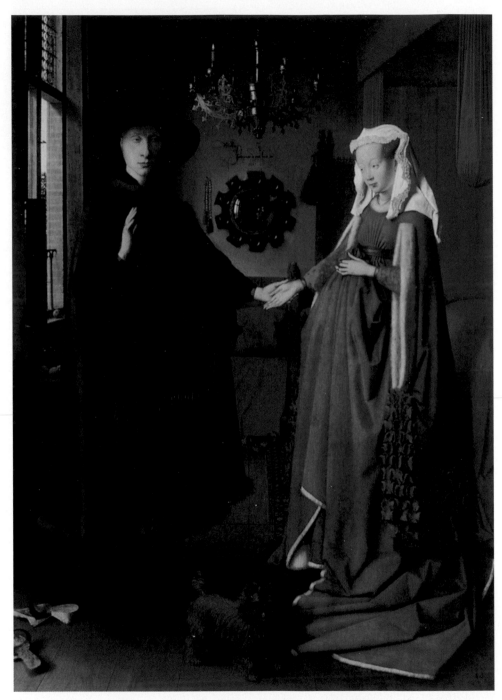

Jan van Eyck, *Giovanni Arnolfini and His Bride,* 1434. This unique portrait was commissioned by an Italian businessman to serve as a record of the couple's marriage and as a kind of wedding contract. It is often discussed by art historians as an example of Christian symbolism in painting. (Reproduced by courtesy of the Trustees, The National Gallery, London)

their dwellings with them to follow the buffalo; the Tlingits of the Northwest Coast lived in a humid, wet, coastal environment and depended a great deal on the sea and their skill with boats; and the Algonquin, Cree, and Ojibwa peoples of Alaska, Canada, and the northern United States lived at the opposite extreme of the Navajos, in the frigid north. Different conditions, languages, and lifestyles among the more than 150 major Indian tribal nations in North America have resulted in a wide range of art forms.

The Northwest Coast Native Americans, for example, carved beautifully designed wooden utensils for everyday use and developed the idea of totem poles as culturally significant symbols of family lineage and characteristics. Navajos are noted for exquisitely designed and woven wool blankets and silver-and-turquoise jewelry. The Pueblo peoples have developed highly prized pottery that is collected and exhibited in art museums. Sioux nations created beautiful clothing, including wedding garments, from tanned and decorated leathers. Many of these objects incorporated designs and symbols that expressed spiritual values and beliefs held within respective cultures, many of which recognized the importance of the sun, the sky, the earth, and of unity between nature and the people. Unfortunately, much of the best art of Native Americans has been lost over the years, and many of the craft forms are not being continued within tribal groups. However, the good news is that in some areas, notably the Southwest, traditional art and craft forms are maintained with vital and creative results, such as the woven blankets, pottery, and silver jewelry of the Hopis and Navajos.[16] The National Museum of the American Indian, Smithsonian Institution, in Washington, D.C., was created to preserve and exhibit the heritage of Native Americans and to provide the public with access to knowledge about indigenous American cultures through its education program. The museum publishes the periodical *Native Peoples,* which is "dedicated to the sensitive portrayal of the arts and lifeways of native peoples of the Americas."[17] The Canadian Museum of Civilization in Hull, Quebec, performs a similar function in Canada.

Renaissance and Baroque

The *Renaissance* began in Europe about 1400 and continued for about two hundred years. This period marked an increased interest in classical learning, philosophy, and art, hearkening back to the thoughts of Greece and Rome. With beginnings in Italy, the spirit of the Renaissance moved throughout Europe, with notable effects in the Netherlands

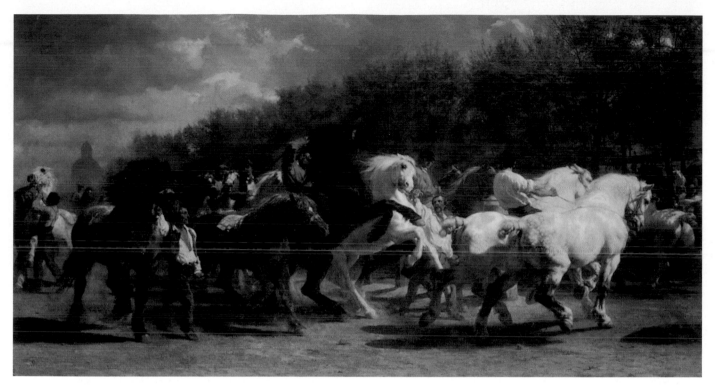

Rosa Bonheur, *The Horse Fair,* 1853. Oil on canvas, 8' 1/4" × 16' 7 1/2". The Metropolitan Museum of Art, New York, gift of Cornelius Vanderbilt, 1887.

French painter Rosa Bonheur employed high contrast, linear movement, and dynamic poses of horses and handlers to create this dramatic, exciting scene from the nineteenth century.

and Flanders. The pantheon of great artists associated with the Renaissance and the list of masterpieces of art from this period are extensive, including works by Michelangelo (the ceiling of the Sistine Chapel, *Pieta, David*), da Vinci (*The Last Supper, Mona Lisa*), Botticelli (*Birth of Venus*), van Eyck (*Giovanni Arnolfini and His Bride*), Raphael, Anguissola, Brueghel, Dürer, Altdorfer, and many others. Numerous artworks during the Renaissance employed symbolism, often expressing Christian concepts or beliefs. For example, van Eyck's painting of the Arnolfini wedding portrays the Italian silk merchant and his shy Flemish bride in a room surrounded by objects with subtle symbolic meanings. The couple standing with shoes off signifies that they stand on sacred ground (the sacred institution of marriage). The dog signifies fidelity; miniature figures of Adam and Eve, the first couple, are carved in the bench; the single candle burning in the chandelier represents the light of Christ; and the convex mirror, symbolic of the all-seeing eye of God, reflects the entire scene.

> The small medallions set into the mirror's frame show tiny scenes from the Passion of Christ and represent van Eyck's ever-present promise of salvation for the figures reflected

on the mirror's convex surface. These figures include not only the principals, Arnolfini and his wife, but two persons who look into the room through the door. One of these must be the artist himself, since the florid inscription above the mirror, *Johannes de Eyck fuit hic,* announces that he was present.[18]

Following the Renaissance, during the seventeenth and eighteenth centuries, came the age of *baroque* art, with painting and sculpture featuring dark and light contrasts, exaggerated emotions, and dynamic movement in composition. Such artists as Gentileschi (*Judith and Maidservant with the Head of Holofernes*), Caravaggio (*David with the Head of Goliath*), and Rembrandt (*The Night Watch*) extended the use of light and chiaroscuro for dramatic effect to the same high degree that perspective was earlier developed during the Renaissance. Later, French artists created the intimate *rococo* style with a profusion of curved ornamentation and intricate decoration. The rococo, as the baroque, was manifest in painting, sculpture, architecture, and interior design, and in the crafts areas of furniture, tapestry, porcelain, and silver.

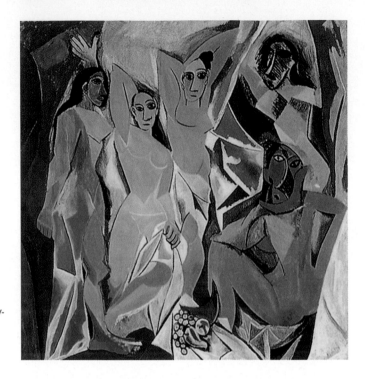

Pablo Picasso, *Les Demoiselles d'Avignon*, 1907. Museum of Modern Art, New York, bequest of Lillie P. Bliss.

Modern and Postmodern Art

Rococo art was replaced in popularity by the *neoclassical* movement, which emphasized straight lines and classical ornamentation in architecture, and by balanced formalism, precise linear drawing (as in Charpentier's *Portrait of Mlle. Charlotte du Val d'Ognes*), and classical subjects in painting, such as David's *The Death of Socrates* and Ingres's *Oedipus and the Sphinx*. Neoclassicism became entrenched in the French Academy and was the style against which the impressionist painters rebelled late in the nineteenth century.

The nineteenth century in Europe was a period of many artistic styles, beginning with the subjective orientation of *romanticism,* which suggested a personal, intensely emotional style. In France, Delacroix (*Liberty Leading the People*) and Géricault (*Raft of the Medusa*) exemplified the romantic movement. Bonheur's monumental *The Horse Fair* lifted animal painting to a high level. The leading landscape painters of England, Constable (*The Hay Wain*) and Turner (*The Burning of the Houses of Parliament*), expressed the fascination of romanticism with untamed nature, country folk in natural settings, and the picturesque or exotic. Turner's huge paintings were prophetic of the monumental nonobjective canvases of abstract expressionism. The following excerpt

from a book about Turner demonstrates how art historical research and writing can enlighten us with respect to an artist's expression.

The old man's [Turner's] request was a strange one. Aboard the steamboat *Ariel,* out of Harwich, preparations were afoot for a bad storm that was brewing. The passenger was persistent. Others might want to go below; he wanted to be lashed to a spar on deck. He was a little man, almost gnome-like, and plainly battered by time. But his sharp gray eyes were impelling, and the crew, in the English tradition of tolerance of eccentricity, complied with his wish. Tied to his perilous post for four hours, Joseph Mallord William Turner, England's leading painter, absorbed and observed the onslaught of the elements.[19]

It is certain that this storm, experienced by the artist in all its force and fury, provided the raw material for some of his bombastic paintings of nature's power, such as *Shade and Darkness: The Evening of the Deluge* and *Rain, Steam, and Speed.*

During the second half of the century, *realism* and social protest followed the French and American revolutions. Artists depicted social themes, the dignity of working people, and the unfairness of some social institutions and practices. Millet (*The Gleaners*), Daumier (*Third Class Carriage*), Morisot (*In the Dining Room*), and Courbet (*Burial at Ornans*) painted ordinary people with a stark realism that was quite different, both in presentation of subject and paint application, from the neoclassical style of Jacques-Louis David and Ingres.

Many innovations or movements in the modern era began in revolutions against accepted artistic tradition or, in many instances, academic dogma. So it was that a group of French painters, including Manet, Morisot, Renoir, and others, rejected the narrow aesthetic views of the state academy of artists and developed new purposes and images in painting.[20] These artists, dubbed *impressionists* as the result of a remark by a sarcastic critic, responded to the invention of the camera as a recording device that surpassed the painter in accuracy and to the new scientific knowledge of optics. They began to concentrate on the creation of images the camera could not achieve as they emphasized mood and visual impression.

The traditional hierarchical organization of subject matter was abandoned in favor of a relatively modern preoccupation with light and color. Flat tones and clear edges were avoided in favor of small strokes of color and indefinite contours, both of which tended to convey a sense of diffuse and often sparkling light. Artists moved their studios outdoors, and such painters as Monet found themselves doing multiple studies of a particular subject as they focused on the light of early morning, high noon, and twilight in relation to a cathedral, a bridge, or a haystack.

The more immediate forebears of twentieth-century art were a group of painters known as the *post-impressionists* because of their close relationship to the earlier impressionist movement. Vincent van Gogh, Paul Cézanne, Suzanne Valadon, and Paul Gauguin, all highly individualistic, contributed their own distinctive perception of art to those who were to follow. The vivid, emotionally charged works of van Gogh left their mark on the expressionists; the broad, flat tones of Gauguin were to find their echoes in the work of Henri Matisse; the unidealized female nudes of Valadon are reflected in contemporary figure painting; and the construction of forms in terms of planes undertaken by Cézanne opened the door to cubism, perhaps the most revolutionary of twentieth-century styles. Cézanne refused to limit his vision to the forms given by the tradition of painting and thus examined the structure beneath the outward aspects of objects. He invited the viewer to study his pictorial subjects from multiple points of view, and he made the space between objects as meaningful as the objects themselves. Cézanne rejected the hazy softness of impressionism and applied his paint in clearly articulated flat strokes of color, which appeared literally to build his paintings as one small passage led to larger areas.

The *fauvists* may be represented by Matisse and André Derain. Matisse was the leader of this group of painters in France who extended the new use of color created by Gauguin and van Gogh, carrying it to the point where the group earned the critically derisive term *fauves,* or "wild beasts." The art-viewing public at the turn of the twentieth century, having just begun to accept the radical innovations of the post-impressionists, could not cope with the fauvists' strident use of pure color, their free-flowing arabesques, purely decorative line, and total disregard of local color (the specific color of a natural object). They were trying to paint according to Derain's clarion call of 1906: "We must, at all costs, break out of the fold in which the realists have imprisoned us."[21] The fauvists were creating their own reality, and they conceived of painting as a vehicle for expression that was totally autonomous, wholly independent of the viewer's perception of the world.

It was in 1907, when he painted *Les Demoiselles d'Avignon,* that Pablo Picasso took Cézanne's ideas one step further toward what is now known as *cubism.*[22] *Les Demoiselles* combined the simultaneous perspective of Cézanne with the simple,

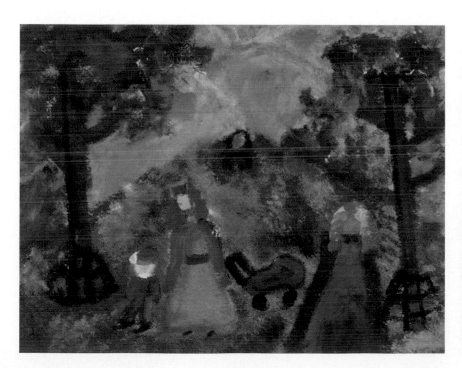

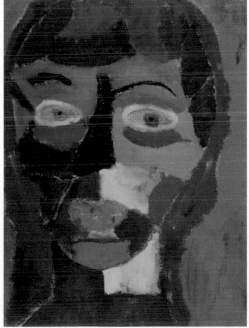

Two ten-year-olds produced these paintings in a unit on expressionism. Their work was preceded by a discussion of attitudes and visual characteristics shared by German expressionist painters. (Young People's Art Studies, Maryland Institute College of Art. Ruth Aukerman, teacher)

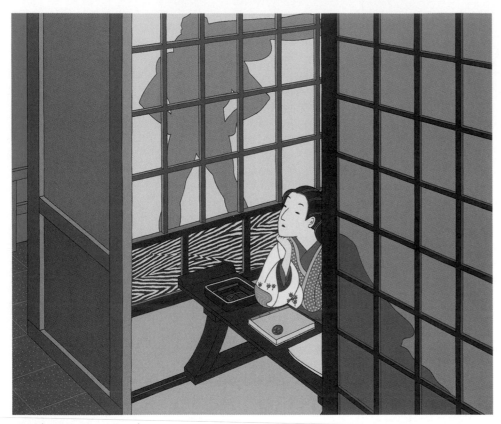

Roger Shimomura, *Diary: December 12, 1941*, 1980, acrylic on canvas, 50 1/4″ × 60″. National Museum of American Art, Smithsonian Institution, Washington, D.C., U.S.A. Art Resource, N.Y.

Shimomura's "Diary Series" of paintings was inspired by the daily journal kept by his grandmother, who immigrated from Japan in 1912. The artist gives visual form to events that deeply affected the Japanese-American community during World War II. Art in the postmodern era often refers to social issues and events.

monumental shapes and sharply faceted surfaces of traditional African and Iberian art. As Picasso developed his ideas along with Georges Braque, the forms of cubism moved continuously away from photographic realism. By 1911, cubist compositions grew in complexity as planes overlapped, interpenetrated, and moved into areas of total abstraction. Space and form were now handled with a minimum of color, in contrast to the rich hues of fauvism and expressionism. Historian Werner Haftmann commented on cubism's lack of interest in color and light in favor of a more intellectual concern for order:

> Cubism embraces all the aspects of the object simultaneously and is more complete than the optical view. From the information and signs conveyed on the rhythmically moving surface, the imagination can reassemble the object in its entirety. . . . Cubism corresponds to that new modern conception of reality which it has been the aim of the whole pictorial effort of the 20th Century to express in visual terms.[23]

Within cubism can be found many of the central concepts of modern art: manipulation and rejection of Renaissance perspective, abstraction to the point of nonobjectivity, emphasis on the integrity of the picture plane, introduction of manufactured elements in collage, and experimentation with different conceptions of reality.

The precursors of *surrealism* were such artists as Paul Klee, Giorgio di Chirico, and Marc Chagall, all of whom dealt with fantasy, dreams, and other states of mind. We may add to these influences the dada movement, whose anti-art theatrics and demonstrations challenged the most basic assumptions about art.[24] André Breton, a poet, first used the term *surrealist* in his own publication, thus reflecting the close connection between an art movement and a literary one, a common situation in the history of art. The artists who were ultimately to be identified with the movement—Salvador Dalí, Joan Miró, René Magritte—all shared Breton's interest in Freud's ideas regarding dreams, psychoanalysis, and the relation of conscious and subconscious experience as the subject matter for art. They strove to divorce themselves from rational and logical approaches to art. Breton, who admired and encouraged the painting of Frida Kahlo, wrote, "Surrealism: the dictation of thought free from any control of reason, independent of any aesthetic or moral preoccupation . . . rests upon a belief in the superior reality of certain forms of association hitherto neglected, in the omnipotence of the dream, in the disinterested play of thought."[25] Influences of surrealism are especially evident in many contemporary music videos.

Expressionism, generally speaking, places emphasis on emotions, sensations, and ideas rather than on the appearance of objects. Expressionist artists convey their views in a form that is almost invariably a pronounced distortion of photographic realism. Characteristics of expressionism often include heightened use of color, extreme simplification of form, and distortion of representational conventions for expressive purposes. Themes of expressionism differed radically from the French preoccupation with form and style, as such artists as Käthe Kollwitz focused on social, emotional, and political subjects. Kollwitz, who lived through both world wars, commented powerfully in her drawings and prints on themes of political corruption, the suffering of women and children, revolution, and the horrors of war. The expressionist stance, like realism, seems to have a universal appeal, as evidenced by the emergence of abstract expressionism worldwide in the 1940s and of neoexpressionism in the late 1970s.

One of the most revolutionary developments in European art of the early twentieth century was the shift toward what was at first called *nonobjective* art. Vasily Kandinsky, a Russian who lived in Germany and France, is considered the father of nonobjective painting.[26] The concepts subsumed under this term are now usually referred to as *nonrepresentational* and cover a much wider range of styles than originally. Nonrepresentational art now refers to many of the artistic styles that developed in the United States after World War II, when the center of the avant-garde in art shifted from Paris, which had been occupied during the war, to New York City.

Art in America

When American humorist Mark Twain remarked, "Whoo-oop! I'm the original iron jawed, brass mounted, copper bellied corpse maker from Arkansas," he was referring to the robust aggressive character of a country pushing its boundaries westward. Twain's view of America in the nineteenth century was the complete antithesis of the way Americans viewed Europe—as a group of monarchical societies with grinding, hopeless poverty at one end of the social spectrum and a wealthy, cultivated elite at its opposite.

American artists rejected European traditions, which drew upon mythological, historical, and religious subject matter, in favor of recording nature. They created a romantic view of America's manifest destiny with landscapes that ranged from the acutely observed to the visionary. Early limners painted stiff, naive portraits that farmers could afford; untrained anonymous itinerant artists painted signs for inns or decorated anything from wedding chests to rocking chairs to household implements. Women of several ethnic origins developed quilting as their own form of artistic and cultural expression.

Art and architecture in the United States during the colonial period and westward expansion largely reflected European styles and tastes. Government and public buildings and the homes of the wealthy were built according to a series of revival architectural styles. Near the turn of the twentieth century, American architect Louis Sullivan expressed ideas (e. g., "form follows function") that were the foundations for design of the American skyscraper. Sullivan's student, Frank Lloyd Wright, developed an architectural philosophy and form that became intrinsically American. Wright gained worldwide attention for his blending of nature and modern architectural form in a series of homes built in several states around the country, notably the Robie House in Chicago and the Kaufman House, *Fallingwater*, built over a waterfall in Bear Run, Pennsylvania.

Early American painting and sculpture reached points of excellence but contributed little to the avant-garde develop-

ment on an international level. Such artists as Albert Bierstadt painted magnificent landscapes of the Rocky Mountains, Yosemite Valley, and the great American West, motivating even more westward migration. Charles Russell and Frederic Remington chronicled the taming of the "Wild West" with their paintings of cowboys, Native Americans, cavalry, and life on the frontier. George Catlin focused his attention on the life and culture of Native Americans and painted many authentic portraits and group pictures. The list of great early American artists is a long one that includes Homer, Eakins, Church, and many others.

In the nineteenth century, such artists as James McNeil Whistler and Mary Cassatt left the United States for Europe to further their artistic education and to enjoy the more sophisticated ambiance of European culture. In the first decade of the twentieth century, a group of artists known as the "Ash Can School" abandoned European traditions to record the seamier

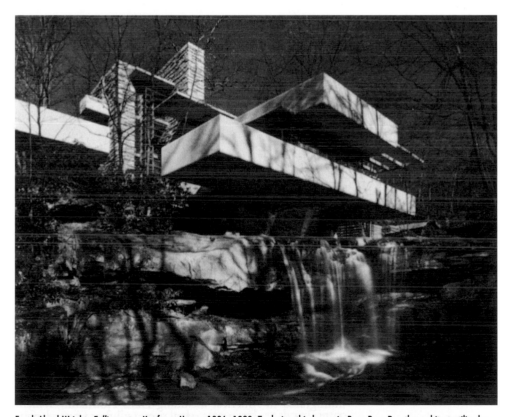

Frank Lloyd Wright, *Fallingwater*, Kaufman House, 1936–1939. To design this house in Bear Run, Pa., the architect utilized a cantilever construction to place part of the house over the natural waterfall, an example of Wright's approach that wedded structure and environment. Chicago Historical Society.

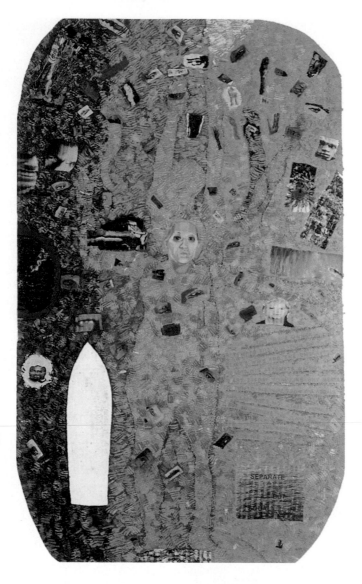

Howardena Pindell, *Autobiography: Water/Ancestors, Middle Passage/ Family Ghosts*, 1988. Acrylic, tempera, cattle markers, oil stick, paper, polymer photo transfer, 1989.17. Wadsworth Atheneum, Hartford, the Ella Gallup Sumner and Mary Catlin Sumner Collection Fund.

In recent decades, artists have turned to social themes and cultural contexts as subjects for expression. This multimedia work by Howardena Pindell includes a sewn insertion of the artist's body silhouette, the blank white shape of a slave ship, and references to the artist's African ancestors and the abuse of slave women.

The Changing Face of Art History

Art history, as we have seen, has its origins in Western thought and has changed in its scope and emphasis since the time of Vasari. The discipline continues to change as new scholars with different points of view criticize the field and suggest, even demand, improvements. The field of art history is responding to current issues, such as an overdue *recognition of the contributions of women artists*. When a woman says that she does not know about significant women artists or that there were none, she is usually reflecting the information that has come to her

through art history textbooks, whose authors have most often been men. Fortunately, this oversight is being corrected through scholarly research and publication of such books as *Women Artists in History, Pioneering Spirits: The Lives and Times of Remarkable Women Artists in Western History*, and more inclusive histories of art, such as Stokstad's *Art History*, and Tansey and Kleiner's *Gardner's Art through the Ages*.[30]

Women are now in the mainstream of drawing, painting, and sculpture; and forms of expression that have been developed primarily by women, such as quilting, are being recognized for their contributions to traditional and contemporary art. Art periodicals, such as *ARTnews* and *Art in America*, recognize, present, and discuss art by women artists on a regular basis.[31] We are seeing exhibitions of art by women in museums and galleries more frequently, providing more of the equity that has been absent for so long. *ARTnews* reported the progress of women as directors of major art museums: "Ten years ago, about one in every seven American museum directors was a woman. Today, it's nearly one in three."[32] Included in the report were the female directors of Yale University Art Gallery, the Los Angeles County Museum of Art, the Philadelphia Museum of Art, the National Museum of American Art, and other important art museums.

Unfortunately, this process is not as rapid or as easy as might be desired or expected. For instance, a 1993 article in *Art in America* identified fifty of the "art world's most powerful people."[33] Of the fifty artists, museum curators and directors, art dealers, and collectors of art listed, only six (12 percent) were women. A 1999 issue of *ARTnews* identified their selection of "The Century's 25 Most Influential Artists."[34] Only two of the artists, Louise Bourgeois and Cindy Sherman (8 percent), are women.

Another area that art historians and other art professionals are attending to increasingly is *recognition of non-Western art*. The Western tradition in art has always been the primary focus of art historians, probably because of the discipline's origins and the European heritage of many scholars in this field. Educators in the public schools are especially concerned about the Western emphasis in art programs because of the non-Western ethnic heritage of so many schoolchildren. The concern of educators and community leaders with respect to all Western culture and thought is that students might gain the impression that this is considered the dominant, preeminent, or highest culture and that others are less worthy of attention and recognition. When nearly all the art exemplars used in school art programs are works by males of European heritage, this misconception is perpetuated.

Americans of color and of various ethnic roots have contributed significantly to contemporary art, including such well-known names as Henry Ossawa Tanner, Romare Bearden, Maria Martinez, Frida Kahlo, Diego Rivera, Isamu Noguchi, Nam June Paik, Maya Ying Lin, and others. Many of the following artists are featured in art writer Lucy Lippard's influential book, *Mixed Blessings: New Art in a Multicultural America:* Jacob Lawrence, Faith Ringgold, Howardena Pindell, Jean-Michel Basquiat, Fred Wilson, Marisol Escobar, Luis Jimenez, Ana Mendieta, Ester Hernandez, Juane Quick-To-See Smith, James Luna, Roxanne Swentzell, Robert Haozous, James Joe, Kay WalkingStick, Fritz Scholder, Margo Machida, May Sun, and many more.[35]

Art historians are also correcting what some have viewed as an *overemphasis on the formalist tradition* of art. All art disciplines have changed during recent years in the direction of broader applications of perspectives from such fields as psychology, politics, sociology, and anthropology. We can read the writings of art critics and historians who apply perspectives of psychoanalysis, feminism, Marxism, and cultural anthropology. Formal analysis of artworks for many is decidedly secondary to the psychological and social issues that surround art. These perspectives influence judgments made about entire styles of art, with formalistic styles, such as abstract expressionism and op art, sliding down the scale and art with social content, such as neoexpressionism, gaining respect. For art education in the schools, an overemphasis on formalism can be seen when curricula fail to go beyond superficial teaching of the elements or principles of art, when the social significance of artworks is ignored, and when functions of objects are ignored and they are viewed exclusively for their aesthetic properties.

Another current issue in art history and art education is a perceived *overemphasis on the fine arts* to the exclusion of crafts and decorative arts, of folk arts, and of applied arts, especially their commercial applications. The very old debate that centers on distinctions between art and craft, the elitist view that finds little significance in applied arts, and the lack of recognition of art in everyday experience are attitudes that are losing prominence.

TEACHING ART HISTORY

Children are fascinated with the content of art history and with the art images when teachers can engage them at levels appropriate for their abilities and interests. Traditional

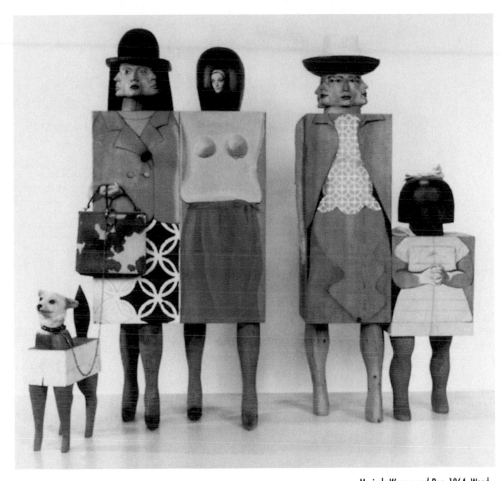

Marisol, *Women and Dog,* 1964. Wood, plaster, synthetic polymer, taxidermed dog head and miscellaneous items, 72 1/4″ × 73″ × 31″. Collection of Whitney Museum of American Art, purchase, with funds from the Friends of the Whitney Museum of American Art 64.17a–g. © Marisol Escobar/Licensed by VAGA, New York, N.Y.

Artists in the 1950s and 1960s combined a variety of materials in their works and challenged traditional distinctions between sculpture and painting. Marisol's work exemplified both of these developments as she drew and painted on the surfaces of sculptures, incorporated ready-made objects, and included plaster casts of her own face and hands.

teaching methods used by university art history instructors (projecting slides and lecturing) are not appropriate for most elementary classes. Showing slides and providing information can be useful in brief sessions, though it is rarely effective for more than ten or fifteen minutes. Children often learn more and perceive more carefully when they are engaged in active tasks that relate to the art being studied.

Organizing Art Images

A visual time line and a world map provide useful reference points for art history. Although young children do not have sufficient concepts of time to comprehend such lengthy periods as centuries and decades, they can understand the

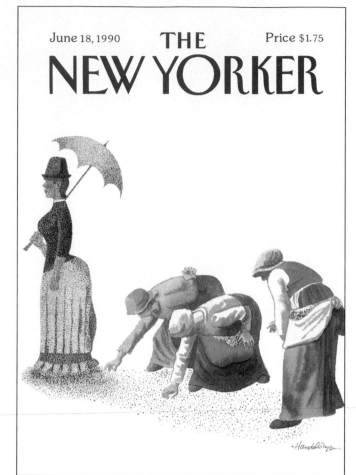

June 18, 1990   **THE**   Price $1.75

THE NEW YORKER

The humor in this magazine cover is dependent on the viewer's knowledge of Georges Seurat's painting technique, known as pointillism, and recognition of the three figures from Jean Francois Millet's famous work, *The Gleaners.* Instead of gathering leftover grain and straw, these gleaners collect the painted dots near a figure from *A Sunday Afternoon on the Grande Jatte,* the large Seurat painting featured in the contemporary musical *Sunday in the Park with Georges.* Original drawing by J. B. Handelsman. Copyright © 1990 The New Yorker Magazine, Inc. Reprinted by permission. All Rights Reserved.

be able to associate differences in art styles with different cultures and their locations.

To increase their understanding of art modes, write terms, such as *drawing, painting, sculpture, ceramics,* and so forth, on strips of cardboard, and place them at the heads of columns on the bulletin board. Using reproductions collected from magazines (or on postcards, etc.), ask the children to categorize the art objects according to mode. They can include examples of their own work as well, placing their artwork in the correct columns. This categorization activity can continue to whatever level of sophistication the age group can achieve; for example, sculptures can be grouped according to materials (wood, bronze, stone, and so on), and landscape paintings can be grouped according to artist (van Gogh, Bierstadt, Münter, etc.). Postcards with a wide range of art reproductions can be purchased at nearly every art museum and can also be ordered from many museums. Some museums publish books of postcards for very reasonable prices. A collection of postcard art images can be one of the art teacher's most versatile resources. Small reproductions of art images can also be collected very inexpensively by cutting pictures of art from art magazines. A magazine that costs $5 might yield more than a hundred good-quality art reproductions, most in color, appropriate for teaching.

In another exercise, design a bulletin board display of a different artist (Mary Cassatt), culture (African masks), style (Gothic architecture), or other art topic every month or more often. Use good-quality reproductions, pictures of artists if available, titles, concepts, names, dates, and whatever information is appropriate for the age levels and interests of the children and your art curriculum. With all these display strategies for teaching art history, provide the information you want children to receive according to your teaching goals. Engage students with questions and discussions about the visual displays, the artists, and the historical contexts. You will note that many will absorb much information and ask for more. They will become able to discuss art with levels of knowledge and understanding that many adults will envy.

Integrating Art History

Defining Purposes of Art

Organize the children in small groups of three or four, seated together preferably at tables. Display four or five art reproductions or photographs of objects at the front of the room where

implications of relative differences in distance from "now" on the time line. Similarly, many primary children are not able to conceptualize the distances involved in world geography and cultures, but they can see different locations on a globe or world map, and their understanding will grow as they mature and as they learn more in social studies.

Show children postcards or larger reproductions of artworks that are culturally distinctive, such as an Egyptian sculpture, an African mask, or a Rembrandt painting, and ask them to identify where each artwork belongs on the world map and on the time line. Display the art reproduction on the bulletin board, and string a length of yarn from the picture to the correct world location and point on the time line. Repeat this process as you teach about different periods and styles of art. Eventually the children will all can see, or provide smaller reproductions for each group. Ask each group to speculate as to the purpose of the object when it was created. You might include a Greek vessel for holding water, a painting of a king in full royal regalia, a Navajo silver-and-turquoise necklace, a cathedral, and so forth. The difficulty and complexity of the tasks should be adapted to the abilities of the grade level. This activity can lead naturally into as much historical content as you wish, as well as into art criticism and aesthetics. The idea that there are different purposes to art is a simple but important idea basic to aesthetics.

Researching Problems

Collect articles, books, pictures, filmstrips, and other materials on a topic, such as Canadian Haida totem poles. Organize a folder with such materials on as many topics as you choose (you can add one or two each year to your files). Divide your class into groups of four or five (this will work best with upper-elementary or middle-school students). Pro-

vide each group with a file, access to whatever audiovisual equipment is needed, and a study sheet asking such questions as: Who were the people who created totem poles? Where did they live? What materials and tools did they use to make the totems, and why? When did they begin doing this? When did they stop, if ever? Why did they make totem poles? What did the totems mean to the people? and How could we make totem poles in art class?

After appropriate class time (and homework?), ask each group of students to briefly report to the class on their topic. When reports have been given (and perhaps displays mounted), let the class vote on which of the reports they would like to pursue with a studio activity. If they choose totem poles, expand the discussion of how this might be done, what materials will be needed, how students might help to collect materials, and what they might learn from making totem poles. In this case, the groups might design, construct, and paint their own totem poles and display them with descriptions of the meanings and symbols that they used in

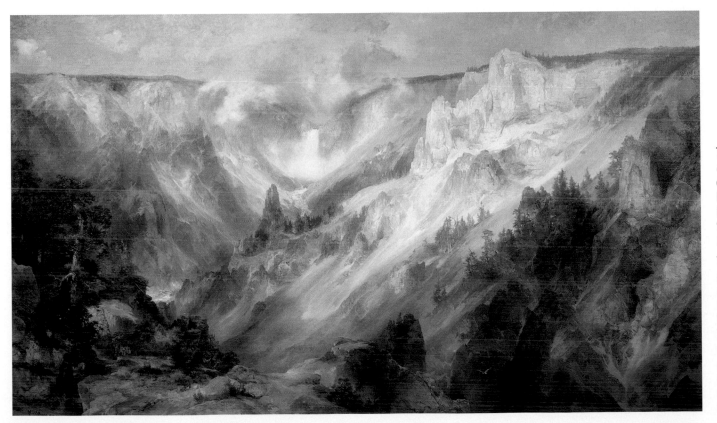

Thomas Moran, *The Grand Canyon of the Yellowstone*, 1893–1901. Oil on canvas, 8′ × 14′. Lent by the Department of the Interior Museum. National Museum of American Art, Smithsonian Institution, Washington, D.C., U.S.A. Art Resource, N.Y.

The tremendous scale and colorful grandeur of the West impressed artist Thomas Moran during his travels in Wyoming and Montana. This monumental painting of Yellowstone Park established Moran as one of America's premiere landscape painters. Compare this landscape with the work of contemporary landscape painter Wolf Kahn (see painting on page 351).

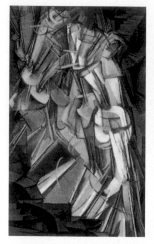

Marcel Duchamp, *Nude Descending a Staircase, No. 2*, 1912. Oil on canvas, 4' 10" × 2' 11". Philadelphia Museum of Art, Louise and Walter Arensberg Collection. © 2000 Artists Rights Society (ARS), New York/ADAGP, Paris/Estate of Marcel Duchamp.

Eliot Elisofon, *Marcel Duchamp*, 1952. From *Life, The Second Decade* 1980). TimePix. Forty years after *Nude Descending a Staircase* was painted, photographer Elisofon captured multiple images of artist Duchamp stepping down a staircase, giving us another example of the illusion of motion on a flat surface.

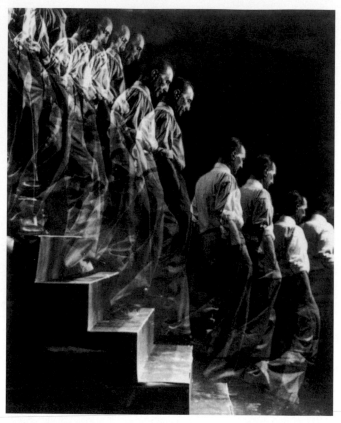

their creations. This type of activity is obviously an in-depth project requiring a number of class periods to complete.

Understanding through Studio Activities

Children become more interested in art historical topics when they are involved with related studio activities. If students are working with the idea of forms in motion, they will likely be very interested to see what the futurists accomplished with the concept. A child struggling with the notion of distortion for expressive purpose can become quite involved in reading about Modigliani and looking at his works. Students who are struggling with composition in their paintings are usually very receptive to a five-minute viewing of slides showing masterworks of composition. In all these situations, the art historical content can be purposefully emphasized by the teacher, or it can emerge naturally in the course of discussions and conversations with individual students and later shared with all class members.

FUNCTIONS OF ART HISTORY AND METHODS OF INQUIRY

Noted art historian Heinrich Wölfflin relates the story of a young artist who, with three of his friends,

> set out to paint part of the landscape, all four firmly resolved not to deviate from nature by a hair's-breadth; and although the subject was the same, and each quite creditably reproduced what his eyes had seen, the result was four totally different pictures, as different from each other as the personalities of the four painters. Whence the narrator drew the conclusion that there is no such thing as objective vision, and that form and color are always apprehended differently according to temperament.[36]

For the art historian, there is nothing surprising in this observation.

Wölfflin made the point that among artists there is no such thing as objective vision. In recent years we have come to realize that the same thing might be said about historians in general and art historians in particular. Art historians have at their disposal today such a range of methods of inquiry that they are able to provide us with many points of view about particular artworks, artists, styles, and periods. We are much richer for this diversity.

Contemporary art historian Eugene Kleinbauer discusses two primary modes of art historical inquiry, the *intrinsic* and the *extrinsic*.[37] Using intrinsic methods, art historians focus on the artwork itself, identifying materials and techniques, establishing the authenticity and attribution, dating and provenance, style, stylistic influences, iconography, subject matter, themes, and functions. In order to perform these operations, art historians must learn a great deal about the artwork and its context, and they must develop the eye of a connoisseur in order to make extremely fine distinctions. A number of scientific tools are employed by art professionals that reveal important facts to assist art historians.

Extrinsic methods of inquiry involve studies of conditions and influences associated with the creation of the artwork, including artistic biography, patronage, and the history of the period. Art historians also apply methods derived from psychology and psychoanalysis and other approaches to learn more about religious, social, philosophical, cultural, and intellectual determinants of the work. The closer we get to extrinsic methods, the closer we are to a postmodern view of both history and criticism (see Chapter 2).

Here is an example of some questions and problems that art historians face: A Rembrandt painting is made available for sale at a reputable New York City auction firm. A museum of art is looking to purchase a Rembrandt painting, which very rarely becomes available, and this work is exactly what the museum director has in mind. There is a question, however, of the authenticity of the painting. Some authorities suggest that it is by a student of Rembrandt, done in the master's studio under his direction, but it is not of the hand of Rembrandt. Should the museum purchase the painting? How can they establish the painting's authenticity and attribution to Rembrandt? If the issue is not clearly resolved, how will doubt influence the price to be offered for its purchase?

All the skills and methods of art historians are brought to bear on such questions, often resulting in definitive information that makes answers to these questions obvious. For example, while investigating the provenance, or history of ownership, of the painting, a scholar discovers a gap of fifty years when the painting was apparently lost. The circumstances of its recent rediscovery suggest that it might be a forgery. The art history scholar, an expert on Dutch painting and Rembrandt in particular, closely analyzes the details of the painting, noting brushstrokes and other painting techniques that are subtly different from Rembrandt's. Scientific analysis of the paint reveals an element that was not available in oil paint until a century after Rembrandt's death. The experts who have examined this painting are able to determine that it is not of the hand of Rembrandt or from his studio, but it is, rather, a copy from a later date or a forgery created with intent to defraud. Methods such as these are applied by art historians not only in conjunction with the art market but also for the purpose of improving our understanding of art and the meaning and significance of artworks.

Methods of Art Historical Inquiry As a Basis for Teaching

Teachers can organize classroom art activities based on art historians' methods of inquiry. Following are some examples.

Style Recognition

Using postcard reproductions (or images from magazines), place about ten paintings on the display board, or arrange them on a table. Place a number beside each reproduction. Tell the students that six of the paintings are by the same artist and four are by other artists. (You might use six landscapes by van Gogh and other landscapes by Gauguin, Monet, and so on. To make the activity easier, select the four to be very different, such as a Japanese landscape, a cubist landscape, or a Grandma Moses landscape.) Ask the children to identify which ones are by the same artist and which are not. Can they recognize and name the artist who created the six? Can they identify the artist(s) who painted the other four? How did they know? Older children can respond with pencil and paper. All ages can enjoy discussing the results and justifying their answers.

Viewing Themes in Art Historically

Using available art reproductions—from books, slides, postcards, and so on—organize a series of artworks on a theme, such as animals in art or people working. Ask children to group the reproductions and identify the theme. For example, with the theme of animals in art, the works might include such items as a Rauschenberg sculpture with a stuffed chicken on top, a Marino Marini bronze sculpture of a horse, a Chinese carved jade dragon, a Japanese woodblock print of kittens, and a Rosa Bonheur painting of horses. (There are thousands of artworks on this theme; other themes include mother and child, flowers, portraits

In a memory exercise, a group of upper-elementary students observed the *Mona Lisa* for one minute and were then asked to draw the da Vinci painting from memory.

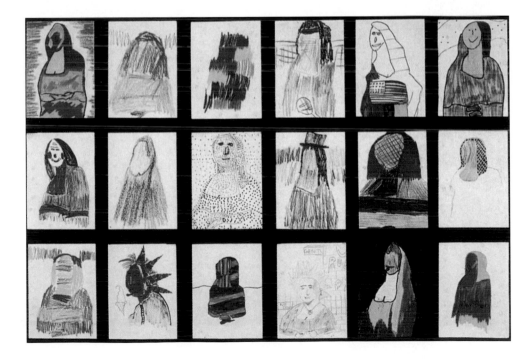

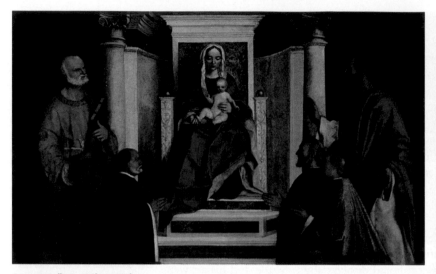

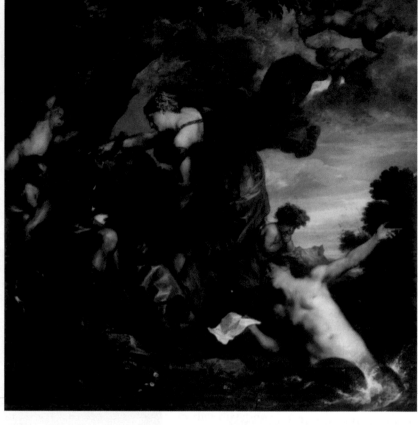

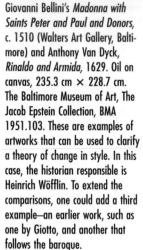

Giovanni Bellini's *Madonna with Saints Peter and Paul and Donors,* c. 1510 (Walters Art Gallery, Baltimore) and Anthony Van Dyck, *Rinaldo and Armida,* 1629. Oil on canvas, 235.3 cm × 228.7 cm. The Baltimore Museum of Art, The Jacob Epstein Collection, BMA 1951.103. These are examples of artworks that can be used to clarify a theory of change in style. In this case, the historian responsible is Heinrich Wölfflin. To extend the comparisons, one could add a third example—an earlier work, such as one by Giotto, and another that follows the baroque.

be sung to a popular tune. The culminating activity was a school assembly to watch a local theatre group perform part of the play *Sunday in the Park with Georges,* which they were presenting in a local theatre at the time. Then everyone sang the Seurat song, to the enjoyment of all.

Dramatizing Art History

Children can often relate better to historical art concepts through dramatization activities. They can collect clothes and props for costumes, scenes, and sets to portray an artist or art event. For example, have children choose an artist and dress in a costume appropriate for the artist, and then have the class try to guess what artist each child represents. This can be expanded by using a "twenty questions" approach, where the child dressed as the artist will answer students' questions about the artist's life and art. This means that the students portraying the artists will have to familiarize themselves with this material.

Here are more dramatization activities:

- The letters of van Gogh when read aloud and supported by slides of his artwork can be an exciting source for a dramatic reading for an assembly, a PTA meeting, or parents' night.

- In 1573, Paolo Veronese was accused of heresy for his painting *Feast in the House of Simon.* The accusations seem utterly groundless today. They included such issues as the reasons for painting someone picking his teeth, as well as objections to portrayals of buffoons, parrots, and even Germans. A staging of excerpts from the transcript of Veronese's trial would interest upper grades and provide opportunity for many roles.[39]
- The following segment of a bombastic futurist manifesto can make an exciting adjunct to the study of this art movement. Simply divide the following passage between alternating groups, and have them read it as they work together for a rousing crescendo.

  Come, then, the good incendiaries, with their charred fingers! . . . Set fire to the shelves of the libraries! Deviate the course of canals to flood the cellars of the museums! . . . Seize pick-axes and hammers! Sap the foundations of the venerable cities! The oldest among us are thirty; we have, therefore, ten years at least to accomplish our task. When we are forty, let others, younger and more valiant, throw us into the wastepaper basket like useless manuscripts. . . . And Injustice, strong and healthy, will burst forth radiantly in their eyes. For art can be nought but violence, cruelty and injustice.[40]

- Sixth-grade students and their teacher produced a videotape featuring paintings by Mary Cassatt of mothers with their infants or children in various intimate and affectionate poses. They recorded the song *Baby of Mine,* sung by Bette Midler, as accompaniment to the series of visuals of the paintings. The result was a delightful and emotionally powerful video for classroom use. Copyright issues were cleared with the district office and presented no problem because of the exclusively educational use of materials. Always check on copyright practices and procedures when using visual or musical artworks for such productions to learn if permissions must be sought.

Using a Historical Theory to Bridge Criticism and Art History

In the critical processes, the stage of formal analysis requires the viewer to focus on the ways the elements and/or the principles of art have been employed. An example of this is noting how certain geometric shapes provide the structure for the composition of the work. (Rubens used S-shapes, circles, and "lozenges" or ovoid shapes; Renaissance painters often used the triangle, etc.)

Higher-level analysis involves comparing stylistic differences among two or more historical periods. Swiss art historian Heinrich Wölfflin attempted to set up some guidelines for comparing major styles of art—in this case, the Renaissance and the baroque.[41] He developed the idea of "intuitive forms"—that is, changes of style that occur according to their own inner laws, independent of social or historical forces that lie apart from art. When we can recognize such differences, then we can apply them to other periods of art. This is important because, through their changes of style, artists often anticipate breakthroughs in the use of formal elements and continue to use them until they are either built on by succeeding artists or abandoned.

Although Wölfflin's guidelines for comparison between Renaissance and baroque painting apply to sculpture and architecture as well, they are most readily recognized in painting. The four concepts of change described here can be identified in the works of van Dyck and Bellini.

Linear/Painterly

The contours of linear forms are clearer in the Renaissance than the softer and more uneven edges in the baroque work. Because these distinctions are not absolute, they may also appear in the same period in different parts of the country. Although Botticelli's *Primavera* is an example of linear painting in northern Italy, Titian, who worked in the south, preferred softer contours, anticipating the work of baroque painters such as Rubens, who appeared much later.

Closed and Open Composition

Renaissance forms were "closed"—that is, they were balanced carefully within the edges of the canvas, whereas baroque painters extended their subjects *beyond* the confines of the canvas into infinite space.

Color

Renaissance painters confined color to the nature of the subjects, particularly clothing. Baroque painters not only used color to describe a part of a subject but also dispersed it throughout the painting. One reason for the Renaissance painters' use of restricted color lay in the accepted convention of the symbolic nature of color, as in the use of the color blue for the Virgin Mary's clothing.

Light

Light was evenly dispersed in the Renaissance style but, as in the case of color, was used by baroque painters for the opportunities it offered to create mood and drama.

The van Dyck and Bellini paintings clarify these concepts. One way to present Wölfflin's distinctions is for the teacher to identify key points of difference and then to show the class examples of styles they are expected to identify based on the teacher's descriptions. Another way is to mount reproductions on the wall and ask students to separate them by Wölfflin's distinctions. Here are some key words and phrases to bear in mind when comparing the Bellini to the van Dyck.

Giovanni Arnolfini and His Bride and compare each interpretation. Do all the accounts agree, or do interpretations differ? Which interpretation do you believe is most authoritative (accurate)? What did the historian write to convince you of that interpretation?

4. Select any art style or genre from the history of art, such as Japanese landscape, Pueblo pottery, the sculpture of Rodin, or cubist painting. Analyze the topic you have selected with the goal of developing a teaching unit for children. What would you like for children to know about the topic, the artist(s), major artworks, and cultural influences? Analyze the formal properties of the art. What are the major stylistic characteristics, media, processes for creation, themes? Decide which important points, artists, works, and ideas you would like children to learn about. Decide what classroom learning activities will help children to learn about and experience this art form.

5. Consult several art history textbooks. Using the table of contents of each book, compare the categories that author(s) have used to organize historical content. How do these outlines differ? How are they the same? Do all of the texts cover the same periods, styles, and artists? Compare the ways several texts or encyclopedias treat the same artist or movement.

6. Choose a topic in non-Western art, such as the architecture of India or Japanese pottery. Using the library, see how many books are available on the topic. Browse through the books to familiarize yourself with the range and depth of content on this topic.

7. Become an authority on a single painting. (There are at least three books written on Picasso's *Guernica.*)

8. Visit two museums, if they are available, and compare the kinds of information on artwork labels. Do labels represent a philosophy on the part of the museum regarding the nature and degree of communication between the museum and the public?

9. If there is a museum in your vicinity, visit its bookstore, and make a list of the art books you think would be interesting to children (see Suggested Readings).

10. On your museum visits and during your readings in general art history textbooks, note which women artists are represented. What proportion of works on display or in publication are by women? How prominently are they featured? How does this proportion relate to numbers of artists by gender? What conclusions or implications can you draw from the data of your study?

Simulations of Rule-Governed Art

The best way to deal with rule-governed art is to assemble at least three examples of style, and ask the class to note the factors they have in common.

11. Create a contemporary icon. Include such traditional requirements as the following:
    a. Subject must face front.
    b. Subject must be a person deserving of homage.
    c. Background must be painted in gold.
    d. Subject must wear appropriate garb.

12. *The art of the academy:* Pretend you are a student of the Academy des Beaux Arts in the nineteenth century. Your examination project is to paint a landscape that includes the following:
    a. A grouping of figures, such as fauns, satyrs, wood nymphs, shepherds.
    b. A group of buildings in the distance.
    c. Groups of trees five times the size of the figures.
    d. Foreground, middle ground, background.
    e. A shaft of light in the middle ground.

SUGGESTED READINGS

Addiss, Stephen, and Mary Erickson. *Art History and Education.* Introduction by Ralph A. Smith. *Disciplines in Art Education: Contexts of Understanding.* Urbana: University of Illinois Press, 1993.

Arnason, H. H., and Marla Prathe. *History of Modern Art.* 4th ed. New York: Harry N. Abrams, 1998.

Brommer, Gerald F. *Discovering Art History.* 3rd ed. Worcester, MA: Davis Publications, 1997.

Cartoon, Caricature, Animation. Special issue of *Art History* 18, no. 1 (March 1995). Oxford, UK; Cambridge: Blackwell Publishers, 1995.

Congdon, Kristin G. "Art History, Traditional Art, and Artistic Practices." In *Gender Issues in Art Education: Content, Contexts, and Strategies,* ed. Georgia Collins and Renee Sandell. Reston, VA: National Art Education Association, 1996, pp. 11–19.

Erickson, Mary. "Second and Sixth Grade Students' Art Historical Interpretation Abilities: A One-Year Study." *Studies in Art Education* 37, no. 1 (1995):19–28.

Fineberg, Jonathan. *The Innocent Eye: Children's Art and the Modern Artist.* Princeton, NJ: Princeton University Press, 1997.

Fitzpatrick, Virginia L. *Art History: A Contextual Inquiry Course.* Reston, VA: National Art Education Association, 1992.

Getty Center for Education in the Arts, Valsin A. Marmillion, Michael D. Day, et al. "Art History and Art Criticism." *Art Education in Action.* Santa Monica, CA: The Getty Center for Education in the Arts. 5 videocassettes. 1995. Video footnotes by Michael D. Day.

Nochlin, Linda. *Representing Women: Interplay, Arts, History, Theory.* London: Thames and Hudson, 1999.

Paul, Stella. *Twentieth-Century Art at the Metropolitan Museum of Art: A Resource for Educators.* New York: Metropolitan Museum of Art, 1999.

Pointon, Marcia R. *History of Art: A Students' Handbook.* 4th ed. London; New York: Routledge, 1997.

Preziosi, Donald, ed. *The Art of Art History: A Critical Anthology.* New York: Oxford University Press, 1998.

Russell, Stella Pandell. *Art in the World.* 4th ed. New York: Harcourt Brace Jovanovich College Publishers, 1993.

Art History Books for Children and Young People

Acton, Mary. *Learning to Look at Paintings.* New York: Routledge, 1997.

Arnold, Caroline, and Richard Hewett. *Stories in Stone: Rock Art Pictures by Early Americans.* New York: Clarion Books, 1996.

Delafosse, Claude, Gallimard Jeunesse, and Tony Ross. *Portraits.* A First Discovery Art Book. New York: Scholastic, 1995.

Delafosse, Claude, Gallimard Jeunesse, and Tony Ross. *Landscapes.* A First Discovery Art Book. New York: Scholastic, 1996.

Delafosse, Claude, Tony Ross, and Gallimard Jeunesse. *Paintings.* A First Discovery Art Book. New York: Scholastic, 1995.

Gallimard Jeunesse, and Jeannie Hutchins. *Paint and Painting: The Colors, the Techniques, the Surfaces; A History of Artists' Tools.* Scholastic Voyages of Discovery. Visual Arts; 2. New York: Scholastic, 1993.

Greenberg, Jan, and Sandra Jordan. *The American Eye: Eleven Artists of the Twentieth Century.* New York: Delacorte Press, 1995.

Greenberg, Jan, and Sandra Jordan. *The Sculptor's Eye: Looking at Contemporary American Art.* New York: Delacorte Press, 1993.

Lawrence, Jacob, and Augusta Baker Collection. *The Great Migration: An American Story.* New York; Washington, DC: Museum of Modern Art; Phillips Collection; HarperCollins, 1993.

Raboff, Ernest Lloyd. *Marc Chagall.* Art for Children. New York: Lippincott, 1988.

Raboff, Ernest Lloyd. *Michelangelo Buonarroti.* Art for Children. New York: Lippincott, 1988.

Raboff, Ernest Lloyd, and Adeline Peter. *Vincent van Gogh.* Art for Children. New York: Lippincott, 1988.

Sills, Leslie. *Inspirations: Stories about Women Artists: Georgia O'Keeffe, Frida Kahlo, Alice Neel, Faith Ringgold.* Niles, IL: A. Whitman, 1989.

Turner, Robyn. *Faith Ringgold.* Portraits of Women Artists for Children. Boston: Little, Brown, 1993.

WORLD WIDE WEB RESOURCES

Hyperlinks to Museum Web Sites

The following World Wide Web sites are among many that provide extensive and regularly updated Web links to museums and art history resources of interest to art educators. In addition to large image databases, the museum sites have excellent hyperlinks to other museums with similar collections.

ArtsEdNet, The Getty's Art Education Web Site. Museums and Image Resources Links. <http://www.artsednet.getty.edu/ArtsEdNet/Links/art.html>

Art Institute of Chicago. <http://www.artic.edu/>

Metropolitan Museum of Art, New York City. <http://www.metmuseum.org/>

Minneapolis Institute of Art. <http://www.artsMIA.org/>

Musée du Louvre. <http://www.mistral.culture.fr/louvre/louvre.htm>

Museum of Contemporary Art, Los Angeles. <http:// www.moca.org/>

Philadelphia Museum of Art. <http://www.philamuseum.org/>

Multicultural Exhibitions and Collections

The Asian Art Museum of San Francisco, Fine Arts Museums of San Francisco. 1999. <http://www.asianart.org/> This Web site is devoted to Asian art and culture. Includes images, commentary, and teaching resources.

Arts and History of Mexico: Virtual Forum of Mexican Culture. 1996–1999. <http://www.arts-history.mx/ direc2.html> This site provides a gateway to resources on Mexican arts. It covers contemporary art, Mexican masters, photography, museology, a featured artist each month, libraries, cinema, and media.

National Museum of African Art, Smithsonian Institution. 1999. <http://www.si.edu/nmafa/nmafa.htm> The National Museum of African Art (NMAfA) fosters and sustains—through exhibitions, collections, research, and public programs—an interest in and an understanding of the diverse cultures in Africa. Web site contains resources for teachers.

National Museum of the American Indian, Smithsonian Institution. 1999. <http://www.si.edu/nmai/nav.htm> The Web site for the Smithsonian's National Museum of the American Indian provides access to exhibitions and collections dedicated to the history and arts of Native Americans.

Art History Curriculum and Teaching Resources

The Art Teacher Connection. *Art History.* 1999. <http://www.inficad.com/~arted> Links to art and museum education resources for classroom teachers.

The Claude Monet Home Page. 1996. "Claude Monet: French Impressionist." <http://www.columbia.edu/~jns16/monet_html/monet.html> This is the site for all things Monet—biography, discussion of methods and techniques, analysis of works, bibliography, and pictures of some of Monet's famous works, including his series of poplar trees and water lilies.

Educational Web Adventures. "A. Pintura, Art Detective." Art and Art History. *Eduweb. Our Adventures.* 1997.

<http://www.eduweb.com/pintura/> A creative way to teach art history. A. Pintura helps visitors solve "The Case of Grandpa's Painting." Is the painting a Raphael? a van Gogh? a Titian? Site also includes a time line, glossary, and teaching resources.

J. Paul Getty Museum and Getty Education Institute for the Arts. "Looking at Art of Ancient Greece and Rome: An Online Exhibition." *ArtsEdNet. Lesson Plans & Curriculum Ideas.* 1998. <http://www.artsednet.getty.edu/ArtsEdNet/Resources/Beauty/index.html> Drawn from the antiquities collection of the J. Paul Getty Museum, this online exhibition features several image galleries of artworks, including detailed and rotating views. Information about individual artworks and background material on the Greek and Roman gods and goddesses they portray. Includes discussion questions and classroom activities developed with both students and teachers in mind.

National Center for History in the Schools at UCLA and Getty Education Institute for the Arts. "Trajan's Rome: The Man, the City, the Empire: A Middle School Curriculum Unit." *ArtsEdNet. Lesson Plans & Curriculum Ideas.* 1998. <http://www.artsednet.getty.edu/ArtsEdNet/Resources/Trajan/> Interdisciplinary history and art unit uses Roman artworks and primary texts as sources to explore life in the Roman Empire during Trajan's reign. Included are worksheets, diagrams and maps, and background material for teachers.

Art History Resources on the Web

Davis Publications. "Artists Biographies." *Web Resources.* 1998. <http://www.davisart.com/ABframe.htm> (November 1999). Short references written for elementary-school teachers. Presented in English and Spanish.

Delahunt, Michael R. "Art History." *ArtLex.* 1996–1999. <http://www.artlex.com/> Visual arts dictionary for artists, students, and educators in art production, criticism, history, aesthetics, and education. Definitions of terms, along with numerous illustrations, pronunciation notes, great quotations, and links to other art history resources on the Web.

Foundation Jacques-Edouard Berger. *World Art Treasures.* 1994–1999. <http://sgwww.epfl.ch/BERGER/index.html> The principal purpose of this site is to offer a different approach to art history via the World Wide Web. The site is multidimensional and multilevel and provides links intended to enrich the study of art.

Harcourt Brace College Publishers. *Art History Resources on the Web*. <http://www.harbrace.com/art/gardner/> This site is designed to use with the art history text *Gardner's Art through the Ages*. The site is organized to supplement the chapters in the book, with extensive links to other image and information sources.

Pioch, Nicolas. "Famous Paintings Exhibition." *Web Museum, Paris*. 1996–1999. <http://www.iem.ac.ru/wm/paint/> *Web Museum, Paris* is an extensive online database of images and information. Search capability with links to internal information and external Web sites. World Wide Web site presents a massive database of world art and art history information.

Women Artists in History. 1999. <http://home.webcom.se/art/index.html> This is an online gallery of paintings by major female artists from the fifteenth century to the present day. Includes brief biographies and a collection of images. There is an index of artists featured on the site and links to other sites featuring women in history and art history.

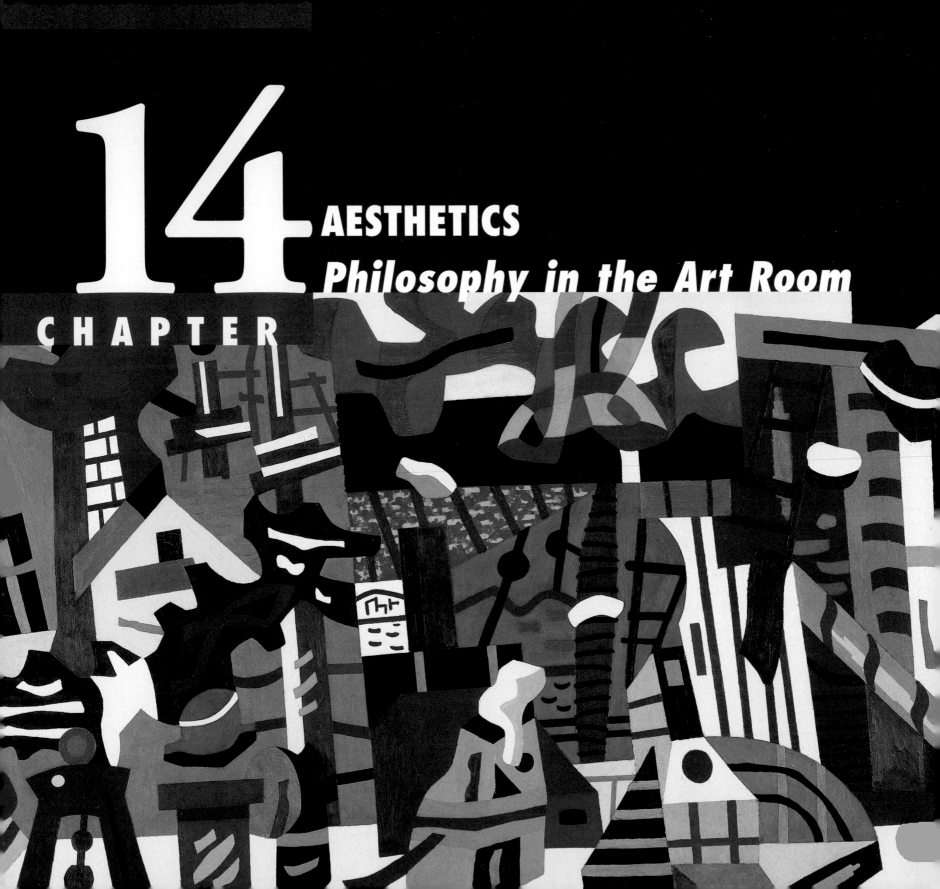

CHAPTER 14

AESTHETICS
Philosophy in the Art Room

> *Artistic products must be seen and thought of in a context of theory to be truly edifying. Framed by the philosophical imagination, they must be captured by the mind as much as by the senses.*[1]
>
> **—Ronald Moore**

Aesthetics is a body of writing by philosophers that poses such recurring questions as these: What is a work of art? How does it differ from other objects? What purposes does art serve? Can art be judged, and if so, how? What responsibility does the artist have to society? Can *nature* be art? What makes an experience aesthetic? Can a mass-produced object be a work of art? How do institutional settings, such as museums, galleries, and art magazines, define art? What is the relation between emotion and aesthetic experience? Why are some artworks labeled masterpieces? These questions are not uncommon, even among children who, during an art museum visit, might ask, "Who decides what to put in the museum?" "Is everything in this museum art?" "Why is that chair art? Is it better than the chairs at school or at home? Why?" Such questions are inevitable from lively children in a stimulating environment, and they require thoughtful responses from teachers at levels appropriate to children's capacities of comprehension.

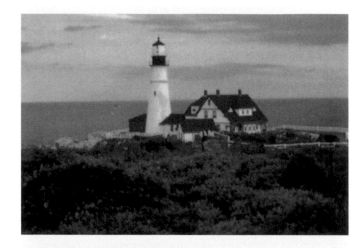

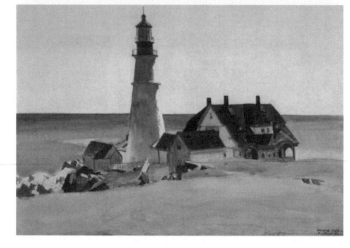

Edward Hopper, *Lighthouse and Building,* Portland Head, Cape Elizabeth, Maine, 1972. Comparing the photograph showing the source of the artist's subject to the watercolor itself, one can see how the artist transformed nature. (Bequest of John T. Spaulding. Courtesy, Museum of Fine Arts, Boston.)

aesthetic fallacy in the following lines from Joyce Kilmer's famous poem "Trees":

> *I think that I shall never see*
> *A poem as lovely as a tree . . .*
> *Poems are made by fools like me*
> *But only God can make a tree.*[11]

Art and Knowledge: How Much Does One Need to Know?

Study Sandro Botticelli's *Primavera.* Without taking the time to describe or analyze its structure, think about your intuitive response to it. If you are like most people, your reac-

tions will be positive; this is one of the most reproduced, hence most popular, images of Western European art. As one writer states:

> Its complete meaning is as elusive as the remote and wistful elegance of the almost transcendental scene which Botticelli sets before our eyes. This is a picture with layers of meaning, layers that shimmer like the diaphanous veils of its dancing figures.[12]

In this bit of evocative description, the writer has already taken a stand on the relative importance of knowledge and appreciation. In order to sense "wistful elegance" and shimmering "diaphanous veils," we do not need knowledge, but if we are to probe the painting's layers of meaning, we are going to need some historical facts that have little or no relation to the realm of intuition. Here are just a few to consider:

- Sandro Botticelli represents a late rather than an early Renaissance style of painting. The painting is executed on wood, rather than on canvas, and bears no signature or title.
- More than forty different plants can be identified in the painting, all of which have a reason for their placement.
- The setting is in a sacred grove, known to everyone who is familiar with Dante's *Divine Comedy* as the boundary between heaven and purgatory.
- Each figure in the painting has its own identity. They are known by their attributes or objects with which they are associated: Cupid with his bow, the myrtle bush with its aphrodisiacal powers with Venus, Mercury with winged heels, and so on. Fewer agree on the meaning of the main figures. Some say one group represents chastity, beauty, and love; others see them as splendor, youth, and happiness.
- The *Primavera* also possesses a musical analogy to some historians. The concept of harmony in human affairs is embodied in the mathematical basis of the use of intervals and in the ratios of smaller to larger units of harmonic relationships. "The figures string out across the painting like the notes of an octave. Mercury and Zephyr are the tonic notes. All those in harmony with them face the same way while the discords, the second and seventh notes, turn the other way."[13]

The writers from whom this brief listing of facts was taken spent a year in Florence studying five paintings, among them

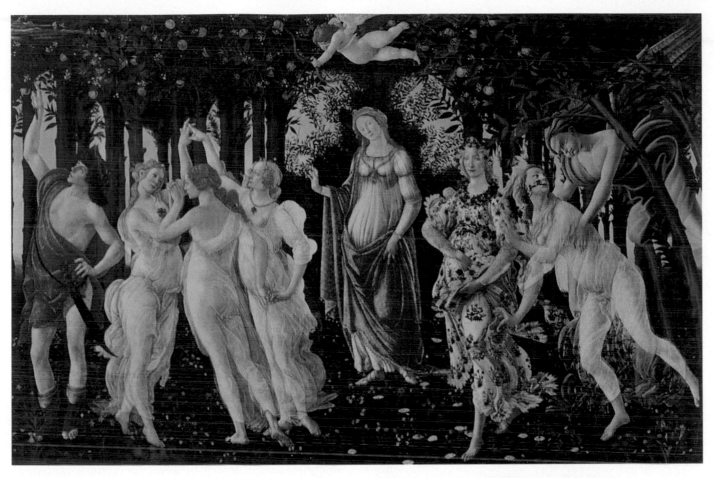

Sandro Botticelli, *Primavera*, 1477. This painting serves to show that a viewer can have both an intuitive as well as a knowledge-based appreciation of an artwork, both of which are unique and valid reactions to viewing the painting. (Galleria degli Uffizi, Florence) Scala/Art Resource, N.Y.

the *Primavera*. This dedication to deciphering the layers of a work is what distinguishes historians from aestheticians. The aesthetic question posed by the work of historians is "How much must one know in order to fully appreciate a work of art? Has the knowledge gained by reading about the *Primavera* in any way affected your relation to it and, if so, how?" Of the thousands of visitors who yearly come to the Uffizi to see the *Primavera,* many seek information about the work and the artist, and others do not feel they need anything beyond what they bring to the work.

A work of art, as demonstrated by the *Primavera,* can reach us on several levels. The first level is accessible to anyone with an open eye and mind, but to reach succeeding levels or layers of appreciation, we may have to call on the insights of art historians, general historians, or anyone who can shed light on the work from the perspective of his or her discipline. Some artworks are like puzzles waiting to be solved.

Aesthetics and Media

The medium selected by an artist is a critical factor not only in the success of a work but also in its material value. Why is it that oil paintings generally enjoy more prestige than the same subject executed in watercolor, and what circumstances could serve to equalize such a discrepancy? For no other medium are aesthetic issues raised more than printmaking; the director of one print workshop poses the following questions:

> Is a computer print an original? Should it be considered alongside etching, lithographs, wood blocks and screen-prints? Some would say no, it lacks the 3-D quality of layering that distinguishes "hand made" prints from mechanical reproduction. And is it mechanical? Just because you cannot distinguish the texture because of the superfine resolution, does that make it any less mechanical? Is the act of originality simply choice and are the means of producing the image irrelevant?[14]

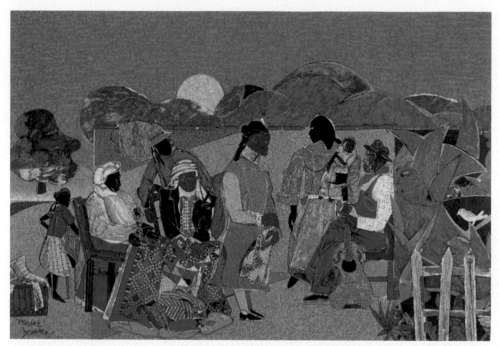

Romare Bearden, *Quilting Time*, 1986. The Detroit Institute of Arts, Founders Society Purchase with funds from the Detroit Edison Company. © Romare Bearden Foundation, New York, N.Y. Photograph © 1990 The Detroit Institute of Arts.

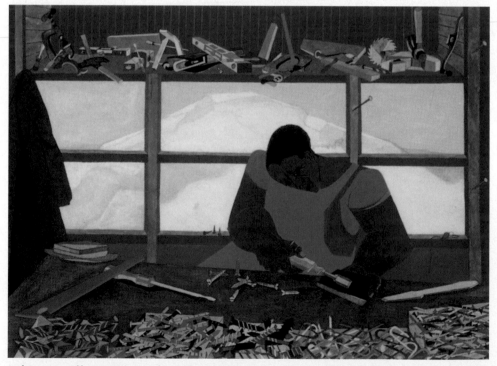

Jacob Lawrence, *Builders #1*, 1972. Watercolor, gouache, and graphite on paper, 22 1/2" × 30 3/4". The Saint Louis Art Museum, Eliza McMillan Fund.

THREE AESTHETIC STANCES: MIMESIS, EXPRESSIONISM, AND FORMALISM
Mimesis: Art As Imitation or Representation of Things As Seen

Must art match what we see? Plato argued that it did not matter how skillful artists were in portraying the physical world; they could never render the true reality—the essence of objects. Artists were therefore imitators or mimics and, because of this, were inherently inferior to poets and musicians. In the beginnings of Western art, people admired the skill it took to create visual equivalents of the world they knew. The notion of art as imitation or representation of life becomes more complicated as one studies it and discovers related movements and theories, such as the realism of Courbet, who once stated, "show me an angel, and I'll paint you one." The idea of realism has also taken the form of *social realism,* which dealt with particular social-consciousness subject matter (the working class); *naturalism,* which overlapped into literature; and *trompe l'oeil* painting, where meticulous handling of detail could deceive the eye. Techniques for imitating nature range from the *illusionistic* devices in perspective developed in the Renaissance and used by both scene designers and painters to the contemporary photorealists' reliance on photographic veracity. Behind all variations of "art as imitation" lies the assumption that art is most meaningful when it can provide some sort of match between the personal experience of the viewer and the work of the artist. As in all aesthetic theories, the questions that inevitably arise are: "Is that all there is to art, and, if not, what are the alternatives? What lies beyond our immediate experience?"

The major alternative approach to the imitation or *mimesis* theory is the expressionist view.

Art As Expression: Emphasis on Feeling and Emotion

The idea that expression can be considered as a major function of art creates a distinction between what we *feel* about something and what we *know* about it. Tolstoy believed that the expressive power of art reached its highest form only when an artwork could successfully communicate its meaning to the *viewer.* The emotive power of art was one of the main ideas behind the movement of *expressionism* that began in Germany during the early decades of the twentieth century. The term has since been applied to any movement or artist whose work puts a high priority on feeling and emotion, and it has also come to be associated with the formal *means* used by the artist to achieve it, such as spontaneity of execution, heavily applied paint, the use of accidents, and, as in the cases of van Gogh and Joan Mitchell, even to certain kinds of brushes and implements for applying paint. The key element is transmission of feeling—the assumption that to be effective, the viewer must receive the feelings of the artists. As Tolstoy described it, "Art is a human activity . . . that one man consciously . . . hands on to others . . . feelings he has lived through so that other people are infected by them and also experience them."[15] This is also related to *empathy*, which we will discuss later.

It is of course possible to transmit deep feeling and emotional conviction *without* stressing the formal aspects just listed; indeed romantic realists such as Rosa Bonheur also direct our emotions through subject matter as well as specific painting techniques. Picasso's *Guernica* is an example of how abstraction treated with a minimal use of color and surface manipulation can also arouse our feelings. Regardless of where one throws one's allegiance, arousing and conveying emotion in the spectator must be taken as a universal condition of the expressive function of art. The current worldwide neoexpressionist movement in art demonstrates again the relevance of this aesthetic stance.

Formalism: the Importance of Structure

Formalist aesthetics asserts that the value of an artwork lies not in its relation to real life or to subject matter—as in a landscape or portrait—but in its use of color, space, rhythm, harmony, and so on. To ask of any artwork that it remind the viewer of something in his or her life rather than be valued as the work itself, say the formalists, is to place a limitation on the work. A love of nature, for example, can only partially prepare us to appreciate a Chinese landscape, a Tiffany scene in stained glass, or an Inuit carving. We must be able to respond to the sensory and formal properties of art as well as to subject matter. The critics who developed the formalist theory thought that a picture representing a subject in a recognizable way is essentially an arrangement of colors and forms and must be judged on this basis.

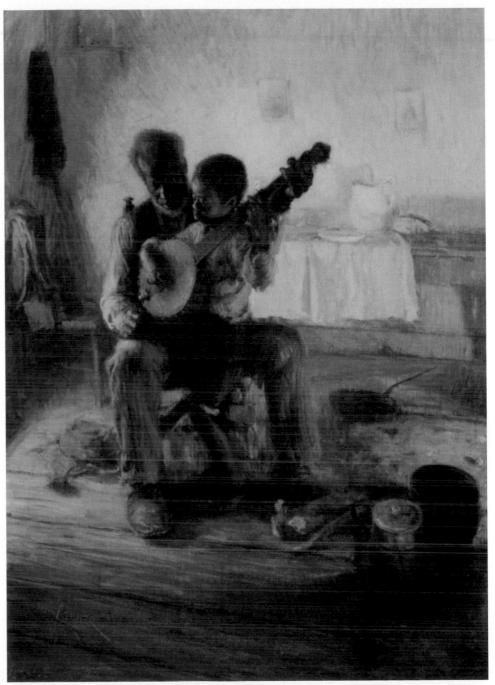

Henry Ossawa Tanner, *The Banjo Lesson*, 1893, oil on canvas, 36 in. × 48 in. (Hampton University Museum, Hampton, VA)

Tanner, Bearden, and Lawrence are recognized for their powerful and sensitive portrayals of everyday experiences in African American communities. Themes of building, working, creating, playing music, family, and inter-generational relationships can be observed in these works. What media were used for each of these works? Compare these works with art by other artists on the same themes. Find other works in this book by African American artists. Which aesthetic stances best apply to each of these works?

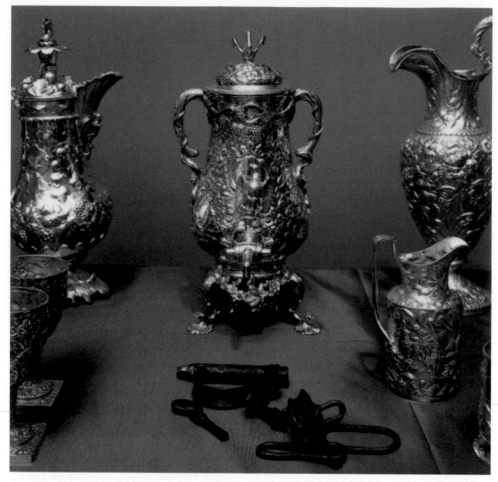

The context of an artwork can change the meaning and the aesthetic response of the viewer. These two examples of metalwork from the same period reflect the violently contrasting social conditions that surrounded their creation. The silver tea service cannot be regarded in the same light when shown in the presence of the slave shackles. (From the exhibition "Mining the Museum," Maryland Historical Society, Fred Wilson, artist-curator)

The formalist artist or critic looks for unity and internal consistency in artworks. Whether the object is a painting, pot, or chair, all parts must relate in a unified way to every other part. In terms of balance, emphasis, and variation, to mention only a few principles, the art object must express the artist's intelligent decisions. When a work is lacking in some aspect, the informed viewer or critic can point to the weakness, because it is apparent in its lack of consistency with the expression of the complete work. The notion of craftsmanship, artistic skill, or competency in technique is often included within the formalistic viewpoint. The formalist keeps his or her eye on this arrangement, while the expressionist is interested in the feelings or emotions the artist wants to convey.

The discipline of aesthetics is an invention of Western culture, as we have noted, and the aesthetic stances discussed here were developed primarily in response to Western art. Although these stances are remarkably useful for viewing art from any culture or, indeed, natural phenomena as well, they are not central to the way art is regarded within many other cultures. Anderson has compared philosophies of art within nine cultures separate from the Western tradition, including the San people of southwestern Africa, Eskimo or Inuit peoples of the Arctic, Aboriginal Australian peoples, inhabitants of the Sepik region of New Guinea, Navajos of the American Southwest, Yoruba people of West Africa, pre-Columbian Aztecs, peoples of early India, and peoples of Japan.[16] Anderson's studies provide a sample of the range of views, purposes, and functions of the visual arts among the diverse peoples of the world.

The Intentional Fallacy

The fallacy of artistic intention is interesting because of the sharp division it has created among critics, philosophers, and artists. Everyone seems to agree that any artist has some purpose in mind when beginning a work, but, from this limited-consensus point on, opinions diverge. The intentionalist critics say that if the goal of the artist is not taken into consideration, we may be looking for the wrong things or expecting more than the artist can deliver. Others argue that we must deal only with what we see, because the artist might not be around to question, and, even if he or she were present, artists are not always articulate with respect to their work. The fallacy lies in the belief that it is necessary to know the artist's intention before we can appreciate his or her work. As an example, although cultural differences may stand in the way of completely understanding some art forms, we can still appreciate and enjoy Haida masks or totem poles without knowing the artists' original intentions. When an intentionalist points to an artist such as Jackson Pollock, whose decision to rely on accidents precludes a clear intention, the opposing side will say that when Pollock decided *not* to plan ahead, that decision in itself is a statement of intent.

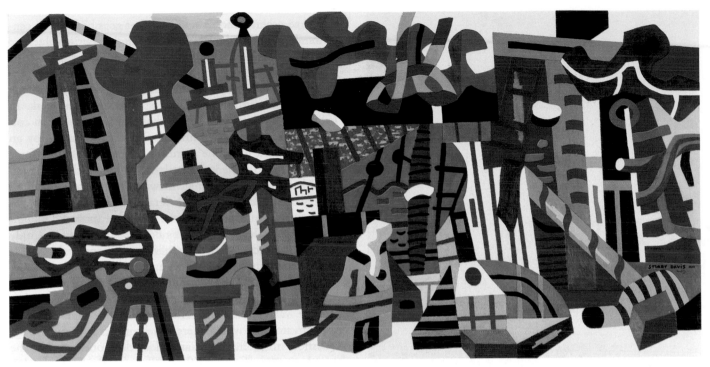

Stuart Davis, *Swing Landscape*, 1938, oil on canvas, 86 in. × 172 in.

© Indiana University Art Museum, photograph by Michael Cavanagh and Kevin Montague. © Estate of Stuart Davis/Licensed by VAGA, New York, N.Y.

One of the most original artists, Stuart Davis combined concepts from Cubism with his unique American vision. Davis' work provides a transition between French cubism and the non-objective painting of Pollock, De Kooning, and Mitchell. Many of Davis' works made reference to musical forms such as swing, jazz, and boogie woogie.

Both sides would have to admit that, in most cases, there is always some element of surprise or discovery even when the artist's intentions are formulated in advance. Artists will often comment on the things people see in their work that have little to do with what they had in mind. Tom Stoppard, the British playwright, likens it to going to a foreign country. The customs officer asks you to describe what you have in your suitcase, and you list such items as clothing, toilet articles, and books, but the customs officer, on investigating, says, "That's odd, I don't see any clothing. I see candy, stuffed animals, and jewelry." The more poetic, personal, or imaginative a style of criticism, the less attention will be paid to the original intent of the artist. When children role-play the critic, they should be aware of these two approaches: interpretation derived from the goals of the artist and interpretation that inspires imaginative or purely literary responses.

Some artists object when asked to explain the meaning of their work and take the position that, if they could explain the meaning, there would be no reason to create the artwork, that the work must speak for itself. Other artists are not articulate and have no interest in speaking and writing about their art or the work of other artists. They feel that they should not be burdened with interpreting their own work. Probably all artists are, to some extent at least, culture-bound, in that they are unable to detach themselves from the influences and conventions of the society in which they live. The idea that only the artist can provide the real meaning of a work of art is, basically, impractical for these reasons and also because many artists are no longer living and able to answer our questions.

Art critics are the professionals who have the greatest responsibility to explain, interpret, and assess works of art. This is not to suggest that the written or spoken ideas of artists about their own work, their motivations and influences, or their personal lives are of no worth. Art historians spend much time and effort searching for such material from artists of the past, and good critics are sensitive to the entire body of work of contemporary artists. Intentionalists and nonintentionalists differ primarily in the emphasis each places on artists' interpretations of their own work.

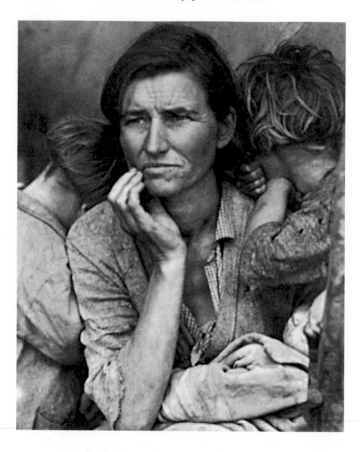

Dorothea Lange, *Migrant Mother, Nipomo, California,* 1936.
© Dorothea Lange Collection, The Oakland Museum of California, City of Oakland, gift of Paul S. Taylor.

Photographer Lange was driving across rural California during the depression years and was drawn to a migrant workers' camp where she discovered this mother and her children. There was no work because the vegetable crop had frozen. One of the most memorable pictures of the last fifty years, this photograph expresses the anguish of extreme poverty, concern for family, and stoical endurance. Is this photograph a work of art? Does it matter that Lange took many pictures of the family and selected this one to publish? Why is this image so enduring?

beyond standards of decency held by most people, do public officials have an obligation to display those works? Are standards of community morality and decency separate from standards of artistic quality? If they are separate, which standards take precedence in the Mapplethorpe case? Should the photographs continue to be displayed because of their artistic excellence attested to by knowledgeable art professionals, or should the photographs be removed because they offend a large number of viewers, including politicians?

- Question for students: Pretend you are a member of a Jewish congregation who discovers that the art committee has scheduled an exhibition of prints by an avowed anti-Semite such as Andre Derain. Would you attempt to cancel the exhibition? If the exhibition were held, would Derain's opinions lessen your enjoyment?

As with many problems in life, there are no easy answers to many aesthetic issues. It seems that each question raises even more questions. Nevertheless, these are real issues that must be resolved in real life, one way or the other. In some ways the study of aesthetics is one of the most useful things we can ask students to do, because it gives them valuable experience in thinking carefully and logically about very "messy" real-life problems and in learning to evaluate different points of view, each of which might have some merit.

Examples of Censorship Issues

- Cartoonists in Nazi Germany depicted Jews as gross and evil, and in World War I Allied artists in their posters treated Germans in similarly unflattering ways. These are examples of art as propaganda and are considered acceptable, indeed patriotic, in times of war. Should the license to demean people in a racist or other hostile way be suspended after peace has been declared? Are there boundaries to artistic freedom? And, finally, a legal constitutional issue arises here—how close does artistic freedom lie to the controversy caused by American Nazi or KKK groups who wish to parade on national holidays?
- If you examine the surface of the Washington Monument, you will see that the color of the stone changes

- Is the issue one of spending public funds on art, or is it an issue of art judgments being made by persons not qualified as art critics? Should politicians, with the dual responsibilities to promote and support the arts and to spend public monies wisely, have the option to judge the quality and significance of the art they support? Can politicians perform the functions of art critics, or should they commission professional critics to make such decisions?
- What problems arise when politicians or other bureaucrats take upon themselves the function of judging the quality and significance of art? Is this practice consistent with the freedom of speech guaranteed in the Constitution of the United States? Are there historical precedents for this practice? What can we learn from these precedents?
- When works of art supported by public funds appear vulgar, disrespectful of some group or institution, or

around a quarter of the way up. This is because some people were so enraged by its design that they dumped hundreds of slabs of stone into the Potomac River. The monument was completed some forty years later when the furor subsided, but, by then, it was impossible to match the original colors of the stone.

- In San Diego, California, the city council voted down funds for a park that featured a sculpture composed of airplane fragments. Why is it that in Israel airplane fragments and other relics of war are accepted by the public as art, while Americans are divided on the use of abstract sculpture in public spaces?
- In Grand Rapids, Michigan, a public sculpture is proposed to commemorate that city's role in fluoridation. The monument suggested is a six-hundred-pound, eighteen-foot-high molar, and its rejection is led by local dentists. Why?

These examples show how truly important aesthetics can be in practical matters. Although it is helpful to have examined a primary source, such as Plato's *Republic* or a commentary on Plato's ideas, this is not needed in order to get a good debate going. Censorship is a particularly effective topic to introduce problems of aesthetics, because at some point all of us must deal with the conflict between reason and emotion. Iredell Jenkins states:

> It behooves the artistic community to accept the responsibility of exercising discrimination and selectivity in its own house. If it does not do this, then an extraneous censorship is sure to be imposed, which will at once touch off movements towards the two extremes of suppression and license.[18]

Is Jenkins suggesting that self-censorship is to be preferred to that of outsiders?

Aesthetics thus has a way of answering one question by posing another. If you can get students to accept this, then they are exercising that "tolerance of ambiguity" that is one characteristic of the sophisticated mind.

Aesthetics Controversy in Museums

The following example of real-life aesthetics is centered on the nature of the art object. We'll call this example "The Question of the Missing Nose."

Situation

Go into any museum that collects classical art, and you will find portrait busts minus their noses. This is understandable since protuberances from any basic form are vulnerable, especially when one considers the hazards of being buried for centuries under debris, dirt, and archaeological fragments.

Problem

As a curator of a museum, you have received a classical sculpture of a portrait bust from a donor. There is one condition attached to the gift, however. The donor insists that the missing nose be repaired so viewers can see it exactly as did the Roman citizen at the beginning of the Christian era. Not all of your staff is overjoyed at the conditions under which the gift is offered. Some flatly reject it on the grounds that no person under any condition has the right to tamper with a work of art, while others say, "Why quibble? Don't look a gift horse in the mouth; our collection needs this work."

What does the class think?

This is a good adversary situation and lends itself to a formal debate. One could also simulate a courtroom setting,

Jaune Quick-to-See Smith, *Rainbow*, 1989. Oil and mixed media on canvas, 66" × 84". Courtesy Bernice Steinbaum Gallery, Miami, Florida.

Quick-to-See Smith's colorful painting of a rainbow combines a number of postmodern elements: The work relates a contemporary ecological theme which is tied as well to the artist's Native American heritage. She uses words in the work, as well as pictographs, and is apparently well acquainted with conventions of modern painting including emphasis on the flat picture plane and paint quality and texture. The combination of ideas, images, and styles is typical of many postmodern works.

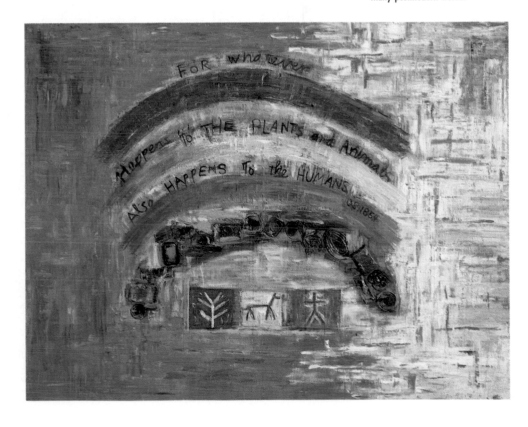

freewheeling one, the same guidelines for discussion apply to both. The following suggestions are not necessarily listed in order of importance.

1. Build your lesson around a few key questions embodied in the concepts you wish to teach. If you wish to stress the concept for third graders that "art is humanmade, not a creation of nature," show them a photo of a city scene and a painting by Edward Hopper and ask, "Which is the painting, which is the photograph, and what is the difference?" Try to stick to your key question, and, to maintain your conceptual focus, resist the temptation to go off into side issues. (This is not always easy with imaginative primary graders.) Although informal brainstorming and free association do have their place, they are not to be confused with the process of inquiry.

2. Try to avoid yes/no questions, since these have limited value and do not open further discussion.

3. Rote definitions repeated from text or dictionary can obscure understanding, since they give the impression that only one answer is correct. Because rote answers represent very little struggle on the student's part, they are also the most quickly forgotten.

4. Complex answers take time; obvious ones do not. Obvious answers do serve one purpose, however—they can get things rolling and involve the shy or reluctant participant. No one likes to keep saying, "I don't know."

5. Avoid asking questions that contain their own answers. For example, "Isn't Barbara Hepworth terrific in the way she simplifies natural forms?"

6. Encourage the role of devil's advocate by having students present counterarguments even when they go against their convictions.

7. Do not get carried away by the brilliance of your question. The longer and more involved the query, the quicker the point will be lost. Be as clear and precise as you can in your questions, since the nature of a question often determines the kind of answer you will receive.

8. Wait for the moment when it is the teacher's job to sum up—to clarify. The summation, a form of Hegel's third stage of *synthesis,* sets the stage for what is to follow.

9. Play off one student's answer to another's. ("Do you agree with Susan? No? Why?")

10. Move the discussion around the room instead of concentrating on a few bright lights. Above all, do not neglect those in the back row, and never underestimate the role that seating plays. Proximity to windows, to friends, or to the teacher can all affect the attention of students.

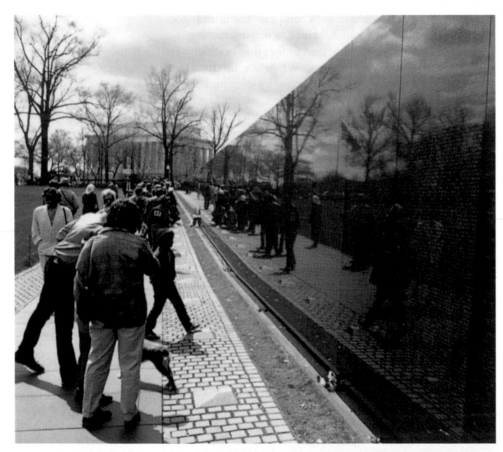

Maya Ying Lin, *Vietnam Veterans Memorial,* 1982, 150 polished and engraved black granite panels 40 in. wide, height from 18 in. to 10 ft. 9 in. (Washington, D.C.) Photo by Michael Day.

Maya Lin's design for this memorial comes from the context of contemporary minimal sculpture. The abstract quality of the black marble "Wall," as opposed to traditional memorials featuring realistic sculptures of combatants, made this work controversial when it was dedicated in 1982. Since then two traditional sculptures have been added, one of three soldiers, another of women military medical personnel caring for the wounded. The Wall has subsequently gained stature as a unique and effective memorial. Visitors to the *Vietnam Veterans Memorial* stand before the reflective surface, viewing their own images as they see the thousands of names of fallen veterans engraved in the stone.

11. There is no point in asking a question if you do not take time to listen to the answer.

12. Try the "pair-share" method as part of your inquiry. Divide the class into teams, and allow two or three minutes for participants to think about an answer. Then have a representative of each group share their answers with the class.

13. Although the truth does not necessarily lie in consensus, try an occasional survey to see what kind of consensus exists. ("How many agree with Bruce? You seem to be in the minority. George, since you don't agree with Bruce, can you come up to the picture and identify what you are referring to?")

14. Since inquiry cannot proceed without guidelines, get the class involved in setting down a few rules before you begin. These may range from the general ("Try to be open to a point of view that's different from yours") to the more specific ("When possible, give some clear evidence, such as pointing to a flaw in an argument to support your statement.")

15. Although aesthetic discussions can proceed on what is said rather than on what is seen, the ideas selected for discussion should, whenever possible, relate to artworks. Can you imagine how much would be lost in a discussion of formalist or expressionist philosophies of art without comparing works of Mondrian and Kokoschka?

16. The general goal of any program of aesthetic inquiry is to develop in students the ability to deal with disagreement and uncertainty, to value ways of viewing a problem that differ from their own.

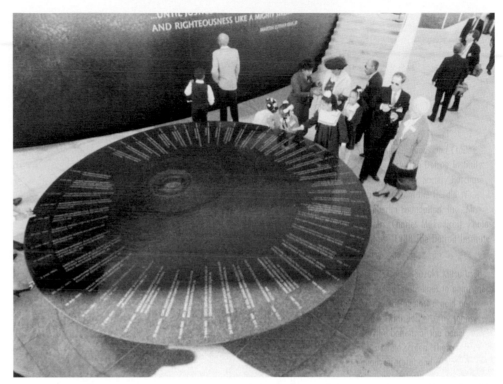

Maya Ying Lin, *Civil Rights Memorial,* 1990, curved, polished black granite wall, 9 ft. high and 40 ft. long, and a circular table of black granite, 11 ft. 6 in. in diameter, 30 in. high, on a base of 20 in., water (Southern Poverty Law Center, Montgomery, Alabama) AP/Wide World.

The use of water that slides down the wall in a thin sheet and wells up onto the circular table is suggested by the quote from Martin Luther King, Jr., inscribed on the wall, "until justice rolls down like waters and righteousness like a mighty stream." The names of men, women, and children who lost their lives in the struggle for civil rights in the United States appear on the round table, covered by a thin sheet of water. Both of Lin's memorials demonstrate how art can communicate social ideals, values, and beliefs in ways that transcend the power of words.

Never underestimate the desire of children to talk about art, particularly in primary grades. The fact is, the younger the child, the more eagerly discussion will be welcomed. Any idea presented as a puzzle or a quandary or that uses a case history has immediate appeal as a means of provoking discussion.

NOTES

1. Ronald Moore, ed., *Aesthetics for Young People* (Reston, VA: National Art Education Association, 1995), p. 8.
2. Leo Tolstoy, *What Is Art?* (Philadelphia: Henry Altemus, 1898), p. 281.
3. Ibid.
4. Ibid.
5. Jon Sharer, "Children's Inquiry into Aesthetics," document presented at the National Art Education Association Convention, New Orleans, 1986.
6. Robert Russell, "The Aesthetician as a Model in Learning about Art," *Studies in Art Education* 27, no. 4 (1986).
7. Margaret P. Battin, "Cases for Kids: Using Puzzles to Teach Aesthetics to Children," in *Aesthetics for Young People,* ed. Moore.
8. *Merriam-Webster's Collegiate Dictionary,* 10th ed. (Springfield, MA.: Merriam-Webster, 1993).
9. An excellent sourcebook for aesthetics discussions is Margaret Battin, John Fisher, Ronald Moore, and Anita Silvers, *Puzzles about Art: An Aesthetics Casebook* (New York: St. Martin's Press, 1989).
10. William Feaver, "Reawakening Beauty," *ARTnews* 98, no. 9 (October 1999): 216.
11. Louis Untermeyer, ed., *Modern American Poetry, Modern British Poetry: A Critical Approach* (New York: Harcourt Brace, 1936), p. 391.
12. Richard Foster and Pamela Tudor-Craig, *The Secret Life of Paintings* (New York: St. Martin's Press, 1986), p. 41.
13. Ibid.
14. Dennis O'Neil, *Lasting Impressions,* catalog, Susquehanna Art Museum, 1993, p. 32.
15. Tolstoy, *What Is Art?* p. 281.
16. Richard L. Anderson, *Calliope's Sisters: A Comparative Study of Philosophies of Art* (Englewood Cliffs, NJ: Prentice-Hall, 1990).
17. *Smithsonian,* (October 1989): 2.
18. Iredell Jenkins, "Aesthetic Education and Moral Refinement," *The Journal of Aesthetic Education* 2, no. 3 (July 1968): 35.
19. Battin et al., *Puzzles about Art,* pp. vi–viii.

ACTIVITIES FOR THE READER

1. Conduct a survey by asking six people, "What does the word 'aesthetics' mean?" Choose from a wide variety of occupations, such as teachers, nurses, lawyers, waitresses, truck drivers, and bankers.
2. A painting of a black circle could be interpreted as the artist's mood, the Black Hole of Calcutta, or just leftover black paint. Apply multiple meanings to Wyeth's *Christina's World* as you try to account for the subject's relation to her house. Is your interpretation as valid as Wyeth's?
3. Select a common object, and endow it with meaning beyond itself. (Warhol did this with his Brillo boxes.) What can you do to transpose the object of your choice? Consider its environment, the lighting. How would you use written material?
4. Select a well-known artwork such as Picasso's *Guernica,* and write reactions to it from the following points of view: a historian, an art historian, an art critic of the last century, and a survivor of the bombing.
5. In *Principles of Art,* R. G. Collingwood makes a distinction between fine art (or art proper) and craft, stating "the craftsman knows what he wants to make before he makes it." This suggests that the potter's or jeweler's relation to their raw materials places a limitation on the process of creation.

   To examine the idea, create a clay vessel with some very clear specifications in mind, such as height, thickness, and shape. As these conditions are met, begin taking some freedom with your vessel by giving it a human reference, adding form, working the surface, and so on. When you do this, have you passed over from craft to art?
6. Review the discussion about artist's intent in this chapter. Discuss the following case with a friend or colleague. Vincent van Gogh's *The Starry Night* is widely appreciated and highly regarded by professionals in the art field. It is considered to be one of his masterworks and, according to

the current art market, is worth many millions of dollars. What if an art historian uncovered a lost letter by van Gogh to his brother Theo, indicating his dissatisfaction with his recently completed painting entitled *The Starry Night*. He wrote in the letter that it just did not turn out the way he *intended,* and he considered it to be a failure. Would such a revelation of the artist's intent and his negative evaluation of the painting change the way we respond to it and regard it?

7. Prepare a bulletin board for an ongoing display entitled "Big Questions about Art." When a question comes up through class discussion or studio activities, such as "Is a pot art?" (or a chair, car, building, African mask), bring in pictures of examples under discussion. Place each picture on the bulletin board under YES, NO, or MAYBE. Students might bring such items as a postcard from a natural history museum that pictures embroidered fishskin boots made by Nanai people in Siberia, a *National Geographic* picture showing jewelry and body scarification in an African tribe, or a picture of a beautifully designed modern toaster. Move pictures from one category to another as more information is gathered. A beautifully shaped piece of driftwood might be moved from the YES category to the NO category after it has been decided that natural objects are not considered art. The driftwood, however, may remain in the NO category until someone discovers Marcel Duchamp's "readymades."

8. Refer to Tolstoy's definition of art presented at the beginning of this chapter. Make a list of what he says art will not be and a list of what it will be. Then look at a range of artworks by such artists as De Kooning, Rembrandt, Kieffer, Clemente, Cassatt, Rodin, Nevelson, and so on, and decide which works you think fit Tolstoy's definition.

9. Try to locate a cheap "airport art" reproduction of a piece of sculpture being sold as African in origin. Take your purchase to a museum or to any collector who has authentic examples. Compare the two, and search for any factors that separate a clumsy fake from what is authentic (nature of material, surface, evidence of age or newness, and so on). Some clever fakes are made of the same materials used in authentic works. Try to locate an example of a work that is difficult to categorize as authentic or imitation.

10. Should the objects depicted in a work be taken literally, at face value, or can we assume that the artist is using unpleasant subject matter to get at an idea that exists beyond what is seen? Set up a debate centered around the withdrawal of financial support of a museum because the public finds certain works offensive.

SUGGESTED READINGS

Anderson, Tom, and Sally McRorie. "A Role for Aesthetics in Centering the K–12 Art Curriculum." *Art Education* 50, no. 3 (1997): 6–14.

Eaton, Marsha M. *Basic Issues in Aesthetics*. Belmont, CA: Wadsworth, 1988.

Getty Center for Education in the Arts. *Art Education in Action. Aesthetics:* Episode A: "The Aesthetic Experience"; Episode B: "Teaching across the Curriculum." Viewer's Guide by Michael D. Day. Santa Monica, CA: Getty Center for Education in the Arts, 1995.

Henry, Carole. "Philosophical Inquiry: A Practical Approach to Aesthetics." *Art Education* 46, no. 3 (1993): 20–24.

Lankford, Louis. *Aesthetics: Issues and Inquiry*. Reston, VA: National Art Education Association, 1992.

McRorie, Sally. "On Teaching Learning Aesthetics: Gender and Related Issues." *Gender Issues in Art Education: Content, Contexts, and Strategies*. Ed. Georgia Collins and Renee Sandell. Reston, VA: National Art Education Association, 1996, pp. 30–38.

Moore, Ronald, ed. *Aesthetics for Young People*. Reston, VA: National Art Education Association, 1995.

Parsons, Michael J., and H. Gene Blocker. *Aesthetics and Education. Disciplines in Art Education*. Urbana: University of Illinois Press, 1993.

Smith, Ralph A., and Alan Simpson, eds. *Aesthetics and Arts Education*. Urbana: University of Illinois Press, 1993.

Stewart, Marilyn G. *Thinking through Aesthetics*. Worcester, MA: Davis Publications, 1997.

WORLD WIDE WEB RESOURCES

Resources for the Study of Aesthetics

American Society for Aesthetics. "Aesthetics Teaching Resources." *Aesthetics Online.* 1999. <http://www.aesthetics-online.org/teaching/index.html>. This site provides information about aesthetics and includes links to other aesthetics, philosophy, and arts-related resources.

Aesthetics and Multicultural Issues

Chalmers, F. Graeme, and the Getty Institute for Education in the Arts. "Aesthetics." *Celebrating Pluralism: Art, Education, and Cultural Diversity: Multicultural Approaches to Art Learning.* 1996. <http://www.artsednet.getty.edu/ArtsEdNet/Resources/Chalmers/aestheics.html> Chalmers addresses cultural contexts of aesthetics and their application to cultural diversity in art and education.

Switala, Kristin. Center for Digital Discourse and Culture, Virginia Tech University. Feminist Theory Website: *Feminist Aesthetics.* 1999. <http://www.cddc.vt.edu/feminism/aes.html> This Web page features an extensive bibliography and provides links to Web sites of feminist scholars, artists, and related online resources.

Curriculum and Teaching Resources

ArtsEdNet, The Getty Art Education Web Site. *Philosophers Forum: Asking Big Questions about Art.* 1998. <http://www.artsednet.getty.edu/ArtsEdNet/Resources/Philos/index.html> In this innovative ArtsEdNet program, two professional philosophers, Dr. Marcia Muelder Eaton and Dr. Ronald Moore, model aesthetic inquiry with commentary by an expert in K–12 art education, Dr. Marilyn G. Stewart. Their discussion demonstrates the application of aesthetic inquiry to classroom settings.

ArtsEdNet, The Getty Art Education Web Site. *Art Education in Action: Aesthetics.* 1995. <http://www.artsednet.getty.edu/ArtsEdNet/Resources/Aeia/aesthetics.html> This online version of the video series *Art Education in Action* (see Suggested Readings) includes lesson plans and video footnotes. Images of art are also provided.

McRorie, Sally, and Getty Center for Education in the Arts. "Questioning the Work of Sandy Skoglund: Aesthetics." 1996. <http://www.artsednet.getty.edu/ArtsEdNet/Resources/Skoglund/mcrorie.html> Provides a working definition of aesthetics for classroom teachers with questions formulated specifically for lessons in art production, art criticism, and art history. Demonstrates a process of inquiry that mirrors what aestheticians do. This material is related to an online exhibition of work by artist Sandy Skoglund.

Van Camp, Julie C., and California State University, Long Beach. *Freedom of Expression at the National Endowment for the Arts: Governmental Determinations of Aesthetic Value,* 1997–1999. <http://www.csulb.edu/~jvancamp/freedom4.html>This Web site is part of an interdisciplinary education project involving aesthetics, law, and education. It covers the controversy surrounding debates over government funding of the arts and presents in-depth information that is useful to any classroom teacher interested in issues of freedom of expression, obscenity, and aesthetic judgments.

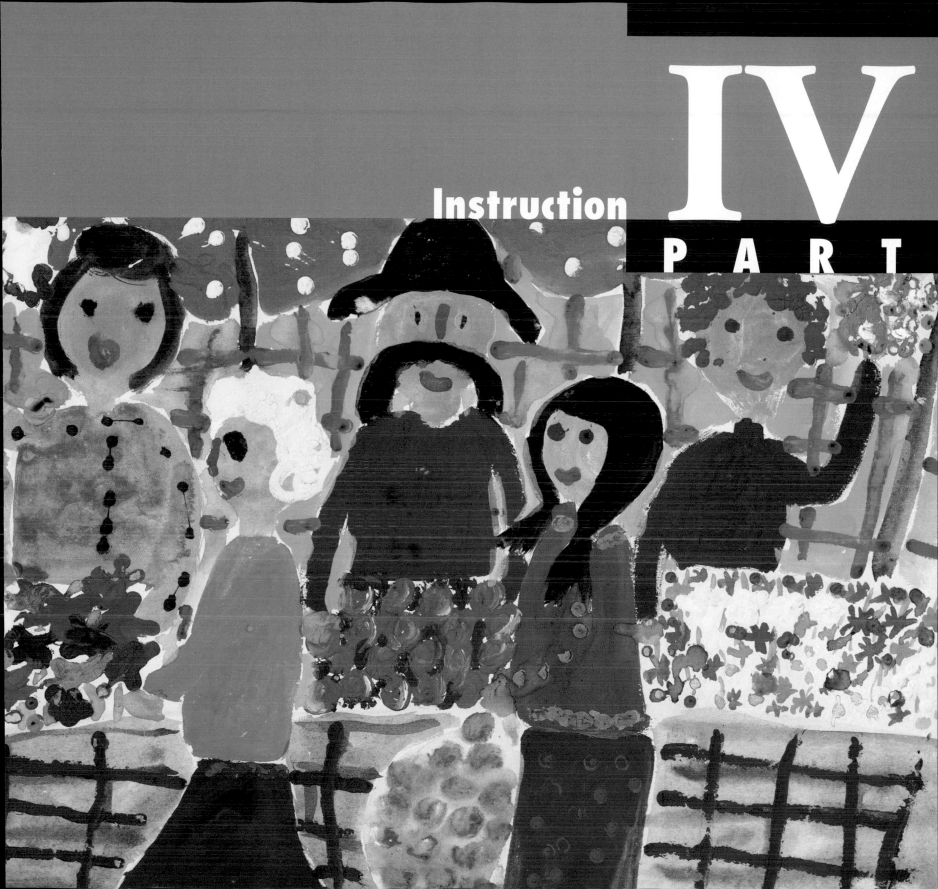

Instruction

IV

PART

15

METHODS FOR TEACHING ART
Classroom Practice

Teaching is intellectual and ethical work. It requires the full attention—wide awake, inquiring, critical—of thoughtful and caring people if it is to be done well.[1]

—William Ayers

How does one go about teaching art? A ten-year-old child watches in fascination as an artist-in-residence throws a pot, the sensuousness of the clay in motion nearly driving him to distraction as he anticipates his turn on the wheel. The attention of a fifth-grade girl is held by a slide of a Mayan temple and by the teacher's account of the rituals that occurred on various occasions, while a second grader is proud to have been chosen by the teacher to help distribute the supplies needed for the first painting session of the year. When children are engaged in situations like these, someone has made a decision regarding the means of learning—one way of defining what is known as *methodology,* or that drier term, *pedagogy.* We noted in Part II that all children are unique individuals and that we encounter a wide range of learning styles and abilities among the children in our schools. We discussed in Part III the extensive content for instruction within a balanced, comprehensive art program. Given the diversity of learners and the breadth and depth of the subject, art teachers need to develop and employ a repertoire of teaching methods. Indeed, the type of art program outlined in previous chapters requires a variety of teaching methods. For example, art teachers demonstrate skills for art making, show slides or prints of artworks, and lead discussions about works of art. In this chapter we will discuss some

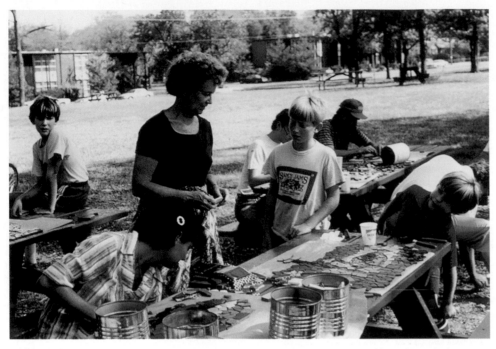

U.S.A.

1. The *directive* method, appropriate for transmitting skills, techniques, or processes.

2. The *Socratic* or questioning method, employed with groups or individuals, is used to *guide* students in finding answers. This method requires certain skills of the teacher and takes more time, but it is particularly appropriate for aesthetics or any realm of instruction that deals with ideas, theories, interpretation, and analysis.

3. *Discovery*, the method in which the teacher sets the stage for lessons that are open ended, speculative, and problem-solving.

Depending on the content of instruction, the teacher may use several styles in the same unit if not in the same lesson. The three general approaches suggest different problems and therefore different methods of presentation, motivation, and styles of pupil-teacher relationships. The problem the teacher faces is to determine appropriate times to use each approach. The introduction of a new medium can be either directive or discovery centered, a discussion of the meaning of an artwork can be Socratic, and calling attention to safety factors should be directive. The approach recommended is flexibility: a teaching style that draws on a number of strategies or methods of instruction suitable for a particular child, material, or idea.

The approaches discussed thus far are general. Another level of methodology deals with the specific aspects of instruction. When teachers suggest a particular way of developing a painting ("Begin large, then work small, and choose your brushes to match the problem," or "Before you mix a color, think of the amount of paint you will need to cover the space"), they are working at the most immediate level of methodology. When two teachers discuss the most effective way of teaching lettering, or when a teacher plans to introduce a new tool in such a way as to minimize waste or accidents, this is directive methodology operating at both immediate and practical levels. In a broad sense, discussions of teaching methods might include such questions as: How does a teacher assist students to become more aware of symbols in works of art? What do teachers say or do to open students' eyes, to heighten their perceptions of the aesthetic dimensions of their environment? How do teaching methods relate to motivation and discipline problems? Before dealing with the specifics of such questions, we must turn our attention to more general contexts for instruction.

of the issues and practices for teaching art in elementary and middle school classrooms, and we will review the range of teaching methods that might be appropriate for different teaching situations.

METHODOLOGY

Methodology is not a rigidly prescriptive series of step-by-step directions on the "how" of teaching. Certainly a multitude of methods can and should be used by a teacher. If curriculum deals with the content of instruction, methodology concerns itself with the most effective means of moving students toward realization of curriculum goals. A program can be well planned and resources plentiful, but if a teacher is unaware of processes for getting children to move in a productive way, then the art program the teacher (and students) envision will probably never materialize.

Methodology brings to mind certain principles and techniques of motivation and control that can be studied, observed, and reflected on. If we concede that methods are determined by the varying nature of the children and the task, then methodology invites an eclectic approach. Here are three general styles of instruction:

Contexts for Art Teaching

Art, like any other subject, no matter how intrinsically interesting and attractive, can be poorly taught. Teachers have failed when students learn to dislike the subject and avoid contact with it in later life. Teachers must never become so concerned with emphasis on subject content that they ignore students' attitudes and feelings about the subject. In general, students will respond positively to art instruction when teachers are well prepared, have learning goals clearly in mind, and are able to explain the goals to children at their levels of understanding.

When art is taught well, children are enthusiastic about learning, and, when such is the case, art can influence the whole atmosphere of a school, and other fields of study seem to benefit by its good effects. Thinking becomes livelier, and children take a greater interest and pride both in their school and in themselves. School halls, classrooms, and the principal's office are changed from drab areas into places of real visual interest, and children proudly bring their parents to school to see exhibitions of work. Principals report a greater degree of cooperation not only among the children themselves but also among members of the teaching staff and between the public and the school. Most of all, *successful teachers bring the student to believe that art matters*. They also help parents understand why art is worth the time and money required, that it occupies a justifiable position in general education.

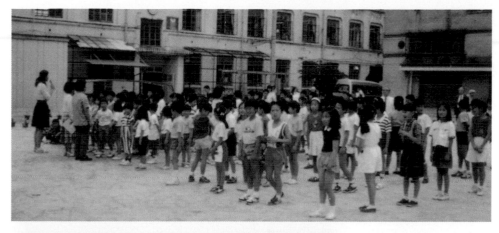

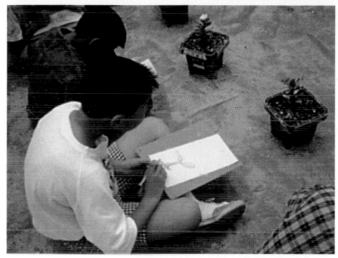

In this method of group instruction (1) the entire school gathers on the playground to receive instructions after which (2) each child completes a line drawing of his or her own plant. After this, the work will be critiqued in each classroom and some will develop their drawings into more complete works using watercolor or mixed media. (Japan)

Who Should Teach Art?

The National Art Education Association states that "art instruction shall be conducted by qualified teachers of art."[2] Advocates for art instruction by specialists at the elementary level argue that most classroom teachers have not had the benefit of a fundamental art education and therefore are not qualified to teach art. Art teachers are specially prepared to implement art instruction. They point out that classroom teachers already carry a heavy burden of instructional responsibilities, and do not need another subject to concern them.

Some states discourage the employment of art and other subject specialists at the elementary level. Advocates of both sides of the issue appear to agree that art specialists, as a rule, can teach art better than classroom generalists, but some point out that other factors must be considered. In some cases, the objection to specialists is a financial one; in other instances, the argument is philosophical. Some educators argue that, for art to be integrated with the rest of the curriculum, for art to become part of the basic curriculum, it is best taught by classroom teachers. They point to art programs where art teachers move from school to school with hundreds of pupil contacts, preventing them from learning the names of children or developing meaningful relationships with them as individuals. In some cases, art programs are limited by what art specialists can bring to classrooms on a cart.

Because some school districts have more autonomy than others, the issue of who teaches art to elementary children becomes a local decision. In some districts, part of the elementary schools employ art specialists, and others do not. There are districts in which art instruction is accomplished cooperatively by art teachers and classroom teachers. Statistics indicate that 85 percent of public elementary schools in the United States offer visual arts instruction. In 43 percent of classrooms, art is taught by art specialists and in 28 percent of classrooms, art is taught by classroom teachers. In the remaining 29 percent of classrooms, art is taught by a combination of art specialists and classroom teachers. The employment of elementary art specialists varies widely in different regions of the country. In the west, 53 percent of schools report art instruction by classroom teachers, while in the northeast, only 7 percent of schools do not include visual arts specialists on their teaching staffs.[3]

Regardless of who is given the responsibility to teach art, effective teachers in all subjects are expected to demonstrate the following abilities:

1. Know the content of the curriculum and be able to identify and generate instructional materials, tasks, and activities suited to specific teaching/learning situations.

2. Be able to create an environment conducive to learning.

3. Accurately observe and record selected aspects of performance to enable the diagnosis of individual and group learning needs.

4. Be able to work effectively and harmoniously with colleagues, parents, and others in the community.

5. Be able to carry out administrative tasks appropriate to the level of appointment.

6. Adopt methodologies consistent with the goals of the curriculum and the intellectual and social backgrounds of students.

Most countries do not have trained art specialists in the elementary grades. (Israel, Canada, and the United States are a few exceptions.) In most countries, it is assumed that art will be taught by the classroom teacher. (Great Britain, Korea, Australia, and New Zealand have very active art programs conducted by non-art specialists.) Japan's solution is to include at least two courses in art education in the preparation of every classroom teacher.

The teacher who has sufficient ability, tact, and liking for children to teach language, arithmetic, or social studies is capable of conducting an art program. Like any other subject, art requires of the teacher some specific knowledge and skills—such as a knowledge of design, an acquaintance with professional artworks, and some ability to use materials such as paint and clay. With the support of a well-written art curriculum, a competent teacher may gain the knowledge and master the skills associated with art education. The problems in teaching art, including classroom management and control, discipline, presentation of lessons, assistance of pupils, and appraisal of the success of the program are, broadly speaking, similar to those in the general school program.

Teachers do not have to be accomplished artists, critics, or historians in order to know how to initiate classroom art activities. If they can handle basic materials and have the aid of a sound art curriculum, classroom teachers can provide children with an art program of value, if not of the same quality as art specialists. Basically three types of teachers can offer some degree of art instruction:

1. The classroom teacher with limited preparation who encourages children to use art by assigning problems and conducting what has been called a laissez-faire program.

2. The classroom teacher who has taken the time to take an in-service course and to study on his or her own and who is able to begin art activities that go beyond making art into studying about art.

3. The professional art teacher who, through training in education as well as art, has the knowledge to advance the child's work.

One of the purposes of this book is to serve all three of these types of teachers.

Even if every elementary school were suddenly to be allotted its own art teacher, there would still be the problem of finding hours in the week for each child to be reached by the art specialist. Under ideal conditions, the classroom teacher should serve as a partner to trained art personnel in planning and should share responsibility for the success of the program.

TEACHING PRACTICES IN ART

The following discussion of teaching methods is based on tried and proven practices. Almost anyone who has taken a course in methods of teaching will be familiar with the ideas presented. The contemporary art program rests on a strong belief in the need for both positive guidance and consistent yet flexible methodologies.

A good teacher begins where the child's natural interests and abilities end. During the progressive era of the early

1930s, teachers were apt to accept everything children did as evidence of their optimal potential. We now recognize that much of what children do on their own without guidance, motivation, or special material is repetitive and not a clear indication of the children's true capabilities. If children are to be challenged, their levels of development should be regarded as plateaus from which the children must advance rather than rest. The teacher, weary of seeing the same array of rainbows, cartoon characters, and other stereotypes, obviously must teach for the capability of the child. A good teacher realizes that one does not take away without giving something in return—that it is possible to build even on stereotypes. Even secondhand images can provide a starting point for original thinking.

Setting the Stage

Methodology begins before the students enter the art room. Classroom teachers send out cues by the way they prepare their rooms. They should *avoid commercial giveaways* from product manufacturers and instead display reproductions of artworks and natural objects, such as flowers, driftwood, or plants. Art teachers with their own rooms can create an environment rich in visual stimulation, well organized, and reasonably clean and orderly. When students first enter, they should receive cues about the potential excitement that awaits them in an art room. The teacher who stands at the door and greets the children, who does not begin the class until order is established, who has a pleasant expression, is teaching. The questions all teachers must ask themselves are quite simple: If I were a child, what set of circumstances in this room would direct my thinking and my attitudes? What will a child feel like in this space?

The Sources of Art

Children can be motivated by their experiences to produce and respond to art. As children live from day to day, they have many experiences that arise from life at home, at play, at school, and in the community in general. They bring to each new experience the insight they have acquired from previous experiences. If, on the one hand, the new experience arouses their interest and if it is sufficiently reminiscent of former experiences, learning should occur. If, on the other hand, children are not interested in the new experience, they will probably not profit from it. The majority of experiences children enjoy, however, do arouse their intellect and stimu-

late their feelings and so may be considered suitable subject matter for artistic expression.

When teachers respect the memories, the imagination, and the life experiences of children, they set the stage not only for studio activities but also for an awareness of history and criticism. To cite an example, when a seven-year-old child wants to draw his or her family, the family pictures and sculptures of Cassatt, Picasso, or Romare Bearden might be of special interest to the child. Themes in art based on everyday life and universal human experiences, such as family, love, conflict, fantasy, and fear, are evident in art from many cultures. The most powerful art often relates directly to the experiences we share as human beings. This is no less true for children.

A major source of motivation, then, is the life of the child, both internal and external. The teacher who can regard students as thinking, feeling organisms who function intimately with both the world of the senses and that of fantasy, imagination, and dreams will have greater insight into the possibilities of motivation. Because the *total* makeup of the child provides sources for motivation, the teacher can go beyond lived experience and probe for what might be called the *inner vision;* that is, the dream worlds, fears, desires, and reveries. *A very real function of the art program is to provide visual objectification for what is felt and imagined as well as for what is observed and directly experienced in the world.*

Motivation

In general, the teacher makes a distinction between *extrinsic* motivation, which consists of forces external to the child (such as contests and grades) that influence the child's level of motivation, and *intrinsic* motivation, which capitalizes on internal standards and goals the child recognizes as having value (such as the desire to perform well). The teacher should avoid striving for the short-term gain of the former, and concentrate on intrinsic sources, which are far more valuable in the long run to the child's development.

The teacher, having decided on the source of motivation, must consider this question: What are the most effective means of getting the children to use their experiences with the materials I have provided? At this point the teacher must be sensitive to the variables of the situation, linking subject to materials with techniques capable of capturing the attention of the class. The teacher may decide to focus on the excitement of untried materials, may introduce the lesson with a new film, or may set up a bulletin board using materials from outside the classroom. The teacher may engage the class in a lively discussion or bring in an animal or unusual still life, plan a field trip, invite a guest speaker, demonstrate how a particular skill might be used, or use an artwork to build their art vocabulary. In some instances, several such ideas may be combined in the same lesson.

When a discussion is planned to provide the basis of motivation, the teacher should involve more children than the usual bright extroverts. She or he should know when to let the class members do most of the talking until *they* have come up with the points to be emphasized.[4] The teacher may find it wise to increase interaction by seating the children close together or by dividing the class into small groups, each with their own reproduction of an artwork. In this kind of instruction, the teacher's personality, enthusiasm for the task, acceptance of unusual ideas, and flair for communication all play an important role. When the energy level is low and the class has to be brought up to a productive level, the motivational phase can be enhanced by a touch of showmanship. This is where creativity and imagination come into play.

In an example of media as motivation, pulling the first print provides a special excitement that is never quite achieved in other stages of the print process. When the print is completed, the student must decide on the size of the edition, the choice of paper, the ground or support—shall it be white or colored, collage or montage?—and the color of the ink itself. In each of these stages, the teacher should try to lead the child toward solving the problem independently.

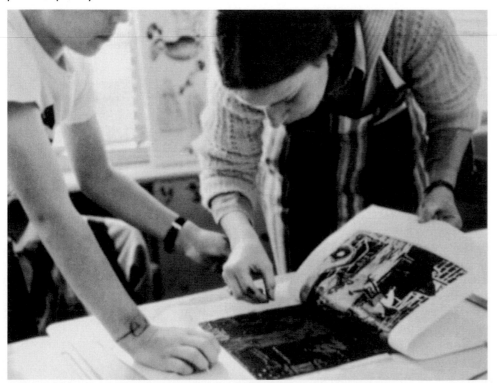

It is important to remember that children do not normally connect their experiences with artistic acts. If a teacher tells children to paint a picture of an experience that appeals to them or to do whatever they like, the results are usually disappointing. Under such circumstances, the children are often at a loss about where to begin. A well-known cartoon of children looking up at a teacher and asking with rueful expressions, "Do we have to do anything we want to?" illustrates the point. It is not that children are incapable of expression but rather that they have not connected total freedom with expressive acts.

A Range of Teaching Methods

It is difficult to discuss teaching methods without referring at the same time to educational goals, curriculum, and evaluation, because they are all interrelated and each influences all the others. The broad range of art content that we have suggested for the art curriculum suggests that a variety of instructional methods should be used. Evaluation, if it is not to appear as an afterthought, must be considered during the curriculum development process. As teachers conduct instruction in their classrooms, they are aware of curriculum goals, content for instruction, activities intended to foster learning, and evaluation processes that will assist teachers to assess student progress and program success. With this point in mind, we will focus attention here specifically on teaching methods, with occasional references to these other interrelated topics. By the same token, the chapters on curriculum organization and evaluation will refer to some of the ideas in this discussion.

The Art in Teaching

Teaching can be considered an art form; although much progress has been made toward improving teaching and learning in the schools, it certainly is not a science with specified actions that guarantee certain responses or reactions. When we observe a great teacher in action, it is not uncommon for us to remark, "She is an artist in the classroom!" or "He handled that situation beautifully," or "What a creative teacher!" These comments are always meant as compliments for a person who has developed into a great teacher. Like artists (actors, poets, dancers, musicians, and visual artists), teachers develop a repertoire of meaningful behaviors and apply them as they see fit according to their experience and goals. One of the differences that marks novices in art or in teaching from those who are masters is their limited repertoires. For this discussion we will review a range of teaching methods that many excellent teachers are able to use fluently and flexibly, according to their teaching purposes and the needs of their students.

Following are a number of methods good teachers use with varying degrees of emphasis.

demonstrations   student reports
assignments   games
audiovisual   field trips
   presentations   guest speakers
lectures   dramatizations
individual work   visual displays
group activities   discussion

Many of these methods have been mentioned in previous chapters in conjunction with suggested activities for teaching art history, criticism, aesthetics, or any of the different modes of art production. They are not listed in any order of effectiveness, and the list is not exhaustive. It is not unusual to observe a good art teacher using several methods during a single class period.

Demonstrations

When the children are prepared to paint with brushes, tempera paints, water containers, paper towels, and old shirts worn backwards for smocks, the teacher demonstrates how to dip the brush into a color, to brush color on the painting surface, to rinse the brush in water, to blot on a paper towel, and to dip into another color. Children like watching demonstrations and particularly enjoy observing the teacher use the chalkboard; indeed, it is almost impossible to ignore the line that is moving on paper or chalkboard. The ability to draw an example can give a teacher added credibility in a relatively short period of time.

Outside the studio classroom, the teacher can show students how to use the resource books in the library to find information on the art history topics they have selected to study. The teacher can show students how to use an encyclopedia, a dictionary of art terms, and a handbook on art and artists.

Assignments

After many discussions of puzzles about art over their years of art instruction, the sixth-grade students are ready to write a paragraph on their own. The teacher gives them a description of a difficult art situation and assigns them to write their response to the puzzle, stating reasons for their decision. This is the situation:

> There is a famous painting by a master artist from the seventeenth century that has hung in a great museum for many years, where it has been seen by thousands of art lovers. The painting has been photographed and reproduced as beautiful art prints sold in the museum shop. Thousands of people have these prints hanging in their homes. During a routine cleaning of the painting, the art conservator discovered by means of an X ray that the famous painting was painted over another painting by the artist. This happened when the artist was poor and could not afford a new canvas. Experts agree that the newly discovered painting is probably as good as the famous familiar work. Should the museum director
>
> **a.** Authorize the removal of the famous work in order to uncover the one never seen before? This would destroy the famous painting but would provide the world with another great painting by the master.
>
> **b.** Keep the famous work as is and leave the underpainting where it is, never to be seen?

For homework, children can be asked to bring a clipping about art from a magazine or newspaper. The clippings can then be placed on the bulletin board and used for discussions of what is happening in the world of art. The chapter on aesthetics provides other suggestions.

Audiovisual Presentations

Children often become bored watching instructional movies, videos, or lengthy slide lectures. Audio and visual presentations need not be uninteresting to children if teachers adapt them to children's capacities for instruction and attention. Rather than showing an entire video, for example, teachers often preview and select only one relevant segment that focuses on the concept, skill, or understanding relevant to the art lesson. Brief audiovisual presentations interspersed with studio activities are often effective.

Interrupting their work on a collage assignment, the teacher can show slides of surrealist paintings, then turn the lights back on so children can resume their work. This need not take more than five minutes.

Or, children can watch a ten-minute segment of a videotape on the stained-glass windows in Gothic cathedrals. After the video presentation, the teacher can hand out worksheets asking questions about the topic. Demonstrations and lectures can be combined to enhance motivation.

Lectures

Before starting the class on a ceramics project, the teacher can give the students a brief lecture about handling clay, including the health hazards and safety precautions that need to be understood when working with clay, glazes, and clay tools. The kiln in the art room should be discussed, and the teacher should preview the firing process, explaining the high temperatures inside the kiln. Lectures can also be combined with demonstrations.

In another lecture, the teacher may show slides of African masks and tell the children about the uses of masks in African societies. Although lectures are often associated with higher education, this method can be effective with all age groups if teachers will control duration and content and use visual aids in conjunction with their lectures.

The lecture method should be used sparingly unless it includes student discussions or participation of some sort. Brief talks, however, can be effective as a review or to emphasize a particular point. Teachers will soon become sensitive to the attention span of the class and how this relates to their ability to control the attention of the group.

Individual Work: Studio Activity

As with other school subjects, most art learning activities involve individual work by students. When children are involved in their own art expression, when they are working on individual reading or writing assignments, or when they are using learning centers during spare time in class, they work as individuals. Good teachers often try to vary the amount of individual work with group activities, providing variety for children in the class. Individual work will always be primary, however, because each child needs opportunities for individual artistic expression, as well as individual response to the artworks of others.

After participating in an art criticism session as described in Chapter 11, each student may be given a worksheet with several questions about a painting displayed at the front of the room and asked to discuss his or her personal response to the work. Each student then completes the worksheet and gives it to the teacher, who may share some comments worth noting after the papers have been read.

During a visit to an art museum, children may have a tour led by a museum guide. After the students have completed the tour and have asked questions, the art teacher can ask each child to take ten minutes to select his or her favorite work (in a large museum, this assignment might be restricted to one or two galleries), suggesting that the children copy the information from the label by the work, take brief notes describing the work, and be prepared to tell why they chose it.

Group Activities

Children can be organized into groups to work on a mural that will be designed and painted on a wall in the school neighborhood. A delegation of children and the teacher will need to identify the wall and to obtain the necessary permission from the owner and the city to paint on the wall. Each group has a task. One group will do library research on murals, especially contemporary murals in community settings. (The teacher can direct attention to the tradition of mural-making by the Mexican muralists Rivera and Orozco, and by some Hispanic artists in the United States.) Another group can be assigned to plan the background, another to work on the buildings, another to work on the vehicles (cars, buses, trucks, etc.), and another to draw and paint the figures.

In the art museum, children can be divided into groups of three or four assigned to particular works of art. The task for each group is to discuss the work using strategies that they have learned in class and to report on the work to the rest of the class when they are back at school. The teacher can show the slide of the work while each group reports (see Chapter 16).

Reports

The method of fostering learning by assigning reports has been mentioned in conjunction with other methods. Teaching methods are often integrated, although they might also be used separately. The same is true of learning activities that integrate content from art history and art production or other combinations of the art disciplines.

In preparation for a unit about architecture, the teacher may ask the children to notice some things about the buildings where they live. Each child is to notice if her or his home is in a one-story, two-story, or more than two-story building. Each child should be given the opportunity to report this information at the next class meeting.

A fifth- or sixth-grade class can be given a library research assignment, in which they select an artist's name from a list provided by the teacher, spend a period in the library, and write a two-paragraph report about the artist. This assignment could be in conjunction with a unit in language arts.

If an evening or weekend television program is scheduled that is art related, students can bring in a report that describes the program, their reactions to it, or both. Another form of report is the personalized autobiography of an artist (see Chapter 13).

Games

If a fourth-grade class has been learning about color—primary and secondary colors—the class can be divided into four groups and assigned to four locations in the classroom. In each location an assortment of art postcards from museums should be provided. The first group to select works of art that match each color category on their worksheet receives a reward (e.g., first group out for lunch).

Teachers often invent learning games based on quiz shows or other well-known games. Art games are available commercially and many promote worthwhile learning as well as the inherent fun of social interaction.[5] Art museums often produce game-like activities for gallery visits. Many of these are adaptable for classroom use (see the Appendixes at the end of this book).

Field Trips

Most teachers are convinced of the value of field trips, but many are faced with limited financial support from the districts where they teach. Whenever possible, however, students should have opportunities to learn about the world away from school. For the art program, field trips to art galleries or

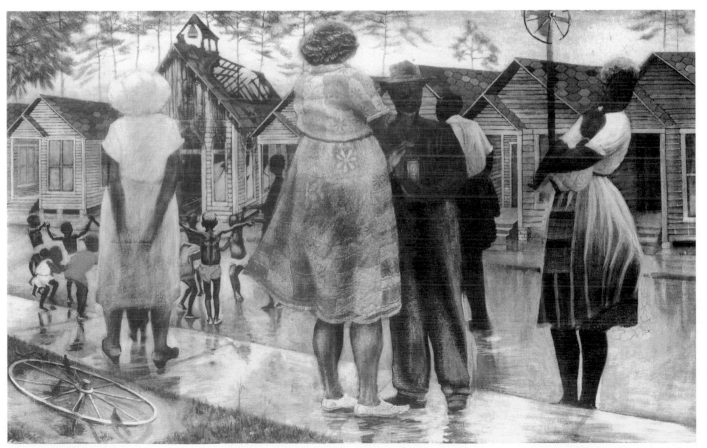

National Museum of American Art, Smithsonian Institution, Washington, D.C., U.S.A. Art Resource, N.Y. John T. Biggers, *Shotgun, Third Ward #1,* 1988, oil on canvas, 30" x 48", National Museum of American Art, Smithsonian Institution, Washington, D.C., U.S.A. Art Resource, N.Y.

This painting depicts a scene from the Houston community where the artist lived, with the row of "shotgun" houses next to the church, which was burned. Reacting to the calamity, the residents gather in the street. The man with a hat holds a lighted candle in a glass, symbolizing a ray of hope for the burned church, which will be restored and continue to serve as a source of inspiration for the community. The circle of children might be seen as the next generation of leaders, the continuing "cycle" of the community.

museums are especially beneficial, because children are able to experience original works of art of high quality and to obtain a needed frame of reference that will help them better understand what the slides and prints they see in school actually represent.

Teachers learn many pointers about supervising children on trips through experience and sharing with one another. Books about visits to museums are also available.[6] Following are a few brief suggestions that might fall under the category of teaching methods in relation to field trips (other suggestions are listed in the section on using museums in Chapter 12).

1. When possible, visit the museum or gallery ahead of time in preparation for the planned field trip to note possible problems, such as parking, limited space for your purposes, and so forth. Contact the education staff and arrange for a guided tour if one is available for your grade level. Learn about the services offered to school groups. *Schedule your visit!*

2. Select several artworks you want all children to see. One problem with museums is that there is too much to see unless the teacher can provide some focus for the children. You can discuss works seen after you return to school.

3. If possible, obtain slides of selected works. You can show slides of some of the works to the children before the trip. This establishes an anticipatory mood and provides the works with "celebrity status."

4. Note such things as where the bus will stop, where students will enter, where they will place their coats, where the bathrooms are located, and so forth. Decide where the group will meet before and after the museum visit. Are there clocks in evidence so everyone will know what time it is?

5. Draw a map (some museums provide maps), and show these items to the children in the classroom before leaving on the trip. Talk the class through the entire trip, using the map to show where everything is, what the time schedule is, and how they should handle any problems that might arise, such as becoming separated from the group (this should never happen, of course, but sometimes does, regardless of precautions).

6. Children may "act up" much more when they are nervous and uneasy because of strange surroundings and situations. By providing all this information, you will place the children more at ease and help them to enjoy the experience and learn from it.

7. Follow up the museum visit with discussion and sharing back in the classroom. Try to consolidate learning that has taken place. Help children to realize what they have learned. Report the successful trips to parents.

8. Enlist the aid of parents as assistants.

Field trips also can be taken in the neighborhood with little or no expense. The art teacher may take the class for a walking architecture tour in the neighborhood, noting some basic features of buildings that relate to the study of architecture, such as how the buildings relate to each other and to the environment, what materials they are constructed with, how old they appear to be, and for what purposes they were built.

Guest Speakers

It is a common practice to invite artists into schools. When the goal of the art program is for children to learn more about the world of art, this makes a great deal of sense. Children have opportunities to see a professional artist at work, to talk with the artist and ask questions, and to observe the materials and methods used to create works of art. It also makes good educational sense to invite other art professionals into the classroom, such as art historians, art critics, and aestheticians (probably more difficult to locate). Often a parent or community figure is happy to help, if asked.

For example, the first-grade teacher wants the students to see what oil paints are like; to smell the paint, linseed oil, and turpentine; and to see an artist's palette and easel. The teacher asks the class if any of them knows of a person who paints. One little girl says her mother's friend is a painter. The teacher contacts the mother, learns the artist's name, and invites the woman to visit the class and demonstrate with her oil paints on a stretched canvas. Although the artist is not a professional, her tools and materials are authentic, and the children learn a great deal from the artist's visit and enjoy it very much.

Dramatization

This teaching method can make experience more vivid for children, who often remember dramatizations for many years. This does not mean the teacher has to be an actor and dramatize classroom presentations, although some teachers have abilities in dramatics and use their talents effectively with children. Rather, this is a method whereby teachers assist children to act out, or dramatize, situations that are educationally meaningful with respect to the art curriculum.

For example, a teacher asks for a volunteer from the class each month to dress up as his or her favorite artist and to present the artist's autobiography as if he or she were addressing the class. One boy chooses Mondrian and, with help from the teacher and from home, develops a costume with primary colors and black vertical and horizontal lines. Another boy chooses Jackson Pollock and has a great time splattering some old clothes with multicolored tempera paints to create his costume. A girl chooses Georgia O'Keeffe. She dresses in black and white like a photograph of the artist and somehow finds a bleached cow skull. Another girl chooses Whistler and dresses and poses like the painting known as *Whistler's Mother* (entitled *Arrangement in Gray and Black* by the artist). As each new month begins, students are asked to guess the name of the artist being dramatized. The child doing the dramatization, having studied the artist's life and works, answers classmates' questions. Some of the artists are more difficult to guess than others. In every case, students are more interested to learn about the artist after the dramatic presentation.

A sixth-grade teacher engaged her students in an aesthetics discussion based on a real-life art controversy reported in the news. The issue revolved around a sculpture that was installed near a county jail, raising questions of use of public money for art versus other needs, appropriateness of the sculpture site, and opinions of the work itself. The teacher assigned groups of class members to represent the points of view of the artist, members of the public, prison guards, prisoners, and state legislators.[7] Students entered their roles enthusiastically and put on a class skit (with many ad libs) that was videotaped in the classroom. The issues were clearly stated and students had the opportunity to examine several valid but competing points of view. Students enjoyed viewing their performances on the video monitor.

Visual Displays

One advantage that art teachers have is the visual nature of the subject. Many children learn visually, and art teachers can see visual evidence of the effectiveness of their instruction in students' art products. We can accomplish much instruction and foster learning without taking any class time, simply through the means of visual displays.

One teacher always includes explanatory material as a component of exhibitions of students' artwork. When she teaches a unit about color, composition, or an art style such as cubism, this teacher displays material about the concepts, skills, and instruction that children have received, along with examples of their work. As other teachers, parents, administrators, and students pass the room, they learn that art content is being taught and learned by students in this teacher's class.

Children in another classroom look forward to new editions of their teacher's puzzle display. The teacher begins a new puzzle every few weeks. The object is to guess the artist, artwork, or culture being depicted on the display. The first item might be a fragment of a picture of a painting, sculpture, pot, or mask, whatever the subject might be. Next a photograph of an artist might appear, next a word, next a date, then the name of a country, and so on. The student who guesses the answer wins extra credit points or some other reward.

Discussion

Although most people think of a teacher as a solitary figure controlling a class from a space between desk and chalkboard, teachers also work on a one-to-one basis or move from group to group in cooperative learning situations, where four or five mixed-ability groups work together toward a common goal. Small groups can collaborate on murals or dioramas, or they can focus on problems posed by a phase of criticism, such as analysis or interpretation. When five groups each work from the same reproduction and are asked to deal with the same problem, a lively mixture of ideas is likely to occur. As one writer has noted,

> Cooperative learning involves every class member. The most skillfully conducted class discussion cannot eliminate the reluctance of the shy and the disinterested to participate. In a class of thirty, the constraints of time may not allow for student input on an individual basis. Cooperative learning makes it easier for a student to state a point of view as a member of a team than as a member of a class. In Slavin's view, "In a traditional classroom, students who don't understand what is going on can scrunch down in their seats and hope the teacher won't call on them. In a cooperative team, there is nowhere to hide." Group art shares with cooperative learning that critical social dimension which can facilitate the ways in which students learn.[8]

Six Levels of Art Talk

First Grade: Flower Problem in Tempera

TEACHER: I like your shapes; they move all over in so many ways. Tell me about this—it isn't a flower, is it?

STUDENT: It's a bug—yes, a bug.

TEACHER: Does it have a name?

STUDENT: A grasshopper.

TEACHER: Grasshoppers are long and skinny, aren't they? How about a different-shaped bug? Can you think of one?

STUDENT: I can paint a snake—

TEACHER: Well, a snake isn't a bug, but a snake is very nice.

Second Grade: "My Pet," Drawing in Felt-Tip Pen

TEACHER: That's a good rabbit, but he looks awfully small.

STUDENT: It's a girl rabbit.

TEACHER: Yes, well, it looks kind of lonely by itself. What can we add to keep it company—you know, to make the picture bigger?

STUDENT: It has a cage.

TEACHER: Cages are good; where do you keep your cage?

STUDENT: Outside, on the porch.

TEACHER: Well, if it's outside, there are other things to draw, aren't there? You put them in, and let me see if I can tell you what they are.

Third Grade: Clay Animal

STUDENT: It doesn't look like a dog; it's all lumpy.

TEACHER: I think you are going to have to decide what kind of a dog—

STUDENT: A German shepherd. I like German shepherds. My uncle has one.

TEACHER: What makes a German shepherd different from, say, a beagle?

STUDENT: The ears stick up.

TEACHER: Okay. Then let's begin there. Pull its ears up, and I think you can smooth out some of those lumps.

Fourth Grade: Box Sculpture

TEACHER: Having trouble, Chuck? You don't seem very happy.

STUDENT: I hate it; it's not turning out.

TEACHER: What seems to be wrong?

STUDENT: I don't know; it's a mess. Nothing seems to go together; I wanted this neat truck—

TEACHER: Well, I think you've been a little careless in joining the sections together (demonstrates joining process with tape). See what I mean?

STUDENT: Yeah, I don't know. It still won't look like a truck.

TEACHER: Look, Chuck, try to think ahead. You have a cereal box and a medicine carton, and they both have pieces of letters and different colors showing. Why don't you join it, then paint it; I think you'll like it better.

Fifth Grade: Linoleum Print

STUDENT: It won't work.

TEACHER: What won't work?

STUDENT: The tool; it keeps sliding and slipping.

TEACHER: Let me try. No, the blade's okay. Here, try standing and let your weight press the blade, and, for goodness' sake, keep your left hand out of the way of the blade, or your mother will be calling me tonight about an accident, okay?

STUDENT: Okay.

TEACHER: Say, I haven't checked your drawing. Can I see it before you continue?

Sixth Grade: Landscape Painting

TEACHER: Very nice, John, very nice.

STUDENT: It all looks the same.

TEACHER: What do you mean?

STUDENT: Well, there was more color—

TEACHER: You mean more kinds of green in the trees—?

STUDENT: Yeah, that's right.

TEACHER: Look, you keep using the same color green. Come on; you know how to change a color.

STUDENT: It will be messier.

TEACHER: You've got your palette set up; try out some mixtures, add yellow, try a touch of black—

STUDENT: Black?

TEACHER: Why not? Try it; it won't bite you. You can always paint over it.

Each teacher in these dialogues had to be sensitive to the range of vocabulary, the nature of the assistance needed, and the tone of address. The role of language is complex and plays a vital part in art education. The best way to learn how to use language more effectively is to observe good teachers in action, either in an art or general classroom situation.

These lessons would have been improved had the teachers included somewhere in the discussion a reference to the work of an artist who dealt with the problem under discussion.

Questionable Methods for Teaching Art

In the absence of sound programs of art education, such as we have discussed throughout this book, some teachers have devised activities that might superficially resemble art instruction but that have little or no educational substance. We mention these questionable practices here, because they have been so pervasive in some locations, and because we believe that they are harmful to the extent that they, like junk food, take the place of something much better.

Mechanistic Production

Every year when spring approaches, Ms. L, a conscientious second-grade teacher, provides the class with yellow and green construction paper. She has designed a pattern of a daffodil in which the leaves are green and the flower yellow. She demonstrates first how to cut the petals and then shows how to make the leaves. "The children," says Ms. L, "love to make a daffodil. It provides a most effective art lesson."

Ms. L is correct in saying that the children love to make a daffodil, but she is incorrect in saying that her assignment constitutes an effective art lesson. The activity is not art: it is "busywork." In producing the flower, no one but Ms. L has done any planning. The children may have developed some skill, but they have done so without thought and feeling. The children have been subjected to a mechanistic form of teaching.

Tidy Art

Mr. W is a tidy person; he presents a neat appearance, and his classroom is a model of order. "I like things to look right," says Mr. W. Mr. W encourages neatness so vigorously that his pupils have grown afraid to experiment. Those who first tried to experiment with ideas and media ran into difficulties with both the media and Mr. W. Now they hold fast to thoroughly familiar materials and well-tried clichés in artistic thought, which pleases their teacher.

Although no one would advocate untidiness for its own sake in a classroom, children must be allowed to experiment freely with ideas and media. Children's lack of skill in organizing both subject matter and materials makes it inevitable that their art production is often messy. Neatness in executing artistic activities will occur only after the children master the skills associated with the activities. To demand extreme neatness at all times is to handicap children in producing creative work.

Formula Art

Ms. Z, the teacher of a third-grade class, is clever at mathematics. One of her favorite art lessons consists of having the children resolve objects into triangles, squares, oblongs, and circles. She admires the precision resulting from this activity. "The children are learning to handle basic forms," she explains. Thus, the children are taught to draw houses by means of a triangle supported by a rectangular oblong; a chicken by using two circles; a young girl, strangely enough, by resorting to triangles and squares.

Ms. Z is another example of a teacher who prevents children from any sort of personal expression. Moreover, the designs she insists on are inaccurate in relation to the objects depicted. The forms of houses, chickens, and girls cannot be successfully arrived at through geometric shapes supplied by the teacher. They can be depicted adequately only by means of personal experience and observation on the part of the children. Ms. Z's system is convenient for her but asks woefully little of her students.

We find that these questionable practices seldom occur within art programs with clear educational objectives and well-articulated art content. This does not mean that teachers never engage students in activities that relate to holidays or seasons. As we have discussed in other chapters, holidays and seasons are legitimate themes for the study of art when presented in imaginative contexts.

TEACHING IN ACTION: PLANNING FOR THE FIRST SESSION

All teachers must plan for the first meeting with their pupils. The taped dialogues transcribed here represent two approaches to this first meeting. The first conversation depicts a teacher's attempt to deal with a basic question of aesthetics: a grass-roots definition of art from disadvantaged children in the third grade; the second demonstrates how a first planning session with middle-class children might appear.

First Dialogue

TEACHER: Do any of you know who I am? (*pause*)
TOMMY: You an art teacher?
TEACHER: That's right. I am your art teacher. Now, can anyone tell me what an artist does?
SARAH: He paints you pictures.

7. Demonstrations convergent on single solution

8. Class is flexible:

   a. Chairs reorganized for viewing demonstrations

   b. Children can come to teacher freely for additional material

   c. Several projects in operation at same time

   d. Children can move freely from project to project

The Class in Action

1. Teacher:

   a. Listens to pupils when asking questions

   b. Asks open questions

   c. Asks closed questions

   d. Praises work of pupils in general terms

   e. Praises work in specific terms relevant to the problem

   f. Uses other forms of verbal reinforcement

   g. Is able to reach pupils who request consultation

   h. Talks at length to some pupils

   i. Relates comments not only to objectives but to pupils' frame of reference

   j. Motivates those who have become discouraged

   k. Remotivates those with short attention span

   l. Is flexible in permitting deviation from assignments

   m. Uses art vocabulary

   n. Is competent in handling discipline problems

2. Pupils:

   a. Are self-directive in organizing for work

   b. Are self-directive in organizing for cleanup

   c. Use art vocabulary

Evaluation Period (for Final Group Evaluation)

1. Evaluation relates to goals of lesson

2. Pupils encouraged to participate

3. Pupils do participate as a group

4. Only one work is evaluated

5. Several works evaluated

6. Range of evaluation devices used

7. No final evaluation given

8. Pupils do not feel embarrassed or threatened by public evaluation

9. Pupils generally negative to evaluation process

Teaching Style (Personality)

1. Teacher takes positive attitude toward instruction

2. Teacher shows rapport with pupils' age group

3. Teacher demonstrates sense of humor

4. Teacher has sense of pace: controls flow of lesson

5. Teacher is innovative in following respects:

   a.   **c.**

   b.   **d.**

6. Teacher is aware of language (vivid phrasing, imagistic speech, clarity of expression)

If a teacher wishes to have an objective profile of her or his performance, an administrator could be requested to use the instrument during an observation period. This may hold some surprises for the teacher, as well as educate the administrator regarding what is involved in conducting an art program.

NOTES

1. William Ayers, ed. *To Become a Teacher: Making a Difference in Children's Lives* (New York: Teachers College Press, 1995), p. 60.

2. See the NAEA's brochure *Quality Art Education* (Reston, VA: National Art Education Association, 1984).

3. National Center for Education Statistics, *Arts Education in Public Elementary and Secondary Schools* (Washington, DC: U.S. Department of Education, 1995).

4. For examples of classroom dialogue, see the seven case studies of art programs in Michael Day, Elliot Eisner,

Robert Stake, Brent Wilson, and Marjorie Wilson, *Art History, Art Criticism, and Art Production*, vol. 2 (Los Angeles: Rand Corporation, 1984).

5. See, for example, Mary Erickson, Eldon Katter, and Marilyn Stewart, *Token Response Game* (Tucson, AZ: Crizmac Publications, 1994).

6. See, for example, Jean Sousa, *Telling Stories in Art Images* (Chicago: The Art Institute of Chicago, 1997).

7. *Art Education in Action, Aesthetics,* Episode B: "Teaching across the Curriculum," Evelyn Sonnichsen, art teacher, videotape (Los Angeles: Getty Center for Education in the Arts, 1995).

8. Al Hurwitz, *Collaboration in Art Education* (Reston, VA: National Art Education Association, 1993), p. 12.

9. Phillip Dunn, "More Power: Integrated Interactive Technology and Art Education," *Art Education* 49, no. 6 (November 1996): 6–11.

ACTIVITIES FOR THE READER

1. Describe any situation you have experienced in which children disliked art. Explain how the dislike arose, and indicate the means you might use to alter the children's attitude.

2. Describe the traits of a personal acquaintance whom you consider to be an effective teacher of art.

3. Observe some art lessons given by expert teachers, and note especially (a) the motivational devices employed; (b) the manner in which themes are defined; (c) the way in which goals are established; (d) the problems that arise and the means by which a solution to them is found. Can you add any items to the analysis instrument at the end of this chapter?

4. Describe how you would motivate a class for a lesson in increased sensitivity to color, based on fall colors in nature.

5. Take a close look at your personality, and try to project your teaching "style" from it. Apply your style to a specific teaching situation—demonstration, evaluation, or selection of topic. In what ways does your style suggest limitations?

6. Describe the steps you might take to improve the following situations: (a) a third-grade art class whose members are outrageously untidy and wasteful of materials; (b) a class of fifth graders who have always been taught to copy during their art sessions and feel they are unable to create; (c) a group of sixth-grade boys who think art is "sissy"; (d) a group of children whose parents or older brothers and sisters have given them formulas for the drawing of objects.

7. Observe an art teacher in action, and document the methods used by the teacher. How many methods mentioned in this chapter did you observe? Was the teaching effective? Did you observe ways that instruction might be improved through the use of a wider variety of teaching methods?

8. Review the list of teaching methods in this chapter. Add to the list other methods you can think of or have observed.

9. Select two of the teaching methods listed in this chapter. Develop lessons that utilize each of these, and try them out in a classroom situation with students. Repeat this process with one or two more methods until you have developed a repertoire of teaching methods on which you can rely as situations arise in your teaching position.

10. Select a topic and teach it to three different grade levels. What decisions must you make to have a successful lesson on all levels?

SUGGESTED READINGS

Ackerman, David B., and David N. Perkins. "Integrating Thinking and Learning Skills across the Curriculum." *Interdisciplinary Curriculum: Design and Implementation,* ed. Heidi Hayes Jacobs. Alexandria, VA: Association for Supervision and Curriculum Development, 1989, 77–95.

Baker, Gwendolyn C. *Planning and Organizing for Multicultural Instruction.* 2d ed. Menlo Park, CA: Addison-Wesley, 1994.

Barron, Ann E., and Karen S. Ivers. *The Internet and Instruction: Activities and Ideas.* Englewood, CO: Libraries Unlimited, 1996.

Delacruz, Elizabeth Manley. *Design for Inquiry: Instructional Theory, Research, and Practice in Art Education*. Reston, VA: National Art Education Association, 1997.

Dobbs, Stephen M. *Learning in and through Art: A Guide to Discipline-Based Art Education*. Los Angeles: Getty Education Institute for the Arts, 1998.

Gregory, Diane C., ed. *New Technologies and Art Education: Implications for Theory, Research, and Practice*. Reston, VA: National Art Education Association, 1997.

Henry, Carole, and National Art Education Association. *Middle School Art: Issues of Curriculum and Instruction*. Reston, VA: National Art Education Association, 1996.

Nyman, Andra L., ed. *Instructional Methods for the Artroom: Reprints from NAEA Advisories*. Reston, VA: National Art Education Association, 1996.

Simpson, Judith W., Jean M. Delaney, and Karen Lee Carroll. *Creating Meaning Through Art: Teacher As Choice Maker*. Prentice-Hall, 1997.

Stankiewitcz, Mary Ann, and National Art Education Association, eds. "Literacy, Media, and Meaning." *Art Education* 50, no. 4 (July 1997). Special Issue.

Susi, Frank Daniel. *Student Behavior in Art Classrooms: The Dynamics of Discipline*. Teacher Resource Series. Reston, VA: National Art Education Association, 1995.

Thompson, Christine Marmé, ed. *The Visual Arts and Early Childhood Learning*. Reston, VA: National Art Education Association, 1995.

Wongse-Sanit, Naree. "Inquiry-Based Teaching Using the World Wide Web." *Art Education* 50, no. 2 (1997): 19–24.

WORLD WIDE WEB RESOURCES

Professional Resources for Teachers of Art

National Art Education Association. *NAEA Website*. 1999. <http://www.naeareston.org/> NAEA provides extensive resources, training, and tools designed to support teaching and learning. NAEA has affiliate organizations in every state and the Web site provides links to these local organizations. Information about NAEA programs is provided on the Web site, including the following: conferences, workshops, and training opportunities; publications; resources for classrooms; news related to policy in education and art; and material concerned with the role and problems of art teachers.

National Parent Teachers Association. *Children First: The Website of the National PTA*. 1999. <http://www.pta.org/> This site is full of helpful resources for teachers on a variety of issues that affect classroom practices.

Meta Sites

ArtsEdNet: The Getty's Art Education Web Site. *Web Links: Education Links*. 1999. <http://www.artsednet.getty.edu/ArtsEdNet/Links/ed.html> This Web site is a rich resource for educators and provides a list of Web links evaluated for their usefulness to teachers of art. The site is regularly updated.

Internet Education Group, Inc. *Inet-Edu*. 1998. <http://www.inet-edu.com/index.html> *Inet-Edu.* is an educational service site provided by Internet Education Group. It offers an excellent gateway to Internet sources for art teaching. The site is full of valuable resources.

Teaching Resources

Classroom Connect. *Classroom Connect's Connected Teacher*. 1999. <http://www.connectedteacher.com/home.asp> *Connected Teacher* is a community service of Classroom Connect. The site presents abundant professional education material for classroom teachers, with excellent and extensive Web links to WWW sites containing curriculum resources and lesson plans for teachers of art.

Lake, Bettie. *The Art Teacher Connection*. 1997. <http://www.inficad.com/~arted> This Web site is designed by an art educator for teachers of art and art students. It provides art education resources, images, Internet art lessons, and advice on how to integrate computer technology into a visual arts curriculum. The site features multidisciplinary, interdisciplinary, or cross-curricular units that fulfill national standards requirements in several curriculum areas, including the visual arts.

National Art Education Association. *Electronic Media Interest Group.* 1998. <http://www.cedarnet.org/emig/nb.html> The purpose of *Electronic Media Interest Group (EMIG),* an affiliate of the National Art Education Association, is to promote informed and responsible applications of media and technology to art education. The site provides support to teachers who wish to develop and incorporate technology resources in their teaching. Open "Tools and Construction Materials for Electronic Media" for links to Internet resources. "On-line Exhibits" and other curriculum resources are included.

New York Foundation for the Arts. *Arts Wire: Online Communication in the Arts. Spiderschool.* 1997–1999. <http://www.artswire.org/spiderschool/1997/content_toc.html> Online resource with tutorials and workshops on Web use in arts education. Provides a database of cultural resources with links.

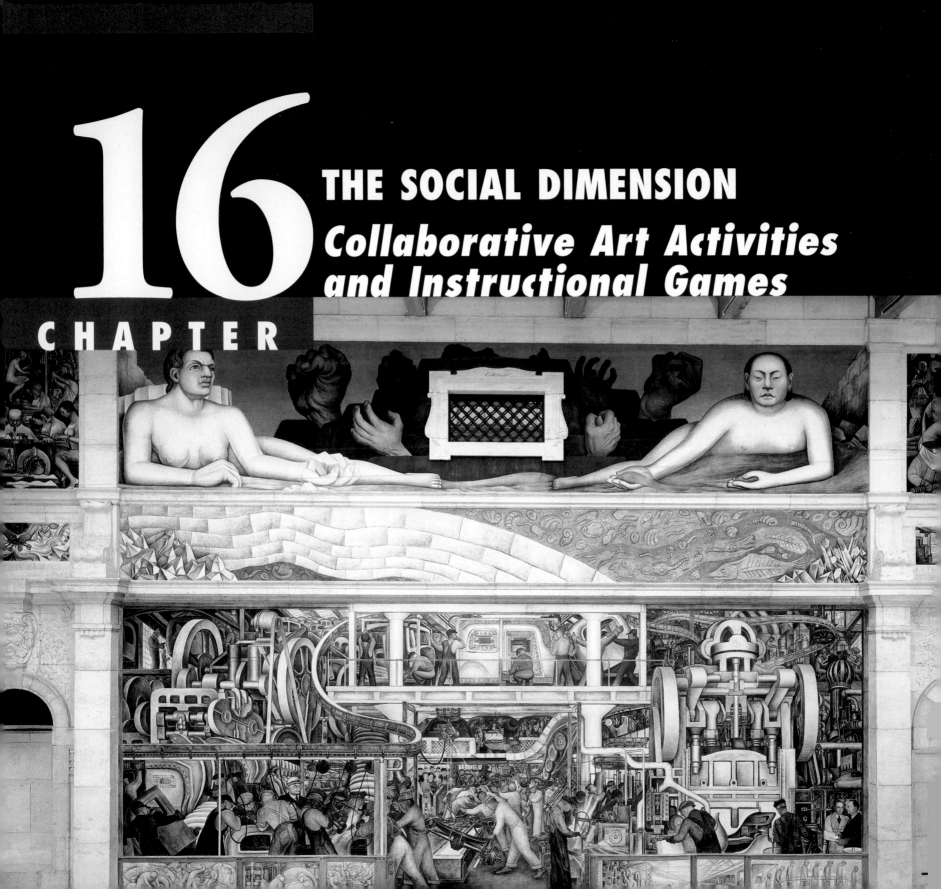

16

CHAPTER

THE SOCIAL DIMENSION

Collaborative Art Activities and Instructional Games

The challenge of raising knowledgeable, responsible, and caring children is recognized by nearly everyone. Few realize, however, that each element of this challenge can be enhanced by thoughtful, sustained, and systematic attention to children's social and emotional learning.

—Maurice J. Elias[1]

A school child, as well as an adult in society, is an individual interacting within groups. Children belong to a class assigned to a teacher, they belong to a grade level, and they are associated with their particular school. Within the classroom, children are often grouped for various reasons. Reading groups are formed, interest groups are organized, and children develop their own groupings according to friendships. Although much of their learning must be accomplished individually, learning and interacting within groups is also very important and beneficial. As they participate in groups, children learn social skills, enjoy making a contribution, share in the excitement of the group, and learn in a cooperative manner about the subject or topic that is the focus of the activity.

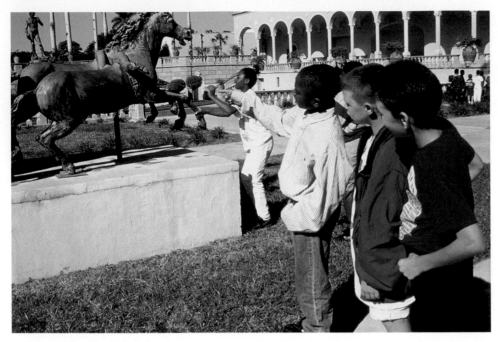

Students at Ringling Museum, Sarasota, FL.

ecological trends."[5] Cooperative learning and collaborative activities can play a central role in such a curriculum.

In this chapter we discuss the expanded role that art education can play in helping children understand social processes as they increase their comprehension of art. We shall describe some art activities that are especially suitable for the development of children's social insights and discuss concepts of art that have emerged in recent years, as well as more traditional forms, such as puppetry and mural making. We will also provide examples of children learning about art through participation in a variety of educational games.

THE ROLE OF THE TEACHER IN COLLABORATIVE ACTIVITIES

Group art can be likened to an amoeba; although outward forms are in a constant state of flux, the essence remains constant. One difficulty in categorizing group activities lies in the ways in which styles borrow from each other. There is really only one condition which must be shared; namely, that

In his book *Democracy as a Way of Life,* Boyd H. Bode stated that "teaching democracy in the abstract is on a par with teaching swimming by correspondence."[2] In a democratic community, Bode says, there is provision for all people to share in the common life according to their interests and capacities. A democratic school promotes the doctrine that people are free and equal by taking proper account of individual differences and by relying on the principle of community living.

SOCIAL VALUES IN ART EDUCATION

Many art educators today advocate a teaching philosophy that encourages students to think about relationships of art, ecology, and community.[3] They emphasize a curriculum that is interdisciplinary, action-oriented, and based on social values. Teaching is aimed at fostering awareness of interconnections between community and environment and focuses on concepts of environmental design, ecological art, and involvement with community.[4] Community and ecological issues "can empower students with the understanding that they, as creative individuals, can have an active voice in protecting their environment and changing current devastating

Cooperative Learning

Individual Accountability
Each student's performance is frequently assessed and the results are given to the group and the individual. Teachers may effect this element by giving individual tests or calling on individuals within the group to demonstrate a skill or respond to questions.

Group Interaction
Students promote each other's learning by helping, sharing, and encouraging efforts to learn. Students explain, discuss, and teach what they know to classmates.

Social Skills
Collaborative skills include leadership, decision-making, trust-building, and communication and conflict management.

SOURCE: Steve Smith, *Active Learning Center: Principles of Cooperative Learning.* December 1999. <http://www.excel.net/~ssmith/cooplrn.html>

two or more participants be brought together to create an object or event which, in some way, exists beyond the effort of a single person.[6]

While realizing the desirability of including group activities in an art program, the teacher may have certain questions concerning the mechanics of this technique. How does group activity work? How should the activity be chosen? What should be its scope? What is the role of the teacher?

W. H. Kilpatrick outlined the steps in what he called a "purposeful activity." These steps, which have stood the test of time, he called *purposing, planning, executing,* and *judging.*[7] Kilpatrick's steps were to be verified much later in the many descriptions of the creative process that came to light as a result of research into creativity. Creative minds in both the sciences and the arts were found to work in a progression of thought and action similar to Kilpatrick's steps.

Group activities, like those of an individual, must begin with some end in mind. This sense of purpose supplies the drive necessary to complete the project. Moreover, it is the children who should share a role in the "purposing." The teacher, of course, may make suggestions, but before these suggestions can be effected, the children must accept them wholeheartedly. Both the "planning" and the "executing," which are outcomes of the purposing, must also be controlled by members of the working group. Finally, the children themselves must ask the general and the specific questions concerning the outcome of the activity: Did they do what they planned? What was learned in the doing? What mistakes were made? How could the activity be done better next time? Children, in other words, should also be involved in evaluating the experience.

In the collective life of the school or classroom, occasions requiring group effort in art invariably arise. "Let's have a play," the children say. "Let's run a puppet show. . . . Let's make a big picture to go in the hallway." Very little suggestion need come from the teacher to set in motion a desirable group project. The children themselves are often the first to suggest to a teacher that a group activity be considered.

It is in this area that the classroom teacher has an advantage over the art teacher, who may see a class for only fifty minutes a week. Children quickly learn that some activities are inappropriate for the typical art schedule and do not even suggest time-consuming group activities. If art teachers are skillful, however, they can sustain interest from one week to the next so a class is able to paint a wall, build a miniature city, or convert a section of the art room into an art "environment." There will always be some children who want to continue working on such a project after school, and release time may even be possible for others to come to the art room as a large project nears completion.

Before encouraging children to proceed with a group project, the teacher must judge not only whether it is sufficiently challenging to occupy the attention of several people but also whether it may be too large for successful completion by a group. In their enthusiasm for art, children are sometimes willing to plunge into a task they could never complete. Once fired with the idea of a mural, for example, a group of fifth graders might cheerfully embark on the enormous task of designing murals for all four walls of a school gymnasium. A group activity in art that comes to a wavering halt because the children have lost interest or lack competence to complete it reflects not only on the group techniques but also on the teacher's judgment. When failure looms, the teacher must help the pupils alter their plans so they can achieve success.

Public mural painting is a popular activity in Mexico, where group activities are often part of neighborhood festivals.

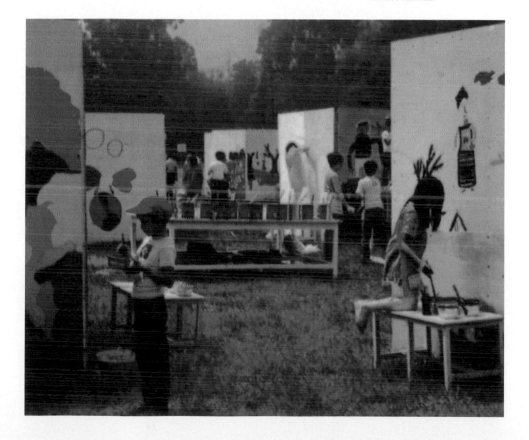

Having a greater maturity and insight into group processes, the teacher must fill the role of counselor with tact, sympathy, and skill. As soon as the need for group work in art is apparent, the children must be urged to elect leaders and establish committees necessary for "purposing, planning, executing, and judging" to take place. The teacher should see that, as far as is practical, the children control these steps. Although teachers have the power of veto, they should be reluctant to use it. If at times the children's decisions seem to be wrong, the teacher should nevertheless allow them to proceed, unless, of course, their chosen course of action would only lead to overwhelmingly disastrous results. It is part of the learning process for people to make mistakes and, profiting from them, subsequently to rectify them.

Because group procedures depend for success largely on the maximum contribution of each participant, *the teacher must see that every child in the group is given an opportunity to make a suitable contribution to the project. A good group project should include a wide enough range of tasks to elicit participation from every member of the class.*

GROUP ACTIVITIES: SIMPLER FORMS
Media and Techniques

A group activity for primary grades may be based on any theme that interests the pupils and may make use of any medium and technique the children are capable of handling. If a kindergarten class happens to be talking about the subject of spring, for example, each child who has reached the symbol stage may select one item of the season to illustrate. The children may draw and paint symbols of flowers, birds, trees, and other springlike objects. After drawing or painting each item, the children cut away the unused paper around the symbol. Then the drawings and paintings are assembled on a tackboard.

Many other suitable topics could be treated in a similar fashion. Among them might be the following:

1. *Shopping:* Various stores may be drawn and painted, together with people and automobiles. This subject also could be handled as an interior scene showing the articles on display in a supermarket.
2. *Where I Live:* Pictures of houses are eventually assembled to form a street or neighborhood.
3. *My Friends:* The outlines of boys and girls are assembled to form a crowd of children.
4. *Spring in the Garden:* Forms associated with gardens, such as bugs, butterflies, flowers, and trees, are gathered.
5. *Above and Below:* Sky shapes (clouds and birds), trees and flowers, and imaginative treatment of what lies below the earth's surface, such as root systems and animal homes, are included.
6. *A Story Everyone Loves.*

Three-dimensional output also lends itself to group activity for early grades. For example, the children can assemble modeling clay and paper constructions on a table to depict such scenes as "The Farm," with barns, cows, and so forth, and "The Circus," with clowns, elephants, and the like.

One of the simplest and most effective group projects is the "chalk-in," which can be executed on a sidewalk or parking lot. This can be done randomly or with sections marked off in a grid, with parts of each section touching adjacent ones at some point.

Teaching

The teacher begins the group activity in the same way as individual picture making or three-dimensional work, supplying motivation and teaching as required. Eventually, when the children have produced their work, the teacher, who has reserved a display space in the room, asks each child to bring a piece of work to the board and pin it in place. At first, a rather disorganized arrangement may result. A short discussion with the class, however, will elicit a few suggestions for improving the placement of the individual drawings. Some of the largest and brightest work can be located near the center of the panel, while smaller drawings of the same symbol drawn by several children might be grouped or arranged in a rhythmic line. When the "mural" is made with cut-out shapes, even a first grader can begin to think of subject matter in relation to organization of masses in space. In such cases, it may facilitate matters to do the initial planning on the floor, where shapes may be more easily adjusted than on the wall.

The finished composition will, of course, have many small areas of interest reminiscent of Grandma Moses and other so-called naive artists. Teachers should not attempt to improve the layout by adding any of their own work. If they are tempted to provide a fence or road in perspective, or even a horizon line, they should not—first, because the children should learn to depend only on themselves in developing a group activity and, second, because only a muddle could result if adult work (however naive) and children's work were assembled on the same panel. Children should not be used as surrogate artists for the teacher.

A "group" may be defined as a team ranging from three students to a complete class, depending on the nature of the project. Small groups work very well on dioramas, middle-sized groups can work in the sandbox, and larger groups can take on constructions like model shopping centers and housing communities. Other projects could include decorative maps or a mural that transforms the entire classroom into a medieval environment, complete with mullioned windows and stone walls.

PUPPETRY

Although puppetry is generally not taken seriously as an art form in the United States and Canada, it occupies a very high position in many other cultures. In Moscow, the National Puppet Theater is intended for adults rather than children, and in Spain and Italy no public park is complete without an adult puppet theatre. In Indonesia, Japan, and other Asian cultures, puppeteers begin their careers in childhood as apprentices, learning not only the intricate processes of construction and operation but also the roles to be enacted, many of which date back many generations. These plays recount the myths of creation and the battles between good and evil carried on by warriors and figures of royalty. Like the so-called fine arts, puppetry has its own history and its unique function as an educational and socializing factor in both developing nations and European societies. Puppetry, from hand puppets to marionettes, has a legitimate place in a balanced art program. Perhaps some of the most effective group activities lie within this art form.

Because it is more complex than most art activities, puppetry is often seen as a threat to other priorities in the curriculum. It is therefore neglected in favor of art experiences that require less time and planning and fewer materials. However, properly conducted, puppetry can carry the children into language arts and history as they gather information, prepare scenarios, and plan and construct a theatre and sets. Work in puppetry is a natural focal point for accommodating various learning styles.

To produce a successful puppet play, the group as a whole must reach decisions, and each member of the group,

although maintaining a personal identity, must give full cooperation if the enterprise is to succeed. Puppets range in technical complexity from the very simple to the very intricate, so groups of children at any particular stage of development may select techniques compatible with their capabilities. The two major types of puppets that elementary-school children in one stage or another may select are fist puppets and shadow puppets.

Fist Puppets

Media and Techniques

Simple stick puppets—the type operated directly with one hand—may be produced in a variety of ways. The beginner can draw a figure on cardboard and later cut away the excess background. The cut-out figure is then attached to a stick. In place of a cut-out figure, the pupil may use a bag stuffed with paper or absorbent cotton, decorated with paint or cut paper, and tied to the stick.

A paper bag also may be used for a puppet that moves its head. A string is tied around the middle of a paper bag, leaving just enough room for inserting the index finger above the middle. A face is painted on the closed upper portion of the bag. To operate the puppet, the hand is thrust into the bag

Diagrams of stick puppets (A and B), a puppet made from a paper bag (C), and a puppet made from an old stocking (D).

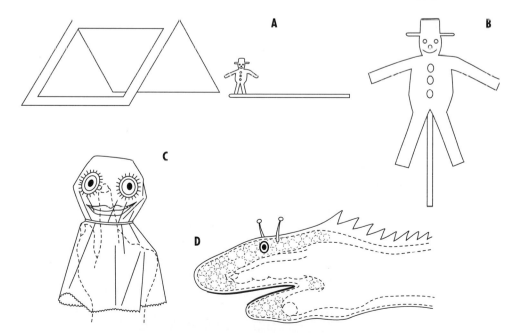

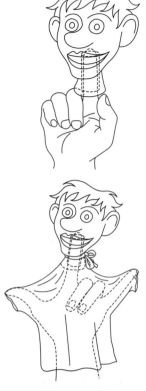

A puppet head modeled over a cardboard fingerstall. The puppet can be manipulated by placing the fingers as shown.

up to the neck and the index finger pushed through the neck to articulate the head.

An old stocking, appropriately decorated with buttons for eyes and pieces of cloth or paper for hair, ears, and other features, also makes an effective puppet when slipped over the hand and arm. Animals such as snakes or dragons may be formed by this means. They become especially fearsome if a mouth is cut into the toe of a sock and cloth is stitched to form a lining to the throat thus formed. Both top and bottom jaws should be stuffed with a material like absorbent cotton. The jaws are worked by inserting the fingers in the upper section and the thumb in the lower. The attractiveness of this creation can be enhanced by making a lining of a color contrasting with the sock, or by adding teeth or a tongue made from bright materials.

A fist puppet may be constructed from a wide variety of materials. Some of the modeling media mentioned in earlier chapters, including papier-mâché, are suitable for the construction of heads; plastic wood also may be used. The bodies of the puppets may be made from remnants of most textiles. These more advanced fist puppets should be capable of articulation in both the head and arms. The thumb and little finger are usually employed to create movements in the arms, while the index finger moves a modeled head.

To model a head, children should first cut and glue together a stiff cylinder of cardboard (preferably light bristol board) large enough in diameter to fit their index finger loosely. The modeling medium, which tends to shrink the cylinder slightly, is then worked directly around the cardboard until the head, including all features, and the neck are formed. The neck of the puppet modeled over the lower part of the cylinder, or "fingerstall," should be increased slightly in diameter at its base to hold in place the clothes, which are attached by a drawstring. When the modeling medium is dry, it should be smoothed with sandpaper and then decorated with poster paint. An attractive sparkle can be added to eyes, lips, or teeth by coating them with shellac or, better still, clear nail polish. In character dolls, attention can be drawn to outstanding features by the same means. Most puppets tend to be more appealing if the eyes are considerably enlarged and made conspicuous with a shiny coating. Hair, eyebrows, and beards made from absorbent cotton, yarn, cut paper, or scraps of fur can be pasted or glued in place.

The clothing covers the child's hand and arm and forms the body of the puppet. The outside dimensions of the clothing are determined by the size of the child's hand. The hand should be laid flat on a desk, with the thumb, index, and lit-

tle fingers extended. The approximate length of the puppet's arms will be indicated by the distance from the tip of the thumb to the tip of the little finger, and the neckline should come halfway up the index finger. To make clothing, fold a single piece of cloth in two, make a cut in the center of the fold for the neck, and then sew the sides, leaving openings for the fingers. Small mitts may be attached to the openings to cover the fingertips. If children wish their puppets to have interchangeable costumes, a drawstring can be used to tie the clothing to the neck. If they plan on designing only one costume for their puppets, the pupils can glue it into place, as well as tie it for extra security.

Lively puppet costumes can be made with bright textiles; men's old ties are valuable for this purpose. The lining of the ties should first be removed and the material ironed flat before being folded over and sewn to make a garment. Buttons and other decorations may be added, of course, as required.

When children make puppets, they expect to use them in a stage production. In presenting a fist-puppet show, the operators work beneath the set. This means that the stage must be elevated so the puppeteers can stand or crouch under it while the show goes on. A simple stage can be constructed from a large topless cardboard carton with two opposite sides removed and an opening for the stage cut in its base. The carton is then placed on a table with the opening facing the audience. The puppeteers stand or crouch behind the table and are concealed from the audience by the carton and a curtain around the table legs. Teachers can capitalize on the popularity of television's Muppets but should avoid using commercially manufactured hand puppets, since children may see these as competing with their own efforts.

The stage settings should be simple. In most cases they may be approached as large paintings, but they should have strong "carrying" power and be rich in a decorative sense. The costumes and backdrops should be designed to provide a visual contrast with each other. Because the stage has no floor, the background is held or fixed in position from below or hung from a frame above. On it may be pinned significant items, such as windows and doors. Separate backdrops may be prepared for each scene. Likewise, stage properties—tables, chairs, and the like—must be designed in two dimensions. Spotlights create striking effects and bring out the features of the presentation. Occasionally, it may be worthwhile to experiment with projected materials like slides.

The manipulation of fist puppets is not difficult; the pupils can teach themselves the technique merely by practice. They should remember, however, that when more than one puppet is on stage, the puppet that is "speaking" should be in continual movement, so the audience may know exactly which puppet is the speaker. The other puppets should be still.

Children have been raised in a video and television environment in which the Muppets and Mr. Rogers' "neighbors" are an important part of their culture. Puppetry activities allow children to become producers and creators rather than passive consumers.

Shadow Puppets

Although shadow puppets are not difficult to make, successful operation of them demands some finesse. In this technique a silk or nylon screen is set up between the operators and the audience. Strong spotlights on the operators' side are then beamed on the screen. The puppets, consisting of cardboard figures attached to a thin control stick, are held close to the screen in the direct path of the light, thus casting a shadow on the screen. Because the puppet appears to the audience only as a shadow silhouette, the figure needs no painting or decorating. Since the technique of operating is similar to that used with fist puppets, the stage for the latter may also be used for shadow puppets.

Children in the earliest phases of the symbol stage can be taught to make shadow puppets. The child simply cuts out a figure drawn on thin cardboard and glues it to a stick. As the children develop their ability to produce symbols and as their skill in using cutting tools improves, they can make much more elaborate puppets. Outlines will become more subtle so such features as shaggy hair, heavy eyebrows, or turned-up noses can be suggested in the silhouette. By punching holes or cutting inside the puppet, the pupil can depict, say, buttons, eyes, and frilly clothing.

Pupils can also make shadow puppets with moving parts. To make a dragon, for example, a number of small sections of cardboard are joined with paper fasteners. Two sticks are attached to the assembly. With practice, a child can make the creature wiggle in a highly satisfactory manner. All stage properties, from tables to houses, must be cut from cardboard, placed on sticks, and also shown in silhouette.

Many teachers begin by holding a general discussion of the problems involved in a project. After viewing a video of *Sesame Street,* children are asked to list the various tasks that must be done before a show can be successfully produced. Eventually, the main items of work are listed: selecting or

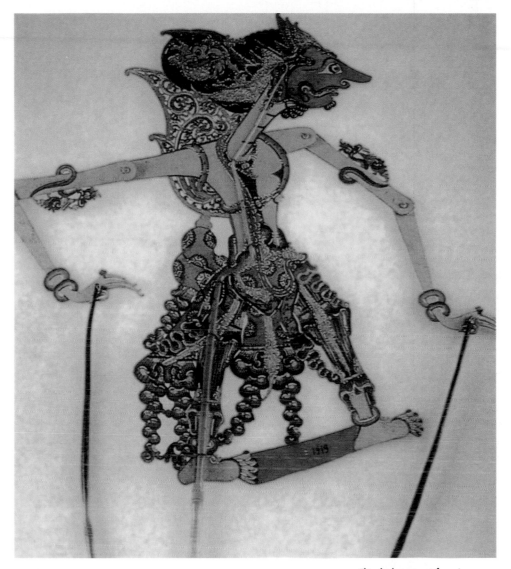

writing the play, making the puppets, making the stage scenery, lighting the stage, practicing manipulation, and deciding on the audience.

Next, committees should be listed to carry out the various tasks. Such groups might include a selecting committee, to recommend suitable plays to the general group, and a production committee, to recommend suitable stage properties and backdrops for each scene, the general size of the puppets, and the costumes.

Often the chairpersons of the committees are elected with the understanding that they will form a production

This shadow puppet from Java, Indonesia, although intended to be viewed lit from behind on a screen, can be enjoyed for the richness of its decorative detail when not in use. It is constructed of leather that is gilded, painted, and perforated. The continuous line beginning with the forehead and moving over the full profile has the flowing grace of Javanese calligraphy.

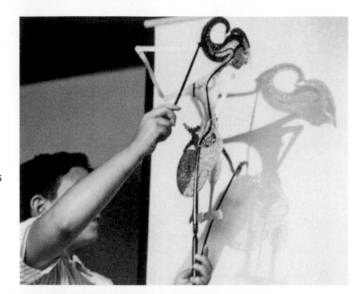

An authentic Javanese puppet, manipulated by a fifth-grade boy. Because the construction principle is simple, children can create a Western version of the same puppet; a sheet and two light sources will be needed to create the performance. Javanese puppetry can provide an introduction to Asian art, mythology, religion, and entertainment.

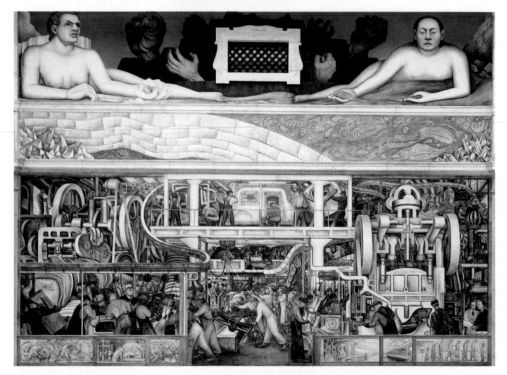

Diego Rivera, *Detroit Industry*, 1932–33. Mural (view of south wall). Gift of Edsel B. Ford. Photograph © 1991 The Detroit Institute of Arts

This is one wall of a very large fresco mural by the great Mexican artist, depicting the automobile industry in Detroit during the first decades of the twentieth century. Murals, because of their large size, provide an excellent format for telling complicated stories or expressing magnificent themes. Murals usually include many details, such as the figures in Rivera's work, each involved in some operation of the automobile factory. This painting and others by Rivera provide excellent focus for the study of politics, economics, industry, technology, and related subjects.

team, with the duty of overall coordination of the project. Either the members of the team or all the children elect a chairperson whose duty is to report from time to time to the children about progress and to seek suggestions for improvement.

Puppetry, like any theatrical activity, culminates in the inevitable presentation of a performance for an audience. The teacher should help the class as a whole to decide who will review the performance—the PTA? The class next door? All the sixth-grade classes? And so on. Once the audience has been decided on, publicity must begin; this may involve preparing posters for bulletin boards, a story for the school paper or PTA bulletin, and mimeographed programs—that final testimonial to all who have had a hand in the production.

It is most important that group evaluation or judging take place as the production proceeds, and, after the show is finished, the time-honored question is raised: "How can we improve the show next time?"

MURALS
Murals and Art History

The tradition of making murals, or very large paintings on walls, as art forms dates back to Egypt, Greece, and other early cultures. One might even claim that the prehistoric cave paintings are murals. During the Renaissance, murals in fresco were very popular, and two of the world's most famous works are murals in churches done during that period: Michelangelo's ceiling of the Sistine Chapel, and Leonardo da Vinci's *Last Supper*. Marc Chagall painted magnificent murals on the ceiling of the Paris Opera House, and American artists such as Thomas Hart Benton painted murals for the federal government as part of an assistance program during the Great Depression. Diego Rivera is perhaps as well known for his murals as any artist; the great Mexican artist painted numerous murals, many of them on highly charged social and political themes, in the United States and Mexico. Hispanic American artists in contemporary communities such as Los Angeles have continued under Rivera's influence with striking public murals on building exteriors.

Although elementary-school children cannot use oil paints or fresco, they can gain familiarity with the terms used in discussing these media. They can also observe how mural materials have changed with advancements of technology: Muralists now use such materials as welded metals, fired enamel plates, ceramics, and concrete. David Siqueiros, for example, used automotive lacquers as well as other industrial materials in his murals. Gyorgy Kepes produced murals using illuminated glass. Muralists today are as likely to be sculptors as painters; children who are exposed to their work may want to participate in a relief mural rather than a painting for their class activity. Children involved in mural-making activities will benefit from learning about these great traditions, and teachers will note that children often demonstrate greater interest, have more ideas, and create better murals when they have been taught them.

The contemporary mural is also a vital means of multicultural expression in inner-city neighborhoods, building community and cultural identity, as well as conveying frustration with existing conditions. Walls are designed and executed by one artist, by teams of artists, or by nonprofessionals working under the direction of artists. For *The Great Wall of Los Angeles,* Chicana artist Judy Baca used more than 200 rival gang members from Latino and African American communities to create a 1,700-foot-long mural.[8] In the artist's words, "Murals belong to no one, therefore to everyone." Funding for this impressive urban project came from a multitude of sources, including the National Endowment for the Arts, the juvenile justice system, and the Los Angeles Department of Recreation and Parks.

Mural Making

Although the term *mural* in its strictest sense refers to a painting made directly on a wall, in many schools it has come to denote any large picture. We have adopted that meaning for this discussion. Murals can be painted or constructed on exterior or interior walls, and we can find examples of both done by children in their schools and neighborhoods. For example, a school in an industrial part of town may be near an abandoned factory surrounded by concrete walls that are an eyesore for the community. With proper permissions, art classes could transform the ugly walls into objects of beauty and community pride.

Media and Techniques

When a school group decides to paint a mural inside the school, it should be considered as part of the scheme of interior decoration and should be integrated with it. The color relationships already established by the interior where the mural is placed should be echoed in the new work. Further-

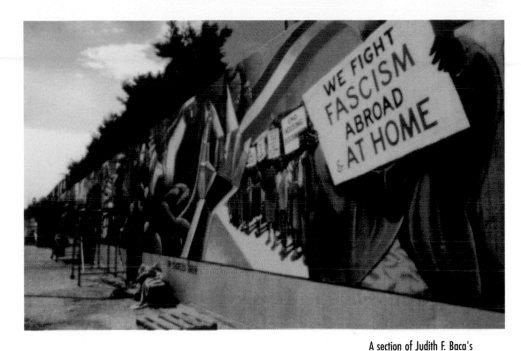

A section of Judith F. Baca's "mile-long" mural in Los Angeles. The artist enlisted the aid of rival youth gangs and, in the process, established a system for assisting the participants in their school studies. The mural is a visual record of Los Angeles history and the personal and social concerns of its citizens.

more, because door and window openings create a design in a room, the mural should be placed so it does not violate the architectural arrangement of these elements but rather tends to maintain the existing plan or even to improve on it. The architectural limitations of classrooms are so consistently severe that most murals will probably be no larger than 4 by 8 feet. Composition-board backing, which can be purchased at lumberyards or building-supply stores, may be used as a light, portable background for direct painting or as a backing for mural paper.

Despite the technicalities involved in the successful production of a mural, most children find that the activity is generally within their capabilities, and find the experience happy and rewarding. Children in the primary grades will have difficulty preplanning their work and will probably see mural making as an activity that allows them to paint on vertical surfaces.

The subject matter for murals may be similar to that used in individual picture making, or it may derive from a broader frame of reference, such as social studies. The most successful murals reflect the children's own experiences and interests. A subject such as the Western Movement, though not a part of the child's personal background, can still be worthwhile if attention is given to motivation by creating the environment of the early settlers with folk music, old prints, posters, and films. Whatever subject is chosen must

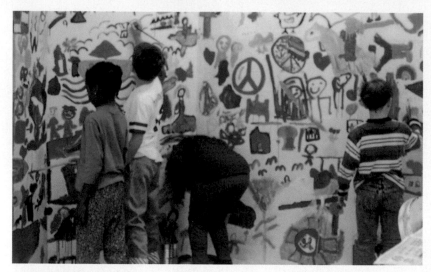

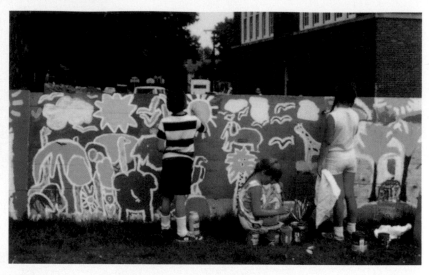

1 An example of a spontaneous mural made up of literally anything that came to mind. Once popular images (flags, rainbows, peace symbols, etc.) were taken care of, children were encouraged to create their own images. Contributions became smaller to fill spaces between the larger centers of attention.

2 A more structured mural using child-sized figures to dress up a building site.

be sufficiently broad in scope to allow several pupils to elaborate on it. A still-life composition, for example, would not be an appropriate subject for a mural.

The distinction between a painting with a limited focus of attention and a mural with multiple focuses must be made. A subject in which there are many objects of related but differing appearance, such as houses, factory buildings, or crowds of people, would be most suited to group activity. An example of a subject that offers a great variety of shapes is "At the Circus." Members of a third-grade class included both circus performers and spectators in the mural. The following are examples of themes that elementary-school pupils have successfully developed:

From the Experience of the Child	From Other Areas of the Curriculum
Our School Playground	The New Millennium
A Trip to the Supermarket	The Rain Forest
Playing Outside in Winter	Books I Have Liked
Shopping	Our Town (Neighborhood)
The Seasons Change	Acting My Age in Ancient Greece

Most of the picture-making media can be used in mural production. The paper should be sufficiently heavy and tough to support the weight of the finished product. Kraft paper, the heavy brown wrapping paper that comes in large rolls, is suitable. Many school-supply houses offer a gray mural paper that is pleasant to use. When ordering paper, a 4-foot width is recommended. The most effective coloring medium for young children is tempera paint. This should be applied with the same wide range of brushes suggested for picture mak-

ing. Some especially wide brushes should be available for painting the large areas of the mural. In applying tempera paint, excessive thickness should be avoided, since the paint will flake off when the mural is rolled up for storage. Chalk may be used, but it tends to be dusty and to smudge badly when several children are working at one time. Colored cut paper also yields effective results from the first grade on; the cut paper also can be combined with paper collage. Wax crayons are not suitable because they require too much effort to cover large areas, but crayons may be used in some areas as a resist with thin tempera.

The technique of planning and executing the mural varies with the nature of the group. The kindergarten child may begin by working side by side with classmates on the same long strip of paper. Beginners all paint on the same topic suggested by the teacher and use the same medium, but each child actually creates an individual composition without much reference to the work of the others. Not until they reach the third or fourth grade are some children able to plan the mural cooperatively. When they develop this ability, they may begin by making sketches lightly in chalk on the area allotted for the mural. Considerable discussion and many alterations may occur before the design satisfies all the participants.

By the time they reach the fifth or sixth grade, many pupils are ready to plan a mural on a reduced scale before beginning the work itself. They prepare sketches on paper with dimensions proportionate to those of the mural. These sketches are made in outline and in color. Later, when the mural paper has been laid over a large table or pinned to tackboard, the final sketch is enlarged on the mural surface. Usually this is done freehand, but sometimes teachers suggest that the squaring method of enlargement be used. By this method, the sketch and the mural surface are divided into corresponding squares. A pupil redraws in the corresponding area of the mural what is in a specific area of the sketch. Such a procedure, though common practice with professional muralists, may easily inhibit elementary-school children and should be used with caution. Only the most mature children are capable of benefiting from this technique.

After the drawing (or "cartoon," as it is sometimes called) has been satisfactorily transferred to the mural surface, the colors are applied. If tempera paint is to be used, it is usually mixed in advance in a relatively limited number of hues. Tints and shades are also mixed in advance. All colors should be prepared in sufficient quantity to complete all areas in the mural where they are to be used. In this way time and paint are saved, and the unity of the mural created in the sketch is preserved in the larger work. If colored chalk or cut paper is used, of course, the class is not likely to run out of a color. Acrylic paint is advisable for murals because it is waterproof, does not flake off if rolled up, and allows sand, paper, and other objects to be embedded in it while the paint is still wet.

When pupils use cut paper, the technique for producing a mural is less formal than when paint or chalk is used. The pupils can move areas of the colored paper around on the mural to find the most satisfying effects. Thus plans may undergo even major revision up to the final moment when the colored paper is stuck to the surface. Colored construction paper is recommended for the main body of the mural, because it gives the background areas added interest.

In carrying out the plan of a mural, the pupils quickly discover that they must solve problems of design peculiar to murals. Because the length of a mural in relation to its height is usually much greater than in paintings, the technical problem arises of establishing satisfactory centers of interest. Although only one center of interest may be developed, it must not be so strong that the observer finds it necessary to ignore portions of the work at the extremities of the composition. On the other hand, if a series of centers of interest are placed along the full length of the composition, the observer may consider the result jumpy and spotty. In general, the composition should be dispersed, the pupils being particularly careful about connecting the rhythms they establish so no part of the mural is either neglected or unduly emphasized. The balances in a mural made by children, fur-

thermore, have a tendency to get out of hand. Not infrequently children become intrigued with subject matter in one section of the work, with the result that they may give it too much attention and neglect other sections. Profuse detail may overload a favored part, while other areas are overlooked.

One problem of design that rarely occurs in mural making is lack of variety. Indeed, with many people working on the same surface, the problem is usually too much variety.

Teaching

As with puppetry, it is not difficult to interest children in making murals. Showing a video and slides or going to see a mural in a public building are two ways to arouse their interest. Pictures of the restored ceiling of the Sistine Chapel, for example, show the tremendous scale of Michelangelo's masterpiece and the complicated foreshortening the artist had to accomplish in the figures so they would look natural when viewed from the floor.[9] Before-and-after photographs show the remarkable effects of cleaning and restoring the vivid colors Michelangelo had applied but that had been dimmed by dirt and deterioration over the centuries. Students can gain some idea of the tremendous size and scope of the artist's accomplishment, the value placed on the work by experts, and the care with which the restoration has been accomplished through the use of computers and other modern devices. Children are also motivated by seeing the murals other children have made. Perhaps the most effective method is to discuss with the class the needs and benefits of making murals as decorations for specified areas of the school, such as the classroom, the halls, the cafeteria, or the auditorium.

Although in puppetry enough work often needs to be done to permit every member of the class to participate in the endeavor, this is not so in mural making. The pupils may all discuss the making of murals, including the various media, the most suitable subjects, and the probable locations where the work might be placed, but eventually the pupils must divide into small groups, probably not to reunite until the

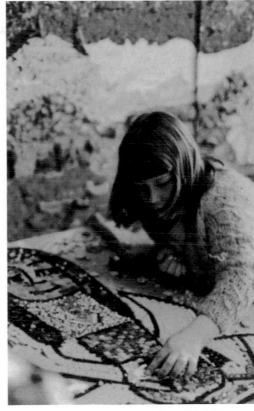

Lily Ann Rosenberg is an artist who divides her time between studio and community. To create her ceramic murals, the artist has students generate ideas that are mounted as they work, then the students and leader organize the ideas into an overall composition. They convert these into flat forms such as tiles or slabs, then color, fire, and glaze them. The "ground" is prepared by fastening chicken wire to plywood, and the various sections are separated by "walls" of clay so that individual sections composed of tiles, sand, shells, etc. can be pressed into sections of wet, colored cement.

final evaluation period. In the elementary school, the small groups may comprise from three to ten pupils each, depending on the size of the mural.

Preadolescents should be able to organize their own mural making. First, all the pupils in a class interested in mural making assemble to discuss what the theme should be. After the pupils' suggestions for the main theme have been written on the blackboard, each pupil selects some aspect to work on. Those interested in the same aspect form a team to work on that particular mural. If too many students elect one aspect, two teams can be created, each to work separately on the same subject. The teams are finally arranged, and each elects its chairperson.

Discussion then takes place within each team regarding the size and shape of its particular mural, the medium, and possible techniques. Sketches are then prepared, either cooperatively or individually. The teams can either choose the individual sketch most liked by all or prepare a composite picture, using the best ideas from the several sketches. The cartoon is then drawn, usually with the chairperson supervising to see that the chosen sketch is reproduced with reasonable accuracy. Next the color is added. This process goes on until each team's mural is completed. Finally, all the mural makers meet to review their work and to discuss the usual topics that arise in the "judging" stage.

During these proceedings the teacher acts as a consultant. If the pupils have previously made individual pictures, the teacher need give few demonstrations. The teacher's tasks consist for the most part in seeing that a working area and suitable materials are available, providing the initial motivation, outlining

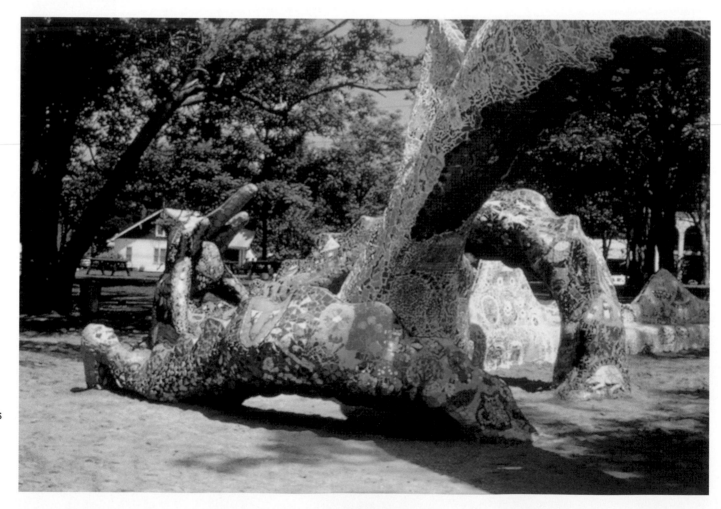

An emerging profession in art is that of the itinerant community activist who serves as an energizer as he or she works with people of all ages within a neighborhood. This photo shows part of a serpent created in Nashville's Fanny Mae Dees Park. It was executed in cement surfaced with mosaic. (Pedro Silva, artist)

some of the technical requirements of a mural, and demonstrating the "squaring" method of enlarging, if it is to be used.

A completely different approach allows the children to develop the mural spontaneously. In this approach the children can choose colors prepared beforehand in order to assure color harmony. The group then gathers around all four sides of the paper placed on the floor and begins to paint. If the group is too large to do this comfortably, it is divided into smaller units. The first children paint whatever comes into their minds, and succeeding groups try to relate their shapes and colors to those that have preceded them. The entire experience should be as open, and the children as immediately responsive, as possible.

Tableau Projects

In the late Middle Ages and into the Renaissance, many artists were called on to provide or design entertainments for their patrons. Even Leonardo da Vinci designed many such projects for the Duke of Milan. Included among the entertainments was the production of *tableaux vivants* (living pictures), in which participant-actors dressed and posed in legendary or historical depictions. Such tableaux could provide an unusual assembly program.

Students working in teams should choose a work of art and "become" the work of art through creating a setting and costumes and posing the figures. They should be encouraged to use the simplest materials, the emphasis of the project being the understanding of the visual aspect of the work they have chosen to portray.

As well as the tableau itself, the members of the group can include an oral presentation of background information on the artist, on the original work, or on the historical context. At the time of the presentation, a slide of the original work can be shown so the spectators can compare it with the tableau.

Ecological Themes

An example of a collaborative art project with a theme based on social values is the Commentary Islands unit taught by Sharon Seim of Nebraska.[10] During this four-week (12-session) art unit, students studied works by several artists who use contemporary landscape forms to make comments about the world in which they live (see Christo, Andy Goldsworthy, and Robert Smithson in this book). Then they formed teams of five and wrestled with decisions about social issues upon which their islands would comment.

The size and shape of the islands were restricted only by the size of the Styrofoam slab each team received. The artworks were created on these bases, which would float and therefore appear as islands on the pond near the school. Students were asked to prepare a written dedication speech (with music or dramatic accompaniment) that would be given on the occasion of launching the islands. Their speeches focused on such themes as "Destruction of the Rain Forest," "How the World Is Solving Pollution," "Urban Sprawl," "Endangered Animals," and "World Peace."

As the islands were launched in an emotionally moving ceremony, they floated out into the pond and floated together in the sunlight. Then they were retrieved with the fishing line attached to each work and taken back to the classroom. It is very likely that all the students who worked in teams and as an entire class to achieve this collaborative effort will fondly recall this experience for many years to come.

Blowups

"Blowups" are another simple way to begin a mural, and the most manageable way as well, since each child works on her or his own section in her or his own space. First, select an interesting image. (Photographs of the facades of older buildings, group portraits, city views, and well-known artworks are good subjects.) Then the master photo should be divided into as many squares as there are students. Each class member should have his or her own section of the photo to enlarge according to scale (a 1-by-1-inch square equals a 1-by-1-foot square, and so on). They then transfer the small segments to the larger space, heeding whatever problem or technique the class has selected for attention. This is an excellent way to apply a particular skill in color, collage, or pencil. In studying color, children can work in flat tones, blend the tones, or try to match the original color purely as an exercise in color control. When the segments are assembled according to the original, nothing quite goes together; the viewer must accomplish the process of making things "fit" via perceptual reconstruction. When this occurs, the viewer becomes a more active participant in studying the final image.

When making blowups, randomness moves closer to control. In this situation, students work strictly on their own but within certain limitations, knowing that a surprise awaits them. For example, a junior high school art teacher wanted to celebrate Washington's birthday in an unusual and memorable way. He cut up a reproduction of Emanuel Leutze's *Washington Crossing the Delaware* into 1-inch squares. Each student

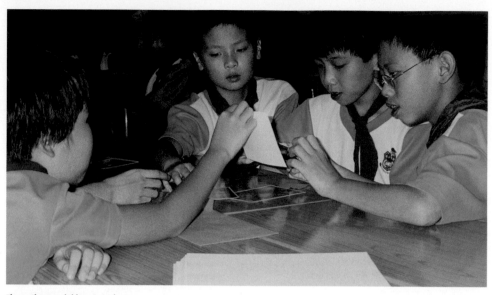

These Chinese children are playing a game using postcard-size art reproductions. This game is designed to challenge and expand the concept of "landscape" in traditional and contemporary art. Students in China often wear school uniforms.

received a square and a large sheet of paper cut to a proportionate size. The class then "blew up," or enlarged to scale, the small segments and transferred them to the large paper. No attempt was made to match colors, because Day-Glo paint was used instead of the standard tempera, watercolor, or chalk. Individual students used whatever colors they wanted without regard for Leutze's painting or the choices of other students. A wall was selected for mounting the project. When the completed pieces were assembled in proper order and fixed in place, a black light was turned on the wall and the effect was overwhelming. The teacher's goal was reached: "Neither teacher nor students will ever forget Washington's birthday."

ART GAMES

Group art activities can be conceptual, visual, and verbal as well as creative. Art games can be a very effective means to get children involved in art content and ideas. Game activities can teach cultural and historical content and philosophical and aesthetic concepts and skills in enjoyable ways. Open-ended games can raise questions and issues about art that students love to discuss and debate. Many games can be played in small groups or by individuals.

Art Images for Games

Art games usually require the use of art images—that is, reproductions of artworks. Teachers can obtain a wide selection of small, good-quality art reproductions by purchasing such art magazines as *ARTnews, Art in America, American Artist,* or *School Arts & Art Education,* and by clipping the reproductions from the pages. We recommend that you record all the pertinent information about each artwork, mount the picture, and place the information on the back. You can collect pictures of paintings, sculpture, prints, architecture, product design, and all modes of art. Another excellent source for small, manipulable art images is the postcards sold in art museums. One of the sources of income for art museums is the sale of reproductions of the works in their collections. Most of these postcards sell for very reasonable prices, and some museums sell postcard portfolios, which result in even lower costs per card. Some games can be played with larger prints, such as those available from companies that sell reproductions (see "Art Teaching and Learning Resources" in Appendix C).

Artists' Names and Styles

An elementary art teacher can organize and involve students in learning art history by using names of artists, styles, or cultures. For example, when students enter the room and sit down, the teacher directs them to look beneath their seats, where a card is taped. Each child finds a card that has an artist's name and possibly biographical information and a picture of a work by the artist. In preparing the cards, the teacher can create any type of category, such as impressionist painters, cubist painters, abstract expressionist painters, and so on. Or the categories might be related to art modes, such as drawing, painting, sculpture, ceramics, or architecture, or to examples of art from various cultural groups.

The teacher can use the card designators in a variety of ways. "Now students, look at your card, and make sure you know who you are. Where is Pablo Picasso? Where is Mary Cassatt? Where is Helen Frankenthaler? I see you notice that your name can be a man's or a woman's; you can trade around later if you want to. The important thing to recognize is your style of painting. I would like all the cubists to sit at this table, the impressionists over at that table, the fauvists here, and the abstract expressionists at the table by the door."

The teacher can use these categories for cleanup and monitor assignments, for dividing groups for games or studio projects, for dismissing at the end of the class period, or for whatever reason group divisions are useful. The teacher can also reshuffle the groups at any time by using other information on the cards. "Will all of you artists please look one more time at the painting on your card. If you used mostly warm colors, sit here; mostly cool colors, sit there . . ." and so forth, using such categories as color selection, dates of birth or death, or the subject matter of paintings, such as still life, figure, or landscape.

The teacher also can use these card designators to encourage class participation. The teacher displays one of Monet's water lily paintings and addresses the class: "Everyone please look at this large print I am showing. Now which one of you painted this?" A boy raises his hand. "Please tell us a little about yourself. What is your name, where are you from, and how did you come to paint this?" The level of these questions and the student's responses will depend on how much instruction has been given and on what information is included on the cards.

Art Collector

Simple children's card games such as Art Rummy can be altered to use art images instead of the traditional pictures. One teacher has devised card games using postcard-sized art images. The goal of one of the games is for the players to obtain entire "art collections" of four matching artworks, such as four by Emily Carr, four portraits, four sculptures, and so on. The cards are shuffled and dealt, and the deck is placed face down for drawing. Each card in a collection has the titles and artists' names of the other three in the collection. Children then ask each other for cards they need for a collection. "Do you have *Waves at Matsushima,* by Sotatsu?" If the child who is asked has the card, he or she gives it to the asker, who then gets another turn. If not, the child draws a card. The next child asks, "Do you have *The Letter,* by Mary Cassatt?" or "Do you have *The False Mirror,* by René Magritte?" As with most of the games, children become increasingly familiar with art images, styles, modes, subjects, and names of artists.

Similar games are available for purchase in some museums and bookstores. For example, Art Rummy consists of thirty-two cards of quality artworks from the Metropolitan Museum of Art, Quartet is a card game with four art images by each of thirteen artists from the collection of the Tate Gallery in London, and Masterpiece is an art game of bidding and selling artworks from the collection of the Art Institute of Chicago.

The following games were devised by the authors and have been used with success in classroom situations. Some

will appeal more to older elementary students, but each game can be adapted by teachers to meet the levels of their students.

Guess the Theme

Using small reproductions or postcard art images, organize five or six artworks according to some theme or idea. For very young children, this might be very simple, such as five paintings of babies, or five sculptures of horses. For older children, themes can be more difficult to detect, such as six works from different cultures, in different art media, all representing some form of violence (which is, unfortunately, very common in history and in art).[11] A theme such as this might also raise questions about what art should depict and what artists should create about the world around them. The number of themes is almost limitless. Some interesting examples might be people at work (using different cultures), mother and child, people with authority, flowers in art, relationships between two people, hats, cityscapes, and so on. Themes can relate to topics in the grade-level curriculum, such as The Sea, or The Westward Movement.

For a variation of this, place the complete collection in one place and have students pick out a thematic set from the whole collection. The teacher may suggest or students can assemble a group of artworks whose theme the class is asked to identify.

Compare and Contrast

For this game select two artworks that are similar in some ways, the more obvious for the younger children. Give the two reproductions to a group of three or four children, and ask them to discuss (to list, if they can write) ways the two artworks are similar and ways they are different. In making the comparisons, children should be encouraged to look at information on the backs of the cards that will give them more of a basis for deciding on similarities and differences. For example, comparing the portraits of two American presidents, George Washington and William Clinton, students can point to both paintings as portraits of men who held the same office, who have dark suits and white shirts, who are looking at the viewer, and who have similar neutral brown backgrounds. From the backs of the postcards, students will learn that both artists are male Americans who lived in different times, as did the presidents depicted. They may learn that both paintings are in galleries in Washington, D.C., both are owned by the people of the United States, both are oil paintings on canvas, and both are approximately the same size, but one is vertical, the other horizontal in format, and so on.

Older children might be able to make comparisons of the two men and their records as president. The contrasting styles of the artists and the differences in level of formality of pose might be related to the different times these men served as president. These paintings would provide teachers with opportunities to relate art to history and social studies, as well as politics.

The comparisons that teachers can organize are limitless, including ideas from architecture, applied design, art materials, and cultures. Examples include an ivory carving from the Congo of an African mother and child, compared with a Raphael madonna; a gold Egyptian statue of the god Amun, compared with the Roman marble sculpture titled *The Apollo Belvedere;* and the geometric nonobjective colored squares painted by Frank Stella, compared with the colored splashes and drips in a print by Sam Francis, both created in the 1970s and both hanging in the National Gallery of Art.

How Are These the Same?

In this game the children are given a series of art images that have something in common, either obviously or more subtly, depending on the teacher's goals and the children's abilities. For example, the six or seven artworks might all be made of bronze, might all be utilitarian art objects, might all be watercolors, or might all be nonobjective art. This activity can be used to push children beyond observation into other means of investigation. For example, a series of seven cards seems to have almost nothing in common on observation of the artworks. One is a traditional portrait painting, another is a nonobjective wood sculpture, another is a floral abstract, another is a watercolor of the sea, and so on. Only by investigating the information on the backs of the cards will the students be able to make the connection that all the works were done by women. Other categories might include artworks that are all religious objects, all in the same museum, or all created by a Dutch artist.

Is This Art?

Postcard images are arranged in small packets of six or seven. The teacher selects these images to raise questions about definitions of art: What objects can be counted as art, and why? This game works best with small groups of children discussing the question and reporting what they decide and why to the entire class. For example, one packet might contain a photograph of an ordinary chair, a picture of a tree, a painting of a tree, a picture of an animal, a picture of a building, and a photograph of a sculpture. The primary question about art in this packet asks if natural objects are works of art or does art have to be made by humans? If art has to be made by humans, which objects should be considered art and which are ordinary objects?

Another packet contains art images that are suspect in the minds of some people. For example, among images that are generally acceptable, such as a Rembrandt painting or Greek sculpture, the teacher places one of the graffiti paintings of Keith Haring, a photograph by Man Ray, and an interior environment by Sandy Skoglund. The variety possible for this game is unlimited, and it can be directed by the teacher to correlate with curriculum goals and objectives.

Where and When?

The teacher displays (maybe permanently) a large world map and a large time line on the wall or bulletin board. On the game table or in a box are several packets of postcards pasted on envelopes (the more substantial envelopes wear better). The information usually found on the back of the postcard, including when and where the works were created, is typed on a card inside each envelope. The task for children is to try to place each art object on the correct continent or island group and/or to place it approximately on the time line. One image might be of an African mask, another a Native American eagle-feather bonnet, another an Egyptian sculpture, another a Gothic cathedral, and so on. Children can look on the card inside the envelope to see if they were correct. The packets of postcard images are arranged according to difficulty.

Connoisseur

Teachers can organize bulletin-board displays that include games. For example, for very young children, the teacher might display three landscapes and a still life and ask, "Which painting doesn't belong?" The task can become more difficult as children progress. The image of the connoisseur is a person who can make very fine distinctions, such as art historians and critics.

In one example of the connoisseur game for upper-elementary children (or adults), the teacher displays twelve images of artworks on the bulletin board, each with a number beside it. Six of the postcards show paintings of buildings by Edward Hopper; three show paintings of buildings by Charles Sheeler, Hopper's contemporary; and three show paintings of buildings by other artists, such as O'Keeffe, Wood, Demuth, or Estes. By selecting works that are either very similar to Hopper's or very different, the teacher controls the difficulty of the game.

To play this game students might be asked to:

1. List the numbers of the paintings they think were done by the featured artist (the one with most works displayed)

2. Name the featured artist

3. List the numbers of paintings by other artists

4. Name as many of these artists as possible

5. List titles of paintings

Students might work individually or in teams. Points can be tallied for every correct response, and individual and team champions can be recognized. To follow up, teachers might ask students to explain how they knew that the six paintings by Hopper belonged together (stylistic characteristics, subject matter, mood, etc.) and how they knew that the other paintings were done by other artists.

Art games can be fun for children and teachers, they can provide variety in teaching and learning, they can motivate and stimulate interest, and they can inspire a great deal of learning. Teachers can use games to raise issues of aesthetics and to teach about history and criticism. In the hands (and minds) of good teachers, art games become another component in the instructional repertoire.

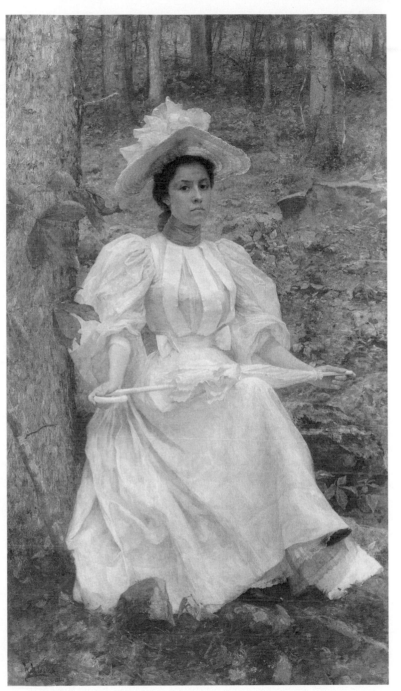

William Robinson Leigh, *Portrait of Sophie Hunter Colston*, 1896, oil on canvas, $72\frac{3}{8}$" × $40\frac{7}{8}$". National Museum of American Art, Smithsonian Institution, Washington, D.C., U.S.A. Art Resource, N.Y.

One of the issues of feminist criticism deals with the representation of women in works of art. Women are often depicted as powerless, subservient, domestic, or as objects of the male gaze. Feminist critics ask for a more diverse and balanced representation including women of power, intelligence, position, and authority. How would you interpret this representation of the artist's cousin, Sophie Hunter Colston? What is this woman like? What is her personality? And what is her place in the world?

NOTES

1. Maurice J. Elias, et. al. *Promoting Social and Emotional Learning: Guidelines for Educators.* (Alexandria VA: Association for Supervision and Curriculum Development, 1997), p. 1.

2. Boyd H. Bode, *Democracy as a Way of Life* (New York: Macmillan, 1937), p. 75.

3. Louis E. Lankford, "Ecological Stewardship in Art Education," *Art Education* 50, no. 6 (1997): 47–53.

4. Ronald W. Neperud, "Art, Ecology, and Art Education: Practices and Linkages," *Art Education* 50, no. 6 (1997): 14–20; and Theresa Marche, "Looking Outward, Looking In: Community in Art Education," *Art Education* 51, no. 3 (1998): 6–13.

5. Cynthia L. Hollis, "On Developing an Art and Ecology Curriculum," *Art Education* 50, no. 6 (1997): 21–24.

6. Al Hurwitz, *Collaboration in Art Education* (Reston, VA: National Art Education Association, 1993), p. 3.

7. W. H. Kilpatrick, *Foundations of Method* (New York: Macmillan, 1925).

8. The Annenberg CPB Collection, *Judy Baca,* videotape. (South Burlington, VT: Annenberg, 1997).

9. For a fascinating article about the restoration of the Sistine Chapel ceiling, including excellent pictures, see David Jeffrey, "A Renaissance for Michelangelo," *National Geographic* 176, no. 6 (December 1989).

10. *Art Education in Action,* Episode A, "Highlighting Studio Production and Student Social Commentary," videotape (Los Angeles: Getty Center for Education in the Arts, 1995).

11. For example, this set might include such artworks as *The Burning of the Sanjo Palace,* thirteenth-century Japanese; *Battle between Zanga and Awkhast,* fifteenth-century Persian; *The Martyrdom of St. Hippolytes,* fifteenth-century Flemish; *The Crucifixion,* Tiepolo, 1700; *Echo of a Scream,* Siqueiros, Mexican, 1937; and an untitled drawing showing two men in business suits struggling, by Robert Longo, contemporary American, 1986.

ACTIVITIES FOR THE READER

1. Study a group activity in a classroom, and analyze it according to Kilpatrick's four stages.

2. Describe three group activities not mentioned in this chapter.

3. Make three fist puppets: a simple stick puppet, a more complicated paper bag puppet, and, finally, a cloth puppet of an animal whose jaws will move. Improvise dialogue around a situation with a fellow student's puppets.

4. Practice manipulating each of your puppets. When skillful, give a short performance for some of your younger friends, and see how they react.

5. Study any professional murals in your locality. Make a note of their subject matter in relation to their location, their design, and the media used.

6. Design a small-scale mural suitable for the interior of your local post office, the foyer of a local theatre, or the entrance of the local high school. Choose subject matter of local interest.

7. Try some of the art games described in the chapter. Look for art games in museums and bookstores. Begin your own collection of them.

8. Collect a large number of art postcards or art magazine cutouts, and invent art games using the images. Make games that will be useful for teaching art concepts, skills, and history.

9. Create a game that involves using the following elements:
   a. Advancing an object, such as a checker or a chess piece, to reach a destination: a museum, a gallery, or a collection
   b. Chance, such as rolling dice
   c. Moves determined by color-coded cards that relate to the numbers on the dice

10. Create a reduction/sorting game. Select eighteen to twenty-four paintings that can be divided into two sets, each of which shares a dominant concern, such as color or line. Take each set of paintings, and divide it in turn into two more sets, following the same selection process. (The "color" set may have one realistic and one nonobjective subset, while the other set could be divided into "active" and "passive" subsets.)

SUGGESTED READINGS

Alger, Sandra L. H. *Games for Teaching Art.* J. Weston Walch, 1995.

Baloche, Lynda A. *The Cooperative Classroom: Empowering Learning.* New York: Prentice-Hall, 1997.

Barthelmeh, Volker. *Street Murals: The Most Exciting Art of the Cities of America, Britain and Western Europe.* New York: Alfred A. Knopf, 1982.

Hurwitz, Al. *Collaboration in Art Education.* Reston, VA: National Art Education Association, 1993.

Hurwitz, Al, and Stanley Madeja. *The Joyous Vision: A Source Book for Elementary Art Appreciation.* 2d ed. Englewood Cliffs, NJ: Prentice-Hall, 1999.

Johnson, David W., and Roger T. Johnson. *Learning Together and Alone: Cooperative, Competitive, and Individualistic Learning.* 5th ed. New York: Allyn and Bacon, 1999.

Rochfort, Desmond. *Mexican Muralists.* London: Laurence King Publishers, 1993.

Slavin, Robert E. *Cooperative Learning: Theory, Research, and Practice.* Trans. 2d ed. New York: Allyn and Bacon, 1995.

WORLD WIDE WEB RESOURCES

Teaching Resources

Lake, Bettie. "Integrating the Web and the Visual Arts." *Art Teacher Connection.* 1999. <http://www.inficad.com/~arted/pages/themes.html> This Web page contains links to Web sites with projects and activities that provide for multidisciplinary, interdisciplinary, or cross-curricular units and that fulfill national standards requirements in several curricular areas, including the visual arts.

The Getty Institute for Education in the Arts. ArtsEdNet: The Getty Art Education Web Site. *Worlds of Art: Mexican American Murals: Making a Place in the World; African American Art: A Los Angeles Legacy; Navajo Art: A Way of Life.* 1998. <http://www.artsednetgetty.edu/ArtsEdNet/Resources/Murals/index.html> This online curriculum consists of four lessons that can stand alone or be used in conjunction with the others. Includes background information and images of key artworks. Abundant teaching resources and links to museum collections are included. The mural unit culminates in an art-making activity that leads students to create their own classroom or school mural.

The Getty Art Education Web Site. Art and Ecology: Interdisciplinary Approaches to Curriculum. 1997. ArtsEdNet. An ArtsEdNet Online Exhibition. <http://www.artsednet.getty.edu/ArtsEdNet/Resources/Ecology/index.html> This Web site provides both a set of resources for teachers and an online exhibition of contemporary ecological art. The discussions and activities focus on understanding contemporary ecological art and community environmental issues. The curriculum is organized to be interdisciplinary with a variety of environmental, social, and cultural issues from different subject areas. A comprehensive DBAE approach supports the material.

Hispanic Research Center at Arizona State University and Gary Keller Cárdenas and Mary Erickson. *Chicana and Chicano Space: A Thematic, Inquiry-Based Art Education Resource.* 1999. Arizona State University. <http://mati.eas.asu.edu:8421/ChicanArte/> This site provides an interdisciplinary approach to Chicana and Chicano art and culture. It includes images of artworks (with ample background information) and thematic instructional units.

Online Group-Based Art Activities

Museum of Modern Art. *Art Safari: An Adventure in Looking for Children and Adults.* <http://artsafari.moma.org/> *Art Safari* presents the painting and sculpture collection of the Museum of Modern Art in the context of an interactive Web site activity. This site encourages learning about art by looking and sharing interpretations.

MOWA. "Kid's Wing." *Museum of Web Art.* 1999. <http://www.mowa.org/about.html> The Museum of Web Art was founded to provide a context for new electronic art. The site is patterned after traditional museums. "Kid's Wing" is designed as an interactive experience for groups or individuals and includes games, art activities, puzzles, and a display of children's electronic art.

Online Classroom Materials for Art Teachers

CRIZMAC Art and Cultural Education Materials, Inc. <http://www.crizmac.com/> CRIZMAC Art and Cultural Education Materials, Inc., is a publishing company dedicated to art education and appreciation. Products are carefully selected to provide curriculum resources for art and classroom teachers. The site includes some online material.

Davis Publications. <http://www.davis-art.com/Default. htm> This publishing company creates K–12 art textbook programs, art resource books, and visual art resources. The Web site provides links to *School Arts* magazine and art lesson plans for elementary classroom and art teachers.

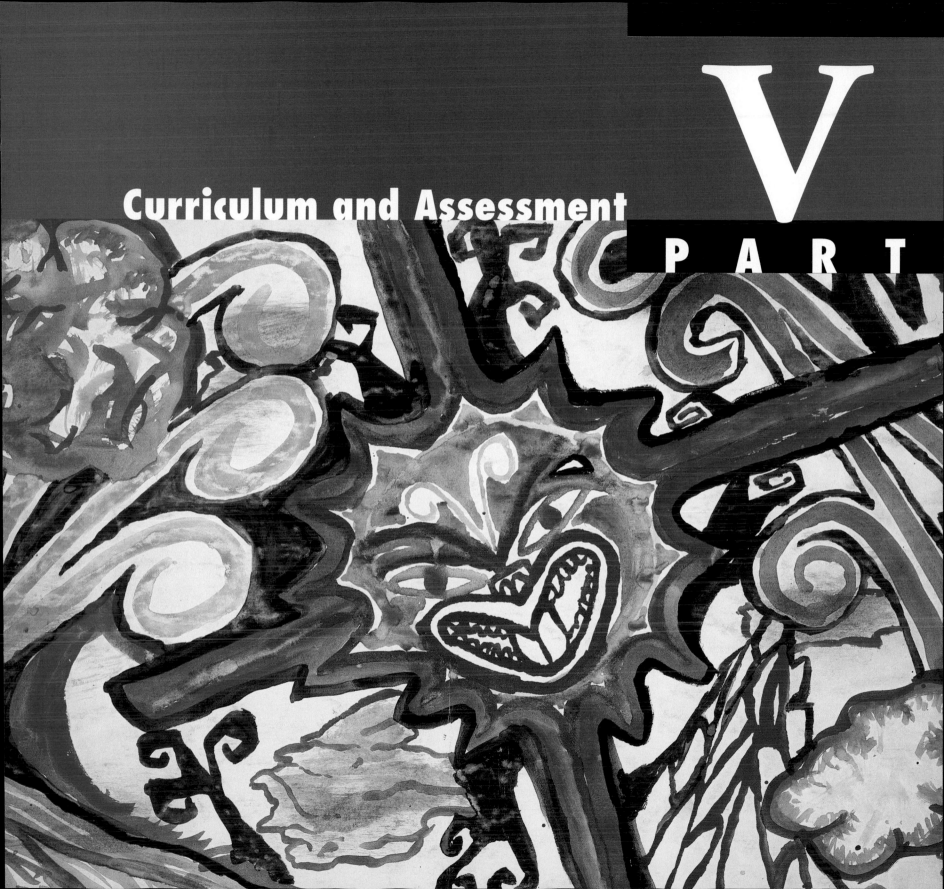

Curriculum and Assessment

PART V

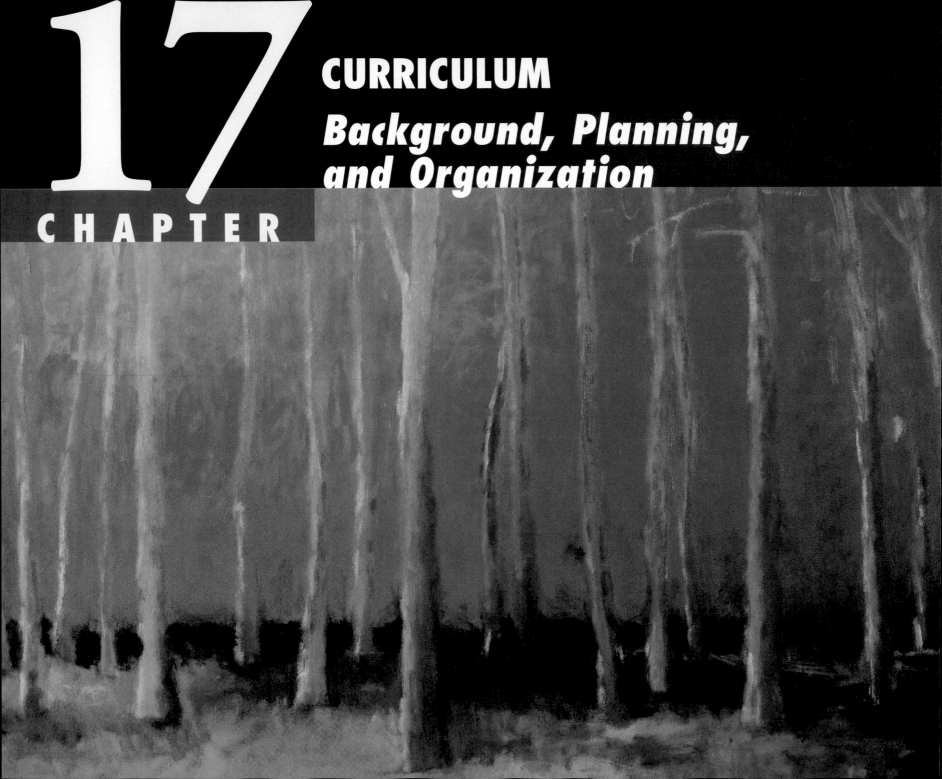

17

CURRICULUM
Background, Planning, and Organization

Curriculum planning is not thought of as a series of distinct and fixed steps. No single pattern, beginning, for instance, with stating objectives, will suffice in solving all curriculum problems. The dynamics of given school situations and the resources provided by interdisciplinary study and practical experience in curriculum planning determine the ways in which problems should be attacked.[1]

—Ronald C. Doll

The term *curriculum* is used to refer to several aspects of the educational enterprise, depending on who is using the term and in what context. For some, the curriculum is the organized content that is planned for students to learn; for others, curriculum refers not to the written plans for learning but to actual instruction as it takes place in the classroom. Other educators might indicate that curriculum refers not to what teachers teach but to what students learn. Still others see the curriculum as the entire experience of children in and out of school. All these connotations are worth considering whenever we set out to plan a program of art education for children and youth. This chapter will focus on organizing art content and on planning art activities to promote learning about art.

As we discussed in Chapter 1, the art curriculum planning process requires that we pay attention to the nature of art, to appropriate conceptions of children and their abilities to learn, and to the values of society.[2]

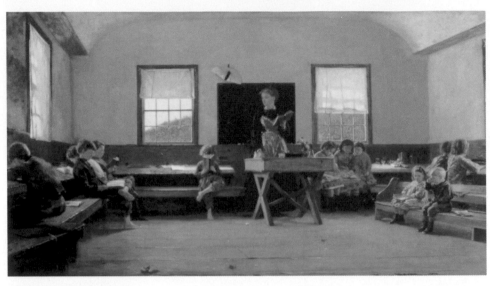

The schoolroom is a familiar scene for children of every generation. Early American artist Winslow Homer created many works depicting childhood experiences, including this informative view of a one-room school in nineteenth-century New England.

Curriculum planners in different states or provinces will be influenced and guided by the values set forth by their respective state frameworks. Within a state, different school districts will shape their state's framework to meet local values, needs, and resources. Within school districts, individual schools will apply their own guidelines according to their perceived needs, and, finally, each teacher will adapt all of the prior educational guidance as he or she sees fit, in the context of the needs and interests of students.

It is difficult, if not inappropriate, to discuss curriculum without referring to instruction and evaluation. The planned curriculum is intended to be implemented through the teacher's direction and instruction. Art curriculum planners must be aware of the realities of the classroom, including the age levels and abilities of children, requirements and duties placed on the teacher by the school, and relationships between the art curriculum and the rest of the school curriculum. Curriculum developers also must consider relationships among the written curriculum, instruction and learning in the classroom, and evaluation of students' progress.

INFLUENCES ON CURRICULUM DECISION MAKING

Children's Characteristics and Needs

One item often mentioned in relation to curriculum development at all levels is "the characteristics and needs" of children. As educators, we know we are supposed to be sensitive to children, but how do we ascertain children's needs, and to what needs are we supposed to respond? How will these needs and characteristics influence the planning of art curricula? Much of what we need to know here is discussed in Chapters 3, 4, and 5, and numerous examples are provided that illustrate how teachers adapt their intentions and classroom activities according to what they know about their students. One authority on curriculum has provided an explicit illustration of what we mean when we refer to general characteristics and needs of children. The following lists were developed by a committee of teachers after close observations of kindergarten and first-grade children.[3]

Characteristics

1. Children begin to lose baby teeth, causing lisping, and so on.
2. Right- or left-handedness is established. No change should be made without expert advice.
3. Bone structure growth is slower than in previous years.
4. Heart growth is rapid. The child should not be overtaxed physically.
5. Eyes are increasing in size. Watch reading and writing habits.
6. Feelings of tension may be evident in thumb-sucking, nail-biting, and mistakes in toilet habits.
7. Motor skills begin to develop and coordination may be awkward.
8. Large muscles are much more developed than smaller ones.
9. The child responds to rhythm—skips, beats time, and so forth.
10. The average child of these ages is full of vitality.
11. Children are interested in an activity rather than in its outcome.
12. Self-dependence and a desire to help others are developing.
13. Children prefer activity—climbing, jumping, running—but they tire easily.

Needs

1. Short periods of activity
2. Twelve hours of sleep
3. Vigorous and noisy games, essential to growth

4. Many opportunities to do things for oneself

5. Frequent participation in organized groups—games, dramatics, puppetry, and so on

6. Chances for the shy child to join in the routine and be important

The characteristics and needs listed are general rather than specific to art education, but they follow closely many of the observations made about children of these ages in previous chapters. For example, children should be encouraged to express their own ideas and feelings in their artwork, rather than using coloring books or copying what other children are creating; given opportunities to release tension through expressive activities; and given art materials appropriate for their physical coordination. Reviewing this list gives us many ideas about teaching art activities to children in kindergarten and first grade. Similar lists can be made for older age groups as well.

Readiness of Learners

The subject content of a balanced art program can accommodate learners of any age, personality type, or experience. Curriculum writers need to recognize that just as no two children are exactly alike, so also do classes or groups of children differ. The written curriculum should provide for differences, allowing teachers to adapt activities to the differences in individuals and groups. The capacities of the children to learn will obviously influence the art program, and variations in intelligence may affect art production as well as general learning about art. Slow learners in other subjects are often also slow to profit from art activities, and the art curriculum must be flexible enough to accommodate such differences. Fast learners must also be considered by curriculum planners, and extensions of the regular activities should be provided for those who are ready to move ahead or work more in depth. The needs, capacities, and dispositions of the children demand diversification of materials to be used, problems to be solved, and concepts to be introduced and reinforced.

Values of Society

The values of the larger society, along with local community values and those expressed within school systems, influence curriculum planning. As noted in Chapter 1, art education in the United States was initiated for the purpose of improving this country's ability to compete internationally in business and industry. Since that time we have seen national and international events and trends assert their influence on American education. Current examples of society's values often mentioned in discussions of education are:

1. The explosion of the Internet as a worldwide interactive source for information and a resource for research

2. Concern for safety in schools

3. Renewed emphasis on the so-called basics of education: reading, writing, mathematics, and science

4. Concern that American education aims too low and does not teach students to develop more complex levels of thinking

5. A desire to recognize and sustain the contributions of other cultures and their legitimate connections to Western ideas and to each other[4]

Issues such as these influence federal support of education, state and local funding, professional meetings and publications, and even the local voting public when school issues are placed on the ballot. Sometimes the complexity of issues that impinge on education is ignored, and simplistic slogans or panaceas are offered to the lay public by reformers in place of sound proposals with sufficient financial support for implementation.

Curriculum planners need to be up-to-date with respect to educational trends and value issues in society. Curriculum writers can contribute significantly toward educational improvement through the content and activities they place in the curriculum. For example, art curriculum planners currently are very aware of the need to provide children with knowledge and understanding of world art as well as of art from the Western tradition. Curriculum planners can also encourage art activities that engage children in more complex levels of thinking.

Thinking Skills in the Art Curriculum

Although considerable variation occurs in what different psychologists and educators mean when they refer to more complex levels of thinking, Resnick and Klopper have developed a brief set of characteristics that we can apply to art curriculum and instruction.[5] Through art education, students can become engaged in

1. Thinking that is *nonalgorithmic*—that is, a path of action not fully specified in advance.

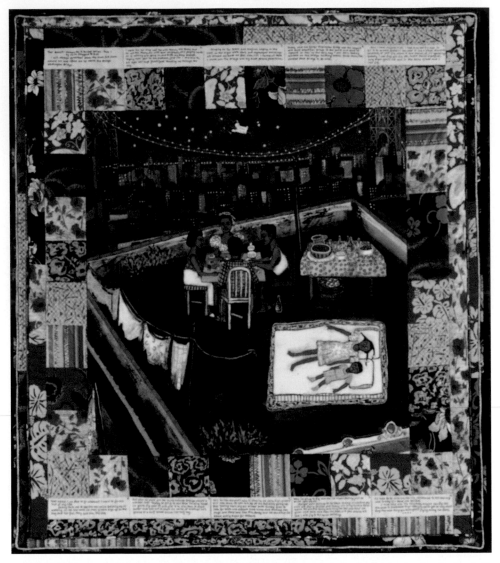

Faith Ringgold, *Tar Beach* (*Woman on a Bridge Series, Part I*), 1988. Acrylic on canvas, bordered with printed, painted, quilted and pieced cloth, 74⅝″ × 68½″. Solomon R. Guggenheim Museum, New York, gift of Mr. and Mrs. Gus and Judith Lieber, 1988, 88.3620. Photograph by David Heald © The Solomon R. Guggenheim Foundation, New York.

Through her use of quilts as a foundation for her work, Faith Ringgold raised questions about supposed hierarchies in art that relegated utilitarian objects to a lower status. Ringgold also wrote and illustrated a children's book on the theme of *Tar Beach*, the rooftop summer retreat for her family during the hot summer nights of her childhood in the city.

2. Thinking that tends to be *complex*. The total path is not "visible" (mentally speaking) from any single vantage point.

3. Thinking that often yields *multiple solutions*, each with costs and benefits, rather than unique solutions.

4. Thinking that involves *nuanced judgment* and interpretation.

5. Thinking that involves the application of *multiple criteria*, which sometimes conflict with each other.

6. Thinking that often involves *uncertainty*. Not everything that bears on the task at hand is known.

7. Thinking that involves *self-regulation* of the thinking process, where students can consider their progress as they work on a problem or endeavor.

8. Thinking that involves *imposing meaning*, finding structure in apparent disorder.

9. Thinking that is *effortful*. Considerable mental work is involved in the kinds of elaborations and judgments required.

When we consider the range of activities that children participate in with a balanced, comprehensive art curriculum, we can recognize art as a school subject that encourages more complex levels of thinking. For example, when children apply a phased approach to art criticism, involving description, analysis, interpretation, and informed preference, they are involved in *complex* mental activity with *multiple potential solutions* requiring *nuanced judgment* (see Chapter 12 on art criticism). When children apply what they have learned about color, composition, proportion, and distortion to the creation of a landscape painting that expresses a mood, they are involved in a *nonalgorithmic* activity with *multiple criteria* requiring *self-regulation*. When children are old enough to discuss and debate basic questions about art, such as the puzzles described in Chapter 14 on aesthetics, they might be engaged in several types of thinking, including *effortful* thinking involving a good deal of *uncertainty*.

Much of the discussion of the thinking curriculum in general education is focused on such subjects as language arts, science, and mathematics, with relatively little attention paid to the potentials in the art curriculum. This is somewhat paradoxical, however, as writers of the stature of Susanne Langer and John Dewey have long recognized the cognitive requirements of making and evaluating art. Dewey wrote:

To think effectively in terms of relations of qualities is as severe a demand upon thought as to think in terms of symbols, verbal and mathematical. Indeed, since words are easily manipulated in mechanical ways, the production of a work of genuine art probably demands more intelligence than does most of the so-called thinking that goes on among those who pride themselves on being "intellectuals."[6]

Nearly sixty years later, such writers as Eisner and Gardner continue to emphasize the cognitive dimensions of art and the existence of multiple intelligences that children and adults bring to bear on developing their understandings of the world.[7]

The Community Setting

The local community often provides the strongest influence on the school curriculum. Local control of education is one of the hallmarks of the American system. This principle is at once one of the most progressive values in education throughout the world and one of the most difficult practices.

When we consider that the many thousands of school districts across North America have the authority to establish the curriculum to be implemented within their own boundaries, we can understand the great strength in such diversity and the likelihood that local programs can respond effectively to local conditions, resources, and needs. On the other hand, the task of moving progressive ideas in education into the schools is multiplied almost by the number of school districts across the land, and at times it seems that needed changes move very slowly to the level of the classroom.

Nevertheless, a number of factors encourage similarities among diverse school populations. One factor is the use of textbook series by large publishing companies in many school districts, which tends to encourage uniformity among the local curricula. Other factors that tend to bring uniformity in school curricula are the establishment of graduation requirements for high school, college and university entrance requirements, and the use of standardized national aptitude and achievement tests. Even though some of these practices apply only to secondary schooling, the effects are seen in elementary schools as well.

Curriculum planners must respect local social issues and values. For example, an art curriculum developed within a school district that serves a primarily Latino community in east Los Angeles might differ significantly from an art curriculum tailored to the needs and interests of students in rural Kansas, northern Minnesota, or urban Philadelphia. Teachers, administrators, and curriculum planners should be aware of local issues that might be sensitive, such as sex education, religious issues, ethnic values, and such specific topics as nudity in art. Michelangelo's *David* and Botticelli's *Venus* may not be welcome in all communities, for example, and curriculum planners should be aware of community mores and standards. Although these two artworks are considered by many experts to be masterworks of Western culture and might be counted essential for cultural literacy in some schools, because of their use of nudity they might be rejected in other communities. Knowledgeable curriculum planners realize that the tremendous range of art content makes the omission of particular artworks a relatively minor problem. There is much more of value to teach than class time available, and excellent art curricula can be developed without nude figures or other problematic issues in recognition of local standards.

Knowing what to include and develop in art curricula is at least as important as knowing what to avoid. Locally developed art curricula can take advantage of local resources, such as architecture, museums, and galleries, art-related industries and businesses, and local experts in the many occupations related to the visual arts.

Sometimes the general character of the community will influence the materials used in an art program. In Oregon, the authors observed a far greater use of wood in art programs than in Miami, where sand casting was popular. Communities such as New Orleans, where there is a well-defined interest in local history, might again influence some of the activities in the art program. In some communities, ethnic groups still maintain traditional arts and crafts of which they are rightfully proud.

Art Museums

Visits to art museums are often vital components of the best art programs. A quality art curriculum requires the development of extensive skills in responding to art as well as in art making, and it is in museum and gallery settings that children often have their most memorable experiences with original works of art. The range of museum resources across the country is very great, from the encyclopedic holdings of the Metropolitan Museum of Art and the National Gallery of Art to modest local museums with small collections, often focused on a particular aspect of the history of art. Many art museums have staffs of professional educators whose major focus is on school populations. Museums today welcome school visitors, especially if they have the preparation for appreciation. Many museums have educational materials for loan to schools, such as films, slides, videos, written materials, art reproductions, and sometimes actual art objects that children can examine. Many local museums and school districts collaborate to form cooperative programs for children and youth, sometimes featuring a planned series of visits to the museum.[8]

Many museums also organize and present educational displays, using objects from their collections to educate around concepts or themes. Most major art exhibitions include educational materials for viewers—sometimes audiotapes for use in the galleries and video presentations to view in the museum before viewing an exhibition. Parents and children are often welcomed to family-centered programs offered after school or during weekends. Hundreds of excellent museums exist in the United States and Canada, a few of which are listed in Appendix C of this book.

Perhaps the greatest resource of a community is its people. Some teachers survey the careers of their students' parents and then send out form letters requesting volunteers to serve on field trips, give demonstrations in class, or speak about their artwork. Other teachers make arrangements with local institutions, such as libraries or banks, for exhibition space. Others work closely with their parent-teacher associations and solicit financial support for the art program. The art curriculum can reflect the nature of the community and at the same time use it as a valuable resource.

The School Setting

The art program is greatly affected by the school setting. In most school districts, the board of education, or school board, is responsible for establishing school policy, for designating the curriculum, and for overseeing the expenditure of funds to run the district. The board hires a superintendent to carry out board policy and to administer the school program. The superintendent usually hires central office staff and often selects principals for individual schools in the district. In this way the community is actually responsible for the school curriculum but often relies on education professionals such as the superintendent for counsel in decision making. It should be noted, however, that the superintendent usually serves at the pleasure of the board of education, so the real power resides with the elected representatives of the community. The relationship of principals to superintendent is important for art educators to note. Most often the principals serve at the pleasure of the superintendent and take cues from their superior with respect to the relative value of various components of the curriculum.

What this established system means in practice varies, of course, from one district to the next, but certain facts are worth noting. First, art usually will not find a significant place in the curriculum unless the board of education formally indicates that it will be taught. Second, even if the board of education formally establishes art as a regular subject, the superintendent might neglect its implementation. This requires careful attention by the board, who might not realize that the art curriculum is not being well implemented. The National School Boards Association and the Getty Center for Education in the Arts have written a useful guide for school board members and interested parents and community members who wish to support art in the schools.[9]

Third, even if the superintendent indicates that art is to be implemented as directed by the school board, this will not occur in all schools if principals are not convinced that regular instructional time should be spent on art education. Full implementation will usually occur only when the superintendent reviews and evaluates art education with the same attention given to mathematics, language arts, and social studies.

The place of art in the school setting is influenced as well by the facilities and teaching resources provided for art instruction. Is regular school time set aside for art instruction? Does the school have an art room with the necessary sinks and display and storage spaces? If art is taught in regular classrooms, what provisions are in place to accommodate a comprehensive art program? Are sinks available? Is storage space available so student work can be set aside and worked on over several periods of instruction? Are adequate funds available for art supplies? Where are art materials stored? Are slide projectors and video players readily available for art instruction? Does the library hold an adequate array of art books and magazines? Are art prints and other visual support materials available for art instruction? Is there a written art curriculum with suggested evaluation procedures and instruments? Do teachers and administrators accept and respect art as a regular subject in the curriculum? The National Art Education Association has published an excellent guide for administrators with similar questions, for recommended practices, and for resources to assist interested administrators who wish to implement strong art programs.[10]

WHO DESIGNS THE ART CURRICULUM?

Several strategies exist for planning and implementing art programs, with wide variations of these approaches from one school district to another. The major issue is one that has been discussed in other chapters—that is: Who shall teach art? And the extension of this question is: Who shall

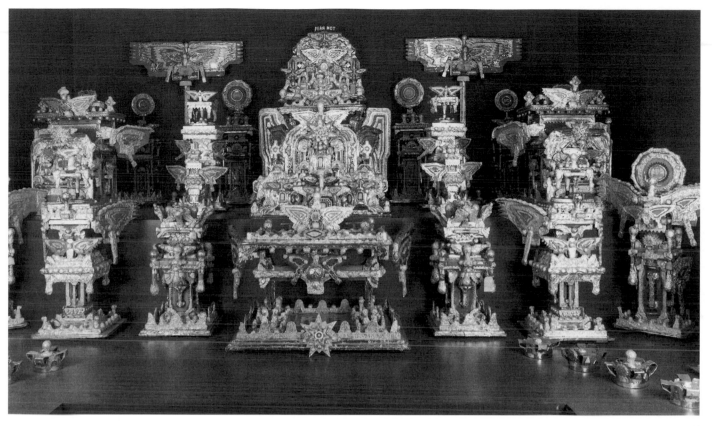

James Hampton, *The Throne of the Third Heaven of the Nations Millennium General Assembly,* ca. 1950–64, National Museum of American Art, Smithsonian Institution, Washington, D.C., U.S.A. Art Resource, N.Y. Gold and silver aluminum foil, colored kraft paper, and plastic sheets over wood furniture, paperboard, and glass, 180 pieces, 10.5 × 27 × 14.5 ft.

James Hampton was a black veteran of World War II who worked for many years as a janitor for the General Services Administration in Washington, D.C. He had an artistic calling that gave him a secret life: Over the years he collected cast-off furniture and government property and fashioned altars, thrones, offertory tables, crowns, lecterns, all covered with silver and gold foil. When he died he left a rented garage full of these wonderful objects, which were immediately recognized as inspired fold art. A tribute to the irrepressible creative force felt by all artists, this work is permanently installed in the National Museum of American Art.

plan the art curriculum? This issue refers basically to two alternatives—either the art program is planned and taught by regular classroom teachers or by certified art specialists. Other important roles in various districts include the district art consultant or art supervisor and community art volunteers.

The Art Supervisor

The art supervisor is an art specialist with administrative responsibilities, usually on a districtwide basis. Some art supervisors have administrative training and credentials. The responsibilities of art supervisors, known in some districts as art coordinators, usually include overseeing implementation of the art curriculum across the district, managing district stores of art supplies, ordering resource materials for art instruction, providing in-service education for teachers of art, and periodically overseeing the review and revision of the district art curriculum. Art supervisors often have more responsibility and authority with respect to the elementary art curriculum than with secondary art education. This person usually provides leadership regarding art curriculum issues, often in consultation with art teachers, classroom teachers, and interested community members.

The role of art supervisors varies a great deal according to the configuration of personnel for art instruction within the district—that is, whether art is taught by art specialists or by classroom teachers. When art is taught by classroom teachers, the art supervisor has the challenging task of overseeing art curriculum implementation by nonspecialists. The written curriculum becomes more essential, and in-service instruction by the supervisor is often focused on basic principles of art and art teaching. The supervisor will likely be able to demonstrate art instruction only in selected classrooms and will of necessity rely on classroom teachers to teach art on a regular basis.

When art is taught by elementary art specialists, the role of the art supervisor is changed to that of providing support for colleagues with art expertise. This also significantly changes the requirements for the art curriculum. If art is

4. Understanding the visual arts in relation to history and cultures

5. Reflecting upon and assessing the characteristics and merits of their work and the work of others

6. Making connections between the visual arts and other disciplines[14]

The National Standards are intended for secondary education as well as for elementary levels and the basic ideas are similar. A curriculum that attends significantly to historical knowledge, to analysis and evaluation of artworks, to art concepts and vocabulary, and to accomplishment in the production of art in several media is a balanced art curriculum. Art curriculum planners need to decide if the art curriculum will be balanced or if it will emphasize a narrower range of art learning.

Scope and Sequence

The term *scope* refers to the extent and depth of content coverage, and *sequence* refers to decisions about the order in which learners encounter content. Scope and sequence documents address such questions as: Will the children learn about African art? If so, during what grade level? A balanced art curriculum requires extensive planning so children will learn as widely and deeply about art as instructional time allows. Decisions of scope will determine what historical periods children will study during their elementary-school years, what different art modes and media they will experience, what cultures they will learn about, and what vocabulary of terms and concepts they will master.

Sequence is one of the keys to cumulative learning.[15] Learning activities organized in sequences that build on previous learning help children develop from naive understandings to sophisticated knowledge. Curriculum sequences can occur within a single lesson, can develop from lesson to lesson in a single unit, and can be written across entire terms or grade levels. For example, as children learn about color, their curriculum activities could progress from identifying the primary colors to mixing secondary and tertiary colors to the use of complementary colors to decrease intensities for expressive purposes. Sequences of activities can be written and placed within a grade level that will take children from simple beginnings in their use of color to more and more complex understandings and applications in their own art production. Curriculum develop-

ers will need to deal with issues of content scope and sequence and to decide how they will utilize these ideas in the art curriculum.

Student Participation in Curriculum Development

Although research indicates that students often have very little to say about curriculum development, this need not be the case. Students are the ultimate recipients of the art curriculum, and their participation at some levels can provide assurance that curriculum writers are at least on the right track. This does not mean that first- and second-grade students are able to tell professional educators what ought to be taught and how it ought to be organized. Rather, it means that students of various age levels can be consulted profitably at several stages of the curriculum development process. For example, children can be asked to try curriculum sequences and express their opinions. Children can be polled for their interests in current events, personalities, music, and other parts of the popular culture, and these interests can be considered as starting points for art instruction. Children can view proposed art reproductions, can give their responses to particular artworks, and can provide curriculum writers with a running assessment of the activities they are planning. In brief, children can provide a reality check for curriculum developers who might be tempted to become pedantic, grandiose, and too academic in their writing and planning. This process can also serve as a form of evaluation.

Published Art Curricula

As the field has moved in the direction of balanced, comprehensive art programs, the role of planned, written art curricula has gained in significance. Publishers of educational materials have developed a wide range of excellent art resource materials, including several series of elementary art curricula that provide local curriculum planners with some options. School districts can choose to *adopt* a published art curriculum and *adapt* it to local goals and resources. This process requires an assessment of the available curricula, trial teaching in classrooms, analysis of content and activities, and a determination of the match between commercial curricula and state or district art guidelines. It usually involves a committee that reviews, tries, and selects a curriculum that is then recommended to the board of education for adoption. When adoption is accomplished, materials are developed to assist teachers to adapt the commercial curriculum to the specific goals of the local schools. This might mean suggested sequences of lessons, the addition of lessons written locally, the development of supplementary teaching materials, and designation of vocabulary and lists of artworks to be studied at each grade level. Prepared curricula, in other words, should be adapted for local needs.

Many districts choose to develop their own art curricula, sometimes based on the belief that teachers are more likely to enthusiastically teach what they have a stake in through their own efforts. The issue of cost is an important one. District leaders who believe that commercial art curriculum materials are too costly and for that reason choose to develop their own might be disappointed as the process of developing an art curriculum is a lengthy, time- and energy-consuming task. And when the curriculum is ready for implementation, released-time in-service support is always required for adequate results. This requires long-term administrative and financial support.

CORRELATING ART WITH OTHER SUBJECTS

Two major choices are reflected in many new art programs: (1) integration within the various arts and (2) integration of art with academic subjects. The conscious seeking of relationships among separate disciplines is assumed to be educationally desirable in any discussion of art beyond its customary function. If one examines the "grass roots of art," to borrow Sir Herbert Read's phrase, the distinctive qualities of visual art become less apparent as one compares the formal characteristics of art to those of its neighbors. As an example, design features such as line, rhythm, and pattern have their counterparts in music, drama, and dance. For this reason, design components are used as the basis for some related art programs. The visual arts all involve perception, emotion, imagination, and the creative processes—a love of manipulation (of both forms and materials), a delight in sensations, and considerable pleasure in the contemplation as well as creation of structured experiences.

It is precisely because of these shared characteristics that art is so suitable as an adjunct of other activities. The major interest in correlating art with the general curriculum lies in

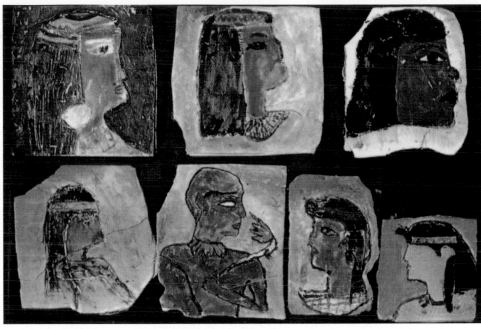

These simulated Egyptian fresco paintings on low, carved relief were done by drawing the faces on slabs of plaster of paris. The lines were incised with a sharp tool and the faces painted in tempera. Sandpaper was then lightly applied to contribute to the appearance of age. The thinner the paint, the more delicate the colors. This activity was part of a class unit on ancient Egypt.

its integration with academic subjects. Before we examine this direction, however, let us look at a few examples of the way art is employed in the first two areas mentioned.

Relationships within the Arts

In a situation where the arts relate in a broad context, some principle or concept is selected, because it is a part of the artistic experience and, at the same time, exists separately from a particular art category. Let us take one concept that many artists face at various times in their careers—*improvisation*—and examine its possibilities as a "connector" among several art forms. Improvisation is borrowed from the professional training of actors and works well with students of any age.

As a rule, improvisations do not allow any preplanning. They are spontaneous acts created from moment to moment, using some stimulus in the immediate situation as a point of departure. Improvisations always call on the inventiveness of the participants, thus developing such attributes as spontaneity, fluency, and imagination. Participants in improvisational situations learn to respond to the moment at hand and

The sixth-grade girl who drew this picture gave it the title, "New dragon riders getting their training." Her human figures are drawn in proportion with articulated hands and arms. The composition is complex with cropping of the large dragons, extensive use of overlap, and texture and contrast to fill the entire picture space. Her series of dragon pictures grew out of a strong interest in books about dragons. The drawings were accompanied by the child's poems and stories about imaginative dragon and human relationships in societies where dragons are friendly and intelligent. Art is often integrated naturally in the lives of children with other means for imagination and expression (see photo page 358).

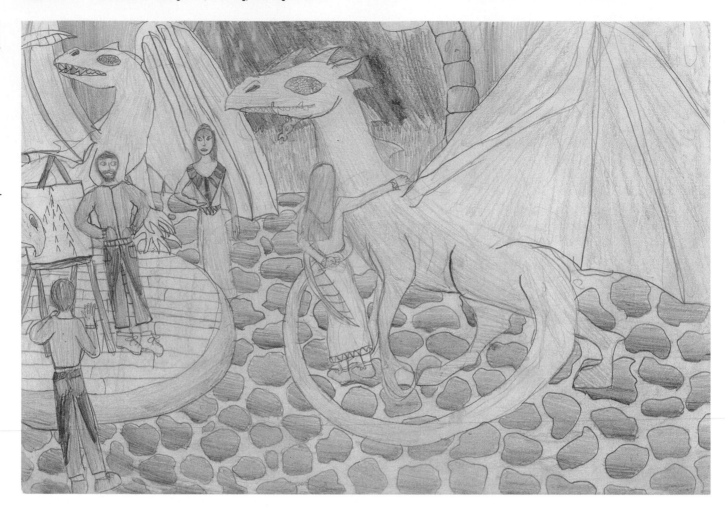

to trust in their ability to embellish, expand, and develop an idea. Following are several suggested improvisational activities organized by category.

Visual Arts

- *Graphic improvisation:* Pupil A draws a line, pupil B counters with another, and pupil C follows suit. The idea is to work from the previous image, relating new images as intimately as possible to the preceding ones, thus provoking each pupil to respond immediately to the partners' work. Have each pupil use individual colors, or have them all use one color as a means of gain-

ing cohesiveness. The criterion for success is the sense of unity attained. When divided into teams, students can also improvise stories and create a series of narratives and events.

- *Musical improvisation:* Select two or three violently contrasting musical pieces (such as rock music, Mozart's *Eine Kleine Nachtmusik,* or Duke Ellington's jazz composition, *Such Sweet Thunder*). While listening to each, pupils can allow their crayons to roam freely over sheets of paper. They should allow themselves to respond completely to the suggestiveness of the music, especially in terms of color and rhythm. When the music has ended, hang the pictures on the wall and discuss differences and similarities in structure, choice of colors, and the like.

- *Word images:* The teacher calls out words that have strong emotional overtones, and the pupils improvise drawings suggested by the words. As an alternative, pupils can respond with their bodies, reacting either physically or pictorially to onomatopoeic words such as *explosion, piston,* and *eggbeater.*
- Examples of improvisation from the arts can be compared and discussed, perhaps with examples from improvisational theatre, modern dance, jazz music, and abstract expressionist art (action painting). Students will note that an expressive vocabulary in an art form is a prerequisite for improvisation.

Movement and Music

- *Sculpture machines:* The class is divided into four groups. A leader is selected for each group and creates a "living sculpture," designing the team for visual interest as well as for the possibility of movement. Each member of the team should adopt a frozen posture showing movement of the torso, arms, or legs. Working to the music of a Sousa march, for instance, the sculpture should activate itself in time to the musical beat. The basic form of the sculpture (the position of the pupils) remains in place while the separate parts (their bodies) move.

Connections and Sequences

Although the arts lend themselves to many styles of related instruction, teachers must learn to distinguish between forced and natural ways of connecting one experience to another. If the planning for sequences of activities can be shared by two or more arts specialists, the pooling of ideas can lead to rich possibilities for arts experiences. One arts area can provide motivation for another and so on, creating a sequential flow of activities. *Exercises* can free the body and attune it to *movement* to music, which in turn can set the stage for a more *formalized dance experience.* Since no dance occurs without *rhythm,* exploration and creation of rhythmic patterns can lead to *creating sound-making instruments.* Rhythm also can be translated visually into *large-scale drawings* based on principles of conducting (imagine holding a brush instead of a baton). Making a spontaneous *graphic* record of a musical experience can then provide the basis for more thoughtful

works, developed with care at the student's own pace rather than that of the music.

Experiences in related arts can also be connected through grouping activities around some common element. For example, *observation* is a skill that actors use in studying characteristics of various kinds of people (toddlers and very old people have their own way of walking, for example—hesitant, halting, insecure). Such observation helps in the actor's creation of a character. Artists use their powers of observation as a means of memory development and analysis of form. *Memory* can be developed, as can visual acuity; many kinds of artists store and call on recollected experience. The actor must learn the lines of *King Lear,* the pianist commits musical scores to memory before a concert, the dancer must recall dozens of minute bodily movements within fixed time frames, and the artist develops a mental storehouse of images. *Improvisation* is part of every actor's training, and the painter who develops an image from each preceding stage without any preplanning or the jazz trombonist who picks up cues from what the clarinetist is playing also is improvising. These are three of the many shared characteristics of the arts that suggest activities.

Overlapping Goals: Social Studies As an Example

Many of the claims art teachers make for their subject are parallel to goals in other subject areas. A group of social-studies specialists specified the goals for which they teach. Their choices indicate some obvious analogies to art. Listed next are seven points they felt were vital for any current social-studies program. These assumptions may be similar to those made for an art program, but the teacher should be cognizant of the art program's unique features, as the comments in parentheses indicate.[16]

1. Humanity in relation to the natural environment and the cultural environment is a proper subject for the elementary-school social-studies curriculum. (This is also proper subject matter for art activities.)

2. Contrast is a powerful pedagogical tool: Look at unfamiliar cultures to understand one's own; look at animal behavior to understand what characteristics humans and animals have in common and what differentiates them. (The art teacher utilizes the contrasts found in works of art to reinforce learnings in criticism

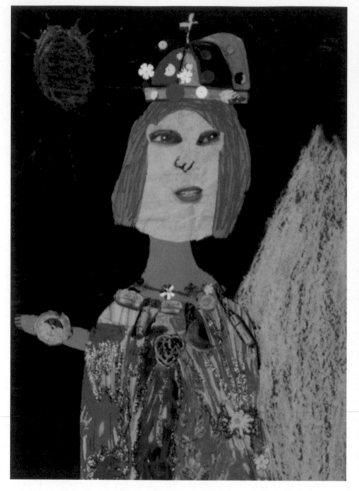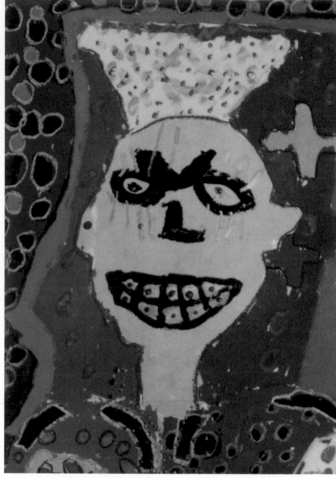

The use of historical sources for picture making need not constrict the child's imagination as evidenced in these portraits of Queen Isabella and King Ferdinand. (Grades two and five, Clark County, Georgia)

and appreciation. Polarities of style and technique are stressed to heighten the child's perceptions of likenesses and differences in artworks.)

3. "Ways of knowing" are important, such as the way of the anthropologist, the archaeologist, and others. ("Ways of knowing" in art implies understanding not only the functions of critic, historian, and artist but also the kinds of "knowing," perceiving, and experiencing that differentiate the painter from the sculptor, the architect from the potter.)

4. Studies in depth provide a thorough foundation and a point of reference around which later learnings may cluster. (An art program that included in-depth studies would give a great deal of time to a few selected

concepts deemed important, such as drawing, color relationships, or Japanese pottery, rather than skipping to a different activity each week without making any connections among the activities.)

5. Discovering how things are related and discovering how to discover are the ends of learning; the end should not be just mastery of the subject matter. (Discovery is a part of the process in art as well. Sensitive teachers are aware of the importance of the changes that may occur when children are taught for discovery as well as for adult-inspired goals.)

6. The students are participants; they can be self-motivated inquirers rather than passive receivers. (The taped dialogues transcribed in this book testify to the value of

interactions between teacher and pupil in discussions of art activities.)

7. Students should find their own meaning in the material, some of which should be the "raw data" of creative studio experiences and original works of art, be they buildings, paintings, or craft objects.

The seven points have been included here to emphasize the need for art teachers to define the special nature of art, even when art appears to be close to other subjects in its ultimate objectives.

Problems of Correlation

The teaching of art has, of course, been affected by both the correlation of subjects and their fusion in the curriculum. In certain circumstances art education has benefited from the grouping of areas of learning; in other circumstances, however, it has suffered.

The four arts-education professional associations are concerned that each art discipline receives sufficient place in the school curriculum and that regular instruction in the arts not be diffused through the guise of curriculum integration. In a joint statement, the associations representing theatre, music, dance, and the visual arts indicated their belief that

when appropriate, instruction in the arts may be used to facilitate and enrich the teaching of other subject matter. The arts must maintain their integrity in the curriculum and be taught for their own sake as well, rather than serving exclusively as aids to instruction in other disciplines. The use of the arts as an instrument for the teaching of nonartistic content should in no way diminish the time or effort devoted to the teaching of each of the arts as distinct academic disciplines in their own right.[17]

Correlation or integration need not debase an authentic art experience. In two pilot programs, both dealing with language development, the resulting artworks reflected as much original thinking as those produced in the regular art program.[18] In group A, children of Italian parents worked on mosaics, simulated frescoes, and created travel posters. They studied Venice and created a city of islands in clay. In group B, children of Cambodian, Vietnamese, and Laotian parents made paintings and drawings of their personal histories. In both cases, language developed out of labeling, naming, and using new language in the art activities. Both programs were conducted by art teachers who felt that, far

from being an inhibiting factor, the thematic use of Italian and Asian cultures actually stimulated art activity. Although certain children might have a cultural affinity for a particular art expression, all children can benefit from learning about Venetian art and the arts of Southeast Asia.

Language Arts

As noted in Chapter 12, experiences in criticism create natural allies between writing and art. Thought processes are clarified when ideas are written as well as voiced. The method of wedding language to art is to encourage a "visual narrative" approach, wherein one activity reinforces the other, using stories as a basis for sequences of drawing involving characters in specific settings.[19] This is a natural alliance, because most children begin schooling with their imaginative skills developed through listening and looking at books, as well as through having consumed countless hours of television. Teachers use myths, poetry, artworks, folk tales, and other literary sources as a basis for children's artwork.[20]

Generally, stories and poems may encourage children in the symbol-making or later stages of expression to make two- and

When a teacher prepares students for a story, they reach back to an ancient mode of communal sharing. Love of narrative exists in all cultures, and television, film, and theatre all draw upon our fascination with good tales well told.

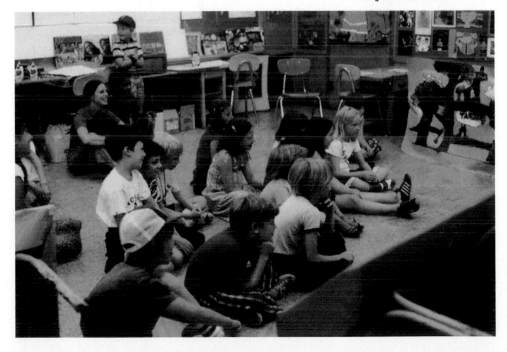

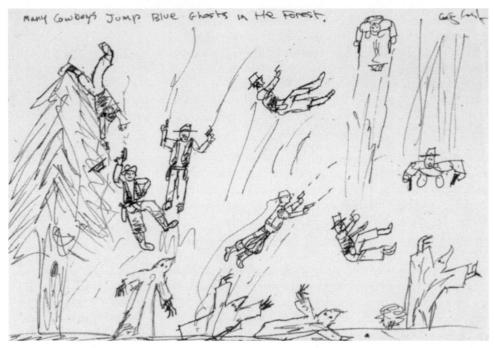

Elements of grammar can serve as sources for art. In this case, students selected randomly from a group of nouns, adjectives, verbs, and prepositions to produce the sentence: "Many cowboys jump blue ghosts in the forest." The problem was to incorporate all the words into one drawing.

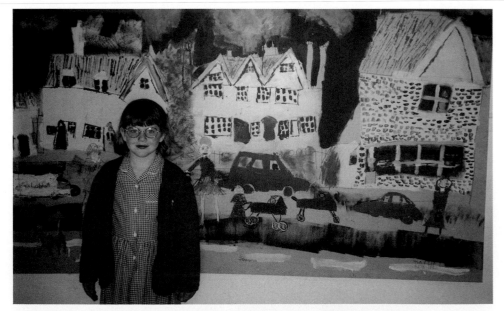

As part of a unit on the history of their village, a class in an English primary school first created a photo essay of their community based upon the architectural styles which made up the village of Cavendish. Since the school had no art specialist, the project was carried out by an itinerant art teacher in collaboration with the classroom teachers. Photograph by Neil Jacobs.

three-dimensional illustrations. One very natural way to relate language, art, and imagination is to ask children to write about what they have drawn. If the subject is selected with care (such as Machines Designed to Perform Unusual Tasks), then the interplay between idea and image grows dramatically. Children can speak and write about things they may not draw and vice versa. Combining the two can enhance the development of both linguistic and graphic forms.

One study demonstrated that higher levels of achievement in reading and writing in the middle grades could be obtained when narrative drawing was used regularly.[21] The teacher began by asking her students to draw the answers to such questions as, "How many kinds of people can you draw?" and "How many kinds of movement and emotions can you draw?" These activities took place before the students created a plot for the characters drawn. Such experiences made writing about sequences of events come more easily. Because writing is increasingly stressed on all levels of instruction, children, particularly in the upper grades, should be encouraged, once familiarized with the critical process, to write on the descriptive and interpretive stages (see Chapter 12 on art criticism).

Social Studies

For children, social studies begin in their immediate environment. The geography, history, and politics they first consider are found close to home. Because children are naturally interested in what goes on around them, few problems arise when their art is derived from this area of learning. Following is a sample of themes for curricular units in science and social studies that might correlate as well with the study of art history, criticism, production, and aesthetics:

Caring about others
Celebrations
Environmental responsibility
Family relationships
Freedom
Justice
Portraits of influential people
Sensitivity to human rights
Spirituality
Suffering and the human experience
Wonders of nature
Working

A primary teacher in an urban environment integrated art and social studies on the theme of Migration, featuring the migrations of black people from the southern states to northern states before, during, and after the Civil War. She focused on the paintings and collages of Romare Bearden, using such concepts and vocabulary as "urban," "rural," and "migration," as well as "collage," "texture," and "contrast." She played blues and jazz music that described the period, including music composed by Bearden. As they studied the life and times of the artist, students viewed, analyzed, and discussed Bearden works in relation to these concepts and students learned in a vivid way about history, culture, and art.[22]

A sixth-grade teacher organized an art unit on the theme of the Caribbean, with emphasis on the Carnival festival and the festival arts of music, dance, and costume, all in conjunction with the museum exhibition of the *Caribbean Festival Arts,* which traveled across the country to several museums in urban centers. Building on earlier art units on textile design, batik, and masks, this teacher engaged his students in a community celebration based on the Carnival festival, with steel drum music, Caribbean foods, dancing, and costumes made by students. The entire school and parents were invited to a community celebration. Students were introduced to an unusual type of art, saw videotapes of festival costumes and dancing available from the museum, noted the multicultural dimensions of the celebration, and enjoyed a vivid, memorable experience that integrated the arts in a natural and spontaneous manner.

Art and Multicultural Understanding

In a democratic society made up of people from every part of the world, it is most appropriate that education in the United States respect contributions of excellence from many cultural sources. The arts provide the most vivid and vibrant means to understand any culture and to reveal its most significant meanings. The visual arts in particular provide our greatest insights into cultures of the past and the present. For these reasons, art education is a focal point whenever multicultural education is discussed.[23]

The term *multicultural* has been used so broadly in discourse about education that clear definition has eluded the education profession. Over the past decades, "even the designation itself has been used to denote terms, such as multi-ethnic, multi-racial, cross-cultural and gender-balanced, as well as representations of global religions, or all age and socioeconomic groups." Tomhave provides some clarity with his discussion of six recognizable emphases for multicultural education.[24] The most relevant of these for this discussion are:

Cultural Separatism: A large infusion of one particular subculture may lead to enough economic and political power for the group to practice cultural separatism. The ethnic school is a "folk school" that disseminates ethnic customs, traditions, and languages that a particular group cherishes and finds worthy of transmission to later generations.

Peter Minshall, designer, *Fly, Fly, Sweet Life,* from *Papillon,* 1982 Trinidad Carnival (The Saint Louis Art Museum).

Caribbean festival arts are perhaps the most integrated of art forms, incorporating dance, costume, music, and the visual arts with literary themes, legends, and stories. Designers appropriate art from an unrestricted selection of world cultures and combine art traditions with the most contemporary images and materials. In this work, the dancer's wings feature the image of Marilyn Monroe created by Andy Warhol, in the guise of Botticelli's famous *Venus* from fifteenth-century Italy. The theme of "butterfly" is mirrored in the work's title.

© Noel P. Norton, Norton Studio with permission of Peter Minshall.

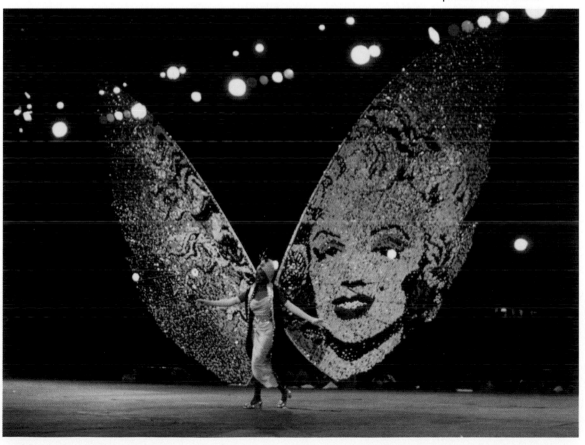

Social Reconstruction: This approach is concerned not only with ethnic and racial perspectives but also with matters of Eurocentrism, sexism, and classism. Sociopolitical change amounting to a restructuring of society is the goal and valued outcome of this approach. Education in art becomes part of or subordinate to the goal of social change.[25] The desire for social change is one of the characteristics of postmodernism (see Chapter 2).

Cultural Understanding: Without losing the ideal of achievement in the present democratic educational system, we can accommodate the concerns of various ethnic groups and also gain appreciation of, respect for, and acceptance of diverse cultures' contributions to the human condition. Attempts are made to translate multicultural theory into multicultural practice.

Although each approach is valid within some settings, the one that seems most useful for general art education is the Cultural Understanding view, which seeks to foster appreciation and acceptance of diverse cultural contributions. Other approaches might serve within local communities with particular circumstances that warrant a more specific focus.[26]

Art and Nature

Although such artists as Audubon and da Vinci were able to bring art and science into proximity, scientific drawings and artistic expressions differ in intent. A scientific drawing is an exact statement of fact, allowing no deviation from the natural appearance of an object.

For children, natural objects evoke feelings and hold meanings that go beyond a scientific statement. The objects in the science corner of the classroom, such as fossils, shells, and rocks, can provide the basis for invention as well as for scientific study. Studying the natural world satisfies the curiosity of both artist and scientist (see da Vinci's notebooks). The studios of many artists, Georgia O'Keeffe as an example, are filled with specimens of rocks, bones, and other natural objects. A middle-school art teacher describes his room as follows:

> My art classroom could be mistaken for an extension of the Smithsonian Institution's National History Museum. Along with children's art expressions on animal themes, there are continuous displays of real and pictured butterflies, seashells, wasps' nests, rocks, and peacock feathers. The children are constantly exposed to color slides, films, posters, photographs, and books about wild animals, tropical fish, beautiful and bizarre insects, various plant forms, and of course—dinosaurs.[27]

Most elementary-school children, of course, are incapable of drawing with scientific accuracy. This does not mean that they should not be exposed to natural objects or that they should not use them for expressive purposes. On the contrary, flowers, birds, seashells, fish, and animals, as stated pre-

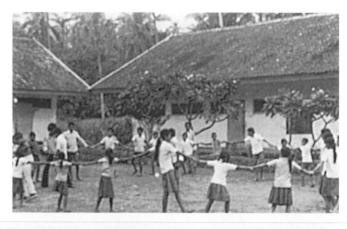

Children can learn from other children through the growing number of exchange programs. These examples of the Bo Train Circle game are from Sierra Leone and are part of an exhibition organized by the Foster Parents Plan Program on understanding the Third World through art. (Compare with circle games in Chapter 3.)

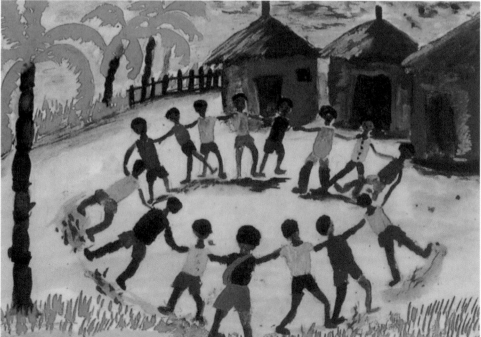

viously, may be used with excellent effect in art. Any natural object may be employed as the basis of design, provided the children are also given freedom to depart from the scientific form they observe. The fact that this freedom is allowed does not retard the children's growth in scientific knowledge.

A correlated art-science project could work as follows for the fifth and sixth grades. The first step would be an *observational phase,* in which students would be asked to draw as carefully as possible an object or specimen, such as bones (skeleton segment), fossils embedded in stone, flowers, or cellular forms viewed through a microscope. The second step, the *design phase,* would involve using the drawing in one of the following ways:

- Fill in areas within outlines with flat tones based on a color theory.
- Blow up the drawing to ten times the original size, and turn it into a hard-edge-style painting.
- Move a piece of tracing paper over the original, allowing shapes to overlap. Fill in with textured pen-and-ink patterns, a color scheme, or a number of shades of one color.
- Select a section for a small linoleum print, and make a repeat pattern.

In such a sequence, the student moves from observation to design judgment and, in making the print, comes to understand how artists use natural forms as a basis for applied design. The entire sequence may take up to four or five class sessions, but it allows the student to "live with" one problem for an extended period of time.

The greatest care, of course, must be taken not to supply children with symbols considered to be artistic that tend to replace or interfere with a study of natural objects. The cutting of paper snowflakes, for example, could be practiced only after a careful study of these forms and only if the activity were entirely creative. The drawing of evergreen trees in the well-known bisymmetrical zigzag design results more often from a teacher's demonstration than from a child's observation of a real tree.

Music

Music and art lend themselves to several types of correlation. As an indirect correlation, a background of music playing is often valuable to children while they are drawing, painting, or working in three dimensions. The music appears to influence the children's visual output in a subtle fashion.

The teacher may arrange direct correlations between music and art for children at any level in the elementary school.

Music with a pronounced rhythmic beat and melodic line may be used as a basis for drawing nonobjective patterns.

Music depicting a definite mood may also lead to some interesting artwork, especially in the fifth and sixth grades. Before playing the piece, the teacher usually discusses the mood of the selection. After hearing the music, the class may discuss possible combinations of colors, lines, and other elements of design to express the mood pictorially. Work then begins, possibly in soft chalk or paint, with the music playing in the background.

Classical music with a literary theme may also assist in developing noteworthy picture making by pupils in the symbol-making or later stages of expression. The teacher gives the outline of the story, plays excerpts from the music, and from time to time draws attention to passages depicting specific events in the narrative.

Varieties of pop, rock, and jazz can be used with equal effectiveness. A wide range of classical and contemporary music can be used to motivate artwork. And record covers can be studied as a popular art form that links the mood and beat of music to visual experience. Musical selections from such cultures as Spanish, African, West Indian, Scottish, or Native American can add interest and variety to this type of experience, especially in conjunction with study of art and culture. Music teachers can be particularly helpful in choosing appropriate works.

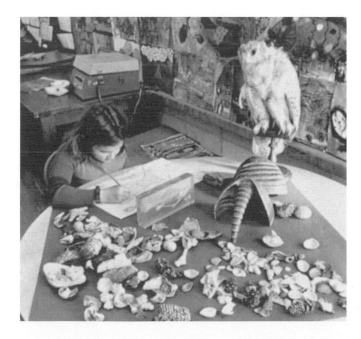

The teacher in this school has provided an array of diverse materials which can be used in science and art. Most objects can be picked up, examined, and used at the student's desk.

Mathematics

As soon as a child is capable of using a measured line, mathematics may begin to enter into some of the child's artwork. Such activities as building model houses, making costumes for puppets, or constructing puppet stages lend themselves to this correlation. Studying the history of art provides ample examples of uses of mathematics, especially geometry. Mathematical foundations exist for some of the great monuments of the world, such as Egyptian pyramids; prehistoric Native American rock art that marks solstices; Mayan art, calendars, and architecture; and Stonehenge. The Golden Mean, for example, was used by the ancient Greeks in architecture and art. Geometry has been applied by contemporary artists who use linear patterns on their canvases to establish balance and centers of interest in their compositions. The geometric works of Piet Mondrian, M.C. Escher, and Op artists Bridget Riley and Victor Vasarely all are examples of creative variations on strict mathematics-based themes.

Some teachers have attempted to combine the two fields by having the children work during art sessions with mechanical drawing tools, such as compasses, triangles, and T-squares, to devise geometric designs. If this type of work is largely mechanical and hence not particularly expressive, there is little reason to recommend it. However, because children do enjoy the clarity and precision that designing with drafting tools provides, in many situations the teacher may establish creative and aesthetic standards to make the design activities worthwhile. These tools might be combined with work in any number of techniques—crayon and pencil drawing, painting, crayon resist, and etching, among others.

If attempts to integrate art across the curriculum avoid the pitfalls of losing time allocated for regular art instruction, they are often very successful. In addition to the values of intrinsic goals for art education are significant benefits for the pupils and for the entire school program.

ORGANIZING AND WRITING ART CURRICULUM

Approaches to Curriculum Development

The shaping of any curriculum must begin by establishing a direction. Although curriculum planners may bring to this problem some knowledge of art, of children, and of sound educational practice, the content of the curriculum begins to take form when they use all their knowledge and experience as a basis for setting down what they hope to accomplish in terms of art goals and objectives.

Ralph Tyler, in his brief-but-classic essay on curriculum planning, cites four questions that are generally accepted as a reasonable place to begin:[28]

1. What educational purposes should the school seek to attain?

2. What educational experiences can be provided that are likely to attain these purposes?

3. How can these educational experiences be effectively organized?

4. How can we determine whether these purposes are being attained?

The "purposes" to which Tyler alludes also may be viewed as goals, and his "experiences" as the vehicles by which goals or purposes are attained. In many cases the new art teacher is presented with a written curriculum or guide prepared by a committee of teachers. The new teacher may not be prepared to carry out all the activities suggested and, in such cases, searches for ways to accommodate the curriculum. Even though teachers are expected to teach from the school or district art curriculum, it is good practice to expend the effort needed to create your own applications.

School districts have two basic options for curriculum development in any subject area: They can purchase a commercial curriculum and adapt it to local needs, or they can develop their own curriculum using district personnel and, possibly, consultants. Regardless of which choice is made, teachers will make many curriculum decisions and will ultimately shape the curriculum to their own personal teaching styles and their own classroom situation. It is important for professional teachers to develop skills in understanding and creating curriculum if for no other reason than to gain greater appreciation for the many curriculum decisions they and others will make during each school year.

Curriculum writing is a complex undertaking with several levels of decision making. The first level appears as soon as instructors begin to organize a curriculum and must decide on an approach to the task. Klein describes four distinctive approaches that appear in theory and practice:[29]

Traditional Approach: Processes reflect a scientific, reductionistic, linear, and rational approach to curriculum development. This position emphasizes the role of organized subject matter, often in the form of disciplines. The outcomes desired deal primarily with predetermined, logically organized skills or bodies of knowledge that all students are to learn and with the development of their intellectual capacities.

Emphasis on Self-Understanding: Value is placed on development of the individual pupil and creation of personal meaning in learning. Organized subject matter is important only insofar as each student affirms its relevance to him or her. Reflection on the personal meaning of content and experience by each student is highlighted. Learning is viewed as holistic, not as hierarchical discrete tasks within specific domains of human behavior.

Emphasis on the Role of the Teacher: The teacher is a very powerful influence on what students learn. Teachers develop practical knowledge and wisdom about curriculum as they make myriad classroom decisions daily. Teachers should be supported in their role as curriculum developers.

Emphasis on Society: The intent of the curriculum is to help build a better society and to improve human relationships—to foster social change through the strong involvement of the surrounding community. Emphasis is placed on the interaction of societal norms, values, and expectations with curriculum and schooling. Organized content fields in the form of the disciplines are important to the extent that they can be brought to bear on issues and problems under study.

Probably no single approach in curriculum will do all that we expect from our schools in helping students grow and develop today and prepare for their lives in the twenty-first century.

As the curriculum development process unfolds, general decisions about content must be confronted. What modes of art making will students experience? What artists, cultures, and artworks will be studied? Will there be a balance of artworks according to gender?[30] What questions and issues in art will be discussed? What skills of creation and response to art will be learned? And, what structure will be used to organize this material? All these decisions and more will be made during the planning process for a single grade level. If the curriculum project includes several grades, the process is even more complex, because content from each grade level must be related and articulated with the grades above and below.

Usually, it is best to organize content in very general ways for yearly plans so individual teachers have appropriate latitude for decision making within their classrooms.

Organizational Categories for Art Curricula

Several ways to organize art curricula deserve the attention of curriculum writers. Many art curriculum guides and curricula have been organized on the basis of the elements and principles of design. Another traditional organizing scheme uses modes of art production. The changing paradigm for art education, however, has caused art educators to consider additional categories suggested by art history, criticism, and aesthetics. Following is a brief list of topics or categories that might be considered for organizing art curriculum content:

Elements and Principles of Design

Units of instruction might be organized according to

line	harmony
shape	rhythm
color	composition
texture	movement
space	contrast
unity	pattern

Art Modes and Media

Units of instruction might be organized according to

drawing	photography
painting	graphic design
printmaking	newer media
sculpture	installation art
architecture	video/computer art
ceramics	environmental art

Periods of Western Art History

Units of instruction might be organized according to

prehistoric art	the Renaissance
art of the ancient world	baroque art
art of the Middle Ages	modern art
medieval art	postmodern art

1
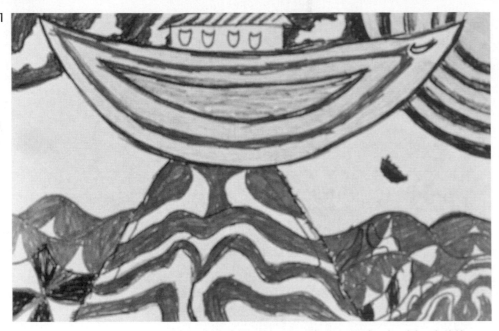

2
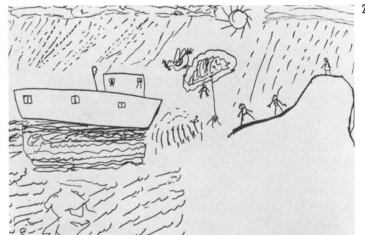

3
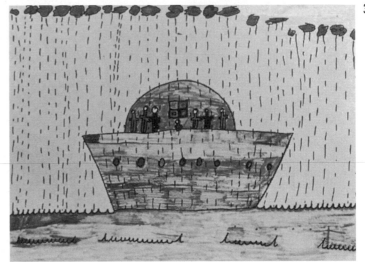

In a study by the author of art inspired by the story of Noah and the Ark, children from various nations produced work reflecting three major influences: cultural, educational, and personal. The children, ages ten to twelve, were told the same story, often through interpreters. 1: A Maori boy in New Zealand integrates designs from traditional Maori wood carving into wave and sky patterns. Strong art program in the school. 2: A Bedouin child in the Negev area of Israel uses linear patterns from Arabic calligraphy to create the sea. The delicate broken lines of rain were also typical of his class. Art teacher not present. 6: A child in rural Kenya emphasizes the path to the ark because of the importance, in the child's homeland, of footpaths. The animals were traced, but the humans and ark were done freehand. No art instructor present. 3: The orderly pattern of rain, waves, and wood distinguishes this rendering of the story by an Australian aboriginal child. Art teacher present. The watercolors (4,7) are from two matched groups in separate schools in Seoul, South Korea. The two groups (like children in Taiwan, Hong Kong, and Japan as well) shared a sensitivity to art media, drawing skills, and an ability to activate the human figure. But the tendency among the Korean children to depict the Noah story in human terms is unique. In one picture, animals dance in celebration at the end of the deluge; in the other picture, Noah and his family are busy at work. 5: A Gypsy girl in a rural settlement in Hungary, considered gifted by her teacher, placed the dove inside another bird and combined the olive branches, Mt. Ararat, and the ark in a forceful, coherent design. From an after-school art program in a special-interest center. Strong art teacher present.

4
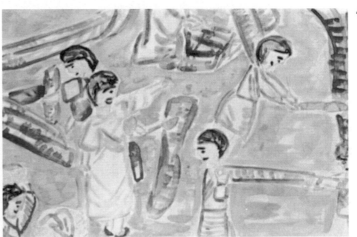

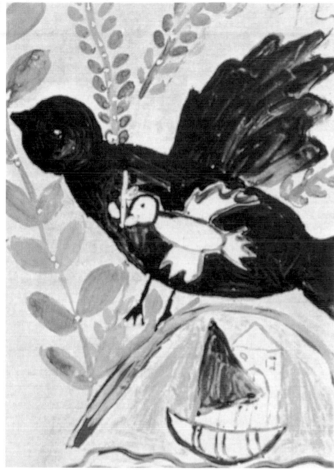

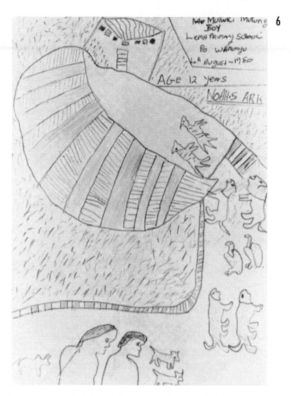

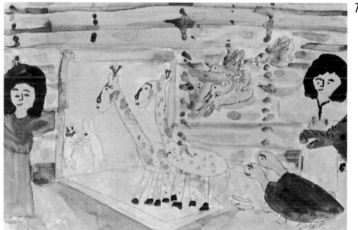

Art from Various Cultures

Units of instruction might be organized according to

Art of China	Native American art
Art of Africa	Contemporary
Art of Italy, Spain,	American art
or France	African American art

Themes

Units of instruction might be organized according to

art and ecology	images of men
art and technology	images of women
the westward movement	art and worship
mythology	the artist as social critic
the horse in art	

Aesthetics Topics

Units of instruction might be organized according to

purposes and functions	the artist's intent
of art	art versus nature
beauty in art	the creative process
What is art?	

Landmark Artworks

Units of instruction might be organized according to

Egyptian pyramids
Michelangelo's Sistine
   Chapel ceiling
the Taj Mahal
Marisol's *The Last Supper*
da Vinci's *Mona Lisa*
Hokusai's *The Great Wave*
Rodin's *The Thinker*
van Gogh's *The Starry
   Night*
Picasso's *Guernica*

Ringgold's *Tar Beach*
O'Keeffe's *Black
   Hollyhocks*
Adams's *Yosemite Valley*
Notre Dame cathedral
Frank Lloyd Wright's
   Fallingwater
Maya Lin's Vietnam
   Veterans Memorial
Frank Gehry's Guggenheim
   Museum, Bilbao

Functions of Art

Units of instruction might be organized according to

spiritual and religious art
art to convey power and
   authority
art as a force for social
   reform
art as personal expression

decorative art
art as narrative
art for celebration
design for human
   needs

Art Styles

Units of instruction might be organized according to

Egyptian figures
baroque style
rococo style
impressionism
cubism
surrealism

abstract expressionism
pop art
African Benin
Chinese Ming
American colonial
German expressionism

Artists

Units of instruction might be organized around landmark artists, particularly if their work reflects periods of change or possesses some element of personal history or artistic content interesting to children.

Pablo Picasso
Romare Bearden
Georgia O'Keeffe
Frank Lloyd Wright
Maya Lin
Frederic Remington

Frida Kahlo
Alice Neel
Mary Cassatt
Anselm Kieffer
Rembrandt van Rijn
Alan Hauser

A balanced art curriculum can be organized on the basis of any of the schemes listed and on the ways they interact. For example, if the elements of design are selected, artworks that exemplify different uses of line can be studied. Specific artists well known for their mastery of color can be studied. The history of color usage in Western art can be investigated and technological advances in the development of natural and artificial pigments noted. Color symbolism found in different cultures can be studied in relation to color meanings in contemporary American society. Students can develop skills in the use of line, shape, and color in their own artwork as a result of instruction and of observation of the works of other artists. Likewise, any of the category systems listed can be cross-referenced to art content from aesthetics, art history, art criticism, and art production. The organizational category usually assures emphasis on its topic.

The Yearly Plan or Course Outline

The main purpose for a broad outline of content and activities is to provide the art teacher with an overview of the entire term or year. This will assist the teacher to develop stronger sequential learning, to build on prior learning, to integrate across the curriculum, and to better use class time. One way for teachers to get their thoughts on paper is to use a matrix as a graphic guide for sorting ideas. The matrix is simply a grid that indicates where key issues intersect. Table 17-1 is a sample, showing several units of a sixth-grade yearly plan outlined in matrix form.[31]

TABLE 17-1

	Unit Title: Coiled Clay	Unit Title: Painting People and Objects	Unit Title: Graphic Design—Imagination and Influence
Art-Making Topics and Processes	*Media and materials:* ceramic clay, clay equipment and tools, glazes *Processes and skills:* coil and slab construction, building with a support mold, burnishing, clay slip for decoration, firing pots. Write description of coil construction process. Discuss coil techniques of several cultures. Learn to work in style of Southwest pueblo potters.	*Media and materials:* tempera, watercolor, acrylics, oil pastels, inks, marking pens *Processes and skills:* drawing and painting skills from previous units, still life from several vantage points, combining versions of still life in a collage, painting expressive face and posed figure	*Media and materials:* marking pens, commercial letters, computer *Processes and skills:* analyze design problem and develop solutions; communicate effectively with combined words and images; create package design; create poster or book cover; illustrate literary work, social issue, or personal experience
Art Criticism: Topics and Processes	Study coil pottery from several cultures. Study symbols used by traditional pueblo potters. Interpret meaning of contemporary ceramic sculptures. Judge quality of pots according to construction and decoration techniques. Critique student pots and sculptures.	Analyze painting and collage techniques in cubist still life. Interpret paintings of human faces and figures. Describe in writing moods or emotions in paintings of faces. Discuss and interpret student paintings. Mount display of student paintings.	Interpret meanings of international symbols. Judge quality of graphic designs. Examine design of common food and household packages. Recognize influence of graphic design on consumer decisions. Write critique and interpretation of an illustration.
Art History/Culture: Topics and Sources	*Learn about:* traditional Pueblo, Mayan, African ceramic works Contemporary pueblo and European-American pottery Study lives and works of selected potters and ceramic sculptors.	*Learn about:* historical Dutch, Flemish paintings Modern Spanish, Mexican, Native American, and European-American paintings Study still life and figure as traditional subjects for painting. Study lives and works of specific artists. Analyze figure paintings for pose, costume, theme, mood, and setting.	*Learn about:* careers in design and commercial art Contemporary design of packages, book covers, posters; computer graphics Study historic role of graphics for communication. Study lives and works of selected graphic artists.
Aesthetics: Topics and Questions	*Investigate questions:* How can scholars interpret meaning and quality of art objects from prehistoric times? Should beautifully designed and decorated functional pots be considered art or craft? Should contemporary Native American potters copy ancient designs or invent new symbols?	Analyze and discuss various meanings of realism in painting. *Investigate questions:* Must art reflect nature? Can abstract art convey meaning? Can an artist change styles and retain his or her individuality?	Recognize and value skills of graphic artists. *Investigate questions:* What is the relationship between fine arts and applied arts, such as graphic design and illustration? Can a poster or book cover be a work of art?

TABLE 17-1 (continued)

	Unit Title: Coiled Clay	Unit Title: Painting People and Objects	Unit Title: Graphic Design—Imagination and Influence
Evaluation: Assessing Student Progress in Specific Activities	Coil construction techniques	Worksheet on expressive faces	Package design
	Technique for clay figure with attention to figure gesture and freedom of attitude	Multistage painting/collage process	Illustration
		Quiz on slides and related information	Poster or book-cover design
	Essay on Southwest Native American potter	Still-life painting	Report on works of graphic design viewed on television
	Display and discussion of student work	Painting of expressive face	
	Written review of ceramic sculpture display	Painting of posed figure	Paragraph explaining example of graphic design
	Identify ceramic works from slides	Essay on expressive purpose of own painting	Effective communications through design
		Display, discussion, and evaluation of student work	Problem-solving techniques expressed through design

Unit Plans

The unit plan outline is similar to a yearly plan but with more detail. A unit plan is a series of lessons organized on a single theme, topic, or mode. The unit plan should provide the teacher with a concise overview of the unit, including information about artworks, art materials, and special preparations that need to be considered. The unit should be organized to emphasize sequences of learning activities. Units vary in length from a few lessons to an in-depth sequence of lessons on a topic that might last as long as six weeks. Following is a sample unit outline for upper elementary grades. The unit consists of four lessons estimated to require six class sessions for completion. It is organized as a sculpture unit.

Grade 6

UNIT TITLE
Sculpture: Materials with Messages

OVERVIEW

In this unit students are introduced to a number of monuments of world sculpture followed by focus on the works of six contemporary Japanese sculptors and two prominent British sculptors. Students will analyze and interpret several sculptures, discuss different purposes for sculpture, and create two sculptures, one made from natural materials and one carved from a relatively soft material.

UNIT OBJECTIVES

1. Students will engage in historical research and report their findings. They will study materials about contemporary Japanese sculpture and the work of two British sculptors, Barbara Hepworth and Henry Moore.

2. Students will practice interpreting feeling and meaning from sculpture. They will respond to slides and pictures of sculpture from various times and places.

3. Students will create two sculptures based on different views of art.

4. Students will ponder and discuss differences in purpose and function of sculpture from a range of cultures and times.

MATERIALS FOR PRODUCTION

1. Notebooks and sketch pads for sketches and ideas

2. Collection of natural materials, such as sand, stones, dirt, cotton, wood in various forms, rope, cardboard, papers, and others stored in plastic buckets or bins

3. Modeling clay

RESOURCES

1. Art books and pictures of sculptures from around the world

2. Slides of designated works by Japanese and British sculptors

ASSESSMENT OPTIONS

1. Written response to designated sculptures

2. Brief papers on sculpture topics

3. Assessment of quality of student sculptures, including their records of the process in notebooks and sketch pads

Lesson Plans

The planning process discussed here is most appropriate for curriculum lessons and units that will be shared with other teachers, probably as part of a district art curriculum. When planning exclusively for their own classes, teachers quickly develop shorthand versions of their plans. The unit plan shown constitutes one of the columns in the yearly plan matrix. In turn, curriculum units are made up of a series of lesson plans. The lesson plan that follows is an example of the type of detailed version that provides sufficient information so experienced teachers could prepare and teach the lesson. It also provides background materials on the artists,

Grade _____

LESSON
Lesson Title

FOCUS *Statement of the generalization about art emphasized in the lesson*

OBJECTIVES Students will:

a

b

RESOURCES *Audio and visual instructional aids and other teaching resources*

•

•

TIME X class session(s)

MATERIALS AND PREPARATION *List of materials and tools students will use for the lesson and preparation tasks for the teacher*

•

•

INTRODUCTION *An introductory paragraph on the topic of the lesson*

INSTRUCTION *Explicit step-by-step guidance for the teacher, including rationales for practice as needed*

1.

2.

EVALUATION *Suggested assessment strategies that correlate directly with the lesson objectives*

a

b

BACKGROUND *Written materials for teachers' use*

Art in Context (art history/culture)

Art and Meaning (art criticism)

Creating Art (art making)

Questions about Art (aesthetics)

artworks, and historical/cultural contexts intended to save teachers time and to assist them to enrich the lesson.

Following is a sample lesson plan using these categories, with each one filled in to demonstrate how a complete lesson plan appears. Not included are the background materials for the teacher, with handouts on selected topics for students. Slides or other art reproductions should be included with the lesson to allow the teacher to implement it. Providing such detailed plans,

LESSON 1
Contemporary Japanese Sculptors

FOCUS Some sculptors emphasize inherent qualities of materials to express ideas and feelings. They believe that direct response to natural materials is aesthetically powerful.

OBJECTIVES Students will:

a. study artworks by contemporary Japanese sculptors.

b. make a list of materials and elements used by the sculptors in their work.

c. formulate several ideas or values that seem to be expressed by the Japanese artists.

d. make a list of materials available for students' own sculpture projects.

RESOURCES
- Slide *Related Effects S-90LA,* by Ebizuka
- Slide *Untitled,* by Tokushige
- Slide *Range of Mountains,* by Toya
- Slide *Silence,* by Tsuchiya

TIME

1 class session

MATERIALS AND PREPARATION
- Students will use paper and pencils to take notes for their notebooks and to make lists of materials.

INTRODUCTION

Japanese sculptors of today combine Western and international understandings and techniques for making art with traditional Japanese cultural values. The notion that natural materials have intrinsic aesthetic value and "life" to be experienced by the sensitive viewer is central to the work of these artists. Students will investigate these values by viewing and discussing sculptures by these artists and by creating their own sculptures with materials available locally. The scale of student work will be limited only by local available space and materials.

INSTRUCTION

1. Show slides of works by contemporary Japanese sculptors and discuss the materials used by the artists. Most materials are evident in the work, but others are mentioned in the background materials. Make a list of materials on the chalkboard as they are identified through class participation.

2. Discuss the list of materials and help students to notice that they are all natural materials and elements (water and fire). The metals are minerals that have been processed by fire.

3. Tell students that you will show all slides again, mentioning titles and approximate size of the sculptures, and ask them to speculate about what messages the artists are attempting to convey in their work. Assist students to note the artists' respect for natural materials, especially wood; the lack of representation of figures or objects; and the large size of many of the works.

3. *Identification of the primary conditions* under which the performance is expected to be measured: These might include restrictions placed on the project during the performance of specified tasks.

4. *Establishment of the minimum level of acceptable performance.* This step is the critical phase and the one that poses the most problems. What is the criterion for success? How will it function in evaluation?

5. *Establishment of the means of assessment,* which will be used to measure the expected performance or behavior. What forms will assessment take? Checklists, informal observations, anecdotal records?

One benefit in understanding these requirements is that we might become much clearer in our thinking when writing curriculum as we focus sharply on exactly what we intend and how we will know when and if students are able to accomplish it.

Obviously, planning a program can be arduous and time-consuming if teachers feel they must do the entire job themselves rather than consult existing models. Most teachers, in any case, will not be expected to plan entire programs on their own. The suggestions described are intended as a brief introduction for readers who suddenly find themselves on a team required to produce a total art program in depth and detail.

The idea of approaching art instruction in a disciplined manner may seem rather extreme to the teacher who feels that art lies beyond careful planning. But every teacher, regardless of philosophy or subject, must face the results of his or her instruction, and planning for art simply requires that the instructor consider the results before beginning to teach.

NOTES

1. Ronald C. Doll, *Curriculum Improvement: Decision Making and Process,* 7th ed. (Boston: Allyn and Bacon, 1989), p. 26.

2. Ralph Tyler, *Basic Principles of Curriculum and Instruction* (Chicago: University of Chicago Press, 1950).

3. Doll, *Curriculum Improvement,* p. 45.

4. Lois Petrovich-Mwaniki, "Multicultural Concerns in Art Education," *Translations: From Theory to Practice* 7, no. 1 (spring 1997).

5. Lauren, Resnick, and Leopold E. Klopper, *Toward the Thinking Curriculum: Current Cognitive Research* (Alexandria, VA: Association for Supervision and Curriculum Development, 1989).

6. John Dewey, *Art As Experience* (New York: Capricorn, 1958), p. 46.

7. Elliot W. Eisner, *Cognition and Curriculum Reconsidered,* 2d ed. (New York: Teachers College Press, 1994); and Howard Gardner, *The Disciplined Mind: What All Students Should Understand* (New York: Simon and Schuster, 1999).

8. Arlene L. Barry and Pat Villeneuve, "Veni, Vidi, Vice: Interdisciplinary Learning in the Art Museum," *Art Education* 51, no. 6 (1997): 17–24.

9. National School Boards Association, *More Than Pumpkins in October: Visual Literacy in the 21st Century* (Washington, DC: NSBA, December 1990).

10. *Elementary Art Programs: A Guide for Administrators* (Reston, VA: National Art Education Association, 1992).

11. National Center for Education Statistics, *Arts Education in Public Elementary and Secondary Schools* (Washington, DC: U.S. Department of Education, 1995).

12. *Art Education in Action,* Tape 3: "Making Art, Episode B: Integrating Art History and Art Criticism," Evelyn Pender, art teacher, videotape (Los Angeles: Getty Center for Education in the Arts, 1995).

13. Music Educators National Conference (MENC), *National Standards for Arts Education: Dance, Music, Theatre, Visual Arts* (Reston, VA: MENC, 1994), pp. 5, 50–51.

14. Ibid.

15. Thomas M. Brewer, "Sequential Learning in Art," *Art Education* 48, no. 1 (1995): 65–72.

16. The list of goals is taken from "Curriculum Study Group: Social Studies" (Newton, MA: Newton Public Schools).

17. Consortium of National Arts Education Associations, "Joint Statement on Integration of the Arts with Other Disciplines and with Each Other," *NAEA Advisory* (spring 1992).

18. "English as a Second Language" (Newton, MA: Newton Public Schools, n.d.).

19. Janet L. Olson, *Envisioning Writing: Toward an Integration of Drawing and Writing* (Portsmouth, NH: Heinemann, 1992).

20. Brent Wilson, Al Hurwitz, and Marjorie Wilson, *Teaching Drawing from Art* (Worcester, MA: Davis Publications, 1987).

21. Olson, *Envisioning Writing.*

22. *Art Education in Action,* Tape 4: "Art History and Art Criticism, Episode B: Art Informs History," Ethel Tracy, second-grade teacher, videotape (Los Angeles: Getty Center for Education in the Arts, 1995).

23. Minuette Floyd, "Multicultural Understanding through Culturally and Personally Relevant Art Curricula," Parts 1 and 2, *NAEA Advisory* (Reston, VA: National Art Education Association, spring 1999); and Elizabeth Manley Delacruz, "Multiculturalism and Art Education: Myths, Misconceptions, Misdirections," *Art Education* 48, no. 3 (1995): 57–61.

24. Roger D. Tomhave, "Value Bases Underlying Conceptions of Multicultural Education: An Analysis of Selected Literature in Art Education," *Studies in Art Education* 34, no. 1 (fall 1992): 48–60.

25. Patricia L. Stuhr, "Multicultural Art Education and Social Reconstruction," *Studies in Art Education* 35, no. 3 (1994): 171–178.

26. Bernard Young, ed., *Art, Culture and Ethnicity* (Reston, VA: National Art Education Association, 1990).

27. Frank J. Chetelat, "Art and Science: An Interdisciplinary Approach," *Art Teacher* (fall 1979): p. 8.

28. Tyler, *Basic Principles of Curriculum and Instruction,* see Chapter 1.

29. M. Frances Klein, "Approaches to Curriculum Theory and Practice," in *Teaching and Thinking about Curriculum,* ed. James T. Sears and J. Dan Marshall (New York: Teachers College Press, 1990), see pages 3–14.

30. Renee Sandell, "Feminist Concerns and Gender Issues in Art Education," *Translations: From Theory to Practice* 8, no. 1 (spring 1999).

31. This matrix outline and the following unit and lesson plans were derived from the *SPECTRA Art Program,* K–8, Kay Alexander and Michael Day (Palo Alto, CA: Dale Seymour Publications, 1994).

ACTIVITIES FOR THE READER

1. Describe in some detail the significant planning decisions that must be made in an art program developed in the following situations: (a) a sixth-grade classroom in a new, wealthy suburb of a large city; (b) a third-grade classroom in a temporary school for the children of construction workers in an isolated part of North Carolina; (c) a mixed-grade classroom (first through fourth grades) in a mission school for Native Americans located in New Mexico.

2. Describe how you would constructively handle a situation in which your principal was more interested in having an art program based on a rigid approach of outdated concepts than on a contemporary, creative approach. Choose a classmate, and do some improvised role playing on the subject.

3. You are elected chairperson of an eight-person ad hoc committee in a city school system to submit ideas to a central authority for the improvement of the art program. You are expected, furthermore, to select the eight members of the committee. State the kinds of people you would choose. Describe the agenda you would draw up for the first hour-long meeting.

4. Because of negative associations with a previous art program, your fifth-grade pupils do not seem interested in helping you develop an art program. Describe how you might improve matters.

5. A former teacher had for two years taught nothing to fourth-, fifth-, and sixth-grade pupils except the copying of either comic strips or picture postcards. How would you proceed in developing an art program in your new teaching position?

6. Improvise the conversation you might have with a parent who thinks teaching art is a waste of taxpayers' money, which should be used for "more important fundamentals." Try this conversation with various types of parents: professionals, lower-middle-class factory workers, local shopkeepers.

7. Plan a sequence of six art activities for the middle grades, all based on a theme of your choice. Try one unit for a limited budget and one for a generous budget.

8. Divide the painting experience into "tight" (performance) objectives and "loose" objectives (more personal interpretations).

9. Review the section on "Thinking Skills in the Art Curriculum," and determine what art activities are suggested by the styles of thinking listed.

10. Create a fourth unit for Table 17-1.
11. Plan a lesson of your choice, using the example prepared on "Contemporary Japanese Sculptors."

SUGGESTED READINGS

Curriculum: Theory, Issues, and Trends

Barry, Arlene L., and Pat Villeneuve. "Veni, Vidi, Vice: Interdisciplinary Learning in the Art Museum." *Art Education* 51, no. 6 (1997): 17–24.

Briggs, Patricia, and Frederick R. Weisman Art Museum. *Cultural Diversity in the Visual Arts: A Collection Inventory and Curriculum Tool.* Minneapolis: Frederick R. Weisman Art Museum, University of Minnesota, 1995.

Dunn, Phillip C., and National Art Education Association. *Creating Curriculum in Art.* Reston, VA: National Art Education Association, 1995.

Efland, Arthur, Kerry J. Freedman, and Patricia L. Stuhr, eds. *Postmodern Art Education: An Approach to Curriculum.* Reston, VA: National Art Education Association, 1996.

Henry, Carole, and National Art Education Association. *Middle School Art: Issues of Curriculum and Instruction.* Reston, VA: National Art Education Association, 1996.

Johnson, Mia. "Orientations to Curriculum in Computer Art Education." *Art Education* 50, no. 3 (1997): 43–55.

McFee, June King. *Cultural Diversity and the Structure and Practice of Art Education.* Reston, VA: National Art Education Association, 1998.

Milbrandt, Melody K. "Postmodernism in Art Education: Content for Life." *Art Education* 51, no. 6 (1998): 47–53.

Curriculum Models and Development

Alexander, Kay, and Michael Day. *Discipline-Based Art Education: A Curriculum Sampler.* Los Angeles: Getty Center for Education in the Arts, 1991. Model curriculum produced to demonstrate DBAE comprehensive approach to art teaching.

WORLD WIDE WEB RESOURCES

Professional Support for Curriculum Development

ASCD. The Association for Supervision and Curriculum Development. <http://odie.ascd.org/> ASCD provides professional development and support in curriculum creation and implementation. Provides a wide array of education information services.

NAEA. The National Art Education Association. <http://www.naea-reston.org/> Professional support and resources for art teachers and administrators. Provides links to state organizations and commercial art suppliers.

Department of Education. "Summary Statement: Education Reform, Standards, and the Arts: What Students Should Know and Be Able to Do in the Arts." *National Standards for Art Education.* 1999. <http://www.ed.gov/pubs/ArtsStandards.html>

Meta Sites for Art Curriculum and Teaching Resources

The Getty Art Education Web Site. *ArtsEdNet.* 1999. <http://www.artsednet.getty.edu/> Provides links to top art education, general education, and museum Web sites. Growing database of curriculum resources provides search capability.

National Endowment for the Humanities. *EDSITEment.* 1999. <http://www.edsitement.neh.gov/> This Web site brings together the top humanities Web sites, lesson plans, and other useful teacher resources. Growing database of online lesson plans and other links. Excellent search ability provided for the site.

U.S. Department of Education: National Library of Education. *Gateway to Educational Materials.* 1999. <http://www.thegateway.org/index.html> GEM is a consortium effort to provide access to collections of educational materials found on federal, state, university, nonprofit, and commercial Web sites. The large database is searchable by subject, keyword, and grade level.

Comprehensive Art Education Curriculum Models, Online Lessons, and Curriculum Resources

Alexander, Kay, and Michael Day. *Discipline-Based Art Education: A Curriculum Sampler.* Los Angeles: Getty Center for Education in the Arts, 1991. Online version: The Getty Art Education Web Site. *ArtsEdNet.* 1999. <http://www.artsednet.getty.edu/ArtsEdNet/Resources/index.html> Model curriculum produced to demonstrate DBAE comprehensive approach to art education. Complete curriculum units with supplementary material. Introduction on curriculum development.

Getty Center for Education in the Arts. Viewer's Guide by Michael Day. *Art Education in Action.* Santa Monica, CA: Getty Center for Education in the Arts, 1995. Online version: The Getty Art Education Web Site. *ArtsEdNet.* 1999. <http://www.artsednet.getty.edu/ArtsEdNet/Resources/index.html> Model curriculum demonstrated by classroom teachers. Online version contains text of curriculum units and the viewer's guide.

University of North Texas. North Texas Institute for Educators on the Visual Arts. *Curriculum Resources.* 1995–1999. <http://www.art.unt.edu/ntieva/artcurr/index.html> The North Texas Institute for Educators on the Visual Arts, developed by the Getty Center for Education in the Arts, creates comprehensive art curriculum content materials for use by art and classroom teachers. These materials include art historical, cultural, and critical content as well as production activities and are adaptable for different grade levels and teaching styles. The site features valuable professional teaching materials.

Killam, Lauren H. *Virtual Curriculum: Elementary Art Education.* 1997–1999. <http://www.dhc.net/~artgeek/index.html> This site is designed for teachers and art educators of elementary-aged children. The lessons include concepts, objectives, vocabulary, materials, procedures, and evaluation. Links are provided to museums and other related resources.

Roland, Craig. *The @rt room.* <http://www.arts.ufl.edu/art/rt_room/@rtroom_home.html> This Web site, designed by an art educator, is patterned after art rooms in schools. It is a place for both kids and teachers. Children are offered opportunities to create, to discover, to imagine, to invent, and to learn. It provides teachers with curriculum models and resources. The graphic look is high quality.

Commercial Web Sites to Support Art Education Curriculum

Crayola. *Art Education: Lesson Plans.* <http://education.crayola.com/lessons/> Provides lesson plans and useful information on art-making products.

Pacific Bell Knowledge Network. *Eyes On Art.* 1966–1999. <http://www.kn.pacbell.com/wired/art/teach.guide.html> This Web site was created to demonstrate the educational value of Internet resources for art education. The site's curriculum is discipline-based and provides links to art museums and other art education resources.

Pacific Bell. Knowledge Network Explorer: *Blue Web'n.* 1995–1999. <http://www.kn.pacbell.com/wired/bluewebn/about.html> *Blue Web'n* is a searchable database, updated weekly, consisting of Internet learning sites categorized by subject area, audience, and type. The site is well designed and features links to quality resources, lessons, and tools for art teaching and technology. The Hot Lists are particularly helpful. Site developed by Pacific Bell as a public service.

Sanford: The Write Site. *ArtEdventures.* 1998–1999. <http://www.sanford-artedventures.com/> Site provides resources and lesson plans, including many that align with the National Visual Arts Standards. Created by Sanford Manufacturing Company, suppliers of art products for classroom teachers.

18

CHAPTER

CLASSROOM ORGANIZATION AND DISPLAY OF STUDENT WORK

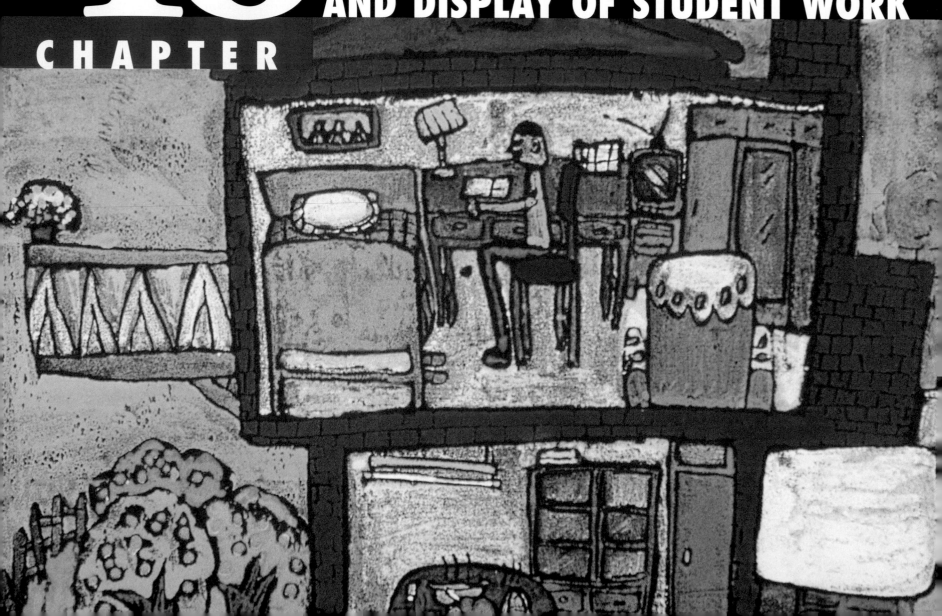

The art room is . . . the teacher's canvas on which ideas are showcased, the curious are challenged, and responses are invited.[1]

—George Szekely

To conduct an art program successfully, the teacher must often plan alterations and additions to the basic classroom provided. In this chapter we will discuss some of the ways a general classroom may be modified to accommodate pupils engaged in artwork. Some attention will be given also to the planning of an art room, if such a separate room is available. We will deal first with the physical equipment and functional arrangements for art activities in different types of rooms. In the second half of the chapter, we will discuss the display of student artwork.

Many of the problems that arise from the task of reorganizing a room for art are unique to the particular situation. The size and shape of a room, the number of children in a class, and the type of activities in the program all will modify the arrangements to be made. Making suitable physical arrangements for art, therefore, presents a challenge that in the long run, only the teacher can satisfactorily meet.

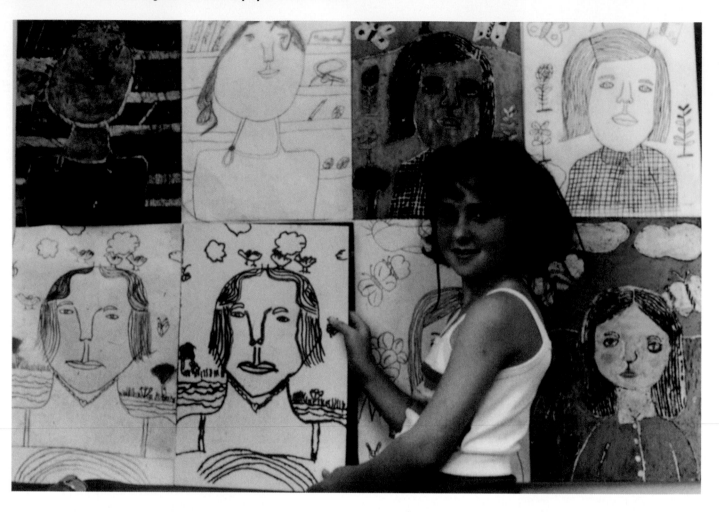

U.S.A.

PHYSICAL REQUIREMENTS
OF THE CLASSROOM

A classroom in which art is taught requires physical provisions for storing equipment and supplies, preparing current supplies for the class, and setting out the supplies for current work. The room should accommodate slide and overhead projectors and a video monitor, as well as the display of large art prints. After children learn what to obtain and where to obtain it and how to move so they do not get in each other's way (all of which they learn through discussion with the teacher and subsequent practice), they must have suitable places to work. Drawing and painting are quiet activities; cutting and hammering are more active. Papers for drawing and painting are usually much larger than those for writing, so surfaces to accommodate them must be larger than most school desks. Certain activities, such as linoleum block printing, demand a special surface on which the materials may be cut. Through use, this surface will roughen and become unsuitable for drawing, painting, and other activities. Two boards, a work board and a drawing board, are necessary. Drying unfinished or completed work, storing unfinished work, and displaying work also require their own spaces. These requirements suggest the following furniture:

1. A storage cupboard with some adjustable shelves, the latter at least 8 inches wide for small items and at least 18 inches wide for larger items. The outside dimensions of the cupboard will, of course, be determined by the floor and wall space available.

2. Two tables, preferably at least 5 feet long and 30 inches wide, one to be used largely by the teacher in arranging and displaying supplies and the other for children's group work.

3. A sink, or a stand for pails of water. The sink should have at least two faucets to hasten the cleanup activity.

4. A drying shelf or battery of shelves near a source of heat. The shelf should be about 12 inches wide and as long as space permits. Shelves also can be placed over windows, since this space is rarely used.

5. Some display facilities, such as cases and bulletin boards.

6. Some chalkboard space—but not so much as to displace needed display areas.

7. Blackout drapes, projectors, and screens for showing slides and videos and for overhead projection.

8. Storage for art prints, slides, and other art resource materials.

9. Walls that can accommodate thumbtacks.

BASIC SUPPLIES AND EQUIPMENT

Although each type of art activity demands particular tools and equipment, and sometimes special room arrangements, the following list of tools and supplies seems basic to nearly any art program. Miscellaneous supplies and equipment, such as scissors, thumbtacks, masking tape, and a paper cutter (18-inch minimum), are not listed, because they are part of general equipment for other subjects. Craft materials are not listed, because they vary so much with each teacher. Paper cutters are potential hazards and require instruction on their use.

1. *Brayers:* available in a variety of widths from 3 to 8 inches. Soft rubber rollers are recommended, and a set for one class can service the entire school.

2. *Brushes:* for painting larger areas—flat, hog-bristle, ¼ inch to 1 inch wide; for painting detailed sections—pointed, sable, large (size 6 or 7) paste brushes.

3. *Chalk:* soft; ten or twelve colors plus black and white; dustless preferred.

4. *Crayons:* wax; soft; ten or twelve colors plus black and white.

5. *Oil crayons:* often known as oil pastels.

6. *Pens:* felt-tip marking pens.

7. *Drawing boards:* about 18 by 24 inches; soft plywood at least "BC" grade (that is, clear of knots on at least one side); Masonite, composition board (optional).

8. *Erasers:* Artgum type.

9. *Inks:* black drawing ink; water-base printing inks in tubes for block printing.

10. *Printing surfaces:* Linoleum is traditional, but may be too difficult for younger children. A number of good alternative surfaces are available in art supply catalogs.

11. *Tempera paint:* liquid in pints or powder in pounds (white, black, orange, yellow, blue, green, and red as basic; magenta, purple, and turquoise as luxuries; probably twice the quantity of black, white, and yellow as of other colors chosen).

    Tempera paints have been the traditional mainstay of painting activity. Acrylic paint is now priced competitively with tempera and should be considered for its distinguishing properties: It is waterproof, and therefore ideal for interior and exterior wall murals; murals on paper can be rolled up without flaking. It will adhere to any surface—clay, wood, glass, and so on. When it is applied thickly, objects can be embedded into it; when thinned with water, it can serve as a substitute for watercolor. When applied with a soft foam brayer, it can also be used for linoleum printing.

12. *Watercolor paint:* Secondary-color selections are preferable.

13. *Paint tins:* muffin tins, with at least six depressions; baby-food jars and frozen-juice cans also may be used.

14. *Paper:* roll of kraft (brown wrapping), about 36 inches wide; or "project roll," 36 inches wide; white and manila, 18 by 24 inches, cream and gray, 40-pound; colored construction, 12 by 18 inches (red, yellow, blue, light green, dark green, black, gray, and perhaps some in-between colors like blue-green and red-orange; about forty colors are available); color tissue; newsprint, 18 by 24 inches.

15. *Paste and glue:* school paste, in quarts; powdered wheat paste for papier-mâché; white glue for wood joining (thinned, it works well as an adhesive for colored tissue).

16. *Pencils:* drawing; black, soft.

17. *Printing plates:* glass trimmed with masking tape for inking brayers.

18. *Firing clay:* 3 pounds per child minimum.

19. Slide and video projectors should be available.

20. A collection of art prints, postcards, and other reproductions.

21. Filing cabinet for item 20.

22. Art books and magazines should be available in the art room or the library.

23. *Recycled materials:* bottles, heavy cardboard, newspapers, wood scraps, corks, string, containers, buttons, etc.

CLASSROOM ARRANGEMENTS
A Primary-Grade Classroom

The teacher's preparation of art materials for young children is often quite different from that for the upper grades. Older children can usually select art materials for themselves, but the primary teachers must, at least at the beginning of the school term, arrange sets or groupings of materials. These vary greatly in the number of items they contain. For example, for crayon drawing, children need only six crayons and a sheet of manila paper each. For painting, they require perhaps aprons or parents' old shirts, a sheet of newspaper or oilcloth to protect the painting surface, two brushes and a sheet of newsprint each, paint cloths, and some liquid colors.

From a necessarily large and convenient storage space, the teacher selects materials and places them on a long table, cafeteria-style. Crayons may be put on a paper plate and set on the sheet of paper. The painting kit may be assembled in discarded "six-pack" cartons, on a metal or plastic tray, or on a wooden work board. The paint should not be included at this point, because children could spill it as they transport the kit to the place where they will be painting. Paint and any other "dangerous" materials should be placed in the work area ahead of time in broad-based containers (jars or milk cartons).

The following suggestions may be helpful in storing tools and supplies so they will be ready for distribution:

1. Brushes and pencils should be placed in glass jars, with bristles and points up. Blocks of wood with holes bored in them, each hole large enough to hold one item, provide another convenient way of arranging brushes.

This manner of storage also allows the teacher to make a quick visual check for missing brushes.

2. Crayons should be separated according to colors. Each container, which might be a milk carton or a cigar box, should hold only one color.

3. Moistened clay should be rolled into balls and placed in a large lidded earthenware jar or plastic bags to keep in the moisture.

4. Paper should be cut to size and arranged on a shelf in piles according to size and color.

5. Paper scraps should be separated according to color and saved in small cartons.

6. Paste should be kept in covered glass jars. The teacher should place paste on disposable paper plates or simply on pieces of cardboard after it has been mixed for use.

7. When oil or Vaseline is spread on the rim or cap of a jar in which tempera has been stored, the paint will not harden and the cap can easily be removed.

It is fortunate that the furniture in most primary rooms is movable, because floors provide an excellent work area for art. If the floor is covered with heavy linoleum or linoleum tile, it is necessary to set down only a thin protective covering, such as oilcloth, plastic sheets, or wrapping paper before work begins.

Some teachers like to hang paintings to dry on a clothesline with spring clothespins. Tables are often used for drying three-dimensional projects.

Because it is desirable for all children eventually to learn how to procure and replace equipment and supplies for themselves, the room should be arranged so children can perform the task easily.[2] In the primary grades, as elsewhere in the art program, the cafeteria system is useful. Children must develop the ability to obtain and replace art materials according to a plan that they themselves help to determine. The teacher should discuss with children the necessity of learning these skills. However, in the primary grades the children will usually follow plans willingly and treat the routine as a game. The game can even include a rehearsal or drill of the routine.

A General Classroom

Many contemporary school plans give considerable thought to suitable accommodation for art activities in general classrooms. A description of the special provisions for art in the general classroom is offered here primarily for those teachers who are provided with a reasonably liberal budget for the furnishing of their art facilities.

In most classrooms desks can be easily arranged to suit the studies in progress. Movable desks are a great convenience for drawing and painting, since they allow a pupil to use a drawing board without interfering with other children. Clusters of desks may be arranged so large flat areas of working space are available for group activities.

In some contemporary classrooms, an entire wall is provided with fixtures that facilitate the teaching of art. These can include a counter covered with Formica or some other suitably processed material, built from wall to wall. This counter houses probably the most important single convenience for art activities—a large sink supplied with hot and cold water. Below the counter are several storage cupboards equipped with adjustable shelves and swinging doors, where all expendable supplies may be stored. A second row of cupboards is suspended about 12 inches above the counter. These cupboards also have adjustable shelves, but the doors are of the sliding variety so pupils will not bump their heads on them when open. Additional supplies or the pupils' unfinished work may be kept in this storage space. Electrical outlets are frequently provided at convenient intervals along the counter. The whole assemblage, which substantially resembles a work unit in a modern kitchen, occupies relatively little floor space. Sometimes an additional work counter is provided along part of the window wall; more cupboards may be built below this counter.

Because the teacher in a general classroom requires a relatively large expanse of chalkboard, it is sometimes difficult to find sufficient space to display art. This is often provided, however, on the side wall to the rear of the room and on two walls above the chalkboards, where a wide strip of tackboard is fastened. But since even these areas are usually insufficient for display purposes, many new schools are being equipped with display boards and cases in the main halls of the building.

To carry out a comprehensive art program, it is also necessary to organize the classroom for use of audio and visual materials, such as slides, overhead projection, video, and computers.

The Art Room

In today's educational world, budgets are not always large enough for accommodating a separate art room in a new school, although this is recommended by the NAEA. If not

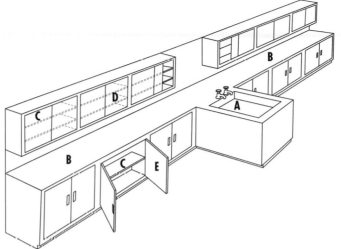

A typical wall fixture for art activities in a general classroom.
a Sink
b Counter
c Adjustable shelves
d Sliding doors
e Swinging doors

all the ideas set forth in this section can be adopted, perhaps some of them may be employed as the teachers gradually improve the working conditions in their school.

Design

An art room should be placed near a service entrance on the main floor of a school building, for convenience in delivering supplies and equipment. In junior high schools, it is preferable also to have the room situated reasonably close to home-economics rooms and industrial-arts shops so pupils may conveniently move from one room to another to use special equipment.

According to standards developed by the National Art Education Association, because student art projects and materials may be bulky and rooms must fulfill multiple purposes for contemporary art programs, art rooms need to be larger than general classrooms.

NAEA recommends 55 square feet per student, not including storage, kiln rooms, and teacher's office, and a maximum pupil/teacher ratio of 28:1. This leads to an art room covering 1,540 square feet, excluding auxiliary space. NAEA recommends 400 square feet for the storage room, 45 square feet for the kiln room, and 120 square feet for the teacher's office.[3]

Lighting in an art room is of the greatest importance. Natural north lighting is recommended whenever possible. Preferably, the lights should be set flush with the ceiling, with the exception of spotlights for important displays. Unless the room has a daylight screen, blackout curtains for the windows should be provided so films may be shown. In all matters

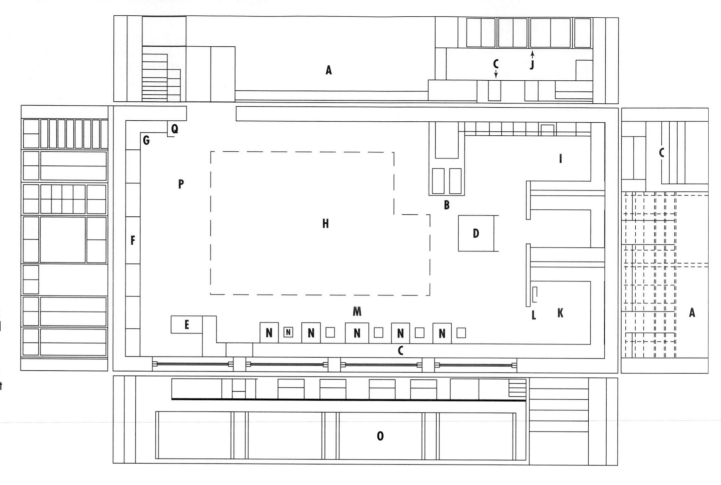

Comprehensive plan for an all-purpose art room.

a Tackboard and screen
b Sinks
c Work counters
d Heavy workbench
e Teacher's desk
f Cabinets and display cases
g Library corner
h Central space for tables and seats
i Clay-working area
j Storage area: expendable art materials
k Library corner
l Stepladder
m Area for three-dimensional work
n Solid desks for three-dimensional work and individual stool for each desk
o Windows (north light preferred): should be provided with blackout curtains for showing slides and films
p Areas for easels, posing models, etc.
q Filing cabinet

pertaining to both artificial and natural lighting, architects and lighting engineers should be consulted. Many excellent materials and arrangements are available, including directional glass bricks, opaque louvers, clerestory lighting, and various types of blinds.

The efficient use of space around the walls also should be considered. Along one of the shorter walls, storage rooms jutting into the room might be planned. Two storage areas are desirable: one to house a stock of expendable art materials and the other to store the pupils' unfinished work. Each storage room should be fitted with as many adjustable shelves as convenient. Since the shelves may rise to a considerable height, it would be well to have at least one light-weight stepladder available. The outside walls of these storage rooms, facing the classroom, can be covered with tackboard. The long wall area opposite the windows should for the most part

be faced with tackboard running from about 30 inches above the floor up to the ceiling. An area of about 20 square feet, however, should be reserved for a chalkboard. Space might be provided for counters and cupboards.

The sink may be located on this long side of the room. Its position should be reasonably central, and it should be accessible from at least three directions (see floor plan, above). It may be placed in a separate cabinet so the pupils can approach it from all directions, or it may be placed at the end of a counter running at right angles from the wall toward the center of the room. However arranged, the sink should be large, deep, acid-resistant, and equipped with hot- and cold-water taps. Clean-out traps should be fitted, and all plumbing leading from them also should be acid-resistant.

Along the entire wall at the end of the room and opposite the storage rooms, storage cupboards might alternate with glass-enclosed display cases. These cases should be provided with adjustable glass shelves and illuminated with hidden or indirect lights.

Beneath the windows, a work counter might run almost the full length of the room. Below the counter, storage cupboards could be constructed, or the space might be left open to house tools. Jutting out at right angles might be a series of small counters for delicate work. Each small counter, which might be collapsible, should be provided with a stool of convenient height. An area might be set aside for the teacher's desk and files.

The placement of electrical outlets is a task for an expert who understands electrical loads, but the teacher must be sure that outlets are placed in correct locations for their use. In addition to outlets for ceramic and enameling kilns and service outlets in general, there should be an outlet for an electric clock. The pupils should always be aware of how much time is available to begin certain phases of their work or to start cleaning up toward the end of the art period.

Furnishings

Certain equipment should be placed in convenient relation to the arrangements around the walls. Such items might include an electric kiln with a firing area of not less than 3,000 cubic inches, a pullout storage bin for clay, a storage box for keeping clay damp, and a spray booth. The clay-working area should be located near the sink. A filing cabinet for storing catalogs, folders containing information about the students, and miscellaneous items useful to the teacher should be placed near the teacher's desk.

Furniture for the art room must be chosen with care. Suitable art desks come in a variety of designs, but a desk with low shelves on which the pupils may place schoolbooks would have optimum utility. Desks with movable tops, by which the slope of the working surface may be regulated, have *not* proved particularly serviceable because the adjusting mechanisms tend to break. For seating, chairs, stools, and benches are all useful. One or two carpenter's benches, as well as desks for drawing and painting, should be provided. The benches should be supplied with vises and have storage space beneath them for tools and other equipment.

The colors used to decorate the art room must be carefully planned. Bright colors are generally to be avoided since they "rebound" and confuse a painter. Tints or neutral colors such as pale grays or off-white are recommended for the walls and ceiling. The ceiling should be lighter in tone than the walls. The floor also should be neutral but mottled. Chalkboards come in pale greens or ivory, as well as black. Natural or limed wood finishes on cupboards and doors are attractive and serviceable. In general, color in an art room must not interfere with the color work in progress, and it must serve as background for the displays of the children's work.

Before an elaborate art room of the type described can be set up successfully, much study must be given to the problem and many experts consulted. Not only should plans of the room be drawn but also a model should be made. Particular attention should be given to the grouping of furniture and equipment to avoid overcrowding in any one part of the room and to locate in an area everything necessary for any one type of work. Obviously, an art room entails costly construction, and whatever arrangements are made, good or bad, are likely to be in use for a long time. One example to study is the accompanying comprehensive plan for an all-purpose art room.

Creating a Learning Environment

Equipment, facilities, and storage have been considered thus far, but functions other than purely practical ones are also essential. The art room should be an environment for learning about art as well as an assembly of hardware. It must contain many stimuli; it must be a place for sensory excitement; it is also the child's link with the world outside the classroom.[4] Here, before painting a favorite animal, a child may have access to slides, paintings, or photographs of animal life. One day the teacher may bring in a live puppy, kitten, or turkey to study. At times the art room may resemble a science laboratory as the teacher attempts to acquaint the children with intricate or hidden forms of nature. The room may contain inexpensive microscopes, aquariums, terrariums, bones, rock formations—anything that can direct the child's attention to visual cues that have bearing on the art experience.

A corner of the room might be reserved for research and supplied with art books, well-illustrated children's books, magazines on a suitable reading level, file material, slides, and videos. Another part of the room might be set aside as a "serendipity corner"—a place for interesting and unusual things to draw. The more provocative these items are, the better. Each teacher creates a unique collection of objects chosen for their shapes, colors, and associations. This collection provides its own stimulus for any lesson that employs observation.

One way to create a learning environment in the art room is to have the children themselves design portions of the

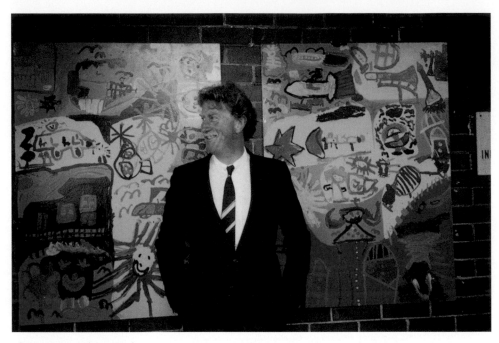

Administrators can play a critical role in the life of an art program. This Australian principal gives students house paints so that large-scale artwork can be attached to exterior walls of the school.

worth observing for their aesthetic qualities. Children's art is often so attractive that it should be brought forth for people to see and enjoy. The production of any art form is not a casual event; it is an offering of heart and mind from one human being to another.

The display of children's art is an effective teaching device. One common method of display is to group the work according to topics or themes. When twenty-five or more pupils in a class present their reactions to one theme, it is highly educative for all to observe those reactions. If art is suitably taught, no two children make identical statements about an experience. After viewing the various statements, the children may gain a broader insight into the topic as a whole.[5]

The display of children's art tends to develop certain desirable attitudes toward the school. When young children see their artistic efforts on display, they tend to sense a oneness with the group. Their participation brings out a feeling of belonging, which often increases the fullness of subsequent participation.

Children's art on display also has its decorative purposes. The classroom is usually a barren place when the teacher enters it before the beginning of the school year. Likewise, the halls of many schools are dull, institutional places until suitable decorations have been arranged. The artwork of children humanizes the character of a school building. Even the most delightful interior architecture of modern schools can be improved by a judicious display of children's production.

More and more, schools are serving as institutions of learning by day and as community centers by night. Parent-teacher groups, night-school classes (in which, among other subjects, art may be studied), and other meetings of interest to members of a community are causing greater numbers of adults to visit the schools than ever before. This is desirable, because it provides the school with an opportunity to show the public what is being done with taxpayers' money. Furthermore, it presents an opportunity to arouse or maintain public interest in education in general and art education in particular.

Art displays operate on three different levels: the classroom, the school, and the community. In the classroom or art room, display is linked closely to instruction and also enhances the environment. In the school and community, however, it should be used to alert viewers to the nature and goals of the art program. No work should be presented with-

room. Wooden crates painted in bright colors and units constructed of wallboard can provide flexibility even beyond purchased components. The teacher who thinks of the child as entering a laboratory of visual delight—a place for looking, feeling, shaping, and forming—will have some idea of what the art room or even a section of the classroom might be. Above all, an art room should have a special character. The moment a child enters should be one of happy anticipation. The art room is a space where creative things happen; it should be the most attractive place in the child's school life.

WHY DISPLAY CHILDREN'S ART?

From the art program come tangible visual results of the learning experience; the art program in fact constitutes the only part of the school curriculum with truly visible results, because they can be exhibited over a prolonged period. As such, art lends itself to display, which serves as the final communicative stage of the creative process.

Perhaps the most important reason for displaying art is simply that the results of children's artistic acts are usually out a label conveying such information as the student's name, school, teacher, and grade, the title of the piece, and—most important—the concept, goal, or unit to which the work is related. Exhibitions should be viewed as a way of educating the public.

SELECTING WORK FOR DISPLAY

Probably the first question in the teacher's mind when exhibiting art is how to choose the work. The criteria for selection should be both pedagogical and aesthetic. Although children will find interest in the art output of others, they are also interested in their own work and are usually proud of it. This means that every child in a class sooner or later during the school term should have some work on display. Since space is limited in a classroom, pupils cannot expect their work to appear very often, but they will accept this fact if they feel that their chances to have work displayed are equal to those of others. Awareness of this tends to make children more active participants in all displays that appear on the classroom walls.

As children mature, they develop an ability to appraise the standards of both their behavior and their artistic output. They are capable of realizing when their output has not resulted in a success commensurate with their effort. An attempt at expression does not always result in success, as every creating person knows. When children realize that their output has not reached an accustomed standard, displaying their work would in all likelihood be an embarrassment to them. Before a particular child's work is displayed, therefore, a teacher would do well to compare it with previous performances and to talk with the child.

If work for display is chosen with these ideas in mind, the child of exceptional ability will not create the problems of selection that might otherwise occur. It would be discouraging for the members of the class to see a more gifted child's work repeatedly occupying a major portion of the displays

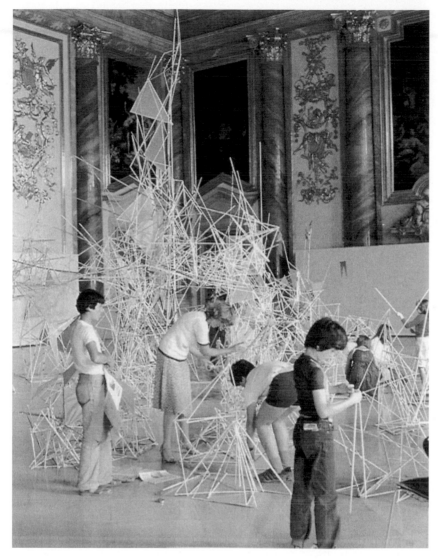

Displays need not be limited to completed works; they can also present processes and involve parents in the subject or media in the exhibits.
(Elizabeth Safer, Museum of Modern Art, Lichtenstein)

to the partial exclusion of the work of others. The gifted child exhibits a range of success just as everyone else does. This being the case, only the most significant items of that child's expression need appear on display.

The teacher will not have to save all the artwork of every pupil during the school year to summarize the general progress of each child. Although some of the work may be kept in a portfolio for reference, the teacher will be able, for the most part, to remember each child's earlier performances. The art output of each child becomes unique in the eyes of an alert and sensitive teacher.

The selection of work for display depends not only on the quality of each piece but also on an intimate knowledge of every child responsible for it. The teacher must be fully aware of each child's potential and must judge the work in relation to the pupil's personal abilities.

In general, it is suggested that the farther the display is removed from the classroom, the more selective should be the process of choosing the works to be displayed. When children's art goes to the front hall or to some location in the community, each piece should be selected for its ability to capture and hold the attention of the viewer. In the classroom, the work of the entire class should be displayed.

ARRANGING DISPLAYS IN THE CLASSROOM
Displaying Two-Dimensional Work

The display areas should not be overcrowded. Each piece should be set apart and mounted in some way. Mounts should be chosen so their color unifies the display but does not conflict with the colors used in the drawings and paintings themselves. Grays, browns, and sometimes black are usually suitable colors for mounts. White is also recommended, since it flatters the picture and gives a clean look to the exhibit. When the display panels are made of soft wood, cork, or composition board, both mount and picture may be most conveniently fastened to the display area by a gun-type wall stapler or clear-headed pushpins. Thumbtacks should be avoided because they distract the viewer's attention from the work.

Mounts or frames may be devised in a number of ways and with several materials. The simplest, cheapest, and, many think, most attractive method of mounting is to attach a sheet of newsprint, paper, or cardboard to the display board and to fasten on this a drawing or painting having smaller dimensions. A variety of effects may be obtained with this method by altering the proportion of background to picture. Another method of framing a picture is to fix the picture to the board, cut a window the size of the picture in a sheet of paper or cardboard, and then, placing the frame over the picture, attach it to the board. Mounts need not be wide: Even a 1-inch border with a 2-inch lower border can be effective, as long as it leaves room for a label.

When a display is arranged, a title is usually required. Titles, of course, become part of the general design of a display. A title may be produced in two dimensions with lettering pens and india or colored inks and felt pens. Although they are beyond the ability of most elementary-school children, three-dimensional titles can be made from cardboard cutout letters. After it is cut out, each letter is stuck on a long pin that holds it away from the display board. Attractive background papers of contrasting color or texture help to make this type of title particularly arresting. Computer-generated titles have become popular, as has the use of calligraphy (often with special pens).

The simplest and most common arrangement of pictures on a display panel is one that follows the rectangular shape of the board. The pictures are hung so their edges are parallel to those of the board. More often than not a formal balance is achieved, so the viewer's attention will be attracted equally around imaginary central axes of the board. The margins established between the picture frames and the outside edges of a display panel that is horizontal should be such that the bottom margin is widest, the top narrowest, and the width of the sides in-between. In a vertical panel, the traditional proportions to be observed reverse the proportions of sides and top: The bottom is the widest, the top is second in size, and the sides are the narrowest. A square panel calls for even margins at top and sides, with a wider margin at the bottom for information regarding the work. These classic arrangements are safe, and by using them one may tastefully display any group of pictures.

If display panels are not available, it may prove difficult to exhibit works of art in the school hall. Curls of masking tape on the back of pictures are often used to attach flatwork to such surfaces, but this is far from ideal because of the expense involved and the tendency of pictures to slip. Two

Some methods of mounting two-dimensional works.

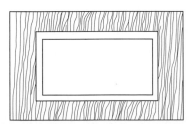
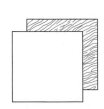
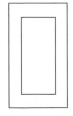
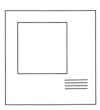

permanent solutions are strips of cork bolted to the wall and/or framed 4-by-8-foot sheets of composition board or any other material that takes staples and pins. Avoid Masonite for this reason. Masonite pegboard, however, is excellent, because bent metal hooks can be inserted to hang shelves, puppets, and other three-dimensional objects.

All exhibitions in a classroom must show an awareness of the display situation and should be considered as designs subject to the discipline of good taste. As each display is added, it must be considered in relation to whatever displays are already on view. In general, it is wise to restrict displays to those areas especially designed for them. A classroom can scarcely appear orderly if drawings and paintings are stuck to blackboards, pinned to chalk ledges, or plastered on windows. Blackboards, chalk ledges, and windows are functional parts of the classroom whose efficiency is impaired by displays of art.

Here are some other points the teacher might keep in mind when setting up bulletin-board displays and exhibits:

1. A bulletin board has somewhat the same function as a poster. Both must capture attention, provide information, and present a unified design through pleasing relationships of textures, masses, subject matter, and lettering.

2. Pins with clear plastic heads are the best fasteners, metal pins next, and tacks last. Staples may be used if a staple remover is available.

3. Background spaces should be uncluttered, to give the eye a rest.

4. Respect the eye level of the viewer. A good average height is 5 feet, 6 inches.

5. Avoid extreme "artiness," such as complicated diagonal arrangements.

6. Bulletin-board exhibits should seldom be on display for more than two weeks. There is no disgrace in occasionally having a blank display area.

7. If possible, use a well-lighted area for the display.

8. Usually tops or sides of pictures should be aligned for consistency and order, and vertical and diagonal lettering should be avoided.

9. Keep on hand a supply of such materials as solid-colored burlap. These make excellent background segments to unite a small group of pictures. Do not

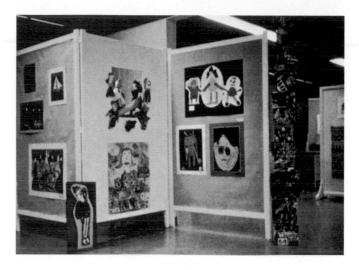

The corner of a classroom has been temporarily converted into a gallery. Display units are dispersed to accommodate traffic and facilitate viewing.

use any material that distracts from the objects on display.

10. When "going public," avoid supermarkets and other busy environments that distract from the exhibit.

11. Avoid large groups of objects that are too similar in either size or subject. Twenty drawings or paintings of different sizes can maintain variety within themselves.

12. Occasionally, break up displays with a sudden shift of scale. It can be quite exciting to have the usual 12-by-16-inch or 16-by-24-inch works set off against a life-size painting or mural.

13. Some works are "quieter" (lower key, smaller scale, less obtrusive) than others. A group of quiet paintings fares better than a row of loud ones, which tend to cancel out one another's effectiveness. Try alternating works of contrasting character.

14. When appropriate, statements by students or teachers or Polaroid photographs of a class in action can add diversity and a documentary effect.

15. Nothing is more barren than a blank wall when the public has become accustomed to a surface filled with art. Leave the walls empty for at least a week before putting up the next show. A never-ending exhibit ends up as pure decoration, and after a while the public may take it for granted.

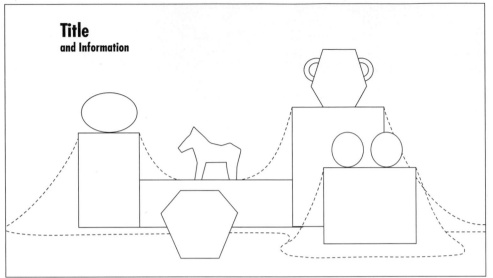

Title
and Information

When designing for a display case, cover an arrangement of boxes with cloth, leaving enough background area for flatwork, titles, etc. For variety, plan at least three levels and sizes of support beneath the cloth.

Displaying Three-Dimensional Work

Most classrooms are not equipped with display cases for three-dimensional artwork. It is frequently necessary, therefore, for the class to improvise other means of display. If space is available, a table may be placed directly in front of a display board. The three-dimensional objects may then be set on the table, and descriptions of the work or related two-dimensional work may be pinned to the board. Should it be necessary to link a written description to any particular piece on the table, a colored string may be fixed from the description to the piece of work.

The objects should be arranged according to their bulk and height. Obviously the largest and tallest objects will have to be placed well in the background so smaller objects will not be hidden. Some groups of objects, particularly modeled or carved forms and pottery, will demand the use of pedestals. The pedestals, which can be made from boxes or blocks of wood, may be painted or covered with textiles. By placing a sheet of glass over one or more of the pedestals, it is possible to arrange a convenient series of shelves of varying heights. Ceiling space can be utilized in many unusual ways, particularly for mobiles and kites. Caution should be used, however, in hanging objects from the ceiling, for certain ceil-

ing surfaces and lighting fixtures must be treated with care. Consult custodians and principals before hanging anything from a ceiling.

Display boards themselves may be used to exhibit three-dimensional work. Metal brackets fixed to the boards with screws are able to support glass shelves, which make attractive display space.

In arranging three-dimensional displays, the exhibitors must give the same attention to design that they would in displaying flatwork. For example, brilliantly colored pieces or those having outstanding structural or textural qualities must be well placed with respect to the centers of interest, the balance, and the rhythm of the design. To bring unity to the three-dimensional display, it may be necessary to use the same background for the objects.

Teaching

Because the display of art is an art activity in itself, it is highly desirable for children to take part in it. Even a six-year-old can see how much better a drawing looks when it is mounted and displayed. A simple act such as this can establish the connection between design and order in a young mind. Moreover, display techniques may lead to excellent group endeavors. Kindergarten is not too soon for children to begin this work. Kindergarten children may participate in quasi-group activities in which individuals bring their work to some central area for display.

The teacher should encourage pupils to experiment with new ways of displaying their art. One method is to have members of the class report on any outstanding display techniques observed in store windows or elsewhere. Another method is to have the teacher from time to time arrange children's work, demonstrating some new ideas for display.

ARRANGING DISPLAYS OUTSIDE THE CLASSROOM

The problems arising from displays arranged in the halls or elsewhere in a school are little different from those related to classroom exhibits. More people and examples of work are involved, of course, so organizational problems are intensified.

Media and Techniques

School architects should give attention to display possibilities. It is not unusual for some elementary schools to have display cases or gallery-type walls designed adjacent to the principal's office.

If no gallery space is available, school authorities may be expected to provide suitable panels. When the panels or cases are being installed, those responsible for the installation must remember to arrange suitable lighting.

On occasion the school may need additional display facilities. Many extra panels might be required on "Parents' Night," for example, when the school wishes to make an exceptional effort to interest the community. The design of panels for extra display facilities has become almost standard. The panels consist of sheets of building board, usually measuring from 4 by 4 feet to 4 by 8 feet, with legs bolted to either end. The legs are usually in the form of inverted Ts, but other ingenious and attractive designs are to be seen. For three-dimensional displays, a boxlike construction having shelves takes the place of a panel.

A second type of portable display board has been designed for space-saving and quick assembly. It consists of panels of building board and sturdy legs with slots cut into two adjacent sides. The panels are fitted into the slots to form a zigzag effect that is pleasing and practical. The panels are made secure by lashing the legs together with cord at the top and bottom of the panels.

Another portable display unit requires 2-by-2-inch wooden rods slightly more than 5 feet in length, with holes bored at approximately 30-inch intervals. These rods will receive 1-inch dowels, on which hang metal rings attached to the pictures. The placement of the holes on the 2-by-2-inch rods determines how the units may be angled so the flow of traffic can be controlled.

THE DISPLAY AS COMMUNITY EDUCATION

The subject matter of art displays for parent and community groups may be different from that of displays for children. Parents and other adults are interested not only in the work as such but also in the objectives and instructional contexts of the work shown.[6] We should remember that, for many adults, the comprehensive program of art in schools today is completely different from the art education they received in their youth. Although ignorance of the contemporary program sometimes leads to disapproval, parents are generally quick to react favorably to present-day trends in art education, once they understand the goals and content of the program. For parents, subjects of exhibitions of children's art might emphasize the instructional implications of the art activities. Display written commentary next to artworks when a problem of critical reaction or art history is involved. Themes of exhibitions may dramatize the overall structure of the art program or a single aspect of it. The following are a few sample topics that have proved satisfactory for "Parents' Night":

The Art Program: A Grade-Level Approach
Looking at Nature
Personal Development through Art
Variety in Artistic Expression
Group Work in Art
Learning from Other Artists
Art from Other Cultures
Art Styles of Today

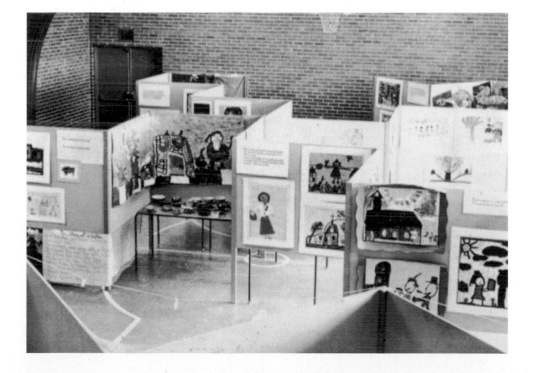

A large zigzag display in a school gymnasium. Activities that normally take place in the gym must be rescheduled to accommodate the exhibit. Moreover, setting up such an exhibit may involve a good deal of the teacher's time and energy, even though the exhibit itself may be on display for only a short time. (Pat Renick, designer)

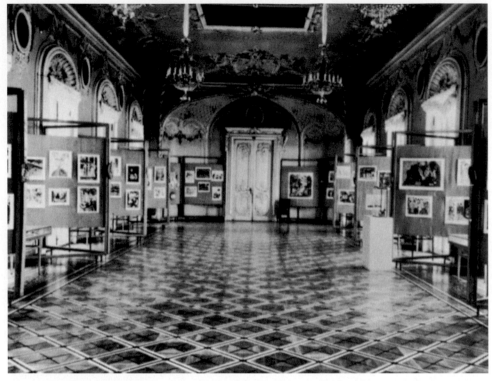

Rarely has there been a more impressive place to set up a display of children's art than in one of the main galleries of the Hermitage Museum, St. Petersburg. The work comes from special children's art classes in the museum.

For each exhibition, brief but effective signs should be made to emphasize the points demonstrated by the children's work. Each show, moreover, should have a clearly marked beginning, a logical sequence of ideas throughout the body of the exhibition, and a short summary, either written or pictorial or both, at its close. The exhibit should be more than merely another chore. It is the most dramatic means of communicating the teacher's role in the school to the public, to the administration, and to other teachers.

NOTES

1. George Szekely, "Visual Arts," in *Kraus International Publication,* ed. John A. Michael, p. 87, 1991.

2. *Art Education in Action,* Tape 3: "Making Art, Episode B: Integrating the Art Disciplines," Sandy Walker-Craig, elementary teacher, videotape (Los Angeles: Getty Center for Education in the Arts, 1995).

3. MacArthur Goodwin, ed., *Design Standards for School Art Facilities* (Reston, VA: National Art Education Association, 1993).

4. Frank Susi, "Preparing Teaching Environments for Art Education," *NAEA Advisory* (Reston, VA: National Art Education Association, winter 1990).

5. *Art Education in Action,* Tape 3: "Making Art, Episode A: Integrating Art History and Art Criticism," Evelyn Pender, art teacher, videotape (Los Angeles: Getty Center for Education in the Arts, 1995).

6. Kelly Bass, Teresa Cotner, Elliot Eisner, Tom Yacoe, and Lee Hanson, *Educationally Interpretive Exhibition: Rethinking the Display of Student Art* (Reston, VA: National Art Education Association, 1997).

ACTIVITIES FOR THE READER

1. Describe the various criteria used by teachers you have observed to select children's artwork for display. Appraise each criterion according to its educational effects on the children concerned.
2. Study and compare the display techniques you have observed in various classrooms.
3. Experiment with mounting and framing a picture on a surface such as a drawing board. Try some of the ways suggested in this chapter, and then devise new ways to display the picture.
4. Sketch in pencil or crayon some plans for a display of five pictures. Select the plan you like best, and use it in an actual panel display.
5. Repeat number 4, this time including at least twelve pictures.
6. Make some plans for the display of three pieces of pottery. Carry out the plan you like best.
7. List some subjects for an art display to be used in the main entrance of a school on "Parents' Night." The entrance hall is about 25 feet long and 12 feet wide. After selecting the subject that most appeals to you, indicate in detailed sketches (a) the type and position of the display panels, (b) the number of and subject matter of the pictures or three-dimensional objects, (c) the captions to be used, and (d) the route visitors should follow to view the exhibition.
8. Collect a number of boxes of varying sizes, and arrange them so that, when covered with one piece of cloth, they provide an attractive setting for ceramics, sculptures, or other three-dimensional objects.
9. As part of a field experience, such as a visit to an art classroom, gifted program, or art museum, work with colleagues to mount a display demonstrating what was learned and encountered on the trip. Take photographs of the completed display, and make a journal entry about its effectiveness in the classroom.

SUGGESTED READINGS

Bass, Kelly, Teresa Cotner, Elliot Eisner, Tom Yacoe, and Lee Hanson. *Educationally Interpretive Exhibition: Rethinking the Display of Student Art.* Reston, VA: National Art Education Association, 1997.

Evertson, Carolyn M., Edmund T. Emmer, and Murray E. Worsham. *Classroom Management for Elementary Teachers.* 5th ed. Boston: Allyn and Bacon, 2000.

Goodwin, MacArthur, ed. *Design Standards for School Art Facilities.* Reston, VA: National Art Education Association, 1993.

Nyman, Andra L., ed. *Instructional Methods for the Artroom: Reprints from NAEA Advisories.* Reston, VA: National Art Education Association, 1996.

Sandholtz, Judith, Cathy Ringstaff, and David C. Dwyer. *Teaching with Technology: Creating Student-Centered Classrooms.* New York: Teachers College Press, 1997.

Spandorfer, Merle, Deborah Curtiss, and Jack W. Snyder. *Making Art Safely: Alternative Methods and Materials in Drawing, Painting, Printmaking, Graphic Design, and Photography.* New York: Van Nostrand Reinhold, 1993.

Susi, Frank Daniel. *Student Behavior in Art Classrooms: The Dynamics of Discipline.* Teacher Resource Series. Reston, VA: National Art Education Association, 1995.

Weinstein, Carol Simon, and Andrew J. Mignano. *Elementary Classroom Management: Lessons from Research and Practice.* 2d ed. New York: McGraw-Hill, 1997.

Witteborg, Lothar P., Andrea Stevens, S. D. Schindler, and Smithsonian Institution. Traveling Exhibition Service. *Good Show!: A Practical Guide for Temporary Exhibitions.* 2d ed. Washington, DC: The Smithsonian Institution, 1991.

WORLD WIDE WEB RESOURCES

Internet Exhibition Sites for Children's Art

ART ala Carte. *Art-Vark*. 1996–1999. <http://artcarte.com/artvark.html> *Art-Vark* is sponsored by Art ala Carte Web Graphics. The intention of the site is to promote student interest in art and to encourage imagination and creativity. The online gallery will post the art of children and students between the ages of three and fifteen. Directions for submission are provided on the site.

The Natural Child Project Society. *Global Children's Art Gallery*. 1996–1999. <http://www.naturalchild.com/gallery/> *Global Children's Art Gallery* welcomes children's artwork from around the world from children ages one to twelve. Only drawings with family-friendly content are accepted.

Craig Roland. The @rtroom. *The @rt Gallery*. 1999. <http://www.arts.ufl.edu/art/rt_room/@rt_gallery.html> This Web site presents exhibitions of artwork created by kids from around the world. Directions for submitting work to the online gallery are included.

Model Online Exhibitions of Children's Artwork

Getty Education Institute on the Arts. The Getty Art Education Web Site: *ArtsEdNet. Kids Framing Kids: More Than Just a Pretty Picture*. 1997. <http://www.artsednet.getty.edu/ArtsEdNet/Exhibitions/Kids/overview.html> This online exhibit presents the work of elementary students, between five and eleven years old, who learned about photography through the four disciplines of art—art history, art criticism, aesthetics, and creating art. The exhibition was installed for the opening of the Getty Center in Los Angeles.

Getty Education Institute on the Arts. The Getty Art Education Web Site: *ArtsEdNet. Cognition and Creation*. <http://www.artsednet.getty.edu/ArtsEdNet/Exhibitions/Eisner/index.html> *Cognition and Creation* examines the cognitive processes used to create art and how these processes are exemplified in student artwork. Elliot Eisner, professor of education and art at Stanford University, devised the concept for the exhibition. This online exhibit provides a model for school art displays that link student learning in art to the stages of cognitive development, shows the use of a student exhibition as an advocacy tool to strengthen the case for arts education, and provides innovative ways to organize and display your students' artworks.

National Art Education Association. Electronic Media Interest Group and Emil Robert Tanay. *Heart in the Middle of the World: Art of Traumatized and Displaced Children*. 1995–1999. <http://www.cedarnet.org/emig/index.html> Exhibit and discussion of artwork by displaced and homeless children from the recent conflicts in Bosnia and Herzegovina. Dr. Emil Tanay, professor of art at the University of Zagreb, Croatia, developed the online exhibition.

Safe Art Materials and Classroom Practices

The Art & Creative Materials Institute, Inc. *Safety—What You Need to Know*. 1996. <http://www.creative-industries.com/acmi/safety.html> ACMI is a nonprofit association of manufacturers of art, craft, and other creative materials. Since 1940, ACMI has sponsored a certification program for children's art materials, certifying that these products are nontoxic and meet voluntary standards of quality and performance. The Web site lists all the art products that are certified as safe for children by ACMI. The site also provides information about art materials.

Office of Environmental Health Hazard Assessment. "Special Concerns Regarding Children in Kindergarten and Grades 1–6 (K–6)." *Guidelines for the Safe Use of Art and Craft Materials.* 1997. <http://www.oehha.ca.gov/art/ artguide.htm> This Web site, maintained by the state of California, provides a section devoted to the use of art and craft materials by children, including some that may have health risks. The site provides information and criteria for evaluation, selection, and use of art supplies. The site addresses other environmental problems associated with art classrooms.

CHAPTER 19

ASSESSING STUDENT PROGRESS AND PROGRAM EFFECTIVENESS

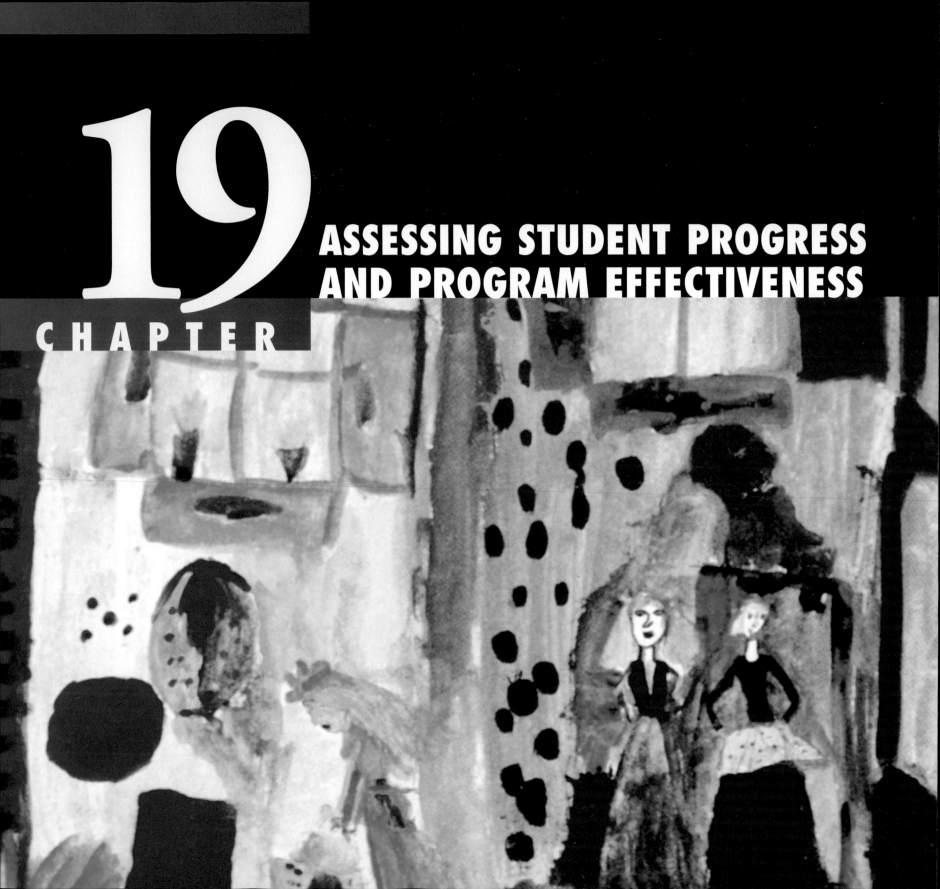

Authentic assessment is an idea whose time has clearly come. If authentic assessment becomes widespread, it will spawn more appropriate instructional emphases in our schools.[1]

—James Popham

Art teachers, like their colleagues across the curriculum, are asked to take full responsibility for evaluation and assessment. Art in today's schools is a subject for all students. Art can be studied, practiced, learned, and understood by all students as an essential part of their general education. Teachers are expected to develop expertise in assessment as part of their professional preparation. Their understanding of assessment in art education should be commensurate with their competencies in curriculum and instruction. Indeed, these three areas of teaching expertise must be fully integrated in practice.

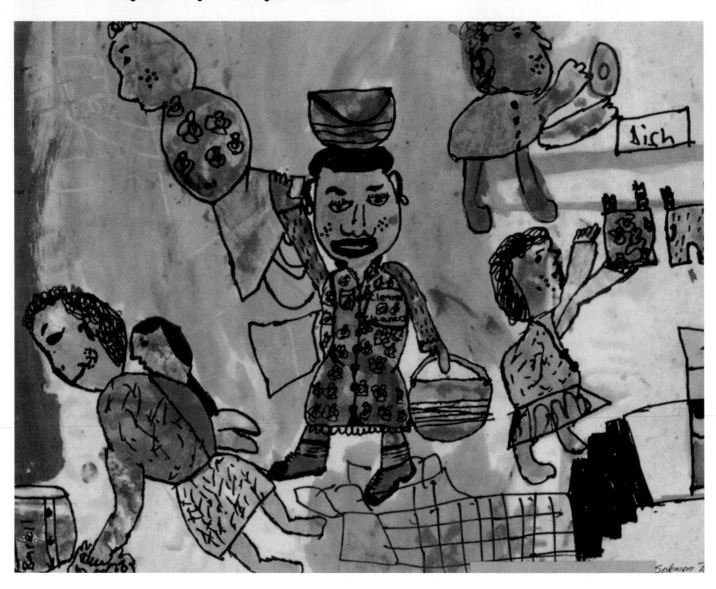

South Africa

The arts contribute unique perspectives within the field of educational assessment. By their very nature, the arts can be seen, heard, and viewed in their particular forms. In the visual arts, teachers have access not only to finished works by students, but also the record of their creation through such media as sketches, plans, notebooks, and portfolios, all part of the rich heritage of art. Art educators have at their command an array of authentic assessment strategies much more meaningful than the traditional paper-and-pencil tests so prevalent in schools.

As often as possible, assessments in art include actual performances in the forms of created artworks, essays and critical responses, interpretations and evaluations of works of art, and other authentic as opposed to surrogate tasks. Authentic assessments are, as often as possible, fully integrated with and consistent with the art curriculum and the instructional strategies employed by teachers.

The terms *evaluation* and *assessment* are often used interchangeably, especially in classrooms where evaluation usually means assessing students' progress in relation to curricular goals. Evaluation sometimes takes on a broader meaning associated with entire educational programs and all their components, from philosophical, social, and financial concerns to curriculum, instruction, and student achievement. Evaluation, in the broad sense, is the practice of placing value within educational programs. Briefly stated, "assessment is the method or process used for gathering information about people, programs, or objects for the purpose of making an evaluation. . . . Effective assessment techniques can improve classroom instruction, empower students, heighten student interest and motivation, and provide teachers with ongoing feedback on student progress."[2]

Although most art educators will probably agree that assessment is a necessary component for responsible education, it might be the least well-developed and most misunderstood part of art education. In this final chapter, we will discuss types of assessment, provide examples of devices and applications, and attempt to dispel some potential misunderstandings about assessment of art learning.

INFORMAL ASSESSMENT

We regularly make value judgments about many aspects of schooling, ranging from the quality of textbooks to the adequacy of school facilities or the behavior of individual students. Most assessment is accomplished informally. On entering the classroom, for example, the teacher notices the room temperature, the lighting, and the arrangement of furniture. The teacher assesses the situation and makes the necessary changes. As the students enter the room and the class period progresses, the teacher makes numerous quick assessments of the students, noting who is engaged in activity and who is not, and adjusts teaching strategies accordingly. The teacher speaks quietly with a student, moves on quickly to a restless group, demonstrates a technique, offers words of encouragement, chastises mildly, and so on, as each situation warrants—all the while noticing in what ways students are encountering difficulties in their work and formulating changes in the plans for tomorrow's activity.

FORMAL ASSESSMENT

Formal assessments are devised to gain important information for educational decision making, decisions ranging from assignment of student grades to program revisions to school policy changes. We will discuss a variety of means for con-

ducting formal assessments of pupil progress, including traditional tests and more authentic devices such as portfolios.

Verification of student learning is the reason for most formal assessment in schools, and since a report of student progress is usually required, this form of evaluation holds a high priority. The basis of appraisal of a pupil's progress in any area of learning often can be found in the objectives of that area. Well-stated objectives can reflect not only the specific contributions the subject has to offer but also the philosophical foundations and educational practices of the school system. An appraisal of the progress of any pupil involves a judgment of the efficacy of the school system in general and of the teacher's endeavors in particular.

Assessment and instruction are both guided by the educational goals and objectives of those who educate (see Chapter 1). Assessment must be made compatible with objectives, and results should be reported in ways meaningful to those who receive them.[3] Five basic questions can be asked about any system of evaluation:

- WHO will do the evaluation—teachers? pupils? some outside agency?
- WHAT is being evaluated—attitudes? curriculum content, such as skills, knowledge, or processes?
- WHO will be evaluated—elementary-school children? teachers? special students?
- WHAT is the range of the evaluation—pupil? class? entire school? art program?

And finally, perhaps the most difficult:

- WHAT is the purpose or function of the assessment?

Eisner states that evaluation in an art program can help the teacher to:

1. Diagnose
2. Revise curricula
3. Compare
4. Anticipate educational needs
5. Determine if objectives have been achieved[4]

For this discussion we refer to assessments conducted by teachers for their own students, classrooms, and curricula and not to the work of professionals. This discussion is intended to assist teachers with the practical problems of assessing both their own work and that of their students.

Concerns about Assessment in Art Education

The use of educational assessment distinguishes between what is traditional and what is contemporary in art education. Art educators in the past were concerned that formal assessment might discourage children from learning and progressing in their own creative production.[5] The evaluation process, of which assessment is a part, might place too much emphasis on children's art products and inhibit their expressions of personal feelings. These concerns have been expressed most prominently in relation to art programs that are nearly exclusively dedicated to children's work with art media.

Few educators would disagree with these concerns about assessment, which must always serve to improve education rather than detract from it. Assessment should not be arbitrary, nor should it discourage children from learning and progressing in their understanding of art. Overemphasis on children's art products should be avoided, and the processes of learning and creating are of utmost importance. Such devices as tests should not dominate the art curriculum, influencing teachers to teach for test results. Such negative aspects are not the inevitable results of educational assessment and are certainly not related to uses within a responsible, comprehensive art program. Assessment can be unobtrusive, interesting for students, and, in some instances, part of learning activities.

ASSESSMENT OF STUDENT PROGRESS IN ART

As with other school subjects, many factors influence the progress of students as they study art. Following are some of the questions that assessment might assist teachers to answer.

1. Are students enjoying a positive experience in class? Is the learning environment compatible with the goals for learning?

2. Are changes in the pace of learning needed? Is a shift in instructional strategy warranted? What about grouping of students versus individualized learning projects?

3. What are students learning? How does this relate to prior expectations for the class? How does this relate to prior performance by the students? And to students' own expectations?

4. How can the teacher become more effective? How can sound judgments about student progress be made?

5. How can the teacher communicate with students about their strong and weak points in art? How can the teacher communicate the accomplishments of students to other teachers, school administrators, and parents?

A Balanced Program of Assessment

Assessment conducted as the school term unfolds can be used for two purposes: first, as feedback about the art class and how things are progressing; and, second, as a basis for end-of-term decisions. Information gained for the teacher's ongoing educational decision making is known as *formative assessment*. Flexible teachers are ready to respond to information obtained while curriculum implementation is in progress and are willing to revise their instructional approaches or reteach areas of the curriculum that students did not understand.

Assessment of student learning that will assist teachers to reach summary statements about student accomplishments and the relative success of the class is known as *summative assessment*. At the conclusion of the school term, often some type of final assessment is conducted to certify student learning and to diagnose areas of the curriculum that might need extra emphasis in the future. This might include a wide range of assessment devices, including final examinations and personal interviews. Often, at this time, teachers are required to report on each student's success in accomplishing the goals and objectives of the curriculum by assigning a letter grade or by providing a more descriptive analysis of the student's work. The teacher can draw on all the information obtained during the school term as well as on postinstructional assessments to prepare this report.

A balanced plan of assessment will provide teachers with appropriate and useful information that will assist them in making sound decisions about individual students, the curriculum, and the overall art program.

Assessment of Children's Creative Work

The prospect of assessing the creative artwork of children is a concern to many teachers. Before discussing this topic, we offer several principles that we hope will make the teacher's task easier and more acceptable.

1. As in all areas of art learning, assessment should be closely related to instruction. This means that teachers can expect children to learn what is taught and that they should focus assessment on those skills and understandings that children have had a fair opportunity to learn. Assessment of student progress then becomes more a measure of the teacher's abilities to foster learning than a means to distinguish students' strengths and weaknesses.

2. We seldom attempt to assess students' creativity or expressiveness. Rather, assessment is focused on what students have learned as a result of instruction. Students' creative and expressive efforts should always be encouraged, whether or not we are able to measure their progress.

3. Students who do not exhibit great natural ability in making art still will be able to succeed because of the diversity of a comprehensive art program. Students who appear to have natural abilities for making art will be rewarded for their efforts but will need to make progress in the other areas of learning as well.

4. Part of instruction in art making deals with clear-cut skills, such as knowledge of color theory resulting in abilities to mix the hues, change color value and intensity, and identify cool and warm hues. Children can learn to apply technical skills and principles associated with any art medium.

When the art program focuses on the learning of art knowledge and skills, students soon realize that art can be taught and can be learned, just as in other subjects in school. If children can learn and practice, they can make progress toward clearly defined, understandable goals. When finished art products reflect the intended learning, the reasons for their excellence can be pointed out, discussed, and related to classroom instruction. As with other subjects in the curriculum, students in art can begin with whatever aptitude is given and can progress at faster or slower rates according to their individual motivation and application. The notion that art is only for the few "talented" stars will soon be dispelled, and the idea that art learning is for everyone will be reinforced.

Many assessment problems in the area of art production are alleviated when teachers realize they have different instructional purposes at different times and that different assessment procedures are appropriate according to the specific instructional purpose. For example, when instructional goals call for the learning of specific production skills, assessment can be equally specific. Teachers can readily learn if students are able to overlap objects to represent space, make a graded watercolor wash, or construct a coil clay pot that will hold water. Students' progress in such skills can be assessed, students and teachers can discuss results, and students can learn how to improve.

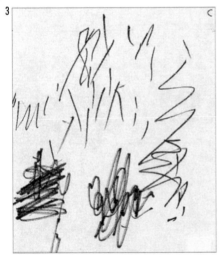
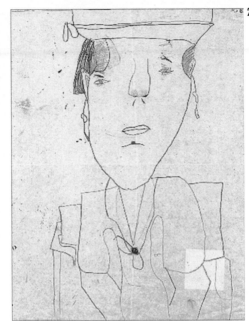
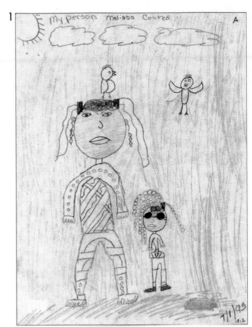
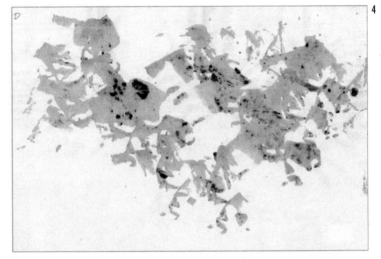

(1) In "My Person," twelve-year-old Melissa draws the human figure from memory. The results indicate that Melissa has received little if any instruction in drawing from observation. (2) Contour Line Method, is the result of one period's instruction using the contour line method discussed in Chapter 6. The advancement in handling, particularly in the neck and shoulders, can provide one clear basis for evaluation, but the assessment problems which exist in a 30-second response to electronic music (3) and the drawing (4) based upon the blot drawings used by the eighteenth-century artist Alexander Cozens presents a different set of problems. (See Cozens' *A New Method of Assisting the Invention of Drawing Original Compositions of Landscapes.*) Da Vinci searched for associations in cloud formations and Cozens studied the accidental effects that occurred when inked wads of paper were pressed onto a surface. Indeed, there is a whole history of artists generating ideas from haphazard events. The question is, how shall one evaluate students who have been asked to emulate such practice? Should accidents be evaluated, and if they can't be, does this invalidate activities based upon the use of chance and randomness?

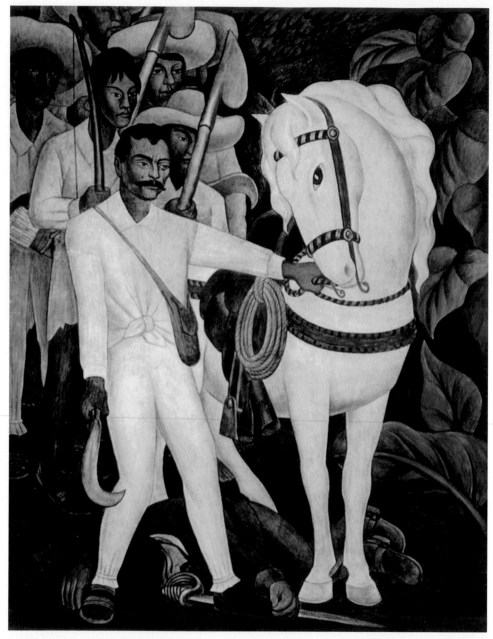

Diego Rivera, *Agrarian Leader Zapata*, 1931. Teachers can gain insight into children's learned abilities to describe, analyze, and interpret artworks through their spoken and written comments. As children view this fresco, how do they explain the fallen man, his drawn sword, and the beautifully appointed, but riderless, white horse? How do they interpret the tool in the central figure's hand, his placement in front of the fallen figure, and his hold of the horse's rein? From their study of art history, what do children know about the white clothing of the men in the picture, their tools, hats, and the agricultural setting suggested on the right side of the painting? Who are these men and what is happening? What is the social theme of the painting? What do children know about Rivera, events in Mexico that he depicted, and the fresco process? (Collection, The Museum of Modern Art, New York. Abby Aldrich Rockefeller) © McRay Magleby.

Not all learning in art falls into this clear-cut relationship between instruction and assessment, however, and time should be maintained for art activities with no specified outcomes other than student participation in the process. For example, students who are given access to water-soluble printing inks, brayers, and a container of various objects that can be used to print are asked to explore the possibilities of the medium. The educational expectation is that the children will learn individually and from one another some of the properties and possibilities of the medium. The appropriate educational assessment would be to note students' participation, the level of serious engagement, the sharing of discoveries, and the quality of the learning environment in terms of noise, activity, and attention to the task.

It would be inappropriate to assess this art activity by testing the children on specific information or skills that might have been discovered by some but that were not presented to all. It would be inappropriate to assess this activity by collecting the results of their experimentation and judging them for aesthetic quality.

Everyone Needs to Care, A Drawing Lesson

Children in second grade are shown paintings by Cassatt, Renoir, and Vasilieff, all on the theme of persons caring for pets. After discussing the artists and analyzing content of the paintings, the children are asked to make a drawing of themselves with a pet or object for which they care, such as a doll or toy. The teacher intends that students will "make a connection between their own feelings for something and similar feelings that can be found expressed in works of art." Assessment is focused on the extent to which pupils are able to:

a. recognize the theme of caring in paintings;

b. verbalize connections with their feelings and those expressed in the paintings; and

c. make a drawing that indicates the theme of caring.

Assessment devices in this lesson included class and small group discussions and teacher's observation of each child's drawing.[6]

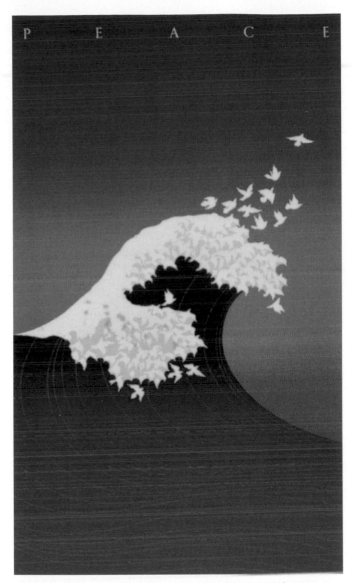

American graphic artist McRay Magleby made significant changes in Hokusai's *Great Wave* to create a different message in his *Wave of Peace*, 1985, serigraph poster, 26 in. × 40 in. © McRay Magleby.

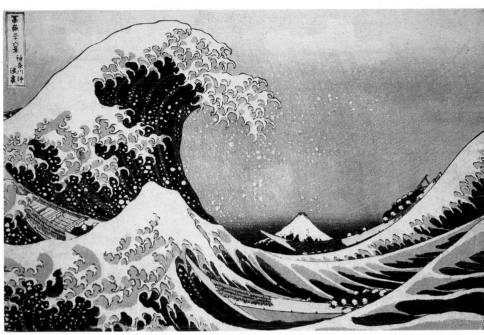

Katsushika Hokusai, *The Great Wave*, from *Thirty-Six Views of Mt. Fuji*, Tokugawa period, c. 1823–1829. Woodblock print, 14 ¾" wide. Museum of Fine Arts, Boston, Spaulding Collection.

This is one of the few traditional Japanese artworks that has become so well known in the United States that it can be used as a recognizable source in the works of other artists.

comprehensive art program will include a variety of instructional purposes and various assessment devices. When students are assessed according to their participation, their successful completion of specific tasks, and the quality of their completed artwork, the teacher has a valid basis for assigning grades as well as for diagnosis and suggestions for improvement.

Assessment of Learning in Art Criticism

As we discussed in Chapter 12, students in a balanced art program will view many artworks, respond to them in depth, and discuss and write about them. They will learn approaches to art criticism, such as the phased approach of description, analysis, interpretation, and informed preference. Assessment within some parts of the critical domain of art learning is obvious. For example, teachers can determine when students might be able to apply such concepts as visual balance, distortion, and emphasis in their descriptions and analyses of artworks. Teachers can note students' progress in analysis of artworks and their understanding of what they are doing and why. Teachers can assess students' progress in developing plausible interpretations of particular

Some instructional activities will foster individual expression, experimentation, and exploration; others will focus on precise technical skills; and still others will call for students to apply art concepts and skills to produce finished works appropriate to their age level and reflective of the art instruction that has taken place up to that time. *A*

The Great Wave, An Art Criticism Activity

This assessment form is part of a lesson for upper elementary students in which they learn to use formal analysis as a means to interpret content in paintings. They are asked to make detailed comparisons of two paintings, one a modern revision of the earlier work. This device can provide the teacher with evidence of each pupil's understanding of formal analysis and ability to interpret meaning in two contrasting works. At the same time, this is a learning activity for students.[7]

The Great Wave

Compare Hokusai's The Great Wave *and Magleby's* Wave of Peace. *Use the back of this sheet for the last answer and if you need more room for the others.*

The Great Wave by Hokusai	*Wave of Peace* by Magleby
1. Color:	Color:
sky	sky
water	water
whitecaps	whitecaps
other color	other color
2. Shape of wave:	Shape of wave:
3. Use of line:	Use of line:
4. Use of texture:	Use of texture:
5. Format:	Format:

6. List ways in which Magleby simplified Hokusai's picture.

7. Do the two artworks express the same feeling or idea? If not, how are they different?

8. Which artwork is more interesting to you? Why?

artworks and their abilities to support them with good reasons. Teachers can ask if the children are able to see and understand how artists control and manipulate their media to achieve the desired effects and meanings. In all instances, the levels of instruction and the means of assessment must be suited to the age levels and abilities of the children.

Finding ways to assess children's critical understandings and skills can challenge the teacher's ingenuity. Teachers strive to ask the most meaningful questions about students' progress and devise means to gather information in response to these questions. Teachers can collect evidence of children's understandings about purposes and functions of art. They can seek to learn more about their students' knowledge of and recognition of religious, political, and social themes in art, such as in Michelangelo's *Pietà*, Rivera's *Agrarian Leader Zapata*, James Flagg's classic recruiting poster "*I Want You*," Maya Lin's *Vietnam Veterans Memorial*, and Judy Chicago's *The Dinner Party*. Teachers will use various methods to assess learning activities that integrate content from the art disciplines.

Teachers also need to attend to some larger questions about children's progress. Is the art program assisting students to respond more fully to works of art and to derive satisfaction in the process? What evidence can the teacher find to inform this question? What evidence can the teacher find that students are developing positive attitudes toward art? Is instruction leading the children to richer and deeper encounters with art and to a broader and deeper understanding of the purposes and functions of art in the lives of human beings? Do the children use valid reasons to inform their art preferences? Do the children seem to enjoy these activities? Several of the methods for assessment discussed in this chapter might assist teachers to answer such questions.

Assessment of Learning in Art History

Art historical learning includes a broad range of topics. Indeed, it would be possible to study much of the history of the world simply through the study of art history. The amount of information and the level of detail in which it is available is nearly overwhelming, making selection of curriculum content a major task.

As noted in Chapter 13, much teaching in art history can be done in a visual rather than in a verbal mode, with visual displays of the artworks and styles of art from various eras and cultures. Topics from art history can be related directly to the interests of children, because the great themes of human experience are available in visual form in the art of the past and present. Reproductions, pictures, slides, videos, magazines, and books about art are readily available.

Assessment methods can be tailored to complement the teacher's instructional approaches. If instruction is intended to assist children to recognize the characteristics of Chinese art, then the assessment should be as general as the instructional goal. For example, children might be shown a series of slides of artworks from various cultures and asked to designate which works are from China. If the children are unable to do this, perhaps the instruction needs to be revised. When instruction in art history is precise in terms of specific information to be learned by students, then traditional objective tests might be appropriate, including identification of specific artworks by artist or style, period or country. When art history is taught to assist children to understand and appreciate the contributions of other cultures and art from different times, assessment must be linked to those purposes. Attitude and preference measures are often as useful in this domain as objective measures.

Assessment of Students' Progress in Aesthetics

A balanced art program includes content derived from the discipline of aesthetics, or philosophy of art.[8] Aestheticians deal with many interesting questions that are raised whenever people begin to talk about art. Even young children ask such questions as, "Why is this object art and that object is not art?" Fundamental conceptions of art, beauty, quality in art, and judgments about art are examined by aestheticians.

Aesthetics questions are often integrated within learning activities that involve other art disciplines. Assessment of student achievement in the domain of aesthetics will depend, as always, on instructional goals and strategies. Some assessment strategies will focus on the use of language by children as they read, discuss, and write about the basic questions identified with aesthetics. They will be asked to contemplate the nature of art and to justify their conclusions at levels

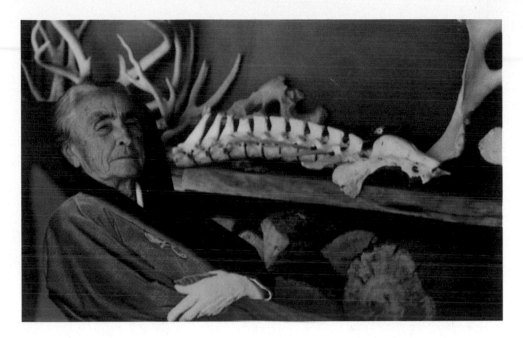

Georgia O'Keeffe at Ninety, photo by Malcolm Varon, New York, N.Y. © 1985, 2000. Who is this person? What is her place in art history? Why is she portrayed with bleached animal bones? Evaluation of cultural and historical learning goes far beyond names, dates, and titles. Teachers can learn from their students how well they understand the roles of artists, how artworks are regarded by society and by art experts, and what artists have contributed to the world through their work. Study of the life of Georgia O'Keeffe will lead children from the bustle of her early career in New York City and her association with other, now famous, artists to her secluded and productive life in New Mexico.

appropriate for their ages. Children in middle grades, as an example, should be able to demonstrate the difference between art and nature by comparing a photograph of a tree to a painting of a tree and an actual tree. Upper-grade students might be asked to give three reasons for supporting or rejecting a philosophical position (e.g., "The purpose of art is to create works of beauty").

METHODS FOR ASSESSMENT OF STUDENT PROGRESS IN ART

Assessment is a central topic in the discourse of general education reform at the turn of the century. A number of highly visible initiatives have come forward, including the president's education agenda, *Goals 2000: Educate America* (which has received billions of dollars of federal funding through the year 2000), the *National Standards for Arts Education,* national professional teaching standards (NBPTS) for art, the 1997 report of the National Assessment of Educational Progress in the Arts, and publication

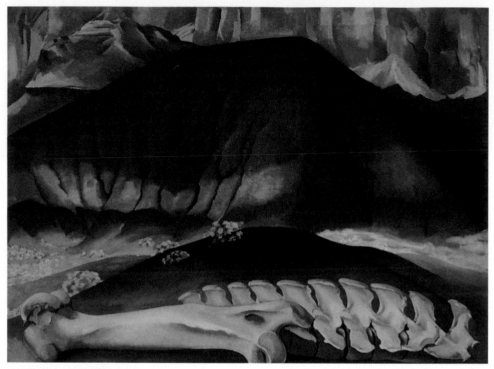

Georgia O'Keeffe, *Red Hills and Bones*, 1941. Oil on canvas. Philadelphia Museum of Art, The Alfred Stieglitz Collection. Historical background about the life of artist Georgia O'Keeffe can help students understand this painting. They can associate the painting of bleached animal bones and the barren red earth with the photograph of the artist. Such learning and associations can be applied in students' own art production as they select subjects or techniques suggested by the study of an artist's life and works. As an evaluation device, teachers might assign students to make a painting in homage to a particular artist, displaying their knowledge and understanding of the artist and her or his works.

Didactic Display, Art History Content

Fifth-grade students participated in a series of art lessons on the painting traditions of still life, landscape, and figure during which they studied works by various artists from several cultures. They also created their own paintings on each topic. This final assessment is a display activity in the school hallway, with the students assigned to convey what they learned visually to the rest of the school. To do this, students had to:

a. select reproductions of paintings exemplifying the concepts of still life, landscape, and figure;

b. make labels denoting these concepts as well as basic information such as title, artist, medium, date, size, and a brief statement about each work;

c. select and mount examples of their own paintings, also according to categories with labels and statements by each student artist;

d. mount the exhibition with the teacher's (and volunteer parents') assistance.

Assessment involves observation of the display itself and how well it meets the assignment. Cooperation, quality of writing, and sense of accomplishment and pride exhibited by students are also evaluated.

of NAEA's *Standards for Art Teacher Preparation*.[9] All these publications and projects view educational assessment as an integral component of education reform. Leaders in art education have been energetically involved in these initiatives, which will affect the content and quality of education on a large scale.

The most prominent means, traditionally, for conducting assessments has been in the form of standardized tests with multiple-choice and true-or-false items. It is the history of paper-and-pencil testing, which many view as too narrow and too readily biased, that has motivated educators to develop alternative forms of assessment. The term *alternative assessment* is often used synonymously with *authentic assessment* and *performance assessment*. Interest in alternative assessment crosses subject content boundaries, and discussions often focus on such items as exhibits, experiments, journals, and portfolios. Alternative assessments require students to generate rather than to choose a response and to "actively accomplish complex and significant tasks, while bringing to bear prior knowledge, recent

learning, and relevant skills to solve realistic or authentic problems."[10] Alternative, authentic, or performance assessments of student learning include:

1. Evaluating students on tasks that approximate disciplined inquiry

2. Considering knowledge and skills holistically rather than in fragmented parts

3. Valuing student achievement in and of itself and apart from whether it is being assessed

4. Attending to both processes and products of teaching and learning

5. Educating students to assess their own achievement in consort with assessments of others

6. Expecting students to present and defend their work orally and publicly[11]

These criteria for alternative assessment are relevant for assessment in art education. In fact, the concept of portfolios of student work collected over time has a long history in the visual arts and is now being recognized within other disciplines (see the section "Portfolio" on p. 409).

In his national study of school programs, Goodlad found that art teachers employ a greater variety of teaching methods in their classrooms than their colleagues who teach other subjects.[12] The same comparison might hold for methods of evaluation, because art, unlike most other school subjects, involves much visual as well as verbal content and includes the creative production of students. Following are some examples of traditional and alternative strategies that might be used in assessment of a comprehensive art program.

Observation

The task is for the students in the class to explore the properties of clay in preparation for learning some of the traditional forming techniques. The teacher observes that most of the students are engrossed in the task and seem to be experimenting with the clay: pinching, rolling, stamping, and marking the clay. Several students appear reticent and seem to need the teacher's attention and encouragement

Interview

The teacher is interested to learn why a boy in the class consistently has trouble with drawing. The teacher talks to the boy privately in a corner of the room, trying to learn more about the apparent problem. Or the teacher wishes to learn more about what the students know about how the works of art are made, how artists work, and how they are educated.[13] The teacher talks with groups of five or six students, showing them a reproduction of a painting and asking them pertinent questions.

Discussion

The teacher wishes to know more about the students' responses to art and their interpretations of what is acceptable as art. The teacher leads a class discussion on a series of reproductions of paintings he or she shows to the students. Each painting shown is more abstract than the previous one.

Performance

The teacher distributes tempera paints in the primary hues, black, and white to the children, along with the necessary brush and water. After distributing a sheet of paper divided into six rectangles, the teacher asks the children to mix and paint in the respective spaces orange, green, violet, yellow-green, brown, and light blue. Or the teacher gives each child a grease pencil and a reproduction of a still-life painting in a clear plastic envelope. The students are asked to circle the main centers of interest and to place a plus sign on the positive spaces and a minus sign on the negative spaces.

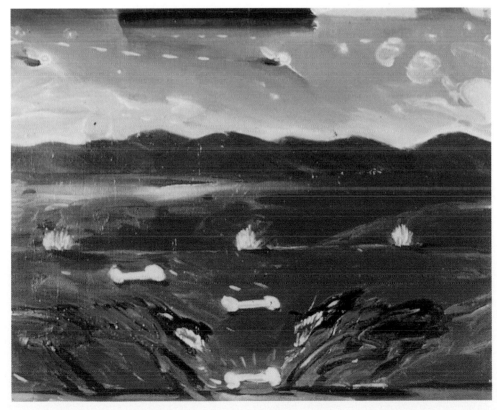

Carlos Almarez, *Greed,* 1982. What is the theme of this painting? How can you support your interpretation? How would you characterize the stance of the two animals? What feelings does the artist arouse through his choice of colors? Describe the colors in terms of hue, value, intensity, and relationship. How does this painting compare with Georgia O'Keeffe's painting of red hills and animal bones? How does the mood of Almarez's painting compare with the mood of O'Keeffe's? Which do you prefer, and why? Teachers can formulate such questions as these and engage children in response to them through various evaluation devices, such as questionnaires, discussions, essays, interviews, and creative art production. (Collection of John and Lynne Pleshette)

I'm on Video, A Lesson on Self-Portrait

The lesson is on the concept of self-portrait in art. Students view many examples from traditional and contemporary art and make a self-portrait collage using pictures, symbols, and images of any kind that would best express their looks, preferences, or personality. The finished collages are displayed and the teacher shows a videotape featuring each student outside of school in a characteristic setting or activity (the videotape is made with the cooperation of parents and other students).

As a peer assessment on a single criterion, the class is asked to match the student depicted in each video segment with his or her self-portrait, noting the relative effectiveness of each collage as a self-portrait, and giving reasons for their statements.

Checklist

As the teacher leads discussions of artworks from time to time in the classroom, he or she marks the class roster by the names of those students who participate. The teacher encourages and invites responses from those who have not participated. In another example, the teacher keeps a list of the several drawing exercises for the drawing unit and checks off accordingly as each student completes the exercise satisfactorily.

Questionnaire

The teacher administers a questionnaire that assesses student learning about architectural styles from various cultures and about the reasons for the development of each style. Or students are required to answer a questionnaire about the details of the copper enameling process. Each student must score 100 percent correct on the technical questionnaire, which includes items on hazards and safety precautions, in order to begin work with actual materials.

Test

The teacher administers a multiple-choice and short-answer objective test with questions from several units of study completed during the school term, including items in the aesthetic, critical, historical, and productive domains of art learning.

Essay

The teacher asks students to write about a sculpture, considering the appropriate level of writing ability for the grade level. Students are to use the skills of art criticism that they have practiced several times in class as a large group and in small discussion groups.

Visual Identification

Students are shown slides of artworks by artists they have studied in class. They are asked to identify the work by artist, by style, or according to other categories they have practiced in class.

Attitude Measurement

The teacher is interested to know how students are responding to the new approach to art education that includes talking and writing about art as well as making art objects. In addition to talking to individual students and holding discussions with the entire class, the teacher develops and administers a questionnaire that asks for students' feelings about specific learning activities that have been completed.

Portfolio

Students' artwork, exercises, written assignments, notes, class handouts—virtually all of what they have produced as they study art—are saved in a folder. Periodically, the teacher reviews this work with each student individually and discusses the student's learning, progress, and aspirations in art.

Judgment of Student Work

When art programs are studio-centered, many teachers assume that the basis for evaluation and grading is the teacher's judgment of the quality of students' art products. Art teachers are aware of the biases and inconsistencies likely to occur as they attempt to render judgments, and they might prefer to avoid evaluation. The making of judgments about art, however, is one of the major aspects of art criticism, which is integral to a balanced art program.

Art teachers are able to make judgments of aesthetic quality with respect to their students' artworks in appropriate contexts. Teachers who have taught specific art skills, principles, and understandings, and who have implemented a balanced program of assessment using a variety of evaluation tools will gain confidence in making judgments of students' artworks. As an example, the curriculum has taken students through a series of learning activities focusing on the use of basic color theory, composition, and basic drawing skills. The completed paintings are judged by the teacher according to aesthetic criteria and evidence that students applied the concepts they studied.

Standardized Art Tests

Techniques for assessment range from the most formal test to the most informal conversation with a child. A number of standardized art tests are available, dating back to the 1920s and 1930s, and include the Meier-Seashore *Art Judgment Test,* the *McAdory Art Test,* and the *Bryan-Schwamm Test.* Although standardized art tests are interesting and provocative, often they are not very reliable and do not apply to the specific needs of classroom situations.[14]

Since the heyday of standardized testing several decades ago, the trend in testing for art ability has been toward specific ends—that is, tests have been designed by teachers or research workers to arrive at limited kinds of information. Tests may be designed for a number of purposes, but in all cases they represent a judgment of the adequacy of behavior as compared to a set of educational objectives. Any test is a reflection of what a teacher considers important in a student's behavior, studio processes, skills, and knowledge about art. The test may be formal or informal, and it may just as easily precede instruction in the form of a diagnostic device as it may follow the instructional period to measure a student's

Video and Advertising, A Unit on Graphic Design

The unit is on graphic design as advertising in magazines and on television. During the unit, children create their own design for a product and make an illustration for a story. To help students recognize the pervasiveness of advertising and begin to make judgments of quality and motive, the teacher asks them to watch a thirty-minute television program she has taped. They are to take notes on uses of graphic design for the television program and in the commercials. The teacher assesses students' abilities to note lettering, layout, illustrations, animation, and computer graphics as they observe the videotape.

As a follow-up or alternative to this assessment, the teacher hands out a collection of popular magazines and asks each student to select what he or she considers a high-quality example of graphic design, package design, or illustration. Students are to cut out the image, paste it on a sheet of paper, and write a paragraph about how the image was created and about their reasons for selecting it as a good example. The teacher is able to assess students' understandings of graphic design and their abilities to make and support judgments of quality.

gain. In any case, the test is but one technique among many to gauge the kind and quality of change in the student.

Formal Tests Devised by the Teacher

In addition to the standardized tests devised by experts, tests are composed by the classroom teacher. Such tests often can be useful, provided the teacher understands their significance. Sometimes the teacher may wish to use a test (usually cognitive) to discover whether or not the pupils have grasped some part of the art program. For example, it may be helpful to present a few questions based on the pupils' knowledge of a specific medium, of facts surrounding an artist's life, or of techniques in using color.

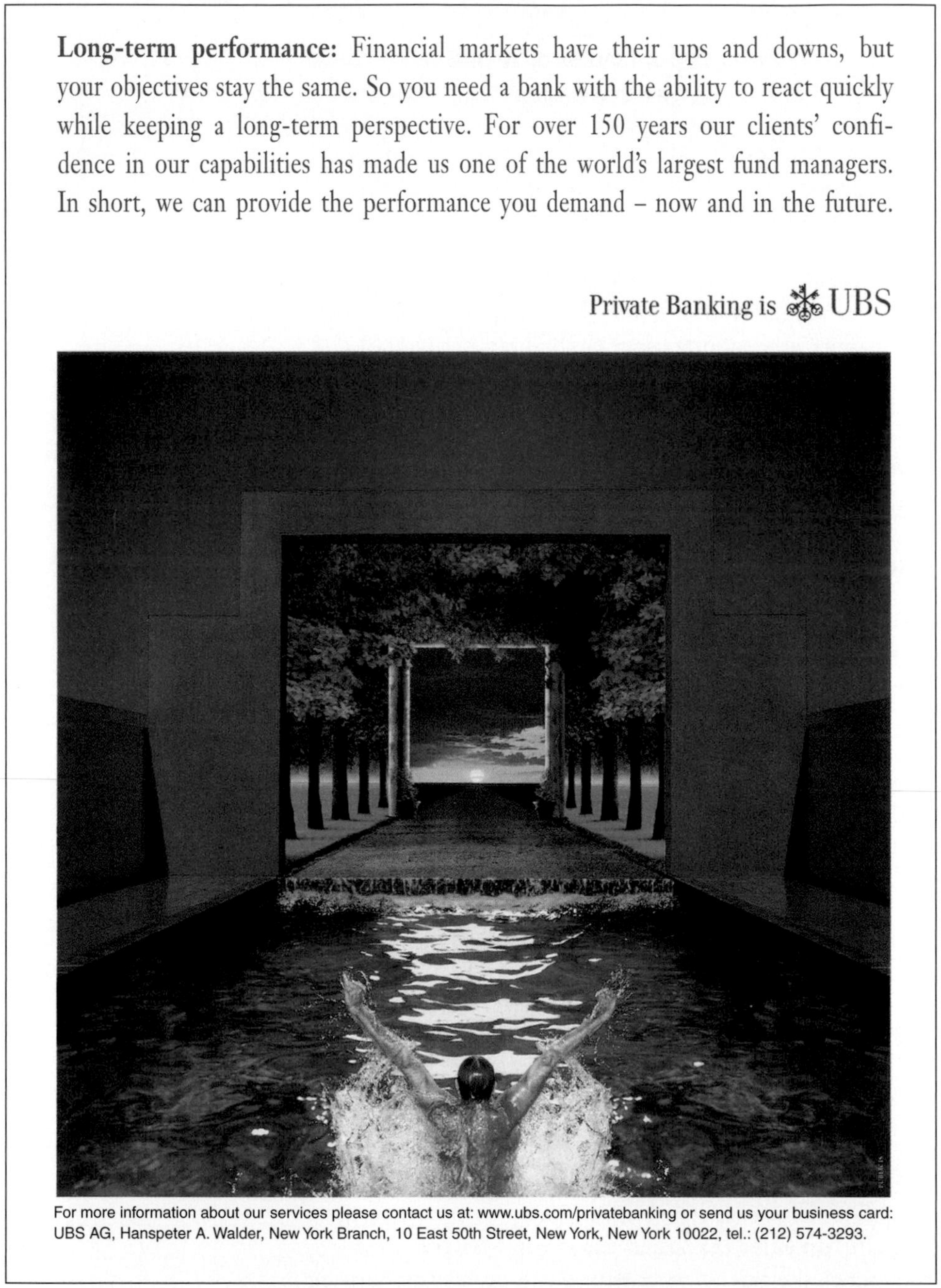

Long-term performance: Financial markets have their ups and downs, but your objectives stay the same. So you need a bank with the ability to react quickly while keeping a long-term perspective. For over 150 years our clients' confidence in our capabilities has made us one of the world's largest fund managers. In short, we can provide the performance you demand – now and in the future.
Private Banking is UBS
For more information about our services please contact us at: www.ubs.com/privatebanking or send us your business card:
UBS AG, Hanspeter A. Walder, New York Branch, 10 East 50th Street, New York, New York 10022, tel.: (212) 574-3293.

Ad from *The New Yorker* (no title), advertisement for UBS. Courtesy UBS, New York, N.Y.

Many ideas, conceived on the fine art level, are eventually appropriated by graphic designers. A postmodern sensibility in this advertisement can be seen in its use of ambiguous relationships among objects—a swimmer, recessive layers of space, and a sunset. Viewers ask, "What does this have to do with banking?" The advertiser assumes that any viewer who asks such a question has a better chance of remembering the product (a banking service) than someone who glances at the ad and turns the page.

The following completion-type problem could be used to test knowledge of color mixing:

Fill in the blanks:

1. To obtain a *shade* of red tempera paint, add ______.
2. To obtain a *tint* of red watercolor, add ______.
3. To turn *blue* to gray, add ______.
4. To turn *green* into gray, add ______.

An essay-type answer might be obtained from the following:

Describe two methods of mixing tempera paint to obtain gray.

Identification and multiple-choice tests are useful for younger children, because they do not require written answers of any kind. For example, one item could be the following:

Which pigment, when added to red tempera paint, will result in a *shade* of red?

a. green
b. white
c. black

Another recognition category might be based on slides and reproductions. After being shown a Rouault and a Rembrandt, a child may be asked the following items:

Art forms that had great influence on Rouault are

a. impressionist paintings
b. stained-glass windows
c. sculptures

Which of the following methods did Rembrandt use to achieve his effects?

a. chiaroscuro
b. impasto
c. glazes
d. all the above

It should be noted that the easiest test items to compose are often technical questions that tend to be trivial compared with the goals of developing personal expressiveness and artistic creativity. The most significant educational objectives are often the most complex and the most difficult to evaluate appropriately. Teachers can develop their own creative strategies for assessment that meet the unique needs and requirements of their students, the art curriculum, and the school setting. For example, Beattie lists fifty-nine assessment strategies for art education.[15]

Informal Assessments

The Anecdotal Method

Another assessment device, known as the *anecdotal method,* is also valuable. With this method the teacher periodically jots down observations about each child, based on the questions in the three categories of criteria. A cumulative record of such specific reactions may become a reliable index of a pupil's progress. It at least furnishes the teacher and the pupil with some concrete evidence of strong and weak points in the pupil's art learning conduct.

As an example, opposite some of the items of a performance checklist, the following remarks might be set down for a six-year-old child in first grade:

The Student:	Comments:
1. Was able to use the concepts of line, shape, and texture in describing a painting by Mary Cassatt.	"Seemed to be very interested in looking at the painting. Good attention span."
2. Participated in class discussions of art reproductions.	"Indicated a special interest in African masks. Made very perceptive remarks about the feeling qualities of the masks. Referred to one of the library books on African art."
3. Participated in group activity of sorting art postcards according to warm and cool colors and primary colors.	"Had some difficulties with sharing and cooperating in group activities. Needs special help to work with group."
4. Completed line drawings done in response to Japanese print and Pollock painting.	"Was not clear about purpose for this activity at first. Was pleased when the drawings were displayed and discussed."

The teacher also might consider commenting from time to time after periodic examination of portfolios. A checklist might be used as a guide in writing these comments but need not be referred to item by item. Such records give general, overall impressions of a large body of work. The following are examples of notes about children that a teacher might write for a personal file.

John A. (6 years, grade 1) John uses a variety of personal experiences in his pictures, and he is certainly getting along well lately in trying to develop symbols of houses. It is strange, however, how his work seemed to deteriorate last week. He works hard, though, and participates well in a group.

Roberto L. (11 years, grade 6) He shows himself to be a sensitive child, and his writing about several sculptures from the museum field trip reflects his feelings. He seems to be fascinated by seeing actual sculptures and especially enjoys the painted wood sculptures of Louise Nevelson. His handwriting is improving but sometimes is barely legible. His art vocabulary is excellent for his age group.

Betty McM. (10 years, grade 5) Betty continues to be careless and untidy; her paints are in a mess, her drawings all thumb marks, her brushes unwashed. As stage manager of our play, however, she worked well. She seems to be more at home with sculpture than she is in drawing and painting. Her last sculpture in clay was quite vigorous. She likes to explore new materials and last week brought to school some wood for carving.

The data derived from checklists and other notations will greatly assist the teacher in appraising a pupil's progress, but it is necessary also to keep a file of the child's actual art production for periodic study and comparison with the written notations. Usually lack of space prevents the teacher from keeping any but the flatwork.

These methods of assessment allow the teacher to summarize the child's progress in only the most general of terms. Once made, however, such a summary will prove valuable to the teacher in making progress reports to parents and others interested in the child's welfare.

Tools for Assessment of Student Progress in Art

Following are some examples of assessment tools that reflect the methods discussed in the preceding section.

This type of schedule can be used by teachers with middle-grade children. The teacher conducts the interview on a recent project, uses the schedule for notes as appropriate, and keeps the schedule for future reference as the term progresses.

Sample Interview Schedule

Student _____ **Grade level** _____

	Yes	No	Comments
1. Did you know what you wanted to do before you began working? What was it?	_____	_____	
2. Did you change your way of thinking while you were working? Why?	_____	_____	
3. When things went right, did you know why?	_____	_____	
4. When things went wrong, did you know why?	_____	_____	
5. Did you discover anything unusual or special while you were working?	_____	_____	
6. Did you solve your problem/theme satisfactorily?	_____	_____	
7. Is there a part you would like to change?	_____	_____	
8. Did you enjoy working on this piece even if you did not solve all your problems?	_____	_____	
9. Would you like to do something like this again? Why?	_____	_____	
10. Now that you are finished, are you pleased about what you have accomplished? Why?	_____	_____	

SOURCE: This assessment device was developed by Donna Kay Beattie, Brigham Young University.

This is an example of a rating scale for art production focused on specific criteria of performance taught as part of the teacher's instruction.

Stipple Drawings
Sample Rating Scale

Student_____ Date_____

DIRECTIONS: Listed below are assessment criteria related to performance in art production (studio activities). Under each are the numbers 1 to 5, which stand for the following:

1. In this respect, the performance ranks *below* most of the performances you have known.

2. In this respect, the performance is *only fair* in comparison with other performances you have known.

3. In this respect, the performance is *competent and compares well with the average* performances you have known.

4. In this respect, the performance is *well above the average* of performances you have known.

5. In this respect, the performance is one of the *most outstanding* performances you have known.

Rate the quality of the performance by circling the number that indicates the category which best describes your judgment on each item.

ARTISTIC ABILITY

1. The pupil's technical skill in rendering strong contrasts in value (deep blacks and white highlights).

      1   2   3   4   5

2. The pupil's technical skill in handling gradation or chiaroscuro in the stipple technique.

      1   2   3   4   5

3. The pupil's technical skill in accurately rendering the subject matter.

      1   2   3   4   5

4. The pupil's technical skill in handling the medium of stipple.

      1   2   3   4   5

5. The pupil's skill in creatively interpreting the theme.

      1   2   3   4   5

SOURCE: This assessment device was developed by Donna Kay Beattie, Brigham Young University.

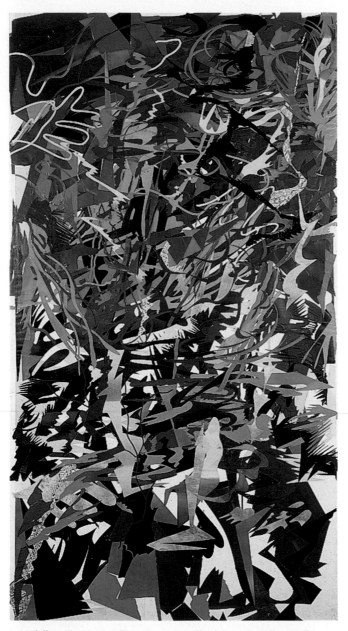

Judy Pfaff, *Voodoo*, 1982. Collage, 98" × 60". Albright-Knox Art Gallery, Buffalo, N.Y., Edmund Hayes Fund, 1982.

The mood, action, or feeling of a nonobjective work of art, such as this large piece by contemporary artist Judy Pfaff, can be discussed and interpreted by children who have learned fundamentals of formal analysis.

Before doing this worksheet, students discussed many artworks and attempted to find words that described their content or feeling. The teacher showed a slide of the large, very bright, nonobjective collage by Judy Pfaff and asked students to respond on this form.

Voodoo by Judy Pfaff

Study *Voodoo* by Judy Pfaff. Circle the words that you think describe the collage.

soft	hard	curved	straight
jagged	blurred	angular	smooth
rough	thin	thick	blended
active	horizontal	dead	rising
drooping	intertwined	friendly	alive
bright	dull	dark	light
layered	confused	organized	jittery
calm	nervous	simple	restful

Write additional words that you think describe the artwork.

What do you think you would feel if you were standing in front of the actual work, which is about 8 feet high and 5 feet wide?

Based on the words you circled and wrote, what mood, idea, or feeling do you think is conveyed by this work?

This worksheet can be used with small cooperative-learning groups or as an individual response. Its content refers to a particular painting by Winslow Homer, *The Fog Warning,* that students discussed in class. It also refers to a critic's written interpretation of the painting, which was given to each student and discussed in class. Students respond not only to the painting but also to the critic's writing about the painting.

The Fog Warning Worksheet

Read Henry Adams's commentary about Homer's painting and answer the following questions, providing reasons and explanations.

1. How does Homer direct our attention to the tiny sailing ship in the distance? [fisherman's gaze, tail of fish points, whitecap points]

2. Why did Homer show the man holding the oars out of the water?

3. How does the viewer know the fog is moving from right to left?

4. Why does Adams think the rower is in danger? What are the signs of danger? [fog advancing, ship moving away, rower misdirected, big waves]

5. In what ways could the rower's experience be like our everyday lives? [we lose sight of goals, become disoriented, feel as if our troubles are like a fog bank, need to realign our course, need to work hard to reach a goal]

6. Do you think Adams's interpretation of the painting makes good sense? Why or why not? Explain.

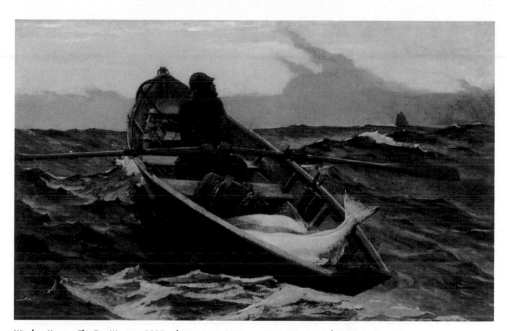

Winslow Homer, *The Fog Warning,* 1885, oil on canvas, 30 in. × 48 in. (Museum of Fine Arts, Boston)

Historical knowledge and the writing of critics can assist teachers and children to interpret meaning in works of art. This work can be interpreted as a metaphor for the human struggle with nature and the task of facing adversity against great odds.

This student worksheet was developed for upper-elementary students who studied the concept of metaphor in art, as distinct from literal representation. For example, what symbols and metaphors can students discover in Keleny's humorous painting (see p. 203)?

Metaphor and Meaning

Study the artwork your teacher shows. Fill in the lines below to identify the artwork. Then describe the literal content of the work and the metaphorical meanings of the work in the spaces provided.

Title_____   Artist_____

Culture or Style_____Date_____ Media_____

Literal Content   Metaphorical Meanings

Based on the content and possible metaphors you have described, write a brief statement about the meanings of this artwork. Use the back of this sheet.

Oath Taker is an African wooden figure regarded by Congo peoples of western Africa as a source of healing and as a judge for ending disputes or attending to civil matters, such as divorce. The nails in the figure mark specific oaths or contracts made by supplicants and are similar in function to signatures on legal documents in contemporary Western society. Children work in groups to discuss the questions, then report to the entire class. Note that questions relate to art history, art criticism, and aesthetics.

Oath Taker Worksheet

View and analyze *Oath Taker,* learn about its cultural context, and answer the following questions, explaining your answers:

1. An *nkisi n'kondi* sculpture, such as *Oath Taker,* is used within Congo cultures for purposes of:

2. Why were nails and blades driven into the wood of the sculpture? How does this relate to the legal system of this society?

3. What have you learned about the culture of Congo peoples?

4. In what ways has knowledge about the *Oath Taker* and its cultural role influenced the way you view the sculpture? Do you understand it better? Do you like it more? Less? What has made a difference for you?

5. Do you think it is appropriate to exhibit an object such as *Oath Taker* out of its original context in an art museum in the United States? Explain your answer.

6. Can people of other cultures who do not use sculptures this way enjoy looking at the *Oath Taker*? Why or why not?

7. Discuss your response to *Oath Taker:* Do you like it? Do you think it is a good work of art? What feeling do you think it conveys? Would you like to see the original? Explain your answers.

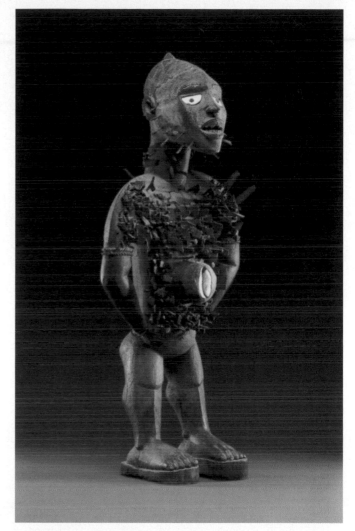

Nail Figure, Congo, 1875–1900. The Detroit Institute of Arts, Founders Society Purchase, Eleanor Clay Ford Fund For African Art. Photograph © 1998 The Detroit Institute of Arts.

Understanding the cultural context in which works are created and the functions of artworks in societies can help us to appreciate artworks from other times and places. Works of art such as *Oath Taker* can help dispel cultural stereotypes and expand children's understanding of the diversity of world art.

SOURCE: Kay Alexander and Michael Day, *SPECTRA Art Program, K–8* (Palo Alto, CA: Dale Seymour Publications, 1994).

This assessment device features open-ended statements that children are asked to complete. It is especially useful for eliciting comments that might not be forthcoming on a form that requires only correct answers to specific content questions.

Painting Review

Complete the following statements.

1. My favorite painting studied in the two painting units was

2. I like this painting best because

3. The most important thing to remember about painting is

4. In order to understand a painting, a person needs to

5. Paintings are best when they

6. Bierstadt was best known for

7. I thought Basquiat's painting was

8. Representational painters tried to

9. The Abstract Expressionists tried to

10. In studying painting, I learned it really doesn't matter that

Students are given a case-study problem in aesthetics and are asked to analyze different reasons associated with debate of the issue and to rate the quality of reasons given in support of particular views.

Evaluating Reasons

Citizens in Allentown are debating whether the city should give money to artists to erect sculpture in the park again this summer. Last year, artists submitted slides of their work and drawings and plans for the sculptures they intended to make. A group of citizens, some of whom were art critics, artists, and art teachers, decided which artists would receive money to help pay for materials. The ten sculptures were put into the park, where they remained for one month, including the 4th of July weekend.

Here are some of the comments offered in the discussion. Tell whether you think the comments include good or not very good reasons. Be prepared to tell members of a small group of classmates why.

a. We should not give artists money to erect sculpture in the park again this year. Artists make art but they can't tell us what to like and what not to like.

GOOD_____ NOT VERY GOOD_____

b. Over time, the great artists will stand out. Even though van Gogh wasn't popular in his own time, his work is very valuable today. We should wait until an artist is accepted as really great before we put his or her work in the park. Not one of the Allentown artists has been recognized as really great, so we should not give any of them money to put their sculptures in the park.

GOOD_____ NOT VERY GOOD_____

c. Some art is really good today, even though the artists aren't well known by most people. The art people who selected the sculptures know what art is the best, so we should put the sculptures in the park and learn about what the experts say is good, even though we don't like it much.

GOOD_____ NOT VERY GOOD_____

d. There are two kinds of art—art for galleries and museums and art for public places. The art for public places ought to be art that everybody likes. In Boston, a sculpture of Mrs. Mallard and her ducklings (from the children's book *Make Way for Ducklings*) was put near the Public Garden lagoon where, in the story, Mrs. Mallard and her ducklings go swimming. All art in public places ought to be like this—art that everybody likes. No artist should be given money unless the sculpture will probably be liked by everybody.

GOOD_____ NOT VERY GOOD_____

e. All art in public places should be art that looks like something we all recognize. It should never be abstract art.

GOOD_____ NOT VERY GOOD_____

f. Since they are putting the sculpture in the park, it should blend in with the natural surroundings. Only give money to the artists who will make sculpture to blend in with nature.

GOOD_____ NOT VERY GOOD_____

g. Art in the park should not blend with the surroundings. It should stand out so that everybody can see that it is art in the park. This way, they will see it and try to understand it. Maybe they might even learn to like it.

GOOD_____ NOT VERY GOOD_____

h. Art only belongs in museums and galleries. Keep it out of the park!

GOOD_____ NOT VERY GOOD_____

SOURCE: This assessment device was developed by Marilyn Stewart, Kutztown State University.

REPORTING PROGRESS IN ART

Every school system reports to parents concerning their children's progress. This is one of the traditional and necessary functions of a school. Regarding the mechanics of reporting to the parents, several points must be kept in mind. First, the method of reporting must be easily understood by all parents. Any report that makes use of complicated symbols or what is considered by some to be highly professional language (and by others to be an undesirable "pedagese") will not be appreciated by most parents. Second, the report should reflect the objectives and practices of the art program and should attempt to comment on the child, both as an individual and as a member of a group. Third, any good report should, of course, be as accurate and fair as a teacher can make it. Fourth, from the teacher's point of view, the system of reporting should not demand a disproportionate amount of clerical work.

Two of the best means of reporting available to teachers of art are *progress reports* and *narrative reports*. The progress report is based on the use of check marks, symbols, or letters. Often only two marks are used—*S* for satisfactory and *U* for unsatisfactory. Sometimes the letter *O* may be employed to signify outstanding progress. The teacher can make subheadings according to content categories (art history, art making), personal behaviors (initiative, social development), or other topics. The parent would then expect to find either *S*, *U*, or *O* opposite each of these subheadings. This system appears to be theoretically sound for reporting art, in that it is based on each child's individual progress rather than on progress in comparison with other pupils.

A teacher might, with the parents' consent, wish to make an initial report to them verbally during a short conference. This method tends to be time-consuming, but because of its flexibility it has some obvious advantages over written reports.

It demands, of course, that the teacher have some ability to report both positive and negative aspects of a child's efforts without arousing the wrath of a parent. No teacher, furthermore, can afford to arrange an interview of this type without first being fully prepared. Parents should be informed of their children's special educational needs. Of course, if the child is gifted, the teacher should make the parents aware of this, so the child can gain support that might otherwise be lacking without this knowledge. Many parents are completely unaware of their children's creative abilities in art making as well as in the other domains of art.

Often the best type of reporting goes on during the academic term, when teachers send items home with students, such as a summary of an art unit with objectives and content, samples of student work with teacher's comments, invitations to exhibits of student work, and other items that convey to parents what the art program is about and what their children are learning. For parent conferences, nothing is as helpful or impressive as a complete portfolio that displays the child's progress and learning. Some teachers use the technologies of video, computers, CD-ROM, and XAP-Shot cameras to record and organize visual images of students at work and students' artwork. For example, one CD-ROM disc can store a student's art production from thirteen years of schooling. In addition, teachers who have used a comprehensive approach to assessment will be able to communicate very specifically to students and parents regarding each pupil's strengths, accomplishments, and areas where improvement is possible. Far from becoming a "chore" for teachers, assessment can be a most rewarding integral part of the art program, and teachers can gain a great deal of personal satisfaction because they have the ability to communicate so clearly and effectively to students, parents, and school administrators about the progress of each student.

NOTES

1. James Popham, "Circumventing the High Costs of Authentic Assessment," *Phi Delta Kappan* 74, no. 6 (February 1993): 473.

2. Donna Kay Beattie, *Assessment in Art Education* (Worcester, MA: Davis Publications, 1997), p. 2.

3. Michael Day, "Evaluating Student Achievement in Discipline-Based Art Programs," *Studies in Art Education* 26, no. 4 (1985): 232–240.

4. Elliot Eisner, *The Educational Imagination: On the Design and Evaluation of School Programs,* 2d ed. (New York: Macmillan, 1985), p. 192.

5. See any of the editions of Viktor Lowenfeld and Lambert Brittain, *Creative and Mental Growth,* 8th ed. (New York: Macmillan, 1988).

6. Mary Lou Hoffman-Solomon and Cindy W. Rehm, "Art Touches the People in Our Lives," in *Discipline-Based Art Education: A Curriculum Sampler,* ed. Kay Alexander and Michael Day (Los Angeles: The Getty Center for Education in the Arts, 1991).

7. Kay Alexander and Michael Day, *SPECTRA Art Program, K–8* (Palo Alto: Dale Seymour Publications, 1994).

8. See, for example, Monroe Beardsley, *Aesthetics: Problems in the Philosophy of Criticism* (New York: Harcourt, Brace and World, 1958); Stephen Pepper, *The Basis of Criticism in the Arts* (Cambridge, MA: Harvard University Press, 1945); and Susanne Langer, *Mind: An Essay on Human Feeling,* vol. 1 (Baltimore: Johns Hopkins University, 1967).

9. W. J. Clinton, "President's Call to Action for American Education in the Twenty-first Century," *State of the Union Address* (Washington, DC, February 4, 1997); Consortium of National Arts Education Associations, *National Standards for Arts Education: What Every Young American Should Know and Be Able to Do in the Arts* (Reston, VA: Music Educators National Conference, 1994; National Board for Professional Teaching Standards (NBPTS), *Standards for National Board Certification: Early Adolescence through Young Adulthood/Art* (Washington, DC: NBPTS, 1994); National Center for Education Statistics, *The NAEP 1997 Arts Report Card* (Washington, DC: U.S. Department of Education, OERI, NCES 1999-486, 1998); and Carole Henry, ed., *Standards for Art Teacher Preparation* (Reston, VA: National Art Education Association, 1999).

10. John Herman, Pamela Aschbacher, and Lynn Winters, *A Practical Guide to Alternative Assessment* (Alexandria, VA: Association for Supervision and Curriculum Development, 1992), p. 2.

11. Enid Zimmerman, "Assessing Students' Progress and Achievements in Art," *Art Education* 45, no. 6 (November 1992): 16.

12. John Goodlad, *A Place Called School* (New York: McGraw-Hill, 1984).

13. For an interesting study of this topic, see Howard Gardner, Ellen Winner, and M. Kircher, "Children's Conceptions of the Arts," *Journal of Aesthetic Education* 9, no. 3 (1975).

14. For a thorough discussion of standardized art tests, see Gilbert Clark, Enid Zimmerman, and Marilyn Zurmuehlen, *Understanding Art Testing* (Reston, VA: National Art Education Association, 1987).

15. Beattie, *Assessment in Art Education.*

ACTIVITIES FOR THE READER

1. Describe some situations in which the art program reflects the educational outlook of (a) a school principal, (b) a school board, and (c) a community.
2. Devise some test items in art as follows:
   a. A true-false type to test third-grade pupils' knowledge of handling clay.
   b. A recall or completion type to test fourth-grade pupils' knowledge of color mixing.
   c. A multiple-choice type to test sixth-grade pupils' knowledge of art history.
   d. A matching-items type to test fifth-grade pupils' ability to use a mixed-media technique.
   e. A recognition type to test sixth-grade pupils' knowledge of art terms.
3. Make checklists for (a) appreciation of sculpture by sixth-grade pupils and (b) skills needed by fourth-grade pupils when doing art criticism.
4. Over a period of two weeks, study the art output of a group of ten children, and write a paragraph of not more than fifty words for each child, summarizing their progress.
5. Describe any results, either good or bad, that you have observed as a result of competitive marking of children's art. How do those who have received a poor grade react?
6. Study the checklist in Table 19-1. Try to rework a portion of it to reflect learning in art history, criticism, and aesthetics.
7. Imagine yourself to be a parent. How would you want art to change your child? List the outcomes that, in your parental view, would demonstrate the effectiveness of art education. Pick a specific age level.
8. Make a checklist of items that would reflect the attitudinal change of the principal and faculty with respect to the art program.
9. Review the works by artists in this book, and select three that would make good subjects for a pictorial-analysis exercise involving the use of an overlay of tracing paper. Can these exercises be assigned according to grade level or experience of children?

SUGGESTED READINGS

Armstrong, Carmen. *Designing Assessment in Art*. Reston, VA: National Art Education Association, 1994.

Beattie, Donna Kay. *Assessment in Art Education*. Art Education in Practice Series. Worcester, MA: Davis Publications, 1997.

Day, Michael D. "Evaluating Student Achievement in Discipline-Based Art Programs." *Studies in Art Education* 26, no. 4 (1985): 232–240.

Eisner, Elliot W. "Evaluating the Teaching of Art." In *Evaluating and Assessing the Visual Arts in Education: International Perspectives*, ed. Doug Boughton and Elliot W. Eisner. New York: Teachers College Press, 1996, pp. 75–94.

Eisner, Elliot W. "Overview of Evaluation and Assessment: Conceptions in Search of Practice." In *Evaluating and Assessing the Visual Arts in Education*, ed. Boughton, Eisner, and Ligtvoet.

Gardner, Howard. "The Assessment of Student Learning in the Arts." In *Evaluating and Assessing the Visual Arts in Education*, ed. Boughton, Eisner, and Ligtvoet, pp. 131–155.

Johnson, Margaret H., and Susan L. Cooper. "Developing a System for Assessing Written Art Criticism." *Art Education* 47, no. 5 (1994): 21–26.

National Center for Education Statistics. *Arts Education: Highlights of the NAEP 1997 Arts Assessment Report Card. The Nation's Report Card*. [Washington, DC]: National Center for Education Statistics, 1998.

Popham, James W. *Classroom Assessment: What Teachers Need to Know*. Needham Heights, MA: Allyn and Bacon, 1998.

Vallance, Elizabeth. "Issues in Evaluating Museum Education Programs." In *Evaluating and Assessing the Visual Arts in Education*, ed. Boughton, Eisner, and Ligtvoet, pp. 222–236.

Wiggins, G. *Educative Assessment: Designing Assessment to Inform and Improve Performance*. San Francisco, CA: Jossey-Bass, 1988.

Wilson, Brent. "Arts Standards and Fragmentation: A Strategy for Holistic Assessment." *Arts Education Policy Review* 98, no. 2 (1996): 2–9.

WORLD WIDE WEB RESOURCES

Meta Sites

Lake, Betti. *The Art Teacher Connection*. 1999. <http://www. inficad.com/~arted/pages/arted.html> Provides regularly updated links to Web sites on general assessment and art assessment.

U.S. Department of Education. National Library of Education. *The Gateway to Educational Materials*. 1999. <http://www.thegateway.org/> Search this database for links to interior and exterior resources on assessment, evaluation, and goals and standards.

Assessment and Evaluation

Education Resources Information Center (ERIC). *The ERIC Clearinghouse on Assessment and Evaluation*. 1999. <http://ericae.net/> This site provides information and resources on testing and evaluation. Resources include provisions for responsible test use as well as standard and model tests. Web site includes full-text library and a test locator.

North Central Regional Educational Laboratory. *Assessment*. 1999. <http://www.ncrel.org/sdrs/pathwayg.html> This site's assessment section contains substantial information and practical guidelines. A search tool is provided that enables one to design a path of inquiry. Furnishes links to Web sites containing supporting resources.

Goals and Standards

U.S. Department of Education. *Goals 2000: Legislation and Related Items*. 1999. See also *Goals 2000: Reforming Education to Improve Student Achievement*. 1998. <http://www.ed.gov/G2K/> The U.S. Department of Education created this Web site to enhance state and local endeavors to develop clear and rigorous standards for what every child should know and be able to do. The continually updated information also provides support for state- and districtwide planning and implementation of school efforts focused on improving student achievement to those standards.

U.S. Department of Education. National Center for Education Statistics. 1999. <http://nces.ed.gov/> NCES collects and reports information on the academic performance of the nation's students. The primary focus of this assessment is what American elementary/secondary students know and can do in academic subjects. This Web site is organized to provide data and information about NCES's surveys and assessments. Data on state or local school districts can be accessed.

Online Journal

ERIC Clearinghouse on Assessment and Evaluation (ERIC/AE) and the Department of Measurement, Statistics, and Evaluation, University of Maryland, College Park. *Practical Assessment, Research and Evaluation*. 1999. <http://ericae.net/parc/> Online journal provides education professionals access to articles with both practical and theoretical material on assessment, research, evaluation, and teaching practice.

APPENDIX A

A Historical Framework for art Education: Dates, Personalities, Publications, and Events

1749   Benjamin Franklin advocates art instruction in the school curriculum for its utilitarian functions, thus establishing himself as a precursor of the Massachusetts drawing provision of 1870.

1761   Jean-Jacques Rousseau, *Emile*. Revolutionary (for its time), *Emile* stresses the nature and interests of children as a basis for education. Through his influence on succeeding educators, Rousseau sets the stage for child-centered approaches.

1746–1822   Johann Pestalozzi follows Rousseau's theories and anticipates those of Frederick Froebel as a member of the triumvirate who set the stage for the Child Study Movement through their interest in the use of objects, the function of physical activity in the process of learning, the rejection of severe discipline, and, above all, respect for the child as an individual, whose development is viewed in context rather than as a flawed adult.

1781   Johann Pestalozzi, *Leonard and Gertrude*. A proponent for the learner as active participant, who is influenced by Rousseau and who, in turn, inspires Herbart.

1816   Johann Friedrich Herbart, *ABC of Sense Perception*. A German psychologist who attempts to systematize the ideas of Pestalozzi.

1827   A course in drawing is offered to students of Boston English High School.

1839   Horace Mann, while secretary of the Massachusetts Board of Education, visits Germany to study the teaching of drawing. He is particularly impressed by one teacher, Peter Schmidt, and publishes Schmidt's lessons. Mann views drawing as a source of pleasure, as well as leading to a vocation. G. Stanley Hall also visits Germany, but unlike Mann, he studies psychology instead of drawing. When Hall develops the idea that is to grow into the Child Study Movement (late 1800s), a marriage between psychology and art education is begun. The enduring nature of this partnership is reflected by the current research of Project Zero, which shares with Hall an association with Harvard University.

1834–1839   Bronson Alcott begins the Temple School in Boston, employing drawing as an adjunct of the imagination, one of three major areas of mental activity.

1835–1850   Friedrich Froebel develops his ideas in his Garden of Children (kindergarten) school devising curricula based on play and on the use of "gifts" designed to develop mathematical and aesthetic relationships through the use of objects, such as woolen balls, geometric forms, and drawing on slate.

1848   Rudolf Toppler, a Swiss schoolmaster and illustrator, devotes two chapters to child art in his book. In 1902, "the father of the Child Study Movement" acknowledges Toppler's insights.

1849   William Minifie teaches drawing in the Boys High School in Baltimore, and, like Benjamin Franklin, Walter Smith, and William Bentley Fowle, uses a "scientific" sequential approach to carry out his belief in drawing as a practical and useful skill.

1860   Wm. Bradley Co., founded in Springfield, Massachusetts. Manufactured Froebel's "Gifts."

1870   Elizabeth Peabody, a former teacher in the Temple School, publishes *A Plea for Froebel's Kindergarten as the Primary Art School*, advocating drawing as a major component of kindergarten instruction.

By 1870   The Oswego Movement of the Oswego, New York, Normal School, following the lead of the Kindergarten Movement, stresses the use of instructional "objects," such as charts, cards, picture sets, blocks, specimens in glass, textiles, and maps, in the classroom. Although intended for general education, the implication of "objects" for art education becomes clearer over time. Related to this are the "type forms" or geometric models of spheres, cones, cubes, pyramids—those basic pure forms Cezanne referred to as the structural components of natural form. Type forms are formally introduced to art education students at the Pratt Institute in 1886. The dominant figure at Oswego is Herman Krusi, whose books on drawing, influence classroom teachers.

1870 Massachusetts passes the Drawing Act, making drawing instruction mandatory in towns with populations of 5,000 or more.

1871 Walter Smith of England is invited to the Massachusetts Normal Art School by the state to help teachers fulfill a new state requirement for the teaching of drawing to prepare students to function as draftspersons and designers. He becomes director of what is now Massachusetts College of Art.

1880s Beginning of Child Study Movement.

1883 The National Education Association (NEA) creates a department of art education, and Carrado Ricci writes the first book on child art, *L'Arte dei Bambini*.

Mid-1880s Fowle publishes the *Common Schools Journal*, introducing the monitorial system—training students to teach other students. Fowle stresses the use of maps and blackboards and eliminates corporal punishment. Fowle writes more than fifty books on all phases of education and translates a European text on drawing.

1888 Bernard Perez, *L'Art et La Poesi-Chez l'enfant*, a poetic approach to child art (France).

1892 James Sully, *Investigation on Childhood*. Sully charts three stages of artistic development and is first to use the term *schema* (Great Britain).

1892 In Boston, art appreciation is introduced into the schools, and Earl Barnes, first psychologist to "discover" child art, publishes *Art of Little Children*.

1890–1905 Study of child art accelerates and James Sully (U.K.) in his *Studies in Childhood* pioneers study of developmental stages in art.

1894 T. R. Ablett, a teacher in the Bradford Grammar School in Great Britain, is a pioneer in the study of memory, the relation of writing to drawing, and the use of shading as opposed to outline. He promotes exhibits of child art and the development of imagination, and he is a successful advocate of art for all children.

1895 Louise Maitland is the first woman to write on child art ("Children's Drawings") for the *Pacific Education Journal*.

1899 The NEA (National Education Association) appoints a committee to report on the teaching of drawing in the public schools. Their report stresses art appreciation, development of the creative impulse, the use of perceptual training for representational drawing, drawing as a vocational preparation, and the rejection of the use of public schools for the training of professional artists.

1899 *The Teacher's Manual (Part IV)* of the eight-volume Prang series of art instruction is designed to serve classroom teachers, using such consultants as Winslow Homer, Arthur Dow, and Frederick Church to develop curricula in aesthetic judgment, art history, nature drawing, perspective, decoration, design, and paper construction.

1899 *New Methods in Education* by J. Liberty Tadd is published. Tadd, the director of the Public School of Industrial Arts in Philadelphia, is the first American art educator whose influence is felt in Europe. (He was invited to lecture in Great Britain.) His book is a marked departure from Walter Smith, stressing working directly from nature.

1900 Lamprecht, another collector of children's drawings, develops a theory that compares the stages of artistic development to the nature of intellectual change.

1901 The publication of *The Applied Arts Book*, edited by James Hall, promotes "projects and activities" that are to lead art teachers away from the "scientific" method of Walter Smith.

A Massachusetts Normal Art School graduate, Henry Turner Bailey, is appointed editor of the newly titled *School Arts Book*.

1904 Franz Cizek, an Austrian artist/teacher, begins his children's classes at the Vienna School of Applied Art. Cizek rejects the idea of realistic drawing and instead draws on the personal reactions, memories, and experiences of students. The pictorial results are so impressive that art educators from America come to study his methods. One observer (Thomas Munro of the Cleveland Museum) comes to the conclusion that the consistently high quality of student work is attributable to the structured nature of Cizek's teaching, a contradiction of which Cizek may not have been aware.

1904–1922 Arthur Wesley Dow becomes the major spokesperson for the importance of composition or structure of art, what is now referred to as the elements and principles.

1905 George Kerschensteirner, *Die Entwicklung Der Zeichner-ischen Begabung*. A superintendent of schools and an art supervisor, who collects a half-million drawings from the children of Munich, stresses freedom from teacher intervention, and is an early advocate of the use of the imagination.

1905 The first seminar on the psychology of children's art is offered by the University of Breslau, Poland.

1908 *Kind und Kunst* (Child and Art), the first periodical devoted to child art, is published.

1908 First symposium on picture study convened by Henry Turner Bailey for supervisors in major cities.

1910 The NEA proceedings of its 46th annual meeting includes Colby's account of his investigations into the nature and causes of children's artistic preferences.

1911 The *Encyclopedia of Education* includes the first article on art education.

1912 Fifty art supervisors are working in New York City.

1912 Walter Sargent (University of Chicago), in his book *Fine and Industrial Art in the United States*, stresses the need to respect the child's needs, interests, and desires to create art, calling attention to the uneven course of progress in a child's ability to draw and recommending the study of conventions established by artists as a means of developing ability in drawing. Some of Sargent's ideas have reemerged today.

1912 Ebeneezer Cooke (U.K.), building upon the theories of Sulley, writes on the relationship between the methodology of institutions and developmental issues.

1914 Max Verworn, *Ideoplastic Art*, stresses the uses of art for the cultivation of sensory experience in education (Germany).

1917 Walter Krotzsch, *Rhythmus Und Form in Der Freien Kinderzeichnung*, makes the first argument for studying the processes as well as the products of creation among children (Germany).

1919 Pedro J. Lemos succeeds Henry Turner Bailey as editor of *School Arts Book*, currently published as *School Arts Magazine*. Over time *School Arts* moves closer to serving art teachers as well as elementary classroom teachers.

1920s As Dewey's ideas begin to merge with other child-centered educators, the era of progressive education grows, lasting until the demise of the movement in the 1930s, during which time the public schools attempt to apply ideas that have had greater success in private schools. The progressives are committed to unit or project learning and the integration of subjects. "Creative expression" becomes a catchword of the movement and continues to be used, although with less regularity. Since the teacher's responsibility is to provide materials and to foster an environment conducive to freedom and exploration, the content of art is not deemed important. One consequence of emphasis on the child rather than on art is a decline in gains made by the Picture Study Movement. Many of the progressives' ideas will resurface in the 1960s in the books of such "radical" critics as John Holt.

1920–1930 The Picture Study Movement thrives as an antecedent of the current discipline-based art education movement. Encouraged by advances in printing technology and the use of color reproductions, art appreciation is taken seriously as part of a balanced program. The goals of appreciation lie on the moralistic as well as the aesthetic side as sentimental narrative works take precedence over contemporary

European exemplars. Pictorial images are regarded as natural vehicles for transmitting society's most dearly held values (patriotism, family, religion, etc.).

1924 Belle Boas publishes *Art in the Schools,* advocating art appreciation through an applied arts philosophy. Margaret E. Mathias publishes *The Beginnings of Art in the Public Schools.*

1925 The Carnegie Corporation supports a report on the role of art education prepared by the Federated Council in its call for greater content in art.

1926 Gustav Britsch, "Theory of Child Art," a systematic theory of the developmental aspects of the art of children, provides a basis for Henry Schafer-Simmern's book (1948, Germany).

1926 Florence Goodnough, *Measurement of Intelligence by Drawings.*

1927 Margaret Naumburg, *The Child and the World; Dialogues in Modern Education;* in 1947, *Studies of the "free" Art Expression of Behavior Problem Children and Adolescents as a Means of Diagnosis and Therapy.*

1927 The NEA, in its annual meeting in Dallas, Texas, recognizes art as fundamental in the education of children.

1927 Oskar Wulff, *Die Kunstdes Kindes.* Wulff emphasizes feeling and affect over the intellect in artistic expression. His views on the limitations among the blind are later to be questioned by Viktor Lowenfeld's research.

1932 *The Teaching of Art* by Margaret Mathias is published, contributing to the growth of serious literature in art education.

1933 The Owatonna Art Project in Minnesota creates an art program that falls not only within the responsibility of the school system but also responds to the needs of the citizenry, promoting and advising on home decoration, art in public places, landscaping, and even window display, thus demonstrating that art can be public as well as private and personal as well as utilitarian, and that art teachers are capable of raising the general aesthetic level of an entire community. One of the teachers is Edwin Ziegfeld, later to become the first president of INSEA; head of the department of art education at Teacher's College, Columbia University; and author of *Today's Art.* The Owatonna Project loses its impact at the onset of World War II but retains its importance as a historic landmark in art education.

1933 While Owatonna is getting underway, teachers from Germany's Bauhaus, an art academy that significantly influenced American art and art education, escape from Hitler and arrive at Black Mountain College in North Carolina, led by the painter Josef Albers. By the time the Bauhaus has to move to a more permanent setting at the Institute of Design in Chicago, the ideas begun in Germany begin to exert an influence in the curricula of a growing number of American art programs. Chief among these is the growth of photography and photograms, a new attitude toward experimentation with materials, and an approach to design based more on the ideas of Johannes Itten than Arthur Dow. Architecture is accepted as a valid part of an art program.

1938 Leon Loyal Winslow, director of art for Baltimore City Schools, publishes *The Integrated School Art Program,* demonstrating a need and method for using art as a catalyst for learning academic subjects.

1940 Natalie Robinson Cole's *Art in the Classroom* reaffirms the importance of creative expression and is one of the few books to deal with the subject from a personal point of view. (Seonid Robertson's *Rose Garden and Labyrinth* is a good example of how an English art educator worked in this limited genre.)

1941 Edwin Ziegfeld with Ray Faulkner, *Art Today: An Introduction to the Visual Arts.* With Mary Elinore Smith, *Art for Daily Living: The Story of the Owatonna Art Education Project* was published in 1944.

1942 Victor D'Amico's *Creative Teaching in Art* states the case for the nature of creativity, moving closer to the artist as model. As director of the children's program for the Museum of Modern Art in New York City, D'Amico creates a laboratory to carry out his ideas and to exercise his power as a creative, charismatic teacher.

1943 Herbert Read, a British poet, philosopher, and critic, publishes *Education through Art.* Like Lowenfeld and Dewey, Read sees aesthetic education as the logical center for education in general. He inventories European and British developmental theories and endows his ideas with a wide frame of references from art, psychology, and philosophy.

1946   Wilhelm Viola, *Child Art*. Forty-two years after Cizek began his classes in Vienna, Viola publishes his recollections of Cizek's classes.

1947   Viktor Lowenfeld's major work, *Creative and Mental Growth*, is published. It is still in use. Lowenfeld (another refugee from Germany) reorganizes the threads of developmental study of child art begun in Europe and relates these to the formation of personality. The authoritative and comprehensive nature of the book establishes it as a classic of enormous influence both here and abroad.

1947   The National Art Education Association (NAEA) is founded, adding three geographical regions to the existing Eastern Arts Association.

1948   Marion Richardson, *Art and the Child* (U.K.).

1948   Henry Schafer-Simmern, *The Unfolding of Artistic Activity*, discusses the title of his book in relation to his work with special groups, such as the aged and retarded. Relies on Britsch's work (1926) as a basis for his theory of artistic development.

1950   Creativity is taken seriously by the psychological community, and numerous research studies are conducted to analyze the creative personality. J. P. Guilford, president of the American Psychological Association, calls the attention of his colleagues to a hitherto neglected area embraced previously by art educators in the progressive era.

1951   The International Society for Education through Art (INSEA) is founded by UNESCO in Bristol, England, with the guidance of Sir Herbert Read. The purpose of INSEA is to provide periodic forums for art educators interested in the philosophy, objectives, curricula, and methodology of art education, within an international framework. Tri-yearly meetings are held on a national and regional basis. Americans who have served as presidents are Edwin Ziegfeld, Al Hurwitz, and Elliot Eisner.

1951   Florence Cane, *The Artist in Each of Us*. Cane's book bridges art therapy and the talented child through a series of case studies.

1951   Mildred Landis, *Meaningful Art Education*, a textbook based on Dewey.

1951   Rosabelle MacDonald (Mann), *Art as Education*.

1956   Thomas Munro's *Art Education, Its Philosophy and Psychology* is the first scholarly attempt by a museum-based educationalist and aesthetician to focus attention on art education.

1957   The Soviets launch *Sputnik*, an event that establishes their lead over the United States in space technology and provokes a reevaluation of American education, beginning with science and mathematics and attempts at curricular reform, and eventually reaching art education.

1957   Miriam Lindstrom, *Children's Art: A Study of Normal Development in Children's Modes of Visualization*.

1958   Congress passes the National Defense Education Act to encourage a reevaluation of curriculum, primarily in the "defense-related" subjects of math, science, and foreign languages. Art education receives limited funding, along with other academic subjects.

1959   Blanche Jefferson's *Teaching Art to Children* is published.

1960   Viktor Lowenfeld dies.

1960–1970   The "greening" or consciousness-raising of America before the end of the Vietnam War results in an awareness of the diversity of American ethnicity and of the environment and an acceleration of interest in technology and collaborative projects in art education.

1961   *Preparation for Art* by June King McFee provides a significant shift toward the importance of perceptual and environmental issues in planning curriculum.

1961   President John Kennedy's Science Advisory Committee recommends that the arts be included in educational reform.

1962   Manuel Barkan's article, "Transitions in Art Education: Changing Conceptions of Curriculum Content and Teaching," published in the *Art Education Journal of the NAEA*, marks the initial stage of a movement toward increased emphasis on art content in art education. This period is also a time of openness toward newer media, borrowed from the revolution of youth culture occurring in higher education. It parallels the more conservative rational methods of the accountability movement, which represents mainstream thinking in all areas of education.

1965 The publication of *Art Education: The 64th Yearbook of the National Society for the Study of Education,* an anthology of essays by leaders in art education, serves as a status report on U.S. art educators. This book should be compared to the fortieth yearbook, published some thirty years earlier. A later, if somewhat briefer, effort is the *Report of the NAEA Commission on Art Education* (1977).

1965 Federal support of the arts in education grows with the passage of the Elementary and Secondary Education Act (Title V), which strengthens the role of art supervision at the state level.

1965 Congress establishes the National Endowment for the Arts.

1965 The "Seminar in Art Education for Research and Curriculum Development," held at Penn State University, is the first conference to bring together artists, critics, historians, philosophers, and art educators in an attempt to reevaluate the nature of the curriculum in art education.

1966 *Journal of Aesthetic Education*, Ralph Smith, ed.

1967–1976 The Central Midwestern Education Laboratory (CEMREL), with Stanley Madeja as director, is the first government-funded project to develop a curriculum ("Through the Arts to the Aesthetic") and to support materials in consultation with artists, historians, critics, and aestheticians.

1968 University City in St. Louis, with the support of the JDR III Fund and under the direction of Stanley Madeja, creates a model for an "arts infusion" curriculum to address the question, "Can the arts be made integral to the general education of every child from kindergarten through high school?" (Kathryn Bloom, Director, JDR III)

1968 Under the direction of Elliot Eisner, the Kettering Project at Stanford University develops a comprehensive elementary art curriculum based on art content.

1968–1979 Kathryn Bloom directs the Arts in Education Program for the JDR III fund for "all of the arts for all of the children." Laura Chapman refers to the role of the new bureaucracies

as the "de-schooling" of art education because of the stress laid upon extra school considerations: the use of noncertified art teachers, liaisons with community agencies, and art councils, all of which can tend to weaken rather than strengthen art education in the classroom.

1969 The National Assessment of Educational Progress (NAEP) assesses the state of art education from a national perspective.

1969 Mary Rouse and Guy Hubbard of Indiana University write *Meaning, Method, and Media,* the first commercially available elementary art curriculum.

1970 Advanced Placement in Studio Art and Art History is offered for senior high school students interested in credit in institutions of higher education.

1970 The decade of assessment or age of accountability begins, wherein art education is defined in terms of behavioral goals and objectives.

1973 The Alliance for Arts Education is formed through a mandate of the John F. Kennedy Center and joins a growing family of support groups attempting to bring arts education closer to the mainstream of American educators. Art education is moving out of isolation and is included in all arts education deliberations. Other organizations that work for the arts as a whole are the JDR Arts in Education Program and the National Endowment for the Arts, with its support of numerous projects, including the Artist-in-Schools program.

1973 The National Assessment of Educational Progress in art (NAEP) is conducted at the request of the U.S. Office of Education. This study examines the knowledge, skills, and attitudes regarding art of nine-, thirteen-, and seventeen-year-olds, using the objectives of art education as a basis of investigation. Brent Wilson is the major investigator.

1978 A second NAEP in art is conducted but without an analysis of data. A third assessment is planned for 1996.

1981 A program on the gifted and talented in art is held at the NAEA convention in Chicago. This is to a large degree art education's response to a general interest in children with special needs and leads to a number of publications and conferences in art education, as well as new programs for children and adolescents, such as the growth of Magnet schools.

1982   The Getty Center for Education in the Arts is created as one of the Getty trust's seven units. Headed by Leilani Lattin Duke, the Getty Center offers support for discipline-based art education in the public schools through a program of research, publications, conferences, grants, and regional institutes. Laura Chapman publishes *Instant Art, Instant Culture,* an independent view of art education policy that includes survey reports and recommendations for future practice.

1984   Dwaine Greer introduces the term *discipline-based art education* in an article in *Studies in Art Education.*

1988   The National Endowment for the Arts publishes *Towards Civilization: A Report on Arts Education,* which attempts to reveal the status of the arts in education in the United States. It recommends that the NAEP be reinstated.

1990   *America 2000,* a status report on education in the country, is issued by U.S. governors and President George Bush. After initial failure to mention the arts and the resultant protest, the report includes arts in national goals statements.

1991   The National Board for Professional Teaching Standards (NBPTS) is formed in order to offer recognition for exemplary or accomplished secondary teachers, art included. Elementary follows later.

1994   National voluntary standards in the arts are developed by the three arts education associations (American Alliance for Theatre & Education, Music Educators National Conference, and the National Art Education Association) in conjunction with a movement for standards in all areas of the school curriculum.

1994   In the largest art education reform initiative in history, six art education institutes established since 1988 in Florida, Minnesota, Nebraska, Ohio, Tennessee, and Texas by the Getty Center for Education in the Arts support discipline-based art programs in more than two hundred school districts in fifteen states, reaching close to a million students in kindergarten through twelfth grades. The institutes are based on findings from the Los Angeles Getty Institute for Educators on the Visual Arts (1982–1989), which served 1,300 teachers in twenty-one school districts in the Los Angeles area.

1996   Secondary art teachers become National Board Certified. By 1999 there are nearly one hundred NBC art teachers in states across the country. National Board Certification is expected to become available for elementary art teachers in 2000.

1997   The second National Assessment of Educational Progress in the visual arts employs a wider range of assessment items, following national developments in educational evaluation that feature authentic approaches to assessment.

1998   Leilani Lattin Duke resigns as director of the Getty Center for Education in the Arts. Getty art education programs are significantly reduced.

1999   NAEA publishes *Standards for Art Teacher Preparation,* a document that discusses requirements for quality art teacher education programs, preparation of faculty, and knowledge and skills new art teachers will need as they enter the teaching profession.

2000   The Creativity Movement celebrates its 50th anniversary.

APPENDIX B

Professional Responsibility and Professional Associations

We all agree that teaching is not just a job, and that preparing future generations of citizens for their place in society is the most important work that we can do. Dedicated teachers who view education as a career recognize their responsibilities as professionals. As citizens in our communities, as well as professional educators, we are often called upon to provide assistance and guidance in developing and maintaining sound programs of education for children and young people. Because of our education and experience as teachers, we have much to offer our communities and many insights about education that are not available to average citizens from other walks of life.

We find that we face several responsibilities as professional teachers. First, we have an obligation to gain the best preparation for teaching by excelling in our undergraduate education so that we will have much to offer our students. As in-service teachers we should keep up with change and innovation in our subject areas, as well as with the issues and trends of education as a field and the place of education in our communities and in society. Like professionals in law, medicine, business, and other fields, we should be active in our professional associations, subscribe to our professional journals, and participate in the educational issues of the day to assure that the children receive the best education that we know how to provide.

If we, as teachers, are to model for our students the excitement of learning and the values and benefits of education, we must be active learners in our own right. We should collect, keep, and add to a professional library of important works in our field. We should be active learners by participating in and enjoying the subject area of our teaching expertise. For teachers of art this means that we seek opportunities to visit art museums and galleries, read the current art books and periodicals, and take time to express our ideas and feelings through our own art production. The excitement and joy that we gain through our participation in and appreciation of art will be conveyed directly to our students. There is no substitute for our own enthusiasm and participation in the life of the mind. Students cannot be fooled; they seem to know which of their teachers are genuine in their advocacy of learning and education.

Too often, teachers feel isolated from their colleagues, as they spend nearly their entire working days with their young students. Like professionals in other fields, teachers need time and opportunities to share ideas and values with their peers. Active membership in local, regional, and national professional associations provides many such opportunities. The following list is provided to encourage interested teachers to participate as professionals, to learn from their colleagues, and to become leaders in the advocacy of sound education for all children and young people.

Professional Organizations

International Society for
  Education through Art
  (InSEA)
cito/InSEA
P.O. Box 1109
NL 6801 BC Arnhem
The Netherlands
cspace.unb.ca/insea

National Art Education
  Association (NAEA)
1916 Association Drive
Reston, VA 20191-1590
703/860–8000
www.naea-reston.org

USSEA
United States Society for
  Education through Art
C/O Dr. Mary Stockrocki
Arizona State University
School of Art
Box 871505
Tempe, Arizona 85287
http://www.public.asu.edu/
  %7Eifmls/ussea

CSEA
Canadian Society for Education
  through Art
675 Rue Samuel-De-Camplian
Boucherville, Quebec
J4B 6C4
Phone: 450/655-2435
http://art education.concordia.
  ca/csea/

APPENDIX C

Art Education Resources

Art Museum Resources

Albright-Knox Art Gallery
1285 Elmwood Avenue
Buffalo, NY 14222
716/882-8700
www.albrightknox.org

American Association for
   Museums
1575 I Street Northwest, Suite
   400
Washington, DC 20005
202/289-1818
www.aam-us.org

American Craft Museum
40 West 53rd Street
New York, NY 10019
212/956-3535
www.fieldtrip.com/ny/
   29563535.htm

Amon Carter Museum
3501 Camp Bowie Boulevard
Fort Worth, TX 76107
Mail to: P.O. Box 2365
Fort Worth, TX 76113-2365
817/738-1933
www.cartermuseum.org

Art Institute of Chicago
111 South Michigan Avenue
Chicago, IL 60603
312/443-3600
www.artic.edu/aic/index.html

Arthur M. Sackler Gallery
1050 Independence Avenue,
   Southwest
Washington, DC 20560
202/357-4880
www.si.edu/asia/

Asian Art Museum of San
   Francisco
The Avery Brundage Collection
Golden Gate Park
San Francisco, CA 94118
415/379-8801
www.asianart.org

Baltimore Museum of Art
10 Art Museum Drive
Baltimore, MD 21218-3898
410/396-7100
www.artbma.org

Birmingham Museum of Art
2000 Eighth Avenue North
Birmingham, AL 35203
205/254-2566
www.artsbma.org

Buffalo Bill Historical Center
720 Sheridan Avenue
Cody, WY 82414
307/587-4771
www.bbhc.org

Carnegie Museum of Art
4400 Forbes Avenue
Pittsburgh, PA 15213-4080
412/622-3131
www.cmoa.org

Cincinnati Art Museum
953 Eden Park Drive
Cincinnati, Ohio 45202
513/639-2995
http://www.cincinnatiart
   museum.org

Cleveland Museum of Art
11150 East Boulevard
Cleveland, OH 44106-1797
216/421-7340
www.clemusart.com

Contemporary Arts Museum
5216 Montrose Boulevard
Houston, TX 77006-6598
713/284-8250
www.camh.org

Cooper-Hewitt Museum
National Museum of Design
Smithsonian Institution
2 East 91st Street
New York, NY 10128
212/849-8400
www.si.edu/ndm/info/start.htm

Dallas Museum of Art
1717 North Harwood
Dallas, TX 75201
214/922-1200
www.dm-art.org

Delaware Art Museum
2301 Kentmere Parkway
Wilmington, DE 19806
302/571-9590
www.delart.mus.de.us

Denver Art Museum
100 West 14th Avenue Parkway
Denver, CO 80204-2788
303/640-4433
www.denverartmuseum.org

Detroit Institute of Arts
5200 Woodward Avenue
Detroit, MI 48202
313/833-7900
www.dia.org

Freer Gallery of Art
Smithsonian Institution
Jefferson Drive at 12th Street
   SW
Washington, DC 20560
202/357-4880
www.si.edu/organiza/museums/
   freer/start.htm

Frick Collection
1 East 70th Street
New York, NY 10021-4967
212/288–0700
www.frick.org

Greenville County Museum
   of Art
420 College Street
Greenville, SC 29601
864/271-7570
www.joel.nu/museums.htm

High Museum of Art
1280 Peachtree Street Northeast
Atlanta, GA 30309
404/733-HIGH
www.high.org

Hirshhorn Museum and
   Sculpture Garden
Smithsonian Institution
Independence Avenue at 7th
   Street, Southwest
Washington, DC 20560-0350
202/357-3091
www.si.edu/organiza/museums/
   hirsh/hrshwel.htm

Hispanic Society of America
613 West 155th Street
New York, NY 10032
212/926-2234
www.hispanicsociety.org

Huntington Museum of Art,
   Inc.
2033 McCoy Road
Huntington, WV 25701
304/529–2701
www.artcom.com/museums/nv/
   gl/25701-49.htm

Institute of American Indian
Arts Museum
1600 St. Michael's
P.O. Box 2007
Santa Fe, NM 87504
http://hanksville.phast.umass.edu/
misc/IAIA.html

J. Paul Getty Museum
The Getty Center
1200 Getty Center Drive
Los Angeles, CA 90049-1679
310/440-7300
www.getty.edu

Joslyn Art Museum
2200 Dodge Street
Omaha, NE 68102
402/342-3300
www.joslyn.org

Kimbell Art Museum
3333 Camp Bowie Boulevard
Fort Worth, TX 76107
817/332-8451
www.kimbellart.org

Los Angeles County Museum
of Art
5905 Wilshire Boulevard
Los Angeles, CA 90036
323/857-6000
www.lacma.org

Metropolitan Museum of Art
1000 Fifth Avenue at 82nd
Street
New York, NY 10028
212/535-7710
www.metmuseum.org

Milwaukee Art Museum
750 North Lincoln Memorial
Drive
Milwaukee, WI 53202
414/224-3200
www.mam.org

Minneapolis Institute of Arts
2400 Third Avenue South
Minneapolis, MN 55404
888/MIA-ARTS
www.artsmia.org

Minnesota Museum of Art
Landmark Center
75 West Fifth Street
Saint Paul, MN 55102
651/292-4355
www.mtn.org/MMAA

Museum of Contemporary Art
220 East Chicago Avenue
Chicago, IL 60611
312/280-2660
www.mcachicago.org

Museum of Contemporary Art,
Los Angeles
250 South Grand Avenue
California Plaza
Los Angeles, CA 90012
213/621-2766
www.moca-la.org

Museum of Fine Arts
255 Beach Drive
St. Petersburg, FL 33701
727/896-2667
www.fine-arts.org

Museum of Modern Art
11 West 53rd Street
New York, NY 10019
212/708-9400
www.moma.org

Museum of the American Indian
470 L'Enfant Plaza Southwest,
Suite 7102
Washington, DC 20560
www.si.edu/nmai

National Museum of African Art
950 Independence Avenue
Southwest
Washington, DC 20560
202/357-4600
www.si.edu/nmafa

National Museum of American
Art
8th & G Streets N. W.
Washington, DC 20560
202/357-1729
http://nmaa-ryder.si.edu

National Museum of Women in
the Arts
1250 New York Avenue
Northwest
Washington, DC 20005
202/783-5000
www.nmwa.org

National Portrait Gallery
F Street at 8th Northwest
Washington, DC 20560
202/357-2866
www.npg.si.edu

Nelson-Atkins Museum of Art
4525 Oak Street
Kansas City, MO 64111
816/751-1278
www.nelson-atkins.org

North Carolina Museum of Art
2110 Blue Ridge Road
Raleigh, NC 27699
919/839-6262
www.ncmoa.org

Oakland Museum
1000 Oak Street
Oakland, CA 94607
888/OAK-MUSE
www.museumca.org

Philadelphia Museum of Art
P.O. Box 7646
Philadelphia, PA 19101-7646
215/763-8100
www.philamusum.org

Portland Art Museum
1219 SW Park Avenue
Portland, OR 97205
503/226-2811
www.pam.org

Saint Louis Art Museum
Forest Park
1 Fine Arts Drive
St. Louis, MO 63110
314/721-0072
www.slam.org

San Francisco Museum of
Modern Art
151 Third Street
San Francisco, CA 94103
415/357-4000
www.sfmoma.org

Seattle Art Museum
100 University Street
Seattle, WA 98101-2902
Mail to: P.O. Box 22000
Seattle, WA 98122-9700
206/654-3100
www.seattleartmuseum.org

Solomon R. Guggenheim
Museum
1071 Fifth Avenue
New York, NY 10128-0173
212/423-3500
www.guggenheim.org

Southwest Museum
234 Museum Drive
Los Angeles, CA 90065
Mail to: P.O. Box 41558
Los Angeles, CA 90041-0558
323/221-2164
www.southwest.museum.org

Textile Museum
2320 South Street Northwest
Washington, DC 20008
202/667-0441
www.textilemuseum.org

Virginia Museum of Fine Arts
2800 Grove Avenue at the
Boulevard
Richmond, VA 23221-2466
804/340-1400
www.vmfa.state.va.us

Walker Art Center
Vineland Place
Minneapolis, MN 55403
612/375-7622
www.walkerart.org

Whitney Museum of American
Art
945 Madison Avenue at 75th
New York, NY 10021
212/570-3676
www.echonyc.com/~whitney

Wichita Art Museum
619 Stackman Drive
Wichita, KS 67203-3296
316/268-4921
www.wichitaartmuseum.org

Commercial Resources

A.R.T. Studio Clay Company
9320 Michigan Avenue
Sturtevant, WI 53177-2425
877/ART-CLAY
www.artclay.com

Artkits, Inc.
743 East Washington Street
Louisville, KY 40202
888/884-4002
www.artkits.com

Art Industries Inc.
151 Forest Street
Montclair, NJ 07042
973/509-7736
www.artindustries.com

Art Visuals
P.O. Box 925
Orem, UT 84059-0925
801/226-6115
www.members.tripod.com/
~artvisuals

AmeXpo Company
Educational Software
P.O. Box 2094
Carlsbad, CA 92018
760/720-1010
www.znet.com/~amexpo

Beckley Cardy Group
100 Paragon Parkway
P.O. Box 8105
Mansfield, OH 44903
888/222-1332
www.beckleycardy.com

Bemiss-Jason Corporation
525 Enterprise Drive
Neenah, WI 54956
920/722-9000
www.bemiss-jason.com

Binney & Smith Inc.
1100 Church Lane
Easton, PA 18044-0431
1-800-CRAYOLA.
http://www.binney-smith.com
Crayola: http://www.crayola.com
Crayola Art Education: http://
    education.crayola.com
Crayola in Canada: http://
    canada.crayola.com
Liquitex: http://www.
    liquitex.com
800/CRAYOLA
www.crayola.com
www.liquitex.com

Deco Art
P.O. Box 327
Stanford, KY 40484
606/365-3193
www.decoart.com

Chroma, Inc.
205 Bucky Drive
Lititz, PA 17543
800/257-8278
www.chroma-inc.com

Creative Paperclay Company
79 Daily Drive, Suite #101
Camarillo, CA 93010
805/484-6648
www.paperclay.com

CRIZMAC
P.O. Box 65928
Tucson, AZ 85728-5928
800/913-8555
www.crizmac.com

Davis Publications, Inc.
50 Portland Street
Worcester, MA 01608
800/533-2847
www.davispubl.com

Dick Blick Art Materials
P.O. Box 1267
Galesburg, IL 61402
800/447-8192
www.dickblick.com

Ed Hoy's International
27625 Diehl Road
Warrenville, IL 60555
www.edhoy.com

Fiskars Consumer Products Inc.
P.O. Box 8027
7811 West Stewart Avenue
Wausau, Wisconsin 54401, USA
715/845-2091
http://www.school.fiskars.com/
    classroom/
www.fiskars.com

Glencoe/McGraw-Hill
1221 Avenue of the Americas
New York, NY 10020
800/334-7344
www.glencoe.com

Golden Artist Colors
188 Bell Road
New Berlin, NY 13411
800/959-6543
www.goldenpaints.com

J. L. Hammett Company
P.O. Box 859057
Hammett Place
Braintree, MA 02185
800/333-4600
www.store.yahoo.com/hammett/

Lerner Publishing Group
1251 Washington Avenue North
Minneapolis, MN 55401
800/328-4929
www.lernerbooks.com

Minneapolis College of Art and
    Design
2501 Stevens Avenue South
Minneapolis, MN 55404
800/874-6223
www.mcad.edu

Museographs
3043 Moore Avenue
Lawrenceville, Georgia 30244
404/979-9618
http://www.thelazargroup.com/

Nasco Arts and Crafts
4825 Stoddard Road
P.O. Box 3837
Modesto, CA 95352
800/558-9595
www.nascofa.com

Sanford
2711 Washington Boulevard
Bellwood, IL 60104
800/323-0749
www.sanfordcorp.com

Sax Arts and Crafts
2405 South Calhoun Road
New Berlin, WI 53151
800/558-6696
www.junebox.com/sax/

School Specialty
P.O. Box 1579
Appleton, WI 54913
920/734-5712
www.schoolspecialty.com

Skutt Ceramic Products
6441 Southeast Johnson Creek
    Boulevard
Portland, OR 97206
503/774-6000
www.skutt.com

Universal Color Slide Company
8450 South Tamiami Trail
Sarasota, FL 34238-2936
800/326-1367
www.universalcolorslide.com

APPENDIX D

Safer Materials for Elementary School Art

Photography

Photochemicals
- Use Polaroid cameras, without transfer manipulation.
- Send film out to be developed.
- Do sungrams with blueprint paper and sunlight.
- Do photocopier art.

Textiles and Fiber Arts

Synthetic Dyes
- Use vegetable dyes (spinach, tea, onion skins, etc.) or food dyes.

Synthetic Fibers
- Use fibers that have not been treated with formaldehyde sizings.

Textile Remnants
- Leftover textile scraps can be used for stuffing pillows or soft-sculpture projects.

Printmaking

Screen Printing
- Use CP/AP water-based inks.*
- Use cut paper stencils.

Relief Printing
- Do linoleum cuts instead of woodcuts.
- Use CP/AP water-based inks.

Sculpture

Modeling Clays
- Use premixed clay or CP/AP modeling materials.

Papier-Mâché
- Use black-and-white newspaper with CP/AP pastes or CP/AP instant papier-mâchés made from cellulose.

Painting and Drawing

Paints
- Use CP/AP watercolors, tempera, and acrylic paints, not adult paints.

Scented Markers
- Do not use, because they teach children to smell and eat art materials.

Permanent Markers
- Use CP/AP water-based markers.

Pastels
- Use CP/AP oil sticks, crayons, chalks, and colored pencils.

Spray Fixatives
- Use CP/AP clear acrylic emulsion to fix drawings.

Woodworking

Woods
- Use only common soft woods.

Glues
- Use CP/AP glues.

Paints
- Use CP/AP water-based paints.

Ceramics

Clays
- Use only wet, premixed clays.

White Clays
- Use only talc-free clays.

Glazes
- Paint finished pieces with acrylics or tempera instead of glazing.
- Use premixed liquid glazes, not powders.

Metalworking

Jewelry
- Use bent-metal wire instead of soldering.

Stained Glass
- Use colored cellophane and black paper to imitate colored glass and lead came.

Commercial Arts

Scented Markers
- Do not use, because they teach children to smell and eat art materials.

Permanent Markers
- Use CP/AP water-based markers.

Rubber Cement
- Use CP/AP glues for collage.

---

*CP/AP refers to the Certified Product (CP) or Approved Product (AP) seal of the Arts and Crafts Materials Institute.

INDEX

Page numbers in italics refer to illustrations and text in captions.